Virginia Woolf's Apprenticeship

For Gary, whose
'we'll find a way' kept me researching,
humour kept me grounded,
belief kept me going,
love kept me warm.

Virginia Woolf's Apprenticeship
Becoming an Essayist

Beth Rigel Daugherty

Edinburgh University Press is one of the leading university presses in the UK. We publish academic books and journals in our selected subject areas across the humanities and social sciences, combining cutting-edge scholarship with high editorial and production values to produce academic works of lasting importance. For more information visit our website: edinburghuniversitypress.com

© Beth Rigel Daugherty 2022, 2024

Grateful acknowledgement is made to the sources listed in the List of Illustrations for permission to reproduce material previously published elsewhere. Every effort has been made to trace the copyright holders, but if any have been inadvertently overlooked, the publisher will be pleased to make the necessary arrangements at the first opportunity.

Edinburgh University Press Ltd
The Tun – Holyrood Road
12(2f) Jackson's Entry
Edinburgh EH8 8PJ

First published in hardback by Edinburgh University Press 2022

Typeset in 10.5/13 Adobe Sabon by
Cheshire Typesetting Ltd, Cuddington, Cheshire,
printed and bound by CPI Group (UK) Ltd,
Croydon, CR0 4YY

A CIP record for this book is available from the British Library

ISBN 978 1 3995 0451 5 (hardback)
ISBN 978 1 3995 0452 2 (paperback)
ISBN 978 1 3995 0453 9 (webready PDF)
ISBN 978 1 3995 0454 6 (epub)

The right of Beth Rigel Daugherty to be identified as the author of this work has been asserted in accordance with the Copyright, Designs and Patents Act 1988, and the Copyright and Related Rights Regulations 2003 (SI No. 2498).

Contents

List of Illustrations	vi
Acknowledgements	vii
List of Abbreviations	xvii
Formatting Note	xix
General Preface: Common Reader Learning, Common Reader Teaching	xx
Preface: Common Reader Learning	xxi
Introduction: Contexts	1

Part I: Student, 1882–1904: Learning at Home

1. Learning at 22 Hyde Park Gate	23
2. Coming into 22 Hyde Park Gate	35
3. Venturing beyond 22 Hyde Park Gate	58
4. Reading and Writing Skills	89
5. Outcomes: Learning at Home	106

Part II: Teacher, 1905–1907: Teaching at Morley College

6. Teaching at Morley College	125
7. Learning from Morley College	135
8. Teaching Skills	156
9. Outcomes: Teaching at Morley College	186

Part III: Apprentice, 1904–1912: Writing for Newspapers

10. Becoming a Professional	211
11. Learning from Editors	218
12. Essay-writing and Book-reviewing Skills	250
13. Outcomes: Writing for Newspapers	272
Conclusion: Implications	300
Appendices	309
Sources	351
Index	393

Illustrations

Figures

1.1	Julia Stephen with Stephen children at lessons	27
3.1	Agnes Muriel Clay in Lady Margaret Hall group photo, 1903	70
5.1	Virginia Stephen's books, three trolleys, one shelf full	108
8.1	Cyril Yaldwyn, 'The Mortality of Feeling', *Morley College Magazine*	176
11.1	Virginia Stephen's review of W. D. Howells's *The Son of Royal Langbrith* in the *Guardian*	226
13.1	Virginia Stephen with Adrian Stephen and Duncan Grant	291

Table

7.1	Morley College Demographics, 1906–14	147

Acknowledgements

My work on this project began decades ago, long before the thought of 'books' entered my mind. Through its long evolution from a vague interest in Virginia Woolf's revisions to a focused exploration of Virginia Stephen's education and its impact on Woolf's essays, many people have supported me and my work, Woolf scholarship, scholarship in general. As a result, my extensive debts to family, schooling, colleagues, friends and communities run deep.

I am grateful to my family – Harry S. Eberle, whose dream of being a journalist was thwarted by the First World War; Margaret S. Eberle, who went to college and made sure I went, too; E. L. 'Bruz' Rigel, whose small restaurant fed a town and train travellers; Irene Carter Rigel, who had a degree and taught me how to cook; E. L. 'Red' Rigel, who taught me to love sports and be a good sport; Mary Ann Rigel, who wrote her Faulkner thesis when I was a baby and whose love for language and literature fostered my own; Sue Rigel Rodi, who showed me learning can never be measured by tests and who taught; and Jane Rigel Royse, who persevered through pain and fatigue until she had her degree. Stories, laughter and love were ours growing up.

So many inspiring and challenging teachers along the way, from Quaker City Elementary to Zane Trace High, to Mount Union, to Rice – Mabel Henderson, who was tough, fair, and oh, so good; Richard Cifaldi, who made me fall in love with history; Betty Fahner, who taught biology while making sure every student learned how to do library research; Mary Ann Rigel, who cared about words, sentences and creativity; Mary Ellen Gilpatric, who offered an Emily Dickinson seminar and suggested graduate school; David Ragosin, who added contemporary drama to the curriculum; Lyle Crist, who loved words and humour; Gloria Malone, who ensured we saw beyond the canon; Robert Patten, who introduced me to the Victorians, George Cruikshank and the joys of archival research; Walter Isle, who studied at Stanford and thus could direct a Woolf dissertation in the late 1970s; and Linda Driskill, who introduced me to composition research and writing labs – all made learning a delight. They loved their fields, their calling and their students.

I am grateful to Union Local High School for the chance to teach and work with dedicated teachers like Alice Mauersberger (English) and Jack Martin (Latin) as I experienced Appalachian schooling from the other side. I am also glad I got to teach Basic Writing in the Writing Workshop at the Ohio State University and Critical Reading and Writing at Ohio Wesleyan University. Susan Helgeson, graduation ceremony honouring women who had received only titular degrees up until 1948. The late Julia Briggs shared her home, garden and work with me during a visit to Oxford, along with a memorable drive to a Cotswold pub. I also fondly remember an overnight stay and the hospitality and calm of an urban garden with Anna Snaith and Dominic Rowland.

I have been the lucky beneficiary of books, gifts of generous friends and strangers: Libby Steele sent me the results of her early and painstaking research into the sources and literary allusions in Woolf's essays; Eileen Barrett gave me Sybil Oldfield's *Spinsters of the Parish* at exactly the right time; Roma Goyder sent me a copy of her *From Hayseed to Harvest* that taught me more about Hayes Court School; Marilyn Schwinn Smith gave me the right words and the right memoir at the right time; Alix Bunyan made her dissertation on children's culture and Stephen juvenilia available to me; Nick Rampley sent me the Morley College 125th anniversary portrait; C. S. Knighton gave me *Dynasty: The Polack Family and the Jewish House at Clifton* and pointed me toward other Clifton histories; David Lisle Crane sent me his *Letters between a Victorian Schoolboy and his Family*; and Sarah Funke Butler sent me the Glenn Horowitz catalogues that revealed other books in Virginia Stephen's library and the Grolier Club exhibit catalogue that led to this book's cover photo.

I am deeply grateful to the Woolf community, which has generated and sustained scholarly and pedagogical conversations throughout my career – I feel as though Woolf Studies and I grew up together. To the scholars, critics, readers and editors who worked on Virginia Woolf when she was dismissed, ignored or denigrated, we owe you a great deal for the foundation you built, often without the support of a community; your work literally made succeeding generations of work possible, including my own. More recently, the Woolf community's efforts to maintain ties and keep the talk going have held pandemic loneliness at bay. I want to lift a glass to the Woolf Salon, the Virginia Woolf Society of Great Britain Woolf events, Elisa Kay Sparks's social hours, Literature Cambridge, Blogging Woolf and the listserv, and the extraordinary work of Ben Hagen and the University of South Dakota at Vermillion to host the 30th Annual International Conference on Virginia Woolf virtually.

I want to thank Hazel Mills for helping me understand Classics at Cambridge, particularly the tripos, and Susan David Bernstein for sharing her extensive library research with me. And I am especially grateful to these Woolf scholars for their generosity: Melba Cuddy-Keane for sharing 'Pedagogical Woolf' and its fuller version of the Lewes Free Library story; Pat Collier for telling me about the existence of correspondence course ads in *John O'London's Weekly* and sharing much additional information about Woolf and periodicals over email; Marion Dell for helping me understand the concept of 'further' education in England; Stuart N. Clarke for sending me the biographical information about R. W. Church that became the impetus for my interest in periodicals and their editors, patiently answering numerous, pestering questions about all things English, Virginia Woolf and the essay, and sharing crucial technological advice; Christine Kenyon Jones and Anna Snaith for their ground-breaking work on Virginia Stephen at King's College London, willingness to answer my archival questions, and Lilian Faithfull recommendation; and the late S. P. (Pat) Rosenbaum for his detailed description of Virginia Stephen's monthly progress as a young journalist, patient answers to my many questions about those early years, copies of Thoby's published essays, and transcriptions of Virginia Stephen's lectures. Not to mention his question, 'Do you know who Miss Clay is?'

I am also deeply grateful to Mark Hussey and Jeanne Dubino for their reading and responding to multiple drafts of this book's chapters over many, many years, their knowledge and advice about publishing, and their encouragement through many ups and downs. They have seen this project through its many incarnations, and I value their support and friendship. I want to thank Helen Wussow for saying to me, as I mourned the loss of lengthy endnotes that I had to cut from an article slated for her edited collection, 'You should write a book.' I would like to thank Anne Fernald for reading a very early draft of an introduction, an anonymous reader of two early chapters who remains anonymous only because I embarrassingly failed to keep the response attached to its email, and Ruth Hoberman for doing research in the London Library on my behalf when I could not travel; she made my later research there so much easier. I also want to thank Diane Gillespie for the inspiring example of her careful scholarship and full life, and Leslie Hankins for her creativity, fun and willingness to try new things. I am grateful to Mary Beth Pringle for countless conversations about teaching, *To the Lighthouse*, our various projects, and memoir over many a diner meal. I also want to thank the many Woolf readers, scholars, and creative writers and artists who ask questions at conferences, respond to requests for their work, follow up with references, and teach Virginia Woolf in all sorts of settings around the world.

I am grateful to Ben Hagen for his recent reading of a partial draft; his cogent comments helped me cut, revise, and edit some more. Edinburgh University Press readers also provided many helpful suggestions for improving the manuscript further. Finally, I must thank common readers, who 'behind the erratic gunfire of the press', create an atmosphere within which literature can survive and thrive; they wrote to Virginia Woolf, testifying to her work's power in their lives, they wrote to Leonard Woolf and to Hogarth Press after her death, or they did not write, but read, pondered and absorbed, keeping her work alive. A story from summer 2018: the British Library Humanities Room security checkers were going through my bags and noticed I had two Virginia Woolf books with me. The man commented that out of all the books he looks at as people go through, ones by her are the most frequent. 'She's popular,' he said. The woman chimed in, 'Well, she's a beautiful writer!' I said I was glad to hear that because when I started studying her in 1976, a professor warned me against writing a dissertation on her. Not enough there, he said. The man said, 'Is that right? Well, she's the most popular author we see here. The most popular. Isn't that right?' he turned to his co-worker, who nodded. Everywhere, quietly and steadfastly, common readers continue her work.

Opportunities to present my work at many annual international conferences on Virginia Woolf, several Louisville, KY, conferences on literature and culture since 1900, and occasional Midwest MLA and MLA annual conferences have contributed greatly to this book's development, and I thank the many conference organisers who made those gatherings, presentations and ensuing discussions possible. As Clarissa Dalloway muses, throwing a party is a gift to those attending, with its effects rippling outward, but it is harder to pull off than it looks. Many excellent conference conversations with Woolfian friends over the years have stimulated my thinking and nurtured this book, and besides those mentioned elsewhere, I particularly want to thank Judith Allen, AnneMarie Bantzinger, Steven Barber, Stephen Barkway, Suzanne Bellamy, Kate Benzel, Ted Bishop, Anne Byrne, Ann Gibaldi Campbell, Pamela Caughie, Wayne Chapman, Melba Cuddy-Keane, Kristin Czarnecki, Jane de Gay, Erica Delsandro, Madelyn Detloff, Anne Fernald, Christine Froula, Evelyn Haller, Suzette Henke, Katherine Hill-Miller, Catherine Hollis, Karen Kukil, Karen Levenback, Jane Lilienfeld, Gill Lowe, George Ella Lyon, Eleanor McNees, Jeanette McVicker, Paula Maggio, Patricia Morgne, Vara Neverow, Lolly Ockerstrom, Bonnie Kime Scott, Drew Shannon, Helen Southworth, Elisa Kay Sparks, Alice Staveley, Julie Vandivere, Pierre-Eric Villeneuve, Kathleen Wall, Leslie Werden, Elizabeth Gordon Willson and J. J. Wilson. In addition, I want to acknowledge Pace University Press and its support of *Woolf Studies Annual* and *Selected Papers* volumes from 1991–2001 and Clemson University Digital Press/Liverpool University Press and its support of *Selected Papers* volumes since then. Those publications and editors, along with the *Virginia Woolf Miscellany* and the *Virginia Woolf Bulletin* and their editors, promote substantial scholarship within a lively community. Their importance cannot be overstated.

The internet has made scholarly detective work much easier. Google gave me my first Miss Clay lead, it and Ancestry.com records helped me learn more about the Buchheims, and Ancestry.com and military records provided possible leads on Cyril Yaldwyn. HathiTrust, Internet Archive, Google Books, Open Library and the Gutenberg Project made it possible for me to delve into books I could not have easily obtained otherwise. *EBSCOhost Literary Reference Center Plus* made biographical and literature summary sites quickly available. Wikipedia often gave me a starting point and sources for additional information and, occasionally, provided the most succinct biographical information. Finally, the online edition of the *Oxford Dictionary of National Biography* has been incredibly helpful. Leslie Stephen would be amazed at what his project has become.

I continue to be grateful to Mark Hussey for editing *Virginia Woolf: Major Authors on CD*. Being able to check Woolf's manuscripts and typescripts at home and do word or phrase searches of her published work has been invaluable.

For believing in this project and for making sure it would happen, my sincere thanks go to Jackie Jones, Publisher in Literary Studies at Edinburgh University Press. Susannah Butler, Assistant Commissioning Editor, and Fiona Conn, Managing Desk Editor, ensured I understood the process and worked to make it go smoothly. My copyeditor, Wendy Lee, cheerfully corrected my grammatical and punctuation lapses and saved me from several embarrassing mistakes. I am grateful for her careful and perceptive reading.

Helpful readers and eagle-eyed copyeditors have done their best to find and remove all errors at many points during this book's gestation, and I have worked diligently to proofread and check and recheck sources and quotations. But long experience with copyediting, transcribing, reading submissions to journals and presses, and revising and editing my own papers tells me that mistakes happen anyway. Any that remain are my own.

Samuel Johnson once observed, 'A [person] will turn over half a library to make one book.' In the process of making this one book, I have turned over not only the Courtright Memorial Library but many other archives and libraries as well, and I am grateful: for their existence, their stewardship and their expert guidance. Far-flung librarians and archivists gave their time and effort to an academic they did not know. I am grateful to Sarah Whale at Collections and Archives at Hatfield House, who sent scans of two letters in their possession; Carolynne Cotton, Local Studies, Archives and Museum Manager at the Central Library in Uxbridge, who sent information about Evelyns School; Ann Barton, Texas Woman's University, Linda McFadden and Lugene Schemper, Calvin College, Carl Peterson, Colgate University, and Meredith Gillies, the University of Minnesota, who provided long-distance reference assistance; Simon Bromley, Local Studies Department at the Central Library in Bromley, who found a copy of Roma Goyder's *Hayseed to Harvest*; C. S. Knighton of Clifton College, who sent information, files and photographs relating to Thoby Stephen, talked with me extensively over email and in person, and helped me understand Clifton, its history and Thoby's time there.

How wonderful it has been to work with archivists and archive staff members over the years devoted to this project. My respect and admiration for those who keep authors' works and institutions' histories alive has only increased; they make scholarly and critical work possible for very little recompense or recognition. In acknowledging the people who helped me conduct my research, the brief mentions below do not convey the warm gratitude I feel for the knowledge, competence, dedication and kindness they bring to their work. I appreciate their patient guidance. And their amazingly quick replies to panicked emails!

For their kind permission to use and quote from their own collections and Virginia Woolf holdings, I want to thank the following archives, libraries and institutions: Archives of American Art, Smithsonian Institution (Marisa Bourgoin, Head of Reference Services); Henry W. and Albert A. Berg Collection of English and American Literature, the New York Public Library (the late Lola Szladits, Stephen Crook, Philip Milito, Josh McKeon and current Curator Carolyn Vega); The British Library (Claire Wotherspoon, Manuscripts Reference Librarian, Zoe Stansell, Manuscripts Reference Services, Bruna Lago-Fazolo, Licensing Assistant, and untold staff members); Eberly Family Special Collections Library, the Allison-Shelley Collection, Pennsylvania State University Libraries (past Curator Sandra Stelts and current Head of Research Services and Collections Curator Rachael Dreyer); Girton College Archives and Special Collections, University of Cambridge (the late Kate Perry, Archivist, Tilda Watson, past Library and Archives Assistant, and current Archivist and Curator Hannah Westall); King's College London Archives and Research Collections (Lianne Smith, past Archives Services Manager, Adam Cox, Diana Manipud, Senior Archives Assistant, and Cathy Williams, current Archives Service Manager); Lady Margaret Hall Archives, University of Oxford (James Fishwick, LMH Librarian, and Oliver Mahoney, LMH Archivist); London Borough of Lambeth, Lambeth Archives, Minet Library (Jon Newman, former Archivist, and Zoe Darani, current Archivist); London Library Archive, London Library (Helen O'Neill, former Heritage and Development Librarian,

Inez Lynn, former Head Librarian, Amanda Corp, Head of Enquiries, Member Services, and Nathalie Belkin, Archivist); Manuscripts, Archives and Special Collections, Washington State University Libraries (Laila Miletic-Vejzovic, former Head, Trevor Bond, Associate Dean for Digital Initiatives and Special Collections, and Julia King, Rare Books Cataloguer); Morley College Library Archives, Morley College (Elaine Andrews, Learning Resources Manager); Special Collections, University of Sussex Library, the Keep (Bet Inglis, former curator of Woolf Papers, Dorothy Sheridan, former Director of the Mass Observation Archive, the late Joy Eldridge, Fiona Courage, Associate Director, Library, and Curator of Mass Observation Archive, Karen Watson, University of Sussex Archivist, Rose Lock, Helen Betteridge, the late Sandra Koa-Wing and many staff members); Times Newspapers Ltd Archive, News Corp UK and Ireland Ltd (Nick Mays, UK News Archivist); and Women's Library@London School of Economics (Gillian Murphy, Curator of Equality, Rights and Citizenship, LSE Library).

Thank you to The Society of Authors as the Literary Representative of the Estate of Virginia Woolf for permission to quote from Virginia Woolf's unpublished work. Photographs of Virginia Stephen and of Julia Stephen with the Stephen children appear courtesy of the British Library, the Berg Collection of English and American Literature at the New York Public Library, and Smith College. The group photograph that includes Miss Clay appears courtesy of the Lady Margaret Hall Archives. The image of Cyril Yaldwyn's poem appears courtesy of the Morley College Library Archives. Full credit lines appear in image captions. I thank David Sutton at the University of Reading, the UK branch of the Harry Ransom Center's Writers Artists and Their Copyright Holders (WATCH) file, who helped me find some copyright holders. Questions about the identity of the copyright holder for the unpublished work of Leslie, Julia and Thoby Stephen remain unresolved, however, according to Sarah Baxter of the Society of Authors. All my efforts, including correspondence with Julian Bell, to find someone with the authority to grant permission to use that material were unsuccessful, as were efforts to reach the copyright holder for Mary Sheepshanks's unpublished manuscript.

Portions of '"Young writers might do worse": Anne Thackeray Ritchie, Virginia Stephen and Virginia Woolf', 2010, Palgrave Macmillan, are used here with permission of Palgrave Macmillan. Some of my previous work, as listed in Other Sources, provided the basis for chapters here; though that work has been cut, much revised or completely reshaped here, I want to acknowledge Pace University Press, St Martin's Press and Contemporary Research Press for the material that first appeared in their publications.

Extracts and quotations from the following volumes by Virginia Woolf are reprinted with the permission of Random House Group Limited: *The Essays of Virginia Woolf: Volume IV* (edited by Andrew McNeillie), The Hogarth Press, Text © Quentin Bell and Angelica Garnett 1925, 1926, 1927, 1928, 1994; *The Essays of Virginia Woolf: Volume 5* (edited by Stuart N. Clarke), The Hogarth Press, Text © Anne Olivier Bell and Angelica Garnett 1927, 1929, 1930, 1931, 1932, 1933, 1938, 2009; *The Essays of Virginia Woolf: Volume 6* (edited by Stuart N. Clarke), The Hogarth Press, Text © Anne Olivier Bell and Angelica Garnett 1906, 1907, 1908, 1909, 1910, 1913, 1916, 1918, 1919, 1921, 1922,

1923, 1924, 1929, 1933, 1934, 1935, 1936, 1937, 1938, 1939, 1940, 1941, 1942, 1947, 1950, 1972, 1979, 2006, 2008, 2009, 2010, 2011.

Published passages, extracts and quotations from the following volumes by Virginia Woolf were deemed fair use by Houghton Mifflin Harcourt: *A Passionate Apprentice: The Early Journals, 1897–1909*, edited by Mitchell A. Leaska (Harvest/HBJ © 1990); *The Letters of Virginia Woolf*, Vol. I: 1888–1912, edited by Nigel Nicolson and Joanne Trautmann (HBJ © 1975); *The Essays of Virginia Woolf*, Vol. I: 1904–1912, edited by Andrew McNeillie (HBJ © 1986); and *Moments of Being: A Collection of Autobiographical Writing*, edited by Jeanne Schulkind (Harvest/Harcourt © 1985).

Abbreviations

Virginia Woolf

AROO	*A Room of One's Own*
CH	*Carlyle's House and Other Sketches*
CR	*The Common Reader*
D1–5	*The Diary of Virginia Woolf*
E1–6	*The Essays of Virginia Woolf*
HPGN	*The Hyde Park Gate News*
L1–6	*The Letters of Virginia Woolf*
MD	*Mrs. Dalloway*
MoB	*Moments of Being*
OED	*Oxford English Dictionary*
P	*The Pargiters*
PA	*A Passionate Apprentice*
'Report' MS	Holograph ms. of 'Report on Teaching at Morley College'
'Sketch' MS	Holograph ms. of 19 July 1939 'Sketch of the Past' version
'Sketch 1'	'A Sketch of the Past' 1st edition (1976)
'Sketch'	'A Sketch of the Past' 2nd edition (1985)
'Slater's'	'Moments of Being: "Slater's Pins Have no Points"'
TG	*Three Guineas*
TL	*To the Lighthouse*
VS notes	Notes for book reviews
Y	*The Years*

Other Authors

K&C	Kirkpatrick and Clarke, *A Bibliography of Virginia Woolf*, 4th edition
LDE	*The Long Day Ended*, Mary Sheepshanks
MB	*Sir Leslie Stephen's Mausoleum Book*
MBN	*Mausoleum Book Notebook*, Leslie Stephen
QB1	Quentin Bell, *Virginia Woolf: A Biography* (volume 1)
SLLS1–2	*Selected Letters of Leslie Stephen*, ed. John W. Bicknell
VB	Vanessa Bell, 'Notes on Virginia's Childhood'

Sources

A1–4	*Atalanta*
AGM	Annual General Meeting
AR	King's College London Annual Reports in *SL* Appendices
AR for LMH	*Annual Reports for Lady Margaret Hall*
BL	British Library
CUC	*Cambridge University Calendar*
CUR	*Cambridge University Reporter*
DLB	*Dictionary of Literary Biography*
DNB	*Dictionary of National Biography*
K&M-V	King and Miletic-Vejzovic, short-title catalogue for LLVW
KA/D/M 1, 7	King's College London Delegacy Minutes
KCM	*King's College Magazine, Ladies' Department*
KWA/R 1, 2, 4	King's College London Archives, exam results, term list registers, matriculated students register
KWA/RAD 3–7	King's College London Archives, Registration records, 1897–1901
LLA	London Library Archive
LLAR	*London Library Annual Reports*
LLM	*London Library Minutes*
LLVW	The Library of Leonard and Virginia Woolf
LMH	Lady Margaret Hall
LWP	Leonard Woolf Papers
MASC	Manuscripts, Archives and Special Collections
MCAR	*Morley College Annual Report*
MCECM1–3	*Morley College Executive Committee Minutes* (includes other committees)
MCM	*Morley College Magazine*
MHP	Monks House Papers
NPD	*Newspaper Press Directory*
ODNB	*Oxford Dictionary of National Biography* (online)
SL [year]	King's College London Syllabus of Lectures, Vols 1–3: 1878–89; 1889–1900; 1900–9 (KWA/SYL 6–9)
TLS	*Times Literary Supplement*
WDENP	*Waterloo Directory of English Newspapers and Periodicals* (database)

Formatting Note

Following the practice of her editors, I retain Virginia Stephen's spelling and punctuation in material written by her. I use MLA Style, 7th edition, but omit colons after volume numbers in parenthetical citations. To further streamline in-text citations, I abbreviate works and sources, and use numbers to indicate volumes and pages without abbreviating words for them. If more than one author has the same surname, I depend on a discussion's context *or* a first name initial to distinguish them. If an author has more than one work, I use a shortened title or an abbreviation to distinguish them.

Parenthetical citations document the location information for mentioned or minimally discussed content from *Atalanta* and periodicals publishing Virginia Stephen's reviews, but such information is not repeated in the bibliography. In the bibliography, I do not provide access dates for book and article pdf files or books found online since I consulted them often.

I separately index Virginia Stephen and Virginia Woolf, as well as Vanessa Stephen and Vanessa Bell.

General Preface: Common Reader Learning, Common Reader Teaching

It was the summer of 1988, I was finally there, in the New York Public Library's Berg Collection, and I asked for it first. I remember holding Virginia Stephen's 1897 diary in the palm of my hand, tears welling. What became days, weeks, years, a lifetime of transcribing began in that moment. Later that summer, I read the holograph draft of Virginia Woolf's talk at Hayes Court School, 'How Should One Read a Book?', transfixed by the teacher I saw there. I didn't know it then, but the seed for what I came to regard as the crucial relationship between Virginia Stephen's education and Virginia Woolf's essays had been planted.

Virginia Woolf's Apprenticeship: Becoming an Essayist is the first of two books about Woolf's essay canon. Virginia Stephen spent her apprenticeship as a common reader learning, working to weave together the disparate threads of her homeschooling, teaching and early writing. Coping with piecemeal lessons, she learned, practised and gained an education, writing the nearly 160 reviews and essays that would transform her into Virginia Woolf, a common reader teaching, an essayist who wrote 500 mature essays that strive to educate others.

Virginia Woolf's Essays: Being a Teacher, the book to follow, will show how Woolf uses her essays to welcome readers and students into the literary conversation as well as how they function as an educational laboratory for teachers. She outlines an educational philosophy, shares a curriculum, models a pedagogy and creates a community, demonstrating all the while how we might teach in our classrooms and on the page. Virginia Stephen's apprenticeship turned Virginia Woolf into an educator compelled to teach in essays that continue to guide, encourage and inspire readers, writers and teachers. In this book, Virginia Stephen, student, teacher and apprentice, studies and practises as a common reader learning; she emerges and flourishes in the second book as Virginia Woolf, essayist, educator and mentor, a common reader teaching.

Preface:
Common Reader Learning

> Now I am going to get out all my books again, after I have written to the Quaker, and I am going to write in my head, where I always write immortal works, an article upon Lady Fanshawe, and I am going to walk round my desk and then take out certain manuscripts which lie there like wine, sweetening as they grow old. I shall be miserable, or happy; a wordy sentimental creature, or a writer of such English as shall one day burn the pages.
>
> – Virginia Stephen to Violet Dickinson [7 July 1907] (*L1* 299)

I am a hillbilly, a hick, a ridge runner, a yokel. I don't think I'm a redneck, though people in my part of the country get called that, too.[1] I'm from Appalachia, the hills of southeast Ohio, a village of 583 people. If I had ended my school days in the Quaker City school I started in, my graduating class would have numbered eighteen. But two schools consolidated and I graduated with forty-six other students. I remember hearing *Julius Caesar* read aloud in the halting voices of my classmates in English class, and we must have read a smattering of short stories and poetry in my writing class, but I don't remember reading any other literature in school. We were, however, repeatedly taught grammar, which seemed to work only for those who already knew grammar.

In graduate school seminars at Rice University, I sat at a table with students from Yale, Princeton and Johns Hopkins, wondering what the hell I was doing there. In fact, I learned much later that the department took a chance on me and my small Ohio college degree. What right did I have to discuss literature with such educated people? What right did I, a hillbilly, have to attempt a dissertation on Virginia Woolf's fiction?[2]

I am a professor emerita now. I continue to do research on Virginia Woolf, and my research focus is Woolf's essays instead of her novels because, at that low time, I happened upon Woolf's *Collected Essays* in the Brazos Bookstore: hardback, a different colour for each volume, $7.50 apiece for Volumes 1 and 2, $6.95 apiece for Volumes 3 and 4. I couldn't resist. I started with the first essay in the first volume, 'On Not Knowing Greek', and didn't stop until I finished the last essay in the fourth volume, 'The New Biography'. I read those essays as though they were a lifeline, and perhaps they were. I hadn't read all the people Woolf wrote about (still haven't), didn't know all the works she referred to, had only begun to grasp many of the terms she used. It didn't matter; I read them as fast as I could, one right after the other.

At bottom, my work ever since has been an attempt to figure out how, as she wrote about authors and works I knew nothing of, she made me feel so welcome in her world. How, when I was feeling so alien in the academy because of what I did *not* know, did she beckon me in? Why is her criticism, as Walter James says, the kind 'that opens doors, not lowers portcullises' and why do her sentences '[aim] to break down barriers' (12)? Jeanette Winterson reacts similarly, writing that

> Of the great Modernist triangle, Eliot, Woolf and Joyce, Woolf seems to me to be the writer most interested in communication. Eliot put his faith in an elite, Joyce put his faith in himself, but Woolf, although a self-confessed highbrow, wants the world in her arms. (84)

How does she *do* that? Could I learn and use that gesture in the classroom, where literature, with its special vocabulary, intensity and foreignness, along with my love for it, intimidated my students and made them feel they had no right to voice their thoughts and feelings? Could Virginia Woolf's essays teach me, teach others, how to teach? Those essays read in grad school led me here, where my background and my present, my scholarship and my teaching, my culture and my profession all intersect. Those essays led me to ask: how did her life influence her writing? How did her education affect her work? How did her apprenticeship shape her essays? Why and how did a literary insider invite this cultural outsider in?

* * * * *

Some of Virginia Woolf's contemporaries admired her essays more than they did her fiction, which may have been one reason Leonard Woolf began publishing new selections of her essays soon after her death.[3] Yet as Beth Rosenberg and Jeanne Dubino note in their introduction to *Virginia Woolf and the Essay*, the academy long dismissed Woolf's essays, either comparing them unfavourably to T. S. Eliot's, deriding them as 'impressionistic' or ignoring them altogether (5–7).[4] The second feminist wave brought renewed attention to, first, *A Room of One's Own* and then *Three Guineas*, but even so, Woolf's posthumous reputation rested almost solely upon her ground-breaking novels. Although many critics understandably used individual essays to illuminate the fiction, such a practice can result, as Leila Brosnan points out, 'in a skewed perception of the range of Woolf's shorter non-fiction and a tendency to dissociate style and content from genre and context' (3). Only a few critics focused solely on the essays.[5]

More recently, however, interest in the essays has grown, stimulated by the annotated editions of *The Common Reader* (McNeillie 1984, 1986) and the six volumes of *The Essays of Virginia Woolf* (McNeillie 1986–94; Clarke 2009, 2011). Pamela Caughie reads Woolf's essays as an attempt to keep art and culture 'out of the control of the few' and keep change unfinished (188–9); Dubino examines the contradictions held in tension within Woolf's essay canon ('Politics'); and Laura Kranzler sees Woolf 'commenting upon her own self-divisions as author and critic' (106). Rosenberg uses psychoanalytical and historical methods to argue that Woolf's reading and writing strategies are part of a fluid, ever-changing conversation she had with Samuel Johnson and Leslie Stephen to allow exploration and contradiction (119). Judith Allen explores how Woolf uses the essay's indefiniteness, freedom and multiplicity to critique her culture's hierarchies and binary oppositions ('Essayistic' 1–8). Jocelyn Barkevicius's own essays weave together personal reactions, critical perspectives on Woolf's less-read essays, and the story of a writer reading to learn 'approaches to writing essays' (v–xii).

As the essay enjoyed resurgence as a genre, Woolf's essays garnered more sustained critical attention.[6] Dubino's essay on Woolf's development from novice to professional writer between 1904 and 1918 ('VW' 25–40) and the collected essays in *Virginia Woolf and the Essay* reflected and stimulated an increasing respect for the essays. Brosnan places Woolf's large non-fiction canon in the context of the literary marketplace and reads Woolf's essays through Bakhtin; for her, Woolf's essays are shaped by genre, textual production and gender (170–1). Elena Gualtieri locates Woolf's practice as an essayist within the broad European tradition of essayism, argues that class prevents Woolf's imagination from 'transcending its own historical situation' (21), and investigates the relationship between Woolf and literary history (146). Allen illustrates how Woolf, with Montaigne, uses the essay to 'subvert any doctrines, treatises, or constraining and totalizing systems' (*VW* 2). Woolf's essays are central to Anna Snaith's portrayal of Woolf's negotiation of public and private (*PPN*), Melba Cuddy-Keane's examination of Woolf's pedagogy (*VW*), and Anne Fernald's study of resonances between Woolf's feminism and her reading (*Feminism*). Randi Saloman portrays Woolf pushing against genre constraints and actively attempting to bring the essay's freedom to the novel in *Virginia Woolf's Essayism*.

In this book, I shift attention to the young person learning to write essays.[7] Virginia Stephen's fragmented and solitary apprenticeship took place in 22 Hyde Park Gate, Morley College and Bloomsbury, and was permeated by larger educational forces affecting girls, the working classes and writers. She learned from family members and professors, magazines and libraries, role models and tutors; from mentors and students; from editors and writers.[8] She absorbed the impact of gender, class and readers on learning, on reading, on writing. Little about her education was systematic, formal or sustained, but it did communicate curricula, convey pedagogies and introduce her to communities. And through it all, she practised her non-fiction craft, honed her skills and worked to move from novice to expert. Why, and how, I wondered long ago, do Woolf's essays invite readers in? Now, I argue, Virginia Stephen's lonely education led Virginia Woolf to counteract isolation and create community through writing, with the 'how' of Virginia Stephen's education engendering the 'how' of Virginia Woolf's essays. Virginia Stephen's apprenticeship taught Virginia Woolf how to teach.

Notes

1. Rednecks originally referred to coal miners resisting the coal companies; they wore red bandanas to signal union membership.
2. Much later, I would discover these words in Virginia Stephen's diary: 'what right have I, a woman, to read all these things men have done? They would laugh if they saw me' (*PA* 178). I wrote the dissertation on Woolf's novels, even though one professor thought

I should write about the Bloomsbury Group since 'not enough has been written about Virginia Woolf'.
3. Leonard Woolf published *The Death of the Moth and Other Essays* in 1942 and *The Moment and Other Essays* in 1948. *The Captain's Death Bed and Other Essays* followed in 1950 and *Granite & Rainbow: Essays* in 1958. In 1967, he published four volumes of what he called *Collected Essays*, but a more accurate adjective would have been *Selected*.
4. Florence Howe's comparison of Woolf and Eliot, along with Michael Kaufmann's in Rosenberg and Dubino, attributes merit to Woolf without dismissing Eliot.
5. Barbara Currier Bell and Carol Ohmann's essay on *The Common Reader* began the re-evaluation of Woolf's non-fiction (Rosenberg and Dubino 7), and Mark Goldman and Vijay L. Sharma insisted Woolf was a literary critic. Goldman analysed the design in her essays to combat the 'stereotyped image' of her work as subjective impressionism (3–4), and Sharma noted the 'vital social commitment' at her essays' heart: her 'solicitude for the betterment of the . . . masses' is at the 'base of her desire to educate the common reader' and 'let him into the locked up sanctuaries' (152). Steve Ferebee argued that Woolf's essay voice 'communicates a sense of a real person speaking' (140); she treats the reader as 'an independent, thinking partner' (122), and the resulting bond between essayist and reader is 'integral' to the 'success' of her essays (105). See also Ferebee's 'Bridging the Gulf'.
6. For example, Rachel Bowlby's selected volumes in the Penguin edition, *A Woman's Essays* and *The Crowded Dance of Modern Life*; David Bradshaw's *Virginia Woolf: Selected Essays* in the Oxford World's Classics edition; a chapter of their own in *The Cambridge Companion to Virginia Woolf* (Lee); and appearances in generic anthologies such as Phillip Lopate's *The Art of the Personal Essay* and Joseph Epstein's *The Norton Book of Personal Essays*. For that reason, and because so many other modernists wrote essays, it seems strange that David Bradshaw and Kevin Dettmar omitted essays/non-fiction from the 'Modernist Genres and Modern Media' portion of *A Companion to Modernist Literature and Culture*.
7. *Virginia Woolf's Apprenticeship: Becoming an Essayist* is the first book in a two-book project devoted to Virginia Stephen learning, Virginia Woolf teaching. The second book, *Virginia Woolf's Essays: Being a Teacher*, examines the impact of Virginia Stephen's apprenticeship on Virginia Woolf's large essay canon: the teaching essayist's experiments, principles and practices and the instructional rationale, content and methods of the essays. It also establishes Woolf's wider relevance, tracing the effect her essays, imbued with an educational philosophy, curriculum and pedagogy, have had on teachers and their practice.
8. See Gillian Sutherland, 'Self-education' 530–1, for a discussion of the lifelong education ('always learning') that young women gained from interactions with various 'institutional structures of their society, whether labelled "school", "college", chapel, club, public library – or family and friends'. This study similarly expands the definition of 'education', detecting teachers and pedagogies operating in contexts outside the usual educational framework.

Introduction: Contexts

> How far, we must ask ourselves, is a book influenced by its writer's life – how far is it safe to let the man interpret the writer?
> – 'How Should One Read a Book?' (E5 576)

I start with these biographical facts: Virginia Woolf had an education of sorts; she was a woman writer; and she was an essayist.

Education

The general parameters of Virginia Stephen's education are well known: no formal schooling, full access to her father's extensive library, some classes at King's College, tutoring in Greek. Woolf's biographers do not ignore her education, although some do little more than assume the reader's knowledge of the basic story.[1] Most flesh it out with some detail and provide perceptive insights, such as Jean O. Love's suggestion that although Leslie Stephen did not censor his daughter's reading, he censored his library as he compiled it (42–3), or Panthea Reid's vivid picture of erratic lessons frequently interrupted by Julia Stephen's nursing absences (3–36).[2] But few biographers emphasise it, and if they see a relationship between it and her work, they describe that connection in general terms. So, Quentin Bell points out that when she began to write reviews for the *Guardian*, she was fluent and at ease because 'She had been training herself to be a writer for a long time. That is to say she had been reading voraciously and writing assiduously' (1 93).[3] Phyllis Rose discusses the effect that Virginia Stephen's exclusion from an education had on Virginia Woolf, stressing Woolf's attempts to 'understand and sympathize' rather than reject (92); for Rose, Woolf's modest, anti-authoritarian and feminine persona as a critic grew out of her lack of educational advantages (42).

Biographers Lyndall Gordon and John Mepham devote entire chapters of their biographies to Virginia Stephen's education, with Gordon describing Stephen's 'extraordinary informal education between the ages of thirteen and about twenty-eight' (68–9) and Mepham taking Stephen's early apprenticeship essays seriously (19–20). Gordon focuses on Leslie Stephen, Janet Case and Clive Bell as mentors, whereas Mepham concentrates on Annie Ritchie, Caroline Emelia Stephen and Bruce Richmond.[4] Louise DeSalvo and Katherine Dalsimer devote full-length studies to the young Virginia Woolf, but DeSalvo focuses on the effects of childhood and adolescent trauma on her and Dalsimer traces Woolf's psychological and artistic development; both assert that writing helped Woolf survive.[5] Some critics, too, investigate specific early influences on Woolf's work, with Katherine Hill's study of Leslie Stephen's training being the most focused on education.[6] Christine Kenyon Jones and Anna Snaith detail her classes, more extensive than previously believed, at King's College.

Even after decades of scholars' careful work, the view persists that Virginia Woolf was an elitist novelist removed from ordinary people and their concerns.[7] Yet Woolf struggled throughout her career as an essayist to reach a broader audience than a 'little private circle of exquisite and cultivated people' (L6 420). When Benedict Nicolson attacks Bloomsbury and Roger Fry for '"allow[ing] the spirit of Nazism to grow without taking any steps to check it"' (L6 413) and for not 'trying to make humanity in the mass understand and appreciate what you know and say' (L6 419), she reminds him that *The Common Reader*, *A Room of One's Own* and *Three Guineas* 'sold many thousand copies'. Movingly, she wishes she could have made 'not merely thousands of people interested in literature; but millions' (L6 420).[8] She tries, in her 658 reviews and essays,[9] by addressing a common reader neither elite nor mass and by using inclusive rhetorical strategies. Why and how did a privileged girl transform herself into a woman writer dedicated to inviting outsiders into the literary conversation? Woolf suggests one reason in 'The Leaning Tower', first presented to a working-class audience in 1940. Does not the education of an era's male writers relate to their work?, she asks. Yes, she answers. A connection exists. Their education explains their work.

Her claim applies to her own work as well, so in this book, the first full-length study of Woolf's education, I concentrate on the connections between a writer's education and work. I examine Virginia Stephen's educational experiences and argue that those experiences influenced the attitudes, strategies and content of Virginia Woolf's essays.[10] Employing a feminist, historical and interdisciplinary framework, I examine the biographical, historical and cultural contexts within which Virginia Stephen's education occurred;[11] delve into that education, its teachers and lessons; explore her apprenticeship's outcomes;[12] and suggest the impact of Stephen's education on Woolf's essays.[13] I use extensive archival research to focus on what Virginia Stephen learns, how she practises and what she gains for her later work as an essayist. Ultimately, Virginia Stephen's apprenticeship compelled Virginia Woolf to become a pedagogical essayist.

Woman Writer

Now, at least in the US and Britain, when education for girls is commonplace, when women often outnumber men at institutions of higher learning and when many women writers have received formal education, Virginia Woolf's education narrative seems unusual. But in fact, it was typical, not differing substantially from those women writers with her talents in the past and not that unusual for women writers of her generation. Marked by gender and class, her education occurred in the broader context of education for English girls and women, which, until fairly recently, did not include schooling for middle-class girls. In fact, before 1870, as Deirdre David notes, middle-class girls had less chance, ironically, of receiving appropriate schooling than working-class girls did (18), though the elementary education received by working-class girls was abysmal.[14] Nigel Cross agrees, claiming that middle-class women and the working classes had 'an utterly inadequate education' in common. However, he continues, 'it was often harder for a woman with brains to acquire an education than it was for the working man with his evening classes, mechanics institutes and working men's colleges' (165). Also, girls generally received an education in working-class servitude or middle-class 'accomplishments', meant to keep them in their domestic places. Pioneering educators thus had not only to educate girls, but also to alleviate the threat of societal change that educating girls posed.[15]

Calls for the education of girls and women began at least as early as the mediaeval work of Christine de Pizan's *Book of the City of Ladies* (1405), spread in England with Mary Astell's *Serious Proposal to the Ladies* (1696), continued with Mary Wollstonecraft's *Female Reader* (1789) and *Vindication of the Rights of Woman* (1792), and persisted with John Stuart Mill and Harriet Taylor's *The Subjection of Women* (1861). By the mid-nineteenth century, the calls had become a steady roar, and women such as Dorothea Beale, Frances Buss and Emily Davies, among many others, finally made inroads into the assumption that only males needed education. In the meantime, some women were in fact educated, against great odds, or educated themselves against even greater ones. For example, in the small database of biographical information collected by Joan Bellamy et al. for approximately 150 women scholars and critics between 1790 and 1900, half included no information about education, and 'about a quarter of the total received their early education at home and about a quarter at school' (Postscript 222). In general, girls and women received little or no education, whether or not they had schooling. Of the minority of middle-class girls receiving secondary education at the end of the nineteenth century, 70 per cent still attended small private schools run by 'distressed' gentlewomen trying to make a bare living in their homes, and such schools often emphasised ladylike skills above all else (Purvis, *HWE* 76, 71–2).[16] As late as 1936, long after the 1902 Education Act and five years before Virginia Woolf's death, Barry Turner noted that the number of girls attending recognised secondary schools was not proportionate to the number of boys attending: 150 boys and 124 girls out of 10,000 of the respective male and female populations (177).[17] Changes, then, were slow.

Cross summarises conclusions based on Richard Altick's study of 1,100 British authors between 1800 and 1935, writing that only 20 per cent of the nineteenth-century women writers Altick could collect biographical details on

> had any formal schooling and less than 5 per cent received higher education and then mainly after 1870. In contrast an average of 63 per cent of male writers attended university and only 7 per cent received little or no schooling. (Cross 165)

While the women writers who left no biographical trail must temper any conclusions,[18] biographical paper trails for canonical English women writers before the twentieth century, popular women writers in the nineteenth century and women writers of Woolf's generation provide specific historical context for Virginia Woolf's education.

Among canonical English women writers before the modern period – Aphra Behn, Jane Austen, Fanny Burney, Charlotte and Emily Brontë, Mary Shelley, George Eliot, Elizabeth Barrett Browning and Christina Rossetti – most were educated at home, by family members or tutors. Many were encouraged by their fathers or brothers, though mothers occasionally played a strong role; many had access to a large, private library; and all took the initiative to study, read and write on their own. Reading, particularly out loud, was often important in these writers' families. Jane Austen did spend two years (age 7 and 9) at boarding schools, though Claire Tomalin's description of what happened there hardly merits the term 'schooling',[19] and Charlotte and Emily Brontë spent brief periods in two schools, one very poor, and then furthered their education at the Héger establishment in Brussels for a year. Only George Eliot was educated in boarding schools from age 5 on, and she had to leave the Misses Franklin's school (with its relatively broad academic curriculum) when her ill mother worsened (Robertson 6–7; L. M. Green x–xi). These canonical women writers, then, depended on their families' encouragement or permission for their education, and took full advantage of any opportunities they had.

Among popular nineteenth-century women writers – Ann Radcliffe, Harriet Martineau, Sara Coleridge, Elizabeth Gaskell, Margaret Oliphant, Sarah Grand, Mrs Humphry Ward and Beatrix Potter – half were educated entirely at home or on their own initiative and half received some formal education, though it was often brief and/or poor and supplemented with extensive reading undertaken on their own. Ann Radcliffe probably educated herself through circulating libraries (Norton 49), Margaret Oliphant had no formal education, Sara Coleridge educated herself in Robert Southey's library, and Beatrix Potter had governesses until she was 15. Harriet Martineau, Elizabeth Gaskell and Sarah Grand were all educated at home and in boarding schools of varying quality, and Mary Augusta Ward combined education at several boarding schools with voracious reading at the Bodleian Library in Oxford.

The educational background of twenty-five women writers of Virginia Woolf's generation,[20] from more diverse class and national backgrounds, with differing levels of popularity and writing in multiple fields for various audiences, understandably varied, with more attending day schools, boarding schools and/or university. Even so, five (20 per cent) were educated at least partially at home, generally until 12 or 14, and seven (28 per cent) were educated primarily or entirely at home. Almost half the writers of Woolf's decade, then, received substantial homeschooling. Seven (28 per cent) attended university for at least a year, with five (20 per cent) receiving a degree or its equivalent and four (16 per cent) having further education of another kind, such as a secretarial course or art school. Some had further studies through private instruction.

Although not comprehensive, these groups provide some comparative data. In the group of pre-modernist canonical women writers, almost all were primarily educated at home, with strong family support; schools were generally poor, and if the women attended school, they did not do so for long. In the group of popular nineteenth-century women writers, half were educated at home and half received some education beyond homeschooling; schools had improved but were still uneven in quality; and more of them attended school and for longer periods. Among Woolf's contemporaries, half still depended upon home education to a large degree; schools continued to improve, the potential for further education was added and formal education began to have influence. More of these writers received what we now call an education.

By Woolf's lifetime, then, although education for girls was more accepted and frequent and university education was possible, home education remained relatively common while university education was not yet so. Carol Dyhouse says women constituted only 16 per cent of the students in higher education institutions by 1900 (NDS 17), and Gillian Sutherland notes that as late as 1914, only 1 per cent of the appropriate age bracket, male or female, were attending universities ('Education' 157). Very few women, then, were gaining further education at the turn of the century and up until the Great War. Q. D. Leavis criticises Woolf for using her own education as typical in *Three Guineas* (273), but my research suggests Woolf was not far off. As Rosemary O'Day notes, even women who attended university sometimes began their education at home: 'As late as 1914, 21 per cent of female academics at Oxford and 8 per cent of female students at Oxford had been educated at home' (93). Queenie Leavis, born more than two decades later than Woolf, entered a vastly different educational landscape, confused potential access with equal opportunity (280–1 n5), and assumed *her* education was typical.[21] Certainly the first half of the twentieth century saw more rapid change in women's education than had occurred in the two centuries before. When Vera Brittain published *On Being an Author* in 1947, a university background for authors, including women, had become prevalent enough that she felt compelled to reassure readers that having to go to university to be a successful writer was a fantasy (7), and listed canonical male and female writers who had not been university educated, including Virginia Woolf. But Woolf's lack of formal education was still common in her generation, and Leavis's formal education was still uncommon in hers.

Also, Virginia Woolf's story allows us to glimpse the experience of women in prior centuries; reminds us our moment represents only a small portion of history and our Anglo-American culture occupies only a very small portion of the globe; shows us the advantages and disadvantages of homeschooling; and reflects the outsider experience everywhere: immigrants, refugees, those who are poor, homeless, imprisoned, oppressed, abused, disadvantaged, anyone trying to piece together an education in the face of obstacles.[22] Virginia Stephen, the daughter of privilege, urges us not to forget the difficulty at the heart of the educational pursuit for *anyone*.

Essayist

Virginia Woolf never saw herself as a critic, defining critics as those 'very rare writers who are able to enlighten us upon literature as an art', writers such as Coleridge, Dryden and Johnson who put forward 'qualities that group books together' and rules that bring 'order into our perceptions' (*E5* 581). She could not call herself a journalist, associating journalism with speed, ephemera and money (Whitworth 87–9). And although we now think of Eliot, Lawrence, Orwell and Woolf as the essayists of the modern age, with Andrew McNeillie claiming that Woolf 'was arguably the last of the great English essayists' (ix), she did not refer to herself as an essayist, either. She presented herself as a reader trying to piece together a flexible framework, open to constant revision, for reading and understanding literature. She practised her craft, revised seriously, and sometimes saw her essays approaching 'some kind of whole'. But she positions herself as a common reader (*E4* 19),[23] an amateur writing for other amateurs, both as a deeply felt response to the insecurity her lack of education provoked[24] and as a strategic move designed to gain a wider readership. She made and maintained that distinction between amateur and professional throughout her career, an identity that resulted in great differences between her persona and implied audience and those of her contemporaries.

Starting in the High Anglican *Guardian*'s women's supplement in 1904, Virginia Stephen launched her career through book reviews and essays, a strategy Leila Brosnan notes was common at the time, particularly for women (43). But long after Woolf's apprenticeship was over, long after she could have given up writing 'journalism', long after she could afford to focus solely on fiction, she continued to write book reviews and essays. Her non-fiction was neither just a source of income, nor just a rest from fiction. Indeed, her decision to keep writing essays long after the financial reasons for doing so were past, her care with individual essays, her creation of two collections of essays, her conscious experimentation with the form, particularly in her longer 'pamphlets', *A Room of One's Own* and *Three Guineas*, and her continued and detailed plans for writing non-fiction right up to her death all show her dedication to the genre.[25]

During her apprenticeship and beyond, her work was only one small portion of a huge journalistic and commercial enterprise that brought the public numerous reviewers and essayists weekly, monthly and quarterly. When Virginia Stephen began contributing to the *Guardian* in 1904 and other papers soon after, she entered a field where an older generation of writers such as A. C. Benson, 'one of England's most prolific, popular, and respected essayists' (K. Wilson 84), Edmund Gosse, Arnold Bennett, Alice Meynell, Max Beerbohm, John Galsworthy and Hilaire Belloc were frequent and influential participants. Virginia Stephen does not mention reading other reviewers and essayists in her early letters or diaries, except when she wrote to Violet Dickinson (before she had published anything), saying she thought she could 'write better stuff than that wretched article you sent me', presumably from the *Guardian* (*L1* 155), but that may be because she could not know names. She certainly implies, in 'The Decay of Essay-writing' (1905), that she was reading huge quantities of them. Montaigne and Lamb may have claimed her attention, but so did her contemporaries. Personal essays were everywhere, in all the papers, and many writers produced them quickly and regularly: 'its popularity with us is so immense and so peculiar that we are justified in looking upon it as something of our own' (*E1* 25). She knows the genre differs from others: 'The peculiar form of an essay implies a peculiar substance; you can say in this shape what you cannot with equal fitness say in any other,' and she names the difference: an essay is 'primarily an expression of personal opinion' (*E*1 25). Contemporary essayists are not too personal, she writes, but not personal enough; their egoism evades rather than honestly and courageously confronts the self (*E*1 26–7).

Woolf may have gravitated toward the essay because it allowed her to communicate both directly and anonymously,[26] but it also allowed her to wander, walk on the page as she did in London or the Downs, try out ideas, be personal, all traits she praised in Montaigne. Further, as Chris Anderson has argued, the essay is 'fundamentally democratic. It enfranchises both the reader and the writer' (303). I suspect Woolf chose the essay as her second major genre over the short story, poetry and drama partly because of its factual basis, partly because of family heritage (even Julia Stephen tried her hand at it), partly because it provided entry into the literary world, but mainly because of its pedagogical value, what Scholes and Klaus call its inherent persuasive quality, its attempt to tell the truth, its more direct relationship between author and reader (1–5). Woolf writes poetic fiction, dabbles in drama in *Freshwater* and *Between the Acts*, and composes intriguing short stories, but she uses the essay to represent her direct thoughts about literature, gender, class and reading, and thus share her education with others. She uses her essays' content, rhetoric and tone to enlarge literature's readership and put literature and the experimentation of modern authors, including hers, into context.[27]

Virginia Stephen Learning

When Virginia Woolf says in 'The Leaning Tower' there must be a connection between the education writers receive and their work, she also notes 'how little stress has been laid upon' that education (*E*6 265). Her insistence that we pay more attention to this link between education and work was the impetus for this study because although she makes these points within an argument about specific 1930s male poets, they also apply to her. When she claims the 1930s poets 'cannot throw away their education; they cannot throw away their upbringing', that their years at school 'have been stamped upon them indelibly' (*E*6 268), she could be talking about her own education, upbringing, lack of schooling. Woolf's remarks about her education make clear that Virginia Stephen's education was stamped upon her indelibly. Experiencing her education as isolated, gendered and fragmented, Woolf could not throw it away. Asserting her education was poor, saying working-class and upper-class men's educations were worse, and wondering what the best education for people might be (*L*6 420), she could not throw it away. Pondering class division and trying to reach various audiences, she could not throw it away. Virginia Stephen's education compelled Virginia Woolf to teach, and it marks nearly every essay she wrote.

This project, then, foregrounds Virginia Stephen's education to assert its crucial influence on Virginia Woolf's work as an essayist. Woolf's claim that writers' educations mark their work means, as she also claims, that writers are taught their art, just as painters, musicians and architects are, but she also notes that a writer's education is indefinite: 'Reading, listening, talking, travel, leisure – many different things it seems are mixed together' (*E6* 266). For her, a writer's education does not mean, and she did not receive, direct instruction in writing. What different things were mixed together in her writer's education? How was Virginia Woolf taught her art? All learning and teaching remain something of a mystery, of course, but here, I try to answer those questions. My study paradoxically aims to do what it cannot: define the indefinite and clarify the indirect in Virginia Stephen's training as a future essayist.

To that end, I have divided Virginia Stephen's apprenticeship into three components: her homeschooling, Morley College teaching, and early reviewing and essay writing. Such an organisation risks implying her education progresses through clear, chronological stages when the reality is more complex. From student, to teacher, to apprentice, pieces of her education overlap, accumulate, merge. She remains a student throughout; she becomes a teacher while continuing to learn at home and beginning to review; she becomes a teacher, then remains one, if only figuratively, for the rest of her life; she becomes a reviewer while teaching; and she remains a reviewer while becoming a novelist and essayist. My investigation into the education of girls and women, working classes, and writers provides wider historical, cultural and literary contexts for Stephen's apprenticeship, and in the resulting 'thick description', some 'lives of the obscure' emerge from the shadows.[28] Extensive archival and primary research allows me to expand and deepen Stephen's educational narrative, particularly about her homeschooling, teaching and first reviews and essays, and five appendices provide a wealth of additional material gleaned from that research. In each of the three parts that follow, I describe the wider historical context, discuss her teachers and lessons, examine her practice and identify outcomes. By and large, Virginia Stephen experienced gender's isolating impact on learning during her homeschooling and learned how she might create community through writing, she observed class's damaging impact on both teaching and learning at Morley College and learned how she might make classrooms more welcoming, and she grasped readers' generating impact on writing during her book-reviewing years and learned how she might develop essays based on a mutual writer/reader relationship. Using the historical and contextual to inform the biographical and critical, I argue that Virginia Stephen's struggle to educate herself between 1882 and 1912 – as a student in her parents' home, a teacher in a college for working-class adults and an apprentice writer in her first assignments – shaped Virginia Woolf into an essayist who believed 'literature is no one's private ground; literature is common ground' (*E6* 278).[29]

As essayist, Virginia Woolf would choose to invoke and address common readers, readers 'worse educated', '[h]asty, inaccurate and superficial', reading for pleasure and guided by instinct 'to create for [themselves], out of whatever odds and ends [they] can come by, some kind of whole' (*E4* 19).[30] Virginia Stephen's education shaped Virginia Woolf into an essayist who reached out to readers like herself. But by herself, I do not mean the public, well-read, highbrow intellectual of popular and iconic legend. No, I mean the lonely girl, mooning among books, longing for argument and conversation; the isolated girl, receiving bits and pieces of education and having to piece it together by herself; the insecure because self-educated girl, fearing her efforts will never win approval. That is why Woolf's essays encourage rather than hamper, foster rather than constrain, inspire rather than discourage.

To discover why and how Virginia Woolf's essays teach, then, we must go back to Virginia Stephen learning.[31]

Notes

1. See Aileen Pippett, John Lehmann and Mitchell Leaska, *Granite*.
2. See also Julia Briggs's use of the word 'mentor' to describe both Janet Case, one of Virginia Stephen's Greek tutors, and Mary Sheepshanks, the principal at Morley College (*IL* 89); and Whitworth's surprise at her decision to teach at Morley College, given 'the unsystematic and informal nature of her own education' (11–12).
3. Winifred Holtby suggests that Woolf's candour and her inability to be shocked came from having 'free rein' in her father's library (18) and that her love of truth came from her study of Plato and other Greeks (19). Both Lyndall Gordon and Holtby note Stephen's advantages, with Gordon saying she was 'born ... to the life of the mind' (69) and Holtby identifying some resulting cultural assumptions (24). Hermione Lee notices that during Virginia Stephen's fifteenth year, 'she developed her feelings about reading at random which would form the backbone of her essays on being a self-educated reader' (*VW* 141), but Lee is more interested in relating Stephen's childhood to Woolf's general traits: '[her] appetite for performance, her vulnerability to criticism and her passionate need for solitude and independence ... had their roots' in the Stephen 'communal, collaborative family life' (*VW* 111).
4. Both Gordon and Mepham discuss contextual background and influences, amplify Virginia Stephen's negotiation through her education as a female, and note the unusual length of her apprenticeship. Gordon relates the work Stephen did on English history for her Morley College students to the role English history would play in Woolf's work and discusses an early story, 'The Journal of Mistress Joan Martyn', as an example (86–8), and Mepham focuses on a 1909 essay to note Stephen's discovery of a kindred spirit in Laurence Sterne (21–2).
5. DeSalvo uses contemporary theory about abuse – its presence, concealment, effect – to read Woolf's life and work. Dalsimer employs the clinician's 'familiar rhythm' of moving backward and forward in time (xvi) to illustrate how, first, Virginia Stephen and then Virginia Woolf used writing as therapy for the repeated 'sledge-hammer blows' in her life.
6. See also Alice Fox's discussion of the Renaissance's power on Woolf's imagination and Perry Meisel's analysis of Walter Pater's shadowy presence in Woolf's work.
7. The following scholars, to name only a few, worked to complicate or refute the class-based rejection of Woolf: Gillian Beer, Naomi Black, Julia Briggs, Melba Cuddy-Keane, Mark Hussey, Karen Levenback, Jane Marcus, Merry Pawlowski and Michael Tratner. John Carey and Tom Paulin attacked Woolf and any scholars who admired her work. Sean Latham and Jonathan Rose offer a more nuanced class critique.
8. These comments appear in a much-worked-on draft, revelations Woolf omitted in the letter she sent Ben; see *L6* 421–2. In publishing and describing this draft (*L6* 419 n1), Nicolson and Trautmann testified to its importance.
9. This total includes the extended essays, *A Room of One's Own* and *Three Guineas*, and the variant versions that differ markedly, broadcast and talk transcripts, and published drafts that appear in the *Essays*. By my count, Virginia Stephen published 158 reviews and essays as an apprentice, and Virginia Woolf wrote and published 500 more.
10. DeSalvo's claim that 'Virginia Woolf was a significant, if often overlooked, contributor to both the history and the philosophy of education, with significant ideas about

pedagogy and curriculum' (*VW* 300), prompted this study's research path, as did Rose's emphasis on Stephen's outsider sense and its effect on Woolf's essays. Cuddy-Keane's convincing case for the 'pedagogical and empowering' impact of Woolf's essays (*VW* 1) and her insistence on Woolf's role in a sphere that 'involve[d] public debates about books, reading, and education' (*VW* 8) animates all my work here.

11. Cultural criticism and New Historicism have grappled with Virginia Woolf's epigraph questions by placing modernist authors in plural historical and cultural contexts, enriching the history and definition of modernism, and combining the formal and biographical in new ways. This redefining impulse and its interdisciplinary energy within modernist and Woolf studies has led to ground-breaking studies such as Melba Cuddy-Keane's *Virginia Woolf, the Intellectual, and the Public Sphere*, Anne Fernald's *Virginia Woolf: Feminism and the Reader*, Susan Stanford Friedman's *Mappings: Feminism and the Cultural Geographies of Encounter*, Christine Froula's *Virginia Woolf and the Bloomsbury Avant-Garde*, Jane Goldman's *The Feminist Aesthetics of Virginia Woolf*, Bonnie Kime Scott's *The Gender of Modernism* and *Gender in Modernism*, and Anna Snaith's *Virginia Woolf: Public and Private Negotiations*. These literary critics thoughtfully use biography, history and culture to illuminate literature, complicate our reception of it and revise our perceptions of Virginia Woolf and her work.

12. Because I am examining Stephen's apprenticeship through an educational lens, the word 'outcome' seems suitable, though in its broad sense, not in its narrow, test-driven, quantifiable one.

13. In my follow-up book, I thoroughly examine the impact of Stephen's education on Woolf's essays, essays that teach genre, literature and education.

14. See Ian Copeland, Pamela Horn, J. S. Hurt, June Purvis (*HL*), Frank Smith, Annmarie Turnbull and David Wardle.

15. See Laura Morgan Green's *Educating Women* for a particularly good description of this tension (1–23). But also see M. C. Borer, Margaret Bryant, Joan Burstyn (*VE*), Rosemary Deem, Sara Delamont ('Contradictions'; 'Domestic'), Carol Dyhouse ('Good Wives'; '"Feminine" Curriculum'), Felicity Hunt, Josephine Kamm and Jane Martin.

16. Turner says, 'Between 1897 and 1902 the number of girls educated in recognized schools increased from 20,000 to 185,000'; recognised schools received support from local authorities. By 1914, he notes, 'the total exceeded half a million' (176). See also Vicinus, *Independent Women*, Chapter 5.

17. See Sue Bruley 198 n39: 'J. Gillot (1968) quotes LEA [London Education Authority] grammar schools as spending 12s 6d for every boy and 8s for every girl in 1959, p. 32.'

18. Nigel Cross explains how many persistent writers were made invisible because they did not 'rate an index entry' in someone else's biography or autobiography and then were not included in standard biographical reference works (1–7). He also vividly illustrates why Woolf believed (in *AROO* and 'The Leaning Tower', for example) that most authors came from the middle class – the biographical paper trail for working-class writers is still difficult to find. Cross uses the archive of the Royal Literary Fund, which gave money to needy authors, so has a larger sample for his study of the common writer, but he does not focus on education. See also Altick, 'Sociology', 100.

19. Jane Austen nearly died from the infectious fever she caught at Mrs Cawley's school; the school she attended at age nine, Madame La Tournelle's Abbey School, barely had lessons of any kind (Tomalin 37, 42–3).

20. Daisy Ashford (1881–1972); Enid Bagnold (1889–1981); Ann Bridge (1889–1974); Ivy Compton-Burnett (1884–1969); Frances Cornford (1886–1960); Clemence Dane (1888–1965); Ethel M. Dell (1881–1939); Eleanor Farjeon (1881–1965); Radclyffe

Hall (1880–1943); Constance Holme (1880–1955); Naomi Jacob (1884–1964); F. Tennyson Jesse (1888–1958); Sheila Kaye-Smith (1887–1956); Mina Loy (1882–1966); Rose Macaulay (1881–1958); Katherine Mansfield (1888–1923); Sylvia Pankhurst (1882–1960); Berta Ruck (1878–1978); Edith Sitwell (1887–1964); Marie Stopes (1880–1958); Alison Uttley (1884–1976); Helen Waddell (1889–1965); Mary Webb (1881–1927); Antonia White (1889–1980); Anna Wickham (1884–1947). This group of writers comes from Janet Todd's edition of *British Women Writers: A Critical Reference Guide*; I added Mina Loy and Berta Ruck. *The Bloomsbury Guide to Women's Literature*, edited by Claire Buck; *The Oxford Guide to British Women Writers*, edited by Joanne Shattock; *The Feminist Companion to Literature in English: Women Writers from the Middle Ages to the Present*, edited by Virginia Blain, Isobel Grundy and Patricia Clements; and *The Oxford Companion to English Literature*, edited by Margaret Drabble, provided the information about writers' educations I base my statistics on.

21. Briggs sees the 'impulse to explain to a younger generation how women's lives had changed during [her] lifetime' as the impetus for *The Years* (IL 294), and such a drive explains Woolf's use of past obstacles in *Three Guineas* as well. As Briggs recognises, Woolf realised women had sustained 'many losses' (IL 294). Victoria Stewart notes that Q. D. Leavis thought women's education should be the same as men's, and women must come up to the mark men set (68, 70). In her *Three Guineas* review, Leavis cites others to suggest that women bear the responsibility for their own lack of advantages: exceptional women students are rare; outstanding women students cannot find 'congenial intellectual company' among their peers; and women students 'make themselves a nuisance' (278–9).

22. See Azar Nafisi's *Reading Lolita in Tehran* and Mary Childers's *Welfare Brat*, for example.

23. Briggs notes that in 'Byron and Mr Briggs', a 1922 essay Woolf never revised for publication, she invents Tom Briggs, a maker of spectacles (gig lamps!) and an avid common reader (RVW 73–4). In that essay, Woolf refers to herself as a reviewer, and claims reviewers are descended from common readers like Briggs: 'The genealogists may dispute this claim; but if one has waited for three weeks to get Byrons letters from the Library, then, according to my definition, one is a grandchild of Briggs' (E3 479–80). Briggs comments that Woolf wanted *The Common Reader* to 'provide an account of the reading process while unobtrusively introducing its readers to a wider canon' (RVW 71).

24. Even in the face of all evidence to the contrary. As Fernald notes, Woolf was 'one of the best-read writers in the history of English literature' (*Feminism* 1).

25. She made her *Common Readers* coherent books by revising old essays and writing new ones (see Johnston and also my 'VW Teaching'); produced two long non-fiction texts; wrote a full-length biography of Roger Fry; and put her essays under the same scrutiny as her fiction, often revising them, as Leonard Woolf recounts in his *Death of the Moth* editorial note, 'eight or nine times' (7). At the end of her life, she had begun her autobiography, had plans for a third book of essays, perhaps the 'Common History book' she conceived while blackberrying (D5 318), and had started a literary history called *Reading at Random* (later *Turning the Page*) that included drafts of two chapters: 'Anon', about the move from communal oral to individual written expression, and 'The Reader' (E6 580–607).

26. See Dubino on one of many unresolved paradoxes in Woolf: 'the essay as self-advertisement vs. self-expression' ('Politics' 57–85).

27. Briggs comments,
    > Woolf had grown up with the view that literature should be accessible – the great Victorians had all reached a large reading public: its extent had been one measure of their success. That ideal was reflected in the title and some of the aims of *The Common Reader* . . . . (IL 119)

28. Clifford Geertz's development of this method for his ethnographical work underlies early New Historical criticism and perhaps most nearly describes what I attempt here. Moreover, Virginia Woolf practises 'thick description' in her focus on the 'lives of the obscure'.
29. For Arnold Weinstein, literature 'discovers for us who we are' (xii), moves us into 'our story, ourselves' (19).
30. The term 'common reader' is contested. See Pat Collier in his Woolf chapter in *Modernism on Fleet Street*. But Cuddy-Keane's argument persuades: Woolf attempts to invoke a reader whose openness, questioning and intelligence exist outside of class, somewhere between the binary oppositions used in her time (and ours) (*VW* 117–19). Besides, Woolf's conscious use of the term and attempt to reach such a reader does distinguish her from many other moderns.
31. In *Virginia Woolf's Essays: Being a Teacher*, I analyse the impact of Stephen's apprenticeship on Woolf as an educator essayist, examine the philosophy, curriculum and pedagogy of the essays in Woolf's essay canon, and discuss the influence of Woolf's pedagogy on contemporary readers and teachers.

Part I

Student, 1882–1904: Learning at Home

> It is perhaps because a writer's education is so much less definite than other educations. Reading, listening, talking, travel, leisure – many different things it seems are mixed together. Life and books must be shaken and taken in the right proportions.
> – 'The Leaning Tower' (E6 265–6)

When students walk into a school, they walk into a context providing structure and support: space divided into buildings and rooms; time divided into smaller units; curriculum naming or implying cultural values and knowledge divided into courses; pedagogy assuming how learning occurs; lessons about agreed-upon topics; and community. Teachers have training and credentials, are assigned to phases in student development, have an overall rationale and goals, and work to create learning situations.

But Virginia Stephen went to school at 22 Hyde Park Gate.[1] There, she absorbed lessons from teachers generally untrained in a discipline or pedagogy, navigated between two positions on education for girls and constructed much of the curriculum and assignments on her own. All students piece together their educations, but Stephen, isolated and coping with fractured instruction,[2] had to work harder to make lessons cohere. But learn her lessons she did.

Virginia Stephen's school at 22 Hyde Park Gate provided context and curricula, reflected pedagogies and represented communities. It provided many teachers in addition to her father, some within the home, some coming in, and some outside. Her primary instructors – Leslie and Julia Stephen; her brother, Thoby; her aunt, Anne Thackeray Ritchie; newspapers; libraries; King's College teachers; and Janet Case, her tutor – all helped educate the girl who became Virginia Woolf. As a student at 22 Hyde Park Gate, Virginia Stephen pieced together various curricula, pedagogies, lessons and communities, mixed 'many different things' together, and learned, above all else, how to create community in and through writing.

Education for Girls and Women

Virginia Stephen had a complex educational inheritance, one that shaped Virginia Woolf into an essayist compelled to leave an educational legacy. Born in 1882 to a father 50 years old and a mother in her second childbearing round, she grew up not in a late-Victorian atmosphere of values, attitudes and behaviours, but in a mid-Victorian one ('Sketch' 147; Gordon 23).³ Decades of tradition and conventional wisdom had shaped the family into which she was born, and beliefs about educating girls and women were far from settled or stable before or during her lifetime. Plus, Leslie and Julia Stephen acted out opposing positions in the nineteenth-century debates about girls' education, greatly affecting their daughters. This context forged Virginia Stephen's education and Virginia Woolf's later attitudes to it.⁴

Although Virginia Woolf's private comments about her education contain relief at not being subjected to what her male relatives were ('Sketch' 146; ['VW & *Euphrosyne*'], QB1 205)⁵ and awareness their education was bad (*L6* 420; 'Sketch' 153), she resented their having a formal education and the informal education she knew accompanied it. Twenty-one and writing to her brother Thoby at Cambridge, she says, 'I have to delve from books, painfully and all alone, what you get every evening sitting over your fire and smoking your pipe with Strachey etc' (*L1* 77). When *The Common Reader* appears, she worries about what university don G. Lowes Dickinson will think because 'I have so little education' (*L3* 182). Writing to Vita Sackville-West, she agrees she lacks 'jolly vulgarity', but then explains why: 'No school; mooning about alone among my father's books; never any chance to pick up all that goes on in schools – throwing balls; ragging; slang; vulgarity; scenes; jealousies' (*L3* 247). In her memoir, she writes that partly because she was never at school and 'never competed' with children her own age, she could not 'compare [her] gifts and defects with other people's' ('Sketch' 65). Near the end of her life, she says her education '(alone among books) was a very bad one' (*L6* 420).

Most disturbing in its pain, however, is Woolf's confession in the draft for remarks made to schoolgirls in January 1926, remarks that became 'How Should One Read a Book?'. Even after the success of *Mrs Dalloway* and *The Common Reader* and in the midst of writing *To the Lighthouse*, she expresses shame in the face of girls' achievements at Hayes Court School: 'In the first place I am going to confess a crime – not my own doing however – I have never been to school' ('an awful' is inserted above 'not my'; 'How Should' MS 179; Daugherty, 'VW's "How Should"' 138).⁶ The sentence's syntax and language capture being a criminal, with guilt at committing a sin that requires confession; being the victim of a crime; and naming the crime: never having been to school. The reader grasps the enormity of that exclusion in Woolf's heart and mind; it felt like 'an awful' crime to her, and it feels like an awful crime to us.

Why *didn't* the gifted Virginia Stephen go to school? True, education for girls at nineteenth century's end was not systematic or widespread. Jane McDermid writes, 'At least until the First World War, the majority of girls in Britain received a crucial part of their education in the home' (107), and Sally Mitchell notes that in 1900, 'there were only 20,000 English girls at recognized grammar schools' ('Children's Reading' 62; see also Vicinus, *IW* 333 n6). But it was not unheard of, either, particularly for girls of Stephen's class. North London Collegiate School and Cheltenham were well established and run by Frances Buss and Dorothea Beale, and young women had been attending Cambridge University since 1869. Perhaps her health served as an excuse (Annan 120), but Leslie Stephen knew Cambridge and his rowing coach years had turned a delicate, sickly, nervous youth into an Alpine climber and a walker famous for distance and endurance (Annan 24–34).⁷

No, Julia Stephen's view about educating girls prevailed over Leslie Stephen's more radical ideas. Noel Annan says 'a ding-dong debate' about the girls' education 'reverberated through [the] household' for years (119; see also Reid 37). Their debate, reflecting their century's, began with a courtship letter exchange. In July 1877, Leslie's daughter, Laura, was 7 years old and Julia's children, George, Stella and Gerald, were 9, 8 and 7. Responding to Julia, who asked him to outline his ideas on women's education, Leslie writes he thinks that

> women ought to be as well educated as men, indeed a very great deal better than men are now. ... Laura ... ought to learn something thoroughly when she grows up, thoroughly enough to be able to make her living at it, if it is of the paying kind, as to be an authority on it, if it is not. (*SLLS1* 214)⁸

Julia replies she does not see how he can care for her, then, because 'you have no idea how utterly uneducated I am' (L. Stephen, *MBN* III 80);⁹ he has, as Jean O. Love notes, 'described an ideal so unlike her actual education' that she 'feel[s] all the more inferior to him'.¹⁰ Julia also comments that even women with particular talents 'were pushed into a different groove and never fit' (*MBN* III 80), suggesting a bitter personal experience (Love 60). Perhaps her desire that Stella 'have many interests in life' (*SLLS1* 215) stemmed from a belief that formal education set a woman up for disappointment. Julia also seems to have thought of Stella as '"part of [her]self"' ('Sketch' 96), expecting her to dedicate herself to a life of service in which women discover 'the highest expression of [their] nature' (['Domestic Arrangements'] 254). In his reply, reassuring her about his feelings, Leslie repeats his belief that a daughter who develops a taste for something

> should go to the best teachers & cultivate it thoroughly, as if she meant to make a profession of it & not a mere amusement. . . . The only real advantage of a man's education is that he learns something professionally instead of being an amateur in everything. And what I want for Laura is that she should have the same sort of advantage in case of need. (*SLLS1* 215).¹¹

He thus reinforces his argument's economic component.

Their liberal and conservative positions were not always consistent. Leslie supported the Girls' Public Day Schools Company (Strachey 247), was friends with Henry Fawcett and Henry Sidgwick, who were associated with Newnham College at Cambridge, and believed in education for women; his niece, Katherine Stephen, was Principal of Newnham (Annan 119). Yet, writing to Thoby in 1897, he could not be bothered to travel to Cambridge to vote for the proposal that women passing a Tripos examination be granted titular degrees: 'I shall not go, because I dont much care . . .' (*SLLS2* 478). As Woolf perceived in 1932, 'he cared little enough for the higher education of women' (*E5* 588). His young daughter noticed, too, when he snubbed Katherine Stephen at lunch 'for presuming to be an intellectual' (Gordon 74; *PA* 48).

Julia signed the 'Appeal Against Female Suffrage' in 1889, but 'never belittled her own works, thinking them, if properly discharged, of equal, though other, importance with her husband's ('Sketch' 37).¹² She also passionately argued for a woman's right to equality in religious belief: 'We will not concede that when a man chooses or rejects a faith from conviction, a woman does so from a desire to please' (['Agnostic Women'] 247). Moreover, although without training, Julia took her nursing duties seriously and performed them professionally. As Diane Gillespie puts it, 'Julia Stephen combined the traditional ideal ... of service to others with the kind of professionalism and independence of mind we associate with less conventional women' ('Elusive' 25–7). Pat Thane would put her among the many middle-class Victorian women who turned to volunteering in the absence of paid employment, seeing their philanthropy as 'a long-term commitment, akin to a profession in the seriousness with which it was undertaken and in the skills required and acquired' (190).[13]

The debate between Leslie and Julia about their daughters' education, with Leslie thinking women should receive the same (or better) education as men and become professionals in a chosen field and Julia thinking they should receive a different education suited for women and 'professionalize their own sphere' (Burstyn, *VE* 21), mirrored England's debate about the education of girls and women, ongoing for at least a century.[14] Mary Wollstonecraft, attacking 'accomplishments' education in 1792, called for women to be educated as men were in the use of reason, and thought such an education would make women economically independent – Leslie's position. (She also added they would be better mothers.) Hannah More, as Olive Banks notes, also critiqued 'the frivolity characteristic of girls' education in the middle and upper classes', but thought they should receive an education 'that would better enable them to fulfil their customary duties as wives and mothers and as guardians of the traditional religious virtues' (39) – Julia's position, though with religious overtones.[15]

When Leslie Stephen married Julia Duckworth in 1878, then, the cultural debate was no longer about *whether* girls should be educated, though the entry of women into higher education had led to medical studies 'proving' that '[c]ontinuous mental effort was a danger to young women' (Burstyn, 'Education' 85; see also Marks 188–9),[16] and Victorians remained 'highly ambivalent' about formal education's value for girls (Dyhouse, '"Feminine" Curriculum' 298).[17] Rather, the cultural debate had shifted to *how* girls should be educated, partly because feminists had succeeded in persuading the Taunton Commission to include girls' education in its 1864 inquiry.[18] The nineteenth-century debate about girls' education was tangled up in class, religion, suffrage and women's employment, but also in and of itself complex. It occurred between feminists who agreed girls should be educated, who knew the Victorian domestic ideology of separate public and private spheres still framed the debate.[19] Should girls receive the same education as boys did? Or a different one? That, basically, was the argument between Miss Buss and Miss Beale, between Emily Davies and Anne Clough, between non-compromising and separatist feminists.[20]

Frances Buss, North London Collegiate School headmistress, and Emily Davies, Girton College founder, represented the non-compromising position. Non-compromisers believed education should not be determined by biological or social differences between the sexes. They thought the traditional curriculum flawed but believed the only way to legitimise education for girls and women was to show they could do exactly what boys and men did. They feared special or different courses would be regarded as inferior (Strachey 143) and lead to discrimination and an intellectual ghetto (Delamont, 'Contradictions' 154); as both Deborah Gorham and Felicity Hunt note, reading lists and curricula designed for girls and women were often clearly used to reinforce women's social role (39–59; 18–21). They also believed such a strategy would not, in fact, lead to curricular reform. Thus, they insisted on the same standards, curricula, exams and even timetable that boys and men had to meet.

Dorothea Beale, Cheltenham headmistress, and Newnham College's Anne Clough, and Henry and Nora Sidgwick, represented the separatist position. Separatists thought education should widen girls' intellectual interests and thus prepare them to be better wives, mothers and companions. Beale disliked competition and its effects, and Clough and the Sidgwicks believed higher education needed reform, so they attacked the dominance of the classic languages and mathematics in the male curriculum and called for the inclusion of the sciences, social sciences, modern languages and English literature. They believed women's entry into higher education could help them achieve such reform. Thus, this group called for modified courses, standards, curricula and exams for girls and women (Marks 185–7; Delamont, 'Contradictions' 154–8).[21]

Non-compromisers presented education as necessary for life and followed the male curriculum closely, but couched their call for equal female education in careful terms and were obsessive about female propriety. Given the reaction to curricula at girls' and women's schools – educated women would decrease the birth rate and thus threaten the British Empire; girls were cracking under the strain of studying and competing in exams; educated women would be contaminated by the public world and, in turn, contaminate the home (Marks 187–9) – such caution was warranted. Separatists presented education as necessary for women's future as 'teachers, nurses and mothers' (Delamont, 'Contradictions' 154) and largely kept the male curriculum, but also inserted courses for a domestic future: cookery, needlework, child care.[22] Both groups presented education as something that would not 'unsex' women (Delamont, 'Contradictions' 141–52). Even now, education historians mirror the earlier debate: Delamont says those who 'held out for equal educational standards and curricula were correct to do so' because separate is never equal ('Contradictions' 159), and Turner says if feminists had joined forces and 'stuck to their own line rather than accept what amounted to male leadership', they might have reformed 'the entire structure and content of higher education' (167–8).[23]

When Virginia Stephen was born in 1882, this argument was culturally entrenched, and whether girls should receive the same education as boys or a different one was embodied in the tension between Leslie and Julia. On the one hand, in traditional fashion, the boys went to public school and then to university, and the girls were educated chiefly at home.[24] Thus, Woolf's anger about 'Arthur's Education Fund' and her claim that her father spent maybe £100 (or perhaps as much as £150) on her education (*TG* 4–5, 145; *L6* 419; *L6* 467). Yet, not so traditionally, Virginia and Vanessa were encouraged to pursue their interests in literature and art, and to give Leslie credit, this encouragement increased after Julia's death. Thus, Woolf's gratitude for the freedom she enjoyed and her recognition that her father taught her to think for herself rather than 'impose his own views or parade his own knowledge' (E5 589). Though he had strict standards of behaviour – he thought smoking was not 'a nice habit in the other sex' – he allowed his daughters the same liberty as his sons to 'follow whatever profession they chose' as long as they took their work seriously. Woolf judged this kind of freedom, the 'right to think one's own thoughts and to follow one's own pursuits, ... worth thousands of cigarettes' (E5 588).[25]

When it came to the Stephen daughters' early education, Julia's conservative views won over Leslie's progressive ones,[26] but their underlying disagreement permeates their classrooms, curricula and pedagogies. Virginia Stephen thus received an education simultaneously suited to her profession and aligned against it. That tension haunts Woolf's critique of women's education in *A Room of One's Own* and *Three Guineas*, leading to some views that seem contradictory.[27]

Notes

1. My discussion goes beyond the home and 1904, supporting my assertion that Virginia Stephen's education does not occur in discrete stages. But Stephen's home base remains 22 Hyde Park Gate until 1904, and the teachers discussed in Part I do most of their work before then.
2. DeSalvo describes Virginia Stephen's loneliness in '1897' (80, 90), writing

    > Deprived of school and of the companionship of peers, [she] had nothing against which to judge herself other than the measure of her family, no way to determine where she stood in relation to young women her own age in terms of social, intellectual, and emotional growth, no mirror outside the family that could reflect a less distorted image of herself and her feelings, no companion who could share that she too experienced rages, disappointments, griefs, and fears. (82)

3. See Geoffrey Best on mid-Victorian contexts such as housing, transport, work, leisure, education, class and crime.
4. Queenie Leavis castigates Woolf for not acknowledging changes in women's higher education in *Three Guineas*, but misses several points: Woolf's father was born in 1832, not 1862; having doors open does not mean one can go through them; Woolf was not alone in being prevented from taking advantage of the few opportunities available to her; and the opportunities for women of her class, let alone women in other classes, had not been (and were still not) equal to the opportunities men in her class had. See Viola Klein 266–7 and Sutherland, 'Education' 157. Leavis does not acknowledge how small the university-attending population was, how even smaller the university-attending female population was or how recently the changes and opportunities she mentions had occurred.
5. In ['Virginia Woolf and the Authors of *Euphrosyne*'], she says being educated at home preserves the sister 'from the omniscience, the early satiety, the melancholy self satisfaction which a training at either of our great universities produces in her brothers' (QB1 205).
6. *Woolf Studies Annual* (2010) used this comment to advertise Christine Kenyon Jones and Anna Snaith's article about Virginia Stephen's attendance at more King's College London classes than previously realised. But Woolf's audience for the talk, Hayes Court School students, means she regretted not attending a secondary school.
7. See Louise DeSalvo, '1897' 81 and Hill, 'History' 352 for similarities between Leslie and Virginia Stephen's childhoods.

8. See also *MBN* III 78–83. Leslie's view of education anticipates Woolf's as stated in a letter to G. L. Dickinson after his response to *A Room of One's Own*. She writes, 'I don't believe, though I'm a complete outsider, that its right for either sex as it is' (*L4* 106). See Annan, 34–47, for Leslie Stephen's attempts to reform Cambridge and why such reforms were difficult.
9. Woolf says Little Holland House was Julia's education, where she was taught to 'take such part as girls did then in the lives of distinguished men; to pour out tea; to hand them their strawberries and cream; to listen devoutly, reverently to their wisdom . . .' ('Sketch' 88). (See Herta Engelman dissertation and Joan Perkin for Julia's poor educational context.)
10. Love also says Julia 'deplored her limited formal education', but did not seem to have worried about her daughters being limited in the same way (60). Love's extensive use of correspondence between and among Jackson, Stephen and Woolf family members and friends, located in the Berg Collection, King's College, Cambridge, the British Library and Sussex University, continue to make her biography useful.
    Helping Fred Maitland write his Leslie Stephen biography, Virginia would have learned her parents' views when she read her father's Calendar of Correspondence, now in *MBN* III.
11. Leslie Stephen's wording, '*as if* she meant to make a profession of it', reveals reality: women could not, in fact, make a profession out of their interests. See Philippa Levine's *The Amateur and the Professional* for a nuanced discussion of the terms 'amateur' and 'professional' during the Victorian Age and T. R. Gourvish for an explanation of the difficulty of defining and counting professionals and a detailed look at the 'emergence of a substantial and powerful professional group' (13). See also Ian Small's discussion of the attributes ('manliness', 'freshness', 'health') and binaries established as criteria for literature when its study began to be institutionalised in the 1880s: '"serious/trivial"; "professional/amateur"; "manly/effeminate"; "healthy/ sick"' (140). Woolf would later work to position herself as an amateur within her essays; at the same time, she was clearly a professional writer.
12. The anti-suffrage position was more complex than commonly supposed, and did not see itself as anti-woman. See Brian Harrison.
13. Thane adds that in 1893, 'around 500,000 women worked "continuously and semi-professionally" in voluntary activities' (190). Noting that such volunteer work required 'courage and resilience', she also reminds us that even with servants, running a complex household 'amid the dirt and pollution of a late Victorian town or city' was 'no trivial task' (189–90).
14. For further histories of female education, see Dyhouse (*Girls Growing Up*); in Digby and Searby, 'The Education of Girls', in *Children* (45–52); Martha Vicinus, *IW*, Chapters 4 and 5; and Elizabeth Eschbach. For primary materials, see Janet Murray, Part III ('Woman's Mind') in *Strong-Minded*, 193–255, and Digby and Searby, 'Documents IV', in *Children* (196–250).
15. Kimberly Palmer, reviewing Lyndall Gordon's Wollstonecraft biography, notes Gordon's distinction between More and Wollstonecraft: More 'believed in suppressing a "bold, independent, enterprising spirit" in girls', whereas 'Wollstonecraft recognised that it was through such misteaching that "daughters" internalized their subjection' (30).
16. Dr Seton's remedy of rest, a garden and no lessons for Virginia Stephen in 1897 and rest, quiet, exile from London and no writing (except for her father's biographical note) in 1904 reflected the cultural belief that intellectual activity was harmful to girls and women. (See Burstyn, 'Education and Sex', for how scientific research was used to support this powerful belief.)
17. They remained ambivalent about education generally. As Sutherland notes, between 1850 and 1914, the government began providing education at all levels, but only after

much debate: 'Half a century after the rest of Western Europe, England at last took to system-building in education' ('Education' 141). State secondary schools were not formed until 1902, Andy Green points out, 'one hundred years after their inauguration in France and Prussia', making England 'the last of the major nineteenth-century powers to create a national system of education and the most reluctant to put it under public control' (209, 208).

18. See Reimer, 'Worlds' 203, for the excitement caused when eight women gave evidence as expert witnesses before the Commission, a first, and the damning summary description of girls' schools in the Commission report. The reformers had observed, Reimer writes, that when 'boys moved from the largely rote learning of fundamentals to the examination of underlying principles, girls typically were set lessons to memorize or diverted into domestic duties, religious devotion, and the acquisition of accomplishments' (202).
19. See Carol Sotiropoulos for how this framework shaped earlier European education debates.
20. See Dyhouse ('Buss and Beale'); see Lucy Bland on various feminisms.
21. Reba Soffer argues the two women's colleges differed very little since Newnham did not develop 'education for women as women', but instead 'deliberately adopted the dominant [male] university culture of civic, national and imperial responsibility' (193). Sutherland, however, in 'Girton', 'Clough' and 'Davies', argues the two institutions fundamentally differed on 'how to construe equality for women' ('Davies' 37). She claims Newnham did consider 'the practical reality of many women's lives and resources in the period' ('Davies' 38).
22. In her 'How Should One Read a Book?' draft, Woolf mentions the girls can mend their own clothes ('How Should' MS 179; Daugherty, 'VW's "How Should"' 138).
23. See L. M Green, Joyce Pedersen's work and Sotiropoulos on the quarrel's complexity.
24. The Stephens argued about Thoby's education, too, with Leslie not wanting to send him away to boarding school (his own public-school experiences had been dreadful [Hill, 'History' 353; Maitland 337]), and Julia thinking he should go. As Love details, Thoby started at Evelyns in January 1891 after Julia again won the argument: she 'decided unilaterally that Thoby should go away to school and persisted in arranging for his departure in the face of Leslie's adamant and poorly reasoned objections' (157).

    J. R. de S. Honey explains the 'transfer of function' from parents to public schools in the Victorian Age and articulates the conflict within public schools between problems (disease, immorality and cruelty) and the value of manliness ('Tom' 20–3), thus explaining both Leslie Stephen's resistance to Thoby's going away to school and his eventual capitulation.
25. Love points out, though, Leslie did not want Thoby to follow his own path and study mathematics at Cambridge or become a writer since writing was a 'womanly thing', more in Virginia's line (156). See also Hill, 'History' 351–2, who quotes a letter not included in Bicknell's edition: 'I don't want him to be an author. That is a thing for ladies and Ginia will do well in that line.'
26. He moved into her house, after all, when they married (Gillespie, 'Elusive' 17), a dark house with black woodwork and Virginia creeper covering the windows ('Sketch' 117; '22 HPG' 164). As Jenni Calder writes,

    > The Victorian interior became increasingly burdened and enclosed. Thick carpets and heavy curtains were in dark colours, net curtains and leafy plants at the windows obscured the light, dark wood was preferred, mahogany in particular, and furniture became heavier, more solid, more ornamented, and sometimes, but not always, more comfortable. (33)

    See also Judith Flanders and Julia Prewitt Brown.
27. Patrick McGee teases out the subtleties in these supposed contradictions, which he names ambivalence, and sees them as Woolf's attempts to represent the Other

and present the unpresentable (229–30). He argues that Woolf 'never essentializes women's writing: she historicizes it', thus forcing 'those of us who write within the university to think and recognize the historical *outside*, the tradition and memory of what has been excluded from its foundation' (234, emphasis in original).

Chapter 1

Learning at 22 Hyde Park Gate

Teachers

Leslie and Julia Stephen were impatient and demanding teachers (QB1 26; Annan 104). Leslie once frightened the 4-year-old Thoby by 'jokingly threatening' to make him read a list of names' (Love 155). Vanessa Bell recalled her mother did not teach them Latin, French and history very well and that it was a relief 'when for a short time she went abroad with my father and we had a harmless, ordinary, little governess. It is much too nerve-racking to be taught by one's parents' (61). Stephen remembers Julia 'took it on herself to teach us our lessons, and thus established a very close and rather trying relationship, for she was of a quick temper, and least of all inclined to spare her children' ('Reminiscences' 38–9). Also, Julia often interrupted her children's basic education with her nursing or by sending them to Maria Jackson, their grandmother, in Brighton (Reid 20–4).

At 22 Hyde Park Gate, the dining-room table was the formal classroom, whereas Leslie's informal evening readings were in the drawing room.[1] But the two most important classrooms were Leslie Stephen's library and Julia Stephen's tea table, reflecting their education debate.

Leslie Stephen's Library

Leslie's library was the private study of a man of letters, but he allowed his daughter access and borrowing privileges. Walking into it, Virginia Stephen entered a space that named a curriculum, reflected a pedagogy, taught lessons and introduced a community. The room was large, with 'three long windows at the top of the house' (E5 585), making it more light-filled than the rest of the building. It was 'entirely booklined' ('Sketch' 119), but some system probably existed since in Woolf's memories, Leslie easily finds and replaces books for her. Books were also scattered around Leslie's low rocking chair, where he reclined, smoked his pipes ('Sketch' 112), rocked and wrote: 'The thud of a book dropped on the floor could be heard in the room beneath' (E5 585). According to Woolf, 'His old rocking chair ... was the centre of the room which was the brain of the house' ('Sketch' 119). Rarely disturbed there, reading and writing for at least two or three hours a day even near the end of his life (Maitland 485), he demonstrated daily the advantages of having a room of one's own. To a girl whose 'back room' could be entered at any time by anybody ('Sketch' 123–4), who read everywhere in the house and was delighted to have 'handed over' a sun-filled back room that, although 'almost entirely made of glass', was somewhat private for reading (VB 63–4), Leslie Stephen's library may have seemed a haven. The library's mere presence communicated respect for reading and writing, represented privacy and safety, and, in Leslie's use of it, unpretentiousness and seriousness.

As J. J. Wilson said of the Library of Leonard and Virginia Woolf, 'the books on our shelves do characterize us' (6), and Leslie's library books reflect the man, his interests and the curriculum Virginia studied.[2] Perhaps the Stephen tradition of giving advice about reading started[3] with Leslie's father, Sir James, whose essay 'On Desultory and Systematic Reading' appears in a collection of various lectures delivered to the YMCA in 1854 (K&M-V 251). In volume 6 of *The Correspondence of Samuel Richardson* (K&M-V 186; Annotations in Richardson), Leslie notes the page numbers where Lady Bradsheigh writes against learning in women and Richardson writes for it. Did Leslie see his argument with Julia on those pages? In six of his eight volumes by John Henry Newman, the agnostic Leslie considers Newman's arguments on matters of religion and faith, and thoughtfully argues with him, though occasionally, he verbally snorts 'pish!' (K&M-V 165; Annotations in Newman). W. E. Henley, booster of country, Empire and masculine vigour, inscribes his *Burns: Life, Genius, Achievement* 'To Leslie Stephen his old Protégé', suggesting influence on Stephen's critical criterion of manliness (K&M-V 102). And Sir Francis Galton's book about roughing it, *The Art of Travel, or, Shifts and Contrivances Available in Wild Countries*, obtained while Stephen was at Cambridge, anticipates the Alpine climber, with its how-to essays on building snow houses, making clothes and creating writing utensils in the wild (K&M-V 83).

Woolf's diary entries, memoir and the library's surviving contents also allow some tentative conclusions about its curriculum.[4] First, Louise DeSalvo, Katherine Hill and others surmised correctly: the library contains numerous histories and biographies (DeSalvo, '1897' 88–9; Hill, 'History' 353–4).[5] Titles such as *The Constitutional History of England from the Accession of Henry VII to the Death of George II* abound (K&M-V 96), and many titles are a variation on *The Prose Works of John Milton, With a Life of the Author* (K&M-V 156). Thus, Stephen's sociological approach, seeing works in the context of an author's life and times, communicates itself in the physical proximity of biography to collected works. Second, it is primarily a humanities curriculum in history and political science, philosophy and religion, and eighteenth- and nineteenth-century literature, such as Goldsmith and Pope, Fielding and Richardson, Coleridge and Shelley, Thackeray and Meredith, Lowell and Emerson. Third, eighteenth-century literature dominates; Leslie owned the eight-volume set of the *Illustrations of the Literary History of the Eighteenth Century*, for example, along with the nine-volume set of *Literary Anecdotes of the Eighteenth Century* (K&M-V 166). Fourth, this curriculum includes very few women writers. Leslie Stephen's library literally illustrates why Woolf would claim in *A Room of One's Own* that there was no women's tradition before Aphra Behn. It existed, as Margaret

Ezell shows,⁶ but not on Leslie's shelves, which reinforces Woolf's argument that material conditions matter. Fifth, Leslie's library represents an adult, not a children's curriculum, and a curriculum unchanged for the female student, thus reflecting Emily Davies's Cardinal Principle at Girton: women must master the curriculum offered men.

Paradoxically, then, Leslie Stephen's curriculum assumes male writers have more value than female ones, reinforcing traditional gender roles; but Virginia Stephen's access to it assumes women do not need a different curriculum, providing a rationale for undercutting such roles. Woolf's first memories of her father reading aloud also show Leslie Stephen presenting her with a curriculum unmodified for the female student – she remembers *Tom Brown's School Days* and *Treasure Island*.⁷ He presents her with an adult curriculum early, too, starting in on the Waverley Novels soon after *Treasure Island* (E1 127–8). Giving her access to his library reflects Leslie's belief that 'women ought to be as well educated as men' (SLLS1 213), but he presents her with a largely male world of letters.

Leslie's many sets of authors' complete works also make a strong pedagogical statement: literature should not be taught from anthologies. Or at least the student should be able to see an individual work within the context of an author's entire canon. He also based his pedagogy in freedom. At first, he assigned books to Virginia, and when she returned one, he gave her another. But soon, 'all his books, "mangy and worthless", ... were to be had without asking'; he gave her, at 15, 'the free run of a large and quite unexpurgated library', telling her to '"[r]ead what you like"' (E5 588).⁸ As many Victorians did, he also put great stock in reading aloud; literature was oral, too.⁹ Woolf recalls, 'Every evening we spent an hour and a half in the drawing-room,' where Leslie read aloud to them (E1 127). Scott's Waverley Novels

> provided reading for many years of evenings, because when we had finished the last he was ready to begin the first over again. At the end of a volume my father always gravely asked our opinion as to its merits, and we were required to say which of the characters we liked best and why. I can remember his indignation when one of us preferred the hero to the far more lifelike villain. (E1 128)

Woolf also remembers his reading all of Jane Austen to them, along with Hawthorne, some Shakespeare and Carlyle's *The French Revolution*. He had many poems committed to memory and enjoyed reciting them,¹⁰ and Woolf recalls hearing poems by Keats, Wordsworth, Tennyson and Arnold, among many others, in her childhood: 'many of the great English poems now seem to me inseparable from my father; I hear in them not only his voice, but in some sort his teaching and belief' (E1 128–9).

That teaching included walking. As part of the four hours of outdoors exercise prescribed by Dr Seton in her fifteenth year, Leslie and Virginia walked in Kensington Gardens (Leaska, Intro xvi). Although she resented the stricture of those walks (Annan 118), she later described him as being 'very simple, very confiding' then, with even his long silences 'curiously full of meaning, as if he were thinking half aloud, about poetry and philosophy and people he had known' (E5 588).

His lessons?

> To read what one liked because one liked it, never to pretend to admire what one did not – that was his only lesson in the art of reading. To write in the fewest possible words, as clearly as possible, exactly what one meant – that was his only lesson in the art of writing. All the rest must be learnt for oneself. (*E5* 588–9)

To encourage such independent thinking, this 'man of great learning and wide experience' (*E5* 589) used a simple teaching strategy: when Virginia returned a book, he asked her 'gently, kindly; "What did you make of it?"' ('Sketch' 157). In fact, Woolf uses 'gentle' twice to describe her father in the library: he is also 'very gentle and pleased' when she comes to replace a book ('Sketch' 112). In contrast to what he did elsewhere in the house, Leslie did not throw temper tantrums in the library. His 'teaching and belief' encouraged freedom, put books in context, assumed literature was oral, incorporated movement and used open-ended questions.

Finally, Leslie's welcome extended to her company: 'Went up to read with father . . . ', Virginia writes in her diary on 31 January 1897 (*PA* 25), and he wrote to Anne Thackeray Ritchie on 21 October 1898 that Ginia 'brought me some Greek to construe for her because she knew I would enjoy it' (*SLLS2* 491). His books, notes and inscriptions too, reflect a community of letters, a world of reviewing, corresponding, sharing with friends.[11] Whenever Virginia Stephen picked up one of Leslie Stephen's books, she joined a conversation. She might read something like: 'All this seems to me to be very like nonsense' or 'What, I think, Hume really meant was . . . ' (K&M-V 160; Annotations in Morley 17, 114).[12] Whenever she chose a book from the many sets he owned, she gazed at a writer's whole career. Whenever she read inscriptions from friends (Henry James giving Leslie a copy of his brother William's *Will to Believe* [K&M-V 114] or Hardy sending him a copy of *Wessex Poems* [K&M-V 98]), she experienced literature as an ongoing process. Every time she stepped into that library, she saw and heard, quite literally, in those books and on those shelves, a literary conversation. It might be a male conversation about a male canon within a male community, but she had access to a literary community at work. She could trespass.

Julia Stephen's Stories and Tea Table

Julia taught her classes in public, in the dining room and at the tea table, and Virginia's presence was required at the latter. When she joined her siblings for lessons or came downstairs dressed for tea ('Sketch' 148, 150), she walked into a space that reflected another curriculum and pedagogy, with different lessons and in a different community. In formal classes at the dining-room table, Woolf remembers her mother's hand, with its opal ring, moving across the pages of a lesson book ('Sketch' 81)[13] and recalls that, after her death, Leslie 'was very anxious to take her place and to teach us as she had taught us' (*E1* 129) (see Figure 1.1). The overt curriculum consisted of Latin, French and history, taught by Julia and begun before Virginia was 7, and arithmetic, taught by Leslie (QB1 26–8; VB 60–3), and although governesses occasionally came, Quentin Bell

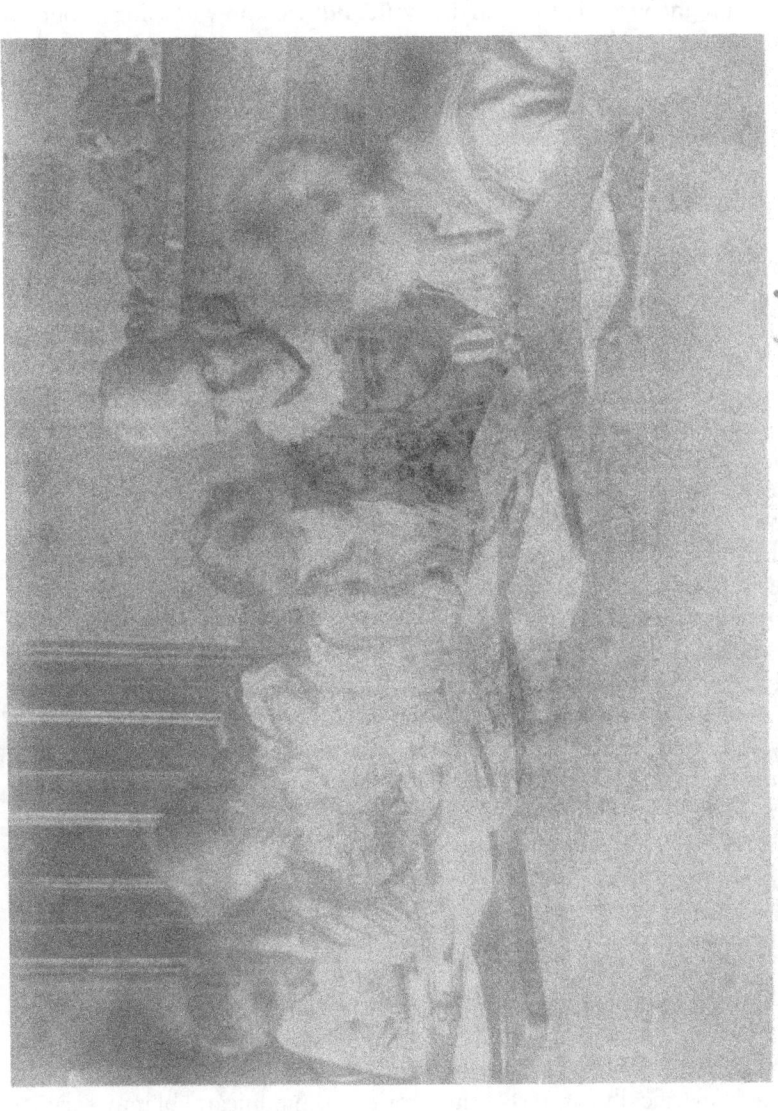

Figure 1.1 Julia Stephen with Stephen children at lessons, left to right: Thoby, Vanessa, Virginia, Julia, Adrian. Leslie Stephen photograph album, Mortimer Rare Book Collection, MRBC MS 00005, Smith College Special Collections, Northampton, Massachusetts.

suspects they learned more English from the children than the children learned foreign languages from them (1 26). There were also classes in music ('naturally, since we were girls' [VB 61]), dance and deportment.

Woolf says little else about her earliest education, and we do not know how she learned to read. (She did 'know all [her] beasts from their pictures in Bewick which were shown before we could listen to reading aloud' [L1 165 and n1]). Julia probably taught Virginia to read and write, but we know nothing about her methods. According to Alix Bunyan, reading, spelling and writing were sequential subjects in the nineteenth century (60), and the 5-year-old Virginia was writing beautifully written letters to her grandmother (78–9), so she was probably reading well before then. Bunyan also suggests, based on a letter from Leslie to Julia about Vanessa's reading 'another page of the fat cat', that a rhyme-based work, perhaps Mrs Mortimer's *Reading Without Tears: Or, a Pleasant Mode of Learning to Read*, was being used in the Stephen household (63 n32). Mortimer's book used rhymes, narrative, the alphabet and illustrations, and she encouraged variety, freedom, reading aloud and enjoyment (Bunyan 63–7). Charlotte Mason, in *Home Education*, advised the mother to play games with the alphabet and sounds, read and repeat lines of simple poetry out loud with the child and then have the child search for familiar words in new lines (135–43), but whether Julia consulted such contemporary texts, or earlier works such as Mrs Barbauld's *Easy Lessons for Children* (1810) or Harriet Martineau's *Household Education* (1849), is not known.[14]

Julia Stephen's stories provide few clues to the Stephen children's schooling, either, and learning references are humourous: the pigs in 'The Wandering Pigs' have not 'been to school to learn geography' (148); Bob and Maggie look at their Latin grammar in 'Cat's Meat' for five minutes and Bob thinks Latin stupid 'if it calls a man the same as a woman' (170); and Poppy in 'The Black Cat or Grey Parrot' compares the funny medical terms in the 'animal' hospital she visits to the *Book of Nonsense*, Edward Lear's limerick book (118).

But surely Julia told and/or read these stories, with their didactic pedagogy, to her children?[15] Annan says Julia's 'children's stories are tales of the disappointments restless, rebellious children suffer who try to escape from the routine of the nursery' (103); Diane Gillespie argues Julia's essays and stories are meant to 'point morals to audiences, young and old, who needed her instruction' ('Elusive' 3); and Elizabeth Steele suggests Julia presented her generally sentimental lessons in a straightforward way to counteract Leslie's more 'mocking and analytical' way of reading literature (31). Julia directs her stories at children (although 'Cat's Meat' criticises her own practice of visiting the poor and sick), and while funny and fanciful, they present two main lessons: strengthen home relationships and be kind to animals (Steele 30).

Not directed specifically at girls, the stories communicate blatant gender lessons: girls serve their brothers and male cousins, waking them 'with a kiss in the mornings and drag[ging] out chairs' for them to sit on at meals, as well as displaying what Steele calls excessive 'tenderness of heart and anxiety to please', often dissolving into 'floods of tears and contorted manners' (31). Boys are allowed, even encouraged, to be rebellious before they learn their lessons. So, in 'The Mysterious Voice', Jem gets to be naughty, make mischief and cause their monkey's death without reprimand or punishment before he decides to be good. In 'The Duke's Coal Cellar', Jim Brown is 'something of a hero' in the neighbourhood for spending the night in the coal cellar, although he has worried his mother sick; indeed, the policeman and a neighbour woman have harsher words for the mother than for Jim (193). Tommy in 'Tommy and His Neighbours' reveals Julia's 'sneaking admiration for devilish ingenuity, especially as practiced by small boys', Steele comments (32). Only Maggie, in 'Cat's Meat', is cleverer than her brother, and then only once, but her 'sum-solving is a relief' (Steele 31). Poppy in 'The Black Cat or the Grey Parrot', though brave enough to follow the parrot to the green gate in the high wall, is a good girl who wants to be a nurse because she is 'sorry for sick people' (122); her Nurse has taught her to 'always do what she was told and never think of what she liked' (123).[16]

Woolf never mentions her mother's stories, but she remembers Julia's 'tea-table training' ('Sketch' 150). If Leslie's library was the 'brain of the house', then Julia's 'oval tea table with its pink china shell full of spice buns', was the 'heart of the family' ('22 HPG' 164; 'Sketch' 118).[17] Leslie's study was full of light, but the tea table was in a 'room naturally dark' and divided by 'black folding doors' ('22 HPG' 164). By 5 p.m., 'father must be given his tea' because in that society, he could not get it himself ('Sketch' 148). Virginia Stephen, therefore, must be in her place at the tea table, changed from a girl with untidy hair trying to 'make out some scene in Euripides or Sophocles' into a young lady 'possessed of a certain manner', following the rules required of a society 'founded on restraint, sympathy, unselfishness' ('Sketch' 148–50). That manner did not come naturally to her, and the training felt imposed, though Julia did not overtly instruct her daughters in it. Rather, Virginia recalls learning it through careful observation, sharp memories of her mother and intense pressure from others – 'if Ronny Norman said that, one had to reply in the same style' ('Sketch' 149–50). In 1869, the feminist journal *Kettledrum* may have playfully used women's rule over the tea table to question male dominance in political affairs (Levine, 'Humanising' 306), but such questioning was not a lesson learned at the tea table over which Julia Stephen had presided, because when Vanessa and Virginia were forced to preside in 1900, the questioning remained inner.[18]

Julia's library also communicates a curriculum devoted to gender lessons. Containing few books she bought herself, it includes scattered gifts and volumes of serious and sentimental poetry. Most of her books were owned by Herbert Duckworth (such as poetry by Coleridge, Keats and Tennyson [K&M-V 48, 119, 223] or Ovid and Virgil in Latin [K&M-V 170, 235]),[19] or given to her by her parents (Aubrey De Vere [K&M-V 59]) or by Leslie (some of his works [K&M-V 215–16]), or presented to her by authors, admirers and well-wishers (*The Angel in the House* given to her by Coventry Patmore in 1866 before her marriage to Duckworth [K&M-V 172] or James Russell Lowell books inscribed with his love to Julia [K&M-V 138]).

The books Woolf associates with Julia, De Quincey's *Confessions of an English Opium-Eater* and first edition Sir Walter Scott works given to her by her father ('Sketch' 86), are in the Library of Leonard and Virginia Woolf (K&M-V 58, 197–8), but not inscribed by or to Julia.[20] As Woolf notes, 'Not very much education came her way,' and although she seems to have loved literature, '[s]he had an instinctive, not a trained mind' – she jumped, Woolf remembers, when Virginia, reading *Hamlet* aloud, read 'silver' instead of 'sliver'. She spoke French 'with a very good accent' ('Sketch' 85–6), and one beautiful book in her library, unmistakably hers, with a JS monogram in the volume's leather, is *French Lyrics*, edited by George Saintsbury (K&M-V 80). An 1858 edition of selected Georges Louis Leclerc Buffon works (*Œuvres choisies de Buffon*) reflects both Julia's love of animals and facility with language; the naturalist's animal descriptions are beautifully illustrated, and her French teacher, J. S. A. Medeney, inscribed it 'Témoignage de ma satisfaction pour le progrès que Mlle Julia Jackson a fait dans l'étude de la langue et de la littérature française' (K&M-V 33).[21]

Julia's stories, her tea table, her nursing and her visits, which Stella continued after her death, introduced Virginia Stephen to a community of women centred around family life, the marriage plot and charitable service. Gillespie notes her stories '[encourage] concern for others not by promising children divine rewards or by threatening divine retribution but ... by promising participation in or threatening exclusion from the community' ('Essays' 200). That community included, Stephen writes in 'Reminiscences', '[p]eople of the most diverse kinds', who 'came to [Julia] when they had reason to rejoice or to weep' (35); in the drawing room, Julia responded, comforting the sobbing Lisa Stillman or Cousin Adeline or poor Mrs Tyndall ('22 HPG' 164). As a result, 'Someone was always interrupting,' and Woolf remembers her mother 'always in a room full of people', surrounded by visitors, young people courting, Stella and her suitors, George and Gerald and their friends, old men ('Sketch' 83–4). That community, in which many middle-class women 'felt a powerful drive to use their time purposefully for the good of others' (Thane 190), required Julia to '[help] people by the light of her judgement and experience' and live at 'high pressure': there were always 'trifling businesses' to transact, difficulties to 'despatch', letters to write ('Reminiscences' 35, 37–8), dying patients to visit ('Sketch' 82). Virginia Stephen absorbed the lesson; membership in that community came at a high cost.

The Stephen Household

The difference between Stephen spaces, curricula, pedagogy, lessons and communities reflects their debate about girls' education, but their household's libraries, aims and behaviours reveal it even more sharply. Leslie's library has over 1,000 volumes in the Washington State University collection, whereas Julia's has a few over fifty. Leslie received inscribed books from friends, editors and loved ones, but he bought many, whereas Julia bought very few. Leslie owned numerous sets of authors' complete works, often with a 'life' attached: Addison, Bacon, Browne, Byron, Eliot, Emerson and way past Q. Julia owned one 'set', three volumes of Abraham Cowley's *Works* combined in one book (K&M-V 52). Leslie owned the five-volume *Works of Thomas Gray*, and he took notes at the end of each volume; the 12-year-old Julia was given *The Poetical Works of Thomas Gray* in one hand-tooled leather volume, and she took no notes (K&M-V 91). Leslie's library represents the canon, a mainly male tradition in a male world, a structure embodying the education of boys in a certain class and aimed at turning those boys into educated, literate, cultured men. Julia's library represents accomplishments, a female tradition in a female world of gifts, a structure embodying the spotty education of girls in a certain class and aimed at turning those girls into dedicated, dutiful, devoted women.

Leslie edited *The Cornhill Magazine* and the *Dictionary of National Biography*; wrote numerous biographical entries for the latter; published important works about the philosophical and literary thought of the eighteenth century; and wrote full-length biographies.[22] Working in a large private space, he modelled the male professional writer's life, with its routines, publications and emphasis on the public sphere. He wrote a pamphlet criticising *The Times*'s coverage of the American Civil War, for example, and put information about US slavery and the North's position into people's hands. His life, and thus his pedagogy, encouraged critical thinking and a professional attitude toward one's work.

Julia was a reader and writer, writing letters almost every evening, 'her hand moving ceaselessly ... as she wrote answers, advice, jests, warning, sympathy' ('Reminiscences' 38), and occasionally writing letters to the editor of the *Pall Mall Gazette*, *Nineteenth Century* or *Cornhill* about issues concerning her (though she did not submit them all), such as her position against the curtailing of beer for workhouse inmates, the servant question and agnosticism.[23] She wrote a long essay, *Notes from Sick Rooms*, revealing humour and professionalism; her entry for Julia Margaret Cameron in the *DNB* illustrates Cameron's professionalism; and she wrote out and carefully reworked the stories she invented for her children (Gillespie, 'Elusive' 2). Writing a lot in a small space – a writing table built 'into a very dark angle of the [drawing] room' – in the midst of family life, Julia published little ('Sketch' 112–13; Gillespie, 'Elusive' 1–2).[24] She modelled the female amateur writer's life, with its 'around the edges' quality and emphasis on the private sphere: letters and stories meant to inculcate family morals. Her life, and thus her pedagogy, encouraged social conformity to a certain *kind* of work, performed in service to others.

How ironic, Gillespie suggests: Leslie was the well-known writer who encouraged Virginia to follow him in the writing profession, but Julia wrote fiction containing playful, even fantastic, elements ('Elusive' 2).[25] In Virginia Stephen's education, then, Leslie and Julia indefinitely '[mix] together', perhaps influencing her later genre choices.

Notes

1. Victoria Rosner 'imaginatively reconstruct[s]' (69) and discusses 22 Hyde Park Gate, its layout, its additions and its meaning for Woolf in her chapter called 'Thresholds', 59–90.
2. The Library of Leonard and Virginia Woolf, comprising more than 4,000 titles and approximately 6,000 volumes because of multi-volume sets, is in Manuscripts, Archives and Special Collections (MASC), Holland/Terrell Libraries, Washington State University, Pullman, WA. With Julia King's help, I sorted out the individual libraries of Leslie, Julia, Thoby and Virginia Stephen contained within the larger Woolf library. See Gillespie's introduction to *The Library of Leonard and Virginia Woolf: A Short-title Catalog*, compiled by Julia King and Laila Miletic-Vejzovic, for

a detailed history and description (vii–xx). See also the Spring 1984 *Virginia Woolf Miscellany* (22), edited by Gillespie and devoted to the Woolf Library.
3. Virginia Stephen reported in the *Hyde Park Gate News* of 11 March 1895 that 'Mr Leslie Stephen went down to Cambridge on Saturday to lecture to the Newnham young ladies upon (we think) "The Choice of Books"' (189), and he gave a lecture called 'The Study of English Literature' at St Andrew's in 1887 (Hill, 'History' 353–4).
4. Tentative because what exists at Pullman is not what existed in Leslie's study. Some of his books were auctioned off, others are still owned by descendants and collectors, some may have been sold when the Woolfs pruned their library for the move to Mecklenburgh Square in 1939, and many were destroyed by the bombs that hit their home in 1940. Some titles on Virginia's 1897 reading list, along with some books she says her father read out loud to them, are not in this collection. There is no Austen, though Stephen took her books to the nursing home in 1902 when he had his operation and began an essay about her afterwards (Maitland 485). There is no Dickens, Shakespeare, Sterne or Trollope, but surely Leslie Stephen owned books by them? Thus, the current lack of an author or title may not have been a lack then. Finally, some titles, in the Library of Leonard and Virginia Woolf and with publication dates or evidence that suggest Leslie's library, lack his inscription, notes or drawings; there is no ownership proof. For example, the book containing Sir James Stephen's essay on reading is inscribed to Sir James and one assumes Leslie inherited it, but in the absence of an autograph or drawings, it has to be labelled contextually convincing and almost surely, but not 'officially', his. Similarly, it is easy to see why Bunyan says the Stephens owned Arthur Acland's 1891 *A Guide to the Choice of Books for Students and General Readers* (171; K&M-V 1), but no inscription proves it, and the handwriting in it does not look like Leslie's or Julia's.
5. See also Theodore Koulouris, who uses Holleyman rather than King and Miletic-Vejzovic to put together his title list (*HL* 41–42). The short-title catalogue compiled at Washington State University makes Holleyman 'obsolete' (Gillespie, Intro xvii), but it sometimes includes information that allows scholars to determine which books belonged to whom.
6. Ezell knows Woolf was 'bound by the limitations of the historiography of her day', but criticises women's literary historians who have taken 'a text designed to be provocative and to stimulate further research into women's lives in the past and canonized it as history' (49–50).
7. Virginia's youthful library reflected this curriculum: Thoby borrowed her copy of R. M. Ballantyne's *Charlie to the Rescue: A Tale of the Sea and the Rockies* to take to his prep school, Evelyns, in 1891. Also, *The World of Adventure* (about the charge of the Light Brigade) must have been in the house since Adrian writes to his mother that he has taken it to school rather than Tennyson, Wordsworth and other authors Virginia recommended (Lee, *VW* 111).
8. Koulouris does not explain why 'we must not think Woolf had unlimited access' (*HL* 42) since she herself said that is exactly what she had.
    See, however, Love, who points out that although Virginia Stephen could read anything she liked in his library, it was a library 'Leslie censored as he compiled' (43), and Janis Paul, who notes that 'While literary England was celebrating *The Yellow Book*, while James Joyce was discovering Ibsen, Virginia Stephen was reading Sir Walter Scott' (20). See also Mary Jean Corbett's 'Hours in a Library' section, 72–9, in her *Behind the Times*.
9. Alison Byerly argues that reading aloud gave Victorians a way to 'domesticate' theatre, 'a compromise for people who wished to be entertained but were suspicious of overt theatricality' (125–6), and Philip Collins comments that 'many people met contemporary literature as a group or communal, rather than an individual, experience' (27).

10. Leslie Stephen loved poetry as a child, reciting it in the streets, and might have become a poet, but a doctor told his mother to stop such habits: send him to a boys' school, deprive him of poetry (a prescription Leslie could barely prevent himself from crying about [Maitland 28]) and prevent him from getting too emotional. Doctors would later deprive Virginia of reading and writing to rid *her* of extreme emotions (DeSalvo '1897' 81).
11. For commentary on Leslie's books not already cited, see Luedeking, Miletic-Vejzovic and my 'Learning VW'.
12. Leslie Stephen frequently wrote and drew in his books. In volume 2 of the first edition *Hours in a Library*, Leslie crammed every free inch of the book's front and back matter and thirty-six pages of his first essay with quotations about books, libraries and reading (K&M-V 215; Annotations in *Hours*), notes that became his second edition preface. Virginia Stephen seems to comment on her father's annotating and its implied coercion in her manuscript fragment ['Writing in the Margin']. Her Colonel Talboy's practice of violently marking in books and declaring his assessments of authors' work to all within hearing distance probably depicts Leslie's marginalia and comments, though perhaps exaggerated, and her Mrs Talboy's resigned reaction to his denunciations, '"Certainly dear" "Of course, of course" while her lips mechanically count the stitches in her knitting' probably reflects Julia's response (2). See also Lee, VW 406, H. J. Jackson on Virginia Stephen's attitude (237–44) and Amanda Golden's transcription and discussion (109–17). Virginia Stephen/Woolf used reading notebooks, except for occasional 'light marks' in books (Gillespie, Intro xviii) and translations in some Greek texts (Golden 109).
13. See also 'Sketch' 117, where Julia's finger 'point[s] its way across French and Latin Grammars', and 'Sketch' 127, with Virginia's memory of 'look[ing] over the grammar in the dining room and see[ing] the lights changing on the bay'.
14. See Christina Hardyment's historical study of baby-care advice, particularly Chapter 3, 'Science and Sensibility, 1870–1920'.
15. Elizabeth Steele also assumes Julia read her stories out loud to the children (31). See Zwerdling, VW 190 and 382 n15; SLLS1 324 n2; and Gillespie, 'Elusive' 2 and 258 n4 on Julia and Leslie Stephen's ultimately unsuccessful attempt to publish her stories, accompanied by his illustrations, with Routledge in 1885.
16. However, Donna Risolo argues that Julia Stephen's 'The Black Cat or the Grey Parrot' is a feminist utopian story that privileges feminine values, promotes the growth of the female character, partners with nature, critiques patriarchy and converts the male character to 'mother consciousness'. Ellen Argyros sees 'Cat's Meat' as evidence that Julia Stephen was 'perfectly aware of her failings as a mother, her unavailability, her devoting as much of her time as she did to poor strangers rather than to her own children'.
17. Rosner discusses the body images used to describe the house (71).
18. Woolf's description of her tea-table lessons and her ability to use the Victorian manner while interrogating it recall Lily's attempt in *To the Lighthouse* to mimic how Mrs Ramsay placated Mr Ramsay before her death (154). Lily remembers, but has not internalised the behaviour enough to use it, whereas Vanessa and Virginia Stephen 'learnt the rules of the game of Victorian society so thoroughly' they never forgot them ('Sketch' 150).
19. According to M. G. Holleyman, *Publius Virgilius Maro* had Herbert Duckworth's bookplate and inscription in it, evidence since covered up by new binding (Victoria Square catalogue, Section I, 55); see also Gillespie, 'Elusive' 8 and 260 n15.
20. Woolf says some Scott first editions were lost ('Sketch' 86).
21. 'Testimony of my satisfaction with the progress that Miss Julia Jackson has made in the study of French language and literature.'
22. See Gillian Fenwick for detailed evidence of Leslie Stephen's prolific writing career.

23. Mrs Ramsay's 'warmth and eloquence' about 'the iniquity of the English dairy system' subjects her to family laughter (*TL* 105); perhaps Julia Stephen's passion about similar issues led to a similar result. The concern about milk was valid. See Tom Phelps, *The British Milkman*, 5–8, for how unsanitary milk was before 1900; even though Manor Farm Dairy introduced pasteurised milk in bottles in 1906, 'unpasteurized milk from 17-gallon churns' was still being sold up until 1914 (11). Ellen Argyros also says Julia Stephen's insistence on an invalid's comfort in *Notes from Sick Rooms* 'might expose her to ridicule from the medical community'.
24. Rosner, using Robert Kerr's *The Gentleman's House* (1864), says the drawing room's folding doors Woolf discusses ('22 HPG' 164) 'preserve[d] a larger drawing room at the expense of a private space for Julia Stephen that would correspond to her husband's study' (75).
25. Gillespie says Julia's story is the kind Woolf says should be told in *A Room of One's Own* ('Elusive' 25), and Argyros suggests we look more carefully at the influence of the mother's pen on the daughter's writing. See also Marion Dell, 'Writing Back' and *Influential*.

Chapter 2

Coming into 22 Hyde Park Gate

Teachers

Luckily, Virginia Stephen's homeschooling was not limited to her parents' teaching. Teachers coming from outside the home, particularly relatives and reading material, brought other curricula, pedagogies, lessons and communities with them: Thoby brought the Greeks, his schools and argument; Anne Thackeray Ritchie brought women writers and their literary community; and *Atalanta* and *Tit-Bits* brought exciting ideas, other girls, other social classes.[1]

Thoby Stephen's Talk

The first time 10-year-old Thoby came home from Evelyns, the prep school he began attending in January 1891, he '[broke] through the schoolboy convention about "work"' and shared with his 8-year-old sister, 'handing it [what he was learning] on as something worth knowing' ('Sketch 1' 108). Although Thoby had started with a 'deficiency in Greek' that put him at the bottom of the school (Love 158), the day after he got home, he 'rather fitfully, but excitedly' told Virginia the Hector and Troy story. '[I]t was through him', Woolf recalls, 'that I first heard about the Greeks' ('Sketch' 125–6). When Thoby brings his story home to his sister, though, they do not sit in the dining room or nursery. Rather, Woolf remembers, 'he was shy of telling it; and so must keep walking up and down; and so we kept on going upstairs and then downstairs' ('Sketch 1' 108). Thoby's talk, his willingness not to become as 'separate' as brothers and sisters 'often become when the boys go to public schools and the sisters stay at home' ('Sketch' 125), occurs in a liminal space, on a threshold between Leslie's library and Julia's tea table.[2] Thoby's shy narrative on the stairs thus bridges his parents' two worlds, existing between their competing curricula, pedagogies, lessons and communities.

Thoby also bridges home and school worlds for his sister. In *Three Guineas*, Woolf rails against Arthur's Education Fund, the system under which Victorian families financed their sons' educations to the detriment of their daughters'. Thoby attended Evelyns Preparatory School (1891–4), Clifton College (1894–9) and Trinity at Cambridge (1899–1903), and Adrian attended Evelyns, Westminster and Trinity, Cambridge. George and Gerald Duckworth went to Evelyns and

Eton (QB1 32; MacGibbon 26) before going to Cambridge, where George went to Trinity and Gerald to Clare. Virginia, on the other hand, attended non-matriculation classes through the Ladies Department at King's College London and had tutors.[3] An 1880 or 1881 household budget in Julia's hand illustrates the monetary disparity.[4] Along with line items for house, clothes and rates, the education line reads: 'boys £280 Stella £55 Laura £50 385' (['Agnostic Women'] verso), the boys being George and Gerald, 12 and 10, at Evelyns. Stella, 11, and Laura, 10, were being educated at home by Julia and presumably governesses. Arthur's Education Fund, then, allotted 73 per cent of the education budget to the boys. But Thoby's talk on the stairs brought the boy's school into the girl's home and undermined the fund's purpose of keeping girls' education separate and inferior.

Thoby's curriculum was heavily oriented toward the classics, as his books in the Library of Leonard and Virginia Woolf indicate.[5] Over half are schoolbooks, with his Clifton books including Homer's *Odyssey*, Plato's *Republic* (Book 10) and R. C. Jebb's *Selections from the Attic Orators* (K&M-V 107, 177, 115). By and large, these texts' prefaces, introductions and notes are in English.[6] But scholarly apparatus could overwhelm a schoolboy edition, as Thoby's Tyrrell edition of Euripides' *Bacchae* (K&M-V 71) shows: its eighty-two pages of front matter (preface thanking or damning other scholars, forty-page introduction and then Walter Pater's extended essay) and seventy pages of endnotes bury the sixty-five-page Greek play and its ten-page English translation.

Although Thoby's library includes seven titles by or from family members, along with Irby's *British Birds*, Thackeray's *The History of Henry Esmond* and poetry by Coleridge, Kipling, Swinburne and Tennyson (K&M-V 112, 224, 49, 122, 220, 223), his books reveal his culture's emphasis on classics in upper middle-class male education, with ten Latin titles and twelve Greek, including two huge, well-known reference works, Liddell and Scott's *Greek–English Lexicon* and Lewis and Short's *Latin Dictionary* (K&M-V 134). His Cambridge books include Aristophanes' *Comedies*, Demosthenes' *Select Private Orations* and Plato's *Phaedrus* (K&M-V 7, 60, 177). Even appended publishers' booklists communicate the supremacy of classics in boys' education. The thirty-one-page George Bell and Sons catalogue at the back of Martial's *Epigrammata Selecta* (K&M-V 147) devotes three and a half pages to English titles and fifteen pages to classics, including translations; it also lists a Public-School Series of Classical Authors, Grammar-School Classics, a Lower Form Series and a set of Latin and Greek Class Books.

Yet Woolf recalls Thoby's curriculum also included Shakespeare, an author he did not study at school, but 'consumed ... somehow or other, by himself' ('Sketch' 138). When Thoby and Virginia began arguing about 'the great William' (*L1* 45), she read and studied the plays, but also watched a common reader at work, someone 'rough and ready and comprehensive' who did not make 'minute comments' or provide specific criticism, but used Shakespeare as 'his other world; the place where he ... took his bearings ... and sized us up from that standard' ('Sketch' 138–9). Writing to Thoby in July 1901, she reveals her lukewarm feelings about Shakespeare as she asks for advice on which Sophocles play to take on vacation, but explains her move from admiring Sophocles to enjoying him means 'there is hope for Shakespeare' (*L1* 42). By November, she admits Thoby is right, confesses she has been 'let in to [the] company of worshippers', and says 'I shall want a lecture when I see you; to clear up some points about the Plays. I mean about the characters' (*L1* 45). As she reads more widely in Shakespeare on her own, she wants to talk to Thoby about the plays and Sidney Lee's *Life*, particularly his sonnet theory (*L1* 77).[7] Julia Briggs suggests that Thoby's possession of Shakespeare, Virginia's sense that Shakespeare was Thoby's inheritance, not hers, and her being 'a little oppressed by his – greatness I suppose' (*L1* 45) all prevented Woolf from writing an essay on Shakespeare (*RVW* 8–11, 21). But as Briggs also notes, Virginia's arguments with her older brother 'created a bond between them' that explains why Woolf would create a literary sister for Shakespeare, not a daughter, and why Woolf could not, in fact, stop writing about Shakespeare, scattering her portrait of him 'throughout her writings – her novels and essays, but in particular her diaries' (*RVW* 20–1).

When Virginia Stephen writes to Violet Dickinson in early 1906 that 'I am reading a Greek play, and Virgil and Shakespeare' (*L1* 215), she summarises her course of study under Thoby's tutelage. But that curriculum may also have included the essay. Leslie Stephen did not encourage Thoby to write,[8] but recorded his son had 'distinguished himself chiefly as an essayist' at Clifton and exclaimed when Cambridge examiners noted his 'general ability specially displayed in an essay upon "living English poets"!' (*MB* 107, 106). Woolf similarly remembers Thoby's Latin and Greek as being 'very rough . . . . But his essays showed great intelligence' ('Sketch' 125). As the 1899 reports unearthed by Vanessa Curtis show (23), his Clifton masters thought highly enough of his work to award him the Schola Cliftonensis Prize for the English Essay. J. H. Fowler, an assistant master and author of *A Manual of Essay-Writing*, said Thoby's English Essay 'impressed me as quite the best school essay I have seen; it showed a remarkable grasp of the significance of historic events and was written in a clean, unaffected style and with scholarly taste and feeling'. Sidney T. Irwin, also an assistant master, said Thoby's 'essays show exceptional ability and are always interesting . . . . I hope he will keep up the practice of English Composition . . . if he keeps it up, he may do with it something very well worth doing,' and W. W. Asquith predicted Thoby's English work 'points . . . to good things in the future' (all qtd in V. Curtis 23).[9] Perhaps his essay writing explains why, when Virginia's stepbrothers gave her jewels for her twenty-first birthday, Thoby, with more foresight, gave her Montaigne and Bacon (*L1* 66).

Given Thoby's habit of sharing work with her, one can imagine them talking about the genre, famous essayists and his own forays into print, 'Compulsory Chapel' and his review of *Euphrosyne* in *The Cambridge Review*. 'Compulsory Chapel' is a well-argued, passionate plea for 'intellectual independence' (45), fitting for a young man studying for the bar and an agnostic's son. It does not help religion to coerce people to practise it, Thoby writes, and he uses his knowledge of audience to provoke freshmen into thinking and acting for themselves, calling their refusal to act on their religious rights cowardly. In his 'Cambridge Muse' review of what S. P. Rosenbaum calls the first (and last) book of Bloomsbury (61), Thoby criticises *Euphrosyne: A Collection of Verse* for being 'oddly named', 'uneven in quality' and 'strangely arranged'; identifies poems he thinks have 'distinctly unusual merit'; and praises those poems for their 'originality of imagination, felicity of diction, skillful technique, and a finely audacious vocabulary'. But he mainly wants to establish the book's decadence through the influence of Swinburne, Verlaine and James Thomson ('Cambridge' 8). When challenged by Walter Lamb, editor of *The Cambridge Review* (Rosenbaum 73), Thoby clarified his position on the decadents, seeing them as inevitably melancholy because they 'possess independence of thought and still care for art' in a society oblivious to art and governed by convention; they show candour, not perversity ('Euphrosyne' 49). In all three pieces, Thoby regards intellectual integrity highly, works with definitions and distinctions and asks his audience to rethink its usual ideas. Whether or not Thoby and Virginia discussed his essays, they shared certain habits of mind.

As Thoby transmitted his Greek, Latin, Shakespeare and essay curriculum, he also indirectly taught the curriculum's underlying 'patriarchal machine', what Woolf would later claim 'stamped and moulded' her male relations into something unnatural ('Sketch' 153). Virginia twice visited Thoby at Evelyns, where cricket, football, butterflies and rabbits figured prominently (*HPGN* 67, 133–4).[10] But Woolf also remembers being an 'eager listener' as Thoby told her 'stories about the boys at Evelyns. Those stories went on all through Evelyns, through Clifton, and through Cambridge. I knew all his friends through those stories' ('Sketch' 138, 126; see also *D2* 308). What Woolf ultimately 'knew' about the patriarchy's impact on the boys and men in public schools and universities started with Thoby's stories. This is why Virginia Stephen questioned the value of the education boys and men received as early as 1906 in her 'Effect of Oxbridge on Young Men', what Quentin Bell calls 'Virginia Woolf and the Authors of *Euphrosyne*' (1 205–6), and why that critique would recur frequently in Woolf's essays and letters.

Tankred Tunstall-Behrens's correspondence, in *Letters between a Victorian Schoolboy and His Family, 1892–1895*,[11] provides a window into public-school life that Virginia probably gained through Thoby's talk and clarifies the unspoken pressures Thoby was probably under at Evelyns, Clifton and Cambridge.[12] (Tankred's last year at Clifton coincided with Thoby's first and both belonged to Moor-Asquith [Brown's] House [Borwick 286, 320].)[13] Boys had to choose between Classical and Modern curricula upon entering Clifton (see 'Educational Course at Clifton College' in Crane, Documentary Appendix XVI–XVIII), a choice reflecting a broader class distinction between classics and science permeating society (Stray, *Classics Transformed* 187; A. Green 286–7, 306–7; Jann, 'Breeding' 88–9).[14] That division might have prevented Tankred and Thoby from having courses in the same 'sets' or from having more than a speaking acquaintance since Thoby was on the Classical side (university), whereas Tankred was on the Modern (business), then Military side, with more science courses. Thoby went to Cambridge, where he placed in the 2nd Classics Class in the Part I Tripos and then began studying law, whereas Tankred went to the Royal Military Academy at Woolwich and became a Royal Engineer, surveying for boundary commissions in Uganda, Peru/Bolivia and Austria/Italy.[15] Tankred finished in the Fifth Form, whereas Thoby spent three years in the Sixth. Asquith begrudgingly noted some improvement on 'the time [Tankred] has taken in the house' (Crane, Documentary Appendix XV); of Thoby, he wrote, 'He has been a good head of the house and will take my best wishes with him when he leaves' (qtd in V. Curtis 23). Thoby took the Classical path when he might have preferred the Natural Sciences, whereas Leu Behrens set Tankred on the Modern/Military path, which made Tankred '*regret* very much not *being able to do greek*' (Tunstall-Behrens 4, emphasis in original).

Clifton had been founded in 1862 on the progressive ideals of John Percival, its first headmaster (1862–78), and though Thoby's Headmaster was Michael G. Glazebrook, 'the Bogey' (Keigwin 148; Winterbottom, *SF* 2; *L1* 17), Percival's presence still pervaded Clifton when Thoby was there from 1894 to 1899.[16] Percival, a democratic radical and authoritarian conservative,[17] insisted that day boys be fully integrated into Clifton's life, instituted a Jewish house and strongly encouraged religious tolerance.[18] He clashed with school governors over his desire to extend a Clifton education to 150 boys who 'would pay little or nothing' and to abolish 'social distinction' in the school's Constitution (Percival 79). Queen Victoria labelled him a 'dangerous subversive' (Potter 5–6),[19] perhaps because he supported the disestablishment of the Wales Church and became President of Somerville, the undenominational institution devoted to women's higher education (Winterbottom, *JP* 10, 7). But Percival was also a 'tough disciplinarian' who wanted boys to remember his birching of them all their lives (A. Howard); his 'immense demands on human nature' (qtd in Winterbottom, *CAP* 26) made Clifton a '*strenuous* school' in which boys and masters alike were driven to 'work hard, play hard, and pray hard' (*JP* 4, emphasis in original).

Letters from Tankred prove that no matter how progressive its ideals, life at Clifton was typical of English public-school conformity and emphasis on games: house masters, praepostors and fags hierarchy; inflexible discipline; and classics dominance.[20] He complains about Mr Hall's rigid mathematics pedagogy and details battles with Clifton authorities (Tunstall-Behrens 6, 12–13, 73; 138–40; 240–6). A Clifton Boy's published 'chat' about his school traces the strictly scheduled school day, as does Tankred (Tunstall-Behrens 5). The Clifton Boy also reports that

> Corporal punishment is administered by all the masters when it is necessary – they cane on the hands. This saves the Head Master a considerable amount of manual labour. It is only on occasions when a boy is not open to persuasion in the matter of canes that he is sent up to the Head Master. This means the birch, and that latter argument is generally conclusive – there is something very persuasive in the nature of a birch. (1892 *Chums*, 103)

Brian Simon's summary of memoirs and biographies makes it clear that boredom and suffering dominated many public-school men's memories (*VPS* 16).[21] Yet Woolf remembers Thoby's equanimity, a 'philosophic' attitude about 'disagreeables', and an enjoyment of school and 'being on his own' ('Sketch' 126);[22] he was head of Asquith's house in 1899, played football and did well enough academically to win prizes.[23] Although Woolf does not remember Thoby's ever saying he was unhappy or bullied ('Sketch 1' 108), 'he could not say a word ever about his feelings', and she remembers 'something melancholy' about him ('Sketch' 126; see also Lee, *VW* 115–16). The biographical evidence suggests he was unhappy at times.[24]

Thoby's pedagogy, however, reflects something hopeful about him; it respects Virginia, her mind and her desire to learn. Thoby does not consider, hesitate or withhold; he simply thinks her capable of reading, studying and discussing what he is reading, studying and discussing.[25] Virginia's letters to Thoby and others show he willingly shared his learning with her throughout his education and beyond: she eagerly awaited holidays, when Thoby could take her in hand with Greek (*L*1 10); held him to his promise to help her with Greek plays (*L*1 42); quizzed him about Shakespeare's characters (*L*1 45–6) and Sidney Lee's sonnet theory (*L*1 77); thanked him for the *Select Epigrams from the Greek Anthology*, with its crib at the bottom, on her twentieth birthday (*L*1 46–7); and scheduled doing Latin with him daily from 10.30 to 12.30 (*L*1 141).[26] Such letters, representing only a few of what they probably exchanged, bear out Bell's conclusion that Thoby was 'her teacher, or at all events an intellectual sparring partner' (1 68). As Lee says, 'A special literary relationship developed between Virginia and Thoby after he went to school' (*VW* 112), one she could not develop with her father (Gordon 74).[27]

Thoby anchors his pedagogy in narrative and argument. Christopher Stray notes the 'grind' boys endured studying the classics, with teaching often becoming 'ritualized. Boys were simply dragged through texts and rules, with little sense that any kind of genuine literary or humanizing experience was possible' (*Classics Transformed* 187). Yet Thoby isolates the Hector and Troy story, starting Virginia on a way of reading Greek that would cause trouble with Janet Case.[28] Virginia listens 'passively' to the story of the Greeks, but when Thoby brings new skills home from Clifton and Cambridge, she becomes 'bubbling, inquisitive, restless, contradicting'. They argue about books, about Shakespeare, and

> He would sweep down upon me, with his assertion that everything was in Shakespeare. He let the whole mass that he held in his grasp descend in an avalanche on me. I revolted. But how could I oppose all that? Rather feebly; getting red and agitated. Still it was then my genuine feeling that a play was antipathetic to me. How did they begin? With some dull speech a hundred miles from anything interesting. To prove it I opened [*Twelfth Night*] and read 'If music be the food of love, play on [. . .]' I was downed that time. And he was ruthless; exasperating; downing me, overwhelming me; with enough passion to make us both heated. So that my opposition cannot have been quite ineffectual. ('Sketch' 138)

Using a pedagogy he had become used to, with friends, if not in classrooms, Thoby pushed her to defend her position, turn to the text, talk back. But he also provided a safe space for becoming heated and trying out positions because she later misses their arguments, writing to him, 'I dont get anybody to argue with me now, and feel the want' (*L*1 77).[29]

Virginia Stephen's notes in some of Thoby's schoolbooks suggest her oral argument practice may have made her a more active reader[30] because she read the classics differently from Thoby. His copy of Lucretius's *De Rerum Natura* from Clifton (K&M-V 140) reflects the contrast between the two note-takers, apparent in several books. Thoby generally annotates with pencil; his handwriting, though similar to hers, is larger, looser. Virginia remembers 'his easy, vigorous, slovenly handwriting' ('Sketch 1' 108), which Gill Lowe calls 'variable' and 'untidy' (Note on the Text xx). He tends to underline, bring brief and literal word translations forward from the editor's notes and jot down things that probably were said in class, such as on page 48, where he has underlined 'varient motus' and written in the margin 'produce varied motions' (Annotations in Lucretius). Thoby was 'not a note taker', Woolf recalls ('Sketch' 138).

Virginia annotates with ink, in a spikier, thinner hand. She works out fine distinctions in meaning, as on the back flyleaf, or jots down cross-references to lines, as on pages 96, 97 and 103 (Annotations in Lucretius). She, too, underlines and translates, but she tends to record longer phrases or sentences, and she takes actual notes. Most important, she sometimes converses with a text, commenting about larger meanings, entering translation debates or even criticising an editor. In a confident, extended response to F. A. Paley's summary of a Martial epigram as 'very elegant' and about 'the death of a handsome youth', she writes

> This is not an epigram about a 'handsome youth', but an ordinary pig keeper during a prosaic occupation. It is *absurdly over elegant* and entirely unlike the rest of Martial's work. It is in fact a parody by Martial on the over elegant work of his contemporaries. This is plain from the epigram itself and is made quite certain by the next epigram. (Annotations in Martial 390–1, emphasis in original; K&M-V 147)[31]

Such notes, along with the contrast between their note-taking styles, make it clear that Thoby read for exams, while Virginia continued to read for story, as he had taught her, whether the narrative originated in the author's text or an editor's notes.

Thoby's curriculum, the Greeks and Shakespeare pervade Woolf's later work, and what she learned from him about education, about gendered education, permeates her essays and anchors *A Room of One's Own* and *Three Guineas*. Perhaps Thoby's essays also taught her to consider audience and its relation to tone. She learned to argue, writing to Violet Dickinson in late 1903 that Thoby 'is always telling me to explain myself clearly, and to say what I mean' (*L1* 103), and to respond actively to her reading, perhaps leading her away from text margins and into notebooks. Most significant, Thoby's talk taught her that conversation is crucial to learning. She groans, 'oh dear – just as I feel in the mood to talk about these things, you go and plant yourself in Cambridge' (*L1* 46), where he was, according to Walter Lamb's obituary, 'the central figure of a small group which used to gather almost every evening in his rooms' (118). She knew delving into books by herself made her knowledge 'scant. Theres nothing like talk as an educator I'm sure' (*L1* 77).

It was consequential, then, when Thoby again brought the conversation home, into 46 Gordon Square's domestic space, introducing his Cambridge friends to his sisters (Annan 159 n1).[32] Virginia Stephen took full advantage of her opportunity:

> Never have I listened so intently to each step and half-step in an argument. Never have I been at such pains to sharpen and launch my own little dart. And then what joy it was when one's contribution was accepted . . . .
>
> From such discussions Vanessa and I got probably much the same pleasure that undergraduates get when they meet friends of their own for the first time. In the world of the Booths and the Maxses we were not asked to use our brains much. Here we used nothing else. ('Old Bloomsbury' 190)

Thoby could not take Virginia to school with him, but his talk opened the door to his education.

Thoby's sharing of educational communities taught Virginia what she was missing, good and bad. As Quentin Bell notes, when Thoby told her about the Greeks, 'a whole new world . . . captured her imagination'. Perhaps then, he adds, she decided to learn Greek; but perhaps then she also sensed 'the Greeks belonged to Thoby in a way that they didn't belong to her' (1 27). Thoby gave her access to the Greeks, to argument, to male friends such as Leonard Woolf and Lytton Strachey. As with her father's library, however, that access paradoxically increased her exclusion. Thoby also provided an example, along with her father, other male relatives and Bloomsbury men, of the English education system's pernicious effects, effects she believed led to the Great War and the next one as well. As Emily Dalgarno bluntly says, 'In [*Jacob's Room*] British education leads to the death of young men' (*Visible* 57; see also Midgley 150–2). Virginia Stephen observed the general patriarchal ethos permeating Thoby's schools and its impact on him and other boys, and Woolf would conclude, knowing her own education was bad, that men's was bad, too (*L6* 420). Thoby made her simultaneously aware of what she was excluded from and the advantages of that exclusion.

Long before tutors, long before classes at King's College, Thoby functioned as a go-between, moving between public and domestic, school and home, Leslie's library, associated with books and isolated study, and Julia's tea table, associated with people and social interaction. Thoby also gave Virginia entry, though limited and vicarious, to his school communities. His talk taught not only particular subjects but also the pedagogical usefulness of talk itself, something she never forgot. In Woolf's hands, the essay would in fact become 'talk as an educator'.

Aunt Anny's Example

Throughout Virginia Stephen's early homeschooling, Anne Thackeray Ritchie frequently came to 22 Hyde Park Gate as a friend to both Leslie and Julia Stephen, and her relationship with Virginia lasted until she died in 1919. The sister of Leslie's first wife, Minny, and close to Julia Duckworth through Julia Margaret Cameron long before Leslie married her, 'Aunt Anny' was William Makepeace Thackeray's daughter, became a successful novelist in her own right and, oddly, lived a life whose pattern Virginia Woolf's would resemble: a father's tutelage and favour, the loss of a mother, mental instability in the family, a late marriage. Also, Anny was an honorary aunt, giving her influence without the need for automatic resistance from her young 'niece'. During the home education that constituted much of her apprenticeship, Virginia Stephen informally studied under Anne Thackeray Ritchie, a teacher who enlarged her world beyond 22 Hyde Park Gate; taught lessons about writing essays and women writers; modelled a professional writing life; and introduced her to women's literary community.

Ritchie published her last novel in 1885, so Stephen observed a writer of introductions, memoirs, essays and biographical sketches. From 1894 to 1899, Ritchie worked steadily on her introductions to the Biographical Edition of Thackeray's Works (MacKay, Intro xv), which Katherine Hill-Miller says 'obsessed her' (382).

Ritchie and her daughter substantially revised those introductions from 1905 to 1910 for the Centennial Edition (MacKay, Intro xvii–xx). No wonder Woolf gently mocked Ritchie's involvement with Thackeray in her portrayal of Mrs Hilbery in *Night and Day* – Ritchie's most intense absorption in Thackeray coincided with Stephen's adolescence (12 to 17) and youth (23 to 28). But the wider extent of Ritchie's interests and career was not lost on Stephen or Woolf. The Library of Leonard and Virginia Woolf contains *The Works of Miss Thackeray* in eight volumes (including *Toilers and Spinsters*, a book of essays), along with many of her individual titles, including *A Book of Sibyls* and *From the Porch*, both non-fiction (K&M-V 187), so they could be consulted when a biographical detail or anecdote was needed: 'Again and again', Woolf writes in 'Lady Ritchie',

> it has happened to us to trace down our conception of one of the great figures of the past not to the stout official biography consecrated to him, but to some little hint or fact or fancy dropped lightly by Lady Ritchie in passing . . . . She will be the unacknowledged source of much that remains in men's minds about the Victorian age. (*E3* 18)

Woolf quotes Ritchie in an essay on George Eliot (*E4* 171–2, 180 n8), and Stephen contradicts her in her essay on Elizabeth Gaskell (*E1* 343, 344 n11) and also quotes Ritchie in that essay (*E1* 344 and n15). Andrew McNeillie identifies two Ritchie sources for Woolf's essay on Julia Margaret Cameron (*E4* 385 n33, 386 notes 35, 37, 38, 40, and 46).[33] Admiring Ritchie, realising Aunt Anny differed from the other old aunts surrounding her (*D1* 247–8) and acknowledging Ritchie's talents for memoir ('she invented an art of her own' [*E3* 17]), Woolf also saw that Ritchie corrected her own tendency to portray the Victorian Age too simplistically: 'Seen through [Ritchie's] temperament, at once so buoyant and so keen, the gloom of that famous age dissolves in an iridescent mist' (*E3* 399).

Ritchie also bequeathed numerous essays filled with linguistic and narrative strategies the novice could adapt to her own concerns and purposes. Stephen realises Ritchie is not 'learned, prosaic, or sentimental' in her essays, but when she tries to discern her method, she falls back on magic to define it (*E1* 228). The clear stylistic links between Ritchie and Woolf show that Virginia Stephen seems to have studied Ritchie's associative language, her scene-making ability and her method of blending anecdote, scene, dialogue, memories and references. For example, both Ritchie and Woolf use lists, piling up phrases or clauses separated by semi-colons. Both use metaphor effectively. One can see in Ritchie's 'Jane Austen' what Woolf meant when she said Ritchie has 'inimitable sentences' that 'rope together a handful of swiftly gathered opposites' (*E3* 401): 'Dear books! . . . in which the homely heroines charm, the dull hours fly, and the very bores are delightful' (Ritchie, *T&S* 85). Examples of the 'apparently simple and yet inevitably right sense of the use of language' (*E3* 15) noted in Woolf's tribute to her aunt also leap out in that essay:

> The charm of friends in pen-and-ink is their unchangeableness. We go to them when we want them. We know where to seek them; we know what to expect from them. They are never preoccupied; they are always 'at home;' they never turn their backs nor walk away as people do in real life, nor let their houses and leave the neighbourhood, and disappear for weeks together . . . . (*T&S* 98)

Virginia Stephen also seems to have read Ritchie's 'assigned' texts by women and her essays about those writers; Ritchie becomes the acknowledged and unacknowledged source for much of what remained in Woolf's mind about the female literary tradition. Esther Schwartz-McKinzie praises Ritchie's efforts to affirm women's achievements in a 'world that relentlessly associated greatness with masculinity. These efforts included documenting the lives of women artists (Mrs Barbauld, Amelia Opie, Felicia Felix [Mrs Hemans], Fanny Kemble and Angelica Kauffmann), who otherwise faced obscurity,' and 'reintroducing the works of her literary foremothers (Mary Russell Mitford, Elizabeth Gaskell and Maria Edgeworth)' (Intro, *Mrs Dymond* x).[34] Stephen observed, then, Ritchie's recovery strategies along with Ritchie's choices for female canonisation: Woolf, following Ritchie, wrote about Jane Austen, Charlotte Brontë, Elizabeth Barrett Browning, Julia Margaret Cameron, Maria Edgeworth, George Eliot, Elizabeth Gaskell, Mary Russell Mitford, Margaret Oliphant and Madame de Sévigné.[35]

Virginia Stephen also learns how to foreground the women's tradition from Ritchie.[36] Carol MacKay and Manuela Mourão note how the content of 'Toilers and Spinsters' anticipates Woolf's *A Room of One's Own*, particularly in its calls for reading/dining rooms for women and in its insistence on lack of money as the cause of the spinster's woes, not spinsterhood itself (MacKay, 'Thackeray' 83 [citing Boyd 87]; Mourão, 'DB' 79). But Woolf may have borrowed Ritchie's use of repetition and piled-up questions and assertions as well, along with her mildly sarcastic tone. At one point, for example, Ritchie facetiously asks, 'But what have the ladies, thus acknowledging their need, been about all these years?' (3), asks eleven more questions, and then proceeds to name women's accomplishments in a lengthy list (4–5). In *A Room of One's Own*, Woolf sarcastically asks her listeners,

> may I remind you . . . that in 1919 – which is a whole nine years ago – she was given a vote? May I also remind you that most of the professions have been open to you for close on ten years now? (111)

Woolf's book may be more focused on obstacles to women's creativity than Ritchie's essay (Maourão, 'DB' 79), but Ritchie does catalogue women writers' achievements in the face of those obstacles and note that 'Old Maids, spinsters, the solitary, heart-broken women of England, have quite a literature of their own' (1), providing, along with Mill, a hint of the phrase Woolf would use for her book title. Perhaps more important, however, Ritchie uses a method Woolf will borrow, doing research into the literature of the unmarried, consulting dozens and dozens of the books on the subject, and then boiling them down into a representative, wry description of the books 'without number' on the 'Moans of old maids' (3).

The evident connections between Ritchie and Woolf suggest Virginia Stephen paid attention to her aunt's lessons. Both Ritchie and Woolf can be called feminists. Both explore what lies beneath the surface of supposedly ordinary women. Both use letters, diaries and memoirs as sources. Both create vivid scenes and capture place, atmosphere and mood. Both bring authors to life to illuminate their art. Both love to exaggerate and use fanciful facts. Both use anecdote, quotation and dialogue to enliven biographical fact. Both work through association or juxtaposition. Both create intimacy with the reader and try to draw the reader into a community. Both muse about the nature of books, the relationship between writer and reader, the experience of reading.

Finally, offsetting a household that catered to a professional man of letters, Anne Thackeray Ritchie was a professional *woman* of letters who showed Virginia Stephen how she might conduct a writing life. Virginia was probably aware of her aunt's habit of writing every morning (M. MacCarthy 80), and it did not escape her that Aunt Anny expressed enthusiasm for the Stephens' new Bloomsbury place (*PA* 228), and thus, by implication, Virginia Stephen's declaration of personal and professional independence. In February 1905, she dropped her severely pruned review of Henry James off at 'Mrs. L's house on my way to lunch with At. Anny at the Sesame' (*PA* 237), a juxtaposition suggesting a possible lunchtime conversation between novice and professional about writing, revising and editing. Woolf later indicates an ongoing conversation between the women about their reading and perhaps their work when she mentions receiving a 'rather dull' letter 'all about books' from Aunt Anny (*L2* 105).

Also, Anne Ritchie went her own way. Leslie Stephen may have chided her about her exaggeration and overspending, but Anny cheerfully laughed at his exaggerated 'glooms'[37] and attitudes about women. Ritchie's 'Toilers and Spinsters' directly refutes Stephen's 'The Redundancy of Women' (MacKay, 'Thackeray' 83), arguing it is simply laughable to be worried about spinsters or characterise them as depressed, with no purpose in life (1–5). As Miss Thackeray, Anny lived contentedly for forty years, and when she fell in love, married a man seventeen years her junior and had two children with him (the second at age 42). Hardly helpless in financial matters, Ritchie handled all her own correspondence with editors and publishers, negotiating her own deals without recourse to Leslie Stephen or Richmond Ritchie (J. Harris 388–9). Moreover, if Ritchie's version of post-it notes on manuscripts condemns her, then many contemporary writers are in trouble.[38] Lillian Shankman suggests Ritchie's famed 'scattiness' was a cover – no one could be that dotty and achieve what Ritchie did (Section 8 265) – and Mourão says Ritchie achieved remarkable independence because she knew how to play the game and keep under the radar ('DB' 75, 87). Schwartz-McKinzie, introducing both *Mrs Dymond* and *The Story of Elizabeth* and *Old Kensington*, shows how Ritchie exposed the debilitating effects of women's relationships with men in her novels, emphasising relationships among women even as she hewed to the marriage plot (xii; xiii–xiv, xvii–xviii; see also Mourão, 'DB', 'N' and 'I'). Stephen noticed and then Woolf commented on Ritchie's adept negotiation with her culture, perceiving that Ritchie may have created 'an atmosphere of tremulous shadows and opal tinted lights' and delighted in 'the idyllic and the rapturous', but underneath, 'the shapes of things are quite hard' and have 'some surprisingly sharp edges' (*E3* 15–16).[39] Thus, Ritchie taught Stephen how to conduct a professional writing woman's life, including how to critique society without calling undue attention to one's rebelliousness.

Anne Thackeray Ritchie had an impact both direct and indirect on the essayist Woolf would become. She taught Virginia Stephen what an independent and professional writing woman looked like and, functioning as a corrective to both Leslie and Julia Stephen, gave her a glimpse into another kind of female community, that of women writers, editors and reviewers. She also bequeathed numerous essays filled with linguistic and narrative strategies the novice could adapt, along with a record of the female literary tradition. When Woolf wrote that 'young writers might do worse' than study Anne Thackeray Ritchie (*E3* 14–15), she acknowledged her debt, the debt of a novice writer to the experienced one, the debt of a student to a teacher.

Atalanta's and *Tit-Bits'* Model

When Virginia Woolf looked back at her home education, its main flaw was her painful isolation. The most important thing Anne Thackeray Ritchie may have done for Virginia Stephen, then, was bring *Atalanta* into 22 Hyde Park Gate. It, along with *Girl's Own Paper* and *Tit-Bits*, introduced the young learner to larger communities of girls, social classes, readers, self-taught people. Although the communities were print, and her access lay only through periodicals, they did enlarge her world beyond her father's library, mother's tea table and brother's stories.

Atalanta was published from 1887–8 to 1897–8 and edited by L. T. Meade for the first six of those years.[40] The Library of Leonard and Virginia Woolf contains bound copies of *Atalanta*, volumes 2 and 4 (K&M-V 9), and 'Miss Thackeray' contributed five articles to the first four volumes, up until 1890–91 – an essay on Jane Austen (A1 226–30), two pieces on Maria Edgeworth (A2 57–61; A3 13–15), a discussion of fashions in manner (A3 336–8) and an essay on fairies in British culture (A4 334–7). Thus, although no inscription says so, it seems likely Aunt Anny, rather than Leslie or Julia Stephen, gave bound volumes to the Stephen girls or gave a subscription whose copies were later bound. One suspects all four volumes with Ritchie's contributions were once in Leslie Stephen's library, with two not surviving the bombing of Mecklenburgh Square. Because the magazine opens a window on to changing attitudes about girls and women in the late nineteenth century, attitudes she would not have learned from her mother, and because it is an autodidact's dream, one hopes Virginia Stephen browsed through or read some issues of *Atalanta*.

More progressive early than late, the first few volumes of *Atalanta* anticipate what Sally Mitchell says about early twentieth-century advice manuals and mainstream periodicals. They

> used the language of moral imperative in precisely the opposite direction [from what it had done for most of the Victorian period]: when a girl leaves school, she 'must find work', either paid or unpaid, which will provide regular duties and teach her essential skills and habits that she cannot learn in the shelter of her family. ('Girls' Culture' 243; citing Elizabeth Sloan Chesser)

For example, L. T. Meade prefaces her first 'Employment for Girls' column with a statement remarkably similar to Leslie Stephen's point in his argument with Julia:

> All girls ought to be so educated that should necessity arise they may be able either to support themselves or to help the family purse. In case of unexpected reverses such girls will be independent . . . .

She must, however, prepare herself for one thing, she cannot expect to earn any steady income as an amateur. The girl who wants to help her family, or to earn her own living, must take up and understand some one calling thoroughly. She must give time and thought, she must give study, and a certain amount of money, to this purpose. (A1 63)

She also notes that girls 'happily' now have more opportunities than just 'the badly-paid and over-crowded profession of teaching', and mentions upcoming papers on Nursing, Wood Engraving, Typewriting, Journalism, Chinapainting, the Civil Service and different professions, among others (A1 63). That year's *Atalanta* (1887–8) also had a column on Pharmacy and two on Medicine. Meade's closing comments reflect the new moral imperative: 'When we work we bring out the best that is in us – when we work we help others' (A1 63). The magazine's progressive nature can also be seen in articles on 'Girls Who Won Success' (Elizabeth Thompson, Elizabeth Garrett Anderson, Florence Lees and Mary Davies in A1 487–93, 572–7, 639–44, 670–4); the dialogue it promotes with readers about 'Brown Owl' essays; and its wide variety of articles, including science ('Birds in London' [A2 139–42]) and sports ('Golf as a Pastime for Girls' [A4 792–4]). Articles on 'feminine' topics like the art of pleasing were in the decided minority.[41]

Atalanta's editors and contributors assumed girls were serious, knowledge-seeking and eager to take advantage of increasing opportunities. They also assumed the girls in its middle-class audience were going to or had been to school,[42] something young Virginia Stephen would have noticed. Mavis Reimer notes *Atalanta*'s coverage of women's education ('Worlds' 206), and articles such as Dorothea Beale's on past and present schools and Lucy Toulmin Smith's 'What America Does for Her Girls' on universities for women appeared frequently (A3 259–61; A3 315–17; A4 755–64). When R. K. Douglas wrote a 'Brown Owl' article arguing that higher education was destroying the feminine graces (A3 459–61), mail flooded the editorial office, almost all in protest. One letter writer, 'An Indignant One', begins by saying 'It does not seem to occur to Mr Douglas that most women do not like the idea of being created solely for the use of man' and adds, 'If Nature does not mean us to cultivate our intellects, why are they given to us?' (A3 587). Mr Douglas was forced to write another article (A3 642–4), which only generated more indignant mail (A3 767–8, n.p. [as though 771]).

Although the magazine discusses the need for girls to find work after school, *Atalanta* also functions *as* a school by bringing schoolroom assignments and questions into the home. The 'Atalanta Scholarship and Reading Union' offered a year-long coherent reading course, along with reading questions, essay topics and a contest. In a volume Virginia Stephen may have read, the reading course includes Maria Edgeworth (written by Miss Thackeray), Walter Savage Landor, Washington Irving, John Keats, Robert Browning, Charlotte Brontë, Tennyson, Thackeray, Nathaniel Hawthorne, George Eliot, John Ruskin and Matthew Arnold. The two 'Scholarship Competition Questions' for Edgeworth were: 'I. Voltaire says, Le style, c'est l'homme. Discuss this with reference to Miss Edgeworth. II. What do you judge to have been Miss Edgeworth's views respecting the art of fiction? Support your answer from any of her books' (*A2* 62). The magazine included articles on art, science, literature, music, history and education (including one on home education), and it introduced readers to different cultures in its 'A Girl's Life in . . . ' series (within 'The Brown Owl'), giving coverage to South Australia, Greece and Russia, among others (*A4* 669–70; *A4* 796–8). It promoted analysis of English literature through its monthly search passages: the 'student's' task was to send in the author's name and title for each quoted passage. References for the September 1888 search passages were from Longfellow, Wordsworth, Bulwer-Lytton, Coleridge, Milton and Hood (*A2* 62).

The magazine counteracted Julia Stephen's library, giving Virginia Stephen access to a community interested in something besides service, and Leslie Stephen's library, giving her access to a literary community of women. It featured 'how-to' articles, like Walter Besant's two-part series on 'The Writing of Novels', Sara Jeanette Duncan's 'How an American Girl Became a Journalist' and Professor A. J. Church's Brown Owl column on what a girl's library should contain (*A1* 163–7; *A1* 370–5; *A3* 91–4; *A4* 475–7), which generated alternative suggestions. Gifts determined Virginia's library at first, and it differed from those proposed in *Atalanta*'s pages, but the assumption that a girl could create her own library and disagree with authorities about its contents was a lesson the young woman may have taken to heart. She may also have found Amy Levy's article on British Museum readers inspiring (*A2* 449–54). In the pages of *Atalanta*, volumes 2 and 4, Virginia Stephen could have found: work by Edith Nesbit, poems by Christina Rossetti, fiction by Frances Hodgson Burnett and essays by Clementina Black, Edmund Gosse and Helen Zimmern, along with Miss Thackeray; a whole year devoted to Shakespeare in the Atalanta Scholarship and Reading Union; articles about birds, seals, spiders and crayfishes; numerous articles about art, including ones on John Ruskin, Raphael, Burne-Jones, brush-marks, and children in modern art. If Virginia opened the pages of *Atalanta*, she entered a middle-class, literate world,[43] but also a world created solely for girls and women.

Atalanta would have made Virginia Stephen aware of what she was missing at the same time as it provided her with some of it, not only curriculum and 'how-to' articles, but also other reading girls. It showed her what women could do in publishing and how a well-established writer like Miss Thackeray could reach out to a new audience. In the home of an eminent Victorian man of letters, a monthly column told her there were English Men *and Women* of Letters and the table of contents told her women like Aunt Anny could, in turn, write about those women of letters. It included numerous examples of a wide range of essays. Finally, its conversational style and democratic inclusion of readers' responses provided Virginia Stephen with a dialogic model that Virginia Woolf could later use in reviews and essays.

The *Hyde Park Gate News* for Monday, 7 December 1891 indicates the Stephen children were also familiar with other popular magazines then available. Answering a question about possible Christmas gifts in the Correspondence column, the 'editor' writes: 'reader. If the child is a girl "A World of Girls" or the "Girls' own Paper" would be suitable gifts. If a boy certainly the "Boy's own Annual"' (*HPGN* 11).[44] Edited by Charles Peters for the Religious Tract Society, *The Girl's Own Paper* followed *The Boy's Own Paper*, developed in

1879 to '[counteract] the spate of "pernicious" publications arising in the wake of the 1870 Education Act' (Forrester 13). Wendy Forrester says the weekly paper style was 'lively and progressive', a 'departure' from the Society's Sunday periodicals, but with a Christian tone nonetheless. *The Girl's Own Paper* did not feature school stories, but focused on gendered adventures: love, marriage, possibly earning a living. Each issue had two serial stories, and the articles were on 'health and beauty, dress, needlework, housekeeping, cookery, hobbies, music . . . , foreign countries, doing good, poems, jokes and anecdotes . . . , competitions and a weekly collection of answers to correspondents' (13–14). It aimed to reach all classes (Forrester 25), but the content often contradicted those good intentions (Dixon 'Deprived'). Terri Doughty explains that its long-lived success probably derived from its ability to help 'New Girls interested in new educational and professional opportunities . . . negotiate the tensions between . . . two mythical creatures, the monstrous New Woman and the sweet Angel in the House' and to respond to a demand for progressive information while appearing to serve conservative aims (8–9).[45]

Vanessa Bell remembers in her memoir of Virginia's childhood that *Tit-Bits*, a popular one-penny paper, was their 'favourite weekly which we used to buy together with threepenny-worth of Fry's Chocolate, taking both to Kensington Gardens to read and eat together lying on the grass under the trees on summer afternoons' (VB 65). Kate Jackson, in 'The *Tit-Bits* Phenomenon', explains that the paper, published by George Newnes, was a miscellany,

> a sixteen page patchwork of advice, humorous anecdotes, romantic fiction, statistical information, historical explanation, advertisement, legal detail, quips and queries, and reader correspondence. Competitions were a central feature. Regular columns and serials were interspersed with short jokes and sallies. (203)

Enjoying a huge circulation – between 400,000 and 670,000 at its height – *Tit-Bits* attracted readers from the 'aspiring' middle class, the 'expanding lower-middle and upper-working classes' (202–3). Yet Jackson notes Newnes's appeal to various audiences, arguing he offered 'the status of the self-educated specialist' to female and juvenile readers as well (*Newnes* 26). The upper-middle-class Vanessa and Virginia Stephen, avidly reading a paper aimed mainly at commuting, working adults, thus gained access to alternate personal and class identities.

Peter McDonald and Kate Jackson make it clear that *Tit-Bits* threatened cultural purists. McDonald describes how W. E. Henley and literary men hated Newnes, Harmsworth, *Tit-Bits* and the *Strand*: *Tit-Bits* stood for the Education Act of 1870, democracy, degradation of literature, loss of culture (9, 34–6, 42–4). Its inclusive nature and personal tone decreased class barriers, Jackson writes, so it was attacked as feather-brained, low, cheap, sensational, irresponsible and ephemeral, 'a transparent attempt to capture the market by playing to the lowest common denominator' ('Newnes' 24; *Newnes* 43, 44, 66).[46] Matthew Arnold, Jackson explains, in trying to lift his own journalism into criticism, pitted literature against the New Journalism of Newnes. In doing so, he 'inaugurated a new critical tradition in discourse about the press, complicated by the fear that "the common reader" represented a threat to both quality and order, that was to persist into the twentieth century' (*Newnes* 46).

However, McDonald and Jackson also understand the newspaper's position and achievement. McDonald notes the continuity between the mid-Victorian penny press and *Tit-Bits*, Newnes's portrayal of himself as 'a socially responsible entrepreneur', and the broadly based lower-middle-class and middle-class families in its audience; the price of the paper put it 'within the budget of many working-class homes' (145–8). He notes its 'entertaining but respectable' (151) and secular and wholesome combination (16), and argues the *Strand* and *Tit-Bits* made the 'established religious monthlies and the more scurrilous working-class weeklies appear outmoded, because they were either too pious, too immoral, or too class-specific for the new homogenous "mass culture" of the 1890s' (16).[47] Jackson defines *Tit-Bits* 'as a source of cultural identification, a supplier of social services, a popular and social educator, a legal and moral bond between readers and editor, and as a pluralistic discursive sphere regulated by a communal sense of mutual responsibility' (*Newnes* 54). *Tit-Bits* was a 'familiar companion', using an 'intimate rather than an authoritative tone' (*Newnes* 53, 66). It attempted to recreate the kind of community lost in the face of urban spread and segregation, promoted mutual responsibility and communal efforts, and encouraged its readers to become writers in a collaborative and democratic enterprise (*Newnes* 74, 16). It also used an educational framework for its 'Inquiry Column', with the editor taking the role of a teacher and answering short, published questions. The column's format, suggests Jackson, 'reflected the familiarity of this kind of exchange, typical of the examination, to an audience that was integrated into a system of compulsory schooling and sought further educational qualifications' (*Newnes* 60). Finally, it mixed light entertainment with instruction (*Newnes* 84).

Tit-Bits gave Virginia Stephen a model and style she could immediately imitate and practice. She learned from and used the *Tit-Bits* formula: *The Hyde Park Gate News*, the family newspaper written mostly by her between 1891 and 1895, looks like it (with drawn columns and headlines) and sounds like it (correspondence, humour, exaggeration and arch jokes). *Tit-Bits* also demonstrated how to reach beyond an exclusive group (*L6* 420), with George Newnes adopting an 'interactive posture' and *Tit-Bits* functioning as a 'popular social educator' (Jackson, '*Tit-Bits*' 206). Under George Newnes, Jackson concludes, '*Tit-Bits* offered its readers engagement, interaction and connection' ('*Tit-Bits*' 213), and in the process, redefined the idea of audience. Thus, Virginia Woolf, in later choosing the term 'common reader', inserted herself into the discourse about audiences on the side of the untutored, not on the side of W. E. Henley and Matthew Arnold. Attempting to create a sense of community in her essays, Woolf reaches beyond her own class, a strategy her younger self may have learned from the transgressive *Tit-Bits*, devoured with chocolate, on those summer afternoons.

Atalanta and *Tit-Bits* gave Virginia Stephen access to two very different worlds, both of which resisted cultural norms while not touting revolution. *Atalanta*, with its strong emphasis on female education and strengths, counteracted her father's library and her mother's views; *Tit-Bits*, with its emphasis on access and speed, allowed her to cross class boundaries and learn about other ways of reading and thinking about literature. The poles these periodicals occupy – literary/popular; middle-class girls/working-class people; serious/fun; lengthy/short – represent the tensions about audience and the nature of literature permeating Virginia

Stephen's culture. From *Atalanta* and *Tit-Bits*, then, she learned about the resistance of outsiders, but also about the tension between quality and access, between professional and entrepreneurial ideals, that Virginia Woolf and other modernists would experience and try to navigate.[48]

Thoby, Aunt Anny, *Atalanta* and *Tit-Bits* broadened Virginia Stephen's curriculum; introduced her to dialogic pedagogies; taught her lessons about society, literature and writing; and widened her communities to include more boys and girls, other social classes and different literary traditions. Even as her teachers shared what they knew with her, however, she was detached from the communities they represented. As these teachers brought much-needed fresh air into the claustrophobic 22 Hyde Park Gate, they also brought with them unresolved tensions, paradoxes and contradictions. Coherence and community continued to elude her.[49]

Notes

1. For Virginia Stephen, many Duckworth and Stephen relatives were oppressive and thus objects of sarcasm, humour, even cruelty. After her mother's death and during her father's illness, their excessive Victorian mourning was burdensome and, to her, hypocritical (Lee, 'How' 119).

   Two distinctive aunts, however, taught Virginia Stephen important lessons: Anne Thackeray Ritchie, actual aunt only to Laura, and Caroline Emelia Stephen, 'the Nun'. Both were matter-of-fact and practical in the face of tragedy, resisted Leslie's manipulative tyranny, lived independent lives and, most important, wrote.

   Even so, they came in for their share of Stephen children's mockery (Lee, *VW* 75), with Hilary Newman suggesting Leslie Stephen's attitude toward Anny was passed down to Virginia (5), but Lee notes Woolf's more considered judgements (*VW* 76–8). Newman insists Woolf never acknowledged her debt to her aunt, but Woolf published three essays detailing Anny's influence (and considered writing a fourth [Newman 6]). See also Dell, *Influential Forebears*, for a nuanced examination of Woolf's ambivalence about her nineteenth-century legacy and what that ambivalence allowed: fluidity, simultaneity, 'a both/and, rather than either/or, approach' (178).

   Caroline Emelia Stephen's influence came after Leslie Stephen's death (Marcus 'Niece'). She provided a haven when Virginia was ill and the capital that brought financial independence and autonomy; furthermore, she 'overturned received opinions with . . . serenity', was comfortable with solitude and exhibited a 'positive spirit of unconventionality' (Mepham 17, 14–15). See also Alister Raby, Madeline Moore, Catherine Smith and Jane de Gay.

2. See Rosner on 'thresholds', 59–90.

3. Even given the number of classes Virginia Stephen took at King's College (Jones and Snaith), her schooling does not come close to the amount or level of her brothers'.

4. Julia Stephen's budget is on the last page (verso) of her unpublished reply to Bertha Lathbury's April 1880 'Agnosticism and Women' in *Nineteenth Century*, ['Agnostic Women'].

5. Twenty are from Clifton, including five prize books, and eight from Cambridge. Thoby's prize books, bound in black leather and embossed by Clifton bookseller J. Baker & Son, include labels signed by M. G. Glazebrook identifying form, date and prize. W. W. Asquith (1851–1918), Thoby's housemaster, known as 'a fine teacher' and 'successful disciplinarian' (Spender and Asquith 18), gave him Omar Khayyam's *Rubaiyat* (K&M-V 169).

See Victoria Larson and Christopher Stray for the importance of classics in nineteenth-century English education for boys and men. Larson argues knowledge of the classics allowed many men 'to obtain worldly power and to justify their right to it' (225), whereas Stray notes that the classics were the 'largest single category of curriculum content' and a 'major symbol of social distinction' (*Transformed* 185; 'Schoolboys' 39).

6. Stray says Greek and Latin grammars were still in Latin, 'the language of learning', in the early 1800s, though autodidacts had some impact in the 1820s and 1830s. R. C. Jebb introduced facing translations in 1870 (controversial because they gave 'too much help to pupils'), which led to books like Mackail's *Select Epigrams* with its 'crib' ('Classics' 264–6).

7. Perhaps she wanted to discuss Sidney Lee's anxiety. According to Bill Bryson,

> Many went into a kind of obstinate denial and persuaded themselves that the sonnets were simply 'poetical exercises' or 'professional trials of skill,' as the biographer Sidney Lee terms them, arguing that Shakespeare had written them in a number of assumed voices . . . . Thus, any reference to longing to caress a fellow was Shakespeare writing in a female voice, as a demonstration of his versatility and genius. Shakespeare's real friendships, Lee insisted, were of 'the healthy manly type' and any alternative interpretation 'casts a slur on the dignity of the poet's name which scarcely bears discussion'. (146–7)

8. Woolf writes, 'His sons, with the exception of the Army and Navy, should follow whatever profession they chose' (*E5* 588), but Thoby's path was in fact set. MacGibbon notes he

> loved open-air activities, beagling, riding, hunting; in the Stephen tradition he was a formidable cross-country walker. He had always been a serious naturalist. At school he had kept caterpillars, observing their metamorphoses. Not for him, on visits to the Bristol zoo, the banalities of camels and great cats; he made for the insect house, or watched lizards being fed live cockroaches, carefully counting the ones that got away. Had he read Natural Sciences in Part II of his Tripos he might have found an occupation more congenial than the law. (35)

In a 23 March 1902 letter to Mary Fisher, Leslie notes Thoby's 'thirst for natural history' and thinks it 'funny' he should have acquired it, given 'how little encouragement he has had' (Lee, *VW* 115; 773 n26). Sadly, because gentlemen studied the classics, it probably did not occur to either Leslie or Thoby to consider the sciences as a career.

9. See also Knighton, 'Thoby Stephen' 25, and *Clifton* 161, where he summarises the reports. Two more form sheets, for Thoby's first two five-week periods at Clifton in autumn 1894, are in the Stephen Family Papers (BL Add MS 88954/3/2). Woolf remembers Sidney Irwin as someone Thoby talked about ('Sketch' 187).

10. Evelyns at Colham Green was founded in 1872 by G. T. Worsley with strong ties to Eton (Leinster-Mackay 81). Virginia also visited Thoby at Clifton, and Thoby and Adrian at Cambridge (*L1* 17, 34, 86). Leonard Woolf first saw Vanessa and Virginia Stephen in Thoby's rooms when they were up for May Week in 1901 (Lee, *VW* 205, citing *Sowing* 182–3).

11. Edited by David Lisle Crane and introduced by Julie Crane, this book is 'a remarkable example of amateur scholarship' (McMahon). Over 100 illustrations, including pictures, maps, drawings and facsimile manuscripts, enrich the text, and the introduction, biographical notes, bibliography and documentary appendices provide even more information. It includes the Behrens family correspondence, but also letters between school and family, reports, exam papers, and so forth. Cross-referenced, indexed and annotated, the letters supply voluminous detail into late Victorian social history, including conflict between Leu and Min Behrens about female suffrage.

12. Not all pressures were unspoken. Repeatedly, Leslie's letters ask for reports, remind and admonish, and push Thoby to do well (Letters to Thoby and Adrian, BL Add MS

88954/1/1). Although Leslie had been miserable at Eton, once he accepted Thoby's being at school, he assumed Thoby would go there on a scholarship. Thoby sat for Eton's entrance exam, but was so low on the list he could not be sure of a spot (Annan 355n [22]). Leslie was 'not sanguine' about Thoby's university examinations, either (*MB* 106), though Thoby won a place at Trinity. When Thoby did not earn the first-class degree in classics needed for an academic career, his father said he took the disappointment 'bravely' (*MB* 111), but Leslie's anxiety about the Tripos beforehand (Letters to Thoby and Adrian, BL Add MS 88954/1/1, #65–69) indicate he may have regretted it more than Thoby did (MacGibbon 34). Thoby's 23 October 1905 letter to C. E. W. Bean about becoming an artist, though perhaps playful, suggests he did not feel strongly committed to the law (Lindsay Appendix IX). Virginia mentions his 'natural, easy gift for drawing' ('Sketch 1' 108), and he frequently drew in books and notebooks; a collection of loose drawings by him are in the British Library (Papers of Thoby Stephen, Add MS 89118).

13. E. N. P. Moor died in March 1895, so Thoby lost his housemaster two months before losing his mother (Crane 236). A 'serious world epidemic' of influenza reached London in 1889, with milder outbreaks from 1891 to 1894 and a 'more serious one' in 1895 (Crane 335). See M. G. Glazebrook's letter notifying parents that boys would be sent home on Friday, 5 April instead of the next Tuesday because of the epidemic (Crane, Documentary Appendix XL).
14. Larson 185–97 and T. W. Bamford 98–101, 168–74, and 218–22 further analyse the class-based classics/sciences divide. Percival hired many scientists, making Clifton 'a pioneer of science teaching' (Winterbottom, *CAP* 22), but reputations depended on classics preparation.
15. His papers, in Archives and Special Collections at Durham University Library, include diaries and journals, correspondence, field computations and maps. He served in France and Belgium during World War I and retired as a Lieutenant-Colonel.
16. After he left in 1879, Percival was on the Clifton Council, serving as Chairman from 1895 to 1917, when he 'was more influential than ever' (Winterbottom, *JP* 13). This later link to Clifton is noted in the 8 April 1895 issue of the *Hyde Park Gate News*; the reporter writes, 'The term ended 4 days earlier than usual because of the influenza, or because Dr Percival has been created an Arch bishop – we cannot make out which; anyhow the extra holydays are very acceptable to every one' (199). Percival became Bishop of Hereford on 20 February 1895.
17. Jeremy Potter subtitles his biography 'radical autocrat'; Winterbottom says he was 'a lifelong liberal' in 'theological doctrine', but 'a puritan' in 'morals and conduct' (*CAP* 26).
18. Clifton has the distinction of opening the first Jewish boarding house at an English public school: Polack House lasted 127 years, 1878–2005. See Winterbottom's *Dynasty* and A. I. Polack. Perhaps Clifton's ethos made it easier for Thoby and Leonard Woolf to be good friends?
19. According to John Sadler, John Percival later promoted the cause of working-class adult education, chairing the first meeting of the Workers' Educational Association in 1903 and then helping Albert Mansbridge, its founder, get the organisation off the ground.
20. See Keigwin; Honey, *Tom* 104–17; and Winterbottom's biography of A. E. J. Collins (*SF*). F. A. M. Webster's Clifton chapter discusses nothing but games.
21. He includes Woolf's description of Roger Fry's Clifton days.
22. Woolf recalls a tolerant, serene and admiring Thoby, who also 'exacted his rights' and was dominant at home and school: 'The Pup had to apologise when he put another boy over him as head of the house; he was not going to be passed over. He was not easy to put upon' ('Sketch' 125–6). Putting this passage with a letter C. E. W. Bean wrote to H. M. Tasker on 18 October 1930, Geoff Lindsay suggests Bean is the boy

Woolf refers to, and Peter Rees agrees. Bean, a Great War correspondent, historian, barrister, and judge's associate in Australia, writes,

> I started near the bottom of the house and finished as the head of it, although my great school-friend, Thoby Stephen, was immediately above me in the school. He was a son of Leslie Stephen, the writer, and had a far better brain than I, but he was very young, and the housemaster (W. W. Asquith . . .) thought it better that I should be head of the house. When I left Stephen succeeded me. (Rees 17; Lindsay 107–8).

Letters from Thoby exist in the Bean papers, and Lindsay wonders if the reverse might be true (109). Virginia Stephen met Bean in August 1897 (*PA* 120 and n4).

23. V. Curtis suggests he played cricket (22), but Knighton says, based on the Clifton 'Annals', he played only football ('Thoby' 26). Since Leslie occasionally asks Thoby about cricket in his letters, perhaps Thoby played it informally.

24. Writing to James Russell Lowell on 7 June 1891, Leslie Stephen mentions what Bicknell calls 'a schoolboy fracas' (*SLLS2* 400-1), also reported in *The Mausoleum Book*, about Thoby's 'allow[ing] a playful schoolfellow to stick a knife into his femoral artery' (84). G. T. Worsley, Evelyns headmaster, wrote to Julia on 18 May, 'Thoby "with almost incredible folly" allowed "another boy to stab with his knife at a book which he put on his leg!" The knife slipped and severed an artery. Thoby lost a lot of blood but watched the wound being sewn up with great interest' (Letters to Julia Stephen, BL Add MS 88954/1/2; see also Carol MacKay, 'Thackeray' 91 n37). Thought of as outgoing, fun-loving, 'sensible, easy-going, dependable' (Annan 118), Thoby was often ill (*MB* 100, 105, 106-7, 107), walked in his sleep (*MB* 84) and was prone to melancholy (Lowe, Biographical Notes 222). Letters from Mr Worsley to Julia Stephen (2 and 20 March and 4 April 1894) cite 'violent attacks', and in an 1894 influenza delirium, he tried to throw himself out of a window (Stemerick 60; MacGibbon 35; also Annan 117, 371n; and Lee, *VW* 114–15). Stemerick notes the difference between Thoby's treatment and Virginia's in 1895–6: Thoby's doctor reassured his parents and sent Thoby back to school, whereas Virginia's doctor decided '[her] one escape, her studies, was probably to blame; his prescription was that all lessons should be stopped' (60-2; see also Jane Marcus, 'VW's Violin' 31-5).

25. Woolf says he had 'an amused, surprised, questioning attitude to me as an individual' ('Sketch' 138).

26. In her journal, she recalls 'Even that little bit of Virgil with T. in the summer, when I was hardly able to use my brains, brought a sense of harmony into them, such as for many months they had not known' (*PA* 238). Thoby was generous with more than his schooling.

27. Woolf would later write, trying to recapture what their young adulthood felt like before his death, that it was an exciting time, when 'we both pushed out from the mists of childhood; and each saw the other emerging; and each felt new qualities, he in himself, me in myself; both in each other. They were days of discovery' ('Sketch' 140).

28. Leslie Stephen also focused on story first: 'His method of teaching language was always the same. He put all grammar on one side, and then, taking some classic, made straight for the sense' (*E1* 129). See *SLLS2* 517 for Leslie's confession of this fault, but also his attempt at grammar instruction. He did notice errors. Woolf remembers his reaction to Lady Strachey's excitement at finding an inscribed first edition of Ben Jonson. He seemed rather grim when Lady Strachey pointed at the title page and exclaimed 'Ex dono Aùctoris.' 'I didn't like to tell Lady Strachey,' she writes that her father told her on the way home, 'but the accent should be on the second syllable of auctòris, not the first' ('J. M. S.' 125).

29. See Koulouris's description of Thoby's abilities and Virginia's sense of loss during his absences (*HL* 36).

30. The notes are probably Stephen's rather than Woolf's because (1) most are in Thoby's Latin textbooks, (2) her Latin studies coincide with Thoby's last year at Clifton and

first year at Cambridge (1898–1900), and (3) she does not continue Latin study as painstakingly as she does Greek. In the Lucretius example, her notes may have been added in 1907; she writes to Violet, in a February 1907 letter (editors' dating), that she is 'stumbling through Lucretius' (*L1* 280). She also seems to have bought a used H. A. J. Munro translation of Lucretius in 1907; according to Julia King, the translation is at the bottom of each page (email message 17 December 2018).

31. Another comment, about Epigram 615, is at the bottom of 391. Thoby inscribed his book J. T. Stephen, Trinity College, Cambridge April 1900, and drew a landscape on the back endpaper. Although not likely, it is possible Leslie wrote in Thoby's 1896 schoolbook. But it is more likely Virginia mimicked Leslie's acerbic tone, perhaps writing the note while studying Latin with Thoby in the autumn of 1904 (*L1* 141). Leslie and Virginia have similar handwriting, but analysis and comparison of their hands at the end of *The Mausoleum Book*, where he dictated the last paragraph to her (*The 'MB'* I, BL Add MS 57920), makes me believe this notation is hers.

32. See R. C. Lehmann's 'Of Sisters' (1891) for a stark contrast to Thoby. John Lehmann's father deals with 'the lighter and less strictly academic side of Cambridge life' (preface n.p.), holding up as funny supposedly engrained gender differences: 'It may be laid down as axiom that no sister ever threw a ball straight' (20; see also 22).

33. McNeillie also suggests 'A.R.' in 'On Being Ill' is Anny Ritchie (*E4* 328 n4). If Stephen read Ritchie's 'Reminiscences' in *Lord Tennyson and His Friends* (Julia Margaret and H. H. Cameron [1893]), she might have observed their footnoted 'unconventional rules for life': the Camerons were peculiar in their 'respect for their own time'. The women in the house did not follow the customary rules, did not 'live in public' and 'utterly ignored' visitors (13).

34. Anne Thackeray Ritchie's *A Book of Sibyls* is a collective biography, a tradition of women's life writing that Woolf does not acknowledge (Booth 229).

35. See also MacKay, 'Thackeray' 83.

36. MacKay argues Ritchie kept herself at the forefront in essays about other women writers, 'almost as if she were providing proof that they lived anew in her' ('Biography' 77).

37. Anny even tried to 'anticipate and dispel the inevitable recitation of misery' he went through during her visits. He may have been dying but she tweaked him about his catalogue of complaints. 'Well, Leslie,' she said on entering his sick room, 'Damn—Damn—DAMN!' (Fuller and Hammersley 156; see also A. Bell, Intro xxv). As Henrietta Garnett notes, she 'succeeded in making him laugh instead of groan. No one else would have dared' (272).

38. Leslie Stephen described her habit of pinning notes to her manuscripts in his *Mausoleum Book* (14); Woolf uses the story and his comparison of Ritchie and Austen in her 1919 obituary essay (*E3* 16–17).

39. Woolf's granite and rainbow combination leaps to mind. See my 'Young writers' for other links between the two writers and the many other critics who note connections.

40. Though Elizabeth Thomasina Meade married Lucy's brother, Alfred Toulmin Smith, she was not Lucy Toulmin Smith as I mistakenly claimed in '"Young writers might do worse"' (30). Reimer says Meade wrote over 280 books in her career, 30 of which were girls' school stories. Having suffered under a father who restricted her access to paper – her 'scribbling' was a bad habit – she often celebrated girls' resourcefulness and portrayed 'plucky but vulnerable children' ('Meade' 193–6). She took over as editor of Routledge's *Every Girl's Annual* in 1887, retitled *Atalanta*, suggesting 'the magazine's celebratory tone toward girls' aspirations' ('Meade' 196–7). Lucy Toulmin Smith, a frequent *Atalanta* contributor, was an antiquarian, scholar and librarian for Manchester College at Oxford from 1894 to 1911 (Porter).

41. Margaret Beetham and Kay Boardman reprinted 'On Housekeeping' (*A4*) in their *Victorian Women's Magazines: An Anthology* (75–7). This column is atypical, given

the preponderance of *Atalanta* articles on non-traditional subjects, but for Beetham and Boardman, its presence shows traditional subjects were still discussed even as 'new activities like sport' were taking up more space (75). The 'strides of the Victorian women's movement can be seen in the definition of girlhood constructed' in magazines such as *Girl's Own Paper* and *Atalanta*: 'Although still in training to be a wife and mother, late Victorian girls are seen as able to consider work opportunities, university education and sport as options for their pre-marital years' (71). They do not note how relatively rare such training pieces were in *Atalanta* or that 'On Housekeeping' was a Brown Owl column meant to invite discussion. They do not note Eleanor Bairdsmith's recommended control of money or the criticism of those who incessantly clean or the matter-of-fact statement that some girls and women do not like housekeeping (76; A4 346–8). They do not note the responses in 'The Atalanta Letter-Bag' (sixth set of letters after 798, back of volume 4 [n.p.]). Some responses reflect traditional attitudes, but others do not: 'La Belle Rose', for example, details how she combines housework with work in a school, study of her own, and private pupils three days a week. 'The Atalanta Letter-Bag', however, may not have appeared in what Beetham and Boardman checked: the letters are in the Ohio State University Library's *Atalanta*, but not in the British Library's.

42. L. T. Meade was a prolific writer of girls' books, establishing the girls' school story in 1886 with her *A World of Girls*. See Reimer for more about Meade, the girls' school story genre, and its explosion during this period ('Meade', 'two irreconcilable things' and 'Worlds'). See also Mitchell, 'Children's Reading', who notes that between 1900 and 1920, the number of girls at recognised grammar schools increased from 20,000 to 185,000: 'L. T. Meade wrote for the first generation in a new world' (62).
43. Its price (6d monthly), pretty covers and lavish illustrations mark its middle-class status (Dixon, 'Children' 139). Reimer calls it 'largely a literary publication' ('Meade' 196).
44. Evidently, the Stephen daughters knew about L. T. Meade's famous school story. Publishers were reluctant to cater to either working-class or middle-class girls before 1880, so many girls read their brothers' magazines. Publishers continued to ignore working-class girls (except in the *Servant's Magazine*) until the mill girl papers began to appear with the *Girls' Best Friend* in 1898 (Dixon 'Deprived').
45. The Stephens apparently knew about these papers and had access to them, but it seems unlikely that Leslie and Julia Stephen, two agnostics, subscribed to Religious Tract Society papers. See Forrester for numerous short excerpts from the paper, organised around large themes such as 'Health and Beauty' and 'Doing Good', which she weaves through her commentary. Doughty also organises her selection around large themes such as 'Household Management' and 'Work', covering more years and reproducing full articles and pages, but with no commentary. See also Bunyan 48–51.
46. See Jackson, *Newnes* 11, for how a 'range of cultural critics from Matthew Arnold to Q. D. Leavis and beyond have constructed an opposition between art and mass culture' that, she argues, is based on a problematic definition of popular culture (32). That definition makes assigning Woolf only to 'art' even more problematic. Anna Snaith (*PPN*) and Melba Cuddy-Keane (*VW*) both show Woolf, in contrast to such cultural critics, demonstrating a complex understanding of her context and her place in it.
47. See Jackson, *Newnes* 54–6, for a critique of the causal connection often made between the Education Act of 1870 and the cheap popular press. As she and others make clear, growth in literacy was well along before 1870, and the reading public had already become increasingly large and diverse. Newnes identified an audience already in existence, whose reading needs, he believed, were not being met.

48. *Atalanta* could not survive financially, whereas *Tit-Bits* lived on until 1956 and has had many imitators, such as *Rare-Bits, Wit and Wisdom, Answers* and *Pearson's Weekly* in the 1980s and 1990s (McDonald 145) and *Reader's Digest* now.

    Jackson, examining Newnes and *Tit-Bits* from the perspective of the periodical press, emphasizes the newspaper's positive features, and sees Newnes straddling culture and profit, whereas McDonald, examining the editor and his paper from the perspective of the literary establishment, emphasizes the fear *Tit-Bits* created in the literati of the day. Interestingly enough, without citing each other, their work together reflects the tension between access and quality experienced by Virginia Woolf and other authors in her lifetime, a tension that has not abated.

49. In 'A Sketch of the Past,' Virginia Woolf remembers feeling what she came to call 'the outsider's feeling'. She was in the Hyde Park Gate drawing room, watching the 'patriarchal society of the Victorian age . . . in full swing', as though she were a child standing outside a tent's flap and 'see[ing] the circus going on inside' (153). Her description captures the outsider's sense of exclusion, but also the detachment. Later discussing the great literary figures who visited her parents, but who were 'looming in the distance', and the world of 'the Post Office, the publishing office, and the Law Courts' that her Duckworth brothers and Jack Hills inhabited, she says she could not

    > make any connection . . . . I could not make them cohere; nor feel myself in touch with them. And I spent many hours of my youth restlessly comparing them. No doubt the distraction and the differences were of use; as a means of education; as a way of showing one the contraries. (158–9)

    Much of Virginia Stephen's education consisted of learning about and absorbing contraries, tensions, lack of coherence.

Chapter 3

Venturing beyond 22 Hyde Park Gate

Teachers

Reading *Tit-Bits* in Kensington Gardens, Virginia Stephen ventured beyond 22 Hyde Park Gate for a momentary escape from its mourning, repression and conventions. As she ventured even further afield – into libraries, classrooms, language – she encountered teachers who encouraged her to go beyond family, beyond Victorian, beyond patriarchal, beyond familiar. Libraries meant new books and research skills; classes at King's College meant multiple pedagogies and an educational structure; and Janet Case meant deepening Greek study and politics. Her new teachers taught lifelong lessons, fostered independence and introduced diverse communities, helping her consider a life beyond 22 Hyde Park Gate.

Libraries' Bounty

In 1938, Virginia Woolf explains asking Lady Tweedsmuir to support the Women's Service Library by writing 'I owe all the education I ever had to my father's library ... ' (*L6* 234). Her request on behalf of the Women's Service Library implicitly acknowledges, however, that she also owed some of her education to the London Library and the British Museum Reading Room; they moved Virginia Stephen away from Leslie's study, Julia's tea table, Thoby's talk and Aunt Anny's influence. She took full advantage of these libraries, using them to fill out reviews, prepare for teaching and explore. Their implicit pedagogy enlarged her curriculum and taught her research skills as she discovered a larger world of readers, writers and books. She also observed how libraries both include and exclude people, facilitate and regulate learning. She experienced, simultaneously, bounty and exclusion, wealth and scarcity, freedom and surveillance.

Although a public library opened in Kensington in 1888 (T. Kelly, *PL* 449), Virginia Stephen does not seem to have frequented it, perhaps because public libraries were new in her world.[1] In 1887, 'only two parishes in all of metropolitan London', writes Richard Altick, 'had rate-supported libraries', and he and Thomas Kelly say London was slower than the rest of the country to establish them (Altick, *ECR* 227; *PL* 24). Altick details why free libraries did not spread rapidly after the passage of the Public Libraries Act in 1850, even as the numbers and kinds of reading materials were exploding: the halfpenny on a pound library rates could often purchase and maintain buildings but not books (228; see also Hammond 89–90).[2] But the association of public libraries with the working classes and the possibility that libraries might reduce the gulf between classes were probably why it took so long to construct a free and public English library system.[3] Seen at first as a handout to classes who would not pay the rates, a force that 'would undermine the independence of the citizen' and '"a shelter for a lot of idle fellows to spend their time in"' (T. Kelly, *PL* 30; see also Altick 233–5), public libraries were scorned by ratepayers who 'could afford to subscribe to commercial libraries' and 'were not convinced that the poor should be "civilized" at their expense' (Inwood 674). The debate about libraries lacked

> any sense of the intellectual and spiritual enrichment – or the simple relaxation – that an individual man or woman, boy or girl, may derive from reading . . . . The old religious and utilitarian prejudices against reading for entertainment still persisted; if the nation were to subsidize the reading habit, it should do so only for serious purposes. (Altick 231; see also Hammond 91–3)

When Woolf's essays promoted public libraries, she strategically subverted 'much of the rhetoric surrounding and subsequent to the Public Libraries Act of 1850' (Snaith, 'Stray' 25). Woolf's working- and middle-class audiences would have heard her sub-text even if we do not.[4]

Although public libraries were not common, fee-paying libraries were available as private, proprietary or commercial circulating institutions, and 10-year-old Virginia Stephen knew about one. A story in the 21 November 1892 *Hyde Park Gate News* reports that Leslie Stephen had become President of the London Library, winning election over William Gladstone; the writer slyly notes Mrs Stephen's joy at her husband's being 'above' the Prime Minister (*HPGN* 144). A subscription lending library for those interested in literature and science, the London Library was founded in 1841 by Thomas Carlyle, incensed because a peasant in Iceland could 'bring home books to his hut better than men can in London' (qtd in Altick, *ECR* 216).[5] The London Library was conceived as a 'large, general, comprehensive' and 'public' Library for the British capital (F. Harrison 89–91), but 'it was never intended to be a popular library' (Altick 216). Rather, it was (and is) a 'scholarly lending library' (Inwood 673) that aimed to 'offer the best books for the general reader and to provide material for all engaged in research' (F. Harrison 92). Because members could take books out and read them at home (F. Harrison 89; Grindea 11; Baker 37–8), Carlyle could read for his *Life of Cromwell* 'undisturbed by the unsavory atmosphere and distractions of the British Museum reading room' (Altick 216), which, before 1857, included 'overcrowding, noise, smells, lunatics, fleas' (Hoberman, 'Women' 495).

Virginia Stephen began her lifelong library use in 1897, if not earlier, with a London Library loan. In a *Diary* entry written on 8 December 1929, Virginia Woolf recollects, somewhat sentimentally, her father's 'tramping over the Library with his little girl sitting at HPG in mind'. She realises she must have been 15 or 16, and that he had 'lugged home' the Hakluyt volumes she would become 'enraptured' by (*D3* 271). Based on the five oversized volumes in the Leonard and Virginia Woolf Library at Washington State University (K&M-V 95), the walk from St James Square to 22 Hyde Park Gate would have indeed tested the 65-year-old Leslie Stephen's stamina.[6] During Virginia's homeschooling, Leslie Stephen was quite involved with the London Library, becoming a life member in 1865, serving on the Library's governing Committee from 1875 until 1892, and being President from 1892 until his death in 1904. The Library's founding documents refer to benefits for its members 'and their families' (LLA; qtd in R. Harrison, Preface viii, 1865 *Catalogue of the London Library*),[7] so her visit with her father on 29 March 1897 was probably typical (*PA* 62). In autumn 1902, when her father was ill, she frequently visited the library, writing to Violet Dickinson, 'I go and rummage in the London Library now. I got into the vaults where they keep the Times yesterday, and had to be fished out by a man' (*L1* 60). When her father died on 22 February 1904, she seems to have feared losing her visiting and borrowing privileges because she applied for her own London Library membership on 26 February, two days after Leslie Stephen's funeral. She took out a £40 life membership, and her application was signed by Robert Giffen, a member of the London Library Committee.[8]

Virginia Stephen refers to the London Library in her 1905 journal frequently, briefly and matter-of-factly, which connotes ease with its environs and policies (*PA* 219 ff.). She consults it as she drafts her note for Maitland's biography of Leslie Stephen, checks out books for the Morley College class she is teaching, borrows a couple of Spanish novels to learn some language before travelling and sits in the Reading Room reading magazines. Between 1897, when Leslie brought her books, and 1905, when she relies on the London Library to prepare lessons and obtain background for reviews, she became comfortable using it. Her habitual usage, not just her father's association with Carlyle and the Library, may have led to her *TLS* review 'Carlyle and the London Library' in 1907 (*E6* 308–10).

Her father's likely instruction and her subsequent familiarity encouraged it, but Virginia Stephen's ease in the London Library may also have stemmed from its homelike atmosphere.[9] Crossing the Library's threshold, Stephen left home and gained some of her education elsewhere, but she did not leave the domestic behind. As Tony McIntyre clarifies, the 'domestic quality' of the Library was important from the start, and the Library was housed in actual houses in Pall Mall and St James's Square (11). He adds, 'Carlyle was explicit in his belief that books should be read at home, and the fact that the London Library itself remains a home-from-home is no accident' (12).[10] At the beginning of the nineteenth century, he writes, many businesses were in houses, but later, as specialised uses seemed to require specialised buildings, many libraries, including the British Museum Reading Room, were built to house books. The 1890 rebuilding of the London Library in what is 'recognisably a house' meant the 'Library ran directly against the increasingly powerful current of the nineteenth century towards specialization' (11–13).

The London Library also had no firm due dates, requiring renewals and asking for a book's return only when another member requested it, and it mailed books to a member's home upon request, making it a national lending library (McIntyre 4; A. Bell, 'LL' 161–2; Phipps 191). Such policies made it easy for Virginia Stephen to navigate between home and library. Plus, London Library staff, particularly Frederick Cox, had an 'encyclopaedic knowledge' of the library's books and its members.[11] Beginning as a messenger boy in 1882 and moving up to the Book Issue counter, where he worked until 1952 (*L2* 303 n2; Wells, *Rude* 123), he replied, for example, when Mrs McColl asked for *The Voyage Out* by Virginia Woolf in December 1918,

> Virginia Woolf? Let me see; she was a Miss Stephen, daughter of Sir Leslie. Her sister is Mrs Clive Bell I think. Ah, strange to see what's become of those two girls. Brought up in such a nice home too. But then, they never were *baptised*. (*D1* 225; emphasis in original; see also *L2* 303 and *L4* 127)

The London Library's homelike quality included monitoring the Stephen daughters.

After 1903, Virginia Stephen could also have consulted at home what amounted to the London Library's card catalogue, an inscribed copy of C. T. Hagberg Wright's alphabetical and catch-word title catalogue (K&M-V 249).[12] In 1903, the Library published his massive catalogue of everything acquired by the Library up until 31 December 1901, 220,000 volumes; members could buy it for a pound before 1 September 1901, and then afterwards at less than cost, £1 and 5 shillings (*LLM* 11 March 1901, promotional pamphlet).[13] Before 1903, shorter catalogues had been published at regular intervals and sold at cost to members (see 31 May 1888 Minutes for 47th AGM, for example), with members also receiving an annual report of additions; probably Leslie Stephen had these at home, too. Members, then, were not forced to consult catalogues 'only inside the Library, as [was] the case at the British Museum' (Baker 94).

Before 1837, admission to the British Museum Reading Room required an introduction by a 'peer, member of Parliament, alderman, judge, rector, or some other eminent man' and the hours were short or non-existent (Altick, *ECR* 215–16; Caygill 18; see also Miller 'BM'), though Susan David Bernstein describes more diverse introductions (*R* 137, 145 n15). But later, policies loosened, giving the public more access, and the new 1857 domed room with its rayed and alphabetised rows of tables and its raised superintending area quickly became overcrowded (Hoberman, 'Bald' 172–3). As Ruth Hoberman and Bernstein detail, the less restrictive policies contributed to women's sense of themselves as public intellectuals and political activists. Up to 1907, 'women ambitious for a role in public life depict themselves and each other as delighting in the reading room's resources.... [They] see the reading room in positive terms, as facilitating women's move from private into public life' (Hoberman, 'Bald' 170; see also 'Women').[14] Readers like Eleanor Marx, Clementina Black and Amy Levy welcomed the public nature of the domed reading room and its workshop atmosphere as opposed to the 'debilitating isolation' of the domestic sphere; for them, the British Museum Reading Room 'figured as a site of commercial opportunity, spiritual illumination, and activist and professional networking for women writers who rewrote the space of knowledge itself' (Bernstein, 'Radical' par. 7, par. 20; see also 'Too Common').

In an essay Virginia Stephen may have read in *Atalanta*, Amy Levy praises the library's accessibility, its book-obtaining ease and its atmosphere of refuge (Levy, 'Readers' 226–7; *A2* 449–54). But Stephen had no childhood experience with the British Museum Reading Room since it did not allow anyone under 21 to have a reader's ticket (Caygill 18). She visited it as a young woman, though, on 4 February 1905 'to get some plan of it into my head', had trouble finding what she wanted and called it a Mausoleum (*PA* 232). Stephen first entered the Reading Room with reader's ticket A82849 on 8 November 1905; Thoby, 46 Gordon Square householder, recommended her, saying '"his sister was interested in "reading works related to English literature & history"' (Harvey 106, 111 n6). We do not know if she sat at one of two tables designated for women readers or did what many female readers did (to the irritation of some complaining male readers) and spill over into the rest of the room (Hoberman, 'Bald' 172–4, 179).[15]

Based on Woolf's portrayals of the British Museum Reading Room, Stephen must not have felt as comfortable there as in the London Library. Hoberman argues that after the dome's redecoration in 1907, with its addition of nineteen male thinkers' names around the perimeter, a later generation of women readers saw their acceptance in public life as 'premised on their identification with the disembodied, implicitly male world of rational discourse' ('Bald' 185). First segregated at specific tables, with their physical presence emphasised, and then overseen from above by great men of the past, women saw 'what had been less evident before: the room was aligned with a model of cultural achievement implicitly gendered as male' ('Bald' 175, 186). Since Virginia Stephen visited the room before and after refurbishing, she would have been keenly aware of the change, and as Anne Fernald shows, the British Library became conflicted space for Woolf, who both admired its breadth and scope and resisted the 'false promise of patriarchal education' symbolised by the domed room ('Memory' 104).[16] The British Museum Reading Room functioned simultaneously as 'a more egalitarian community' catering to a 'socially diverse body of readers' (Bernstein, 'Too Common' 101, 103) and as an architectural symbol of a male mind wielding vast institutional power (Fernald, 'Memory' 104), 'command-central for this late-nineteenth-century knowledge-control industry' (Hoberman, 'Bald' 169).[17]

With the London Library, Virginia Stephen went from her father's private library to the more public one he 'energetic[ally]' presided over (A. Bell, 'LL' 164). Metaphorically and literally, it was a home extension. With the British Museum Reading Room, she walked into a 'confident [monument]' to her culture's knowledge and treasures (Fernald, 'Memory' 94), a space devoted to preserving the nation's identity, displaying the spoils of Empire (Hoberman, 'Bald' 169) and 'influenc[ing] the imagination of its readers' (Fernald, 'Memory' 98). Both were patriarchal. The London Library seemed like a home, the Museum a tomb. A private space with personal knowledge of its members, the London Library required the reader to pay for borrowing and visiting privileges, deal with its limitations and search for books idiosyncratically arranged in cramped quarters. A public space with public surveillance, the British Museum Reading Room required the reader to consult catalogues, request books, wait and take notes according to certain rules at certain hours.

Both claimed openness toward women, welcoming women members and readers in increasing numbers, but operated with unwritten restrictions against them. The London Library, much more so than other libraries, had its collection and governance shaped by its members through a Committee elected from its ranks (Phipps 191; Wells, *Rude* 3), but it had only one female Committee member, Mrs Alice Stopford Green, from 1894 to 1916, and then none until 1937, when Professor Eileen Power was elected (*LLAR* 8 July 1937).[18] In 1929, G. F. Barwick reported on the ever-increasing numbers of women in the British Museum Reading Room – 'In 1906 it was found that the lady readers were about one-fifth of the daily average; in 1913 they had increased to about a third and are at present rapidly approaching the half' (144) – yet not a single woman appears in the 1929 pictures of the Senior and Junior Staff of the Department of Printed Books (P. R. Harris, *History* plates 87 and 88, following 794).

When Virginia Stephen went to the London Library or the British Museum Reading Room, she entered communities of seekers, other readers and writers exploring texts on their own for their own purposes, thus decreasing her solitude. But those communities, defined by class and gender, also excluded others.[19] From the start, the London Library was open to both men and women, with fifteen women members in 1841, and it had no separate reading rooms. But its fee, though a 'small annual sum' compared to buying books and reference works, made it impossible for lower-middle-class or working-class readers to use it (Popowich 6; McIntyre 4), and its system of having current members nominate new members meant the membership stayed class bound (Bernstein, 'Too Common' 103). The British Museum Reading Room system of granting readers' tickets allowed those in all classes to nominate and become readers after 1857 (Bernstein, 'Radical' par. 3; see also *R* 7), but it attempted to literally segregate women before 1907, and after 1907 figuratively segregated them with dome inscriptions (Hoberman, 'Bald' 170–1, 186).

Still, both libraries conveyed a sense of bounty, enlarging Virginia Stephen's contact with books, readers and writers.[20] Learning how to use the London Library and then extending her experience into the British Museum Reading Room, Stephen took more control of her own education and moved beyond her father's curriculum into one that at first seemed infinite, so much so that she yearned 'to read through whole libraries', even though she knows she will not (*L*1 370). As Woolf would later write, 'I used to feel that the British Museum reading room was going on for ever' (*D*4 208), and Fernald confirms the 'ambition of completeness' underlying the reading room ('Memory' 95). In practice, libraries restrict,[21] communicate boundaries and create sometimes quirky categories, but they also represent content full of potential and replete with possibility. Such riches, though not actually infinite, allow the learner to create her own curriculum and syllabus from a much larger set of options.[22]

Libraries gave Virginia Stephen new content to explore, including lives of the obscure. As Judith Chernaik says, only in the London Library 'can a reader sit undisturbed day after day among the original bound volumes of *The Times*, totally immersed in the minutiae of the past' (24), and Stephen records doing just that in 1902 (*L*1 60) and Woolf in 1938 (*L*6 276). Stephen clearly learned how to use a library, and frequent references in Woolf's diaries and letters attest to lifetime use. Woolf used the London Library, 'stale culture smoked place' though it was (*D*1 25), throughout her life; she continued to visit the British Museum Reading Room, liking its 'dusty bookish atmosphere' and its potential for book creation: the readers 'believe in the necessity of making books, I suppose: verify, collate, make up other books, for ever' (D3 80).

The London Library taught Virginia Stephen how to rummage, explore, wander. The British Museum Reading Room taught her system. As a result, Virginia Woolf could use other libraries, not only subscribing to Mudie's and Day's, giving her access to contemporary fiction, but also applying for a ticket at Dr Williams' Library to read history, visiting the Kingston Library, using the Lewes Free Library and depending on the Fawcett Library. Without receiving any formal lessons, Stephen learned effective research strategies and methods that stood Woolf in good stead during her career. Her ability to check authorities and facts, learned in the British Museum Reading Room, underlies *A Room of One's Own* and *Three Guineas*. Her preference for rummaging, exploring and wandering, learned at the London Library, feeds her essay style, allowing her to move bounty from library shelves into essays and create a memory palace there (Fernald, 'Memory' 93). Gathering materials to write an essay on Hardy in August 1921, Woolf writes, 'I ransack public libraries & find them full of sunk treasure' (D2 126).

Library pedagogy supports the garnering of facts, the practical use of information to meet particular aims, but it also promotes the 'creative laziness' Noel Annan describes:

> reading the books one ought not to be reading, and becoming so absorbed in them and following the trails along which they lead you so that at the end of the day you still have most of the reading to do that you had before you that morning. (qtd in McIntyre 3)

Libraries also inherently employ Leslie Stephen's pedagogy of individual initiative: 'All the rest must be learnt for oneself' (E5 588–9). The learner decides to take advantage or not, selects or rejects, and uses whatever and however suits. The London Library, with its open stacks and odd classification system, promotes unorganised learning and serendipity. Woolf's common reader, running up 'some rickety and ramshackle fabric' (E4 19), may owe something to its shelf-marking system, where Science & Miscellaneous includes 'its Dreams, Dress, Drink and Drugs; its Oaths, Occult Sciences and Opera; its Pleasure, Poaching, Poisons and Police; its Wine, Witchcraft, Women, Wool &c. and Wrestling' (McIntyre 16; Phipps 191, Chernaik, and Wells, *Rude* 139).

Virginia Stephen also learned the value of libraries for the outsider. She grew up when W. E. Henley's 'men of letters' saw themselves as literary purists and circulating libraries and their middle-class patrons as 'the blight of the nineteenth century', responsible for changing England's great and aristocratic literary tradition into a 'smug and fat' bourgeois travesty. Their outrage extended to the popular press (McDonald 35–6), and, one assumes, public libraries and their patrons.[23] In contrast, Stephen observed and Woolf claimed a link between libraries and democracy, seeing that libraries could open up education to more people, and a better education at that. Affected by class and gender they might be, but libraries still made entry possible. As Hermione Lee puts it, all her life, Woolf 'celebrated the function of the public library as a necessary resource for a democratic culture', seeing the public library as the 'university of the non-specialist, uninstructed reader' ('Crimes' 132). Thus, Woolf's injunction to the working classes to 'trespass at once', to borrow books and read them critically (E6 278), makes the library a radical space in which they can transform literature, cross boundaries and decrease class division. She challenges them: if relegated to public libraries, turn the insult on its head and steal the culture. For Stephen and then Woolf, libraries and their books represented the power of literature, the potential for self-education and the force a well-read citizenry could become.

Libraries figure prominently in Virginia Woolf's life, fiction and non-fiction – she scatters library content and research methods throughout her essays – revealing how large they loomed in Virginia Stephen's education. In 1940, Woolf discovers her *Common Reader* 'all spotted with readers' at the Lewes Free Library (*D5* 329), which Cuddy-Keane discovered meant literal 'marks of everyday life' made by readers: 'smudges that appeared to be thumb marks but also orange spots, brown spots, pink spots – looking like tea, marmalade, jam, and lipstick' ('Pedagogical' 8).[24] Woolf's readers were using the library, borrowing books, 'teach[ing themselves] to understand literature' (*E6* 277) just as Virginia Stephen had done all those years before.[25]

King's College Classes and Teachers

On 6 May 1897, Virginia Stephen wrote in her journal that

> We went to High St & bought some braid & something else which I cannot remember – a catalogue of the classes at King's College – that was it – which I may go to. After lunch I talked to father about it, and decided to begin next autumn if I begin at all. (*PA* 82)

Her entry uncannily anticipates not only Virginia Woolf's memory lapses about her King's College classes, but also her young, tentative educational desires and her father's influence over them. It envisions a move away, from house into official educational space: she did not go far, but she did go to school. That move away from home exposed Virginia Stephen to new curricula, pedagogies and communities, introduced her to a systematic educational framework and broadened her knowledge. At King's College Ladies' Department, she not only learned Greek, history, Latin and German, she also experienced teachers' methods and observed a women's community. Crucially, Virginia Stephen learned these lessons as a non-matriculated student, contributing to her later adoption of an amateur stance. But her time at King's College also prepared her for Janet Case's Greek tutoring and sowed the seeds for her Morley College teaching.

On the afternoon of 11 October 1897, the 15-year-old Virginia Stephen left 22 Hyde Park Gate, went to King's College Department for Ladies at 13 Kensington Square and entered a classroom for the first time.[26] Three days a week that ten-week autumn term, until 17 December, she took classes in Greek from Professor George C. W. Warr (Mondays at 2–3.30), Continental History from Professor J. K. Laughton (Tuesdays at 10–11) and English History, also from Professor Laughton (Fridays at 10–11). (See Appendix 1 for Virginia Stephen's 1897–1901 King's College course schedule.) No wonder the journal she began keeping in 1897 peters out in October and has only a few more entries before 1898 – Stephen was busy adjusting to classes and instruction outside the home.[27]

Virginia Stephen had talked with Thoby about his classes at Evelyns and Clifton and with Vanessa about her painting classes, and she had heard her father lecture. But she had never taken classes herself. Eager to begin, she was 'very anxious' for the class, her father said (Letter to George Warr), but 'anxious' can also connote apprehension. Dr Seton still forbade lessons in spring 1897 (*L1* 7; *PA* 83), and Stella died in July of that year, which may explain why Leslie Stephen wrote to Professor Warr on 1 November 1897 that he was allowing his daughter to attend the Greek class and asking him to 'let her off with light work' (Letter to George Warr).[28] This letter, which almost surely would have enraged Virginia if she had known about it, makes me wonder: was she or the anxious Leslie responsible for the decision she notes in a letter to Thoby dated 5 December 1897: 'My studies end with an examination, which I shant go in for' (*L1* 12)?

Indeed, who decided her registration status at King's? As Jones and Snaith point out, Stephen was not enrolled as a matriculated student leading to a degree (6). King's College divided the students in the Ladies' Department into matriculated and non-matriculated, according to Alice Zimmern's 7 September 1904 *Guardian* article on women's higher education in London:

> The latter can attend any classes they please, and are under no restriction except that they must conform with the college regulations while actually in attendance. Matriculated students are those who are admitted to the regular course of study in their respective departments. They must take the prescribed examinations, attend the weekly divinity lectures given by the Principal, must put in regular attendance at lectures, and consult the tutor of their faculty about their work. (1486)

Given the weekly divinity lecture and his concern about his daughter's health,[29] Leslie's permission probably included the assumption Virginia would register as non-matriculated.[30]

If Virginia Stephen was nervous about going to classes for the first time, however, her letters and journal do not suggest it; she treats her attendance as routine. Under a journal entry headed 16 October, she acknowledges it is 13 November ('What a skip!') and comments, 'I go to King's College, Nessa to her studio'; on 12 December, she writes, 'My studies have almost come to an end' (*PA* 132–3). She does not seem to have felt stress or needed protection. She writes in a matter-of-fact way to Thoby on 24 October, 'I am beginning Greek at Kings College and two history Lectures – We have got as far as the first verb in our Greek, and by the Christmas holidays you will have to take me in hand.' She does seem surprised that 'I have to write *essays* upon historical subjects for my history class, and on Tuesday I am going to have my first essay given back to me with the masters corrections' (*L1* 10–11; her emphasis), and she exclaims over Miss Holland, who works two hours a day preparing her Greek 'and thought that too little!' (*L1* 13), but neither statement reflects any of the strain her father feared. Perhaps Professor Warr did 'let her off with light work'. But more likely, Virginia Stephen's eagerness to take classes and work hard carried her through – she was one of those students Vice-Principal Lilian Faithfull said had never been to school, was self- or home-taught, and had 'a keen appetite not blunted by text-books, but rather sharpened by browsing in a library' (113).

Certainly, Virginia Stephen's steady enrolment pattern suggests her schoolwork at King's fed an intellectual hunger. According to Jones and Snaith, the King's

College London archives show that between October 1897 and March 1901, she usually took three courses, occasionally two, each term (Michaelmas–autumn; Lent–spring; Easter–summer) for a total of thirty-one courses – twelve in Greek, eight in history, six in Latin, and five in German (41) – and she also registered three times for private Greek lessons. As Jones and Snaith correctly comment, this evidence makes it clear her education outside the home was far from sporadic, 'intermittent, brief, or even non-existent' (1–4). They also carefully point out that 'the pattern and type of Virginia's studies' fit the transitional stage the Ladies' Department then occupied 'between fulfilling a leisure role and providing a basis for university qualifications' and that '[d]istinctions between institutions of "secondary" and "higher" education were less clear in the nineteenth century than they are now' (6, 4).[31] Their meticulous scholarship reveals (1) Stephen took a range of subjects (three languages and two kinds of history) from four main instructors (Professor Warr, Professor Laughton, Miss Pater and Miss Buchheim); (2) her classes were generally survey, introductory or intermediate; and (3) her more advanced work in Greek led to tutors rather than to a degree. Although the classes she took were subjects prescribed for various entrance/university exams or degrees, meant to give students more than 'a taste of a liberal education' (Oakeley 494), and were becoming, under Faithfull's leadership, 'the stern and serious studies necessary for the securing of London University degrees and Oxford or Cambridge diplomas' (Hearnshaw 378), they would have required professors teaching them to meet the needs of both non-matriculated and matriculated students, the latter of whom were still a very small minority in 1904 (Jones and Snaith 5; Zimmern 1486).[32] The solution? Pitch the lectures at degree level; assign work to both types of student, but assign matriculated students 'a considerable amount of further reading and written study' so they could achieve passes in the various local or degree exams (Jones and Snaith 15); and require course exams only for matriculated students.[33]

If Virginia Stephen had enrolled as a matriculated student, she could have used her King's course work to pursue a degree or move toward the Cambridge examinations. According to Zimmern, students pursuing a degree needed to take 'an approved course of study extending over a period of not less than three years from matriculation' and could take longer than three years to complete it. Admission to the Intermediate Examination in Arts required a minimum of 270 hours' lecture attendance; admission to the Final Examination required 540 (1486).[34] If she attended all her lectures, then, Stephen had more than enough attendance hours for the Intermediate Examination by the time she left: 31 non-tutorial courses, times 10 weeks, times 1 hour/week = 310.[35] But she had not taken those hours in an approved course of study, did not do the extra work associated with matriculation and did not take course exams except twice in German.

Enrolling as a non-matriculated student thus put her on a different path from her brothers and a few young women. Indeed, it put her on a different path from Leslie Stephen, who had used King's College courses in 1848–50 to prepare himself better in maths before going to Cambridge (Annan 23; Jones and Snaith 4–5). Leslie Stephen's concern for his daughter's health may have stemmed from his own memories of the Cambridge 'grind', but it obscured the real nature of Virginia Stephen's choice at the time. Any nascent desire or ambition she may have had to prepare for Cambridge examinations was nipped in the bud at registration. Further, passing up the opportunity to end her studies that first autumn with course exams prevented her from comparing her abilities and shortcomings with those of other students ('Sketch' 65) and thus more consciously considering whether to work toward the Cambridge exams.

Without having the information Jones and Snaith unearthed in the King's College Archives, Phyllis Rose (37) and Noel Annan (120) questioned whether Virginia Stephen could have passed Girton or Newnham entrance examinations. With that information, her chances look better. The 1896 *Handbook of Courses Open to Women in British, Continental and Canadian Universities* for Bryn Mawr graduates says the classes at 13 Kensington Square, though taught by King's professors, were 'of a very elementary nature' (Maddison 86), but those compiling the handbook may not have caught up with Faithfull's curricular revisions. And the intelligent and disciplined Virginia Stephen was, even as a non-matriculated student, attending degree-level lectures at a younger than degree-level age, suggesting she could have handled the content and rigour of the matriculated student's curriculum and thus passed the Cambridge entrance exams. Whether she would have thrived under the restrictions of needing an approved course of study, being required to take courses to 'catch up' (in maths, for example), having to take course exams and needing to pass qualifying exams, however, is another question. Being a non-matriculated student allowed her to range through several subjects, pursue breadth rather than depth, learn what she wanted to and not be tested. But did *she* consider and then decide between the two options? Did she even know she had a choice or what that choice's implications were?[36] Her later resentment at not having the same opportunities as her brothers suggests no.

Whatever her status, Stephen's teachers, male and female, were committed to women's education, their subjects and teaching. Faithfull remembers that offers for 'more lucrative posts' often came, but 'men preferred to stay in a place that somehow gripped their hearts by its very poverty and need of them' (103). We can see, and probably Virginia Stephen could, too, that Professor George C. W. Warr (1845–1901) supported women's learning of classical languages. Appointed lecturer in Classical Literature at King's in 1874 and then Professor in 1881 ('Warr' 743), Warr had worked with Mrs William (Maria) Grey, Emily Shirreff and other women's education leaders to found the Ladies Department in 1877 (Oakeley 491). His support of a Department 'house of its own' led him to arrange fund-raising performances of his adaptations: 'The Story of Orestes', an abridged English version of Aeschylus's Oresteian trilogy in 1886 (an 'attempt to bring Aeschylus' trilogy to the general public' [Hall and Macintosh 465]), and *The Tale of Troy, or Scenes and Tableaux from Homer*, in Greek and English, in 1883. Favourably reviewed in *The Times* on 30 and 31 May, this masque raised £650 (*King's College Magazine, Ladies' Department*, Easter 1899, 16–27; Oakeley 492–3; Jones and Snaith 15); among the performers were Jane Harrison as Penelope and J. K. Stephen as Hector. When Warr published the two plays together as *Echoes of Hellas* ('Professor' 12), he donated a share of book profits to the Department (Hall and Macintosh 470). The *Annual Report 1900–1901* author said, 'No one person did more to make possible the establishment of this Department of King's College upon a permanent basis' (*SL 1901–2* 48). Hall and

Macintosh say Warr 'was a radical who rubbed shoulders with the Establishment' (486), working to extend access to higher education for the lower middle and working classes as well as for women (470).[37] He saw translation and commentary as 'vital to widen the audience of the ancient texts' (473) and worked to popularise the classics, finishing a verse translation of *The Oresteia* of Aeschylus right before he died in 1901.[38]

Thus, Virginia Stephen's first Greek instruction outside her family was under a teacher who overtly promoted women's education and wanted to make Greek and Latin accessible to all.[39] We know Warr used J. B. Mayor's *Greek for Beginners* and David Morice's *Stories in Attic Greek* in his Elementary Greek class and that he 'asked most tenderly after Marny [Vaughan]' when she missed the first class of the term, offering to correct her late exercises (*L1* 13). He seems to have been consistently kind, since Stephen always refers to him as her 'beloved Warr' or 'dear old Warr' in letters and her journal (*L1* 20, 21; *PA* 412), and she mentions his 'courtesy & deliberation' in a deleted phrase in her journal sketch of Miss Case in 1903 (*PA* 182, 412). She seems to have signed up for Miss Pater's class in Intermediate Latin in the autumn of 1898 only because Professor Warr's Latin class met at an inconvenient time (*L1* 20).

Stephen became familiar with Professor Warr's encouraging pedagogy because she took at least five Greek classes from him, three elementary and two more advanced. Ascertaining whether she took more from him is difficult. In Michaelmas 1900, for example, she took two advanced Greek courses (KWA/RAD 6). Although unlikely, given her previous registrations (see Appendix 1), she could have signed up for Miss Pater's Intermediate Grammar and Professor Warr's Advanced Reading and Composition; it is more likely she signed up for Professor Warr's course and Miss Pater's Intermediate Reading (Jones and Snaith 26 Fig. 2k; *SL 1900–1* 16), even though they were scheduled to meet at nearly the same time on Mondays. In a letter dated Tuesday, 23 October [1900], Stephen mentions her 'first class with Miss Pater tomorrow' (*L1* 39), so perhaps Miss Pater's class was changed to Wednesdays. More puzzling, the King's College London Register lists neither Professor Warr nor Miss Pater as having taught in Michaelmas 1900. Instead, it lists Miss Lucas for Greek (two classes, four students) and Latin (two classes, four students) (KWA/R2 79). Perhaps Stephen signed up for Professor Warr and Miss Pater but Miss Lucas stepped in because Professor Warr became ill (he died the next term) and Miss Pater continued to be ill (she looked 'very white and shriveled' in October [*L1* 39]).[40]

In Lent Term 1901, Stephen registered for one Greek class (KWA/RAD 6), so she may have planned to read Aeschylus with Miss Pater or Herodotus with Professor Warr, though Miss Pater's class seems more likely, given three pieces of evidence: (1) Miss Pater resigned as classical tutor at King's in February 1901 (AR 1901–2, *SL 1902–3* 50); (2) the Register lists Miss Pater and Miss Clay together as teaching two classes in Greek, with seven students (KWA/R2 82); and (3) Stephen mentions a Miss Clay in the sketch of Janet Case she wrote in 1903 (*PA* 182). See Figure 3.1 and Appendix 1 318 n10.

Even if not in the 56-year-old Professor Warr's class, Stephen was probably shocked by his sudden death on 21 February. Indeed, Virginia Stephen lost both her King's College Greek teachers in February 1901, which may be one reason her

Figure 3.1 Agnes Muriel Clay in Lady Margaret Hall group photo, 1903. She is seated on the ground in the first row, fourth from the right. By kind permission of the Principal and Fellows of Lady Margaret Hall, Oxford.

attendance at King's dwindled and ended soon thereafter.

Stephen took courses in both Latin and Greek, at least ten in all, from Clara Pater (1841–1910), whose teaching, according to Jones and Snaith, 'fostered Virginia's lifelong engagement with Greek literature' (35). As Laurel Brake points out, Clara Pater was an 'advanced woman'. Without much formal education, she used her skills in languages to develop her career and lived an unconventional sexual life. She pioneered change for women and advocated classical education for them but did not identify 'unreservedly' with the mainstream of the women's movement (Brake, 'Pater'; 'Moment' 145). Most often labelled the sister of Walter Pater, she began studying Greek and Latin at age 33 and helped found Somerville College at Oxford in 1879 (Brake, 'Moment' 145, 148, 147; see also Jones and Snaith 34). There, she tutored in Latin, Greek and German for fifteen years, but ironically, her lack of formal qualifications meant the first graduates of Somerville overtook her (Brake, 'Moment' 153)[41] and she moved to London and worked as a Lecturer in Latin and Greek in the Ladies' Department at King's College from 1898 up until February 1901 (AR 1901–2, SL 1902–3, Vol. 3 50). Self-taught, Clara Pater seemed less 'professional' to Virginia Stephen than Janet Case (PA 182), but Stephen also comments to Emma Vaughan that 'Miss Pater was perfectly delightful' when they read some of the Apologia (L1 26). The Ladies' Department certainly appreciated her 'individual interest in her students' (SL 1902–3 50) and called her resignation 'a great loss', with students 'speak[ing] warmly' of her influence and their debt to her (King's College Magazine, Ladies' Department [Easter 1901, 6–7]; qtd in Jones and Snaith 35).

We know Virginia Stephen read Socrates and Plato with Miss Pater in her courses, and perhaps Lysias and Aeschylus as well, though we do not know what she read during her private lessons with Miss Pater in Michaelmas 1899. However, the autobiographical traces of the tutor/student relationship Woolf portrays in 'Moments of Being: "Slater's Pins Have No Points"', The Pargiters and The Years, noted by Leaska (PA 182n24), Brake ('Pater'), Jones and Snaith, and others, suggest (1) Miss Pater was often disappointed in Virginia's work and the excuses proffered for it (*Y* 61; *P* 101–2); (2) Stephen admired Miss Pater's independence, fighter's spirit and 'disinterested passion' for her subject ('Slater's' 219; *P* 112); and (3) Miss Pater challenged her to work harder and use her 'original mind' to form her own opinions (*Y* 61; *P* 117). In these works, we also see the tutor not allowing the student to confide in her (*Y* 62; *P* 103, 114), the student trying to flesh out the tutor's life by making up scenes ('Slater's'), and the student considering how 'curious' the term 'uneducated' is and questioning the reasons for the tutor's poverty, angrily wondering why on earth the 'old buffers' at the university did not 'give Lucy Craddock whatever it is that Lucy Craddock wants' (*P* 113–14, 119–20).[42] In Miss Pater, Stephen observed a woman who had struggled to educate herself then having to struggle as a learned woman to work within a predominantly male arena.

Virginia Stephen also had classes with an influential history teacher, Professor J. K. Laughton (1830–1915), who is still remembered for establishing and building naval history as a discipline. His impact, spread more through his teaching than through published work, even now influences naval policy (Callender and Lambert).[43] Laughton had served as a naval instructor, and while on active duty, had written two textbooks. He developed naval history as a discipline and meteorology and marine surveying as a department at the Royal Naval College, Greenwich, where he retired in 1885. King's College appointed him Professor of Modern History soon after. There, he became a professional historian who had 'a comprehensive grasp' of general history ('Death'). He probably required some reading of matriculated students, along with the writing he assigned, but he listed no textbooks for his Continental and English History courses in the syllabus Stephen consulted.[44] He provided detailed chronological outlines for the three time periods he covered in both Continental and English History, though (1660–1702; 1702–48; and 1748–89). As Clara Jones points out, Laughton disseminated 'a Whiggish narrative of history to his students' in what G. P. Gooch called 'rather uninspiring' lectures (31). But hearing lectures the same term about the same eras in both England and the Continent did take Virginia Stephen's historical perspective beyond her father's library.[45]

Virginia Stephen branched off into something new during her third year at King's College: German with Miss E. S. Buchheim. Although she mentions doing some German in her 1897 journal (*PA* 40, 42, 46), it and other modern languages never captured her imagination the way Greek did, so its addition seems surprising. However, she took Elementary German classes in 1899–1900 and German Grammar classes for two terms in 1900–1; even more surprising, she sat the course exams in both Michaelmas Term classes, earning a Class II pass each time, a 60–74 per cent mark (*King's College London Calendar, 1899–1900* endpaper). Perhaps Miss Buchheim motivated her to take the exams?

Emma Sophia Buchheim (1861–1951) worked with her father, Professor C. A. Buchheim, in the Ladies' Department at King's College, where she was appointed a Fellow at the College for Women in 1913 (KA/D/M1 398, item 794). She probably learned to teach from her father, who truly cared that others learn German: he was still teaching a week before his death during Easter Term 1900 (Virginia was in Miss Buchheim's Elementary German class then) (E. S. Buchheim, 'Biographical Sketch' ix).[46] He was well known for his annotated editions of

Lessing, Goethe, Schiller and Heine,[47] translations of some Dickens into German, and the *Modern German Reader*, a companion to a grammar with selections from modern German authors that a student could use 'as soon as he has mastered the alphabet' (Buchheim, C. A. v).

Emma Buchheim also worked to make German accessible to English speakers, publishing *Elementary German Prose Composition* (passages from English-speaking authors for translation into German) and *German Poetry for Beginners*, both recommended for her classes (Jones and Snaith 25 Fig. 2j). The scholarly daughter, Miss Buchheim helped finish her father's edition of Goethe's *Hermann und Dorothea* after his death and provided its biographical sketch. Her mother, Pauline, also did scholarly work, editing Schiller's correspondence for her husband's series of Schiller texts.[48] Having married in 1857 and borne four children in the 1860s, Pauline Buchheim waited until she was 50 to edit her edition, though she may have assisted her husband with his.

Emma, perhaps noticing the impact of marriage and children on her mother, did not marry.[49] She translated *Poland: An Historical Sketch* by Count von Moltke in 1885 when she was 24, published her textbooks using German poetry and prose extracts in 1889 and 1893 and then a collection of short German plays for reading in 1895, and translated a book on attracting and protecting wild birds in 1912 (Hiesemann, K&M-V 103). She also published several juvenile works, including *Holidays at Sandy Bay* (1898) and 'Stories from the Edda' for *The Land of Enchantment* (1907), illustrated by Arthur Rackham, to which Bella Woolf also contributed. All Miss Buchheim's published work appeared prior to 1915, except for reprints. Did her German roots prevent later publishing attempts? But she continued as Lecturer at King's (Delegacy Minutes reveal a calm approach to refugee and 'enemy alien' students and faculty), retiring at the end of the 1929–30 academic year; together, she and her father had 'an unbroken connection with the College for 67 years' (KA/D/M7 356, item 456).

Virginia Stephen never mentions Miss Buchheim in the letters or journals we have, but her influence may have extended beyond suggesting course exams, perhaps even as one model for Miss Kilman in *Mrs Dalloway*. Stephen must have continued working on German for at least a while since Leslie mentions 'trying to get a little German into Ginia' in a letter dated 1 June 1901, after her classes with Miss Buchheim had ended (SLLS2 517). She decided to accompany Saxon Sydney-Turner to the Bayreuth Festival in 1909, renewed her German language acquisition under Miss Daniel and bought *Cassell's German Dictionary* (L1 288, 323, 331; K&M-V 39). But she admits to Vanessa she can read the German only 'with great difficulty' at the festival (L1 404). Stephen's pre-King's College German work, Miss Buchheim's classes and Miss Daniel's tutoring sessions also did not prevent Woolf's 1935 reply to a German woman's fan letter about *The Waves*: 'I must apologise for not answering your letter before. I have to confess that I do not read German, & thus had to get a friend to translate it for me' (Letter to Dear Madam, Allison-Shelley Collection).[50] Either she was using a pretended lack of German to excuse her delay or she did what many of us do: take courses, pass exams and then promptly forget the language. As Sandra Stelts, then Curator of Rare Books and Manuscripts at Pennsylvania State University commented, taking courses and studying a language are two very different things (email communication). Virginia seems to have successfully taken German courses at King's College, whereas she *studied* Greek.

Virginia Stephen's curriculum at King's College London, then, deepened her knowledge of Greek, Latin, history and German while it introduced her to four teachers, perhaps more, and their pedagogies. During the time she attended, even though many professors were men, she also saw the King's College Ladies' Department develop into a community of women. Lilian Faithfull encouraged staff and students in community-building efforts, holding what she called 'At Homes' every two weeks (115) and proudly writing in her autobiography,

> We were, I believe, the first Women's College to have an annual College dinner. Others had contented themselves with a soirée and what was contemptuously described as 'a cold buffet', but we dined magnificently, and ended with toasts proposed and responded to in the most approved fashion, and witty enough to have deserved perpetuation. (114)

As Jones and Snaith document, it opened its first residential hall in 1897, had a small library, to which Jane Harrison and Leslie Stephen contributed books, published a magazine, had laboratories, classrooms, studios, music rooms and a common room, and provided extra-curricular activities centred around physical activity, music, discussion and service to the Women's Settlement in Stratford (35–7; see also Oakeley 498). Because of scant evidence in letters, journals and memoirs for this period in Stephen's life, we do not know how much she interacted with Lilian Faithfull,[51] whether she read Faithfull's pieces in the college magazine, whether she used the library or sat in the common room, whether she participated in the available college community life. Jones and Snaith say Stephen does not seem to have made any lasting friends while there (38), which suggests minimal time at the college; as Faithfull acknowledges, 'The number of girls who could devote time to [corporate games and societies at] the College was of necessity comparatively small' (114). Letters we do have from this period suggest Stephen was more interested in encouraging friends she already had to attend classes with her (L1 13, 26). But Jones and Snaith also point out that *A Room of One's Own* and *Three Guineas* echo the 'details of the environment' surrounding Virginia Stephen at King's (35–40), which suggests awareness and observation of the community around her, if not participation in it.

Thus, at the King's College Ladies' Department, Virginia Stephen absorbed new and more complex content, experienced at least four different pedagogies and soaked up a women's community atmosphere. Leaving 22 Hyde Park Gate for the classrooms at 13 Kensington Square gave her a taste of an educational system – she registered for courses, attended classes, read material and engaged with teachers and other students. Significantly, however, for her intellectual development, later writing and essayist persona, she went to school as a non-matriculated, casual student. She remained an amateur, an outsider.

Janet Case's Tutoring

Virginia Stephen's Greek course work at King's College led her from Professor Warr's Elementary Greek classes through Intermediate and Advanced classes with him, Miss Pater, and others to one-on one work with Miss Case. With her tutor,

Virginia Stephen strengthened her understanding of the Greek language, extended her knowledge of individual Greek texts and increased her ability to study Greek on her own. Through Janet Case, she encountered yet another pedagogy, one influenced by Jane Ellen Harrison, and although she again watched a learned woman struggle to establish herself within a predominantly male arena, she also saw a more feminist, activist and community-based response to those struggles.

As many have noted, Greek represented an upper-class male fortress, one Virginia Stephen was determined to enter and move comfortably in, thus joining other intellectual women engaged in similar efforts. But Greek's importance to her education went beyond this motivation. Greek challenged her in ways her other studies did not: its strangeness, difficulty, position in another space, time and culture, even articulation through drama – all mentally stimulated her; 'I wish', she writes, 'something would tear away the veil which still separates me from the Greeks,' but immediately wonders, 'or is it inevitable?' (*PA* 250). As Woolf writes later, Greek's 'unlikeness ... perpetually rouses our curiosity' (*E2* 116). Indeed, the energy she expended on trying to understand Greek language, culture, literature and ideas compares to our attempts at multicultural understanding. Stephen struggled with Greek, she knew she would never fully understand or master it (*PA* 250), but she revelled in grappling with a literature that reflected 'the supreme example of what can be done with words' (*E2* 118); as she wrote to Violet, plunging into 'tough Greek' attracted her (*L1* 177). Through Greek, she also honoured her family's appreciation of ancient languages while simultaneously defying its basis; she could search, as Jean Mills argues, for Greek counter-narratives about women, particularly those capturing 'a world conceived upon values of "both/and" thinking, rather than an insistence on hierarchies, competition, and jealousies' (Mills, *SMC* 54). Finally, she took pleasure in its aesthetic beauty, literary sensuality and provocative portrayals (Mills 54–5). Janet Case nurtured all these quests.

Based on diary evidence (*PA* 181), Virginia Stephen started private lessons in Greek with Janet Case (1863–1937) in winter 1902 (see also *L1* 58 n1), after, Case writes to Marion Rathbone on 3 April 1937, 'a terrifying interview w. Sir Leslie Stephen down his ear trumpet' (Letter MASC), and continued regularly until the end of 1903 (*PA* 181 n23; *L1* 98, 108). It is unclear from Stephen letters written to Case in February 1904 when Leslie Stephen was dying whether she was trying to keep up with lessons (*L1* 124). But a letter from Virginia to Violet dated 8 December [1904] mentions hammering out relatives' lives she has sent Violet when she 'ought to have been doing Greek grammar – and having to stop writing of a sudden when Case came into the room' (*L1* 164), and Case remembers Virginia's telling her 'she'd been asked to write an article for the Times or Times Lit. Sup^t' at one of their lessons (Letter). These letters indicate she probably continued her lessons with Case off and on in 1904 and 1905 – she was ill in summer 1904, recovered at her Aunt Caroline's Cambridge house that summer and early autumn, and began writing for the *Guardian* in December 1904 and for the *TLS* in March 1905. The shift from tutor to friend that Stephen hints at in her 1903 sketch ('she had too, I think, a fine human sympathy which I had reason, once or twice to test –' [*PA* 184]) and that Woolf suggests in her 1937 obituary draft ('Her old pupils owe her more than the Greek' ['Janet Case' MS n. pag. 5] probably began when the young woman persuaded her tutor to talk about connections between Greek and English literature (*E6* 111) and confided in her about George Duckworth (*L1* 472). Virginia Stephen expressed a friend's gratitude when Janet Case gave her the gift of conversation in visits during Leslie Stephen's last days in February 1904, which was 'as good as a lesson' (*L1* 124), and when Janet Case helped her recover from her breakdown in the early months of 1914 when Leonard had to be away. '[N]o one, not Leonard even,' Woolf later wrote to Margaret Llewelyn Davies when agreeing to write Janet's obituary, 'knows how much I have to thank Janet for' (*L6* 145). Lessons evidently continued after the Stephen move to Bloomsbury, with references to Miss Case appearing in letters to Violet Dickinson dated [May 1907] and [April 1909] (*L1* 294, 393), but how regularly cannot be determined.[52]

Janet Case was educated at home, but within her parents' co-educational school, Heath Brow (Perry, *ODNB*), where 'she received a more comprehensive classical education than was usual for girls at that time' (Perry, *DBC* 161) and thus entered Girton College in 1881 well prepared in the classics. A December 1882 *Girton Review* article makes it clear how unusual that was: the writer contrasts young men who have attended public schools and thus spent 'the last six years ... studying little else but Classics' with the girl coming from a High School 'with the usual small allowance of Latin and utter ignorance of Greek' – that young woman will 'find herself, at the end of three years' hard and discouraging work, in the position she ought to have been in when starting her work on the Tripos' (4–5, GCCP 2/1/1; see also Long 41, GCCP 2/1/3). Janet entered Cambridge at an exciting time, too; on 1 February 1881, the university determined women could be admitted to the Honours Examinations (Tripos), results being published in the *Cambridge University Reporter* along with men's, even though women could not obtain the accompanying degree (*CUR* 1880–1 334–5). Few women (or men) took Part II of the Tripos, so when Janet Case earned a 2nd class in Part I (div. 4) of the Classical Tripos in 1884 and then a 1st class in Part II (Philosophy) in 1885, she had done something extraordinary. In 1907, she received BA and MA degrees from Trinity College Dublin, which allowed female students at Oxford and Cambridge colleges to graduate there between 1904 and 1907.[53]

Janet Case played Electra in an 1883 Girton College production and the goddess Athena in an 1885 Cambridge University production of *Eumenides*. Christopher Stray quotes the *Illustrated London News* on her mastery of Greek, which '"would have been considered a miracle in a girl some twenty years ago"' (*Transformed* 160–1), and Kate Perry says she was 'singled out in reviews for her "excellence of elocution"' (*DBC* 162). Stray further notes that after that unprecedented performance, 'no parts were taken by women in the Cambridge [Greek] plays until 1950' (161).[54] She and Alice Zimmern founded the Girton College Classical Club (Thomas 50) to promote, reported the March 1884 *Girton Review*, 'acquaintance and mutual help among the classical students' (19; GCCP 2/1/1). Yopie Prins says Case also 'hosted regular reading and discussion of classical texts in her rooms at college, focusing in particular on Greek tragedy' (170). Janet Case's tutoring was grounded in performance and group discussion.

She also adjusted her tutoring based on the student and the desired outcome (*E6* 111–12; 'Janet Case' MS). If students were studying for examinations, she could help them survive the 'grind' leading up to the Tripos. She knew the Tripos was an endurance test[55] and that young men entered it after years of grammar exercises, rote memorisation and translation tests. But for the pupil 'destined to remain an amateur', she freely and humorously structured her tutoring around storming 'the masterpieces of Greek drama' so 'out they shone', whole, meaningful, beautiful even if not marked by impeccable grammar or proper accents (*E6* 111). Janet Case honoured the efforts of both scholars and 'worldlings', appreciated both 'the nymph and the noun' (*E6* 112).

Even for those wanting 'to read Greek for their own amusement' (*E6* 111), Janet Case did not neglect grammar, using her experience as a Girton student and her teaching experience at Maida Vale High School from 1887 to 1896 (Perry, *ODNB*) to push Stephen to learn the rudiments of the language and strengthen her Greek foundation, 'procur[ing] a Grammar' and insisting Stephen start again with 'the very first exercise – upon the proper use of the article' (*PA* 183; see also *L1* 58). Case was as 'regular as a Clock' (*L1* 100) in her bi-weekly lessons ('Sketch 1' 127), marked up Virginia's exercises and told her 'with perfect good humour that [they] were detestable' (*PA* 183). When Virginia Stephen writes to Violet in July 1903 that she has sent an incorrectly added-up bill for her lessons back to Miss Case with the following comment on it, '"Corrections are useless. I can only put notes of exclamation" – which I did, all over the page,' and then asks, 'Wasn't that witty?' (*L1* 89),[56] we see her acknowledge her tutor's 'undaunted courage' in saying once to Virginia, '"I haven't even attempted to correct this one"' (*PA* 183). Case was cheerful, patient and firm ('I never once made her lose her temper', Stephen writes in 1903, 'amazed at the amount [Case] stood from me' [*PA* 183]). Koulouris says Janet Case was perhaps the first teacher to demonstrate to Virginia Stephen how grammar contributes to the 'overall atmosphere and aesthetic value of Greek texts' (*HL* 197 n119). Woolf would later write that beauty in Greek literature was not 'an ornament to be applied separately' (*E2* 117); from Janet Case, Stephen learned grammar could not be separated from that beauty.

As Mills makes clear in her book on Woolf, Harrison and modernist classicism, Case patterned her pedagogical style after Jane Ellen Harrison's, using 'invitation, collaboration, and interaction' to immerse students quickly in Greek plays. Neither of them started with isolated language components or easy works; rather, they plunged students immediately into difficult works such as Aeschylus's *The Libation Bearers* (45–9). Virginia Woolf later recalls her excitement before lessons, her anticipation of interpretive discussions – what were playwrights saying or teaching? what were their views on life and fate? – and theoretical arguments (*D4* 11). She even had strategies for drawing her tutor into such discussions, advancing 'life long opinions on the spur of the moment' (*PA* 182) and leading Case to compare Euripides and Meredith or Aeschylus and Wordsworth (*E6* 111). Case had 'clear strong views' and communicated them openly and eloquently, sharing with Harrison a view of teaching 'as one scholar sharing something new and vital with another' (Anabel Robinson qtd in Mills 47). But she also had 'the rare gift of seeing the other side' – she stimulated Stephen to think hard, to consider what writers were communicating through their work, particularly to readers in another culture and many centuries later, and to 'see her point of view' about the philosophical, religious and pedagogical underpinnings of Greek tragedians. Stephen confesses she 'had never attempted anything of this kind before', protesting that 'Miss Case carried it too far,' and then commenting, tellingly, 'yet I was forced to think more than I had done hitherto' (*PA* 184, 183). Most important, Janet Case took Virginia Stephen and her opinions and contradictions seriously. Case, a classically educated Cambridge woman, thus reinforced what Thoby, her classically educated Cambridge brother, provided: passionate argument, an assumption of worthiness and the need to support one's views while understanding others'. No wonder Stephen says she was an 'excellent teacher' who 'taught well' (*PA* 183, 182).[57]

Janet Case also reinforced Professor Warr's attitudes about Greek in her scholarship – it should not be the sole possession of upper-class males – aspiring 'to bring classical literacy to the common reader' (Prins 174). In Prins's discussion of *Prometheus Bound* translations by Elizabeth Barrett Browning, Janet Case and Edith Hamilton, she points out that the play, with its 'long history of political readings', is also about 'the politics of reading and writing, since Prometheus proclaims he gave the Greek alphabet to humanity along with the gift of fire' and since Greek letters are written on, imposed on, the female body of Io (164–5). Prins notes Lorna Hardwick's observation on the result – translating this play 'became a rite of passage for women, who discovered various kinds of empowerment and subversion in writing their own versions' (165) – and praises Case's 'Promethean effort to teach the Greek alphabet to the common man and so bring classical literacy to the masses' (172). Case's 1905 translation of the play was the only book in the Temple Dramatists Series, aimed at the working classes, to have a foreign-language text (Perry, *DBC* 162). It was inexpensive, pocket-sized, 'designed for amateurs who were lovers of Greek but not philologists', and featured Greek and English text on facing pages (Prins 171).[58] Virginia Woolf would later praise Loeb Library editions for that format because it gave the 'very obscure but not altogether undeserving class' of amateurs the 'gift of freedom' – being able to 'read a whole play at a time, with [their] feet on the fender' (*E2* 114).[59]

Robin Bond, in a University of Reading presentation in June 2017, discussed Stephen's annotations of Sophocles' *Antigone* as she studied it with Miss Pater at King's College London in Easter Term 1900 and argued that those annotations were exactly (and understandably) like those of current students learning Greek at the intermediate level: heavily dependent on text notes and Greek lexicons such as the one Stephen used, Liddell and Scott. However, as Stephen took lessons from Case and learned from Case's translation practice (and A. W. Verrall's),[60] she became more independent, producing 'The Libation Bearers Notebook' in 1907 (Mills, *SMC* 101–3) and what Koulouris calls her 'Greek Notebook' between 1907 and 1909.[61] Mills describes a facing translation notebook, one in which Stephen takes guidance from Verrall but translates on her own, creating a 'product that relies on . . . lively improvisation' (102). The Greek and Latin Studies notebook at Sussex, on the other hand, is a reading notebook, containing Stephen's brief notes on three of Juvenal's *Satires* and Virgil's *4th Georgic*, fragmentary notes on Aristophanes' *The Frogs* and Plato's *The Phaedrus*, and extensive notes on the *Odyssey*'s twenty-four books, Euripides' *Ion*, Plato's *Symposium* and Sophocles' *Ajax*. Still relying on facing translation editions (in his transcription, Koulouris cites Brenda Silver, but cannot always determine which editions Stephen used),

Virginia Stephen may still be an amateur, but she no longer haltingly and literally translates. Rather, she has become a reader of Greek, a note taker, skills Virginia Woolf would use in her work.[62]

Moreover, as Woolf later comments, Janet Case connected Greek to the modern world – suffrage, politics, reform (E6 112). Perry notes Case's work on improved maternity care and divorce law reform, support of Home Rule for Ireland and membership in the Peace Pledge Union (Perry, ODNB), and it was Case to whom Virginia Stephen wrote about joining the fight for women's suffrage in 1910 (L1 421). Case's 'passion for Greek was informed by her passion for politics, and vice versa' (Prins 171), so Case modelled a different use of Greek for her young student: Greek did not inherently reinforce a patriarchal, imperialist world view (Koulouris, HL 1–17). In fact, it could support radical beliefs in women's capacities and social justice (Mills, SMC 1–37). Evidently not seeking an academic post after her Girton achievements, Case taught as a visiting 'classical mistress' in a secondary school until 1896 (Perry, ODNB) and then pursued different kinds of expertise, becoming a student at the London School of Ethics and Social Philosophy and then a University Extension student (KWA/RAD 3, 1897–8 and KWA/RAD 4, 1898–9), for example.[63] Case 'strayed enough from grammar' to let Stephen see 'a really valiant strong minded woman' (PA 184, 183),[64] and through her, through Greek, Stephen encountered groups and communities passionate about social reform, not philanthropy: 'Her Greek was connected with many things' (E6 112). Thus, as Virginia Woolf later asserts, Janet Case was a 'rare teacher' and 'remarkable woman', a pioneer who operated in the background as a counsellor rather than as a champion (E6 111–12). In Janet Case, Virginia Stephen witnessed a woman whose politics did not involve coercive loudspeakers but seamless integration with life.

Although Janet Case came to 22 Hyde Park Gate (and later Bloomsbury) to tutor Virginia Stephen, her work with Virginia figuratively took the young woman out of the house, teaching her how to continue her Greek studies well beyond her apprenticeship, enlarging her concept of Greek beyond its male 'possession' and giving her the language's discipline, power and strangeness. Moreover, Case prodded her to integrate research and life and to use what she had learned from Thoby, passionate argument about texts and ideas. Stephen had had Greek instruction before, but Janet Case taught rather than instructed her: the relationship between grammar and meaning, the relevance of a dead past to a living present, the limits of knowledge, the ability to use one's mind with strength and purpose. More personally, Janet Case modelled professional independence, fostered courage, affirmed Virginia's interpretation of family experiences and introduced her to communities, causes and quiet activism.

Using two different libraries, attending more than thirty classes, and being tutored in Greek widened and deepened Virginia Stephen's curriculum; increased the pedagogies she was encountering; taught her lessons about inclusion and exclusion, the nature of schooling for women, and the mystery of language; and put her in virtual or actual touch with communities of readers and writers, students, and political activists.

Over the course of Virginia Stephen's homeschooling, then, 'many different things [were] mixed together' as she learned from the teachers discussed here

– Leslie, Julia and Thoby Stephen, Aunt Anny, *Atalanta* and *Tit-Bits*, libraries, King's College London instructors, Janet Case – and from many others as well – siblings, relatives, other tutors, friends. From these teachers, Virginia Stephen absorbed various subjects within implied curricula, learned multiple lessons, experienced several pedagogies and became acquainted with many communities. But she probably felt bombarded occasionally as the teachers increased and the learning sped up. Tensions and complexities did not diminish, either, and she remained isolated – she continued to struggle to make the fragments of her education cohere 'in the right proportions' (*E6* 266).

Notes

1. Virginia Woolf did use the public library in Kingston on 12 January 1915 (*D1* 17). Funded by Andrew Carnegie, it opened 11 May 1903.
2. An 1849 Public Libraries Select Committee witness said the country was giving people '"an appetite to read", but failing "to find them any books"' (Miller, 'PL' 126). William Ewart's compromises to get the Act passed curtailed library purchasing; the halfpenny rate was increased to a full penny in 1855, but no further increases occurred between then and 1919 (Altick, *ECR* 228).

   Alistair Black writes that public libraries did increase in London from the late 1880s onward, partly because foundations sprouted up then for several reasons, which he summarises, but mainly because of gifts from philanthropists like John Passmore Edwards and Andrew Carnegie (28).
3. E. J. Miller says Public Libraries Act enemies feared libraries would become 'mere schools of agitation and sedition' ('PL' 125). Kate Flint consulted public library annual reports to determine library users' class and occupational background and notes that, until after the Great War, public libraries 'primarily served the skilled working classes and tradespeople, the middle classes continuing to patronize circulating and subscription libraries' (173). But Mary Hammond argues restrictions meant to protect books actually functioned as social control, excluding many working-class people. If dirty patrons could be kicked out, then manual labourers with no way to clean up at work could not stop at the library on the way home. Plus, the complex process of consulting the catalogue and checking out a book could deter the poor or shabbily dressed, as did 'embarrassment over "not knowing" which books to ask for and how' (96–9).
4. However, public libraries, like US publicly funded schools, have recently come under attack.
5. Carlyle was also angry that Antonio Panizzi, Keeper of Printed Books at the British Museum Reading Room, had denied him a private study room (Grindea 10). But Carlyle's argument was valid: a *Westminster Review* writer said in 1827, 'We cannot believe that any nation under the canopy of heaven can equal, much less surpass us in locking readers out of libraries; we are unrivalled in all exclusions' (qtd in Altick, *ECR* 216). Eight years after the London Library founding, Public Libraries Select Committee witnesses agreed with Carlyle: 'on the whole things were done better abroad' (Miller, 'PL' 126). Some Committee public library recommendations reflect London Library procedures, perhaps because Ewart was a member (Wells, *Rude* 147).
6. Volumes with AVS (Adeline Virginia Stephen) bookplates, edited by R. H. Evans, published in 1809–12, match the volumes listed in the 1888 *Catalogue of the London Library*, 5th ed. (LLA), duplicating what Leslie Stephen lugged home. Although

7. The Committee discussed this policy several times over the years since the Library wanted to accommodate members and their families and yet avoid excessive 'free' use. In 1899, it settled on not permitting 'more than one member at a time of a member's family (who must reside with the members) to use the Reading Room' (LLM 9 January 1899 meeting).
8. Leslie Stephen must have known Robert Giffen, economist and statistician, but he does not appear in any Stephen or Woolf indices. Perhaps Virginia Stephen ran into him in the Library and on the spot asked him to introduce her. See O'Neill for a description and pictures of Stephen's application form, where she describes her occupation as 'spinster'. Ruth Adam's frequent use of the term, in her book *A Woman's Place: 1910–1975*, reflects its common and pervasive use in British society; see especially 'The Superfluous Women', 16–31. Plus, it echoes Ritchie's 'Toilers and Spinsters'. In 2021, a life membership for someone joining at between 18 and 24 years old costs £23,700; annual fees are £510 for individual adults and £255 for partners and young people 16–29, but Supported Memberships help defray a percentage of the cost for those who cannot pay full membership fees (London Library, 'Join Online').
9. Snaith says Woolf's later support of the Fawcett Library stemmed partly from the 'politics of space crucial to Woolf's thinking'. The Fawcett Library 'held significance purely as a building' because it provided a comfortable room where women could meet ('Stray' 23).
10. Carlyle believed a man needed to be alone with a book: he 'can do more with it in his own apartment, in the solitude of one night, than in a week in such a place as the British Museum'. Thus, the London Library's goal: being useful 'as a lending library for home usage and consumption' and emphasising 'suitable stock and not . . . suitable buildings' (Baker 12).
11. Lady Galway recalls

    having been asked by a friend to look up some interpretation of an obscure passage in the Apocalypse: I had of course forgotten the name of the author. Mr Cox instantly informed me that Canon X was the one and only authority; then he looked at me severely and, referring to my father, added: 'Sir Rowland would have known.' (qtd in McIntyre 8)

    Nicholas Basbanes tells about Simon Winchester asking, in 1988, for a book on Royal Navy intelligence in the Pacific, and having the staff member answer, '"I think I do know who has it, a woman who lives in Devon, and she's had it since 1958. I'll ring her up"' (213).
12. 'To Sir Leslie Stephen K.C.B. in gratitude for many kindnesses fr. C. Hagberg Wright' (K&M-V 249). Wright, an extraordinary librarian, had prodigious energy, sometimes working eighteen hours a day (Wells, 'Some' 169). Starting completely again and taking pains to check authors' names, he 'examined, marked, recatalogued . . . and re-placed' each book in a little over three years, then revised and edited the slips for three and a half years (A. Bell, 'LL' 164). In four more years, he and one assistant completed the subject catalogue (McIntyre 16; Wells, *Rude* 137–8), which Judith Chernaik calls 'one of the first of its kind'. Miron Grindea calls him 'the undisputed builder of the modern L.L.' (3n). He was Librarian from 1893 until his death in 1940, just months before the Library's centenary.
13. Wright's catalogues and subject indexes 'enjoyed a circulation beyond the subscribers' (A. Bell, 'LL' 164); the public could buy the title catalogue for £35 from Williams and Norgate.
14. Reimer says L. T. Meade was grateful to the British Museum, where 'she was taken seriously as a writer and provided with the desk, books, blotting paper, pens, and ink she required for her work' ('Meade' 194).
15. Based on complaints in periodicals, Bernstein suspects these seating arrange-

ments were never policed by reading room supervisors (*R* 5–8); women clearly did not stay at their designated tables, and perhaps men sat at the women's tables, though Ruth Hoberman quotes men who felt prevented from doing so ('Bald' 172). It is possible, too, that such British Museum Reading Room divisions had disappeared by 1905. Chris Baggs has a nuanced discussion of contemporary arguments for and against separate accommodation for women in public libraries between 1850 and 1914. See also Flint, 172–9. According to Hoberman, women were never forbidden to use the British Museum Reading Room, but very few patronised it before 1857: 'From its earliest incarnation, the British Museum Reading Room was largely a male domain' ('Bald' 171). Woolf uses *Literary Anecdotes of the Eighteenth Century* to argue 'Women were apparently excluded from the British Museum Reading-Room in the eighteenth century' (*TG* 206 n6), although Arunell Esdaile names three women readers in the late eighteenth century and says, according to Barwick, 'as late as the eighteen-thirties it was the practice, though under no regulation, to admit women in pairs' (53, 355 n37; see also Hoberman 'Women' 494, 'Bald' 171).

16. On 7 May 1926, Woolf says she went to the British Museum, 'where all was chill serenity, dignity & severity. Written up are the names of great men; & we all cower like mice nibbling crumbs in our most official discreet impersonal mood beneath' (*D3* 80).

17. P. R. Harris implies the Reading Room Superintendent affected how readers felt. Superintendents George Bullen (1866–75) and Richard Garnett (1875–84) 'turned the Reading Room into a much more friendly place' (*Reading* 21), and Bernstein says Garnett was a literary mentor for many women ('Radical' par. 5). Harris describes Superintendent F. D. Sladen (1919–29) as 'a martinet and a stickler for the proprieties', whereas the next Superintendent, A. I. Ellis (1929–46), could not have been nicer: 'he probably held the world record for the number of acknowledgements to him by grateful authors in the prefaces to their books' (*Reading* 28).

18. The London Library never had a written policy excluding women from its Committee, which was used to argue against the resolution moved and seconded by Miss Ellen Cahill and Dr Pankhurst on 29 May 1890 – 'That so many Members of this Library are ladies there ought to be at least one lady on the Committee' – and '[a]fter some discussion the Motion was withdrawn' (*LLM* 29 May 1890 Report of AGM; 'LL', *Times* 31 May 1890 9; Wells, *Rude* 115–16). Members put forward Miss Shaw-Fefèvre and Miss Beatrice Potter the next year, but they were defeated (*LLM* 28 May 1891 Report of AGM; Wells, *Rude* 118). The Committee added Mrs Green's name to its slate and submitted it to members for approval on 19 June 1894 (*LLM* 9 May 1894 Committee meeting and 14 June 1894 Report of AGM; Wells, *Rude* 119).

Leslie Stephen did not seem concerned when she joined the Committee (*SLLS2* 429–30). She outlived him and served until 1916, and he helped her edit her husband's letters, writing, 'I have come to think better of her. She is a singularly generous woman and a staunch friend who has been very good to me' (*MB* 108). But he supposedly declared about women on the Committee, 'never again. She was so troublesome,' which E. M. Forster reported when he told Woolf the Committee had 'been discussing whether to allow ladies' and says they would not consider it because '"No no no, ladies are quite impossible."' Woolf, surmising Forster had mentioned her name and imagining the Committee's negative phrase in response, was furious – about the statement, Forster's thinking she would be grateful to be a token woman, her father's attitude (*D4* 297–8; Wells, *Rude* 121; Snaith, 'Stray' 23–4; Pawlowski, Intro 6). Forster talked to Woolf in April 1935; Committee Minutes for 14 January 1935 and the usual rotation of members suggests H. A. L. Fisher, Desmond MacCarthy, E. M. Forster, Colonel Karslake, Osbert Burdett, E. Marion Cox, H. M. Hake, Frederick Pollock (Leslie Stephen's friend) and W. G. Spencer were on the Committee when this discussion took place. Burdett and Pollock died in 1937, which paved the way for change; the Committee elected Professor Eileen Power and Lord David Cecil as replacements (*LLAR* 8 July 1937). Power served until her premature death in August 1940, and Forster again approached Woolf about joining the Committee in November. This conversation brought up her 'London Library complex' (*D5* 358), and she refused. The Committee then elected Professor Lillian Penson to replace Power (*LLAR* 16 July 1941).

Unfortunately for Virginia Woolf's opinion of her father, as Carol MacKay points out, Forster 'may have confused Leslie's reaction with that of another board member', and she cites 'Leslie's letter to Julia, 7 Sep 1894, Berg' ('Thackeray' 88–9 n17). No letter from Leslie with that date exists in the Berg Collection, but Josh McKeon, then Librarian, confirmed my suspicion that MacKay may have misdated the letter based on the difference between American and British dating styles because a letter from Leslie to Julia dated 9 7 1894 is, in fact, in the Sir Leslie Stephen Collection of Papers in the Berg Collection, and it appears in Bicknell's collection of Stephen's letters as noted above (Josh McKeon, 31 July 2018 email; *SLLS2* 429–30). Clearly, Leslie Stephen had no problem whatsoever with Mrs Green's election to the Committee: he writes to Julia, 'We had a very peaceable Committee meeting at the London Library. One old gentleman, Dr [W.] Munk, has resigned in wrath, it is supposed at Mrs Green's election,' which had occurred on 14 June 1894. According to Bicknell, the minutes of the 9 July meeting 'record that the Secretary "was instructed to write and ask Dr Munk to reconsider his decision"; apparently he refused, as he was replaced by Sidney Low on 23 July 1894' (*SLLS2* 430 n1). It is possible Leslie Stephen changed his mind about including women on the Committee, but later minutes do not record any irritation with Mrs Green or any controversial votes involving her. In a letter to Charles Francis Adams, Jr, dated 2 February 1899, he calls her 'a very bright, clever lady' (*SLLS2* 496–7).

19. See Bernstein, who writes 'Woolf did not locate herself comfortably in either class-accented space' (*R* 135).
20. That expansion can feel heavenly, as Woolf confesses in her letter to Lady Tweedsmuir about the Fawcett Library: 'I perhaps endow libraries with more divinity than I should' (*L6* 234). It is an experience Woolf wants to share. Thanking Lady Rhondda for her Fawcett subscription, she writes that 'books have always been so prolific in my life that I can't help being shocked to think that there are those who go without' (*L6* 236).
21. Comparing Alison Booth's list of collective women's biographies (347–87) against the London Library 1903 catalogue shows that of the fifty-two titles in her early examples list, the Library had thirteen; of those thirteen, two were not translated. Sometimes the Library had works by authors of those fifty-two titles, but not the biographies Booth lists. Of Booth's 930 entries, 497 were published before or in 1901. Of those 497 titles, the Library had ninety-six, or 19 per cent. Again, the Library sometimes had the author, such as William Henry Davenport Adams, but titles by him were all about men (10). Or it had the author, such as George Barnett Smith, but many of his titles were not collective biographies, such as the *Life of Gladstone* (1364). Jessica Berman bluntly asks in her review of Booth's book, 'who knew?', and thus confirms one of Booth's important points, the need to renew demands for female presence every generation (39). As prevalent as these biographies were, their absence in the London Library may explain why Woolf remained ignorant of them. If libraries privilege the single life over collective lives, readers may also.
22. See Bernstein's *Roomscape* chapter on Virginia Stephen's use of the London Library and British Museum, and Virginia Woolf's 'dome consciousness' in *A Room of One's Own*, for a delightful perspective on this and other paradoxes. For example, Bernstein says, notwithstanding Woolf's title, her 'creative refashioning of writing in

the Reading Room evokes both solitude and community'. Bernstein details what she calls Woolf's cartwheeling poetics and describes how the narrator somersaults her way through the text in 'an innovative response to [Woolf's] anger over women's marginality in the canon of English letters' (180). See also Devin Griffiths, who shows why the British Museum's *Catalogue of Printed Books* 'was a more radical agent than we have recognized' (158) and how *A Room of One's Own* emphasises those 'radical implications' rather than critiques them (153).

23. Strong pro-public library and museum movements also existed, however, spearheaded by Thomas Greenwood and others, who argued, as Hoberman notes, that such institutions would '[provide] the working classes with moral and intellectual enrichment' (*Museum* 11).

24. During her apprenticeship, Stephen used libraries requiring fees or tickets such as the London Library, British Museum Reading Room, Dr Williams' Library, Day's and Mudie's, although she mentions their returning books to a Bognor library on the Bognor trip with Stella (*PA* 35). Woolf seems to have begun really using free or public libraries in Hampstead and Sussex, and then continued to do so the rest of her life (see *D1* 8, 11, 17, 300). In an email discussion, Ruth Hoberman perceptively noted the difference between Victorian ideas of working-class self-improvement and Woolf's proposal that the working classes become critics and transform literature (16 August 2011).

25. Cuddy-Keane continues,

> I was delighted that Woolf – who so frequently used a metaphor of eating to describe her reading – should have been herself delighted by the literal tokens of eating on her page. And I could think of no better sign for her work as a public intellectual, working for the integration of literature into our daily lives. (8)

In 2017, I was teary-eyed at seeing four full shelves of well-worn books by and about Woolf on the Literature floor of the London Library; I like to think Woolf would have been pleased about that, too.

26. I have relied on Jones's and Snaith's discoveries and description of Virginia Stephen at the King's College Ladies' Department in 'Tilting at Universities' for my discussion of Stephen's life during this period, and Gwyn Jenkins's article on Clara Pater at King's College helped me review and check their work and my own. Jenkins ensured another review of previous work, including mine, here.

27. Barbara Lounsberry agrees: the challenge of her studies 'might explain her neglect of her struggling diary' (40). See Gill Lowe ('locked up') for a perceptive analysis of Virginia Stephen's struggles in her 1897 diary.

28. Leslie Stephen allows her to attend, with the emphasis on allows. As Jane Fisher writes, 'Although [Virginia Stephen] attested to her father's generosity in his role of cultural benefactor, she was sensitive to the threat inherent in it as well: what he had power to give he also had power to deny' (40). He closes by saying, 'Of course, it does not come to much by itself in any case, but I have to be exceedingly careful for the present' (Letter to George Warr; qtd in Dalgarno, *Visible* 41 and in Jones and Snaith 31). Dalgarno suggests he thinks a daughter could not become proficient in Greek (42), but perhaps he meant he had to be careful, even though one course by itself would not add up to much Greek learning or produce much strain. The word 'easily' has been omitted from Stephen's third quoted sentence, which should read 'She has been in a very nervous state, wh., though easily explicable, has given me some anxiety.' Apparently Garnett McCoy made the original transcribing error; see *Reading Records* 25 (Letter to George Warr).

29. Perhaps Leslie Stephen also wrote to Professor Laughton. Callender and Lambert say Laughton wrote almost all the naval memoirs, 900 lives, for the *Dictionary of National Biography*, making him the 'third most prolific contributor' and thus someone Stephen knew, if only through his work. In addition, since Ladies' Department policy stipulated students needed the 'special sanction of the Vice-Principal' to attend courses if

younger than sixteen (*SL 1897–8* 2), Leslie Stephen probably wrote to Lilian Faithfull as well.

30. Non-matriculated students were also called casual students; see n32. The current usage with a similar connotation in the US is 'auditing' a course, which allows the student to attend without the pressure of earning a grade or credit. An auditing student's required level of participation varies according to the college or university, but it never includes final exams.
31. See also Gillian Sutherland, '"Girton for Ladies, Newnham for Governesses"', for how complicated the 'question of where school ends and university begins' (140) was for women's colleges at nineteenth century's end. At Cambridge and King's College London, instructors faced students who might or might not have attended a secondary school, and if they had, might or might not have studied Greek or history, and if they had, might or might not have had the sustained focus on them that young men would have experienced (148).

    The British newspapers were not nearly as careful, with the *Independent* connecting their announcement of the Cambridge University Press edition of Woolf's works to Matthew Bell's impression, gained from erroneously interpreting Jones and Snaith, that Virginia Stephen 'was educated to degree level'. Academics, Holly Williams wrote, had suddenly discovered 'a more clearly politically astute, historically aware, educated, playful and precise author than she is widely thought to be'. The Cambridge edition communicates editors' recent discoveries, but it also builds on work done by British and American scholars who have insisted on those exact Woolfian traits for decades. If readers have 'widely thought' that Woolf was a 'fey, apolitical author in an ivory tower', who was 'delicate, ethereal, and utterly out of touch with the real world' (H. Williams), it has not been for lack of academics trying to correct that impression.
32. The King's College registration books distinguish between the number of registered course entries and the number of enrolled students – in Michaelmas Term 1897, there were 572 entries, but 398 students; Virginia Stephen, one student, took three courses. Approximately 200–400 students attended the King's Ladies' Department in any given term between Michaelmas 1897 and Michaelmas 1901, with Michaelmas Term typically having the highest enrolment and Easter Term the lowest (KWA/R2 265). But the total number of enrolled students in any given year was higher – 543, for example, in 1900–1 (KWA/RAD 6). Jones and Snaith correctly estimate 500–600 students in the Ladies Department (5, 6), but that number represents the total of individual students enrolled over the year, not the number of students there from term to term.

    Zimmern, writing in September 1904, noted the Ladies Department had aimed, 'until quite recently', to provide London girls with 'opportunities for general culture', and the 'casual student still predominates'. But 'the number of those preparing for degrees is increasing', with twenty-nine students reading for degrees out of the previous year's fifty matriculated students (1486), which probably represents the total during the year since the Register for Matriculated Students, begun in 1902 after Stephen left, records seventeen matriculated students on 28 March 1902 for the upcoming Easter Term (KWA/R4). At the most, then, given these numbers, only 5–10 per cent of the students were matriculated at any time during Stephen's time there.

    The ratio in any given classroom or discipline would have varied, though, so Faithfull's efforts – as women's education reformer, Vice-Principal and literature professor – probably meant a higher number of matriculated students pursued a degree in English literature than in other subjects (Jones and Snaith 14; Faithfull 104–5). But Virginia Stephen (or Leslie?) evidently never considered literature courses (Hill, 'History' 353–4; Fisher 38–9).
33. Professor Warr dealt with various expertise levels in his Elementary Greek class by reserving time for those 'prepared for less elementary work' (Jones and Snaith 19, Fig.

2d), thus his classes lasting an hour and a half. His course, then, was geared toward the casual student with supplements for the matriculated.
34. Zimmern describes these requirements in the University of London part of her article, but they would have applied at King's College because of the administrative relationship with the University of London (1487; see also Jones and Snaith 4 and Faithfull 103–4).
35. A student enrolled in one course with a weekly hour-long lecture in each of the three ten-week terms would, with perfect attendance, log thirty hours. In 1900–1, a sizable majority of students (332 out of 543) attended for twenty-five hours or under (KWA/ RAD 6).
36. Stephen probably soon understood the distinction between degree-seeking and casual students that Zimmern identifies. Jones and Snaith suggest Woolf's silence about her course work in later life meant she may have 'preferred to think of herself as an autodidact and felt that her real learning had taken place outside institutional walls' (41). Their persuasive conclusion does not negate other possibilities, however. Being a non-matriculated student may have meant Virginia Stephen and then Virginia Woolf did not think of her course work at King's College, entry- and intermediate-level in several areas rather than sustained study in one (the exact opposite of her brothers' schooling), as formal education. For one thing, she did not go away to school. She attended a non-residential college, and as Faithfull points out, 'there is for the keen student the difficulty of satisfying the claims of home and College'. Any girl with 'the instincts of a scholar' needs 'freedom from home ties for a time' (106–7), something Stephen did not have. (See *P* 113 for Miss Craddock's awareness of Kitty's difficulty in shifting from domestic to academic and Woolf's 'Sketch' 156 for memories of social distractions during studying.) No matter how excellent and conscientious her work, no matter how many courses she took at whatever level, Stephen was still a casual student among many casual students, so it is not surprising she may have internally defined her education as informal, thus not really schooling, thus not worth mentioning. See Koulouris 'Greek' 5 n8, for a similar suggestion, and his insightful comparison of Jane Harrison's and Virginia Stephen's educations in *HL* (169). Finally, Virginia Woolf later called 1897–1904 'the seven unhappy years' and shrank from revisiting them ('Sketch' 136), so she may have subsumed her King's College courses in a much greater erasure.
37. After his death, his wife founded the Warr Memorial Prize in Classics, a £30 annual prize for books, which continues to be awarded to a student in the King's College London Classics Department (Warr Memorial Prize). J. A. Venn's Warr entry notes that Mrs Warr also bequeathed £5,000 for a Cambridge scholarship bearing his name (356).
38. Hall and Macintosh compare Warr's life and work to Gilbert Murray's (471–3) and argue that Warr's stage experiments, use of adaptation and performance, emphasis on gender and insistence on interpreting Aeschylus's trilogy as a whole had a great impact on modern drama, 'reason enough to write Warr back into theatre history, and to restore his efforts and those of his students at King's College, London, to the public memory' (487). See J. Michael Walton for a less complimentary view of Warr's translations (61–5).
39. It bothered him that the classics were 'sealed books for all but students of Greek and Latin' (Preface to the *Oresteia*, qtd in Hall and Macintosh 472–3).
40. Gwyn Jenkins's '"Pater's Pins Stuck": Virginia Woolf and Clara Pater at King's College Ladies' Department' appeared just as I was preparing this study for the press. Wanting to 'rescue Clara Pater from obscurity' (23), Jenkins also compares syllabus plans to staff register realities to construct tables that show Pater's increasing involvement at King's College during Virginia Stephen's time there. Jenkins suggests Virginia Stephen took Intermediate Greek and Intermediate Grammar in Michaelmas Term 1900 (31), both from Pater, which also seems plausible except for Stephen's 23 October 1900

letter. In any case, as we both note, the staff registers indicate Miss Lucas took the courses.
41. Philippa Levine says first-generation women academics 'had little training available to them' and were qualified for their positions only because of their 'commitment and a strong practical humanism' (*Feminist* 134). See also Isobel Hurst's study of Oxford women and the classics.
42. See Jenkins on other ways Pater's influence on Stephen is encoded in Woolf's work.
43. One of Laughton's students and eventual friends was Alfred T. Mahan, United States Navy, who wrote two of Thoby's Clifton prize books (K&M-V 144).
44. Virginia Stephen did not take Continental History in 1899–1900, but that year, these texts were recommended: Kitchin's *History of France* and Jervis's *Student History of France* (SL 1899–1900 16). As Clara Jones notes, the same syllabus recommends these texts for the English History course: Gardiner's *Student History of England* and Ransome's *Advanced History of England* (31). The syllabus also recommends Warburton's *Edward III* and Gairdner's *Lancaster and York* in the Epoch Series and Church's *Henry V* and Oman's *Warwick, the King Maker* in the Men of Action Series. None of these books is in the Library of Leonard and Virginia Woolf.
45. Jane Fisher says Leslie Stephen's initial reading list in history and biography was dominated by works by or about Virginia's literal fathers or strong individuals who reflected their historical times, all promoting 'the undesirability of large-scale social change' (39).
46. Charles Adolphus Buchheim (1828–1900) was born in Moravia, educated in Vienna and fought for reform there in 1848; he fled a death sentence when Imperial forces retook Vienna. In 1851, he left Paris during the coup d'état and began his life over again in England (A correspondent 9) with very little English, almost no money and no references (E. S. Buchheim vi-vii). In 1857, he married Pauline Hermann ('Buchheim' 99), originally from Hamburg (1861 England Census, Ancestry.com), they had Emma in 1861, and he became Professor of German Language and Literature at King's College in 1863.
47. Arthur N. Leonard calls Professor Buchheim a 'pioneer editor' (58).
48. Pauline Buchheim's edition was published in 1886 and received two favourable notices, in *The Princetonian* and the *Nation*, whose reviewer calls the notes 'concise and well-written' ('Rev. of *Schillers*' 139).
49. Charles and Pauline were married in a parish church and baptised their four children in parish churches (Ancestry.com marriage, birth, baptism, census, immigration and death records), and Buchheim contributed a historical introduction to Professor Henry Wace's edition of Martin Luther's works. Although the *Jewish Encyclopedia* includes C. A. Buchheim in its entries (Rhine), Rabbi Calisch includes him in his list of Jewish authors without the asterisk used to denote converts (232) and C. C. Aronsfeld mentions him as one of two 'principal Victorian teachers of German literature' in his article on German Jews in Victorian England (320), the Buchheims fit Aronsfeld's comment about many German Jews who came to Britain during the nineteenth century: they were Jews 'only in name' (321) and 'thoroughly identified themselves with their new citizenship' (325). They did well in their new country until war loomed, when their fight to prevent it was often viewed as treasonous by journalists like Leo Maxse (Aronsfeld 326–7).
50. This letter appeared only in the Palmer Museum presentation of the travelling exhibit, *A Room of Their Own: The Bloomsbury Artists in American Collections*, at Pennsylvania State University, State College, PA, 6 July to 26 September 2010.
51. Jones and Snaith note the 1899–1900 syllabus says private tuition had to be arranged with the Vice-Principal (34 n30), so Stephen had to have talked with Faithfull to register. If, as Leaska and others have suggested, Miss Craye in 'Moments of Being: "Slater's Pins Have No Points"' resembles Clara Pater (see 70–1), then perhaps Miss

Kingston resembles Lilian Faithfull. Kingston 'gave little character sketches' of the faculty 'on the first day of term while she received cheques and wrote out receipts for them,' and she shared something of her childhood with Fanny along with the hint that there was something 'odd' about Miss Craye's famous elder brother ('Slater's' 215–16).

52. Mills (*SMC* 44) cites Alley (292) in describing Case as being 'somewhat intimidated' by the 'new odd Bloomsbury life'. The latter phrase comes from a Janet Case letter Quentin Bell cites in explaining Case's presence in his list of people attending Adrian and Virginia's Thursday evenings in Fitzroy Square after they moved there in March 1907. In her letter to Violet Dickinson, 19 April 1937, just three months before her death, she remembers 'having tea with you one day after the Greek lesson time was over and done with' and thinking Virginia would have no 'further use for me' in her 'new odd Bloomsbury life'. Case says she 'felt shy of going', which Bell surmises means to Fitzroy Square for the Thursday evenings, but '*you* told me to stick to her. She'd like it – so thank you for that' (*QB1* 120–1n; her emphasis).

Several tentative conclusions can be gleaned from this comment. First, it does not clear up exactly when Stephen ended her Greek lessons. Case does not specify a date (the Stephens were at Fitzroy Square until November 1911), and the brief 'Old Case comes on Monday' in April 1909 (*L1* 393) could refer to a visit as well as to a lesson, particularly since Stephen still called her Miss Case in May 1907. Second, Janet may have felt intimidated or shy, but on Violet's advice, she evidently did not stop visiting Bloomsbury, something she is later glad about. Third, her grateful comment captures the awkward transition from teacher and student to equals and friends, a transition sometimes requiring outside help.

53. As S. M. Parkes explains, such students were nicknamed 'steamboat ladies' because they took steamboats to Ireland to receive their degrees. See Claire Breay for further context, history, and information about teaching and achievements in the Classical Tripos.

54. See Prins 170–1 and 178 n5 for information about illustrations of Miss Case in Greek costume for the first issue of *The Woman's World*, edited by Oscar Wilde, in 1888.

55. Part I of the Classical Tripos extended over six June days, from 9 to 12 and 1.30–4.30 on five days and from 9 to 12 on the sixth. On four mornings composition (that is, translation) was required, from: English into Latin prose; English into Greek prose; English into Latin verse; and English into Greek verse. There were four papers of questions, to be answered in an hour and a half each, on Greek history (including literature) and antiquities; Roman history (including literature) and antiquities; Greek grammar and criticism; and Latin grammar and criticism. Finally, five papers contained passages for translation from 'the best Greek and Latin authors, together with questions arising immediately out of any such passages' (*CUC* 1885 33–4).

Part II of the Classical Tripos had five sections. All students had to take section A, which included four translation papers, one from: English into Latin prose; Latin into English; English into Greek prose; and Greek into English. These examinations covered two days, from 9 to 12 and 1.30 to 4.30. The remaining sections (B = ancient philosophy; C = history; D = archaeology; and E = language) were scheduled over the next ten days and had five papers each. Students had to take one or two other sections than A (*CUC* 1885 34–5).

Students were given information ahead of time about which texts would be featured in which exams. So, in 1885, Part II of the Classical Tripos, Section B, had these texts listed: Plato (*Theatetus, Parmenides*); Aristotle (*de generatione et corruptione, metaphysical Z and H*); and Diogenes Laertisu (X [Epicurus in Lives of Eminent Philosophers]) (*CUC* 1884 x).

56. As Jean Mills notes, Virginia Stephen paid for her Greek lessons with Janet Case out of her own pocket (*SMC* 12).

57. Virginia's lessons with Miss Case did not begin well, though. She writes she 'was bored at being taught, & for some time, only did just what was asked from me, & hardly looked up from my book' (*PA* 182). Perhaps her comment reveals another reason she stopped enrolling in King's College classes?
58. Prins notes Case's translation was tied to the Greek text and included a scholarly apparatus, so it probably did not appeal to as broad an audience as she intended; Hamilton's later translation had more popular success. However, Prins admits some of Case's contemporaries thought she 'had found a balance between literal and free translation that was neither completely bound to Greek nor completely unbound from it' (174, 173).
59. She wishes Saxon Sydney-Turner would 'bring out the classics facing an English translation' in a 13 April [1911] letter (*L1* 460).
60. See Mills on the influence of A. W. Verrall's editions on her 'Libation Bearers' notebook (1907) and her 'Agamemnon Notebook' (1922) (*SMC* 49 and n8).
61. See Koulouris's explanation for the title and his annotated transcription of 'VS, Greek and Latin Studies', housed in the University of Sussex Library, the Keep, SxMs–18/A/21, in 'Virginia Woolf's "Greek Notebook"', 1–72.
62. In addition to those already cited, see Dalgarno (*ML*), Fernald (*Feminism*), Rowena Fowler, Amanda Golden ('Textbook'), William Herman, Gerhard Joseph, Vassiliki Kolocotroni, Rebecca Nagel, Sybil Oldfield ('Antigone') and Angeliki Spiropoulou for discussions of Virginia Stephen's Greek studies and Virginia Woolf's lifelong use of Greek in her work.
63. These registrations are at the back of the two Registration books, after the alphabetical tabs. Nothing specific about Case's course work could be found. The London School of Ethics and Social Philosophy was a short-lived experiment launched by the London Ethical Society in 1897 to 'provide university-level education in philosophy to those unable to attend a university' (Gordon and White qtd in Ashton and Colville). Supported by philosophers such as Bertrand Russell, it did not succeed in reaching the working classes; many of its lecturers joined the London School of Economics after the restructuring of the University of London.
64. See Oldfield, 'Antigone' for the relationships among Virginia Stephen/Virginia Woolf, Antigone and Janet Case, all women who thought against the current.

Chapter 4

Reading and Writing Skills

Practice

As Virginia Stephen learned from these and other teachers, she also practised skills. She learned shorthand well enough to do some for her father (*PA* 43, 50). She listened, observed and discussed. She did research and took notes. She translated texts, using a lexicon and keeping a Greek and Latin reading notebook. She read and read and read, reporting a common occurrence on 25 January 1897: 'Reading four books at once' (*PA* 22). When she tapped on her father's study door, asking for another volume to replace one she had finished, his pleased response was '"Gracious child, how you gobble!"' (*L4* 27). Her reading prepared her, after her mother's death 'unveiled' her perceptions, for this interpretive epiphany on a hot spring night:

> [Nessa and I] lay down . . . in the long grass behind the Flower Walk. I had taken *The Golden Treasury* with me. I opened it and began to read some poem. And instantly and for the first time I understood the poem (which it was I forget). It was as if it became altogether intelligible; I had a feeling of transparency in words when they cease to be words and become so intensified that one seems to experience them; to foretell them as if they developed what one is already feeling . . . . no one could have understood from what I said the queer feeling I had in the hot grass, that poetry was coming true. ('Sketch' 93)

Virginia Stephen also wrote and wrote and wrote, though we have only a fraction of what she seems to have written in her youth: letters, journal entries, travel sketches, literary exercises and pieces for the *Hyde Park Gate News*. Written before she turned 22, in the juvenilia we have – approximately 150 letters, three diaries kept until 1904, and the 1891, 1892 and 1895 volumes of the *Hyde Park Gate News* – Stephen mentions or the texts imply the existence of additional work, and Woolf, in her diaries and memoir, also refers to other juvenilia. Such work has a ghostly and teasing presence – we know about it, but it is absent.[1]

None of the following writing mentioned by Stephen or Woolf, for example, has come to light. In a letter to Thoby editorially dated 14 May 1897, she mentions having written their Aunt Caroline a 'vehement letter (in shorthand)' (*L1* 7).[2] In a 25 August 1897 diary entry, Stephen says a visit has not materialised after all her letter writing to Madge Vaughan (*PA* 124). She mentions an 1896 diary (*PA* 16), and on 6 August 1899 writes of 'turn[ing] to my diaries of past years to compare their records' (*PA* 137). Woolf remembers writing an essay, 'the only essay I ever showed father, upon the Elizabethan voyagers' ('Sketch 1' 118), and she recalls her pleasure at discovering her mother 'had sent a story of mine to Madge Symonds; it was so imaginative, she said; it was about souls flying round and choosing bodies to be born into' ('Sketch' 95).[3] She mentions losing her 'precious MS. book' in the move to Bloomsbury in 1904, and it 'would have given me hints for dozens of articles' (*L1* 155). On 8 December 1929, Woolf remembers the 'obscure adventurers' in Hakluyt whose style she 'no doubt practised ... in my copy books' and recalls 'writing a long picturesque essay upon the Christian religion, I think; called Religio Laici, . . . & I also wrote a history of Women; & a history of my own family – all very longwinded & El[izabe]than in style' (*D3* 271). On 19 December 1938, she remembers 'scribbling a story in the manner of Hawthorne on the green plush sofa in the drawing room at St Ives while the grown ups dined' (*D5* 192). In her memoir, she recalls her writing table with its Greek lexicon, her Greek plays, the 'many little bottles of ink, pens innumerable', and 'sheets of foolscap covered with private writing in a hand so small and twisted as to be a family joke' hidden under blotting paper ('Sketch' 122). Though these sheets could have been letters or journal entries, letters are more public and she kept diaries in notebooks, so they were probably literary pieces or exercises, perhaps even the pieces described in 1929.[4] If, to the juvenilia we have, we add (1) the letters she wrote during the gaps in the published *Letters*; (2) the juvenilia we know about and do not have; (3) the juvenilia we do not know about because she neither mentions nor remembers it; and (4) the writing exercises she did for lessons ('Sketch' 82), we see someone practising all the time.[5]

Reading *Tom Brown's School Days* and *Three Generations of English Women*

In Virginia Stephen's note for Frederic Maitland's 1906 biography of her father, she says when the Stephen children were old enough, he spent an hour and a half each evening in the drawing room 'reading aloud to us. I cannot remember any book before *Tom Brown's School Days* and *Treasure Island*' (*E1* 127–8). Years earlier, on 5 January 1897, she writes in her journal, 'Got up at half past 10, and stayed in and read the whole morning . . . . Finished vol I of Three Generations of English Women, and began vol 2'; on 7 January, she adds, 'Finished Three Generations of English Women' (*PA* 6–7, 8).

Thomas Hughes's *Tom Brown's School Days* is the first book Virginia Stephen remembers hearing in her father's voice, and Janet Ross's *Three Generations of English Women* is the first book she mentions in the first diary we have. Leslie Stephen probably read other books to his children before *Tom Brown's School Days*, and we know Virginia was reading widely before her fifteenth year.[6] These books are debatable 'firsts', then, and neither Stephen nor Woolf ever mentions them again.[7] Yet they shed light on the hundreds of other books that taught her to 'read' oral and written language, traditional and evolving gender attitudes, different genres. They also illustrate the nebulous link between an author's education and work that Woolf calls attention to in 'The Leaning Tower' because traces of these books linger in Woolf's work as an essayist, reflecting her ambivalent relationship with Leslie Stephen's library. She both voyages out from his library and never leaves it, creating new literary history by incorporating the old.

Tom Brown's School Days is the more familiar book, its portrayal of a boy's public-school life still part of our culture. George MacDonald Frasier's historical fiction, for example, has kept its villain alive in Flashman. But George J. Worth called its status 'questionable' in 1984 (121). Perhaps it is more known about than read. On the other hand, it was re-issued in the Oxford World's Classics series in 1989, and Andrew Sanders says it has never been out of print since its first publication in 1857 (vii). It was immensely popular and influential, and Hughes is still credited with creating 'a new form, the public-school novel' (Worth 25).[8]

The novel tells about a young boy who leaves the Berkshire Vale of the White Horse to go to a private preparatory school and then to Rugby in the 1830s (when Thomas Arnold was reforming it). Sanders says Arnold's spirit 'pervades the book, but its effect is felt through the experiences of an average boy, not an extraordinary one' (viii): Tom represents 'the commonest type of English boy' (Hughes qtd in Sanders ix), not the intellectual or cultural elite. Arnold's system aimed 'to transform the dull boy into the responsive one' and 'mould that responsive boy into the responsible adult' (Sanders ix). But readers expecting a sappy hymn to 'the virtues of respectability' that Lytton Strachey attacked Arnold for in *Eminent Victorians* (qtd in Sanders vii) will discover a more complex, even surprising, text. The squire, glad his son plays with village boys, hates class separation; environmentalists can appreciate the loving description of the Vale of White Horse; and the account of the school's system does not ignore its abuses. The reader gets caught up in the tale and wants Tom Brown to learn how to give to others and become a good man; besides, the reader learns a lot about class relationships, 'muscular' Christianity, schoolboy games and the schoolboy code. Readers probably suspect Tom will win his struggle against evil forces, but he could go either way until the wise schoolmaster intervenes: he asks Tom to mentor a younger boy, one with more intellectual gifts and more integrity. Hughes thus describes an ordinary boy's social and moral education – intellectual growth is not emphasised (Matthew Arnold was horrified by this portrayal of his father's work [Worth 26]). Moreover, Tom learns his lessons – the schoolboy code (do not tell on anyone [Clark 'Cracking Code']), courage (life is a struggle, and one must fight when necessary), honesty (pass tests without cribs) and Christian values (protect the weak) – from another boy, not an adult. As Beverly Clark notes, Hughes 'empowered children', revealing 'opposition between student and teacher' (*Regendering* 11).

It is ironic to think of Leslie Stephen, the agnostic who hated his public-school days, reading a novel to his children that extols a public school committed to developing Christian virtues; Squire Brown wants Tom's education to turn him into 'a brave, helpful, truth-telling Englishman, and a gentleman, and a Christian' (Hughes 74). But Thomas Hughes shared with Stephen a friendship with James Russell Lowell and public support of the North in the Civil War.[9] A Christian Socialist, Hughes helped found the Society for Promoting Working Men's Associations, the Central Cooperative Agency, the London Emancipation Society and the London Working Men's College, where he was principal from 1872 to 1883. He represented the working-class London constituency of Lambeth from 1865 to 1874, where Virginia Stephen would teach at Morley College in the early years of the twentieth century (Worth viii–ix, 6–12).

Perhaps Leslie read *Tom Brown* to prepare Thoby for school, but his choice suggests girls and boys can appreciate the same texts. Plus, hearing the novel with her siblings indicates it, too, not just Thoby, introduced Virginia to English boys' education. When Woolf writes about not having experienced 'throwing balls; ragging; slang; vulgarity; scenes; jealousies' (*L3* 247), her list could have come straight from *Tom Brown's School Days*. Listening to her father read, she may have noticed the boys' camaraderie, the joys of late-night conversation and food, and the tests of character Tom had to face and pass within the context of support and friendship. As Clark points out, 'A story about school *is* a school' (*Regendering* 7; my emphasis).

If she ever thought about it, Woolf might have seen Hughes's novel as representing the advantages she resented losing because of 'Arthur's Education Fund'. But Stephen may have noticed Tom Brown's other education, in bullying, fagging that becomes hazing, gleeful fighting that Hughes gives 'little sermons in praise of' (Worth 27). The novel reveals public schools' nasty side, particularly their power hierarchies, and may have fed Woolf's relief at not having been 'shot into that [great patriarchal machine] at the age of ten' and having to emerge 'at sixty a Head Master, an Admiral, a Cabinet Minister, or the Warden of a college' ('Sketch' 153).

Tom Brown's School Days may be one text lying behind *Three Guineas*, then, but Hughes's novel may also have contributed to Woolf's other non-fiction. Woolf's use of Mrs Brown as a representative English woman may be a feminist response to Hughes's long opening tribute to the Browns, generations of sturdy, typical English men. When Tom discovers he will have a study, he thinks, 'was he not about to become the joint owner of a . . . home, the first place he could call his own? One's own', he continues, 'what a charm there is in the words!' (Hughes 94). Perhaps Hughes's description of public-school boys routinely using cribs to prepare their Greek and Latin exercises gave Stephen permission to use anything at her disposal in her own lessons and then pass on that permission to the working-class people listening to Woolf's 'Leaning Tower' lecture (*E6* 277). Hughes's critique of the class system may have contributed to Woolf's later perception in *A Room of One's Own* that being locked in may be worse than being locked out (24). Finally, perhaps this novel, in which women are almost entirely absent, starts Virginia Stephen on her voyage toward the British Museum, Professor Trevelyan's *History of England* (1926) and Woolf's conclusion that women are 'all but absent from history' (*AROO* 43).

Perhaps hearing *Tom Brown's School Days* was also why the almost 15-year-old girl later read the two volumes of Janet Ross's *Three Generations of English Women* so voraciously. Much more on the margins than *Tom Brown's School Days*, this book has long been out of print, and although sometimes mentioned in accounts of Virginia Stephen's education, is not looked at or read. Yet we know it journeyed from Leslie Stephen's library to Virginia Woolf's,[10] and it may have had more impact. Partly because Stephen read it herself as an adolescent, but mainly because it reverses Hughes's emphasis: *Three Generations of English Women* focuses on women, including the education of girls, and men are in the background.

The book's title seems to promise a general history of English women over three generations (DeSalvo, '1897' 88) or a gender's history (Fisher 39), but instead traces a family's history through the lives of three particular women, heightening awareness of how individual histories become lost to 'history'. Janet Ross, the fourth generation, writes about her great-grandmother, grandmother and mother: Susannah Taylor, Sarah Austin and Lucie Duff-Gordon.[11] Among the chosen few in Leslie Stephen's *DNB*, with Susannah under her husband John's entry, and Sarah and Lucie with entries of their own, these women would have been familiar to many readers when *Three Generations* was published in 1888. The subtitle, *Memoirs and Correspondence of Mrs. John Taylor, Mrs. Sarah Austin, and Lady Duff Gordon,* reveals Ross's sources and method. Providing little narrative, she relies heavily on journals, memoir sketches, and letters to and from the women to construct her matrilineal heritage's biography, to 'think back through [her] mothers', quite literally (*AROO* 76).

What an inspiration this book probably was for the girl who had grown up under the traditional Julia Stephen's tutelage, watched her mother play the 'Angel in the House' and was seeking, even if unconsciously, new role models now her mother had been dead for over a year and a half. Three women educated mainly at home, teaching their daughters Latin and other languages, focused on the life of the mind. Three women with unconventional lives, strong political views and families they considered important but not all-consuming. Three generations of independent thinkers and brilliant conversationalists. Three generations of readers and writers. Two generations of professional writers, making money from translations, book reviews, travel narratives and letters, and other non-fiction. These volumes may have opened Virginia Stephen's eyes to possibilities – for a woman's life, a self-educated woman's life, a professional woman's life in letters. In reading it, she met three women who had struggled against poverty, depression and illness, but who sustained intellectual vigour, lively salons and vital work. Their negotiation between talent and family, intellect and duty, ambition and angel, differed from her mother's, showing her what else intelligent, self-taught women could do.[12]

Susannah Cook Taylor (1755–1823) was 'not ashamed of being poor', was at the 'centre of the circle of remarkable people who frequented the provincial Athens [Norwich]', 'found time to read and appreciate poetry, and to think for herself', and 'possessed the pen of a ready writer . . . ' (Ross 1 iii, 4). C. Fell Smith says she shared her husband's liberal opinions and evidently 'danced "round the tree of liberty at Norwich at the taking of the Bastille"' (444). Imagine Virginia Stephen reading this excerpt from a letter Susannah Taylor wrote to Henry Reeve, who later married her daughter Susan:

> Nothing at present suits my taste so well as Susan's Latin lessons . . . When we get to Cicero's discussions on the nature of the soul, or Virgil's fine descriptions, my mind is filled up. Life is either a dull round of eating, drinking, and sleeping, or a spark of ethereal fire just kindled. (Ross 1 12)

Taylor writes, in 1807, 'The character of girls must depend upon their reading as much as upon the company they keep. Besides the intrinsic pleasure to be derived from solid knowledge, a woman ought to consider it as her best resource against poverty' (Ross 1 16). Virginia, making the rounds with Stella, was probably delighted to read that 'Systematic visiting is a great consumer of time, and in general, it affords but little recompense. The art is, not to estrange oneself from society, and yet not to pay too dear for it' (Ross 1 21–2). After her death, Basil Montague wrote that Susannah Taylor combined '[m]anly wisdom' with 'feminine gentleness' (qtd in Ross 1 27).

Sarah Taylor Austin (1793–1867) received a 'liberal and thorough education' from her mother: Latin, French, Italian and German, along with the excellent conversations she heard (Ross 1 30). Her diary reading list between 1815 and 1821 (Ross 1 31) looks like one of Virginia Stephen's. Many diaries and letters of the time mention the spirited Sarah, including those of Sir James Stephen, Carlyle and J. S. Mill (Ross 1 37–8). She observed other countries' educational systems, writing to Gladstone about creating an English national education system (Ross 1 128, 133–7, 295–6); criticised the English 'imbecility' about training women (Ross 2 165); and in Malta, broke with British society by visiting and receiving the Maltese and working to create elementary schools for both boys and girls (Ross 1 104–5; 121). Her marriage to John Austin was difficult. He had a brilliant judicial mind but suffered from depression, so she worked prodigiously, supporting them with her pen, editing, translating many German works and writing *Germany from 1760 to 1814*. John Macdonell says she was a rigorous translator, made 'the best minds of Germany familiar to Englishmen', and had a literary reputation based on her 'conversation and wide correspondence with illustrious men of letters'. After John's death, she brought out a new edition of his *The Province of Jurisprudence* with an introductory memoir and prepared 'a large mass' of his manuscript lecture notes for publication as the *Lectures on Jurisprudence, or the Science of Positive Law* (Macdonell 271). She taught her daughter Latin, took her with them to Bonn and sent her, for a time, to a small mixed-sex school (Ross 1 62–8). When Lucie was 10, Sarah writes,

> She seems chiefly to take to Greek, with which her father is very anxious to have her thoroughly imbued.... I am quite willing to forego all the feminine parts of her education for the present. The main thing is to secure her independence; both with relation to her own mind and outward circumstances. (Ross 1 68)

Lucie Austin Duff-Gordon (1821–69), best known for her *Letters from Egypt, 1863–1865*, edited by her mother, and *Last Letters from Egypt*, edited by her daughter, also began her literary life by translating: Neibuhr's *Studies of Ancient Grecian Mythology*. Rescuing a boy called Hassan el Bakkeet from street life (cast out because he was going blind), she established him in the Duff-Gordon household at 8 Queen Square, where he became Janet's playmate. Ross writes she 'perfectly recollect[s] Mr Hilliard, the American author, being much shocked at seeing me in Hassan's arms, and my rage at his asking how Lady Gordon could let a negro touch her child; whereupon she called us to her, and kissed me first and Hassan afterwards' (Ross 2 196–7). She met Heinrich Heine as a girl in Germany, opened her home to a circle that included Lord Lansdowne, Dickens,

Thackeray, Tennyson and Henry Taylor, and established and superintended a working-man's library and reading room in East London (Boose 220). Suffering from consumption, she moved to Egypt for her health while her husband and children remained in London. There, she learned about English bigotry through the Egyptian gratitude for her willingness to eat in the Arab style and interact with them (Ross 2 270, 262–3). Commenting on the social equality prevailing in Egypt, she noted

> The English would be a little surprised at Arab judgements of them. They admit our veracity and honesty, and like us on the whole, but ... are shocked at the way Englishmen talk about [women] among themselves, and think the English hard and unkind to their wives and to women in general. (Ross 2 257)

Her kindness to the sick and oppressed became legendary, and 'she was known as "Sitt el Kebeer", the great lady, who "was just and had a heart that loved the Arabs"' (Boose 220).

Reading *Three Generations of English Women*, Stephen learned about sustaining an intellectually active writing life. Besides giving Virginia Stephen a glimpse into professional writing women's lives, however, *Three Generations of English Women* may have helped spark Woolf's lifelong interest in memoir, letters and diaries as literary forms, her concern with rescuing the lives of the obscure, her interest in acknowledging anonymous but important contributions to literature and her critiques of British patriarchy and Empire. Reading about translators who tried to rid their cultural encounters of British bias may have led to her own attempts in 'On Not Knowing Greek' and 'The Russian Point of View'. Their struggles to establish professional writing lives may have begun her journey to 'Professions for Women'. More than a thin thread connects this book to Woolf's ideas in *A Room of One's Own*: we think back through our mothers if we are women, masterpieces grow out of an atmosphere that encourages the work of many unknown toilers, a connection exists between money and the freedom to write, discovering and constructing a tradition is necessary and worthwhile.

These two books, then, encapsulate the Stephen household tension over the era's female education debates. *Tom Brown's School Days*, with its insider assumptions, and *Three Generations of English Women*, with its outsider portrayal, both come from an insider's shelves. No wonder Woolf ultimately embodied a simultaneous insider/outsider position; Woolf carried traces of books from Leslie Stephen's library with her because they propelled Stephen out of it.

Writing for the *Hyde Park Gate News*

Virginia Stephen's writing origins are also marked by ambiguity – we do not know exactly when she began writing or what she produced at the start – although we know she was an avid writer from a young age. On 19 December 1938, Woolf says writing has been 'absorbing ever since I was a little creature' (*D5* 192), and Vanessa Bell could not 'remember a time when Virginia did not mean to be a writer and I a painter' (63; see also QB1 23). Virginia Stephen 'loved to write for the sheer joy of passing pen across paper' (DeSalvo, 'Miss Jan' 103), and her family saw and abetted her writing interest early, as she reports being 'the happy possessor of a beautiful inkstand the gift of her Grandmother', along with 'a blotter a drawing-book a box with writing implements inside' on her tenth birthday (*HPGN* 27).

Although the *Hyde Park Gate News* dates from 1891 and is thus our first example of Virginia Stephen's work outside a few letters, the first eight issues of the Stephen children's newspaper are missing. Plus, authorship of the pieces in the *Hyde Park Gate News* is murky. Most commentators mention the paper's collaborative origins and nature while also noting Virginia's major role. Christine Alexander writes that Woolf's early literary efforts 'developed from collaborative play and storytelling sessions in the nursery' ('Victorian' 228) and describes how the Stephen children 'swapped and shared notes on their reading', making 'literary play [come] naturally to them all, a collaborative practice' ('Play' 42). Lee names the *Hyde Park Gate News* a 'collaborative family journal' (Foreword vii), calls the serial narratives in the paper 'group efforts' (*VW* 106) and notes how little privacy Virginia had in the Stephen household: 'Everything was shared' and '[a]ll story-telling was collaborative' (*VW* 111). In her edition's introduction, Gill Lowe carefully attributes everything in the paper to 'the children' and in 'A Brief History of the *Hyde Park Gate News*', acknowledges attribution arguments (xvi–xvii; 16). In a letter to Panthea Reid, Anne Olivier Bell writes that transcribing the paper led her to believe 'the greater part was actually written out by Vanessa', and Reid says Bell thought Vanessa 'was sometimes the editor as well as the scribe, although not necessarily the author, and that the paper was often a collaborative effort, organized by Vanessa' (483 n39). But Alix Bunyan claims Virginia wrote more of the earlier issues than Bell and Lowe think, pointing to what she sees as 'small and subtle' but 'discernible' differences in the two girls' similar handwriting (187 n108); she is convinced 'the children wrote out the earlier issues of the paper collaboratively, as hands sometimes change in mid-sentence'. Bunyan also uses the jokes made at Virginia's expense and Thoby's absence to suggest that 'some form of collaboration was involved in the composition' (173 n45). Lowe thinks the existence of two copies of one particular issue may indicate 'fair copies were made from drafts' or that 'more than one copy may have been made for distribution to several family members' (Note xx), but such copies could also mean drafts were written by Virginia and then copied by Vanessa, as Lowe, too, indirectly acknowledges when she points out that just because much of the extant edition is in Vanessa's handwriting does not mean 'she was the author of all that she wrote or *copied*' (Note xix, my emphasis). Vanessa flat out says, 'Virginia wrote most of it' (64), and Quentin Bell says Vanessa always denied 'making any contribution to the text' and assumes Vanessa played the role of amanuensis (1 37). Lowe, too, says 'It is possible that Vanessa acted as an amanuensis while articles were dictated to her' (Note xx) and notes Vanessa is called the 'Editor of this pamphlet' in the 14 December 1891 issue (*HPGN* 12; Notes 203 n5).

Assuming Vanessa Bell told the truth when she said she contributed no content and assuming Thoby wrote only the parts in his handwriting or those directly or indirectly attributed to him (see *HPGN* 124; Notes 203–4 n39), then either Virginia wrote pieces that Vanessa copied, or Vanessa acted as amanuensis (QB1

37), or both. One can imagine Virginia trying out different versions of stories, as God does with worlds in the dream reported on 11 February 1895 (*HPGN* 179), asking Vanessa for her opinion or using Vanessa's reactions to revise as she spoke. Reid's examination of the manuscripts leads her to argue, 'Clearly, Virginia was the genius behind the production' and notes a 'penciled reference to her as "Editor" is crossed out and "Author" is substituted'. For Reid, although Thoby and Vanessa contribute, the newspaper is almost entirely Virginia's creation (30).[13] Leila Brosnan, too, after summarising the reasons for suggesting collaboration, recalls Vanessa's comment, points out the paper's news items that say 'much of it was composed when Thoby and Adrian Stephen were at school', and concludes 'there is ample scope for arguing that the *Hyde Park Gate News* is largely, but not exclusively, the work of Virginia Stephen' (19).[14] The *Hyde Park Gate News*, then, reflects authorial ambiguity, but also a more complex and realistic paradigm for authorship in general: collaborative roots that support individual growth and achievement but never completely disappear.

Virginia Stephen's uncertain writing origins make any conclusions about her juvenilia provisional. Yet, her juvenilia tantalise and lead us to conclude because, as Alexander notes, juvenile writings 'offer a window onto the development of self, uniquely documenting the apprenticeship of the youthful writer' ('Victorian' 224).[15] In the early letters, diaries and newspaper we have, Stephen creates both stories and essays. Within the pages of *The Hyde Park Gate News*, she practises other genres as well, recording the Stephen juveniles' activities in a diary of sorts, but also creating characters who write letters about courtship, money and philosophical topics and keep diaries such as that by Sarah Morgan (*HPGN* 167–70; 172–4). Sarah has a distinctive voice and moral tone; understands the worth of a daily diary kept for sixty years (as the diary's real author mocks the 'diversion and instruction' gained from perusing such a document [*HPGN* 167]); is stern about 'women who wear trousers' (*HPGN* 169–70); and has a keen sense of social class (*HPGN* 168). Stephen simultaneously lets her creation have her say and humorously critiques Sarah's narrowness. Thus, Lee sees not only the 'raw material for Virginia Woolf's novels' in the *Hyde Park Gate News*, but also, 'in its vivid, ebullient, attentive flow of comment, [the] early symptoms of one of the world's great diary-writers' (Foreword x).

But the *Hyde Park Gate News* is also the seedbed for the later essayist, as Brosnan shows in her chapter on Virginia Woolf's juvenile journalism: 'Part of the ease with which [Virginia Stephen] entered the world of the *TLS* and maintained her position in it may be attributed to the youthful training gained on the *Hyde Park Gate News*' (23).[16] Practising observation, scene-making and comment in *Hyde Park Gate News* pages, Virginia Stephen begins learning how to write the essays Virginia Woolf would become famous for.

The *Hyde Park Gate News* reveals a childish sensibility, but also a strong awareness of genres, forms and conventions, an observant and imaginative mind, and a disciplined writer: the paper came out almost weekly for approximately five years, from the time Virginia Stephen was 9 until she was 13 and Julia Stephen died. Not only does she start writing at an early age, but she starts training herself early as well, literally practising a writer's routines and imitating what she was reading while developing a distinctive voice and style. Further, Stephen not only moves between collaboration and individual work in the paper, but also navigates between oral and print expression and parental and wider audiences.

Virginia Stephen's articles in the *Hyde Park Gate News* build on her earlier storytelling:

> Virginia had told stories from early childhood – of Jim, Joe and Hary Hoe, 'three brothers who had herds of animals and adventures'; of Beccage and Hollywinks, evil spirits who lived on the rubbish heap at Talland House in St Ives, and later, of Clémont and the Dilkes, the family who actually lived next door to the Stephens at Hyde Park Gate, and who they imagined to have discovered a hoard of gold under their bedroom floor. (Briggs, *IL* 111)[17]

If Vanessa generally acted as amanuensis (Lowe, Note xx), then Virginia, creating and dictating newspaper items, experienced words going from spoken to written. She gained a deeper sense of literature's oral foundation, the feel and rhythm of words in the mouth and on the tongue, and the power of the spoken word to provoke a response. Most important, she was practising the move into print culture, learning how words change as they move from spoken to written, from imagined to 'published'; Virginia Woolf's pleasure in setting type for the Hogarth Press and her desire to control her publications may stem from this early experience (Lowe, Note on the Text xxi). Stephen's strong oral tradition background, gained from listening as Leslie Stephen recited and read and from telling stories herself, meant Woolf never lost her ties to the actual sound of words.[18] As 'written' as Woolf's prose is, it also remains 'oral', and her essays' conversational tone may owe something to this early interplay between oral and written.[19]

Although Virginia Stephen definitely wanted 'the good opinion of the grown-ups' and her mother's approval, as Vanessa reports (64–5) and Woolf remembers ('Sketch' 95),[20] her audience awareness goes beyond family in the *Hyde Park Gate News*.[21] Certainly, the paper's main readers were Leslie and Julia Stephen (Alexander suggests they functioned 'rather like a general editor or owner of the newspaper' ['Play' 44]), and the 'special correspondent' directs her news items and stories at them. But Lowe's comments about fair copies indicate members of the extended Stephen family may have received copies as well (Note xx), as does the humorous comment in the 7 December 1891 issue: 'The Circulation increases weekly' (*HPGN* 11). Also, some guests probably read the editions 'published' at St Ives. Stephen's references to readers and even a 'dear reader' hints at a dawning awareness of a broader audience (*HPGN* 38, 121, 135, 144, 156). When she writes, 'We leave the rest [of the scene of Mr Fisher's arrival at St Ives] to imagination's vivid course as we are sure dear reader that you possess that faculty in it's highest degree' (*HPGN* 96), she not only takes a student's common way out, but also posits the possession of an active imagination in readers other than her parents, who had been present and observing the scene. When she creates three definitions of a gentleman in a village doctor's invented correspondence (*HPGN* 186–8), does not include the definition nailed over the Hyde Park Gate fireplace ('Sketch' 117) and has her narrator admit three definitions do not settle the question, she sets up opportunities for discussing definitions beyond what her parents might provide (*HPGN* 188). She may create the Author and Editor in the last *Hyde Park Gate News* issue for her family's amusement, but the author in the piece must consider an editor and the readers that editor represents, so Virginia Stephen has begun to think about the world she sees 'out of the open window' (*HPGN* 199). Finally, in imitating *Tit-Bits*, Stephen practised extending her 'acute awareness of audience' (Lowe, Intro xvi) since *Tit-Bits* used inclusive strategies for reaching a wide audience, such as children like the Stephens who were not its primary market (Jackson, 'Newnes' 18, 20, 24; Alexander, 'Victorian Juvenilia' 230–1).

Moreover, in writing for the *Hyde Park Gate News*, Virginia Stephen was anything but well behaved; one suspects she used writing there to counteract the official womanhood lessons she was receiving in her 'graceful deportment' classes (*HPGN* 152). Playful and slyly observant about relationships between sexes and generations, she pokes fun without being openly rebellious or hostile,[22] perhaps already practising the stance she would take as Virginia Woolf, using a 'surface manner' to 'slip in things' ('Sketch' 150; see also Brosnan 23). Quentin Bell tentatively attributes 'An Article on Chekiness' to Thoby (1 29), perhaps because it mentions being 'licked for cheek almost 50 times' at school and because it advises mothers to nip all impertinence in the bud, hoping 'no children are impertinent to their Mothers or any body else' (*HPGN* 26). But Virginia is often and decidedly cheeky in the paper's pages. Alexander agrees, maintaining the 'Article on Chekiness' might have been 'offered as a sop to the adult audience, since most of the early entries are bubbling with cheek' ('Play' 44), including the 'Chekiness' article itself. Yes, Stephen craves her audience's approval, but she also thumbs her nose at it, pushing hard at adult tolerance with the diverse techniques the children had in their arsenal: 'pastiche, slapstick, comedy, satire, euphemism, hyperbole, whimsy and suspense' (Lowe, Intro xvi). In one example, she describes Millicent Vaughan's visit and then comments, 'But we are wandering from our point like so many old people' (*HPGN* 42). Virginia Woolf would later note about Jane Austen's juvenilia, 'Girls of fifteen are always laughing' (*E4* 147). So, if the *Hyde Park Gate News* is any indication, are girls of 10.[23]

As she tries out personae, genres, voices and parodies, Virginia Stephen grows as a writer. Lowe says the 1895 volume includes longer pieces on 'abstract questions about reality, existence, morality and religion' in an 'experimental, more complex and literary' style (Intro xvii). In the 18 January 1895 issue, Stephen wishes she could 'take possession of other people's minds, for a short time, with all their knowledge' and ponders the implications of such power, especially if others had it and could occupy her mind as well (*HPGN* 175–6). In the 4 February 1895 issue, she targets upper-class people's desire to avoid unpleasant facts when she creates a sympathetic piece about Mr James, who devotes his life to others and makes society uncomfortable by saying 'if the clergy would turn their minds to the drains, of their parishioners and left their souls alone, the world would become a much happier place', and 'the people who built improved cottages for the poor, did just as much good, in a common place way, as Jesus Christ' (*HPGN* 177–8). In the 25 February 1895 issue, she writes a professional, detailed account of the meeting held to raise funds for buying Carlyle's Chelsea house (*HPGN* 183–5).

Evidence of her growth is most apparent, however, in two descriptions of the Cambridge–Oxford boat races written three years apart, for the 11 April 1892 and the 1 April 1895 issues (*HPGN* 53–54; 195–8). The first, one paragraph long, simply reports: 'The Cambridge and Oxford boat-race took place on Saturday.' The article includes other information – 'more than usual excitement as the crews were reported to be about the same' and the support for Cambridge stemming from its 'being the place where both their father and brothers have been to' – but says nothing else about the race itself except 'alas, Oxford won' (*HPGN* 53–4).

But the description supposedly sent by the Editor's cousin in 1895,[24] over three pages long and complete with frame, is full of scene-making, observation and commentary. Virginia Stephen's writing has matured. She captures the excitement and fun of the 10 March race day with her spectator's focus on the crowd's actions, behaviours and talk. She describes the crowded train (a third-class smoking compartment with 'an atmosphere, 1 quarter smoke, 2 quarters animal odour, and a fourth quarter of mixed germs)', the crowd on the Putney Bridge ('lined with people walking on the road and on the pavement, while omnibusses and hansoms forced their way through', and the atmosphere ('everyone was talking and pushing and struggling at once' [*HPGN* 195–6]). In a move Woolf would often use later, Stephen then shifts perspective: 'Indeed the only living creature who showed no sign of excitement or interest in the race was a stolid black cat . . . squatting upon a roof and blinking lazily at the sun' (*HPGN* 196). Stephen includes an overheard conversation between two old ladies, who then report on the gun shot beginning the race. She comments on her own point of view, the crews, the press and two babies in a perambulator, who were 'philosophically munching a spongy biscuit and wisely declined to partake of something which looked like milk' (*HPGN* 196–7). She humorously describes two sisters, 'straining to catch a sight of the river', mounting the perambulator and thus appearing 'to be standing upon the legs and bodies of their charges. The babies, as I have said, were philosophers, and showed no outward signs of suffocation.' She notices that everyone cheering for Cambridge obviously thinks they are ahead while those rooting for Oxford 'were equally positive that Oxford was leading' (*HPGN* 197), and when the crowd eventually learns Oxford has won, 'One of the young ladies below us who was wearing [Cambridge's] light blue took of the ribbon immediately.' A list-like summary ends the account: 'The rain began to fall, the crowd left the river banks for the public house, the babies and the perambulator began to toil along home, and the race was over' (*HPGN* 198). Full of description, suspense, dialogue and humour, the article is engaging and very well written.[25]

Three other Stephen pieces in the *Hyde Park Gate News* qualify as possible sources of specific ideas about gender, education and writing Virginia Woolf developed and used later. Numerous stories and statements in the *Hyde Park Gate News* reveal the strength of traditional gender roles in the Stephen household.[26] In 'Miss Smith' (164–6), however, appearing on 7 January 1895, Virginia Stephen 'sport[s] with infidel ideas . . . of a life different from [her mother's]' (*TL* 10). In this piece, Miss Smith has a 'remarkable' intellect – 'At 12 she delighted in Virgil, at 14 she wrote sonnets, at 16 she declared that life was not worth living and retired from the world' – and soon realises that 'society must be entirely reorganised' because the 'position of men and women towards each other was altogether disgraceful', but is disappointed when the world takes no note of her reforming ideas. Feeling plain and ordinary, she settles down at 30, preparing 'to live her life alone' and accepting herself as 'only a woman' (*HPGN* 164–5). Though aware of the independent woman option, Stephen succumbs to the marriage plot promoted by her mother because, at that very moment, 'a gallant gentleman appeared', and 'so lonely had Miss Smith become, and so much did she feel the need of someone stronger and wiser than herself that she consented to become his wife'. The piece ends with Miss Smith proving to be 'an excellent wife, and later on a devoted mother' (*HPGN* 164–6). The almost 13-year-old Virginia Stephen can imagine herself or another young girl as remarkably intelligent and committed to re-envisioning the relationship between the sexes, but cannot yet project that brilliant girl into a successful or happy future that does not include matrimony or children.[27] Or, given her audience, she cannot yet go public with such a vision.[28] Only the older Virginia Woolf can imagine Chloe and Olivia liking each other and sharing a laboratory (*AROO* 84).

The Stephen family newspaper is full of news about the Duckworth and Stephen boys going and coming from school (*HPGN* 45–6, 50, 53, 69, 88, 111, 175), Thoby's prizes and accomplishments (*HPGN* 38, 82, 160) and Leslie Stephen's achievements (*HPGN* 9, 72–3, 75, 144, 183–5, 189; Lee, Foreword ix). So, the imaginary letter from a girl at school in the 9 May 1892 issue stands out. The 'model little girl' thanks her mother for her praise, especially since it comes 'so seldom' and is thus more 'sweet' (*HPGN* 61).[29] But as Stephen tries to imagine a young girl rather than a young boy at school, the marriage plot intervenes again, this time with a troubling twist: Lucy complains about a young male teacher trying to court her, refers to his £40 salary and poor manners, and asks to be removed from the school (*HPGN* 61–2). Her mother's reply mixes advice ('[y]ou must ... put forth all your powers of snobsnubbing'), blame ('if you go and get engaged to this young Mr Archibald Monkman I and your father will make your home pretty hot for you'), protection ('I should like you to tell the head school mistress that she had better expell the young master at once as perhaps he will make love with another of the pretty girls of the school') and praise ('his is the sort of nature which only thinks of beauty and not of real moral worth which all the same you pocess [sic] my dear daughter'). Writing 'I shall most certainly remove you from your school' (*HPGN* 64), Mabel Bareham gives Lucy a way out of school and Stephen a way out of a created situation she cannot sustain. Her inability to open the door to a girl's schoolroom anywhere in the newspaper (as far as we know) epitomises the exclusion Woolf felt in later years and that fed essays like 'Miss Ormerod', 'Two Women', 'The Leaning Tower', *A Room of One's Own* and *Three Guineas*. Also, tellingly, as the young Virginia imagines various reactions to a daughter's revelations of an inappropriate relationship, she has the mother rescue the daughter from an abusive situation.

In the last issue of the *Hyde Park Gate News* before Julia Stephen's death, which halted publication and Virginia's writing, Stephen overtly portrays herself as a writer, creating a scene with an Author and an Editor. Lowe writes, 'The Editor is surely a projection of Vanessa, and the anonymous apprentice Author an avatar of an older Virginia' (Intro xviii), though Brosnan thinks Virginia is both 'author and editor, both in their capitalised and lower case manifestations' (38).[30] The Author and Editor portray a writer's internal voices: (1) one who 'wishes to be poetical', 'thinks about her childhood' with 'a most disagreeable expression' on her face, is 'about to be angry' and 'likes to be terse and if possible, dramatic' when she faces a blank page; and (2) one who holds out a variety of subjects – 'History – Philosophy – Woman's Suffrage – Vivisection – and Poetry', knows the Author 'very well', understands 'a sufficient amount of persuasion would induce the Author to believe in anything' and genially reminds the Author of obligations, deadlines and payments (*HPGN* 199–201). The Author and Editor also exhibit tensions between writer and commerce that Virginia Woolf would address in 'The Patron and the Crocus' and 'Reviewing' (Brosnan 38; Collier, *Modernism* 73–9). Stephen already realises material circumstances contribute to a writer's freedom, a point Woolf would make in *A Room of One's Own*: the 'some hundred verses' made 'with the help of the rhyming dictionary' (and not worth reproducing) are created not because the Author loves and wants to write poetry (indeed, she disdains it, considers it 'indelicate' and has never written it before), but because the Editor has offered her a 'shilling a stanza' (*HPGN* 201).[31] Dinah Birch says Stephen has begun to 'acknowledge the demands and rewards of authorship as a profession rather than a pastime', and Alexander and McMaster see movement 'from the periphery of her highly literary family to the centre, showing her grasp of the professional literary scene and its politics' (7).

Although perhaps other papers such as *The Girl's Own Paper* and *Punch* had some impact (QB1 30; Bunyan 176; Alexander, 'Victorian' 230), *Tit-Bits* provided the chief model for the layout, tone and content followed by Virginia Stephen in the *Hyde Park Gate News* (Lee, Foreword vii; Lowe, Intro vii; Lowe, Note xxi; Bunyan 176; Alexander, 'Victorian' 230–1). Imitation is practice, of course, and in the *Hyde Park Gate News*, Stephen learns from it. As Alexander maintains, though, children do not simply imitate. In the 'play' of creating a family magazine, they also appropriate: 'the child is not simply being colonized by the teaching adult, but is colonizing the adult world itself by remaking it in the image of self' ('Play' 31). Particularly for the Victorian adolescent girl, Alexander argues, the sanctioned context of the family magazine allows her to 'appropriate at will the style, voice, and subject of the adult world' ('Play' 47). The *Hyde Park Gate News* 'provided practice in literary role-playing and a licensed outlet for the subversion of Victorian family values' ('Play' 32) – Stephen does not just copy and emulate, she imagines, creates, edits, reviews and designs ('Play' 47). Zestfully using her freedom, she establishes a regular routine, meets a weekly deadline, tries out genres and voices and considers her audience. Already, we can see a fascination with letters, diaries, fantasy and irony. Already, so embedded in literature, so aware of and comfortable with forms, Stephen can parody them. Already, Woolfian traits and topics have appeared: sense of humour, satire, words as weapons, scene-making ability, anxiety about money, ambiguous endings, mix of facts and narrative, emphasis on psychology or the inner life, and awareness of differences and divisions between groups of people. In this lively, energetic newspaper's pages, we glimpse Virginia Stephen practising the essay.

Listening to *Tom Brown's School Days*, gobbling *Three Generations of English Women*, producing pieces for the *Hyde Park Gate News*, Virginia Stephen reinforced, practised and honed her reading and writing skills. Little was required or assigned, none was graded. Despite fragmentation, loneliness and gaps, she used her freedom and discipline to improve her future craft's skills. Quentin Bell's comment about her newspaper articles applies: 'very clearly the work of a girl making a deadly serious study of English literature' (1 37). Virginia Stephen knew what to do with any education she received or cobbled together: practise, practise, practise.

Notes

1. Some materials may exist in archives or attics, as Tony and Teresa Davies's discovery of a brown paper-wrapped 1909 notebook in a bottom drawer shows (Bradshaw, Intro xxviii). This list of absent works is not exhaustive.
2. We seem to have nothing of Virginia Stephen's in the shorthand her father taught her (see *SLLS1* 19), which John Venn says was the Gurney method (*Annals* 150). Maitland calls shorthand one of Leslie Stephen's 'minor accomplishments', and says his mother, Jane Venn, taught him. Many of his notebooks contain the script, as do letters to his sister (51–2).
3. Brosnan, 35 n7, suggests this story may be the [28] January 1895 piece in which the writer asks a fairy godmother to grant the temporary power to possess other people's minds (*HPGN* 175), but that piece seems more musing than story, and it does not involve multiple souls, flying, bodies or permanent choices. Of course, Woolf's memory of what her mother sent to Madge Symonds could be faulty. Alternatively, since the Stephens labelled the newspaper volume I (1891), volume II (1892) and volume V (1895), leading Quentin Bell to assume it continued to appear weekly in 1893 and 1894 (1 28), perhaps the story about souls flying round was in a missing volume.
4. The 'private writing' could also refer to shorthand, though hiding it under a blotter suggests not. It is possible one such hidden piece was the 'wildly romantic account of a young woman on a ship' that Virginia Stephen sent to *Tit-Bits* and had rejected (VB 65); Vanessa Bell kept it secret until her reading at the Memoir Club on 16 May 1949 (A. Garnett, Prologue 9–10). Or maybe Virginia was hiding her work from George?
5. Except for after her mother's death, when Woolf remembers, 'For two years I never wrote [. . .] The desire left me: wh. I have had all my life, with that two years break. Never wrote a story or an essay, never wished to' ('Sketch' MS n. pag. 11; see also QB1 45).
6. Bunyan lists what 'the young Stephens read, or had read to them' based on *Hyde Park Gate News* articles, letters from Leslie to Julia and letters from Thoby and Adrian (170–1).
7. In 1909, when Stephen meets Janet Ross, she neither likes her nor recalls reading *Three Generations of English Women* (PA 397–8). Indeed, she 'suppose[s] she writes books', given the number of manuscripts all around the room (L1 393).
8. Beverly Lyon Clark's debunking, exalting and deconstructing approaches to the novel in her *Regendering the School Story* introduction complicate Worth's assessment (6–22).
9. Leslie mentions Thomas Hughes's death in his *Mausoleum Book*, and says they were friendly, though not close (100). He also suggests Hughes's younger brother, Harry, whom Leslie had as a pupil at Cambridge, was the model for Tom Brown (30–1 n).
10. *Tom Brown's School Days* is not in the Library of Leonard and Virginia Woolf; *Three Generations of English Women* is (K&M-V 190). George Meredith was Leslie Stephen's friend, and Ross was Meredith's mistress, basis for many of his heroines (Hussey, AZ 90), which may be why Leslie had a copy. Ross was also one model for Alice Flushing in *The Voyage Out* (Hussey, AZ 159).
11. Sarah Benjamin's book about Janet Ross is part biography, part Tuscany travelogue and part cookbook. She does note the reality Ross left out of her somewhat 'popular

feminist biography': many 'problematic details' about the Austin and Duff-Gordon marriages (88–9).
12. The book fits Booth's definition of a female collective biography that helps the reader figure out 'how to make it as a woman' and is number 687 on her list.
13. Lowe says the 'Crismas Number' poem is in Thoby's hand (Notes on Ms. 202 [18]), and that 'Advertising for a Wife' (*HPGN* 76–8) shares with his schoolboy stories 'the same rapid, picaresque, unpunctuated carelessness'; he is co-author of 'A Cockney Farmer's Experience' (*HPGN* 98 ff.), and 'The Experiences of a Paterfamilias' shares the earlier serial's '[p]hysical violence, slapstick and crude plotting' (Note xx).
14. I assume Virginia Stephen wrote the pieces included in this discussion.
15. Brosnan discusses the dangers of mining the juvenilia simply for biographical facts or 'direct correlations between earlier and later works' (18), though she, too, cannot resist the hermeneutic impulse Lowe discusses ('HPGN' 43) and often notes connections between works by Stephen and Woolf, as do I. Bunyan advocates openly defining late nineteenth-century juvenilia as 'apprentice writing, by children who saw themselves as writers already, and who believed they would continue to develop their writing as they grew up' (195).
16. Brosnan's ground-breaking work influenced my reading of this text: taking the *Hyde Park Gate News* seriously as apprentice work for a journalism career. She discusses Stephen's stylistic and formal development (18), production of journalistic language, including irony (23), and use of different perspectives on the same event (32); she argues Stephen emulates the world of letters in the paper (20); and she, too, notices Stephen is learning to encode her judgements and criticism without offending her audience (26). For Brosnan, 'the techniques and strategies [Stephen] developed while experimenting with different voices in her early writing contributed to her subsequent practice as a mature writer,' and the newspaper 'provides a valuable resource for the methods by which Woolf negotiated the theoretical and practical implications of writing essays, both critical and autobiographical, as well as professional journalism' (34).
17. Briggs uses material from 'Sketch' (76–7, 79) here, but Woolf uses the pronoun 'we' in her discussion of the 'dull' walks in Kensington Gardens, so these efforts may have been more collaborative than individual. Also, these walks, in contrast to the later ones she took alone with her father, seem to have occurred when she was quite young, and included siblings, Nurse, and Sooney (a pet?).
18. Woolf Conference-goers often testify to the pleasure of listening to her words being read aloud when the Woolf Society Players perform.
19. Louie Mayer remembers being startled at overhearing Virginia Woolf talking to herself in the bath – 'I thought there must be two or three people up there with her' – but Leonard explained that 'Mrs Woolf always said the sentences out loud that she had written during the night. She needed to know if they sounded right and the bath was a good, resonant place for trying them out' (155).
20. She also remembers being proud when Leslie 'found [her] reading some book that no child of [her] age could understand. I was a snob no doubt, and read partly to make him think me a very clever little brat' ('Sketch' 111–12).
21. Bunyan sees the need for parental approval as typical of nineteenth-century home magazines (166–96). She argues the Stephen children's attempt to be mature, act as though they are adults and even parody their parents were all expected by the time's 'developmentalist' audience. For Bunyan, Leslie and Julia are 'key to the paper's existence' (166), 'distinctly part of the production' (175), and Lee says, 'It was written under parental influence' (*VW* 107). But since Stephen pushes at boundaries in the paper, both practising adult behaviour and parodying it (Alexander, 'Play' 46), she inevitably expands her ideas about audience.
22. Critics' descriptions of the writing in *HPGN* suggest placating parents is not the only aim. Lee calls the paper 'an escapade for the writers, a licensed outlet for rudeness

and aggression, and for a subversion of family sentiments' (*VW* 108); Brosnan adds 'subversion of the rhetoric of sentimentality' to that list (24); Lowe notes the Stephen children enjoyed 'the transgressive nature of this new experience' ('HPGN' 38) and uses the words 'impertinent' and 'effrontery' to describe their audacity in daring to write in such a literary household ('HPGN' 39); and Alexander claims 'literary play provided the Stephen children with the license both to act out adult roles and to satirize them' ('Victorian Juvenilia' 229).

23. See also Monica Latham, who comes to several similar conclusions in '"Virginia Woolf Practising": *Hyde Park Gate News* and the Beginning of Woolf's Career as a Writer, Critic and Reader', part of an edited collection published in France (2011) that is not readily available in the US. She calls the Stephen children 'little ventriloquists', for example, as they 'ridicule ... and criticize' the adults by 'adopt[ing] their voice' (144). I developed my arguments independently of hers, having read Latham's work only recently.
24. Lowe admits a cousin could have sent the story but says it is 'more likely that this is a device to allow another "voice" to be used by Virginia, the "Author"' (Notes 204 [n55]). The asides and commentary sound like Stephen throughout, and portions are in her handwriting.
25. The account also includes what we consider a racial slur, indicating its unthinking, casual use at the time. See 'Negro, New Negro' and 'Race' in Cuddy-Keane, Hammond and Peat, 147–54 and 184–91.
26. Some examples: the courtship rituals reported in the letters, the music lessons girls must take (*HPGN* 153), Mrs Stephen as the 'Good Angel' to the St Ives poor (118), Mrs Stephen settling things with 'all the despatch of womankind' while Mr Stephen sits with the children (*HPGN* 128) and the male speakers at the Carlyle's House fund raiser (*HPGN* 183–5).
27. See Mary Pipher's *Reviving Ophelia* for a detailed examination of this phenomenon.
28. See Alexander, 'Play' 44 and Lee, who notes Julia's views and sayings 'are devotedly echoed' in the newspaper (Foreword viii); those views included anti-suffrage, a scorn for New Women and assumptions about matrimony for girls.
29. Lowe describes a 'remote' and 'undemonstrative' Julia (and Leslie) Stephen (Intro xi). Reid says the paper 'reveals a Julia who was very stern about household regulations but very permissive toward her sons', with 'no scenes of affection between Julia and her daughters' (33). Marion Dell, however, catalogues how Julia encouraged her daughter's creativity and talent, particularly through gossip, anecdotes, laughter and fun ('Writing Back' 20–3).
30. Dell suggests the Editor is Julia ('Writing Back' 23).
31. Bunyan implies the verses were written and not shared (193), but the hundred verses are probably imaginary. Brosnan agrees, calling them fictional (39).

Chapter 5

Outcomes: Learning at Home

Virginia Stephen learned many lessons during and from her home education, and she began practising the skills needed to become a writer early, at first unconsciously, reading for enjoyment and to please her father, writing for fun and to gain her mother's 'Rather clever, I think' (VB 64–5), but then more purposefully and diligently. As Virginia Woolf was aware, education is not easily sorted into clear-cut outcomes, but two important results of Virginia Stephen's homeschooling, among many others, were a tangible library and an intangible worldview, just coming into focus, coloured by observations of and perceptions about access and gender. Eventually, her books and her worldview, along with the crucible of isolation she was educated in, would compel Virginia Woolf to converse with others in writing.

A Library of Her Own: Virginia Stephen's Books

When Virginia Stephen leaves Hyde Park Gate in 1904,[1] she leaves behind a place 'tangled and matted with emotion', a narrow and crowded house filled with a 'rich red gloom', and starts anew in 46 Gordon Square, where the light, air and 'extraordinary increase of space' exhilarate her ('Old Bloomsbury' 183–5). Her room, with windows looking out over plane trees, is at the top of the house (Lee, VW 201), mimicking her father's library location. She leaves her home school and begins an apprenticeship phase in which teaching at Morley College and writing book reviews predominate. What she takes with her, along with a home education consisting of fragments, lessons learned and memories of various teachers, are books: countless books that take her days to unpack (Lee, VW 201); all her father's 'mangy and worthless' books (E5 588), including his sixty-three annotated volumes of the *DNB*; Julia's books; Thoby's, Vanessa's and Adrian's books; various Stephen books; even some Duckworth books.

And *her* books. Virginia Stephen went to school in Leslie Stephen's library and took that library with her when she moved, but she also left Hyde Park Gate with a library of her own.[2] Small, but her own, one she continued to build during her apprenticeship.

At Washington State University in Pullman, Virginia Stephen's library can be isolated from the Library of Leonard and Virginia Woolf, but it is impossible to know in all cases what books were hers. Some books, either in the Manuscripts,

Archives and Special Collections part of Holland/Terrell Libraries or in other collections, are certainly hers: they have a monogram, bookplate or inscription that identifies them as Adeline Virginia Stephen's, AVS. Some books, with no identifying marks, have contextual features that make them almost surely hers, such as Janet Case's edition of *Prometheus Bound* or the copy of F. W. Maitland's *The Life and Letters of Leslie Stephen*, in which her memories of her father appear. Other books we can surmise are hers, such as the Francis Bacon *Essays*, Thoby's 1903 birthday present (*L1* 66) – one copy listed in the Woolf Library short-title catalogue could be that gift, though no inscription proves it. Other books were in her library at some point because she has identified them as gifts or purchases in her journals or letters, but they are not in MASC, meaning either they are owned by other collectors or they disappeared: in later moves, through attrition or lending, in the bombing of Mecklenburgh Square. For example, on 13 March 1905, Stephen says she is going 'Out to Hatchards to buy Stevenson & Pater' to help her learn book reviewing (*PA* 251). Numerous Pater volumes belonging to Stephen exist in MASC, so it seems reasonable to assume she bought some Stevenson essays as well, but no such volumes are in LLVW. Or the book she received from Violet Dickinson for her birthday in 1904 but does not identify: 'Your little Book lies by me, very fragrant' (*L1* 122). When, in December of 1908, she asks her friend for *The Oxford Book of French Verse* edited by St John Lucas (*L1* 375), Violet almost certainly gave it to her for Christmas because Virginia thanks her for a book in late December (*L1* 377) and Violet gave her another specifically requested book on another Christmas, poems by John Keats (see *L1* 263, 269, 272), but we have no proof.

Other books are in a more dubious category, books that contextual or textual evidence suggests may have been Virginia Stephen's, such as the 1706 edition of Mary Astell's *Reflections upon Marriage* labelled in her hand and rebound, but Virginia Woolf could have done the labelling or binding (K&M-V 9). Or the books published before or in 1912 with 'VW' designations, used by cataloguers for attributions unless a direct reference to 'AVS' was made, that seem appropriate for her youthful library, but for which we have no date of purchase or gift, such as *The Collected Works of Henrik Ibsen* (volumes 1–10 out of 12, 1906–12) with possibly VW annotations on 'A Doll's House' and a separate Ibsen volume, *The Master Builder*, published in 1901 and bound by VW (K&M-V 111). Or the Greek texts with notes in her hand: we do not know if Virginia Stephen was working on them, with or without a tutor, or if Virginia Woolf was taking notes for 'On Not Knowing Greek'. Her *Antigone* notes are dated 7 May 1900, and Stephen signed Jebb's 1904 edition of *The Tragedies of Sophocles*, but other textual notes are not dated. The following numbers and conclusions must be understood as tentative, then, but even a blurry snapshot of Virginia Stephen's library provides a glimpse of this tangible outcome of her home education.[3] See Figure 5.1. Appendix 2 lists the books in her library.

Virginia Stephen's library is both an educational tool and an outcome. When James Payn gave Leslie Stephen a *Thesaurus of English Words* (presumably Roget's – it is not in MASC), Leslie was insulted and passed it on to his 15-year-old 'poor scant languaged' daughter so her 'sentences [might] not jar' (*L1* 5–6). Yet the library's existence also illustrates a belief: books can provide an education.

Figure 5.1 Virginia Stephen's books, three trolleys, one shelf full. Part of Library of Leonard and Virginia Woolf, Manuscripts, Archives and Special Collections, Washington State University Libraries, Pullman, WA. Personal photo.

It reflects her mentors' views, and tentatively and increasingly, her own. The library reveals the lessons others tried to teach her and traces her growth as a reader. Like Virginia Woolf's essays, then, Virginia Stephen's library grows out of her education.

Virginia Stephen's youthful library of almost 160 titles (with some of those titles multi-volume works) has much Greek in it and some Latin, but also Foxe's *Book of Martyrs* and Gibbon's *Decline and Fall* (K&M-V 79, 85).[4] Some of her father's publications are there, along with the Rosettis and Wordsworth and Tennyson (K&M-V 190, 248, 223). There is a Baedeker for Northern France and a dictionary of birds by Howard Saunders (K&M-V 12, 196). Browning and Burton, Hakluyt and Hardy, Pater and Poe, Wilde and Wells – a fascinating kernel of a library that would eventually become enormous.

A library reflects not just one's own taste, but the taste of others, the taste others think one should have, the culture's beliefs and attitudes. Since family members and friends transmit the culture's lessons and assumptions through gifts and inscriptions, Virginia Stephen's library often reflects late nineteenth- and early twentieth-century cultural norms. How much and what she learned about the state, religion, the patriarchy and the canon depend upon what she read and retained, but the presence of certain books in her library shows what forces swirled about her. In June 1897, she says her father 'lent' her his twelve volumes of Froude's *History of England* because he did not have room for them, writing 'they have a whole new bookshelf for themselves' and that she is to 'read 'em some time' (*PA* 108–9).[5] She must have started quickly since on 29 July she writes 'I attacked Froude again (I have the 12 vols here!)', indicating she took them with her on their Gloucestershire holiday to Painswick (*PA* 117). She may have learned about traditional views of the state or the state's traditional views when she turned 15 and received Mandell Creighton's *Queen Elizabeth* from Mrs F. W. Gibbs (*L1* 3). For Christmas 1898, she received James Anthony Froude's *Short Studies on Great Subjects* with her father's annotations (K&M-V 82). In summer 1899, Gerald Duckworth gave her an early title published at his new publishing company, her cousin Harry Lushington Stephen's *State Trials, Political and Social* (1899) (he would be in India from 1904 to 1913), and for her birthdays in 1899 and 1900, her father gave her John Richard Green's *The Making of England* (Barkway, Front matter xvi) and Goldwin Smith's *The United Kingdom: A Political History* (K&M-V 214, 206). These volumes illustrate Leslie's 'plan to educate Virginia in history' (Hill, 'History' 353), but they also communicate standard English patriotic views. Smith begins his 1899 book,

> England has taken the lead in solving the problem of constitutional government; of government, that is, with authority, but limited by law, controlled by opinion, and respecting personal right and freedom. This she has done for the world, and herein lies the world's chief interest in her history. (1)[6]

Perhaps attempting to counteract the agnostic Leslie's influence, her religious Aunt Caroline gave Virginia her own *Quaker Strongholds* in 1899 and Dante's *Divine Comedy* for her eighteenth birthday (K&M-V 214, 55); she also sent her *Light Arising: Thoughts on the Central Radiance* when she published it in 1908 (*L1* 331). Her cousin Dorothea gave her George John Romanes's *Thoughts on*

Religion, and she received a *Holy Bible* from Violet Dickinson for her twenty-fifth birthday in 1907 (K&M-V 190, 21). She had already received, as a birthday present in 1900, an oversized 1683 *Book of Common Prayer and The Holy Bible* that includes the Apocrypha and the Book of Psalms collected into English metre by various poets. In it, she pasted a heraldic bookplate that includes her printed initials, AVS, and a printed Latin phrase: *In tali nunquam lassat venatio silva*, which roughly translates 'In such a forest as this the hunt never wearies' (K&M-V 20; Kopley 83, Figure 2.1). In 1905, after Virginia's illness in 1904, Violet Dickinson gave her *These Thoughts Were Written by Anthony Harte*, a small handheld book on sickness, pain and depression that ultimately recommends the ill person 'turn thy thoughts to thy Maker' and 'place all thy trust in His Mercy' (18); she inscribed it 'A tract for the Sp[arroy]' (K&M-V 99). Stephen writes on 13 January 1905 that 'Anthony Harte is [Violet Dickinson's] own writing!' (*PA* 221), and a request for another copy reveals Violet 'published' it as well, given that it 'is all wrongly bound, and numbered, and the same pages are repeated' (*L1* 174).

Some of the patriarchy's unconscious assumptions can be seen in Leslie Stephen's 1892 edition of *Hours in a Library* (K&M-V 215), which, out of thirty-two essays, includes only two on female authors, Charlotte Brontë and George Eliot (an improvement over the 1874–9 edition with only Brontë). Adrian gives her Gibbon's *The History of the Decline and Fall of the Roman Empire* for her twenty-third birthday in 1905 (K&M-V 85), the first volume of which so bores and oppresses Rachel Vinrace in *The Voyage Out* (212). All these gifts reflect the political, religious and patriarchal norms of her time.

Perhaps Virginia Stephen's library most clearly taught her through its canonical literature. On her thirteenth birthday, Virginia received the *Pocket Volume of Selections from the Poetical Works of Robert Browning* from George Duckworth, who did not realise she already had an earlier edition belonging to J. K. Stephen (K&M-V 32). Vanessa and Thoby gave her Samuel Johnson's *Lives of the Most Eminent English Poets* (K&M-V 116), inscribed with quotations they chose from Dickens, Bulwer-Lytton and Johnson himself; the latter inscription reads 'The chief glory of every people arises from its authors.' When she turned 15, she received the ten volumes of J. G. Lockhart's *Memoirs of Sir Walter Scott* from her father (K&M-V 136). In 1899, Thoby gave her *The Rubaiyat of Omar Khayyam* for her birthday (a title he would receive from his housemaster that spring [K&M-V 169]), and for her birthday in 1902, Mackail's *Select Epigrams from the Greek Anthology*, which she calls 'a real addition to my library' (perhaps the first time she refers to her books as a library?) and appreciates because it has a crib at the bottom (*L1* 46–7) (K&M-V 143). For her 1903 birthday, Thoby gave her an edition of Montaigne she had been hunting for for three years and a copy of Bacon that looks 'as though it had worn its corners round in some coat pocket' (*L1* 66) (K&M-V 158, 11). Violet Dickinson gave her Burton's *Anatomy of Melancholy* in 1902 (K&M-V 34), and right before his death in 1904, her father gave her his *English Literature and Society in the Eighteenth Century* for her birthday (K&M-V 215). Family and friends, then, encourage her literary pursuits, but also shape her attitudes about literary value. She unconsciously learns who is important, writing to Violet Dickinson in December 1906,

If there is one book that I want more than another – no, its *not* the Bible – it is the Poems of John Keats, in a brand new edition complete in one vol. published by the Clarendon Press at Oxford. Give me that and I shall dream all day beneath leafless trees. (L1 263; her emphasis)

Violet inscribed the book 'A.V. S. from V. D. 1906' (Funke and Beekman 20), and Virginia mentions opening this present in a letter to Violet on 22 December 1906 (L1 269).

Stephen's library reflects her young interests and her growth as a reader, but also occasionally anticipates future interests and work. She continued her youthful curiosity about the natural world, making a list of London birds in Howard Saunders's *An Illustrated Manual of British Birds*; her books include Gilbert White's *The Natural History and Antiquities of Selborne* and Richard Jefferies's *The Life of the Fields*, containing a chapter on country literature. Her interest in walking can be seen in Augustus Hare's *Walks in London* and Arthur Hamilton Norway's *Highways and Byways in Devon and Cornwall* (K&M-V 196, 242, 115, 98, 167). When she is 14, Madge Vaughan gives her Charlotte M. Yonge's *The Little Duke: Richard the Fearless* (Funke and Beekman 87), children's historical fiction about the great-grandfather of William the Conqueror,[7] but by her mid to late twenties, she buys for herself a different kind of fiction, obtaining all of Thomas Hardy's Wessex novels (Funke and Beekman 21).[8] (Much later, Virginia Woolf would mock Yonge and excoriate her in 'Two Women' for her insistence upon women's inferiority [E4 420].) Hindsight allows us to see Woolf's interest in the letters genre in Stephen's copies of *The Life and Letters of Lady Sarah Lennox*, the *Letters of John Keats to Fanny Brawne*, the 1903 edition of *The Love Letters of Dorothy Osborne to Sir William Temple*, the 1901 edition of *The Paston Letters* (Funke 22–3), the edition of the *Letters of John Richard Green* her father edited and a privately printed copy of the *Additional Letters of Mary Sibylla Holland*, along with her review copies of Percy Lubbock's book on *Elizabeth Barrett Browning in Her Letters* and *The Family Letters of Christina Georgina Rossetti* edited by William Michael Rossetti (K&M-V 133, 119, 169, 92, 106, 139, 190).[9]

As she matured, Stephen made the library more and more hers. Thoby helped her to make a start with Greek and Latin, but her inscribed AVS indicates she bought Plato, Sophocles ('for the Use of Schools'), Euripides, Herodotus, Lucan, Lucretius and Virgil on her own in her efforts to break into that male preserve (K&M-V 71, 102, 139, 140, 235). She also purchased books by Edward FitzGerald, J. B. Bury and S. H. Butcher, all of whom attempt to make the classics more accessible (K&M-V 76, 34, 35). She finds her own way in.

She also used her bookbinding and her bookplate designs and labels to make books her own. Virginia Stephen bought books, received books, loved the physical nature of books – Lockhart's *Memoirs of Sir Walter Scott*, she writes to Thoby after her fifteenth birthday, 'came the evening I wrote to you – ten most exquisite little volumes, half bound in purple leather, with gilt scrolls and twirls and thistles everywhere, and a most artistic blue and brown mottling on their other parts' (L1 4). Her fascination with the physical product led her to design bookplates with AVS in a heart monogram and several other bookplates, and to try her hand at bookbinding, so that near her birthday in 1903, she writes to Thoby she has 'invented a new way of bookbinding' (L1 67). According to Nigel Nicolson, she was taking bookbinding classes from Annie Power as early as 1901 (L1 45 n1), and Alan Isaac says she took lessons from Sylvia Stebbing, both of whom were trained by Douglas Cockerell, who had been trained by Cobden-Sanderson (9). Although her inscription is not in it, Isaac thinks she probably bought Cockerell's classic text new in 1901 (it was still being printed in 1978). *Bookbinding and the Care of Books, A Text-Book for Bookbinders and Librarians* (K&M-V 46) made a good candidate for a Stephen purchase because of its helpful how-to language; drawings, illustrations and photographs; and glossary and table of specifications. Though it cannot always be discerned which books were bound by Stephen and which by Woolf, the binding for volume 4 of Edward Arber's *An English Garner* has an AVS heart on it (K&M-V 7). Her early fascination with the physical nature of books makes it easy to imagine Woolf setting type with inky fingers at the Hogarth Press.

A trip to an old curiosity shop with 'tempting bundles of old books' prompts the comment, 'I cannot say what acute pleasure it is to me to buy books' (PA 158), so her own purchases accumulated. Shelley, Keats and Wordsworth temper her father's eighteenth-century rationalism. Other than the twelve volumes of Hardy, eight Pater titles and five Leslie Stephen works inscribed to or by her, the only other author represented by more than three volumes is poet James Thomson ('B.V.', 1834–82), a melancholy, rebellious, Poe-like figure who suffered from insomnia and died of a haemorrhage after a drunken bout (Rich). Thoby got her started, inscribing Thomson's *Biographical and Critical Studies* to her with the phrase '"There is no God" J. Thomson', but Virginia bought four other books by him in 1905, probably soon after she mentions him as someone she wants to buy '[i]f I am taken on by the Times' (PA 223). Enthusiastically promoting William Blake and Walt Whitman, Thomson also wrote for the Free Thought movement, publishing many essays in freethinker journals such as the *London Investigator* and the *National Reformer*, so one can see ties to Leslie Stephen. But Mark Rich also argues that 'in both subject and literary tone, Thomson expressed a sensibility more akin to that found in the poetry of the twentieth century than in that of the nineteenth', and says some critics consider his best-known work, 'The City of the Dreadful Night', a precursor of T. S. Eliot's 'The Waste Land'. He also singles out a poem called 'In the Room' as a 'tour de force in which the objects of a room speak to one another, as though animate beings equipped with speech and memory'.[10] Isobel Armstrong calls him an atheist, blasphemer and anarchist and places him outside not only the conservative tradition but also the century's radical poetry (450).

Near the end of her apprenticeship, Virginia Stephen bought other books that nod toward Virginia Woolf's modernist rebellions, such as Samuel Butler's *The Way of All Flesh*, a book bolstering Woolf's argument that human character changed around 1910 (K&M-V 36). She also bought *Waste: A Tragedy in Four Acts* by Harley Granville-Barker (K&M-V 90), banned by the British Lord Chamberlain, 'ostensibly', Anne Wright comments, 'because of its reference to an abortion but also, perhaps, because of its explicit political content' (27). It features corruption in government, the struggle for the disestablishment of the

Church of England, sex scandals, suffrage, birth control and suicide. A revised version reached the London stage in 1936, and it was produced more recently, by the Theatre for a New Audience in 2000 and by the Almeida Theatre in 2008, perhaps because, as director Samuel West said, 'The events of *Waste* could have happened this morning' ('Harley'). Or because, as Stella Maloney and Gerald S. Argetsinger argue, the protagonist 'becomes the plaything of the Edwardian political oligarchy that controls government policy by Machiavellian infighting and that deliberately uses the bogey of public morality to destroy the threat posed to it by the able man with the good cause'. Perhaps more important to Stephen would have been Granville-Barker's 'subtle psychological insight' into characters' inner lives (Wright 30).

Much of Virginia Stephen's library reflects her upbringing and homeschooling, revealing her youth's cultural context. It also reflects her education's fragmented and piecemeal quality. But most important, this library of her own reflects the first steps Virginia Stephen took beyond her father's library. Ironically, as Jane Fisher comments, '[Leslie's] intervention in her education gave her the means of refuting him . . . ' (46). Stephen's books reveal her 22 Hyde Park Gate roots, but also her leave-taking.

Virginia Stephen's Lessons: Access and Gender

Undeniably, Virginia Stephen had access to a wonderful resource in her father's library. At first he regulated that access, but soon it was unrestricted. Her mother opened foreign and ancient languages to her, and both parents assumed knowledge of other languages was important. She was privileged, too, in her access to the London Library – her family had the means, and her father had the good sense, to make its resources available to her. She was fortunate her brother Thoby did not hesitate to share what he was learning with her. She had a front row seat to her aunt's professional life and at least two stimulating periodicals at her disposal. She enrolled in classes at King's College London Ladies Department, which gave her access to teachers who cared about the education of women. Her family, then she, could pay for tutors who increased her knowledge of Latin and Greek. Virginia Stephen did not have to contend with obstacles to learning that many have contended with, both then and now; she was not denied an education.

And yet. And yet. Virginia Stephen also learned that being a female curtailed access. The patriarchal pressure to use one's gifts to serve men, to serve others in general, was brought to bear. She was several steps removed from all Thoby gained at school, including camaraderie, self-evaluation, physical activity and friendships. She observed her father's disparaging treatment of her aunt and other intelligent women. She could see assumptions being made about female readers, both their educational opportunities and their interests. She could feel the patriarchal atmosphere surrounding her at the British Museum Reading Room. She understood the different educational paths open to young women at King's College and realised her own was casual, not purposeful. Her tutors, blocked from academic careers, had to be private tutors to earn a living. Her reading often told her the same story: women could certainly achieve, and did, but only with extreme effort and a convergence of circumstances: luck, means, support, resources. That was her story as well. Virginia Stephen had an education; she had homeschooling; she did not confront direct or blatant obstacles. But she felt, and was, shut out: from school, from Greek and Shakespeare, from opportunities, from communities.[11] The obstacles were subtle and internal, as Virginia Woolf would later point out. The Angel in the House's

> fictitious nature was of great assistance to her. It is far harder to kill a phantom than a reality. She was always creeping back when I thought I had despatched her. Though I flatter myself that I killed her in the end, the struggle was severe; it took much time that had better have been spent upon learning Greek grammar; or in roaming the world in search of adventures. (E6 481)

Indirect the obstacles may have been, but real, damaging, pervasive nonetheless. Mixed into her education, the education in which life and books are shaken together, the education that would affect her worldview and thus her work as a writer, was this reality: gender hobbles; inhibits; stifles; thwarts.

As bright girls do, Virginia Stephen absorbed her schooling, the specific approaches to education taken by her teachers in their respective classrooms, curricula and pedagogies, and she internalised the nineteenth-century non-compromising and separatist positions in the debate about girls' education. She both did and did not have an education just like a male's – she had access to the male's library, but at home. She both did and did not have an education suited to a female – she received training at the tea table every afternoon, but after studying Greek many mornings. Woolf later worried that training had compromised her integrity, blaming it for the 'suavity', 'politeness' and 'sidelong approach' of her *TLS* articles, yet also knew its disguise allowed her 'to slip in things that would be inaudible if one marched straight up and spoke out loud' ('Sketch' 150). She resented the isolation of her education, 'mooning about alone among my father's books' (*L3* 247), and envied Thoby the camaraderie of his friends (*L1* 77), but labelled the intellectual and the social moulding men endured at Cambridge and Oxford 'bad' (*L6* 420). She could both mock Anne Thackeray Ritchie's devotion to her father's work and follow Ritchie's lead in writing essays about women writers. She vicariously experienced being addressed as a working-class adult while living the life of an upper middle-class girl. She attended classes at King's College, but as a non-matriculated student who observed but did not participate in a women's intellectual community. She saw two very intelligent tutors come up against the patriarchal wall of you 'shall not, shall not, shall not' (*TG* 124). Virginia Stephen experienced access and exclusion, was inside and outside, felt restriction and value in each position. No wonder Virginia Woolf's writings on education have that strange conjunction of privilege and deprivation. She experienced and felt both.

What was Virginia Stephen's homeschooling like? In curriculum, her father passed on the male literary tradition, and her mother passed on the edifice of Victorian manners, knowledge of traditional gender roles, a smattering of languages and an introduction to fanciful literature. She learned some of the Greek curriculum from Thoby, along with Shakespeare and perhaps the essay. From her Aunt Anny, she gained knowledge about Victorians, women writers and non-fiction. From *Atalanta* and *Tit-Bits* came general knowledge, specific literary knowledge and a look at her exclusion from school and isolation from other girls. Libraries opened up a wider world of knowledge and the pleasures of doing research. Her King's College teachers gave her organised history and an introduction to a modern language while they and her tutors gave her disciplined study methods and enough knowledge of Greek and Latin to read authors' works.

In pedagogy, Virginia Stephen observed a questioning and analytical attitude from Leslie Stephen and a didactic one from Julia. Thoby illustrated how knowledge could make one shy, but could be imparted through conversation, either in letters or actual talk. Aunt Anny used humour and indirection as she provided a role model for the woman of letters. *Atalanta* was direct in its instructional approach, while *Tit-Bits* encouraged interaction. Libraries assumed a world in which everyone who could read had access. Her King's College teachers modelled lectures, and her tutors provided direct feedback and correction, with Janet Case including discussions about what texts and authors were teaching or saying.

She learned many lessons. Her father taught her critical thinking and honesty; her mother taught her creative thinking and kindness. Both taught her gender roles and what it feels like to be excluded. Thoby taught her what boys' schools did to the boys in them, while Anny taught her what a woman writer could do to put together words and sentences and to negotiate within a patriarchal world. *Atalanta* and *Tit-Bits* taught her about different audiences and the stances writers could take toward them. The libraries taught her how to explore, search and take notes. Her King's College teachers showed her how to organise material into lectures and what it felt like to be lectured. Her tutors, especially Janet Case, taught her discipline and an attentive, respectful and welcoming attitude toward learners.

Through her father, Virginia Stephen was introduced to a British and American male literary community of a certain class. Her mother introduced her to a female network. Thoby gave her insight into the world of public schools and elite universities. Anny provided access to a professional community of girls and women. *Atalanta* revealed a world of literate girls and schools, whereas *Tit-Bits* introduced her to a lower-middle and upper-working-class world. Through libraries, she met writers and other readers. At King's College, Virginia Stephen observed a community of women learners, and through her tutors, glimpsed women's entry into a predominantly male network of scholars, Greek editions, translations and interpretation.

Although Virginia Stephen took courses at King's College and had lessons come into the house from outside, although she had a curriculum, encountered pedagogies, learned lessons and was exposed to communities, much of her education and community was on paper. Not only must all the rest 'be learnt for oneself' (*E5* 589), but her parents decreed, at least for her, it must be learned *by* oneself. In an 'earlier version' of what becomes a long section Schulkind uses in the published 'Sketch' (Schulkind 63), Woolf describes her narrative perspective as being 'myself though fr the pt of view of a child who did no lessons; was allowed to read, and write; had no companionship; was absorbing books; terribly alive to the family presence . . . ' ('Sketch' MS n. pag. 10). As Perry Williams notes, what meant the most to the pioneer women students at Cambridge, beyond their intellectual work, was gathering at evening cocoa parties, which 'rapidly became virtual institutions at both colleges'. There, they could meet, talk and be valued, not for who their relations were, but, as one student wrote, 'entirely for what [we] are' (177–80). Virginia Stephen's experience of how painful and lonely it is to piece an education together by oneself, her isolation 'among [her father's] books' (*L6* 420), her feeling deprived even amidst wealth, compelled Virginia Woolf, more than the ideas and approaches suggested by her curriculum's content and lessons, to provide context and conversation in her own essays. 'Theres nothing like talk as an educator I'm sure,' Stephen wrote in 1903 (*L1* 77), and Woolf never quit trying to talk her way out of loneliness and into a learning community in her essays. Ironically, Virginia Stephen's lonely efforts to educate herself may have taught Virginia Woolf, essayist, her greatest lesson: how to create community, 'talk as an educator', through writing.

Notes

1. Virginia Stephen's illness after her father's death meant she took a detour through her Aunt Caroline's home, the Porch, in Cambridge. Vanessa orchestrated the Bloomsbury move, writing joyously about their new life and making Virginia, who felt exiled, envious (Lee, *VW* 200). Virginia began moving into her room at 46 Gordon Square on 8 November 1904 (*L1* 153) and moved between there, the Porch and a holiday in Hampshire up until December.
2. Virginia Stephen's library bears little resemblance to the library A. J. Church proposed in the Brown Owl column of the *Atalanta* in 1891 (*A4* 475–7), or to the different libraries proposed by four young women in subsequent correspondence (*A4* 605–6).
3. To isolate Virginia Stephen's library (Appendix 2), I used Holleyman, the MASC card catalogue, and my eyes to determine if a VW descriptor might be concealing an Adeline Virginia Stephen book. I have included books that are clearly hers and those that seem almost certainly to have been hers based on contextual evidence; have checked my work against the short-title catalogue, against the online catalogue of the Leonard and Virginia Woolf Library, and with Julia King; and have perused the *Letters, A Passionate Apprentice* and *Moments of Being* for other titles. Since other titles almost certainly exist, as catalogues and other collections continue to reveal, and since human error plagues all such endeavours, I welcome any information others have about additional books that were or might have been in her library.
4. By my count, she had 159 titles, with six additional titles almost surely hers and fourteen additional titles possibly hers.
5. Her room has a library's physical qualities, with a whole new bookshelf presumably joining others. I assumed her father never took them back and thus listed them in Appendix 2.
6. See Brian Harrison for Goldwin Smith's place in the 'The Anti-Suffrage Leadership Network' (94–5).
7. Quentin Bell writes, 'Virginia would read aloud from Charlotte M. Yonge – [she and Vanessa] kept a score of the number of deaths in those very necrological novels' (1 28–9). In the *Hyde Park Gate News*, for the alphabets produced on 30 November and 7 December 1891, Y is 'for Miss Yonge Who many things can tell' (*HPGN* 8, 11); in the news item about Thoby's homecoming on 19 December 1892, Leslie Stephen's 'Bravo' at the announcement of Thoby's prize is compared to 'Dr May in the "Daisy Chain" who generally conveyed his meanings by warm pressures of the hand or some

beautiful smile' (*HPGN* 160). Kelly Hager, Simmons College, describes Yonge's *Daisy Chain* as a Victorian bestseller about female education.
8. Perry Meisel's thesis about Pater as an unacknowledged father figure might have differed if he had known about the numerous Hardy volumes in Stephen's library. But such speculation reminds me that conclusions about Woolf based on what seems to have been in Stephen's library must remain tentative, grounded as they always are in incomplete evidence.
9. Only these two books, along with Henry James's *The Golden Bowl* and Anne Thackeray Ritchie's *The Blackstick Papers*, remain from her early reviewing days. By my count, she received 144 other review copies during her apprenticeship. In late April 1906, she asks Madge Vaughan to return a Brontë book 'as it belongs to the Times' (*L1* 225), suggesting papers routinely had authors return review copies, which would explain the absence of other review books.
10. Amy Levy also comments on these two works in her 1883 essay, 'James Thomson: A Minor Poet', reprinted in *The Complete Novels and Selected Writings of Amy Levy, 1861–1889*, edited by Melvyn New.
11. Her 12 March 1897 journal account of her excursion with Adrian to the Natural History Museum, where they encountered 'a notice directing [us] to an insect room open to students from 10 to 4', could stand in for her persistent sense of being denied entry: 'but as we did not feel sufficiently student like to enter, we came home' (*PA* 53).

Part II

Teacher, 1905–1907: Teaching at Morley College

[W]hy lecture, why be lectured? ... Why not let [your elders] talk to you and listen to you, naturally and happily, on the floor? ... Why not bring together people of all ages and both sexes of all shades of fame and obscurity so that they can talk ... ?'
— 'Why?'(E6 31, 33)

When Virginia Stephen was recovering from the depression and strain of care-taking, the death of her father and a suicide attempt in 1904 (QB1 89–90), Frederic Maitland asked her to write about her father for his biography of Leslie Stephen; Violet Dickinson suggested she write for the *Guardian*'s women's pages edited by Mrs Arthur Lyttelton; and Miss Mary Sheepshanks, 'a large kindly & rather able sort of woman' who was serving as the de facto Principal of Morley College, asked her to 'start a girls club at Morley, & talk about books &c!' (*PA* 217). Virginia Stephen gladly cobbled together this freelance work, but it probably puzzled some relatives and family friends – should she not be searching for a husband (L1 274, 296)? It was just what she needed, though, a mix of memory, writing and something new. Work.

Morley College, an institution on London's South side, Lambeth, attempted to provide what we now call a secondary education to working-class adults woefully underserved by England's educational system. The young, painfully shy, upper-middle-class Virginia Stephen began working at Morley on 18 January 1905 and taught her last class there in autumn 1907. This teaching experience, combined with her earlier homeschooling and her concurrent reviewing, made for a distinctive apprenticeship and contributed to Virginia Stephen's perspective on education, which in turn shaped Virginia Woolf into an essayist with an inclusive pedagogy.

Virginia Stephen's education gave her some limited experience as a student, but when she arrived at Morley on Waterloo Road after a ten-minute cab ride and walked into a 'great dreary room with tables & chairs & flaring gas jets' (*PA* 224), she did so with little preparation for teaching there, no teaching experience and no understanding of the working classes. Her knowledge of the latter was limited to workhouse visits with Stella (*PA* 42–3; 56), some exposure to Miss Octavia Hill and Stella's future cottages (*PA* 8 and n, 21, 42, 94), and the servants living in the Stephen household. But neither charity extended to the extremely poor nor the employer/employee dynamic of the mistress/servant relationship modelled by Julia Stephen could have encouraged much understanding of working-class life.[1]

Perhaps more important, Stephen would have known little, if anything, about the education her working-class students had received prior to their taking classes at Morley. So, self-taught and suddenly responsible for educating others, Virginia Stephen was on her own. Again.

During her homeschooling, Virginia Stephen was exposed to curricula, experienced pedagogies, learned lessons and observed communities. Her own learning continued at Morley College, but simultaneously, she had to encourage learning in her students and thus create curricula, use pedagogies, teach lessons and introduce communities. As she learned, she taught, and as she taught, she learned, furthering her education as an essayist. When Stephen moved into classrooms, spaces in which teaching and learning occur, she also moved into a world unfamiliar to her, another social class, and our knowledge, awareness and theoretical and cultural understanding were unavailable to her. Gender marked her homeschooling, but class marked her Morley teaching.[2] What Virginia Stephen learned from her primary instructors at Morley – the college, Miss Sheepshanks and her students – was how to reach out, seek common ground, momentarily cross barriers and share. In other words, she learned how to teach.

Education for the Working Classes

In studies of education for the working classes, education historians point out that, traditionally, education for working-class children began at home. R. K. Webb and David Vincent both note literacy rates for the working classes were rising before elementary education became more available in the 1870s and 1880s (348–51; 54–5), indicating parents and/or various informal schools were teaching their children to read. But schools provided for the working classes by middle-class reformers and the Church Societies in the early and mid-nineteenth century dismantled this working-class 'domestic curriculum' rather than building on it (Vincent 73–84). They subordinated the three Rs to religious and moral training, taught reading by rote learning and oral recitation of long lists of meaningless syllables, attacked students' pronunciation, tried to wipe out dialects and imposed a Latin-like grammar, serving only, as Vincent says, 'to complete the transformation of written English into a foreign language' (82).

Before the 1870 Education Act, working-class children might attend a dame, charity, plait and lace, factory, workhouse, ragged, industry, church, Sunday (secular or religious), or day school sponsored by Church Societies (promoting either Church of England or nonconformist views) (Purvis, *HL* 72). According to David Wardle, most charged a small weekly fee, from a few pence to 2 or 3 shillings (61), and children attended when they could. Children commonly left school at 10, after having spent an average of under two years there (44–5).

Such brief schooling can be easily explained. According to a study cited by E. J. Hobsbawm, in 1867, 77 per cent of the 24 million inhabitants of Great Britain fell into the manual labour class, which was narrowly defined to exclude all shopworkers, shop-keepers, foremen, supervisory workers and so forth. Of these, 15 per cent formed a kind of aristocracy with wages of 28s. to £2 per week (Wardle 41). (It is more accurate to speak of the working classes than the working class, with some of the gradations, particularly those between skilled, semi-skilled and unskilled workers, more rigid than the line between skilled artisans and clerks in the lower middle class.) The average pay of unskilled workers, who formed more than half of the working class, was 10–12s. per week (Wardle 41). As J. S. Hurt explains, children who could earn a few shillings a week thus made a big difference to the working-class family economy, and school attendance cost parents twice, in fees paid and wages lost (34). Also, elementary education was not seen as leading to further education or social mobility (Hurt 29–30). Rather, as John Burnett puts it, 'Education was seen as being for work rather than for life, for producing efficient, manageable workers and law-abiding citizens rather than for developing individual personality, intellectual or emotional independence' (*Destiny* 168). Elementary education was meant to educate the working classes for their station and to control the knowledge they gained (Wardle 89), and according to Burnett, 'The view long persisted that elementary and secondary education were quite distinct systems, appropriate for different social classes, not successive stages in a single process to which all children had a right' (*Destiny* 170). Such brief or bad schooling kept the class system intact.

In the latter part of the nineteenth century, elementary education for the working classes in England underwent several transitions: from voluntary to compulsory, from fee-paying to free, from some parental involvement to more government control. In Virginia Stephen's time and place, though, the idea that the working classes deserved an education, let alone that the nation needed educated workers as citizens, was relatively new. Education had been for ruling an Empire, not for participating in a democracy. As Jane McDermid points out, 'the Church of England was extremely wary of education for the poor, fearing a potential threat to the social order' (117). What education there was for the working classes was almost always subtly or not so subtly geared toward keeping them in their place, not toward their questioning those places or moving out of them; education for working-class girls and women was geared toward improving their homemaking skills and education for working-class boys and men was aimed at improving their technical skills (McDermid 116–20; Altick, *ECR* 163–5, 194; Digby and Searby 47). Education for the working classes was not supposed to contribute to personal enrichment, social or political betterment, or upward mobility (Altick 141–4). Indeed, the increased availability of education for the working classes was creating anxiety, as Stephen Arata points out (56). He quotes Robert Buchanan, who complained that because of the Reform Bills and the Education Act, 'the great waters of Democracy' were 'arising to swallow up and cover the last landmarks' of superior Victorian culture. Buchanan believed that 'After the School Board has come the Deluge' (qtd in Arata 57). Education of the working classes was a threat, not an opportunity.

Ian Copeland says the 1870 Education Act meant communities could form local non-denominational school boards and establish schools to 'supplement' provision by existing church schools (379), which up until then, according to Eric Hopkins, had a 'near-monopoly' on working-class education (122). Schools could receive government rates, so the slow move away from church schools and toward a national system began,[3] with the aim being an elementary education available to all (Copeland 379). However, as Joseph McAleer explains, the Education Act of 1870 did not make elementary education 'mandatory or free' (14). Under the Education Act of 1880, school attendance became mandatory from the ages of 5 to 10, which then caused financial problems for working-class families and, thus, attendance problems for schools.[4] Fees were abolished in 1891, but until 1918, employers could make part-time arrangements for hiring children who were also attending school (Hurt 188). When Woolf began teaching, then, many working-class children had left school at 12 or younger, had worked part-time before they left, and had been taught from the narrowest of curricula.

That narrow curriculum, the Revised Code of 1862, was first applied in day schools run by Church Societies and then after 1870, in local board schools; it was enforced by government inspectors and remained officially in place until 1897, though its indirect effects lingered longer (S. J. Curtis 267; Wardle 69, 107). Under this Code, the Payment by Results system, a school's annual grant amount from the government (and thus teachers' pay), depended on pupil attendance and passed examinations in each of six Standards. As a result, teachers instructed working-class students only in reading, writing and arithmetic, and the instruction was mechanical, geared toward examinations (S. J. Curtis 258–67); students had to memorise answers in constant drills, and exams 'became artificial performances by students for the Inspectors, with anxious teachers standing by nervously' (Heyck 208). The literacy level expected in each Standard was low by today's norms, revealing the level at which many students started, or the expectations of those devising the Standards, or both. In the Standard VI exam, the highest standard, a child 'was expected to "read a short ordinary paragraph in a newspaper", write a similar passage of prose from dictation, and calculate "a sum in practice or bills of parcels"' (Hurt 8).[5] The term writing meant being able to literally write, not composing. Although composing a short letter was added to Standard VI in 1871 and although the Code was later expanded to make it possible for a school to add other subjects and for students to take one, only one in forty students did so; the emphasis on teaching and learning by rote and for an exam remained (Hurt 183).[6] As late as between the wars, according to both Kay Sanderson and Ida Rex, most working-class children received training only in the three Rs (146–7; 29).[7]

The move toward compulsory education in 1880 also tripled the number of children in the schools. Classes were huge, with a pupil to teacher ratio of 123:1 in 1870, 67:1 in 1891 and 62:1 in 1899. For the first time, children with no formal teaching in their backgrounds, no tradition of attendance, and no family members with any history of schooling were present in the schools (Copeland 379). As a result, David Vincent reports, in 1882, just over 3½ million children were at the annual inspection; of these, 'only 47 per cent entered and passed one of the first four Standards in reading and 43 per cent in writing'. During the 1880s, 'there were on average no more than four Standard VI passes a year in each inspected institution' (90–1).

Yet some working-class people educated themselves, carving out ways to study. J. F. C. Harrison says Joseph Barker 'kept a book propped open on his loom' and Thomas Cooper 'got up at 4 a.m. to study' and read at breakfast and dinner (292). Adult education historians tended to focus, until recently, on the tradition of providing education for the working class (university extension lectures,

Workers' Educational Association and so on) rather than the self-help tradition or independent working-class education developed by the working classes themselves (Simon, *Search* 9–10), but Harrison describes several working-class efforts, including mutual improvement societies in which workers 'taught themselves reading, writing, grammar and arithmetic' (292–4). John Burnett argues the presence of so many well-written working-class autobiographies indicates the impact of self-help agencies and the growth of literacy outside formal education (*Annals* 9–14; see also *Useful* and *Destiny*). Paul Thomas Murphy proves the working classes used their own periodicals to establish a working-class canon of literature, Martha Vicinus includes a chapter on self-educated poets in her study of nineteenth-century British working-class literature, Cassandra Falke examines five working-class autobiographies (written and published between 1820 and 1848 and chosen from the fifty-two she annotates in her appendix) as literature, and Jonathan Rose uses many such autobiographies in his work. These narratives and studies make clear a working-class person could in fact acquire some education, but they also make clear going beyond one's basic and often bad schooling demanded great initiative, motivation and discipline.[8]

Notes

1. Woolf remembers Julia being 'a little perhaps ashamed' that someone saw 'what must have been [the servants'] rather shabby rooms' during a pipe bursting emergency ('Sketch' 119); she also recalls her mother's reaction to a servant's outburst during their lessons, '"It's like hell,"' about the 'dark insanitary' basement the maids lived in: 'My mother at once assumed the frozen dignity of the Victorian matron; and said (perhaps): "Leave the room"' ('Sketch' 116). Woolf, knowing the whole system was unfair and yet depending on servants, had a fraught relationship with them. See Alison Light and Mary Wilson.
2. See Mary Childers ('Outside'), Sean Latham (*AIS*) and Elena Gualtieri for critiques of Woolf's class attitudes. For differing views, see Christopher Reed, Mark Hussey ('Thatcher') and Melba Cuddy-Keane (*VW*). For studies of working-class culture, see Jonathan Rose and Christopher Hilliard. For insightful examinations of privilege, class, and the difficulty of speaking about, of, for and to others, see Laurie Quinn and Linda Alcoff.
3. Eric Hopkins says the Education Act, which included a clause requiring any religious instruction to be undenominational, 'really signaled the beginning of a state system of schools in [England], yet it was not done by abolishing the church schools' (123).
4. As Jenni Calder explains, 'For the subsistence wage earner the slightest alteration could make all the difference between survival and starvation.' Change, as she further notes, was 'a threat to basic needs rather than an improvement to prospects' (154).
5. Current concerns in countries like the US about public education's quality are rarely accompanied by any historical analysis of literacy, though such information is available. Not all students in US grade 6, for example, meet the standards expected of them today, but they must do much more than read a newspaper paragraph, copy a dictated passage and do sums. Beyond the earliest elementary grades, US teachers use the term 'writing' to mean composing sentences, paragraphs and essays rather than forming letters on the page. It is simply not historically accurate to say standards have been 'dumbed down'. What we now mean by literate in the US, the UK and many other countries includes more knowledge, more complex abilities and more higher-order thinking skills, including technological ones, than in the past.

6. See 'The Education of Girls', Digby and Searby, 45–7, for how standards differed for boys and girls.
7. See also P. H. J. H. Gosden, Alexander Paterson and John Burnett for first- and second-hand accounts of how working-class children experienced their schooling.
8. They also make it clear that some working-class people of the mid-nineteenth century demonstrated the literary interest and excellence Woolf would later search for in the papers collected for *Life as We Have Known It* ('Introductory Letter to Margaret Llewelyn Davies').

Chapter 6

Teaching at Morley College

Virginia Stephen's education was in part extraordinary, tailor-made for her profession, and better than most young women at the time received: rich in resources and with considerable freedom. On the other hand, it was terrible: erratic, narrow, lonely. She educated herself, receiving informal instruction from various teachers, but like the working-class students she would teach, she had to provide initiative, motivation and discipline on her own. Her education, no matter its strengths and weaknesses, gave her no preparation for teaching at Morley College. She lacked experience with numerous teachers, institutional training or guidance, and cultural awareness about difference. She also, one suspects, lacked knowledge about Morley College or its place within the educational debates of the time. She walked into a rough section of town, into a building which had its classes behind a stage, and into a situation for which nothing in her life or education had prepared her. When she entered her first Morley classroom, Virginia Stephen, just shy of 23, faced the task of negotiating the difference between her own educational background and that of her students. Those negotiations had a lot to do with class, and they influenced the strategies for reaching readers she would eventually develop as an essayist.

Morley College's History, Mission

Morley College's origins make a fascinating story. As Sybil Oldfield puts it in her biography of Mary Sheepshanks and F. M. Mayor, 'There has never been an institution of further education like it' (*SP* 65).[1] Thomas Kelly notes how Emma Cons changed the Old Vic Theatre, known for melodrama, prostitutes and thieves, into the Royal Victoria Coffee Hall in 1880, started offering classes in 1885, and established Morley Memorial College in 1889 with Samuel Morley's help (*AE* 193–4).[2] As Denis Richards tells it (17–85), Cons moved south of the river to Lambeth to manage a struggling block of 'model' dwellings for Octavia Hill. For her, though, better housing was just the start; the poor also deserved educational and recreational facilities, and the latter should not tempt them to drink, which brought even more poverty, physical and mental deterioration, and brutality against women and children. She was determined to create a 'centre for innocent and wholesome recreation' (T. Kelly, *AE* 193), and she succeeded, with the Royal Victoria Coffee Hall offering not only inexpensive tea, coffee and meals, but also lectures, entertainment, concerts and temperance meetings. Scientists gave illustrated lectures, the first on 'The Telephone, or How to talk to a man a hundred miles away' (Richards 58).[3] These lectures proved popular, but the penny to a few coppers charged for beverages, food, lectures and entertainment meant operating at a loss. Thus, Cons approached Samuel Morley, a wealthy Bristol hosiery manufacturer and Liberal MP known for his integrity, clean, well-lit and ventilated workplaces, and high wages and pension scheme.[4] Morley's pledge, along with those of many anonymous women donors, was enough to purchase the building's lease and cover operating costs, which laid the foundation for offering evening classes (at the request of science lecture attendees) and then opening a college, which continued to operate in tandem with Victoria Hall. Indeed, until 1924 and the move to 61 Westminster Road, Morley's recreation rooms were under the Hall's stage, a library above it and classrooms behind it.[5]

Morley College, on Waterloo Road in Lambeth, only a few yards from Southwark, was an urban institution offering an education 'of a more advanced character' to working-class adults (Richards 18, 96).[6] Its official mission was

> (1) To promote by means of classes, lectures and otherwise, the advanced study by men and women belonging to the working classes, of subjects of knowledge not directly connected with or applied to any handicraft, trade or business.
> (2) As subordinate or ancillary thereto, to assist in acquiring the requisite elementary instruction those whose age prevents them from making use of the ordinary elementary instruction.
> (3) To promote social intercourse among those following the above-mentioned pursuits. (Richards 92–3)

In the context of the time's debates, Morley offered a liberal education, not just the three Rs, to its working-class students (M. E. Sadler 138; Richards 91, 96). In 1901, when Morley listed fifty-five classes in thirty-two subjects, it offered courses in science, literature, history, classical and modern languages, music, botany and many other liberal arts subjects (T. Kelly, *AE* 194). As Harold Nicolson notes in his foreword to Denis Richards's 1958 history, 'the dominant demand [from students] has been, not so much for practical instruction, as for the humanities and the arts' (xv). But Morley, like the Mechanics' Institutes and some other adult education institutions, also had to offer courses to help its students catch up (Altick, *ECR* 193; Richards 93), though such elementary instruction was 'from the start regarded as a purely temporary measure' (Richards 96). Given that it started offering classes in 1880 and was officially established in 1889, when there was barely a link between a 'newly organized system of elementary education and the older unsystematized institutions dispensing higher education' (Richards 87), most Morley classes would have been secondary. Such courses were advanced for those enrolling in them, going beyond students' elementary schooling, and Morley did offer some university extension and matriculation courses to help prepare students for university exams and possible admission. But most Morley courses would have fallen between basic elementary and higher education.

Also, as funding for institutions like Morley became more complex, the college had to deal simultaneously with as many as three inspecting entities – the Science and Art Department, the London County Council (LCC) Technical Education

Board, and the Education Department – to earn grants (Richards 118). To receive grants, the college needed strong enrolment, steady student attendance and good reports from these organisations based on course exams, course certificates earned and inspection visits. In other words, as Elaine Andrews, Morley's current Librarian and Learning Resources Manager, explained, students earned certificates for individual courses, not for courses of study, and course exams would not have been too difficult since the college was operating within what was, in effect, a 'payment by results' system (conversation 7 July 2016).

Morley College did not even have courses of study; as Richards writes in 1958, 'Morley College is not concerned with Degrees, and never has been' (85).[7] Florence Acton, the Vice-Principal from 1894 to 1899, in response to a student request,[8] created a voluntary course of study that students could spread out over three to eleven years. This framework provided 'the ideal of systematic and continuous study on a coherent plan in opposition to the easier practice . . . of attending unrelated lectures and classes' (Richards 108). Students were to try out 'the four great branches of education' – English, Mathematics, Languages and Science – by taking introductory and intermediate courses in each branch in the first two stages and then focusing on their chosen branch during the last stage, and students had to pass examinations in each course at each stage before moving to the next (109–10). It was comprehensive and structured, but most who began it found it 'too exacting to follow in its entirety', with only one or two 'toil[ing] almost to the end' (110). Morley, then, offered a broad range of humanities, arts and science courses, which ran the gamut from economics, foreign languages and chemistry to literature, music, and electricity and magnetism, along with courses geared toward helping students catch up (reading and writing, arithmetic), and early on, technical courses in subjects such as cooking and dress-making, typewriting, shorthand and bookkeeping, and wood carving and clay modelling, but it did not require students to take those courses according to any kind of system.[9]

Morley aimed to serve the local population surrounding the Old Vic. In 1890, Richards notes, Lambeth had a nine-tenths working-class population, with half of that population under the poverty line (18–24, 95). Thomas Kelly calls the Lambeth/Southwark area a slum (*AE* 193), Oldfield describes the district as 'the worst poverty blackspot in London . . . with its 200 people per acre' (*SP* 47), and Richards says some of Southwark's worst quarters appeared in Dickens's novels, including *Oliver Twist* (18). Basing his information on Charles Booth's *Life and Labour of the People in London,* Richards notes above the poverty line in Lambeth and Southwark were the working class in regular employment, foremen and artisans. Below the line were four groups: the lowest (no family life, no work, crime, alcoholism); the very poor, with small and irregular earnings; the poor with well-paid but irregular work; and the poor with low regular wages (22–3). J. S. Hurt notes the effect such poverty had on Lambeth students in the Johanna Street Council School, where none of the fathers had a regular job: a third required free meals; boys could not last through a full-length game of football; 92 per cent of those in Standard I were older than they should have been, as were 85 per cent in Standard II and 80 per cent in Standard III; and only 8 per cent ever achieved Standard V (130).[10] At least those children were in school, as Oldfield says 'as many as five thousand children were estimated to be walking the streets of

Lambeth in 1900 without any schooling at all' (92). Such backgrounds led Altick to write that 'the working class was so completely unprepared for higher education that all but the most indomitable spirits soon lost hope' (*ECR* 210; see also 193). Emma Cons's vision was to make further education not just available but truly accessible to the working classes,[11] and Oldfield praises Morley for being 'a radical, innovative college', commends the women who worked for its success (Octavia Hill, Emma Cons, Caroline Martineau and Mary Sheepshanks), and notes its egalitarian structure and humanistic curriculum (65). But as Caroline Martineau, Principal from 1891 to 1902, knew, its many achievements then and since, indeed everything about the College, its operation, its character, its ethos, 'depends after all on the students' (qtd in Richards 144).[12]

Morley College's Students

By December 1890, one year after its founding, 1,270 students had enrolled at Morley, most of them men (Richards 100). Morley was unusual in admitting women on equal terms with men (98), but women's longer working hours, both inside and outside the home, made it harder for them to attend evening classes, scheduled between 6.30 and 10.30 p.m. (Oldfield, *SP* 66), even when they began at 8 p.m. (Richards 97, 101).[13] As Sheepshanks says in her autobiography,

> It was distinctly a school for tired people.... Very many of the students left home early in the morning by the workman's train, came straight from work to their classes and arrived home late, not having had any solid meal all day. (*LDE* 29–30)

Those enrolled represented a wide range of occupations: clerks, engineers, printing and carpentry trades, warehousemen, general labourers, teachers, porters, maids, waiters, cab-drivers, milliners, tailors and so on (Richards 100–1). Although Morley College founders wanted to provide the working classes with an education, the College also attracted students from outside the manual labouring class, such as clerks and shop assistants. Not all Morley students would have fit the definition of working class used at the time, but all Morley students worked for a living; its description of itself as a college 'For Working Men and Women' was accurate (Richards 94–5).[14]

In subsequent years, an overwhelming majority of students enrolled at Morley listed themselves as clerks; sizable numbers of female students were occupied or employed at home or in occupations related to clothing; other large occupational groups included engineering-related jobs, shop assistants, warehousemen, teachers, typists and so forth.[15] Many occupations were represented by only one student, but overall, Morley students were occupationally diverse, ranging from servants to artists, from nurses to porters, from fishmongers to cinematographers, and thus ranging from the labouring working class through the lower middle class. Stephen's classrooms reflected this occupational diversity. Her history class included Miss Williams, a religious paper staff reporter who knew shorthand, did typewriting and wrote book reviews ('Report' 202); one composition class included a Dutchman, an older Socialist and anaemic shop girls (*L1* 210, 212); her advanced composition class included a milkman (*L1*

281); and her reading circle included someone who may have stuttered, an Italian and a young poet who knew shorthand and was good at accounts (*L1* 313, 321). Morley College's occupation lists for its students show a reporter was enrolled in 1904–5 (*MCAR* 1904–5 9), but not in later years – perhaps Miss Williams left Morley or changed occupations – a dairyman was enrolled in 1906–7, as were twenty-one assistants (shop girls) (*MCAR* 1906–7 10), and in 1907–8, four accountants and eight shorthand clerks were enrolled (*MCAR* 1907–8 17). Given Morley's occupational lists, Stephen almost certainly had several other occupations sitting in her classes.

Insight into Morley's efforts, Virginia Stephen's challenges and students' determination can be gleaned from understanding how shop girls and clerks, two large occupational groups, lived and worked. Stephen's description of some of her composition students – 'anaemic shop girls who say they would write more but they only get an hour for their dinner, and there doesn't seem much time for writing' (*L1* 210) – accurately defines their situation. In the late nineteenth and early twentieth centuries, shop girls averaged between seventy-five and ninety hours a week, often starting their day at 7 a.m. and not ending it until 9 p.m. or later, with a half-day off that began at 4 p.m. (Pagnamenta and Overy 108). Work hours were the shop's opening hours; shifts did not exist. Girls had to 'live in', which meant cramped living conditions with no privacy (huge dormitory rooms lined with beds either over or next to the shop), lodging and meals deducted from wages low to begin with (some resorted to prostitution), and fines for not following rules aimed at creating conformity if not subservience (workers rarely made it through a week without being fined for something [Hosgood 335, citing 1893–4 Royal Commission on Labour, Minutes 426]).[16] They had health problems caused

> by poor sanitary facilities and inadequate ventilation.... Miss McDonald, a doctor at the Hospital for Women in Euston Road, concluded that standing [nearly all day], insufficient time for meals, and confinement in close atmospheres precipitated anemia and general nervous debility. (Hosgood 327)

Their occupation required nice clothes, so they were scorned by the working classes for trying to maintain a sheen of respectability and viewed by the middle-class women using their services as doing well; as Hosgood puts it, 'Ironically, shop assistants, who lived uncomfortable, institutional lives, worked in a shop environment that, by catering to the needs of customers, suggested that they enjoyed a privileged lifestyle' (330). They feared dismissal more than anything else because they considered their work better than being a domestic servant and because being fired meant they suddenly had no lodging. Many sought the job because it seemed to promise independence and the chance of managing or owning a shop one day, but the situation created dependence instead, and chances of moving up were almost nil (Hosgood 341–2). Shop assistants, trapped in a perpetual adolescence by paternalistic employers who maintained the pretence of everyone's being part of a family, could not negotiate for better working conditions or pay, Hosgood writes, and 'while not imprisoned, enjoyed few opportunities for broader social engagement and led an isolated existence' (325–6, 335). Escaping isolation may have motivated some shop girls at Morley as much as gaining some education.

Clerks were the largest single job category on Morley's lists, with 175 clerks enrolled in 1904–5 and 220 enrolled by 1907–8. While most shop assistants in the Edwardian period were women, most clerks were men, though women had begun to seek and obtain such work. The term clerk, Geoffrey Crossick explains, 'mask[s] a huge range of occupational status and income' (17–18), ranging from barely above the income tax minimum to over £160 a year,[17] and clerks worked in commercial, bank, insurance, law and railway entities. They most often required mathematics and handwriting skills since work involved taking notes, copying, indexing, ledger entry, delivering and receiving messages, receipts and invoices (Wild 14; Bullock 139), though some clerks did more advanced work involving shorthand, bookkeeping and composing letters.

They, too, were caught between the scorn of the labouring man (a 'soft' job) and the disdain of the middle class (little schooling, no 'connections', imitating middle-class appearance and manner); attempts to become educated, cultured or higher in class were mocked or thwarted deliberately (Crossick 30). They, too, saw their non-manual jobs as a step up and aspired to rise to a partnership, set up in business or rise by merit in a clerical scale (Crossick 21), but might see those ambitions blocked by forces outside their control: cracks in the promotion ladder, increase in scale of capitalisation, work becoming 'routinized and impersonal' or 'increasingly menial' (Crossick 22). They, too, feared losing their jobs because beyond their office work, often tailored to a specific firm, 'the white collar employee had no skill, no ability' (Crossick 23). They had more independence than shop girls because they were not required to 'live in' and could marry and have families. But if they wanted to be seen as more like their middle-class employers, they, too, did not organise for better wages or working conditions; trade unions were seen as beneath them (Crossick 24–6). Self-help, not political response, was the solution, and thus, Crossick notes, the 'upsurge of interest in commercial education ... Adult education became the individual's chance for salvation' (28).[18]

Virginia Stephen's students in 1905, if like Richards's 1890 demographics (101), were between 15 and 35 years old and thus born between 1870 and 1890. The 1870 Education Act meant they probably received an elementary education geared to the working classes (see 120–2). Secondary education was not possible for other than the privileged classes until 1902 (S. J. Curtis 193–4; Arata 56; Richards 88), and even after 1908 and the introduction of the free place system, A. Little and J. Westegaard note that

> only relatively small numbers of pupils from humble homes were to enter the secondary schools. Of boys and girls born before 1910 an estimated 37 per cent from professional and managerial families received secondary education, whereas only 8 per cent came from the classes below; for the 1910–19 age group the proportions were 47 and 17 per cent respectively. (Read 34–5)

Access to higher education at the established universities was also impossible for all except the most extraordinary working-class student.[19] Early in the nineteenth century, when Oxford and Cambridge were the only institutions of higher learning in England, they shared about 1,500 students between them (Heyck 195); the classics or mathematics education they offered was reserved for upper-class males and was meant to prepare them for service to Church or State. But such severely limited access to education had created a strong desire for it – Mechanics' Institutes, the Working Men's College, the Workers' Educational Association, the University of London (a secular alternative to Oxford and Cambridge), the university extension system and institutions like Morley College were all part of a burgeoning adult education movement attempting to feed people hungry for knowledge.

Because Virginia Stephen's students with an elementary education would have been taught under the mechanistic and rote-driven Revised Code of 1862, their encounters with Morley College's liberal arts curriculum were probably difficult or unsettling at first. Richards notes how eager and hardworking the students were and how many succeeded; he speaks with justifiable pride about student achievements, particularly in university extension courses (118–19, 114). But he also says one examiner noticed a 'common failing', the 'inability to marshal information adequately and direct it to answering a particular question'. The answers, wrote the examiner, were what

> might be expected from intelligent persons who had taken a real interest in the lectures, but had little general knowledge, and less intellectual discipline [. . .]. Questions requiring a knowledge of history or of institutions naturally were not so well answered as questions relating to the special interests of the working class . . . . (Richards 114–15)

The examiner's statement is remarkably like Virginia Stephen's July 1905 perception that her students have 'no power of receiving [a set of disconnected lectures] as part of a whole, & applying them to their proper ends' ('Report' 204). Her students were willing and capable, but lacked a general context in which to put new knowledge, and she faulted Morley for not doing more to provide such intellectual scaffolding.[20] As Melba Cuddy-Keane puts it, Stephen saw 'little problem with basic literacy'; rather, problems stemmed from 'class and circumstance: lack of opportunity, lack of time, and lack of comfort and familiarity with knowledge' (*VW* 83). No matter how bright or eager, many students lacked the prior knowledge and intellectual foundation for easily incorporating new learning. They not only needed knowledge; they also needed frameworks, the ability to acquire context, and skill in connecting their new learning to those contexts.

Virginia Stephen's students would also have had limited, if any, access to a library, since libraries in England were not truly free or public until 1919 (McAleer 48; Altick, *ECR* 213–39). Most of the libraries that existed charged a fee. The great Victorian commercial circulating libraries like Mudie's charged readers a guinea a year to borrow books (Altick 295), and libraries that functioned as 'side lines to the barbering, confectionery, news-vending, stationery, and tobacco trades' in London charged a penny a volume rental fee (Altick 217). Even after World War I, as Ida Rex, a teacher in Hackney notes, poor children had very little access to books: 'children borrowed books to take home, although there was a very poor library at the school. I don't remember much about the public libraries – there wasn't one in Hackney Wick' (29). And as Cuddy-Keane explains, even when free libraries began to make books available to the working and lower middle classes at the beginning of the twentieth century, 'methods of book borrowing were still nothing short of intimidating' (*VW* 109; see also Hammond 96–9).

Thus, when Miss Stephen walked into her class to teach 'anaemic shop girls', she confronted not only class difference, but the extraordinarily wide gap between educational backgrounds that class had created and reinforced for centuries. Her education may have been poor, but her family's class and her father's support of her reading meant she possessed a wealth of contextual knowledge her students simply could not have had.[21] She had to learn about the gap itself and its nature – what did her students not know? – and then how to decrease that gap. Her teachers on this new educational journey would be the experience at Morley itself, the principal who hired her, Mary Sheepshanks, and her students.

Notes

1. Denis Richards calls it 'something of a landmark in the history of the women's movement, as well as in that of British adult education' (98), and Oldfield notes women served both on the college's governing body and as administrators (*SP* 65).
2. See Andrea Geddes Poole on Emma Cons's 'subversive' work (14).
3. Cons was responsible for the Coffee Hall project, theatrical management details and the South London Dwellings Company management at one point (Richards 55–6). Tireless, she would have insisted Morley was 'the creation of many hands', but Richards says Cons deserves the name founder; she 'contributed the ideas, the determination, and nine-tenths of the work' (79). Richards calls her 'one of the greatest women of the nineteenth century' and recounts a story that captured her attempts 'to bridge the gulf between the classes': at Emma Cons's death in 1912, Lilian Baylis received a message of regret from a representative of the King and Queen and from a Lambeth scavenger (whose job was to clean streets by sweeping, scraping and removing dirt) on the same day (174).
4. For more on Samuel Morley, see Parry, Hodder.
5. See also Janet Sacks, *Morley College: A 125th Anniversary Portrait*, particularly 9–39.
6. At Morley's founding, evening classes for working people were available in four formats: village schools for younger adults in the three Rs; Mechanics' Institutes focused on 'scientific principles and their practical application'; socio-politically motivated institutions offering liberal, humanistic studies, such as the Working Men's College in London; and university extension lectures (Richards 89–91). Thus, Morley's 'advanced study' filled a different niche. Being a college did not mean it offered higher education leading to a bachelor's degree, but that it had an organised collegiate atmosphere, with flourishing clubs and societies (its third mission). Morley offered its students a wide range of opportunities, from elementary to university-level classes (Richards mentions a university extension class in astronomy, for example [102]), but as Mary Sheepshanks writes in *The Long Day Ended*, her unpublished autobiography, 'Very few of the students had had any secondary education' (*LDE* 30).
7. In 1956, Richards says no students were coming to Morley for qualifications or certificates or degrees; they were coming for love of learning and fun (5).
8. Nicolson notes students could 'play a definite part in the administration of the College, in the choice of subjects, and in the emphasis given to those subjects' (xvii); Morley was not governed democratically, but it had 'sufficient democratic machinery to allow the views and feelings of the teachers and students to be expressed and considered' (Richards 94).
9. Sheepshanks says technical courses like those in electricity were abandoned as the Polytechnics grew, though general and commercial courses were still offered. Oldfield

claims 'Most students entered for a three-year course and wrote weekly papers' (*SP* 66), but Sheepshanks says that about Workers' Educational Classes, not about Morley in general (*LDE* 33–4).
10. See Alexander Paterson for additional details about the area's extreme poverty.
11. As Richards notes, Emma Cons did not believe in giving up on anyone (36, 74–5).
12. Morley College still thrives. Now a 'specialist designated institution', Morley recently exhibited printmaking, bookbinding and ceramics in its gallery, specialises in textile design, jewelry and various book arts, and in its spring/summer 2017 magazine featured student poetry written after a visit to the Vanessa Bell exhibit at the Dulwich Picture Gallery (17–18).
13. Lindsay Martin calls attention to the change in the gender make-up of Virginia Stephen's classes over the course of her tenure at Morley – they were filled entirely by women at first and entirely by men at the end (25, 22). Her classes, whose type changed as she continued teaching, began at 9 p.m.
14. Many well-intentioned educational institutions for the working classes, using teaching methods from middle- and upper-class institutions, attracted lower-middle-class students, and then the working classes for whom the institutions had been intended stayed away. See Altick, *ECR* 191–4, 209–11. By the time Richards published his history, Morley students were more and more middle-class in 'virtues, vices, outlook and income'. In 1949, Eva Hubback's proposal to drop 'for Working Men and Women' from official documents was implemented (273–4).
15. These lists provide a fascinating glimpse into changing technology. There was one 'typewriter' in 1894–5; by 1904–5, seven typists; by 1906–7, eleven. Telegraphists were not on the list in 1894; there were nine in 1904–5 and twelve in 1906–7. Telephonists appeared in 1906–7.
16. See Hosgood, 328–9, for details about the complex wage structure for shop assistants. Lorna Poole notes that part of the income for running the small recreational libraries created by employers for live-in shop assistants sometimes came from fines levied on residents (42–3). For other information on shop assistants, see P. C. Hoffman, Wilfred B. Whitaker, Joseph Hallsworth and Rhys J. Davies. For a literary treatment of shop girl life, see Cicely Hamilton's *Diana of Dobson's*.
17. Jonathan Wild notes the two-tier reality portrayed in Walter Besant's *All in a Garden Fair*: 'ambitious rising clerks' with friends, influence and money, and 'hopeless clerks' who rarely 'progress beyond letter copying, ledger work and limited salaries' (14). Interestingly, in two letters written after her Morley teaching ended, Virginia Stephen mentions writing like a clerk. In the first, she labels such writing 'quite harmless' (*L1* 336), perhaps meaning the ineffectual attempts of a writer trapped in a business job. In the second, she says she has been writing 'like a Bank Clerk' (*L1* 397), suggesting a clerk's drudgery in a monotonous job. See Wild for an analysis of the late nineteenth-century literary portrayals of the clerk (9–32).
18. Crossick discusses the antagonism between the working and lower middle classes, reasons for it, and its impact on social and educational institutions (48–52). See also G. L. Anderson, Michael J. Childs, Jonathan Wild and Michael Heller. Heller disputes some of Crossick's and Anderson's conclusions.
19. Donald Read writes that 'Four or five late Victorian working-class children out of a thousand could hope by winning a series of scholarships' to climb up the narrow ladder from elementary school to grammar school to university (34).
20. Compare, too, Emily Davies's insight about middle-class girls' schooling in 1863: 'women "have never been instructed in general principles"' (qtd in Reimer, 'Worlds' 202).
21. In a 1999 account, *A Hope in the Unseen: An American Odyssey from the Inner City to the Ivy League*, Ron Suskind records a heartbreaking moment when the gap between Cedric Jennings's extremely poor Washington, DC, high-school education

and that of his new Brown University peers becomes startlingly clear to him. Cedric wanders around the bookshop and gazes at 'Sylvia Plath's *The Bell Jar*, Hemingway's *For Whom the Bell Tolls*, a biography of Theodore Roosevelt, another of Woodrow Wilson', all of whom might as well be 'people from another country'. When a stack of new biographies that put 'Churchill's bulldog mug right in [his] face' confronts him, he thinks he should know who it is and surreptitiously looks through the book: '"Churchill," he whispers after a moment, committing it to memory. "Prime minister of England during World War Two." Then he gently replaces the book, looking up to make sure no one has spotted him' (184).

Chapter 7

Learning from Morley College

Virginia Stephen's education gave her no framework for understanding the working-class students she was asked to teach. She was a novice, with no theoretical information at her disposal about class difference and little experience with it. Her everyday experience of class was anchored in an unconscious maintaining, not erasing; hierarchies were accepted as a matter of course; attitudes about difference were not identified, discussed or questioned. Given her prior experience, knowledge and context, it is not surprising her comments about students sometimes seem detached or condescending. We still struggle to create equitable social policies and living arrangements, even with a wealth of information about class, difference and diversity.

Information Virginia Stephen did not have. Recent scholarship tells us early twentieth-century London was home to a great variety of people: tens of thousands of people in London in 1901 had been born in Czechoslovakia, Italy and Germany; the Irish Catholic population was around 435,000; and by 1900, the Jewish population had risen to around 135,000 due to Europe's pogroms (Schneer 7–8). Other kinds of difference were inaccurately perceived as being located in the Empire, not in London (J. Whitaker 481). Jonathan Schneer estimates around 1,000 Indians lived in London in 1901 (184); says over 1,300 Chinese lived in England and Wales by 1911 (the *Westminster Gazette* mentioned Chinese laundries in 1900) (266 n9); and notes 'a sprinkling' of African and West Indian immigrants 'organized the world's first Pan-African Conference' in 1900 with W. E. B. Du Bois as opening speaker (8).[1] Yet conscious awareness of this diversity was minimal. Whitaker's Almanack for 1917, for example, lists separate demographic information for only the Jewish population (Whitaker 290) and 'foreigners' (486–7). Thus, Stephen had little knowledge of other peoples in London and no awareness she should have it. The concept, let alone any resulting obligation, was not on the cognitive map. Activists had been working to make class inequity and solutions visible, but such efforts were easily confused with Victorian middle-class moral pronouncements and, for Stephen, with her mother's charitable service, making it difficult for her to consider, let alone confront, class assumptions. Woolf would later wrestle with class, if not always successfully,[2] but in 1904, Stephen had much to learn.

When Virginia Stephen began teaching at Morley, she knew little about teaching, her students or their context, but as at home, she learned from teachers – a mentor and her students – about the nature of education, the forces of class and the craft of writing. Miss Sheepshanks taught her about institutional constraints, Morley's philanthropic character and, indirectly, her writing. Her students taught her about classroom possibilities, pedagogy, educational barriers and dialogic exchanges. As Virginia Woolf, she turned those lessons into pedagogical strategies in her essays: creating a space in which the potential for growth exists, providing context that lowers barriers to learning, and identifying with readers and anticipating their needs.

Teachers

Virginia Stephen was a volunteer at Morley, teaching for free. When Denis Richards compared the Morley College of 1923–4 to the Morley College of 1889–90, he explains that whereas 'unpaid tutors had been the backbone of the staff' when the school opened, by the later date, only two 'voluntary' teachers remained (213).[3] Stephen worked at Morley between those two extremes, from 1905 to 1907, when the 'Thanks of the Council' column in the annual reports acknowledged seven voluntary teachers in the 1904–5 and 1905–6 academic years and ten voluntary teachers in the 1906–7 and 1907–8 years (*MCAR* 1904–5 6; *MCAR* 1905–6 7; *MCAR* 1906–7 8; *MCAR* 1907–8 15). Salaries of thirty-one teachers (nineteen men, twelve women) were in the 1906–7 budget (*MCAR* 10), so one-quarter of Morley teachers were volunteers that year.

Stephen was at an institution that was one small square in a patchwork quilt of efforts to educate the working classes better. She was untrained. She had experienced excellent individualised Greek instruction from Janet Case, and she and her father had had almost daily discussions about literature at times. She knew how it felt to have a lecture go over her head: in 1897, her father's 'lecture [on Pascal] was very deep rather too deep for the audience; very logical & difficult for the ignorant (i.e. Miss Jan [Virginia herself]) to follow' (*PA* 79). She had also talked with Thoby about his Clifton and Cambridge classes. She had not watched many teachers at work, though she had learned from four to seven different instructors in her non-matriculation classes at the King's College Ladies Department. She had some experience of regularly sitting in a classroom with a group of students, but no experience of working through a sequenced curriculum. Morley did not provide any training, either, other than a College party where she discussed a class with 'nice enthusiastic working women who say they love books' (*PA* 218). Morley was not unique in this regard; many educational institutions for the working classes depended on volunteer untrained lecturers. Some who lectured at the Working Men's College were eminent in their fields, such as Leslie Stephen, John Ruskin, Dante Rossetti and Edward Burne-Jones (T. Kelly, *AE* 185), but no one thought such lecturers might need orientation or training to reach their students.[4]

Indeed, in Virginia Stephen's world, teaching had only recently begun to be considered a profession requiring training and standards. Because elementary school teachers were recruited from the working classes and were needed in such great numbers after the 1870 Education Act (Holcombe 34; Heyck 209), the state required professional status and created training standards. Certified teachers had a secondary education and training at a teacher-training college affiliated with a university by nineteenth century's end (Holcombe 37). But the huge need for teachers to handle the growth in pupils from 1,873,000 in 1875 to 5,392,600 in 1914 (Holcombe 34) meant the numbers of untrained teachers with certificates and uncertificated or pupil-teachers also grew, the latter by twenty-four times between 1870 and 1895 (Tropp, cited in Heyck 209). Secondary teachers did not professionalise as quickly because only a small number of children had access to a secondary education and the chief qualification for a public-school teacher 'was simply to be a gentleman' (Heyck 202). As more public schools were created, particularly for girls, and the move toward a national system of secondary education gained momentum, secondary teachers, generally middle-class, demanded professional status and higher education (Holcombe 47–50).

The early twentieth-century assumption that England's teachers needed little professional training meant Morley did not give its instructors, voluntary or paid, much guidance. Morley did not have departments, and Executive Committee minutes do not mention requirements such as regular teacher meetings or pedagogical discussions. Some effort was made to have an annual voluntary teachers' meeting since the group could elect a member to the governing Council (*MCECM3* 57 [13 July 1905]), but early minutes record nothing more than those present, a vote, and an occasional issue with student level or attendance at social events (*MCECM2* 10–20 [reverse order]). The Executive Committee minutes of the 11 June 1906 meeting note 'The annual meeting of volunteer teachers to elect a member of Council postponed till October as no date can be found to suit the teachers at present' (*MCECM3* 79). In 1907, however, a meeting of voluntary English teachers was held in March (*MCECM3* [reverse order, twelve pages in]).[5]

Also, Virginia Stephen did not seem to have been required to participate in Morley's social life.[6] The Principal, Charles Roden Buxton, wrote in the 1905–6 Annual Report

> True education involves the intercourse of mind with mind; and such intercourse is promoted by Social Evenings and Soirées, by free and easy conversation with the teachers, by College Societies and Clubs, and by the Common Room, where students, before and after the classes, can find a comfortable seat, books and papers, and the chance of a talk. (*MCAR* 3)

Mary Sheepshanks felt obligated to attend many such functions, even on Saturdays and Sundays (Oldfield, *SP* 94), but the College did not require teachers to help create a collegial atmosphere. In 1899, at a voluntary teachers' meeting, it was agreed that if teachers 'attend[ed] the New Students' Teas, whenever possible, it would be a very good thing and would perhaps do more than any formal meetings to bring teachers into touch with each other and with the social life of the College' (*MCECM2* 18), but the phrase 'whenever possible' indicates the request was not codified.[7] Perhaps realising it needed to communicate expectations directly, the Executive Committee on 3 May 1907 suggested asking that teachers 'be given to understand that part of their duty was to keep the club or society connected with their class' (*MCECM3* 108). That proviso, though, was directed only at teachers supervising organisations, and paid teachers were probably more likely than voluntary ones to supervise the Chess Club, Debating Society, Magazine, Photographic Society, Women's Gymnastic Club or Field Club, to name just a few of the social opportunities available to students (Richards 125–7, 157–61; Oldfield 93–4).

Thus, Stephen seems to have operated like many adjuncts do now, coming to campus to teach class, then departing.[8] Her work at Morley occurred in a vacuum, with no support and few chances to talk with other instructors, which may be why she asked others to join her. 'There is work of all kinds going', she writes to Emma Vaughan, 'and they are perfectly *delighted* to find helpers' (*L1* 199, her emphasis).[9] Virginia Stephen's Morley College education was fragmented and lonely, just as her homeschooling had been. She learned valuable lessons about institutions, learning and class from Mary Sheepshanks and from students, but the process was not formalised or coherent.

Mary Sheepshanks's Mentorship

Julia Briggs calls Mary Sheepshanks one of Stephen's 'earliest mentors' (*IL* 89), but direct evidence about the Vice-Principal's interactions with the younger woman is slim. The evidence we do have – comments by Stephen about Sheepshanks's criticism, Stephen's July 1905 draft report to Morley, Sybil Oldfield's Sheepshanks biography, Morley archival information, and teaching information from the time – suggests Mary Sheepshanks, in trying to direct Stephen's teaching, ended by teaching the young writer what she did not want to do, either in the classroom or in her essays. Even so, Sheepshanks taught Virginia Stephen a great deal about education and class and also recognised and communicated a crucial component of Stephen's pedagogy to her, thus contributing to Virginia Woolf's development as an essayist.

Mary Sheepshanks, fairly well known in her day, might be almost totally forgotten now were it not for Oldfield's biography, *Spinsters of This Parish: The Life and Times of F. M. Mayor and Mary Sheepshanks*.[10] Her Morley College job offer proved pivotal to Virginia Stephen, though, because as Stephen wrote reviews and essays for newspaper readers she had to imagine, she also interacted with real working-class adult students at Morley. The relationship Stephen developed with them in the classroom led Woolf to develop a particular relationship between writer and reader in the essay. Teaching at Morley taught Woolf how to teach – in print.

Mary Sheepshanks went to Newnham, where she read Mediaeval and Modern Languages, received a Second Class and stayed for a fourth year when she realised she should have read Moral Science or History. While at Cambridge, she taught adult literacy classes in the Barnwell working-class district on Sundays (Oldfield, *SP* 36), which led to her true calling. At 23, she devoted herself to working in Southwark, where Alice Grüner, an ex-Newnhamite, had founded the Woman's University Settlement (Oldfield 47). She received professional training at the Settlement, which a scholarship paid for since her father would no longer support her, did social work and taught history at Morley (Oldfield 51).[11] When the Vice-Principal at Morley left, she applied for the job and was successful. She was 27 years old. Principal Caroline Martineau became ill with cancer a few weeks after Sheepshanks began her work there, and although Sheepshanks's title remained Vice-Principal when the school hired Charles Roden Buxton as Principal, he was often absent because of his political and social reform efforts on behalf of the working class (Richards 148–9), and she became, in effect, the 'highly competent Principal of the college for the next fourteen years' (Oldfield 67). Oldfield adds that Mary Sheepshanks had been a pioneer woman social worker and became a pioneer woman educational administrator (67), guiding Morley through troubled times. Sheepshanks later held important positions in the National Union of Suffrage Societies, the International Woman Suffrage Alliance, and Women's International League for Peace and Freedom.[12] She fought to make the UK accept Belgian refugees, helped send medical assistance to Republicans in the Spanish Civil War and spoke and wrote for various causes.

She was also very good at her job – 'able' as Virginia Stephen and later Woolf consistently said (*PA* 217; *L2* 76–7; *D1* 225–6) – and Richards says she was an administrator of 'great intellectual and administrative ability', possessing 'exceptional breadth of culture and determination of character' (142). But Sheepshanks later saw 'serious drawbacks' to her work:

> I earned very little money [£100], there were no avenues to promotion and, worst of all, the work being in the evenings cut me off from London social life. I had many friends and many invitations and could have had a gay time, but evening work made it impossible. One evening a week I had free . . . Week-ends too had often to be sacrificed to Saturday evening fixtures at the College. (*LDE* 32)

Oldfield says Sheepshanks, trying to maintain some social life, often grabbed a cab after classes were over at 10.30 and raced to the Stephens' on Thursdays or the Sangers' on Fridays 'just when her hosts were hoping that their guests would soon leave' (96).[13] Sheepshanks cared about Morley and its students, particularly the women, whom she noticed were less confident than the men, and Oldfield notes her special efforts on their behalf: relaxing rules about dress to prevent self-consciousness, encouraging participation in clubs and debates to increase verbal skills, and offering single lectures on literary and social history topics to provide humanities education without a commitment to an entire course. But her dedication to Morley's mission meant six or seven nights a week at the college and little balance in her life (93–4).

Mary was competent, intelligent, caring and hardworking, but had difficulty connecting to people; her 'severe and somewhat unexpressive features as well as her unbending posture' made her hard to approach (Oldfield 97). Neither parent had seemed interested in her – she was one of seventeen children (thirteen survived) – and when she went to university, her sister wrote, she developed 'very advanced views' that their father frowned on, increasing her isolation from family (Muir 179). She suffered from an unrequited love for Theodore Llewelyn Davies,[14] and when he died, was deeply miserable for quite some time. Flora Mayor, visiting a soirée in 1903, noticed no one from Morley talking to her, and Oldfield says though Sheepshanks yearned to be on easy terms with students, she never was (97, 96). Oldfield adds that

> Mary Sheepshanks was a tall [6 feet!], upright woman with bespectacled, brilliantly blue eyes and a brusque manner. Incomparably articulate, her exceptional intellectual competence masked deep personal insecurity; she found it difficult to believe she was liked.... All her life she lacked [her friend] Flora's attractiveness and magnetism – and knew she did. (97)

When she did reach out to others, including Virginia Stephen, they sometimes perceived her as cynical or discontented, and after Davies's death, she became a 'byword in her own circle for being a bitter, self-pitying depressive' (Oldfield 97–8, 141; *L1* 439; see also *D1* 225–6 on her 'bitterness').

Mary Sheepshanks was ten years older than Virginia Stephen, but the two women had many things in common: struggles within the patriarchal family, feminism, suffrage, education's importance, pacifism, agnosticism.[15] Oldfield, Anne Olivier Bell and Julia Briggs all say she and Virginia were friends (*SP* 96; *D1* xxiv; *IL* 112), and she was indeed an occasional guest at the Stephen Thursday evenings in Bloomsbury. Their interests make a friendship likely, yet Lee comments, Sheepshanks 'was one of the public-spirited women for whom Virginia had such mixed feelings .... Morley College linked Virginia Stephen to her mother's and Stella's world of late-Victorian good works for women' (*VW* 218). Because Sheepshanks's Morley administrative work kept her from becoming an integral part of the Bloomsbury set, Stephen interacted with her chiefly through a philanthropic rather than an intellectual nexus of relationships, beginning with Ella Crum through Charles Roden Buxton, who became a Labour Party politician.

Ella Crum, a friend of Violet Dickinson's, a painter, and Stephen's introduction to Bruce Richmond and the *TLS* reviewing world (*PA* 224, 234), devoted a great deal of time to Morley College, both as Ella Sieveking (Vice-Principal from 1891 to 1894 and Vice-President and Council member in 1895) and as Mrs Crum (Vice-President, Council member, or Honorary Secretary between 1895 and 1913). Ella may have been why Miss Sheepshanks approached Virginia Stephen in the first place, and crucially, Sheepshanks tried to persuade the young woman to teach at Morley by telling her she would 'be of the greatest use' (*L1* 172). Framing Virginia Stephen's teaching as a charitable service rather than as a pedagogical, intellectual or creative enterprise may have created tension between the two women, a barrier difficult to cross when it came time to discuss teaching and learning.[16] Ironically, Miss Sheepshanks's attempts to welcome Miss Stephen into her world may have served only to push Stephen away.

When, for example, Sheepshanks asked Stephen to attend a dinner with Mr Buxton, she 'plunge[d]' Stephen into a 'philanthropic society', a 'society' that made her feel 'odd', as though she were 'living on the other side of the river of a sudden'. She felt compelled to discuss her 'good – would be good at any rate – works' (*L1* 198), and perhaps felt pressure to give more to the College, to move literally and figuratively into another space, although tellingly, not as a writer, but as a philanthropist. At this dinner, she was nearly finished teaching her English History course and did not have any books to review, so described herself to Violet as 'rising in philanthropic circles, as I sink in literary ones' (*L1* 193). Perhaps the difference between social and literary concerns seemed particularly stark at the time because everything was changing, everything was new: the give and take of Bloomsbury evenings, her Morley teaching, her entry into reviewing. Virginia Stephen's discomfort with that philanthropic society may have made her devotion to literature seem opposed to her teaching.

It was unfortunate, too, that Stephen read Sheepshanks's confessions about her early life as 'vapid and melancholy' rather than as attempts to confide or find a friend (*L1* 378).[17] After Stephen's Morley years, she mentioned Sheepshanks less frequently: she and Leonard asked 'Miss Harris the great and Miss Sheepshanks the able' to dine in 1916 (*L2* 76–7),[18] and when she came to dinner in 1918, Woolf writes, 'she comes out abler, better informed, more rational than I remembered her in the days of Fitzroy Square' (*D1* 225–6). In 1923, Woolf asked her to talk about Peru for the Women's Cooperative Guild and visited her in Golders Green, where she 'beat up the waters of talk, as I do so courageously, so that life mayn't be wasted . . . . Somehow, extraordinary emotions possessed me' (*D2* 246). But she never mentioned her after that, and the elderly Sheepshanks recalled that both Woolf and Bertrand Russell 'had the habit of dropping former friends about whom they no longer felt curious, "down an oubliette"' (*LDE* 42). Mary Sheepshanks was important in Stephen's life, their paths crossing frequently for a while at Morley and in Stephen's acquaintances network. But the relationship seems to have been more professional than friendly.

When Mary Sheepshanks broached the idea of teaching at Morley to Virginia Stephen, she mentioned two options, a 'social evening' or teaching English grammar ('I have had to tell her that I am not sociable, and I dont know any grammar,' Stephen writes to Violet [*LI* 171]).[19] But Stephen's first term at Morley sounds more like the social evening assignment Sheepshanks outlined, combining 'amusement and instruction – a little gossip and sympathy, and then "talks" about books and pictures' (*L1* 172). Indeed, Stephen calls her class her 'girls club' several times (*PA* 217, 231, 238)[20] and describes preparing to talk about a wide range of subjects in Lent Term 1905.[21] Stephen taught well enough to have some students follow her since she taught English History in Easter Term 1905 because her students 'beg[ged] me to lecture steadily at [it] . . . "from the beginning"' (*PA* 255). Next, she was assigned to English Composition, which she taught in Michaelmas Term 1905 and Lent and Easter Terms 1906,[22] and in Lent and Easter Terms 1907, Advanced Composition. In her last teaching term, Michaelmas 1907, she taught a literary Reading Circle on Keats, Shelley and Browning (L. Martin 24).[23] Thus, Virginia Stephen taught every term at Morley between January 1905 and December 1907 except for Michaelmas 1906, when the Stephens travelled to Greece and Constantinople and Thoby died of typhoid fever in November. She taught eight courses, five in English Composition (see Appendix 3 for her Morley College teaching schedule).

Although Mary Sheepshanks had given classes for Lambeth pupil-teachers, she did not, apparently, give Virginia Stephen any teacher training. Probably Miss Sheepshanks conveyed some sense of expectations and student level when Stephen went to 'see her, and talk over my views' (*L1* 172); perhaps a line crossed out in Stephen's draft report reflects that conversation. Stephen cancelled 'In spite of warning, I found them of a higher standard on the whole' ('Report' MS; C. Jones 215), which suggests the assumption about her students' intelligence in the revised sentence was not entirely her own: 'On the whole they were possessed of more intelligence than I expected, though that intelligence was almost wholly uncultivated' ('Report' 203). Someone – Miss Sheepshanks, another at Morley or a friend – 'warn[ed]' her about Morley students' supposed intellectual level, perhaps as preparation. Miss Sheepshanks did, all the same, encourage the beginner, so Stephen wrote to Violet, 'I dont mind trying' (*L1* 172). However halfhearted a pledge that seems, Stephen did more than try; she committed herself to teaching and took her responsibility seriously. Jane Dunn comments on the 'characteristic thoroughness and wit' of her approach (136). Quentin Bell says she seems to have given 'considerable thought' to the preparation of her classes (1 105). The notes she took about English history from Freeman's *History of the Norman Conquest* in her 1904–5 journal (*PA* 278–80); the English history outline in a notebook labelled 'Authorities, The English Kingdoms';[24] and two surviving lectures (see Appendix 4) certainly bear him out. Phyllis Rose notes Stephen chose to teach before Leonard, with his socialist politics, was on the scene, and she planned her lessons 'dutifully and at great length in advance' (90). 'It is hard work', Stephen writes, not sure what her students know already or how much they are absorbing (*PA* 246), but also 'really interesting' (*L1* 199). Without training, without experience, without really knowing what she was doing, Virginia Stephen gave a great deal of time, thought and effort to her teaching.

Perhaps most important, at the same time as she was preparing and teaching classes, she was learning and practising her craft as a writer. On 15 February 1905, for example, she finished both a lecture on Cellini for her class and an article on essay-writing for *Academy & Literature*. Then she revised a review for the *Guardian*, 'read 2 review books sent by the Times – & to my girls club' (*PA* 237–8). A brief letter reveals how teaching wove through her life:

[January? 1905]
My Violet,
   Of course come any time – dinner, tea, lunch.
   Mrs L: asks for articles. I hope you didn't drop a hint?
   A mercy to see you in this weary world.
   Just off to Morley
                        Yr. AVS (*L1* 175)

It is all there: social life, work in early journalism, friendship with a woman, teaching.

Stephen's early letters indicate she and Mary Sheepshanks discussed her classes twice, though possibly they had more such conversations. In both, Sheepshanks criticised her teaching, first in late June 1905 when Stephen was teaching English History and then in November 1905 when she was teaching English Composition. The letters do not say exactly what instigated the criticism or what it consisted of; they only describe Mary's behaviour. On 29 June 1905, Virginia wrote to Violet that 'We have six people dining here .... I have been doing entirely the wrong thing at Morley – Sheepshanks showed wolf's fangs' (*L1* 194). Why Sheepshanks showed 'wolf's fangs' just then is a puzzle. Although miserable for most of 1905, Mary always maintained a 'strictly professional' stance toward Virginia (Oldfield, *SP* 142–3). We cannot be sure what the 'wrong thing' was, either, or why it drew such sharp comment, though see Chapter 8. Stephen was doing what students had asked, lecturing on early English history (*PA* 255), she had a colourful teaching method (*LI* 191), and she probably was approaching the course differently from how Miss Sheepshanks would have (Oldfield 67).

Virginia Stephen's draft report on teaching at Morley, dated July 1905, directly follows Sheepshanks's showing of 'wolf's fangs' on 29 June. The report probably continued the earlier 'sketch' she cited in her journal on 25 March 1905, in which she reflected on 'how I started, & which girls came' because it 'may be of interest in future terms' (*PA* 256);[25] Stephen describes a 'class of working women whom I have already mentioned', says she had 'already described' the four working women who attended, and notes her 'remarks this time' merely develop that 'tentative sketch' ('Report' 202). Such language might mean these reports were regular requirements of her position;[26] if so, would they not have been turned in to Miss Sheepshanks? Her report points out that history does not please 'those in authority [Sheepshanks?]' because it was the 'least popular subject in the College', but defends it as 'one of the most important' and defends her approach of (1) including 'one good "scene" upon which I hoped to concentrate their interest'; (2) talking from notes rather than reading a lecture; (3) trying 'to make the real interest of history – as it appears to me – visible to them'; and (4) sending her students home 'with a sheet of hard dates' so they would 'have something solid to cling to' ('Report' 203). If, in fact, this report responds directly to Sheepshanks's criticism, it implies Sheepshanks critiqued both the course subject and Stephen's pedagogy. In turn, Stephen criticises Morley (and by implication, Sheepshanks) for saying it preferred having 'a great number' in 'a less valuable subject, like English Composition' than having a few students study English history. She also chastises Morley for not providing students with the context and framework necessary for receiving courses as 'part of a whole, & applying them to their proper ends' ('Report' 203–4).[27]

Mary Sheepshanks and Virginia Stephen clearly wanted the same thing, to educate Morley students, but Sheepshanks may not have understood Stephen's unconventional approach and Stephen certainly did not understand the administrative pressures on Sheepshanks. Since, as Harold Nicolson says, Morley was unique because its curriculum was 'suggested from below rather than imposed from above' and students often demanded the humanities and arts rather than 'practical instruction' (xv; see also Oldfield, *SP* 65), it is puzzling that Sheepshanks seems to have perceived a student-requested history course as being the 'wrong thing' for Virginia Stephen to teach. To Stephen, being told she must 'stop at King John' and tell her students if they wanted to continue learning history, they 'can hear eight lectures on the French Revolution' ('Report' 203) abdicated Morley's responsibility: the lectures would be 'dropped' into her students' minds 'like meteors from another sphere', experienced as 'disconnected fragments' by students who had no way of integrating them into a whole ('Report' 204). Stephen's comment reflects the reality of her students' prior education (Cuddy-Keane, *VW* 83). Her anger at Morley and Sheepshanks about what she perceived as Morley's lack of coherence – the College was not doing enough to help students put the pieces of their education together or to experience their education as a cumulative process ('Report' 204) – may also have stemmed from her own fragmented education. She probably did not know about the Acton Plan or students' difficulty in following it. She could not have known Sheepshanks had kept social history and the humanities alive at Morley (Oldfield 93) or that she had been forced to pay attention to numbers during an earlier catastrophic enrolment drop, when she fought to 'inject renewed vitality into Morley' and 'almost single-handed' got numbers back up (Richards 141, 149–51; Oldfield 92–3).

Then, in a 9 November [1905] letter to Violet Dickinson, Stephen reports Mary Sheepshanks's second expression of dissatisfaction during a visit to her English Composition class: 'It is I suppose the most useless class in the College; and so Sheepshanks thinks. She sat through the whole lesson last night; and almost stamped with impatience' (*L1* 210). Stephen suspects her particular course (or composition itself?) is useless and thinks Sheepshanks agrees, conveying displeasure with it or her teaching. Virginia Stephen defends herself to Violet by using a familiar excuse, the mixed nature of her class and students' working hours:

> 10 people; 4 men 6 women . . . . But what can I do? I have an old Socialist of 50, who thinks he must bring the Parasite (the Aristocrat, that is you and Nelly [Lady Robert Cecil]) into an essay upon Autumn; and a Dutchman who thinks – at the end of the class too – that I have been teaching him Arithmetic; and anaemic shop girls who say they would write more but they only get an hour for their dinner, and there doesn't seem much time for writing. (*L1* 210)

Having been ordered to 'turn [her] mind' away from history and toward 'essay writing & the expression of ideas' ('Report' 203), Stephen may have struggled in the classroom and projected her own sense of being useless on to Sheepshanks's supposed opinion of the course. Or perhaps what Sheepshanks perceived as Stephen's struggle with English Composition reflected an uneasy position for the course within Morley's curriculum (see Chapter 8).

What Virginia Stephen could not have known was that Mary Sheepshanks had written a miserable letter to Bertrand Russell on 6 November 1905 about work's cold comfort. Pining for affection and feeling deserted, she writes, 'Everyone else seems to have their life full of people and interests, and I have failed to fill mine' (qtd in Oldfield, *SP* 140). Two days later, she 'almost stamped with impatience' in Stephen's English Composition class. But a professional rather than personal reason for Sheepshanks's behaviour may be that Stephen's teaching method simply was not what Sheepshanks expected or wanted. Such a reason may underlie Sheepshanks's suggestion a year later that Stephen become Morley's Librarian because, Virginia writes to Violet, she 'thinks my gift is rather influence than direct intellectual teaching' (*LI* 264).[28] It is unclear what 'direct intellectual teaching' of composition would have looked like as opposed to 'influence' – perhaps prescribing rather than guiding, dictating rather than coaching, lecturing rather than suggesting? In any case, Sheepshanks or the Executive Committee asked Virginia Stephen to teach Advanced Composition in 1907 rather than become Morley's librarian.

Perhaps without meaning to, Mary Sheepshanks taught the young teacher the reality of institutional constraints. No matter what a teacher wants or what students ask for, sometimes the institution needs something else, or cannot allow experimentation, or has external demands that prevent flexibility. Ironically,

Morley's administrative structure was indeed more responsive to students than many other educational institutions were, though Stephen could not have known that. Virginia Stephen's Morley experience, however, probably contributed to Virginia Woolf's antipathy to the institutionalisation of English in essays such as 'A Professor of Life' and 'Why?'

In addition, Mary Sheepshanks may have unwittingly reinforced Virginia Stephen's dislike of philanthropy. Morley College, by not offering its voluntary teachers a pedagogical paradigm within which to perceive their work, made it harder for Sheepshanks to be an effective mentor and for Stephen to hear and learn from the Vice-Principal's interventions. Neither Mary Sheepshanks nor Morley can be faulted for this emphasis. They existed within a culture that valorised middle-class attempts (especially by women) to improve housing, education and working conditions for the lower classes. And in fact, Morley College made impressive gains by offering further education to working-class adults. But it, along with many other institutions, assumed untrained middle-class volunteer lecturers' desire to help would make them effective, that they knew how to teach and reach working-class learners. By emphasising philanthropy rather than pedagogy, Mary Sheepshanks implicitly kept the focus on class rather than on teaching and learning. As a result, she paradoxically prevented Virginia Stephen from examining her class attitudes and from seeing how literary and social interests might intertwine.

Ultimately, though, Mary Sheepshanks, by offering Virginia Stephen the opportunity to teach at Morley College, had a great impact on the young writer. Sheepshanks may not have been the teaching mentor Stephen needed at Morley, but she was one of the young woman's writing mentors, even if inadvertently. Her expectations about the nature of teaching, whatever they were, caused Stephen to reflect on her classroom work and defend her methods, which in turn affected how she later incorporated pedagogy into her writing. Sheepshanks's description of Stephen's gift as 'influence rather than direct intellectual teaching' also captures another kind of successful teaching, the sort of embedded pedagogy Woolf would later use in her essays. Mary Sheepshanks may have helped Virginia Stephen see what she did not want to do – didactically lecture, impose views, outline facts, insist on what and how to think – while simultaneously suggesting an imaginative alternative. Virginia Woolf would later use that lesson to create a subtle but powerfully effective pedagogy in her essays.

Students' Influence

If Sheepshanks unintentionally hindered, Morley students literally enlarged Virginia Stephen's world and thus her sense of audience as a neophyte book reviewer, and Virginia Woolf never forgot her work there or what that experience taught her. In a 1940 draft of a letter to Ben Nicolson defending Bloomsbury's efforts to reach beyond its circle, Woolf remembers trying to share what she had learned from her own 'very imperfect education' with the working classes at Morley (*L6* 419), and sixteen days before she died, she recalls 'very happy memories of Morley College' in a letter to Morley's Principal (Letter to Eva

Hubback 5). At the time, Stephen learned about institutional limitations from Miss Sheepshanks while her students confronted her with both educational deprivation and educational potential. Paying attention to them, Stephen learned about classroom possibility, flexibility and strategies for reaching students. Most important for the future essayist, Stephen's students engaged with her, teaching her about teaching and thus shaping Woolf's definition of the common reader and her interactions with her essay readers.

Not many numbers exist to describe Morley's student body when Stephen started, though later demographics suggest she faced a stubborn fact: her students' educational deprivation. Annual Reports for 1906–7 and 1907–8 document only numbers related to age and gender and the distinction between students enrolled and students attending (the latter determined grant monies). In 1908–9, it began recording numbers indicating previous elementary and secondary education, though without completion numbers. See Table 7.1, Morley College Demographics, which covers the period from 1906–7, when documenting began, up until 1913–14, when Ella Crum and Mary Sheepshanks retired.

These demographics suggest Virginia Stephen had many students her age or older, with most having no more than basic elementary schooling, an education, as noted in Chapter 6, focused on the three Rs and rote learning. When she writes, 'I have been teaching a Milkman to write English for 2 hours; and the effect is so singular that I had better say no more. It is like floating your brains in cold mist' (*L1* 281), she does not express sympathy for him or his struggles. But she captures the exhaustion of working with a student who almost certainly had no experience in composing sentences, paragraphs and essays in his previous schooling and who may have been years beyond that schooling. Her comment, though not empathetic, is not really directed at the milkman (was she giving him individual attention?). Rather, it reflects the reality of her students' educational background, her lack of training and experience, and the fatigue of working to get through, to cross barriers. Teaching can feel futile.[29]

Morley students gave Virginia Stephen practical pedagogical information about what they lacked – contextual framework, background for making sense of everything their intellects could take in, method for synthesising – but also about what they possessed – intelligence, desire, curiosity, wonder, ability, all influencing Stephen's pedagogy and purpose. Although Stephen did not understand much about the working classes or her students' lives before she began teaching, she respected their efforts to learn. She mentions to Madge Vaughan that the working women she meets 'are much too keen to let [her] off' – they want to be taught (*L1* 173). Similarly, she says her history course's regular attendants 'came with one serious desire in common' ('Report' 202).

She is convinced 'it would not be hard to educate them sufficiently to give them a new interest in life', and in a cancelled phrase immediately following, adds 'whether it were history, language, music or' ('Report' MS). She recognises their intelligence, though calling it 'almost wholly uncultivated' ('Report' 203). 'Uncultivated' often functions as a class-marked word suggesting lack of culture, good manners or refinement, but Stephen's gardening metaphor for her task, 'to prepare the soil for future sowers', supports an alternative interpretation ('Report' 203; see 15, 47, 163).[30] Perhaps the word functions more as a fact about

Table 7.1 Morley College Demographics, 1906–1914

	1906–1907	1907–1908	1908–1909	1909–1910[b]	1910–1911	1911–1912	1912–1913	1913–1914
16 yo		9M, 0W	13M, 1W	20M, 5W	14M, 10W	9M, 2W	7M, 5W	6M, 5W
17 yo	33M, 13W[a]	33M, 15W	32M, 11W	45M, 18W	50M, 26W	55M, 27W	49M, 30W	37M, 41W
18 yo	26M, 18W	27M, 13W	36M, 15W	33M, 15W	49M, 31W	43M, 22W	46M, 22W	46M, 43W
19 yo	29M, 8W	38M, 11W	32M, 22W	47M, 17W	54M, 17W	48M, 16W	38M, 23W	44M, 34W
20 yo	29M, 15W	31M, 10W	38M, 22W	44M, 25W	40M, 23W	35M, 18W	43M, 22W	45M, 46W
21+ yo	347M, 241W	385M, 236W	383M, 294W	490M, 229W	441M, 333W			391M, 387W
21 yo						30M, 21W	39M, 27W	
22 yo						38M, 28W	27M, 29W	
23 yo						34M, 26W	38M, 28W	
24 yo						34M, 25W	37M, 11W	
25+ yo						255M, 239W	249M, 235W	
Total M/W	464M, 295W	523M, 285W	534M, 365W	679M, 379W[d]	648M, 440W	581M, 424W	573M, 432W	569M, 556W
Students	759	807[c]	900[c]	1058	1088	1005[e]	1005[e]	1125[e]
Grant	386	427	476	Not recorded	526	611	567	708
Elem			All	548M, 317W	519M, 355W	475M, 334W	330M, 231W	414M, 403W
Sec			Not known	131M, 62W	129M, 85W	125M, 91W	154M, 129W	165M, 154W

a. Reports used the words men and women, and then boys/men and girls/women, so this table uses M & W.
b. Language used beginning with this report: Number of Students who received their previous education at Public Elementary schools only; Number of students who have attended Secondary Schools (earlier, report language combined the two levels of education: Number of Students who have received their previous education at Elementary Schools or at Secondary Schools).
c. Totals as recorded in MCAR; correct totals are 808 and 899 respectively.
d. Based on numbers in age categories, W total should be 309; however, numbers for elementary and secondary total 1058, so perhaps mistake made in recording the numbers for age categories.
e. In each of these three years, a discrepancy exists between total number of students and the total implied by the elementary and secondary level numbers. Gathering data about prior schooling may have been difficult and/or erratic in those years, or perhaps students reported incorrectly or not at all.

MCAR 1906–07 9
MCAR 1907–08 5
MCAR 1908–09 10
MCAR 1909–10 12
MCAR 1910–11 7
MCAR 1911–12 8
MCAR 1912–13 9
MCAR 1913–14 11

class-determined background than about inherent ability, with Stephen seeing that her students' brains had not been nurtured or fostered, an accurate observation: past teachers or institutions had not helped her students develop their intelligence or synthesising abilities. As Ursula Howard comments in her study of nineteenth-century writing literacy, 'For practitioners, under-education was not about failure by individuals but about individuals being systemically failed by schooling' (14–15). Seeing her students' potential, Virginia Stephen blames their prior education, determined by class, for leaving that potential fallow.

And Morley. Stephen's draft report suggests she gave her students more credit than Morley did, that at least some students could do more, were eager to do more. Even when she wondered if the past always 'remain[ed] a spectre' to them and asked herself 'how is it *possible* to make them feel the flesh & blood in these shadows?' ('Report' 203, her emphasis), her questions have more to do with their lack of education or the conditions of their lives than with their ability. She understood her task lay near the beginning of a gradual process of accumulating contextual knowledge. She sensed she needed to give them a historical skeleton, not flesh out a non-existent one. She noticed that even without a strong scaffolding upon which to hang additional knowledge, they did not always 'gape' in 'mere impotent wonder', but had begun to try 'to piece together what they heard; to seek reasons; to connect ideas' ('Report' 203). They had, in other words, begun to create what Virginia Woolf would call the common reader's contextual structure, however decrepit or shaky (E4 19).

Virginia Stephen's students also taught her about the fluid possibilities of growth inside a classroom, even classrooms that hold out little physical promise. Going to her first Morley class, Stephen went to the area behind the stage 'cut off by fire-proof walls and floors from all direct communication with it ... in order to shut out the sound of the entertainments from the classes' (Caroline Martineau qtd in Richards 84) and waited alone for fifteen minutes in a dismal room filled with tables and chairs, 'meditating how on earth to discuss Sir T. [Thomas] Browne under these conditions' (*PA* 224). Dreary though the rooms were (see also her draft 'report'), she seems to have learned how to focus on the potential within the classroom space, the students.

Little evidence exists for what students directly expressed to Virginia Stephen in the classroom; they taught her indirectly. Clues about what they taught lie in her reactions, which though few, indicate she heard her students, adapted accordingly and developed strategies for reaching them, all of which implies a belief in the possibility for learning inside a classroom. Stephen could not excise the class distinctions she had internalised over a young lifetime in her family, and when writing letters to friends, who were upper class and would have expected certain attitudes, she affirms class barriers rather than undercuts them. But her students seem to have taught her that within a classroom, the potential for more equitable relationships exists.

For all her shyness and supposed snobbishness, Virginia Stephen also seems to have been more at ease with students than Mary Sheepshanks. Surely her appearance, clothes and speech marked her as upper-middle class, and surely her brilliance was evident? But she apparently did not intimidate students. Quite the contrary. Stephen's journal entries and letters, full of remarks about her Morley classes during her first two terms, provide glimpses of her ability to listen and talk with students. They talked openly in class, consulted her about writing outside of class and asked her to teach history after her first teaching attempt. Not everything she tried worked: the Westminster Abbey excursion attracted only one student on a Saturday, leading her to say tiredly she was 'grind[ing] at my history with a sense of utterly unrequited energy' on Sunday (L1 192–3). Once, in a later composition class, everyone cut (L1 292). She wondered what six working women thought about when they looked at paintings (PA 246) and doubted they knew whether the Greeks or Romans came first (PA 255). Not sure what her students already knew or how much they were absorbing, Stephen revealed both awareness of real knowledge gaps and frustration about how to reach students who had not already inhaled contextual knowledge through reading. But perhaps what Sheepshanks meant by Virginia Stephen's 'influence' was her classroom ease, what Dunn calls her 'basic confidence' and 'enthusiasm' (136), a charismatic quality.

Even before her Morley work began, students told her what they wanted, 'a course of lectures', and although Stephen demurred (L1 173), she responded, putting together a series of lectures about a variety of subjects (see Chapter 8). Virginia Stephen was understandably nervous when she began teaching for the first time in January 1905, but the two women (who eventually became eight, perhaps through word of mouth) seem to have helped her relax; she rapidly became more comfortable in the classroom, 'reading' signals students sent and making extraordinary progress as a teacher over Lent and Easter Terms 1905. Those first two students were 'readier to talk than listen' (PA 224), so she abandoned written-out lectures, began talking from notes, and constructed her classes so they mixed lecture with conversation and discussion, including material from student lives. Student reaction in the classroom meant she increasingly considered their response to material, wondering if they would think it boring or dry. Although personal interests and experiences dictated many of her first-term lecture topics, she also chose subjects she thought they would be interested in (Venice, PA 225) or ones they may have suggested (Greek myths, L. Martin 22), and she followed through on their request for a course in English History in her second term ('Report' 202). She also seems to have realised that variety stimulated interest because, over the course of two terms, she invited a guest speaker, planned a field trip, encouraged students to write, prepared handouts, used vivid scenes to anchor lessons, showed pictures and maps, and lent books. Her extensive preparation, notes, letters and journal entries all point to a novice genuinely interested in reaching students.

Stephen's interactions with students taught her to change her approaches to both them and her subject matter. Her responses to them in her first two courses make it safe to assume she would have continued to change as necessary in subsequent classes. Indeed, Miss Sheepshanks's assessment of her 'gift' in December 1906, after Stephen had taught three Composition classes and right before she started teaching Advanced Composition, suggests her inclination to use indirect and lively approaches had continued to develop in response to student feedback.

From conversations with Burke and Miss Williams discussed in her draft 'report', Virginia Stephen learned her most important strategy for reaching students, crossing barriers, and communicating with readers: identify some common ground upon which to stand. She learned to negotiate difference by at least partially identifying with her students. Glimpsing a similarity between their struggles to learn and her own, she saw Miss Williams was the 'germ of a literary lady' and Burke could have been a writer under different circumstances ('Report' 202–3). She thus forged a link with others trying to educate themselves; they, too, were outsiders, having been excluded from a good education (resulting in an 'almost wholly uncultivated' intelligence or in 'wits sharpened by the streets'); they, too, desired learning, but were often overwhelmed by it (having 'tentacles languidly stretching forth from their minds' but gaping in 'mere impotent wonder'); and they, too, struggled to 'piece together' what they were learning, 'to connect ideas' into some cohesive whole. Her impulse, in her teaching and later in her essays, in the classroom and on the page, was to guide students and readers to 'substance' they 'could really grasp', to connect ('Report' 203–4).

Virginia Stephen did complain about students who did not show up, the time it took to prepare her weekly classes, and the school. Lindsay Martin thinks resentment about the time teaching takes or irritation at one's institution constitutes ambivalent commitment (25),[31] but no evidence exists for questioning Stephen's commitment. Indeed, many of her comments reveal a teacher taking her responsibility seriously, open to trying things and adjusting. Although not as many letters and journal entries exist for when she taught composition and the literary reading circle, and although her reviewing work increased, making it more challenging to balance class preparation and writing, the early evidence suggests Stephen would have continued to work hard to prepare for classes and be an effective teacher. Her being entrusted with teaching the first-ever Advanced Composition course at Morley after three terms of teaching the regular Composition course suggests institutional acknowledgement of her ability and commitment to teaching.[32]

Miss Sheepshanks gave Virginia Stephen opportunity, experience with an educational system and an assessment of her talent for subtle pedagogy; her students taught her the relationship between audience awareness and teaching. By their very presence, Stephen's students opened her up to different perspectives, attitudes and values. They taught her to pay attention, to consider the needs of those different from her, to think about the contextual framework necessary for learning. They taught her about barriers to learning: confusion and the lack of previous education, practice and intellectual or experiential contexts for new learning.

Real similarities exist between Virginia Stephen's education and her students' schooling: begun at home, erratic and fragmented, and narrow in some way; dependent on taking the initiative, maintaining motivation and developing discipline. What Stephen had that her students did not was the wealth, structure and context of her father's library. Her criticism of Morley College for not providing an overall framework within which students could fit their individual lectures and classes ('Report' 204) indicates her students made her aware of her privilege. As fragmented as her education had been, her father's library and guidance, a foundation all her other homeschooling could build on, gave her contextual advantages her students did not have.

Her students' desire to learn, make connections and be included, taught Virginia Stephen that within classroom space, barriers could be momentarily crossed and relationships formed; Virginia Woolf later realised classroom space could become the essay's 'room'. The necessity of paying attention to her working-class students and their learning taught Stephen and then Woolf to think beyond the audience she knew and create a learning space in which the essayist 'sting[s readers] wide awake and fix[es them] in a trance which is not sleep but rather an intensification of life' (*E4* 216). Inside the classroom, everyone can become a learner, including the teacher, so that for a while, labels and divisions can become less pronounced. Relationships grow out of shared learning experiences and possibility weaves in, over, through and around barriers within that space. No guarantees, no promise of permanence, just potential transformation. A good essay, Woolf writes, 'must draw its curtain round us, but it must be a curtain that shuts us in, not out' (*E4* 224). The essay becomes a potentially classless space in which writer and reader can temporarily cross barriers, within which learning and rambling and talking can occur. Virginia Woolf would later work to create essays that functioned like Virginia Stephen's classroom spaces, places where writer and reader could focus on learning together.

Notes

1. See Peter Fryer's *Staying Power: The History of Black People in Britain*, however, for a much more thorough study of Britain's Black population. See also Jane Marcus, *HD*, Michael Diamond, Gretchen Holbrook Gerzina and Deborah J. Rossum. W. E. B. Du Bois's 1903 third edition of *The Souls of Black Folk: Essays and Sketches* is in the Library of Leonard and Virginia Woolf with annotations by Leonard (K&M-V 66).
2. Woolf's class attitudes are complex; see Caughie (113–42) on her vacillation between insensitivity and inclusion. In some of Stephen's comments about Morley students, for example, her 'student bashing' seems almost *de rigueur* (and familiar to anyone who has worked in an educational institution); moreover, they simultaneously reveal acute awareness of how difficult learning is for those who lack contextual frameworks. See also Hermione Lee's 'Virginia Woolf and Offence' for a list of Woolf's offensive remarks and an astute analysis; see Lee's biography as well, along with Patricia McManus, who analyses Woolf, class and Lee's assessment of both. Woolf often found her own attitudes abhorrent; what a friend calls her meta awareness sometimes flashes on in the midst of a disgusting sentence. Woolf rationally understood the damage the class system had done in England: she knew no one, in any class, had escaped the corrosive effects of being either locked out or locked in, and she worked intellectually to cross and pull down barriers. But she found it difficult to understand working-class concerns and desires emotionally or to modify her auto-pilot reactions, behaviours or statements. She understood what Leonard and some friends did not, that abolishing capitalism probably meant their class would no longer have a secure income:

   > L. gave us a great many reasons why we should keep what we have, & do good work for nothing; I still feel, however, that my fire is too large for one person. I'm one of those who are hampered by the psychological hindrance of owning capital. (*D1* 101)

   But she did not understand why the working-class women in Margaret Llewellyn Davies's collection (*Life as We Have Known It by Co-Operative Working Women*) had conventional rather than rebellious or subversive views (*D5* 289; see Ruth Adam for some historical and sociological explanations, 99–109, 157–66).
   Her ideas about restructuring society were actually more radical than those of her

friends, and yet, as Mary Wilson argues, she chafed at having servants while simultaneously depending on them to maintain her writing lifestyle (55) (just as I, a privileged academic, protest against capitalism's cruelties while counting on invested funds for retirement). Caughie argues Woolf provides 'no one answer' to the question of how to change a system we are implicated in: 'Indeed, she shows us that we cannot answer this question once and for all but that we must answer it again and again' (136). Mary Madden perceptively notes the relationship between experiencing extremely stressful psychological trauma and relying on class boundaries and identifies something crucial about Woolf's class attitudes: '*Woolf was conscious* of a deep contradiction between her desire for radical social reform of constricting class codes and her own complicity (and enjoyment) in maintaining and sustaining the privileges of class' (56, my emphasis). Furthermore, she communicates rather than hides that awareness.

3. Executive Committee minutes indicate a variety of teacher types: volunteers, trained and paid teachers, lecturers in the university extension and London County Council organisations, and occasional guest lecturers.
4. Many such volunteers gave university-level lectures, making no concessions to their working-class audiences (Altick, *ECR* 194, 212).
5. Volumes 2 and 3 of the Executive Committee Minutes are organised as Volume 1 is, chronologically from page 1 onward, with pages numbered and an Index at the front. Closing the volumes, however, and turning them over (bottom to top with the spine remaining on the left), means discovering the Education Committee Minutes. In Volume 2, these reverse order pages are numbered. In Volume 3, they are not, although the meeting minutes are dated in chronological order. Thus the designation 'twelve pages in'.
6. Richards is justifiably proud of Morley's efforts to foster the 'corporate spirit' and create community at Morley (see particularly Chapter 7 on 'Play', 120–39). See also Poole, 168–72, for a discussion of Emma Cons's emphasis on citizenship and participation, and particularly her desire that 'the College's elite benefactors, by meeting "minds essentially like their own", [would] realise their kinship with working men and women' (171).
7. No indication is given, either, about how these expectations might have been communicated to teachers in later years.
8. Andrea Geddes Poole contrasts Virginia Stephen's and Gustav Holst's attitudes about Morley and its students and faults Stephen for not understanding Morley's mission (187–8), but no evidence exists to suggest anyone ever explained Morley's mission to her. Poole also does not discuss one other reason for the difference she describes: the contrast between Holst's and Stephen's Morley positions. Stephen was an unpaid, part-time volunteer. Holst applied for the position of music director, was interviewed along with two other applicants, and hired into a permanent position he held for years; his dedicated efforts to create reputable music programmes at Morley were wholeheartedly supported by Morley's administration. Understanding institutional mission is easier when fully *part* of an institution.
9. Emma Vaughn worked in the library for a while and then served Morley's Council as Honorary Secretary up until 1910 (L. Martin 25). Both Lindsay Martin and Quentin Bell use the verb 'roped in' to describe the efforts to induce friends and family to work at Morley, but Martin says Stephen did the requesting (25), whereas Bell attributes the work to Miss Sheepshanks (1 105). Bell mentions a class in Drawing from Vanessa, a class in Latin from Thoby, and a class in Greek from Adrian (1 105); Martin mentions a gift of pictures from Vanessa and classes in Greek and history from Adrian that did not last long (25). Stephen Barkway says the Morley College Staff list has Adrian down for Greek in 1906 (V. Woolf, Letter to Eva Hubback 5). The Council thanks Mr A. L. Stephen in the 1905–6 annual report (7) and Adrian Stephen in the 1906–7 one (8).

10. Oldfield frequently uses the unpublished autobiography Sheepshanks wrote in her eighties, *The Long Day Ended* (*LDE*), housed in the Women's Library@LSE archives. Sheepshanks's letters are scattered in other collections, including that of Bertrand Russell.
11. Mary Sheepshanks had a formal education and had acquired knowledge and experience about class difference and inequality; Stephen had neither.
12. As Sibyl Oldfield details in her article about Mary Sheepshanks and *Jus Suffragii* (the official journal of the International Woman Suffrage Alliance), Sheepshanks took controversial positions during the Great War, expanding beyond women's voting rights to ask readers in neutral countries for news about women in 'enemy' countries and to make arguments for pacifism. She was strongly criticized by some suffragist leaders, including the IWSA president, but after the War, her 'fair-mindedness and vision of women's solidarity' was noted in New Zealand and 'messages of thanks and praise' came to her and the journal 'from the USA, Canada, Rumania, Sweden, Italy, Germany, South Africa, Denmark and Austria as well as from British women's groups such as the Women's Freedom League' (128).
13. Charles and Dora Sanger; he was a barrister and a Great War conscientious objector.
14. Margaret Llewelyn Davies, General Secretary of the Women's Co-operative Guild and friend of Leonard and Virginia Woolf, was Theodore's sister.
15. The 86-year-old Mary Sheepshanks, almost blind, paralysed, and refusing to consider an institution when her daily help quit in 1958, also committed suicide (Oldfield, *SP* 289–90).
16. Virginia Stephen's objection to philanthropy may have been the gendered assumptions underlying it. As Lydia Murdoch notes, reformers believed women needed 'to apply domestic skills outside of their immediate homes' (193) and thought 'elite' women 'particularly qualified for work helping children and the poor, the sick and the elderly – in sum, any group traditionally associated with woman's care within the home' (193). The ideal uniting many female philanthropists 'was the notion that the ideal bourgeois home should serve as the model for all social structures', which often translated into efforts to make the poor or working classes adopt 'strict definitions of middle-class femininity' (197, 196). See also Clara Jones, 18–19 and 55–6 n2, and Jane Lewis, whose study of five female philanthropists explores the complexity and variety of their roles. She notes middle-class men 'tended to give more generously of their money than of their time' and the motives for middle-class women's 'extensive involvement in a variety of charitable endeavours ... were complicated' (10).
17. Lee says Adrian Stephen described Virginia as 'winking and making horrible grimaces at me' behind Sheepshanks's back during a visit (*VW* 218, 786 n21), but his 1909 diary describes a more complex scenario in which Adrian, burdened by Saxon Sydney-Turner's presence, thinks Miss Sheepshanks's arrival something of a relief. He is sure both Miss Sheepshanks and Saxon see Virginia's faces and 'trust they each thought she was commenting on the other' (Diary 1). Virginia diverts Miss Sheepshanks to her room, and after a while, Mary leaves, but Saxon stays on until 2 a.m., after a visit, Adrian writes, of 10½ hours! This entry, focused mainly on Adrian's irritation at Saxon's monopoly of his time, is at the beginning of a short diary that reveals mockery of others was a Stephen trait, not just Virginia's.

    After her Morley teaching was over, Virginia responds to Clive Bell's criticism of her handling of a social snafu with Mary Sheepshanks at tea time; she regrets having to spend time with Mary rather than Clive, but defends her polite behaviour (*L1* 439). Sadly, Mary's earnestness and discontent made it easy for Bloomsbury to make fun of her.
18. Lilian Harris was the Assistant Secretary of the Women's Co-operative Guild.

19. Lindsay Martin says Stephen is listed for composition (22), but the class list at the end of the 1904–5 annual report is headed October 1905, and is thus for the upcoming Michaelmas Term.
20. Stephen never refers to the people in her classes as students, though she uses the word elsewhere, including for a theological student she had to interact with when she holidayed in Wells, Someset, in August 1908 (*L1* 339). A clear distinction was made between 'pupil' and 'student' in the UK, pupil being used for those in primary and secondary grades and students being used for those in universities. (Interestingly, Woolf uses 'pupils' for Janet Case's students in her obituary draft ['Janet Case' MS].) Perhaps Morley's in-between status – people attending were older, and yet not at university or even necessarily secondary level – explains her avoidance of the term. The possessive 'my' grates, particularly when used with terms denoting social class, yet is commonly used by teachers to refer to people enrolled in their classes.
21. In England, eight- to ten-week terms were labelled Lent (January to March), Easter (April to June) and Michaelmas (October to December), comparable to an American winter, spring and fall quarter system.
22. Lindsay Martin reads letters to Violet Dickinson and Emma Vaughan in which she complains about having to leave Giggleswick and be back in London for Morley near the end of April (*L1* 221, 224) as reflecting 'increasing irritation' at her Morley responsibilities (24), but they might just as easily be read as the usual thing one says to friends at the end of a holiday.
23. Richards says she 'took classes in composition and poetry from 1904 to 1908' (154), but Stephen's letters and journals make clear she began teaching in 1905 and ended in 1907. The 18 May 1908 Executive Committee Minutes include this plan – 'Mr Trevelyan & Miss Stephen to be again asked to conduct reading circles in English Literature' (132) – but she did not teach after 1907.
24. The location of this list, in all likelihood related to Stephen's work for the Morley English history course, is puzzling: in the Leonard Woolf Papers, at the rear of a bound account book with Leonard's 1903–13 press cuttings in the front ('Notes ["Authorities"]'). Woolf had no reason to create such an outline in 1913 or after, so perhaps she used the back of the book in 1905 and then Leonard frugally added his press cuttings to the front after they married (email from Eleanor King, the Keep, 6 December 2017). The existing outline consists of 34 pages, 30 of them numbered, but pages 23 and 24 are missing, and the first has been torn out; however, a running list of dates is partially legible down the left-hand side of the ripped-out page. Her notes seem to be following J. R. Green's *A Short History of the English People*. On 29 April 1905, she writes that 'Green for some reason runs off my mind like water' (*PA* 269), which perhaps explains her extensive notes.
25. Stephen's comment reveals she expected to continue teaching at Morley. It also shows pedagogical awareness: those who train teachers recommend logging perceptions about students, teaching and reactions because such logs can help one improve in 'future terms' (*PA* 256).
26. Many Morley College records were destroyed in the Blitz. The new building, at 61 Westminster Bridge Road, was hit by a bomb on 15 October 1940; of the 195 people on the premises, eighty-four were unhurt, fifty-four were injured and fifty-seven were killed (Richards 252–3). Night classes had become impossible, given blackouts and nightly bombings, so Morley planned to reduce the College's programme further and hold classes during weekend days, which had been scheduled to start on 19 October (Richards 249–51). If such descriptive and/or evaluative reports were required and filed, they would have been lost then. Given the detail of Stephen's report, it is regrettable we cannot consult any others, especially the 'sketch' she refers to as written earlier. But since it is a draft, we do not know whether it was required or submitted or ever revised. Given Morley's lack of formal procedures, probably Stephen's report was

not a job requirement. Although Stephen uses the word 'report' in her first sentence, she does not title her draft 'Report on Teaching at Morley College'; Quentin Bell does (C. Jones 23). She called her first such effort a 'sketch', and perhaps, even though it responds to Sheepshanks's criticism, this continuation fulfilled the same function.

27. Stephen may also have felt incensed about the 'official' view of history because of her father's training and her stated interest in writing a history (*L*1 190, 202).
28. Quentin Bell reports Duncan Grant's memory of a Bloomsbury evening when Mary Sheepshanks 'put her down with the devastating enquiry: "Miss Stephen, do you *ever* think?"' (1 121–2, 267n, her emphasis).
29. Teachers at Morley struggled with different levels of preparation in their classes, a familiar struggle. At a meeting of voluntary teachers on 4 June 1898,

> Mr Descours mentioned the difficulty occasioned by students joining a class for which they were not fit. It was agreed that a teacher could refuse to receive such students, and should refer them to Miss Acton to find a suitable class. (*MCECM2* 16)

It is unclear what the line between 'fit' and 'not fit' was, what procedures were followed when Stephen taught, or if procedures were regularly communicated to all teachers. It is unlikely the milkman's prior education had prepared him for an advanced composition class, and it is certainly possible he had not taken the earlier composition course since Morley did not then attempt to guide students into sequenced courses.

30. In discussing books that can 'broaden and deepen our capacity for pleasure – or at least comprehension', Damon Young, in *The Art of Reading*, uses the word 'cultivation' and describes the process this way:

> it is easier to cleave to Aristotle after Plato and, in some ways, Dante after Aquinas. Not because the first authors are simplistic, but because they helped to create the materials from which the later masterworks were wrought. They are introductions to a certain community of problems, or conception of the universe. Progenitors, not primers. (60)

31. Such complaints sound more obligatory in context than expressive of ambivalence.
32. She began teaching this brand-new course in the term following Thoby's death.

Chapter 8

Teaching Skills

Practice

Based on what can be gleaned from her letters and journals and from annual reports, the *Morley College Magazine* and minutes of various Morley College committees, Virginia Stephen taught one course a term at Morley College in eight different terms over a span of four academic years, 1904–5 until 1907–8.[1] In 1904–5, she taught a lecture series in the 1905 Lent Term and English History in the Easter Term. In 1905–6, she taught English Composition all three terms, Michaelmas, Lent and Easter. In 1906–7, she taught Advanced English Composition in Lent and Easter Terms 1907. And in 1907–8, she led a Reading Circle on Keats, Shelley and Browning in Michaelmas Term 1907. (See Appendix 3 for her Morley teaching schedule.) Her teaching threaded through four academic years but spanned three calendar years, from January 1905 to the end of December 1907. Plenty of time to practise.

Current teacher training in some countries such as the US includes learning a discipline and studying education history and theory, particularly theories about how people learn and how social, cultural and economic circumstances affect learning. It also includes discussion, feedback, experimentation and reflection on a lot of supervised experiential, hands-on application – observations, conversations, field experience, student teaching. As one learns in the classroom, one practises teaching with the support of classmates and experienced teachers. Virginia Stephen, without any disciplinary knowledge,[2] any education history or theory, or much guidance, learned entirely by doing.

Although Miss Sheepshanks twice criticised her teaching, Morley's continued requests indicate Virginia Stephen must have been at least competent. Soon after Miss Sheepshanks told her she was doing the wrong thing in June 1905, Ella Crum wrote a long letter to tell her 'what a wonderful thing' it was to have her at Morley (L1 201), perhaps flattering her into continuing. At the Executive Committee meeting on 3 May 1907, it was reported Reading Circles were to be taken by Mr Trevelyan and Miss Stephen for Michaelmas Term 1907, but that teachers were still wanted for 'Literature circles after Christmas' (108), indicating Stephen may have turned down a request or a request was coming.[3] Even after she gave up teaching in December 1907, May 1908 minutes say she and Mr Trevelyan were to be asked to take Reading Circles (*MCECM3* 132). We do not know whether she was asked (no record of a reply), but the plan illustrates respect for her teaching ability. Stephen evidently improved as she practised.

Virginia Stephen did not seem motivated, as her mother was, by altruism or a belief that women have an obligation to serve others. Perhaps a belief in education motivated her to devote the time, energy and thought to teaching that her letters and journals show she did. She taught four kinds of classes at Morley: a cultural lecture series, history, composition and literature. Stephen learned to teach these varied courses as she went, practising something different in each: choosing content and lecturing in the lecture series; building context and using scene setting in the history course; nurturing a skill in the composition courses; and focusing attention on language's oral nature in the literature course. As Chapter 7 details, Miss Sheepshanks taught her about institutional expectations, and her students taught her about their intellectual capabilities. But she learned the most about teaching from simply practising it weekly. Her work taught her about the nature of learning: its inherent difficulties, dependence on context and sequence, and reliance on being heard and understood. Virginia Stephen's growing understanding of the nature of learning would influence Virginia Woolf's choice of persona and strategies in her essays.

Teaching Culture, Lent Term 1905

The exclamation marks Virginia Stephen used to tell her friends and journal about being asked to teach at Morley reveal her excitement (or disbelief) about the job (*L1* 171, 173; *PA* 217). But her assignment is confusing: was it a social evening, girls' club, English grammar, English literature or '"talks" about books and pictures' (*L1* 172)? When she met some equally excited working women at the beginning-of-term soirée, they 'begged [her] to give a course of lectures', which she tried to veto, but they insisted (*L1* 173). So that is what she taught.

Stephen became a Morley teacher with extraordinary speed: she received Sheepshanks's request to teach there around 30 December 1904, met some Morley students at the soirée on 7 January 1905, informed Miss Sheepshanks she could go ahead after receiving Dr Savage's approval on 14 January, and walked into a classroom on 18 January. Normally, her name and a course title would have appeared in the 1903–4 annual report List of Classes and Teachers for the upcoming year or perhaps in the autumn 1904 issue of the *Morley College Magazine*. But the request came at the last minute, and evidently Miss Sheepshanks was not concerned about covering a specific class.

Stephen's other comments show she assumed she needed to prepare lectures. Miss Sheepshanks described her job as giving 'talks' about books and pictures, and before she knew what Dr Savage would say, she 'got a book about the relations of poetry & music' at the London Library because it 'may come in useful for my Morley lectures, if I give them'. Once she accepted, she wrote she must now 'cudgel my brains for a lecture' (*PA* 221–2). She was used to lectures, after all – from her father, from King's College London classes, from public events – as were her students, as their begging indicates. Indeed, Morley College grew out of Old Vic evening lectures, occasions combining social events with learning. Colin

Evans writes that in 1993, the 'forms in which teaching and learning occur are surprisingly few in number and highly traditional' in British universities: lectures, tutorials and seminars (54). It would never have occurred to Virginia Stephen to try anything else. Teaching meant lecturing.[4]

In her first term, therefore, her teaching practice centred around content – finding topics she could talk about and students might like – and pedagogy – reading for, organising and delivering lectures. Her students had no textbook and no reading or writing to do outside class. They came and listened to a lecture. Before Stephen started, she did not 'see any limit to the things I might talk about' (L1 172), but she discovered choosing topics was more difficult than it looked, commenting later in the term that she was at her 'wits end for a subject' (PA 237).

What became Virginia Stephen's 1905 Lent Term lecture series reflects an eclectic, interdisciplinary approach: it covers cultural content ranging from genre to individual writers and artists, from travel to art and history.[5] Her journal and a smattering of letters show she did not plan her lecture series ahead; rather, she identified a subject a few days before she headed to Lambeth to teach. Her course implicitly defined learning as wandering or exploring, then, and though her schedule can be determined, such organisation emerges after, not before, the fact:

W, 11 January: no class (not 'booked' yet) (PA 220; L1 175)
W, 18 January: Prose (Sir Thomas Browne) (PA 223–4)
W, 25 January: no class (PA 227–8; 23rd birthday, went to see *Peter Pan*)
W, 1 February: Italy journey: Venice (PA 225, 231; L1 177)
W, 8 February: Florence (PA 233–4)
W, 15 February: Cellini (PA 237–8; see Appendix 4)
W, 22 February: Vanessa lectured (PA 241)
W, 1 March: no class (PA 245; plans for a 9.30 p.m. housewarming party)
Sat., 4 March: Early Italians at National Gallery (PA 246)
W, 8 March: Greek myths (PA 248, 249)
W, 15 March: [Dramatic in life and art *or* no class]; (dines w/Cecils; does not mention a Morley class, PA 252; see Appendix 4)[6]
W, 22 March: Greek history (last class; students beg for English history course; PA 255)

Reaching for lecture ideas from her interests, experiences and acquaintances, Stephen gave two lectures about the Greeks, one on myths and one on history. If she lectured on Wednesday, 15 March about 'the dramatic in art and life', she probably included something about Greek drama since it would have bridged Greek myths and history, and she was reading Aristotle's *Poetics* between February 21 and March 2 (PA 240, 245) and *Oedipus Tyrannus* between 3 and 10 March (PA 245, 250). Stephen also mined the Stephen trip to Italy, talking about the journey and Venice one week, then moving to Florence, and ultimately to Cellini's *Autobiography* because it 'has some relation to Florence' (PA 237). She asked Vanessa to lecture, likely on Italian painting, since they took students to the National Gallery to see Early Italian paintings (PA 241, 246).[7] Her other lecture topics indicate genre questions may have occupied her. She does not seem to have used the book about the relations between poetry and music, but she chose Prose as her first subject and focused her remarks on Sir Thomas Browne (PA 223–4); featured Cellini's autobiography; and may have lectured on drama's difference from life and fiction (see Appendix 4 for facsimile transcriptions of these lectures). Connections do thread their way through this lecture series, but whether she emphasised them, or students perceived them, is another matter.

More crucial than her topics, Virginia Stephen evolved on the lecture format's usefulness as a teaching method. From the start, she worried about engaging students. Working on her Prose lecture[8] amused her because she could 'say what I like without fear of criticism' and she was interested. But, she added, 'Heaven knows if it will interest them' (*PA* 223). She mocked herself a few days later, saying the note she sent to Fred Maitland about her father was 'all cobblestone sentences brisk & matter of fact, without an atom of beauty or swing about them. And I write about prose!' (*PA* 226). She doubted whether they would like her Cellini lecture (*PA* 237), predicted her Greek history lecture would be 'dry' and thought they were 'bored by my history and dull maps'. However, since her students implored her to 'lecture steadily at English History next term' (*PA* 255), perhaps they had not been as bored as she feared.

By then, too, she had modified her approach, which perhaps increased her enrolment: she started with two women on 19 January, four came on 1 February, seven attended on 8 February and she ended with eight ('Report' 202). When she began, Stephen was nervous and convinced her Prose lecture 'must still be written out, as I cant trust my self to speak from memory – & with writing before me, I cant go far wrong' (*PA* 223). Noting the women at her first lecture 'were readier to talk than listen' (*PA* 224), she wrote 'an odd kind of lecture!' on the Stephen trip to Italy, perhaps odd because she created something different from what she thought a lecture should be or less overtly didactic. She continued, 'This is the kind of thing they really enjoy I know – whether there were fleas in the beds at Venice. I shall have to invent some – &c&c.' Such a lecture was easier to write ('though not instructive'), and she 'rattled off 12 pages' (*PA* 225). Three days later, she commented she had just finished the note on her father for F. W. Maitland, so had 'cobbled my lecture a little' and planned to 'try to write a pot boiler – as I have time' (*PA* 227). Writing to Violet, she described what she had done to interest students:

> we discussed Venice, and I showed them pictures, and they were nice and friendly and full of interest, and told me about their Aunts who said that there was water in all the streets in Venice, and was it true, and the Clergyman at home (Yorkshire) had been to Rome, and shown them pictures of it. You will have to come down and talk to them one week – lots of jokes is what they like – and then they blossom out – and say how they have written poetry since the age of 11! (*L1* 177)

Even given Stephen's penchant for exaggeration in her letters, she clearly moved to a more interactive class that included pictures, talk, humour, and student questions and comments. She seems to have learned she need not choose between instruction and 'get[ting] to know them' (*L1* 173). Miss Sheepshanks's teaching tip, to 'combine amusement and instruction – a little gossip and sympathy' (*L1* 172), was on target, contributing to a lively classroom. Stephen's description also indicates her students' growing ease with her – a traditional lecturer would not have inspired such confidences – along with her delight in them. Stephen also reveals her growing awareness of teaching's performative nature, a performance anchored in authenticity. She took her students seriously enough to consider what might help them engage in learning, and they responded.

She wrote her Cellini lecture out, though she identified main points and used interesting detail, but for her 8 March lecture on Greek myths, something she knew nothing about, she again adapted to student response and tried 'the experiment of only writing short notes, which I shall put into words on the spur of the moment. Directly I begin to read, their attention wanders.' She reported the experiment worked: she 'managed the speaking all right. It is certainly better than reading' (PA 249). On 21 March, she tried to pick out not 'wholly dry' facts for her lecture on Greek history, and on the 22nd, said she did as much as she could and got to the Peloponnesian War. She did not think she would make much of an impression, acknowledging her students' lack of contextual background (PA 254–5), but she worked to find historical events that would interest them and took maps to help them see the geographical implications of those events.

Over the course of her first term, then, Virginia Stephen practised choosing topics – developing content or a course curriculum – and lecturing – trying the most common method for presenting content to students. She covered a variety of topics and gained pedagogical skill, learning to focus on a few main points and use humour and visual aids to enliven those points. But she also learned dialogue worked better than lecturing; simply talking and involving students in discussion helped them learn and enjoy learning. She began to question the lecture's pedagogical usefulness, a question she would ask more loudly as the years went by.[9]

Teaching History, Easter Term 1905

At the end of her Lent Term lecture series, Virginia Stephen's students asked her to start at the beginning of English History and steadily lecture about it (PA 255). Their request suggests they wanted more than exploration, perhaps background and context in a chronological structure. The request also reveals their comfort with her – they can say what they want her to teach and confess their lack of historical knowledge, which, according to Jenny Keating's study of Board of Education documents in the History in Education Project, was extensive. Even though history had become a class subject[10] in the 1875 Code, it could only be taught in Standard V and above (11–12-year olds) after 1882; by 1890, she writes, 'out of 22,516 departments for older children, English was taught in 20,304, Geography in 12,367 but History in only 414' (1). By 1899, she continues, the situation had improved, but even so, only 5,879 schools were teaching History compared to 13,194 teaching English and 17,872 Geography (1). Few inspectors' reports mentioned history, other than to complain about the 'indiscriminate use' of 'dry bones' readers (5). To take a couple of examples, William Collier's *History of the British Empire* (1884) and Cyril Ransome's *A Short History of England from the Earliest Times to the Present Day* (1899) not only bear out this complaint but also target secondary schools rather than elementary ones, though Ransome also aims at pupil and assistant teachers in elementary schools (Collier iii, Ransome v). In the General Reports of HM Inspectors for the Board of Education in 1902, Mr Oliver says the basis of instruction was a 'brief outline of main events for the lower classes, and a more detailed knowledge of a period – usually the reign of Victoria – for the upper classes' (J. Keating 6). Morley students probably had no or next-to-no history education, then, so their desire to start at the beginning and gain a chronological framework makes sense.[11]

History did not have a secure place in Morley's curriculum, either, so students were asking Stephen to fill a curricular gap. Richards says Morley added history in 1892 (110–11), but in April 1900, an Executive Committee member asked about such a course, and though Sheepshanks says she will obtain information (*MCECM2* 106), minutes do not reveal a follow-up. Lists of Classes and Teachers in Annual Reports from 1901–2 to 1904–5 show no history courses offered, perhaps because, as the writer of the 1900 annual report notes,

> It is a curious fact that when we submit a list of various subjects to be voted on by the students, historical or social subjects usually get the largest number of votes, but when the lectures actually take place, the scientific subjects usually draw the largest audiences. (3)[12]

History also did not have a clear identity. On the List of Classes and Teachers, it is sometimes grouped with Literary Courses, other times with Occasional Courses; sometimes it is listed as History with no specifics, other times listed with quite specific titles. Only after Stephen's English History course, in the list for 1906–7 classes, was a Division called History and Social Science added (*MCAR* 1905–6 15).

In any case, Virginia Stephen had learned from her first teaching experience. In contrast to her somewhat hit-or-miss list of lecture topics, her English History course provided a clear chronological scaffolding, starting with early Britain and the Celts (*L1* 191) and moving up through King John, signer of the Magna Carta in 1215 ('Report' 203). She made the framework clear, and given her students were not reading textbooks, but relying on her weekly lectures, and given the fragmentation of their education, worse than hers, her pedagogy depended on story: one good, vivid scene a week (not 'dry bones'), an overall narrative driving the whole, and a list of important dates to walk away with. Learning was implicitly defined as absorbing a narrative.[13]

In Easter Term, Virginia Stephen again did not teach something assigned or on the Morley books; rather, she taught what her Lent Term students asked her to, something she loved and had background in. As Katherine Hill has argued, Leslie Stephen 'trained [his daughter] extensively in history and biography' so she could 'become his literary and intellectual heir' ('History' 351) and have the tools necessary for being a novelist or an essayist (353). During the term, she mentioned her plans to write history, said to Violet she 'always did love it', and talked about studying it at Dr Williams' Library in the same letter in which she worried that although she had been 'pouring my life blood into the grim bones of early English history all the morning', her students 'wont care for it' (*L1* 190).[14] In July, she wrote she wanted to 'produce a real historical work this summer, for which I have solidly read and annotated 4 volumes of medieval English' (*L1* 202), indicating she realised her teaching work could prepare her for history writing.

As discussed in Chapter 3, Virginia Stephen also took courses in Continental and English History from Professor J. K. Laughton at King's College; his emphasis on chronological order probably influenced Stephen's approach and her choice of source material (Jones and Snaith, 16–18, 20).[15] At the back of her 1904–5 journal, Stephen has notes from Chapter 22 in Volume 5 of Edward Augustus Freeman's *History of the Norman Conquest*, and she mentions taking Green's *Conquest of England* with her on the holiday she took to Spain with Adrian in late March and April (*PA* 257). When she returned from holiday, she 'got down to the L.L. & changed some books. I must now solidly drudge through the beginnings of English history & with this purpose I have got Freeman & more Green' (*PA* 269), which is when she probably took notes from J. R. Green's *A Short History of the English People*.[16] On 10 May 1905, she wrote she had begun work on her English History lectures for her class:

> I have read Green, & Freeman's first volume, with copious notes; & I now boil these down, into something as readable as I can make it. It amuses me, as English History always does, & Freeman is a good manly writer with no nonsense about him. (*PA* 272).[17]

J. W. Burrow, intellectual historian, criticises Freeman and Green for having

> views of the present which were Romantically historicised and who [were] drawn to history by ... an antiquarian passion for the past, as well as a patriotic and populist impulse to identify the nation and its institutions as the collective subject of English history.

In their work to flesh out and make more democratic 'older Whig notions of continuity', Green made that view 'popular and dramatic' and Freeman emphasised narrative history (Burrow qtd in 'Edward').[18] Freeman and Green were well respected in 1905, however, and Stephen knew her father had helped edit Green's *Letters*.[19] William Hunt claims Freeman advanced history study in England by insisting on the unity of history and the importance of primary sources (77). Thus, Stephen's admiration for Freeman and Green may have stemmed from what Burrow criticises, a sense of unity supporting a meaningful and unbroken story.[20]

Stephen's sources suggest she wanted to convey the historical context for her students' lives and engage them with a narrative of the past that connected them to it. With guidance from her father, she had gathered contextual wealth in her rambles around a large library; as Hill notes, Leslie Stephen recommended in his St Andrew's lecture a history and biography reading list 'very similar to the one Virginia records in her diary' when she was 15 and she read, among others, Thomas Carlyle's *Cromwell* and Macaulay's *History* ('History', 353). Her King's College London classes supported and reinforced this independent reading. But her students, lacking such contextual resources, told her they needed to start at the beginning, suggesting they wanted to grasp the basic story before attempting to flesh it out, complicate or question it.[21]

Stephen's pedagogical methods suggest the same contextual aim. Freeman and Green had winnowed masses of detail from primary documents and shaped them into national narratives, which Stephen then boiled down even further into something understandable, readable, perhaps even amusing (*PA* 272). She worked from source notes: 'I talked from notes, with as little actual reading as possible.' She knew full well that she 'administer[ed] each week' only 'some semblance of English history', that her talk, although fluent, was superficial. But she tried to make her students 'feel the flesh & blood' in the shadowy past and 'make the real interest of history – as it appears to me – visible to them' ('Report' 203). So, for example, she writes to Violet Dickinson, 'I have been making out a vivid account of the battle of Hastings. I hope to make their flesh creep!' (*L1* 191).[22] Her goal was to 'nourish' her students (C. Jones 213; cancelled in 'Report' MS), giving them a foundation on which they could build future historical study.

She taught the history course, according to her report,[23] even though Morley authorities 'looked rather coldly on it', calling it 'the least popular subject in the College' ('Report' 202). Did Miss Sheepshanks (presumably) communicate that judgement to Stephen before the course, after the course (perhaps at the 29 June 1905 dinner, when Miss Sheepshanks told her she was doing the wrong thing [*L1* 194]), or when Stephen may have asked if she might extend the course beyond King John ('Report' 203)? In April, she assumed she would be teaching an English History sequel the next autumn; she had taken notes up to 1815 and the Battle of Waterloo ('Notes ["Authorities"]' n. pag., after 30) and said in a letter to Violet she supposed she would spend part of her summer 'making English History lectures for my women' (*L1* 188).

At report's end, as noted in Chapter 7, Stephen accuses Morley of compromising, of preferring to enrol large numbers in English Composition rather than encourage a few to study English History ('Report' 203). Clara Jones suggests Stephen's anger might have stemmed from dislike of G. M. Trevelyan, someone Woolf would criticise in *A Room of One's Own*, because his eight French Revolution lectures were presented as the option for students who wanted to continue in history (32–3).[24] But Stephen's description of these lectures as 'dropped into their minds, like meteors from another sphere' and as 'disconnected fragments' ('Report' 204) suggests her anger stems from her sense that her students sought context, coherence, connection. Topic and instructor were not the problem; the problem was assuming students could connect the French Revolution to early English history. Her focus on narrative had, she hoped, assisted them in their efforts to 'piece together what they heard; to see reasons; to connect ideas' ('Report' 203). Instead, having to leap from the Magna Carta to the French Revolution (different time, country and national narrative) meant her students were cut off in mid-story, interrupted, subject to further fragmentation.[25]

Stephen would later bolster her conviction about sequential narratives and connections in an English teachers' meeting on 15 March 1907. Her recorded comments indicate her objection to being told she could not continue her English History course was exactly what she said it was:

> Miss Stephen suggested that a Literature class should be held in connection with History & Composition, some definite period of English literature being studied each term. For instance 1st term, Elizabethan Literature, 2nd term, 18th Century & 3rd term, 19th Century Literature and that someone from outside the College should be asked to lecture once a month on the period dealt with at the class. She also considered that the students should be encouraged to write papers on the authors they were studying. (*MCECM3*; reverse order, twelve pages in)

According to the minutes, Vice-Principal Miss Sheepshanks was at this meeting and would have heard this suggestion, an even more forceful argument for coherence than Stephen had made in her draft report (which Miss Sheepshanks may never have read).[26] Stephen spoke confidently about an overall curriculum that coordinated history, literature, writing and outside speakers – such coordination, she believed, would help Morley students make connections and see the larger picture.[27] She wove her own fragmented educational experience together with her students' pleas for a coherent study of English history into a proposal for an integrated curriculum.

Furthermore, her accusation that popularity was more important to Morley than acquiring interconnected knowledge had some basis. Numbers were indeed important to Morley. They had to be. Much Morley funding came from grants, which depended on inspectors' examinations and/or attendance (Richards 115). Essentially, Morley got money for the number of students in courses; without popular courses, the operating budget was insufficient. Annual reports regularly printed attendance numbers and expressed concern about making classes more 'successful' (three or fewer students meant a course was dropped in Michaelmas 1903) (*MCECM2* 32). The school's existence was also threatened by competition from the Borough Polytechnic and the London School Board: enrolment numbers dropped from the 1,100s to the 700s in the period between 1898 and 1903, right before Stephen began teaching there. Miss Sheepshanks had worked diligently to increase numbers, 'safely negotiated' the 'troubled waters of the early years of the century' and saved the school (Richards 149; Oldfield, *SP* 92–3). Stephen's observation about Morley's compromises is accurate, though based on partial understanding. She argued from educational principle – she wanted to encourage those interested in integrative learning – against college officials who argued from necessity – it had to have numbers to survive.[28]

Perhaps Miss Sheepshanks's assessment – Virginia Stephen was doing 'entirely the wrong thing' (*L1* 194) – had something to do with methods, since Stephen defended them in her draft. After having her numbers drop from eight to four, she wrote, those young women came every week, with 'one serious desire in common'. Thus, she worked to make the 'spectre' of the past thicken their present and help them move 'through Early British, & Romans, & Angles Saxons & Danes, & Normans, till we were on the more substantial ground of the Plantagenet Kings'. She saw their intelligence, struggles and ability to grasp more 'substance'. She engaged with her students, two of whom she acknowledged had writing talent, showing them pictures and lending them books; worked hard to condense masses of primary material into representative vivid scenes within a sequential narrative; supplemented her talk's 'vagueness' with 'a sheet of hard dates'; and attempted to make history's 'shadows' take on 'flesh & blood' ('Report' 203).

More likely, however, Stephen's 'wrong thing' was teaching a course that had only four students in it. She needed to teach courses that would enrol greater numbers of students. Thus, after practising context building, scene making and narrative to teach English History, she was asked to 'turn [her] mind to essay writing & the expression of ideas' ('Report' 203), and in the 13 July 1905 Executive Committee meeting minutes, under the heading Volunteer teachers, it was '[r]eported that Miss Virginia Stephen would take Composition Class' (*MCECM3* 57).

Teaching Composition, Michaelmas, Lent and Easter terms 1905–6; Teaching Advanced Composition, Lent and Easter Terms 1907

In Michaelmas Term 1905, Virginia Stephen had to transition from student-driven courses to an administrator-assigned one, from content-based courses to a skills-based one, and from a course she considered 'one of the most important' to one she considered 'less valuable' ('Report' 202–3). Later in the term, she supposes her composition course is 'the most useless class in the College' (*L1* 210). Today, many argue composition courses have value, help students learn to think and teach students writing skills they can transfer to other courses and their working lives: useful. Stephen's comments puzzle us, especially since she was struggling to become a writer herself.[29]

Clues to this puzzle must remain speculative because little direct evidence about Stephen's teaching of composition survives. Nothing like the 1904–5 journal exists for the period between autumn 1905 and spring 1907, and although some letters exist from that time, few mention Morley. Between September 1905 and January 1906, when she taught her first composition course, only seven letters, three of which mention Morley, appear in the *Letters*. Surely Virginia Stephen wrote more letters than that during those four months, and surely a comparable proportion contained Morley references, but we do not know. No other drafts or sketches about her Morley teaching experiences exist, either. Other than these few letters, then, only indirect evidence about her composition teaching survives: Morley documents; textbooks from the period; general studies of the subject; and her reviews related to writing.

That indirect evidence suggests Virginia Stephen may have viewed composition courses as useless because they did not centre on skills Morley students needed. Courses (1) may have skewed heavily toward grammar; (2) encouraged facile treatment of meaningless topics; (3) had little relationship to students' work; and (4) offered nothing to students serious about writing. She might have preferred to anchor her composition courses in autobiographical writing because that would have served Morley students more usefully, but she may not have been able to do so.

Accepting the composition assignment, Virginia Stephen could no longer rely on quickly reading sources, choosing main points to cover in a lecture and discussion, and devising a story to engage students. She had to move toward a practical, hands-on course, and her experience with tutors and King's College London teachers may have helped her assign and mark papers, though apparently, she did not have to assign a grade to them.[30] As with her earlier courses, she did not seem to have received much guidance, if any, about how to teach composition, what skills should be emphasised, or what the course should help students achieve – correct usage, success in matriculation exams, improved workplace writing, journalism careers, creative writing support, self-reflection, all or none of the above? Perhaps it was assumed Stephen would know what to do since she wrote herself, yet it seems unlikely she could construct the course as she saw fit.

Some historical background for Morley's composition courses can be found in its records. In 1889, Morley offered a course in reading and writing (Richards 101), and in 1894, English Grammar was the English foundation course in Acton's course of study plan (Richards 109; *MCAR 1894* 12–13). Later, English courses were divided into two Literary Classes levels, preparatory (Reading and Writing; Writing and Dictation) and English (Grammar and Composition). The Reading and Writing and Elementary Arithmetic preparatory courses were sometimes scheduled one right after the other (*MCAR 1897* 11),[31] and in Lent Terms 1899 and 1900, they were counted together as one class (*MCAR 1898* 10; *MCAR 1899* 11). Later still, Correspondence and Handwriting was added to the English classes (*MCAR 1903–4* 11) but dropped the next year. When Stephen taught Composition, the other English classes were Grammar, Elocution (Elementary and Advanced), and English Literature (*MCAR 1904–5* 15); Elementary Reading and Writing continued to be offered for many years. When Stephen taught Advanced Composition the next year, other English classes were Grammar and Elementary Composition; Elocution (Elementary and Recitation); Elocution (Advanced); and English Literature (University Extension) (*MCAR 1905–6* 15). English for Foreigners and English matriculation courses were offered after Stephen left, starting in the 1908–9 academic year (*MCAR 1907–8* 24), and a new sequence, Grammar, Composition and Essay, appeared in 1911–12 (*MCAR 1910–11* 18).

In a rare description of what the courses aimed to cover, the 1900 annual report List of Courses says the Reading and Writing course included 'Reading and Dictation'; the Grammar and Composition course consisted of 'Parsing; Syntax; Analysis; Essay Writing; etc.' (13). Dictation's presence shows that writing, for some students, still meant being able to form words on the page (and was perhaps related to clerks' work?), and grammar-related items have a substantial presence in the Grammar and Composition course. In the Programme of Classes for 1911–12, the English course description informed students that the classes were to be 'divided into three grades', with the first-year English course covering 'Elementary Grammar, Reading aloud, Parsing, Simple Analysis, Rudiments of Writing'; the second-year Elementary Composition course covering 'Letter-Writing, Summary and Précis, Paraphrase, Easy Composition'; and the third-year Essay Class including 'Criticism of Students' Essays, Style, Criticism of Authors with examples – Home-work obligatory. Only advanced Students are eligible for this class' – students had to consult the teacher before enrolling (Programme 11). Morley's composition offerings had evolved into a sequence that reveals both its continued devotion to students lacking strong educational backgrounds and its attempt to provide more skilled students with a chance to improve further.[32] The note about obligatory homework indicates writing outside of class was not generally required in other courses.[33] But Virginia Stephen taught her courses in Composition and Advanced Composition between these two descriptions. A student writing in the November 1905 *Morley College Magazine* that Stephen's class in Composition 'should prove useful, as we constantly hear of students with literary aspirations who wish to improve their style' (*MCM* xv.2 19), suggests yet another purpose.[34] It is simply difficult to know how Composition and Advanced

Composition differed or what the two courses meant to Morley, to her or to her students.

However, textbooks from the period show composition courses, at Morley and elsewhere, did not seem to have that hopeful Morley student in mind. They contained very little essay-level or stylistic instruction and a great deal of sentence-level grammar instruction. Students planning to take the Grammar and Composition course in 1900–1 were informed they should acquire either Davidson and Alcock (*English Composition*) or Morris's Primer (*English Grammar*) (MCAR 1900 12–13), influential texts that went into many editions.[35] Davidson and Alcock, Part I, The Structure of Sentences, contains 118 pages; Part II, Letter and Precis Writing, has twenty; Part III, Style, contains thirty; and Part IV, The Paragraph and Essay, has sixteen. Authors relied heavily on exhausting-to-read numbered lists; for example, Davidson and Alcock's style section includes rules like these: '173. III. Precision.--To attain precision of style, avoid: (1) Superfluous expressions; (2) Tautology, or the needless repetition of a word or idea in the same sentence; (3) The improper use of what are termed synonymous* words' (148). The asterisk sends the reader to number 188 for more on improper synonym use. In the paragraph and essay part, Davidson and Alcock ask students to outline sample paragraphs on topics such as truthfulness or the screech owl; they then present lists totalling 250 possible 'Subjects for Essays'. To name just a few, students might write about: Sunshine, Blowing Bubbles, Memory, Cruelty to Animals, Summer, Joan of Arc, Cleanliness, The Crusades, Hypocrisy, A Taste for Reading, The Liberty of the Press, Religion, Novel Reading, Autobiography of an Oak or The Necessity of Submission to Teachers (182–6). Perhaps students turned these topics into concrete, interesting or even personal essays, but one suspects they often produced banal, fake or rote responses instead.

Morris's English grammar primer is short, 115 pages, has introductory chapters on the nature of English as a language and on the parts of speech, then individual chapters on each part of speech, on borrowings from Latin, French and Greek, and on syntax; it ends with a chapter on sentence analysis with a model table of grammatical parsing. In his parsing example, he dissects a four-line verse. Here is the analysis of just the first line:

My father lived at Blenheim then,
My ... Pronoun, personal, possessive, 1st person, singular number, common gender, attribute of *father*.
father ... Noun, common, singular number, masculine gender, nominative case, subject of *lived*.
lived ... Verb, intransitive, weak conjugation, active voice, indicative mood, past tense, 3rd person, singular number, agreeing with its subject *father*. Parts: *live, lived, lived*.
at ... Preposition, joining *lived* and *Blenheim*.
Blenheim Noun, proper, singular number, neuter gender, objective case, after *at*.
then ... Adverb of time, qualifying the verb *lived*. (112–13; his emphasis and ellipses)

These textbooks indicate Composition courses overwhelmingly emphasised grammar and grammatical terms.[36]

We do not know if these textbooks continued to be recommended to Morley students or if Virginia Stephen used them. But a recommendation from Miss Sheepshanks indicates another textbook may have influenced her advanced course. Miss Sheepshanks, perhaps because of her desire to help students build verbal ability (Oldfield, *SP* 93), thought students might benefit from some instruction in oral composition and suggested at an English teachers' meeting that Miss Binning (Grammar and Elementary Composition), Miss Stephen (Advanced Composition) and Mr Howard (Elocution) try incorporating it in their 1907 Easter Term classes as an experiment (*MCECM3*, reverse order, twelve pages in).[37] In the secondary schooling of the late 1860s and 1870s, oral composition meant learning how to pronounce difficult words and answering questions about informative passages before completing written exercises (Hodgson 34). We do not know if, decades later, Miss Sheepshanks meant pronouncing words properly, answering questions about a written passage, brainstorming and outlining out loud, discussing revision or corrections, or practising speech.[38]

But the textbook title appearing most often in search engines for 'oral composition' is J. C. Nesfield's *Oral Exercises in English Composition* (1901). If she meant what J. C. Nesfield covers in his book, Miss Sheepshanks had concerns about students' ability to use basic sentence elements, not their ability to compose essays. The textbook asks students to complete sentences with the correct word (according to various grammatical and syntactical principles Nesfield explains), combine sentences and so forth, at sight and out loud, because 'promptness and facility must be acquired for composition' (3n), presumably for exams.[39] Exercises, made up of long numbered lists of sentences, follow explanations of grammatical principles, also numbered, ranging from simple to complex. In the 'number and person of the verb' section, he explains how to use 'is, am, are, was, were, have, has, do, does', provides sample correct sentences, and then presents an exercise to be done orally. The student must read the sentence out loud and insert the correct verb on the spot: '1. Bread and butter ___ a good kind of food at tea-time . . . . 7. The black and white kitten ___ asleep. . . . 21. My pen ___ been lost; ___ you seen it?' (4–5; underlining in original). In 'use and discrimination of words' (Ch. 7), Nesfield includes exercises asking students to substitute equivalent words without changing sentence sense; they can substitute verbs in 147 sentences, nouns in 158 sentences, adjectives in 150 sentences and adverbs in forty-eight sentences (156–72). It is hard to imagine a teacher using such exhaustive lists or a student listening to or reading a lesson about a grammatical rule and then standing, reading a sentence out loud and supplying a missing word, all with no advance preparation. But we do not know if such a text was what Sheepshanks meant when she asked Composition and Elocution teachers to include oral composition in their courses.

If Morley's Composition course was meant to help students '[acquire] the requisite elementary instruction' they needed for more advanced work (Richards 93), it might have depended on the more prescriptive exercise and model approach used in textbooks like those already discussed or Theophilus Dwight Hall's *A Manual of English Composition, with Copious Illustrations and Practical Exercises* (1880). Even J. M. D. Meiklejohn's *The Art of Writing English: A Manual for Students* (1899),[40] which distinguishes between composition, a 'constructive, or creative, or synthetic act' and grammar, a set of 'critical, examinatory, or analytic acts of the mind', and asserts grammar is 'a corrective after a composition has been produced' (15), does not reach the twelve-page 'How to Write an Essay' until Chapter 12. There, his minimal instructions (three pages) seem geared to students writing essays for examinations, and most of the chapter is filled with detailed outlines for short essays (159–71). The primary focus for the student is not on composing, but on fleshing out teacher-chosen topics and outlines. Such texts define learning to write as following the rules and filling in templates.

But perhaps Morley's course was supposed to fulfil its humanistic mission. Principal Buxton said Morley aimed 'to turn out, not the specialist or the skilled workman or clerk . . . but the man or woman with developed faculties all round; with an interest in life' and 'an intelligent outlook upon the questions of the day' (*MCAR* 1905–6 2). Perhaps it followed the Working Men's College model described by Ursula Howard. According to her, adult education movement leaders understood the need to teach composition long before it was part of the school curriculum, and their approach foregrounded writing, not grammar. The Working Men's College, People's College and later the Workers' Educational Association advocated for writing short essays, reading work aloud, and discussing the writing's subject along with corrections and reasons for them (64–5), and R. H. Tawney suggested beginning with autobiographical pieces (66). If this method, resembling today's workshops, was what Morley encouraged, perhaps Stephen had the freedom to define learning to write as discovering self and world through writing.

But Morley had no stated rationale for the Composition courses it consistently offered. We know Virginia Stephen's composition students did in fact write essays: in a November 1905 letter, she mentions an essay on Autumn (*L1* 210), a subject listed in Davidson and Alcock (183). If she had to use teacher-generated templates or pre-ordained topics, she might have questioned the course's value, particularly given her critique of frequent glib newspaper essays in her February 1905 'The Decay of Essay-writing'.[41] Stephen had sarcastically targeted oracular pronouncements about trivial topics developed out of a 'mechanical act of writing' and writers who were churning out essays because they had deadlines to meet and columns to fill, not because they had ideas they wanted to investigate, explore or develop (*E1* 25–6).[42]

Perhaps the course attempted to straddle the humanities and practical divide and aimed to promote knowledge not directly connected to a trade but also help students gain 'ancillary' skills (Richards 92–3)? Or perhaps Morley more directly linked work or job advancement to writing skill? But students in the occupations most heavily represented at Morley at the turn of the century – the shop assistants and clerks described in Chapter 6 – did not need such skills for current or future employment. Possibly, however, students viewed learning to write as a way of moving up in class. Andrew Miles notes, citing David Vincent and D. F. Mitch, that 'mobility chances were strongly correlated with literacy' – being able to read and write made you more upwardly mobile than those who could not – but he also points out that 'to be literate was neither a guarantee of success nor a prerequisite for it' (87). According to him, over 90 per cent who grew up working class but managed to achieve middle-class status had reached the lowest literacy bar, signing their names in the register. But, he says,

> while literacy was a skill which could be useful even when not strictly necessary, less than a third of those making this transition did so by entering employment in which the ability to read and write was a formal requirement.

Success depended more on acquiring capital than on acquiring credentials (88).[43]

Some Morley students may have wanted to express themselves better or may have been like the *Morley College Magazine* writer who saw such a course as 'useful' because of their 'literary aspirations' and a desire to 'improve their style' (*MCM* xv.2 19). But in her review of Adam Lorimer's *The Author's Progress* on 15 July 1906, Virginia Stephen wrote 'There is so little you can tell a writer about writing' (*E1* 116), a claim reflecting a cultural belief that writing could not be taught: writers coming of age in the early twentieth century had almost no formal or informal writing instruction. If Stephen believed writing could not be taught, she might have believed even students serious about literature and writing would not gain anything from a composition course, or that a course privileging correction of grammatical deficits over growth of ideas would hinder students wanting to become literary writers. Although Stephen calls the 'confusion' between art and trade 'inevitable' in her review of Lorimer (*E1* 117), she may have come to understand that students like Miss Williams could not think about art at all, could not possibly put the two in even the uneasy tension she herself later would.[44] While teaching, Stephen was reviewing books, writing the occasional essay and trying out short stories. She had read literature and history extensively. She was serious about literature and about becoming a writer. Meeting Miss Williams and Burke in the culture and history classes showed her that class status had given her, and was still giving her, the luxury of time to develop skills. Burke did not have Miss Stephen's circumstances, and Miss Williams had to be a 'writing machine . . . set in motion by the editor' and thus 'made no pretence that her work was of any higher nature' ('Report' 202–3). To earn her living, Miss Williams had to treat journalism as a trade, not an apprenticeship. If Stephen suspected students with literary hopes, talent or initiative would often be forced by class circumstance to become writing machines, then she might have viewed a course focus on the development of facile responses to clichéd topics as a steppingstone to trades emphasising speed and wages over literary value.

Given our cultural belief – writing skills are important – it seems inexplicable that Virginia Stephen labelled composition as 'useless' or 'less valuable'. But she may have viewed it that way if she thought an emphasis on grammatical sentences and simplistic essays would not help Morley students gain skills they either needed or desired, would actually keep them trapped by class circumstances, and would certainly not help them learn to write. Some evidence hints that she might have considered an autobiographical writing course more suitable. For one thing, as Stephen said to the young working women at the Morley soirée in January 1905, she would rather get to know them than teach them (*L1* 173). She was, many friends remarked, insatiably curious about other people, 'so intensely interested in facts that she had not come across before' (Grant 20). Woolf recognised her trait in 'Middlebrow', writing 'I always sit next the conductor in an omnibus and try to get him to tell me what it is like – being a conductor' (E6 471), which recalls Stephen 'corner[ing]' Miss Williams 'to make her reveal herself' ('Report' 202). An interest in her students' lives suggests teaching an autobiographical writing course might have come more naturally. As Woolf would write in *A Room of One's Own*, 'there is a girl behind the counter too – I would as soon have her true history as the hundred and fiftieth life of Napoleon or seventieth study of Keats' (89). She knew about such girls; she had met them in her classes.

Second, her draft report reinforces the idea that Stephen could discuss autobiographical writing with ease. She says Burke, a student in both the lecture and English History classes, 'had been as I found, writing that account of her own life which I had suggested before' ('Report' 203). This story implies: (1) Stephen had a conversation with a student about writing before she was teaching writing; (2) Burke was comfortable talking with Stephen outside of class; (3) Burke asked Stephen for advice; (4) Burke shared the account of her life with Stephen; and (5) Stephen encouraged Burke at the time, given her report's assessment: 'in other circumstances, she would have been a writer' ('Report' 203).[45]

Third, Stephen's essay on the 'Decay of Essay-writing' supported autobiographical writing that promoted the self-exploration Montaigne practised. She protested at the contemporary personal essay as practised by some newspaper essayists because it was, paradoxically, not personal enough: it did not do the difficult, courageous work of confronting the self.[46] Instead, it pretended an infallibility (E1 27) about topics it knew or cared nothing about, an attitude the increase in schooling seemed to have encouraged. She deplored the egoism that evaded the self rather than expressed it, an insincere, routine employment of the personal that turned 'individual likes and dislikes' into declarations about 'the great mysteries of art and literature' (E1 26). A composition course encouraging students to confront themselves and their lives honestly might not only support student growth, increase skills and affirm literary treatment of ordinary issues, but also convey important knowledge to other classes about working-class lives and reality. Such an approach would have unknowingly followed R. H. Tawney's recommendation for teaching composition, and compilations of working-class autobiographical writing in John Burnett's *Useful Toil* (1974) and *Destiny Obscure* (1982) reveal it would have built on knowledge, skills and desires working people already had.

But we do not know what Virginia Stephen was expected or allowed to do in her weekly hour and a half-long composition classes[47] or what her students were supposed to learn. We do not know if Morley composition courses implicitly defined learning to write as following grammar rules and filling in templates or as exploring self and world through writing. We do not know if Stephen thought practising autobiographical writing skills would have served Morley students better, or if so, she could have taken that route in her course (though her reference to the 'Autumn' essay suggests not). We do not know if she was supposed to lecture about rules and lead oral and written exercises that inculcated those rules, if she should provide writing exercises or essay models, or if she should assign some writing, coach students as they worked on it and then mark it on the spot.[48] Our only clue to Stephen's actual instruction in an English Composition class appears in a letter to Violet when she wryly comments about her own previous sentence, 'make that sentence clear, as I say to my class, to which I go this instant' (*L1* 219).[49]

Stephen's transition to teaching composition was probably difficult. She struggled; teaching a milkman to 'write English' beat her (*L1* 281); and classes did not always show up (*L1* 292). We know she went into her Composition teaching assignment thinking the course was useless and we can speculate about why. We can assume she had to focus on basic skills, not ideas. We can wonder if she practised being more interactive in class, assigning, working with individual students, coaching, responding and correcting during sessions. And we can suspect she learned a great deal about writing through her efforts to teach it. But exactly what she taught and practised in the courses remains a mystery, as does what she thought about composition as she wrapped up her stint of teaching it.

Teaching Literature – Michaelmas Term 1907

Virginia Stephen ended her teaching career at Morley College teaching poetry when she led a Reading Circle on Keats, Shelley and Browning. Courses in reading and writing and composition were on Morley Course Lists from its founding, but literature courses existed on the fringes for quite a while. Interest in the humanities and arts, from school and students, often took the form of extracurricular initiatives in Morley's early years. So, for example, the 1902–3 Annual Report notes a literary society had been established to continue the study done in a class taught by Mr Buxton; they read and discussed eighteenth-century authors, and discussions alternated with 'papers on various subjects of literary interest' (4). The author of the 1903–4 report, under the heading Educational Clubs, wrote that a Reading Circle organised by students had focused on 'The Puritan Revolution of the XVIIth Century' and 'Some Modern Novels and Essays' under the auspices of the 'National Home Reading Union' (3). According to Robert Snape, the National Home Reading Union 'was in essence a British replication of Chautauqua'; members read the same book at the same time according to recommended lists from the Union, circles met fortnightly or monthly, and voluntary leaders led discussions (90–1).[50] In the July 1906 issue of the *Morley College Magazine*, A. Johnson reports their Reading Circle concluded its meetings on 12 June; they had 'spent many pleasant and interesting evenings in 'takin' notes' and discussion' about Shelley, Keats, Wordsworth, Coleridge, Lamb's Essays and J. H. Shorthouse's novel, *John Inglesant*; and they had 'neared the borderland of history and ethics' several times in their literature study (*MCM*, xv.10 153). The 1904–5 Report mentioned University Extension classes in Shakespeare; such classes were generally funded by external sources, led by lecturers affiliated with a university who came to the educational location, and required students to attend, take notes, participate and write (R. D. Roberts 747).

For the first time, a broadly titled 'English literature (University Extension)' was on the List of Classes for the 1906–7 academic year (*MCAR* 1905–6 15), and the 1906–7 Report mentions University Extension lectures on life and literature in the nineteenth century, presumably the specific topic covered in that lecture course (*MCAR* 1906–7 5). Virginia Stephen's Reading Circle on Keats, Shelley and Browning, and G. M. Trevelyan's Reading Circle on Shakespeare are on the List of Classes for 1907–8 and seem to follow Mr Rickett's suggestion at the 15 March 1907 faculty meeting that groups 'be formed for the consideration and discussion of certain specified writers' (*MCECM*3 reverse order, twelve pages in). In the 1907–8 Annual Report, Morley stated that the college had been selected by the London County Council as one of the 'centres for special courses in English literature', and English literature lectures were on the List of Classes for the 1908–9 academic year, along with a Shakespeare Reading Circle and an English matriculation course (*MCAR* 1907–8 4, 24). From then on, English Literature lectures and English matriculation courses appear on the upcoming year's schedule, though some may have been offered through the London County Council (*MCAR* 1912–13 2; *MCAR* 1913–14 3–4). What began as a course led by the new principal with follow-up by a student-initiated study group in 1902–3 had become a routine part of course offerings by 1908–9. Yet again, Virginia Stephen's tenure at Morley coincided with a curricular transition.

Though the distinction between English literature lectures and Reading Circles is not certain, annual reports and the college magazine indicate the lectures focused on historically based literary periods or genres, whereas the Reading Circles focused on individual authors. Lectures were probably just that, whereas reading circles were probably more informal, perhaps a mix of lecture and discussion, entirely discussion, or a mix of discussion and the writing or reading of papers: in the National Home Reading Union model, members received questions about the next reading and 'were invited to prepare short essay answers to be read aloud and discussed at circle meetings' (Snape 91). In any case, Virginia Stephen again faced a different kind of class. Stephen evidently practised bringing students' attention to the biographical and historical context for literature and the aesthetic and emotional qualities of literary works, and her pedagogy highlighted poetry's oral quality. In this course, she may have tried to pass on to her students some of what she had gained from hearing and reading literature as she grew up. In her most extended comment about this class, she writes to Violet Dickinson on 1 October 1907:

> I gave a lecture to 4 working men yesterday: one stutters on his ms – and another is an Italian and reads English as though it were mediaeval Latin – and another is my degenerate poet, who rants and blushes, and almost seizes my hand when we happen to like the same lines. But I dont have any notes – I can tell you the first sentence of my lecture: 'The poet Keats died when he was 25: and he wrote all his works before that.' Indeed – how very interesting, Miss Stephen. (*L*1 313)

We can glean from this description that her four students were male; one had a disability, one was not a native speaker, and one was a poet. Allowing for her letter's combination of mockery (of others and herself) and exaggeration, it also reveals the circle included reading aloud, discussing lines, and communicating some contextual biography in a brief lecture. Her account hints at interpretive activity as well, since noting favourite lines implies explaining why. Given her own literary upbringing and her father's focus on biography, Stephen's attention to how a poet's life and work interrelate is not surprising. Neither is her focus on the oral quality of literature. She grew up hearing her father reciting poetry from memory, writing 'as he lay back in his chair and spoke the beautiful words with closed eyes, we felt that he was speaking not merely the words of Tennyson or Wordsworth but what he himself felt and knew' (E1 129). It seems likely she both read aloud herself and asked her students to read out loud, focusing attention on language, interpretation of lines and the relationship between oral and written. Given two students' reading difficulties, she may have found it difficult to sustain that emphasis all term, but her last poet was Browning, the master of dramatic monologue, so one suspects she tried. Her literature course implied that literary learning involved attending to language and connecting life and books.

Although Stephen's decision to quit teaching at the end of Michaelmas Term had a lot to do with her increasing absorption in writing her first novel and perhaps with the increasing length of her *TLS* reviews, it is at least possible she also faulted Morley for its piecemeal offering of literature lectures and reading circles. As mentioned earlier, she had suggested in March 1907 that a specific period of English literature be offered each term, connected to history and composition, and supported by outside lecturers (*MCECM3* reverse order, twelve pages in). And although Morley began to offer English literature lectures more systematically after she left, nothing indicates they did so in the sequenced and coordinated way she recommended. Perhaps Virginia Stephen saw something in some Morley College students that officials there did not, a hunger for a more purposeful, integrated, even literary education.

A hunger that mirrored her own? It cannot be a coincidence that the students Stephen remembers by name and we know most about, Miss Williams, Burke and Cyril Yaldwyn, are also the students interested in writing. Virginia Stephen would have instinctively picked up on their presence in her classes just as they would have instinctively responded to her as a fellow writer. She saw the desire for something more in Miss Williams and Burke, and she observed the hunger for literary education in her 'degenerate poet' [51] who 'rant[ed] and blush[ed], and almost seize[d her] hand' when they liked the same lines (*L1* 313). He left a lasting impression on the young teacher. As several have noted, he became a model for Virginia Woolf's Septimus Smith, whose experiences 'made him shy, and stammering, made him anxious to improve himself, made him fall in love with Miss Isabel Pole, lecturing in the Waterloo Road upon Shakespeare' (*MD* 83; Daugherty, 'Taking a Leaf' 39; Daugherty, 'Morley College' 133; Cuddy-Keane, *VW* 84–5; Lee, *VW* 219–20). Miss Pole wonders whether Septimus is like Keats and 'reflected how she might give him a taste of *Antony and Cleopatra* and the rest; lent him books; wrote him scraps of letters' while he dreams of her, thinks her wise, and 'wrote poems to her, which, ignoring the subject, she corrected in red ink' (*MD* 83).

At the time, Stephen asked her friend Nelly, Lady Robert Cecil, about giving Yaldwyn a job in two December 1907 letters. She writes,

> I want also to bother you with my good working man – who is a socialist, of a kind, and a poet; but also very clever and enthusiastic, and he can write short hand, and is a good man at accounts, and has a testimonial. His name is Cyril Zeldwyn, 29 Montagu St. – But I'm afraid there is no chance that you will want him – and dont bother –

and then later writes,

> I am very grateful to Lord Robert for offering to see [him]. I will certainly tell him. I dont know what job he is after now – I dont think he is really very exciting; but what you call a deserving case. (L1 320–1)

In both, she puts Yaldwyn forward and then diffidently pulls back, as though she has a high opinion of him but wonders if others might not – perhaps she suspects others may see him as strange, or worries Lord Robert will not give Cyril a chance or recognise his skills. Perhaps she wants the Cecils to see underneath what she thinks they might see on the surface. She clearly understands the conditions put on upper-class generosity: Cyril is what 'you call a deserving case'.

Lord Robert Cecil was a lawyer, politician and diplomat who would go on to help build the League of Nations and receive the Nobel Peace Prize in 1937. With Joseph Hurst, he collaborated on the *Principles of Commercial Law* (1891; 1906), was appointed a Queen's Counsel in 1899, and up to 1906 practised civil law ('Robert'). When Stephen wrote to Nelly, he was a Conservative member of Parliament. It made sense Stephen would have thought of him in relationship to a job for Yaldwyn, a clerk with shorthand, writing and bookkeeping skills.[52]

Cyril Yaldwyn, the Cyril Zeldwyn of the *Letters*, had poems appear in the *Morley College Magazine* several times between 1907 and 1910.[53] The magazine published his December 1907 'The Mortality of Feeling' in its January 1908 issue, so Virginia Stephen might have seen it before it was published; the flickering fire description of Septimus's feelings about Miss Isabel Pole faintly echoes the poem's imagery, and the line 'Death is feeling ended' also seems apt for Septimus (*MCM* xvii.4 59). See Figure 8.1. The magazine prints his sonnet, 'Two Ways of Love', dated January 1908, in its February issue (*MCM* xvii.5 73) and 'Love's Best Way', dated 17 February 1908, in its March issue (*MCM* xvii.6 89). In the next year, C. Y. has a poem called 'The Passing of Swinburne' in the June 1909 issue (*MCM* xviii.9 143), and he signs 'In Memoriam: George Meredith' with his full name in the July issue (*MCM* xviii.10 151). In 1909–10, Cyril Yaldwyn appears three times, all in the January 1910 issue: a poem, 'Three Poets' (*MCM* xix.4 57–8); a report of his reading a paper called 'The Poetic Principle' on 18 December 1909, which had been followed by an intense discussion about the difference between 'art for art's sake' and 'poetry for man's sake' (*MCM* xix.4 65); and a programme listing for the United Clubs' Tea on 8 January – he gave a recitation of 'Fra Giacomo', a dramatic monologue by Robert Buchanan (*MCM* xix.4 68). Might the latter have grown out of studying Browning in Stephen's Reading Circle?

In *Mrs Dalloway*, Woolf writes that Septimus Smith went off to France 'to save an England which consisted almost entirely of Shakespeare's plays and Miss Isabel Pole in a green dress walking in a square' (84), but Yaldwyn is not on Morley's list of men who served in the Great War British forces. Google and Ancestry.com investigations turn up (1) a Cyril Yaldwyn byline on a 19 October 1913 *Montreal Herald* article about a home owned by Clarence Isaac and Belle Goldsmith DeSola (Kirkland 50–1); (2) a Cyril Ernest Grosvenor Yaldwyn, who was born in India on 31 August 1883, grew up in Sussex, married Grace Stanton Titcombe in 1912, gave his profession as journalist and his address as Richmond, Surrey, when he signed up for service in the Canadian Over-Seas Expeditionary Forces

MORLEY COLLEGE MAGAZINE.

THE MORTALITY OF FEELING.

WHILE we live, we spin
    Webs of fleeting fancies;
    Sounds and colours weave we in,—
Virtue's music, evil's din;
    Thus we build romances.

When we feel, we live;
    Sleep, with no dream blended,
Is the mind's restorative
For the wounds desire can give:
    Death is feeling ended.

Ah! desire, desire!
    When we pass the portal
We shall feel thy fickle fire
Faintly flicker and expire;
    Thou art Life—and mortal!

Soul! couldst thou destroy
    Knowledge of thy being,
Grief would join the flight of joy,
Nought would soothe and nought annoy—
    All with knowledge fleeing.

Call them what ye may,
    Feeling, love, desire,
All are one, and wane away
Till we cool to coldest clay
    Or flash out in fire.

December, 1907.   CYRIL YALDWYN.

CONSULTATIVE COMMITTEE.

THE monthly meeting of the above Committee was held Monday, December 2. There was some discussion re the Saturday afternoon excursions; it was remarked that the excursions arranged by the club secretaries were often unsuccessful because such a small number of students took part in these excursions. It was thought that if the club secretaries would meet to discuss this matter, and each in turn arrange an excursion open to members of all clubs, the excursions would become more popular.

It has been decided to arrange a visit to Buckingham Palace towards the end of the month.

The Council are going to consult with the Borough Polytechnic, with a view to arranging joint expeditions with this institution.

                                                        A. G.

Figure 8.1 Cyril Yaldwyn, 'The Mortality of Feeling', December 1907. *Morley College Magazine* xvii.4 (January 1908): 59. With permission of the Morley College Library Archive.

on 23 September 1914 (he had served in South Africa for two years); he served as a private in the F Company of the 13th Battalion, 3rd Infantry Brigade of the Canadian Contingent of the British Expeditionary Force (*List* 124, No. 24778) and received Star, War and Victory medals (but those list him as 17th Canadian Infantry); (3) a C. E. G. Yaldwyn who was a 2nd lieutenant in the Durham Light Infantry, served in France and confusingly, received the same medals, which he had sent to a Cavendish Square address; and (4) a journalist who left Britain for Gibralter in August 1920, age 36, with a first-class ticket. Any of these men might plausibly be the Morley College poet (and could the first two be the same man?), but whether any or none of them is the person Stephen knew cannot be determined, and no other clues have surfaced to explain what happened to Cyril Yaldwyn after his Morley College days.[54] As a poet, he seems to have disappeared after his promising *Magazine* publications.

During a time of curricular transitions, Virginia Stephen taught four kinds of Morley classes and practised different teaching strategies. At first, she focused on content, delivered in a lecture, but she learned to relax and become more interactive. Then she told vivid stories in a chronological context. Next, perhaps she became more of a coach, interacting with students as they practised and demonstrated writing skill. Last, she focused students' attention on poetry's oral quality and its connection to poets' lives as they practised reading and interpretation. She seems to have instinctively understood that different courses and different student needs called for different strategies, and she adjusted her pedagogy accordingly.

Stephen's practice of these teaching strategies nurtured her non-fiction writing. Not only would she come to write essays in which she surreptitiously coached her readers in reading, researching and writing, but she would also create detailed scenes, call attention to favourite passages, draw her readers into conversations, and most brilliantly sometimes, weave in her version of literary history. Teaching at Morley and practising a variety of pedagogies with her students taught Virginia Stephen, in a visceral and immediate way, to consider her audience. The common readers Virginia Woolf would come to imagine, personify and speak with in every essay she wrote were deeply rooted in Morley College students.

Notes

1. I incorrectly stated Virginia Stephen's career span and number of courses in earlier publications.
2. Stephen's history knowledge, though extensive, cannot be called disciplinary, and neither composition nor literature was a disciplinary field yet.
3. Stephen did not give notice until December (*L1* 320).
4. The two terms seem interchangeable in the 1913–14 annual report when Morley thanks Mr Niemeyer for his 'lectures on English Composition and Essay Writing' and Miss Giles for having 'taught Latin and Greek' (*MCAR* 1913–14 6).
5. Stephen's rather freewheeling class mirrors Morley's curriculum – perhaps an underlying coherence, but one students had to discover.
6. Stephen does not mention a lecture on the dramatic in her journal or correspondence, and unusually for this term, she does not mention a class on 15 March. Rosenbaum does not hesitate to label the holograph titled 'The Dramatic in Art and Life' a lecture (165, 166): it is with the Cellini lecture in her papers and highlights 'rudimentary

ideas on literary matters'. He also suggests she 'had not yet read her Aristotle' when she writes it (166), but see 158, and she was working on an article she called 'Magic Greek' (*PA* 252), so she is immersed in drama.

Rosenbaum is right: these notes do seem to be for a lecture about basic genre differences, differences between art and life. But puzzles remain. It seems unlikely, but perhaps she gave this lecture on 15 March and dined with the Cecils on another date (*PA* 252). Or perhaps she dined with them early and then went to class. Perhaps she gave the lecture some other time during the term, but if so, when? Her journal records her last class meeting on 22 March, and the other dates seem accounted for in the 'syllabus'. Perhaps she gave the lecture in another Morley course, possibly the Reading Circle, yet the Circle's topic is three poets. Perhaps these are lecture notes she sketched out before the term and did not use, which would validate Rosenbaum's Aristotle comment. Or maybe the notes are not for a lecture at all.

7. Some relatives and acquaintances donated to Morley in other ways: Ottoline Morrell gave books by 126 authors (*MCAR* 1902–3 6); Violet Dickinson gave money (*MCAR* 1903–4 10); Vanessa gave pictures (*MCAR* 1906–7 9); and Virginia and Adrian gave funds to the orchestra after she had finished teaching (*MCAR* 1909–10 21).
8. She puts quotation marks around the word lecture in this 16 January 1905 entry.
9. See Ann McClellan, particularly 89–91. Morley began investigating the Workers' Educational Association Tutorial Class teaching method for the working classes in 1910–11, and Richard H. Tawney, who promoted student participation and engagement, joined the Morley College Council in 1912–13. See *MCAR* 1911–12 about this pedagogy's support of working-class learning through more camaraderie in classes (2). Stephen's experiences led her to similar conclusions.
10. The others were grammar, geography and plain needlework; small grants were given if whole classes, not individual students, met the required standard (J. Keating 1).
11. J. T. Murphy writes in his memoir that his working-class schooling was meant to give him 'a little history without understanding' (qtd in Childs 34). See also John T. Smith's detailed study of textbook research, inspectors' reports, rationale, and extent of history teaching from 1862 to 1900. He cites H. L. Withers, who claims in 1899 '"that for practical purposes, even at the beginning of the twentieth century, [history] might be called a new subject in London schools"', and L. J. Roberts, who in 1901 said '"no subject ... has been more neglected in our elementary schools than the history of our own country"' (148).
12. Virginia Stephen experienced this phenomenon: she started her English History class with eight students who had begged for the course, but enrolment dropped to four immediately. She did not care because the remaining students were serious and always attended, but the drop reinforces the 'curious fact' noted in the Annual Report.
13. Interestingly enough, Jenny Keating says the authors of the Board of Education's 1905 'Suggestions for the Consideration of Teachers' recommended an emphasis on the telling of 'vivid and dramatic' stories for young students, with story remaining a foundation as instruction moved toward important historical figures, chronology, and impact of the past on the present. They also recommended the use of maps, illustrations, diagrams, chronological summaries and so forth to give 'vividness and reality to the teaching' (13–15).
14. Nicolson and Trautmann say she is reading Alice Stopford Green's *Town Life in the Fifteenth Century* (*L1* 190 n4), but she read that book in January 1905 (*PA* 274). More likely, she is reading J. R. Green's *A Short History of the English People*; see n16 below. Describing herself as a 'journalist who wants to read history' to obtain a ticket for Dr Williams' Library, Stephen expresses pride in 'feel[ing] a professional Lady' (*L1* 190).
15. See Clara Jones, 28–37, for a discussion of Stephen's dependence on Whig narrative in her course, and especially Laughton's influence: 'Something of Laughton's conception

of "history as a record of events" is surely identifiable in Virginia Stephen's desire to teach English history "from the beginning"' (32). But that desire is her students', not hers (*PA* 255), though a teaching novice could be excused for relying on her father's training, her reading, her King's College courses and the sources she had handy, as Jones acknowledges. She probably was not aware she was a 'custodian of a quite particular historical narrative' (29). Sabine Hotho-Jackson enumerates how historiography changed in the beginning of the twentieth century, but those changes occur in texts written in 1910 and after (293–4, 312 n5–10). Jones shows that in 'The Journal of Mistress Joan Martyn', written in August 1906, Stephen questions grand historical narratives and historians' practices (40–4), but Stephen knew the narratives and had historical knowledge her students did not if F. W. Maitland's gently realistic assessment of Morley's English Citizen students a decade earlier is to be believed: 'I consider the subject a very difficult one for those who have had no previous training in history or law' (*MCAR* 1893 12).

16. Leaska suggests Green's *History of the English People* (*PA* 269 n28), and Emily Kopley points out that three of the four volumes of Green's *History* exist in the Library of Leonard and Virginia Woolf (137; 319 n6). But that title's signer is Julian Bell (K&M-V 92), so it seems more likely Stephen got whatever Green she used for her Morley classes from the London Library when she was there on 29 April. The 1903 *Catalogue of the London Library* lists an 1874 edition of *A Short History of the English People* (LLA), and her notes align with the 1877 edition on *HathiTrust*, including her heading, Authorities: The English Kingdoms, other divisions, subdivisions and details she lists, and even her use of Green's exact words for his first 'Authority' in the English Conquest section: the 'Only extant British account is that of the Monk Gildas' (7; 'Notes ["Authorities"]' title page). In *The History of the English People*, Green uses Early England as his first large heading and writes, 'The only extant British account is the "Epistola" of Gildas, a work written probably about A. D. 560' (5).

17. Like her plans to write history, Virginia Stephen's use of the term 'manly', one of her father's favourite evaluative terms, illustrates his influence at the time. Based on her notes in *PA* 278–80 and its organisation around reigns, it is likely she was using Freeman's *History of the Norman Conquest*, not his textbook, *Outlines of History*, as Kopley suggests (319 n6). Freeman's *History* makes sense as well, given her reading and taking notes on '4 volumes of medieval English' (*L1* 202).

18. Green aimed to produce a history 'not of English Kings or English Conquests, but of the English people'. For him, 'constitutional progress' was 'the result of social development' (*Short History* v, vi). But Burrow criticises Green by implying he was an amateur. See Rosemary Jann's epilogue, however, in which amateur remains a positive term: 'The animating ideals of the amateur, the sage, the man of letters, the "literary" historian, lived on in their twentieth-century successors who continued to measure historical knowledge not in terms of expertise alone' (233). Audrey Johnson's paper on Woolf's resistance to professionalising history in *A Room of One's Own* reveals the fuller implications of Burrow's critique of Green. As history became an academic discipline and its methodology more standardised, the scientific, factual, professional and archival-based approach to history worked to root out the romantic, literary, amateur and narrative-based approach. According to Johnson, Woolf's conscious use of story in writing a women's history reveals her awareness that gender pervaded the dichotomy between the two approaches. See also Juliet Dusinberre, 1–29.

19. Leslie Stephen helped Alice Stopford Green with the project; she was the Mrs Green on the London Library Committee.

20. See Hotho-Jackson and Jann, Chapters 5 and 6.

21. See Chapter 6, 131, for the inspector's comments about Graham Wallis's students in university extension lectures on 'The English Citizen, Past and Present' in 1894 (Richards 114–15). Contextual frameworks matter.

22. In the same letter, she writes, 'Aint it ridiculous—teaching working women about the ancient Britons!' (*L1* 191), a cringe-worthy remark. But this comment, made early in the term, possibly reflects the kind of too-easy dismissal teachers might make in an unthinking moment, particularly to a friend, whereas the draft report comments, made at the end of the term, reflect greater understanding of her students' capabilities and efforts. Her hard work and actions, along with the more carefully considered words of her report, convey respect for her students and awareness of how educational institutions fail them, whereas the words in her letter express a stereotypical assumption between two women of the same class, which, she might have realised at term's end, was not accurate. As Cuddy-Keane points out, 'Woolf's private correspondence, crafted for her addressees and often highly performative, cannot be taken as a reliable indicator of her professional work' ('VW' 242). Stephen's references to her students may sometimes be more addressed to her recipients' assumptions than reflective of her own.

23. Clara Jones notes Stephen does not give her manuscript the title used in Appendix B; Quentin Bell does (23). Jones calls it the 'Morley Sketch'. However, Stephen does start by writing 'This is the season for another report,' which could indicate such reports were routine once classes were over. Nothing in the Morley records remaining from this period suggests that, however, and Stephen did not mention such a requirement when she wrote 'a kind of sketch' after her first class (which Leaska incorrectly assumes is what Quentin Bell published in his biography) (*PA* 256 n53). Whether Stephen drafted her 'report' for herself as a teaching log or revised and submitted it to Miss Sheepshanks or someone else is impossible to know.

    Jones says it does not have the formal quality one would expect from a 'mandatory institutional exercise'. She emphasises the text's 'playful performative' quality and says July 'would hardly be the month when reports were required' since it would be in the 'middle of the Morley College summer holiday' (22–3). But Easter was on 23 April that year, followed by a bank holiday on 24 April, which is when the Stephens returned from Spain (*L1* 186), and Stephen mentioned working on history on 29 April and 1–3 and 10–11 May in her journal (*PA* 269–72). If Easter Term in 1905 was similar to 1907, when the opening and closing dates were 8 April and 1 July (teachers established their lecture schedules within those College dates), and if Stephen did not begin teaching until after 24 April, then early July would be the start of the summer holiday, not the middle. Also, the College opened a week after Easter in other Easter Terms, which might have made the 1905 opening day as late as 1 May.

    The draft's timing, word choice and angry, defensive tone make another kind of sense if Virginia Stephen is responding to Miss Sheepshanks's criticism. Although Jones is almost certainly correct in surmising it is not an official report – it seems written to follow up on an unsatisfactory encounter – it is at least possible Stephen revised and submitted it, or used it as the basis for a letter.

24. Annual reports, meeting minutes and magazine articles show Trevelyan was woven into Morley's fabric early: he taught there, and at the Working Men's College, for years, gave books to the library, participated in College social life and allowed his lectures to be published in the *Magazine*. As a professional academic historian, he also had status the amateur Stephen did not, and if he could include Morley in his schedule and draw high enrolment, requests for English history would not have persuaded Miss Sheepshanks to risk having two history courses compete for students in the same term. Whether Stephen understood that underlying dynamic is debatable – references to her course assignments in Executive Committee minutes did not mean she attended those meetings (in fact, they imply she did not) or was 'aware of the institutional workings of Morley College' (C. Jones 56 n130). Trevelyan's autumn lectures 'received special recognition from the University Extension Board' (*MCAR* 1905–6 2) and appeared on the list of classes as 'Special Lectures' on Thursday evenings, and students paid a small

fee (*MCAR* 1904–5 16). Presumably, he functioned as a paid lecturer in the University Extension programme that term, not as a Morley volunteer.
25. Jenny Keating (see Cannadine et al. xiii) says those remembering their early twentieth-century elementary classrooms frequently criticised the lack of coherence in their history lessons, recalling 'no sequence of chronological progression or sense of intellectual development'. She cites Jack Common, who received a secondhand biography of Dr Johnson but could make little sense of it because he had never reached the eighteenth century in his classes. Jack remembers starting over and over again with the Plantagenets but then suddenly encountering 'a teacher who dropped us quickly down a ladder of classes into an era he had been reading up on' (50).
26. According to her autobiography, Mary Sheepshanks understood the need for more coherence at Morley, writing that the Workers' Educational Classes were

> an important development. The students chose the subject and the lecturer. Each class lasted two hours, the first devoted to the lecture, the second to questions and discussion. Students entered for a three year course, and wrote weekly papers. Thus, continuity and thoroughness were insured, instead of what was sometimes a haphazard and superficial changing from one subject to another. (*LDE* 33–4)

This tutorial class, partially introduced in 1909–10 (*MCAR* 1909–10 3), was fully introduced the next year as 'Industrial History' (*MCAR* 1910–11 2). Much of its expense was defrayed by London University and Workers' Educational Association representatives who had chosen Morley as a tutorial centre. The Fabian Society lent books, the Library purchased reference books and textbook copies, and the class used Goldsmiths' and London University libraries.
27. Clara Jones says Stephen's last sentence suggests her 'commitment to the Whig values of continuity and progress' (34), but perhaps 'whole' and 'proper ends' refer to holistic knowledge construction instead. In her 1903 'The Country in London', Stephen writes:

> I read some history: it is suddenly all alive, branching forwards & backwards & connected with every kind of thing that seemed entirely remote before. I seem to feel Napoleons influence on our quiet evening in the garden for instance – I think I see for a moment how our minds are all threaded together – how any live mind today is of the very same stuff as Plato's & Euripides. It is only a continuation & development of the same thing. It is this common mind that binds the whole world together; & all the world is mind. Then I read a poem say – & the same thing is repeated. I feel as though I had grasped the central meaning of the world, & all these poets & historians & philosophers were only following out paths branching from that centre in which I stand. (*PA* 178–9)

As Virginia Woolf, she would say something similar in 'A Sketch of the Past' (72).
28. In her transcription of the 'Morley Sketch', Clara Jones indicates an illegible word between '{larger &}' and '<great>' (213 last par.). The crossed-out partial word may be 'profita', perhaps the start of 'profitable,' which would fit the context.

This conflict and its ensuing pressures continue to plague higher education. Numbers are important, especially at tuition-driven schools. Enrolment numbers, though no longer tied directly to grants from regulatory bodies, still drive budgets, salaries, offerings, class size and so forth.
29. These comments come before she teaches it and then after being observed in her first composition course. Her thoughts about composition may have evolved over the course of teaching five classes, as her thoughts about teaching and lectures seem to have done as she taught her first two classes, but we do not know.
30. It is possible Stephen marked up student essays the way Professor Laughton and her tutors Clara Pater and Janet Case had marked up her work, though she never mentions doing so. (Differences between the King's College courses she took and the

Morley courses she taught probably struck Stephen, just as the differences between her 'casual' King's College path and Thoby's 'official' Clifton one probably did.) But Morley teachers did not grade student writing, and students did not receive coursework grades. Course certificate exams were held on a certain day after classes were over. Students who wanted to take those exams paid a small fee to do so, and if they passed, they received certificates in an annual public ceremony and were listed in the September *Magazine*. Course instructors did not construct or administer these exams; regulatory bodies did. Six students passed the English Grammar examination with a Class 2 in September 1907, though two did not earn certificates because they did not meet minimum attendance requirements (*MCM* xvii.1 10), and five earned English Grammar certificates in September 1908 (*MCM* xviii.1 1). The first certificate given for English Composition was reported after Stephen left, in the September 1909 *Magazine* (*MCM* xix.1 7). Elaine Andrews suspects these exams were not difficult, especially in the early years, but in any case, instructors had no role in them.

31. Although not the case in 1905, it had been the case in 1904, so perhaps the Dutchman's thinking he was in an Arithmetic class stemmed from confusion about times based on having the wrong schedule or from receiving faulty guidance (*L1* 210). Arithmetic, History, Geography, Elocution, Literature, Foreign Languages, Algebra, Euclid and Logic were all grouped under Literary Classes as opposed to Scientific Classes.
32. Perhaps the Essay Class was closer to what Thoby seems to have taken at Clifton?
33. On the other hand, shop girls in Stephen's class say they would write more if they had more time (*L1* 210), which suggests out-of-class writing, although they could be commenting on their writing in general. As with much else related to composition at Morley, it is difficult to know whether Stephen assigned homework or had students write in class or both.
34. Did students know she wrote?
35. Richard Morris (1833–94), English scholar and philologist, edited twelve volumes for the Early English Text Society, among other scholarly projects, but his book on historical English grammar and the primer, written out of his schoolmaster experience, 'place[d] the teaching of English upon a sound basis': from them, 'tens of thousands of boys and girls have learnt their earliest knowledge of their own tongue, which they will never need to unlearn' (Cotton).
36. Mark Hussey remembers such parsing exercises when growing up in England.
37. Perhaps this request was one reason Stephen did not teach Advanced Composition again after that, shifting to a Reading Circle for what would be her last term at Morley.
38. In a 1914 article for *English Journal*, 'Oral Composition a Basis for Written', E. E. Chiles describes student storytelling, instruction in rhetorical principles while discussing those stories, student outline preparation, student writing in everyday speech, the recording of mistakes in notebooks, and drilling to correct those mistakes (354–61). However, *English Journal* is an American publication. Anne Ruggles Gere, studying the history of US writing groups, discovered articles about their use at Yale, Penn, MIT and so forth, as early as the late 1890s (16–18), yet British sources seem focused almost solely on sentence-level error at this time.
39. Nesfield also wrote *Junior Course of Composition* (1901), *Senior Course of Composition* (1903) and *Manual of English Grammar and Composition* (1905), all geared to examination and matriculation standards. The junior book has instructions on essay-writing and letter-writing and is for 'Oxford and Cambridge Local Examinations (Preliminary and Junior), Preceptors' Examinations (Third and Second classes), and the Government Examinations of Pupil Teachers' (vi); it includes sample essays by 15- and 16-year-olds. The senior book covers more examinations and certificates, including those for the Indian Civil and Home Civil Services.

40. The second subtitle is: *With Chapters on Paraphrasing, Essay-Writing, Précis-Writing, Punctuation, and Other Matters.*
41. Any interpretation of this essay has to be qualified: the editor, without her consent, cut it by half and changed the title and some words (*E*1 27 n1; *L*1 180–1).
42. As Caroline Pollentier clarifies, Stephen's essay appeared during a 'wider controversy on the decline of the essay in the context of mass culture', and commentators like Orlo Williams, a *TLS* contributor, pointedly blamed the journalism trade. She adds, 'Tellingly enough,' Stephen 'associated the decline of the form with its transformation into a school exercise' (138–9).
43. See Vincent 130–4 for a more detailed discussion of the relationship between social mobility and literacy.
44. Clara Jones says Stephen's description of her conversation with Miss Williams was motivated by what she 'clearly felt was an uncomfortable and invasive parity' between herself and her student; her calling Miss Williams a 'writing machine' and defining her work, as Jones puts it, as 'mindless and mechanical', conveys a 'class-based snobbery about religion' (27). The reader of Stephen's draft does not know whether Miss Williams herself was religious, but the description of her reviewing practice fits what many women, not just those at religious papers, had to do to break into the male world of journalism, according to Barbara Onslow: write 'mere summaries padded out with extracts', reviewing that could be 'wearisome because of the sheer weight of reading, even had one perfected the art of skimming' (63, 66). In other words, huge quantities of work were produced at high speed (short notices about new books might appear almost immediately after publication [Onslow 63–4]) for little to no pay. It is hard to determine if Stephen judges Miss Williams's work as like the 'manipulat[ion] of bottles of patent mouth wash' ('Report' 202) or if that judgement, if not the words, comes from Miss Williams as she describes her situation. (Nigel Cross uses the title 'The Female Drudge' for his chapter on female novelists trying to break through.) One thing is certain: *Virginia Stephen* does not use the word 'hack' to describe her student (Jones 27).

Some of Jones's conclusions about Virginia Stephen's conversation with Miss Williams and the 'Morley sketch' depend on her transcription. The difficulty of Stephen/Woolf handwriting is legendary, and disagreements about words abound, especially with cancelled words or phrases. Jones's work is solid – my transcription certainly benefited from hers – with a few minor quibbles: in the 'subterranean passages' sentence, Stephen specifically strikes out 'rather' before cancelling the whole, for example. But in two places, the difference in transcription affects interpretation. In the draft's third paragraph, Quentin Bell's transcription reads 'Here was literature stripped of the least glamour of art' (1 202), whereas Jones reads 'Hers was literature stripped of the least glamour of art' (211). Close examination shows Bell is probably correct about the last letter being an 'e', not an 's'; Stephen/Woolf sometimes, not always, uses an 'e' looking more like a capital letter at the end of words like 'here' or 'there'. That one letter makes a huge connotative difference. In Bell's transcription, Stephen makes a straightforward claim; in Jones's, Stephen implies this literature belongs to Williams. Similarly, in the draft's last paragraph, Bell reads 'like meteors from another sphere impinging on this planet' (1 204), whereas Jones reads 'like meteors from another sphere infringing on this planet' (213). The ascenders, descenders and dotted 'i's are the same in both words. But an 'r' does not seem present, and the word seems to have nine letters, not ten. The words can be synonyms, but the first implies a sharp collision whereas the second implies a violation or defeat of rights; the first seems more logical in context.

In two transcriptions of cancelled phrases that Jones marks as questionable, my questionable readings differ. Jones tentatively reads '{So we made much of this [having]}' (211, l. 13; 214), but perhaps the cancelled phrase reads {So we made much from this basis}. Jones also tentatively reads '{that these remote stories should have one meaning}' (212, l. 4 from bottom; 215), but 'one' might be 'any'. Finally, Jones suggests the 'profuse' revisions, the 'mess of deletions and insertions' in the section on Miss Williams, reveal Stephen's discomfort with her student's class and career. Stephen's revisions in that part of her sketch are indeed heavier than elsewhere in the draft, but no heavier than in many other drafts, so although Jones may be correct about the meaning of specific changes, their heaviness in and of itself is not that 'revealing' (24).

Jones surmises Miss Williams might be Annie Williams, who received a first-class certificate for elocution in 1905 (43), which is possible but unlikely unless Miss Williams changed her profession. No reporter attends Morley after 1904–5, and the certificate winner is probably the Miss A. Williams in Mr Howard's elocution class playing Lady Macbeth in scenes on 3 February 1906 (*MCM* xv.5 84 and *MCM* xv.6 94) and reciting a passage from *David Copperfield* at a literary class tea on 11 January 1907 (*MCM* xvi.5 69). A reporter doing what Miss Williams said she was doing could not possibly have participated at Morley in these additional ways.

45. Jones astutely notes that 'Virginia Stephen was preparing her students to intervene' in the national narrative 'with their own personal histories' (36).
46. Anne Fernald makes a similar distinction in '*A Room of One's Own*, Personal Criticism, and the Essay'. 'The odd result of Tompkins's and Gallop's experiments', Fernald writes, 'is a self-centered criticism that is also impersonal' (167).
47. Morley held classes until 10.30 p.m., according to Oldfield (*SP* 66, 96), but see *L1* 292, where Stephen says she 'spent 2 hours there on Wed: and no class came'. Perhaps she was exaggerating, perhaps she went early to meet with students or perhaps her classes generally lasted until 11.
48. Teaching her first-ever Composition class, Stephen jokingly asks Nelly Cecil on 10 November 1905 'Do you know I lecture on English Composition at Morley?' (*L1* 212); she seems to be denigrating her own writing style in this letter rather than reliably describing what she does in class, especially since it comes a day after she experiences Sheepshanks's impatience. Did that impatience indicate lecturing was expected in Composition and Stephen was not lecturing (*L1* 210)? Does Sheepshanks's assessment a year later, identifying Stephen's 'gift' as 'influence' rather than 'direct intellectual teaching' (*L1* 264), indicate Stephen was trying something different in Composition, or failing at lecturing?
49. Brief as this comment is, it recalls her father's 'teaching' about writing: 'To write in the fewest possible words, as clearly as possible, exactly what one meant – that was his only lesson in the art of writing' (*E5* 588).
50. The General Course cost 3 shillings a year, the Artisan's Course 1 shilling and sixpence, and processes for borrowing books at a low cost were put in place (Snape 91).
51. Lee suggests Stephen's use of 'degenerate' signals instability or homosexuality (*VW* 219). But given the subjects of his poetry and article, the blurring of the terms 'degenerate' and 'decadent' at the time, her purchase of James Thomson's works, and Thoby's review of 'Euphrosyne' in which he defended decadents as poets working against convention, perhaps she saw him as part of that aesthetic movement. Jonathan Wild claims that in *All in a Garden Fair*, Walter Besant reveals the 'incompatibility of the poet and the clerk' and 'makes plain the unsuitability of the City for the type of sensitive, artistic youth whom he felt was increasingly likely to be produced by the Board schools' (16).
52. We do not know how this story ends, if Lord Cecil saw Yaldwyn, if he hired him, or if so, for what or for how long. A mass of archival material exists for Robert Cecil (BL Add MS 51071–204 contains 134 volumes), mostly government letters with individual correspondents. Skimming through a few of these British Library papers did not turn up Yaldwyn.

53. When I discovered the poems by Cyril Yaldwyn, I wondered if Virginia Stephen had misspelled his name or if the editors had misread her handwriting. Sarah Whale, Collections and Archives at Hatfield House, kindly allowed me to examine scans of these letters, and it was immediately evident the latter was the case: Stephen clearly uses a 'Ya' at the beginning of his name, not a 'Ze'.
54. The *Montreal Herald* morgue and Canadian archives might be worth exploring.

Chapter 9

Outcomes: Teaching at Morley College

Once Virginia Stephen said 'yes' to Mary Sheepshanks and agreed to teach at Morley College, she confronted the task of negotiating the difference between her own educational background and that of her students. She also, as with her homeschooling, walked into a school of sorts, one that had a curriculum guided by a pedagogical theory where she learned lessons about particular topics within a community of teachers and learners. In the process of teaching her classes there, Stephen learned about institutions, education, pedagogy and class barriers from teachers: her mentor, Mary Sheepshanks, and her students. In a tangible outcome, she created lectures and learned to distrust their usefulness. Intangibly, she saw what lack of access had done to her students and worked to develop strategies for helping them learn.

Although her Morley College teaching was time-consuming, sometimes frustrating and often difficult, Virginia Stephen ended her work there having gained a wealth of pedagogical strategies that Virginia Woolf would consistently use in her essays. Most important, Stephen redefined her audience to include Morley students, whose exclusion, desire and struggles helped engender Woolf's concept of the common reader. Her uneasy class heritage[1] would continue to trouble her life and work, but at Morley, she momentarily crossed class barriers in a classroom. As a result, Woolf sought to create classrooms in her essays, spaces permeated with the 'understanding of a teacher'[2] whose main goal is to motivate students to read, discuss and learn, spaces where the teacher/writer and student/reader can talk.

A 'vain and vicious system': Virginia Stephen's Lectures

Virginia Stephen quickly abandoned an adherence to formal lectures at Morley, as Chapter 8 details. In *Three Guineas*, Virginia Woolf would call the practice of lecturing a 'vain and vicious system' (46) and call for a university that promoted conversation about the 'art of understanding other people's lives and minds' (43).[3] In her essays, she often inveighed against the practice as well, having a woman ask in 'Why?', for example, 'why continue an obsolete custom which not merely wastes time and temper, but incites the most debased of human passions – vanity, ostentation, self-assertion, and the desire to convert?' (E6 33). About the popular and famous Professor Walter Raleigh, she writes,

He made the undergraduates rock with laughter. He drew them in crowds to his lecture room. And they went away loving something or other. Perhaps it was Keats. Perhaps it was the British Empire. Certainly it was Walter Raleigh. But we should be much surprised if anybody went away loving poetry, loving the art of letters. (E4 344)

She also turned down many requests to lecture, including an opportunity to tour the US for three months and give three lectures a week, as proposed by her American agent, Ann Watkins (D5 94–5). And how could she accept the invitation to give the Clark lectures at Cambridge, she asked in her diary, 'without becoming a functionary; without sealing my lips when it comes to tilting at Universities', without becoming a 'time serving pot hunter' (D4 79, 80)?

Virginia Woolf's dissatisfaction with the lecture format and her resulting attempts to circumvent what she saw as the form's difficulties seem to have begun during Virginia Stephen's time as a teacher at Morley College. Stephen's 1897 diary shows she attended lectures as a matter of course during her adolescence without labelling them pernicious. She mentions hearing a lecture on the Rontgen Rays, one by Fridtjof Nansen on his explorations and one by her father, Leslie Stephen (PA 10, 59, 79); about the latter, she writes 'Not quite as good as I have heard from him,' indicating she had heard him lecture several times. These lectures were cultural entertainment, but during her classes at King's College, she listened to academic lectures. Only when she herself has to teach does she begin to question the lecture's efficacy.

Yet she says she prepared full or partial lectures, at least for a while,. We know her topics for the lecture series, but our only clues to specific content rest in two holograph manuscripts S. P. Rosenbaum identifies as lectures (165–6).[4] One is headed 'Autobiography of Benvenuto Cellini'; the other is titled 'The Dramatic in Life & Art' (see Appendix 4 for transcriptions). Both use lecture-concluding language: 'In summing up' for 'Cellini' [91] and 'To sum up then' in 'Dramatic' [95].[5] Stephen refers to her Cellini lecture on 14 and 15 February 1905, writing in her journal that (1) she has been frantically searching for a subject; (2) there are 'a great many plums which it is no trouble to pick'; and (3) she has spent two mornings on it, commenting she needs to find another time for 'doing these lecture jobs' since 'mornings are too precious' (PA 237). It may take her two mornings because she does not rely on J. A. Symonds's extensive introduction to his translation; instead, she reads or at least skims the entire two-volume text to form her own views. Stephen begins her lecture on Cellini's *Life* by commenting on Symonds's translation; after all, she has just begun her reviewing career and is practising review writing at the same time she is learning to teach.[6] But after her praise for Symonds's work, noting his translation focuses the reader's attention on Cellini, not on the language used [85], she shifts to her assertion that were it not for the autobiography, we would know very little about Cellini the goldsmith or sculptor. She also does for her students what she will often do in essays and reviews: focus on a somewhat unusual situation, detail or image (Bishop 576). Here, it is Cellini's reaction to the mad prison warden who thought himself a bat, took a dislike to Cellini and locked him in a dark cell except for two hours a day: Cellini scrapes powder from the bricks in his cell to make ink so he can record the visions he starts to have as the result of solitary confinement.[7]

Whether consciously or not, Stephen also focuses on titbits elucidating how Cellini and his context differ from artists working in 1905 and their context: he had murdered at least two people, which seemed to make little difference in how he was viewed, and yet he was thrown into prison for some obscure reason having to do with the Pope (whom he had pleased earlier) [89]; he must rely on courts and patronage to find work [90–1]; he often gave his work away rather than demand payment [91]; and he combined art and violence in his person [86–7]. His hot-bloodedness meant he 'had a turn for picking quarrels' [87] – he 'dashed into his brawls without any reckoning of costs to himself or anyone else' [89] – yet that hot bloodedness turn[s] into 'a fine kind of courage' in prison [90]. She praises his portrayal of himself, saying he 'remains a full blooded sensual man of genius, practised in many arts – expert in some – & through all time vigorous & convincing – very palpable flesh & blood in the midst of shadows' [91], words she would later use in her 'Report' about teaching history. Stephen's lecture emphasises how Cellini embodied a devotion to objects created on a small scale (except for his Perseus statue) and a life lived physically, even violently, on a large emotional scale, and in so doing, subtly introduces her students to another time, place and approach to life, one that contrasted greatly with Thomas Browne's in *Urn Burial*, subject of her first lecture, and certainly with her own. As such, the lecture illustrates her ability to identify with or at least evenhandedly portray someone quite different from herself.

In 'The Dramatic in Art & Life', Stephen, as Rosenbaum notes, tries to 'connect life, fiction and drama', and distinguishes between fiction's 'shape of thought and feeling' and drama's 'plotted action' (166), efforts that make sense in a lecture for students.[8] It aims to make generic differences understandable, paint differences between two genres and life in broad strokes, and clarify the workings of fiction and drama for the theoretically uninitiated. Life is one thing; fiction another; drama yet another. Virginia Stephen asserts that not much happens in life, that often, thought and emotion do not get expressed or acted upon.[9] Fiction works to reveal hidden thought and emotion, what people ponder internally, and sometimes, thought and emotion lead to action. But in drama, such thoughts and emotions must be made dramatic or acted out; drama embodies thought and emotion through action, so the form's exaggeration is inherent. Basic ideas, then, but clearly stated. Perhaps she was stating something about genre for herself while explaining it to students, or perhaps she was pondering Aristotle (though she said he was clear and not at all 'abstruse' [*PA* 240–2]). But she seems interested in thinking about the differences among thought, emotion and action and how those differences play out in life, fiction and drama. Stephen also uses a specific and racy situation – a woman caught with her lover in the bedroom when her husband arrives home – to illustrate her distinctions [96].

Her movement from lecture to notes, from written to conversational, the result of facing actual students in a classroom, can be seen in these two drafts. Stephen's work on the Cellini autobiography is a standard lecture: it is six pages long, heavily revised and written out in full sentences. She covers Symonds's translation, then focuses on Cellini: his accomplishments in many fields, his jewelry art, his aggressive personality, his determination to keep writing even when imprisoned. She indirectly nods to his writing's power when she claims we would not know him if it were not for his *Life* – his description of himself, his high opinion of his own perspective and worth, and his combination of artistry in silver and propensity to pick violent quarrels all make him memorable. She reveals her own interest in autobiography, notes Cellini's lack of concern about profit and praises his ability to portray himself as 'full of life & heat', creating a forceful and credible portrait of himself [91]. Virginia Stephen clearly summarises Cellini's 'violence and versatility' (Rosenbaum 165), but does so in a written-out presentation.

In 'The Dramatic in Life and Art', on the other hand, she works with notes and points, not sentences, barely revises it, and uses a vivid (though clichéd) example to demonstrate the differences between the 'liver: the novelist: the dramatist' [92]. As Rosenbaum notes, she 'distinguishes between three "processes": life, fiction, and drama' and thus the draft could be called Virginia Stephen's 'first public statement of what is now called literary theory' (166, 165). She thinks on paper, positing ideas and then, realising she may be exaggerating, pulling back; she is a young person trying to be theoretical and not quite having the wherewithal to do so. But she moves away from the long and complicated lectures of the nineteenth century and tries to make her subject easier to understand. She also writes herself into pithy insights: the playwright has to give 'invisible dramatic emotions a form – a body' [92], and '[t]hought which does something becomes dramatic' [96]. This lecture also includes repetition and circling back to reiterate points already made, though expressed somewhat differently. It thus reflects an awareness of listening students. The format is more informal yet constructed to make sure listeners walk away understanding how life, fiction and drama differ from each other.

Rosenbaum claims 'there is little in [these lectures] to suggest Woolf's later mastery of the lecture form' (166), but hints of her later disaffection appear in the contrast between the two. In the Cellini piece, her summary is emphatic; it reduces a complex man to just two starkly opposed sides ('How I loathe lectures – all the same; always so emphatic' [*L6* 130; see also *L4* 131]). Because it is a lecture, Stephen avoids the complex wandering, setting up of possibilities only to overturn them, that we see in Woolf's essays. She skims the surface rather than digs beneath it. In the drama piece, we can see Virginia Stephen moving away from lecture and toward conversation. She attempts to create a scene, uses detail, wants to both define genre and resist defining it, and talks to herself, noting when she exaggerates for effect. Showing herself in the process of thinking, her tactic invites students to participate in the process.

As a mature writer, Woolf lectured only six times, always to women, students or the working class,[10] and within those lectures, she used what she learned at Morley to work against the dismaying tendencies of the form. She attempted to put herself in the listener's place, indeed, bring the listener into the talk; worked for a conversational tone; shared how-to strategies; incorporated questions; used colourful detail and narrative; commented on the form to undercut it (she cannot fulfil the 'first duty of a lecturer – to hand you after an hour's discourse a nugget of pure truth' [*AROO* 3–4]); and provided a great deal of context. Virginia Stephen's Morley lectures on Cellini and the dramatic may not suggest her later expertise, but her practice with lectures in Morley classrooms contributed to the form and tone that expertise would take.

Virginia Stephen's Lessons: Access and Class

Class inequalities permeated Virginia Stephen's world. Even Morley College's admirable efforts to provide working- and lower middle-class people with further education implicitly reinforced middle-class assumptions. Breaking free of such assumptions is difficult, so it is hardly surprising that neither Stephen nor her world had done so. But teaching at Morley and working with students who had been denied access to a true education because of their class made her examine some of those assumptions. It also literally expanded her world to include people different from her. Most important for her as a budding writer, when faced with real students desiring an education, Stephen discovered a space where class differences, thoroughly embedded in her thinking by her upbringing, could be temporarily muted.

As Jean Baker Miller explains, we form the teacher/student relationship to remove inequality, not keep it in place. Although still surrounded and permeated by institutionalised inequalities – educational systems often maintain social and racial barriers – the teacher/student relation ideally aims to make the student equal to and independent of the teacher (Miller 4-5). The classroom, then, can be a place where teacher and student momentarily suspend 'class'. In Morley classrooms, Virginia Stephen seems to have been her more inclusive self. As she taught in Morley classrooms and learned from Morley students, Stephen developed a pedagogy: she learned to avoid lectures and promote conversation, but she also learned to provide a great deal of context, create entry points into learning through narrative or biography and vivid scenes and details, and identify with and reach out to students. That outcome, a welcoming pedagogy gained at Morley College, would serve the essayist Virginia Woolf well.

As discussed in Chapter 8, Virginia Stephen's evolving pedagogy emphasised providing students with sequenced historical context. She observed her fragmented education writ large in her students' attempts to pull together bits and pieces of knowledge, and she understood her students' background hampered them; she saw their lack of preparation for putting new knowledge into a contextual whole, whether or not she knew that lack stemmed from rote learning of the three Rs. That pedagogical outcome shaped the organisation of Virginia Woolf's *The Common Reader* and *The Common Reader: Second Series*: the two volumes provide a crash course in literary history with the tables of contents looking like course syllabi (Johnston; Daugherty 'VW Teaching'). Realising common readers may not have wide-ranging literary and historical contexts, Woolf uses chronology, historical essays written for the volumes, and transitions and comparisons between and among essays to transform collections of potentially random pieces into coherent volumes that literally model *how* to build literary knowledge.

At the same time Virginia Stephen saw the importance of having a context for new knowledge, she also realised students needed a variety of entry points into any framework they might be trying to build. As a result, she used story's power in her history class and centred each narrative around a dramatic scene. In her reading circle, she enlivened the examination of poetic lines with biography, thus connecting aesthetics to a poet's lived life. In a class about Cellini's autobiography, she focused on the intriguing details of his drive to write while in prison. Although we do not have much evidence about Stephen's actual teaching, and certainly not in all her classes, what we do have suggests she intuitively understood that students needed different ways of approaching material; from what we can tell, she worked to create interactive, lively and engaged classrooms. Supporting such a speculation is Ann Stephen's memory of her aunt, Virginia Woolf. Ann's Newnham friends had been 'pester[ing her] to arrange a meeting at which [Woolf] would expound her ideas about The Novel, but equally obvious was the fact that this was not Virginia's style'. So, Ann invited a few people to come around to her room after dinner 'for coffee and round-the-fire conversation'. She thought the evening went well, with some of the conversation 'predictabl[y]' centring on education – Woolf thought they were lucky to be in university, they thought she had been lucky to avoid it. But, Ann continues,

> Virginia's lack of pretentiousness and her natural interest in what we young women were thinking and doing brought out the best in all of us. Even those guests who, beforehand, had seemed to me a bit mouse-like and dull found their tongues and had something interesting to say. (A. Stephen 17)

Virginia Woolf employed her Morley pedagogy in her essays, too, incorporating fiction into her non-fiction, for example, most notably in *A Room of One's Own*, and attracting readers' attention with colourful scenes and striking details. Also, in her *Common Reader* volumes, she turns the writers (and readers) she discusses into human beings and literature into a living, vital force by frequently using diaries and/or letters, biography and autobiography. Whether it is John Paston reading Chaucer, Sir Thomas Browne describing himself, the Duchess of Newcastle venturing out, Mr Edgeworth visiting the mad clergyman and the lovely girl, Laetitia Pilkington hungrily reading and descending the social scale, Dorothy Osborne writing to Temple, Jonathan Swift juggling Stella and Vanessa, Geraldine Jewsbury and Jane Carlyle arguing, or George Gissing rushing off to school, their lives and times open up before our eyes, indirectly making the point over and over again, that lives and books are interwoven, that literary history was created by and happened to people, flesh-and-blood interesting people.

Probably the most important pedagogical tool Virginia Stephen left Morley with, however, was her impulse to identify, however briefly, with her students. In her draft, Stephen noted she was forced to 'reconsider' an earlier judgement – Miss Williams regularly attended class and no longer seemed 'inattentive and critical' ('Report' 202). (Perhaps her work had been particularly onerous the term before?) Part of what may have caused her to revise her opinion was finding 'we had a good deal in common'. Stephen cancelled that phrase, and the set-up, 'we made much of this' (or 'much from this basis', in my reading), but her words suggest mutual realisation, not just her own. She also cancels 'A journalist in a humble way in short!' and substitutes 'The germ of a literary lady in short!' while adding '& a curious one' above the revised sentence; the humble journalist grows in stature to a budding literary writer ('Report' MS; C. Jones 211, 214). She also comments on Burke's 'account of her own life': flawed as it was ('floundering among long words, & involved periods, with sudden ponderous moral sentiments thrown into the midst', like many novices' autobiographical rough drafts), it suggested that 'in other circumstances', 'she would have been a writer!' ('Report' 203). Both times, Stephen marks her recognition – that Miss Williams is the 'germ of a literary lady' and Burke might have been a writer in other circumstances – with an exclamation mark, signalling both the shock of having an assumption overturned but also the force of the insight's reality. Stephen does not report she voiced these connections to Miss Williams and Burke during their conversations. Rather, she records, perhaps for Miss Sheepshanks, certainly for herself, a perceived connection between her own creative work and that of two students. Only social class prevents them from sharing a label that could and would be applied to her.[11]

Virginia Stephen is not pretending when she sees how different material circumstances might have made them more like her (or vice versa). Just as real differences existed between her education and theirs – she is an insider, with access to the world of letters through the structure, coherence and contextual wealth of her father's library and other avenues – real similarities did, too: irregular home education; reliance on oneself; fragments and interruptions. She identifies with the outsiders in her classes, who, like her, have little money for education (Stephen money was spent on sons) and must struggle to educate themselves ('my own education [alone among books] was a very bad one' [*L6* 420]).[12] Recognising their efforts connect them even as circumstances separate them, Stephen forges a link with others trying to educate themselves: they, too, are outsiders, excluded from a good education (resulting in an 'almost wholly uncultivated' intelligence or in 'wits sharpened in the streets'); they, too, desire learning, but are often overwhelmed by it (having 'tentacles languidly stretching forth from their minds' but gaping in 'mere impotent wonder'); and they, too, must struggle to 'piece together' what they are learning, 'to connect ideas' into some cohesive whole ('Report' 203-4).

Woolf would often duplicate this crucial association with the outsider (Daugherty, 'Taking a Leaf' 37-8) – near the end of her life, for example, in 'The Leaning Tower', given to the Workers' Educational Association in Brighton, she aligns herself with the working-class people in her audience rather than with the university-educated men of her milieu – and it had important consequences for her common reader. When Woolf borrows the common reader from Samuel Johnson and recreates it in her opening essay to *The Common Reader*, she incorporates Morley student traits: exclusion from education, desire for learning and attempt to form wholes out of scattershot reading. The common reader is 'worse educated', less generously 'gifted', and '[h]asty, inaccurate, and superficial'; the common reader loves to read 'for his own pleasure'; and the common reader instinctively attempts to 'create, . . . out of whatever odds and ends he can come by, some kind of whole' (*E4* 19). Woolf writes that 'Every writer has an audience in view' (*E5* 356), and Stephen's Morley students became part of her view. Woolf creates her essays with common readers in mind, an audience linked to her Morley students.

Virginia Stephen, divided from her students by class, identified with her students enough to see that different circumstances, and only different circumstances, separated her from them. Understanding the frustration, desire and struggle associated with being excluded from a good education, she admires the 'regular attendants' who come 'with one serious desire in common' ('Report' 202). When

Stephen began working at Morley, she was a novice teacher confronting class difference. By the time she left, she had developed a pedagogy that could cross class barriers inside the provisional equality of a classroom. That pedagogy – use conversation rather than lecture; provide context; communicate with vivid detail and narrative; and most important, identify with readers and acknowledge their presence and value – would permeate all of Virginia Woolf's essays (Daugherty, 'VW Teaching' 63–5).

Virginia Stephen's comments about Morley working-class students often reflect class assumptions (or uncomfortably frequent misinterpretations of students): they lack persistence, interest, grammar, intelligence, knowledge. It is worth recalling how young she was, 23, and how little experience she had had with the working classes within an educational setting: zero. Also, she had received no formal training in pedagogy or taken academic classes in sociology or cultures. But she learns her assumptions do not always match reality. When Stephen reveals in a crossed-out report phrase that she had been warned about her students' capabilities ('Report' MS; C. Jones 213, 215), she stops, revises and owns the assumption while simultaneously realising its inaccuracy: 'On the whole they were possessed of more intelligence than I expected' ('Report' 203).

Some of Stephen's comments about her students are awful, but her experience of putting fragments of learning together meant she criticised Morley even more; it did not do enough to help students see a large educational framework within which to make meaning. She does not see why Morley College does not encourage the coherent study of history or a sequenced study of literature. Few students chose Morley's unified curriculum option, opting instead for a more hotchpotch approach (Richards 109–10), yet Stephen observed her students 'trying to piece together what they heard; to seek reasons; to connect ideas' ('Report' 203).[13]

Virginia Stephen enacts insider/outsider contradictions at Morley, sometimes between assumptions, sometimes between assumptions and actions. So, she can mock a student in one letter and try to find a job for one in another. Or she can wonder about her students' abilities ('how is it *possible* to make them feel the flesh & blood in these shadows?') and then affirm their potential ('it would not be hard to educate them sufficiently') ('Report' 203, her emphasis). She complains about the time teaching takes yet takes the time to figure out how to engage her students. Sometimes her language distances herself from students, other times she suggests common experiences. As Clara Jones wisely notes, such contradictions also reflect teaching anxiety (29).

Virginia Stephen's Morley teaching both reflects and contributes to insider/outsider contradictions.[14] For one thing, Stephen's (and Woolf's) identity as a reader and a writer extended and deepened the insider/outsider tension of being both of and outside a class. No matter the social class, being a reader and a writer can make you suspect, lead to your being labelled outsider, traitorous or odd (Cyril Yaldwyn is a degenerate poet). Reading and writing increase awareness of your own and other social classes, make you question your class identity and assumptions, lead to your feeling like an outsider in the class you grew up in as well as the class you have moved into or to which you aspire. Many writers of different classes, backgrounds, faiths, races and ethnicities have recorded the painful experiences of being torn between two worlds.

However, feeling like an outsider as a reader and writer may also connect you to other readers and writers, no matter their class, as evidenced by Virginia Stephen's noticing the readers and writers among her students. Perhaps readers and writers embody what Virginia Woolf means by the Outsiders Society. Perhaps social class cannot be totally transcended, but readers and writers can temporarily suspend it, briefly cross boundaries when they fleetingly meet in a space, classroom or otherwise, where knowledge, ideas and thinking are paramount.[15] Stephen's Morley experiences contributed to Woolf's texts, which, as Cuddy-Keane notes, encourage readers to think, speak, read and write for themselves ('Inside' 172, 177).[16]

So, what was Virginia Stephen's Morley education like? Her Morley curriculum included an introduction to an educational institution from within, a hard lesson in the limitations placed on such an institution by the need to survive, and most important, observation of and experiences with social classes different from her own. Plus, Stephen gained more knowledge about barriers to getting an education than she already had, especially about curricula that thwart or support that quest.

Morley took a hands-off pedagogical approach to its teachers, leaving them to find their own way or discover unspoken assumptions. As a practitioner, Virginia Stephen learned a great deal about pedagogical strategies and methods: she saw learners respond to multiple approaches, more open and inviting classrooms, and participatory methods. She learned the importance of discussion, narrative and context. Finally, she may have learned the frustration of having to teach the way others expect or require rather than the way one might prefer.

Virginia Stephen learned a crucial lesson about the effect of class on education and achievement: circumstances, not inherent ability, hamper people. She observed the effects of a scattershot curriculum on those who sought coherence and larger visions. She became more intensely aware of obstacles to learning at the same time as she saw and admired the desire of those working to surmount such obstacles. Most significant, Stephen learned a key lesson about audience: when she saw working-class people striving to be readers and writers, she had a flash of recognition and saw a similarity between their endeavours and her own. Stephen's crucial insight at Morley enlarged her definition of outsiders and fostered Woolf's development of the common reader as a badly educated, '[h]asty, inaccurate, and superficial' amateur intuitively creating a whole out of 'odds and ends' (*E4* 19).

Finally, her Morley work introduced Virginia Stephen to a community of learners within an institutional context, a community she had responsibility for fostering, not one she entered. She saw what attention, respect and openness could do in a classroom, so Virginia Woolf's essays become classrooms. In 1940, Woolf reflected on her essays' aim, to create readers, and wished she could have interested millions of people in literature (*L6* 420). That purpose, desire and attempt to form a large reading community crystallised at Morley College.

Virginia Woolf's essays would resonate with great learning, but crucially, she developed an ideal reader who is common and a strategy to share knowledge, to open literature up to more and varied readers.[17] Those who come to the essays with a 'serious desire' to read and learn, as her students came to Morley classrooms, can educate themselves in one English literature that opens up space for other English literatures. Sometimes accused of being an elitist writing for a coterie,[18] Woolf persisted in reaching out, working to widen the readership not only for modern literature, but for literature in general: 'I did my best to make [some of my books] reach a far wider circle than a little private circle of exquisite and cultivated people' (*L6* 420). When she urges the 'commoners and outsiders' with whom she identifies to 'trespass' on the 'common ground' of literature, she does so because she dares to hope that teaching ourselves 'how to read and how to write' will not only transform literature, but transcend the gulf between classes (*E6* 277–8).

While teaching at Morley College from 1905 to 1907 and trying to negotiate class difference for the first time, Virginia Stephen also began serving her apprenticeship in essay writing. That double education – concurrently teaching a real audience she faced weekly and writing for an audience she could only imagine, preparing and teaching classes for working-class adults at Morley at the same time that she was learning and practising her craft as a writer – reverberates throughout her career, because what Morley College taught the young Virginia Stephen about reaching an audience permeates the essays written by Virginia Woolf.

Notes

1. See my 'Virginia Stephen's Uneasy Heritage: Lessons, Readers, and Class'.
2. Jeanne Dubino, in conversation.
3. Interestingly enough, see Lillian Faithfull on how 'the lecture habit' can be 'vicious', particularly if it 'soothes and satisfies, and leaves [listeners] content with inaction' (116–19). Nicholas Midgley addresses Woolf's attitudes about lectures in *Three Guineas* and his resulting discomfort at being invited to give a lecture on English literature to the Virginia Woolf Society of Japan. He wonders, and asks his listeners to wonder, 'Rather than considering Woolf's comments as the truth *about* education, could we not see them as a form *of* education? ... Is Woolf not demanding that we consider from the very beginning what it means to teach, to lecture, to engage in literary criticism itself?' (149, his emphasis). Two obsolete meanings of 'teach' may be relevant to how Woolf works in her essays: 'to show (a person) the way' (*OED* I.3.a.) and 'to give in trust, commit, entrust, commend to the keeping of some one' (*OED* III.9.a.).
4. S. P. Rosenbaum generously shared his clean transcriptions with me, allowing me to check mine against his. The lectures are in 'Early Writings by Virginia Stephen' in the Monks House Papers (SxMs–18/2/A/26/B and 26/C).
5. These holograph transcriptions are published for the first time in Appendix 4. Stephen's page numbers in her 'mutilated exercise book' begin with 73; perhaps other lectures were torn out. The 'Autobiography of Benvenuto Cellini' runs from 85 to 91 (88 is missing, but the manuscript runs smoothly from 87 to 89); 'The Dramatic in Art & Life' runs from 92 to 96. Bracketed numbers in the text refer to Stephen's holograph page numbers.
6. Rosenbaum says the lecture has to be about the edition of 1901 since it was not reissued until 1910; he argues this draft cannot be a book review because its tone is 'quite unlike that of her reviews at this time' (165), which is true once she turns to the Autobiography itself.
7. Bishop writes, 'Almost all of the essays take shape around figures: Woolf will open with an image, which she then explores discursively, and then she will close with another, perhaps related, image which encapsulates the argument' (576). In this image

of Cellini's tormentor as a bat and his ink-making response, we see Cellini's determination to create, no matter his circumstances, and Stephen returns to his courage and the unusual forms it takes several times in the lecture.
8. See Chapter 8 for a discussion of this draft's puzzling lecture status.
9. Virginia Woolf would be accused of writing works in which 'nothing happens'.
10. These six lectures – 'Mr Bennett and Mrs Brown', 'How Should One Read a Book?', 'Poetry, Fiction and the Future', *A Room of One's Own*, 'Professions for Women' and 'The Leaning Tower' – become some of her most famous essays and all have a pedagogical sub-text. For example, 'How Should One Read a Book?' takes the question seriously and attempts to answer it, and 'The Leaning Tower' and *A Room of One's Own* provide extensive reading lists.
11. Mary Sheepshanks records a similar point about the effect of circumstances, noting one young man who

> was a born scholar. He taught himself Latin and Greek with very little help, and university men with whom he came in contact said that, if he had had a good school education, he could have risen to a university teacher. (*LDE* 32)

I use the word 'identify' not in its psychological sense of becoming one with someone, but in its sense of feeling affinity with another or relating to someone else's problems or feelings. Mitchell Leaska comments that Virginia Stephen's 'preoccupation with pleasing others' made her 'expert in identifying herself with her audience. Carried over into her ordinary life, it made her overly sensitive to what other people were feeling' (Intro xxxviii). Clara Jones does not think Stephen's reported interactions with her students reflect an 'unproblematic identification'. Yes, though perhaps no identification is ever unproblematic. Jones acknowledges Stephen's interest and awareness of 'surface similarities' with Miss Williams, but also describes the conversation as marked by curiosity blended with hostility and competition (24–7). In Stephen's draft, though, it is hard to tell what is reported, what is interpreted, and by whom. Williams, an intelligent woman dealing with journalistic reality, could be judging her own work, with the resulting phrasing belonging to Stephen, Williams or both; or Williams could be describing her work with the implied evaluation coming solely from Stephen; or some shading in between. Stephen may project 'subterranean passages' on to Williams's work, or recognise her own work's underside, or see something inherent in both. (Laurel Brake says 'the subterranean practices of the journalist's trade . . . emerged to become one of the important issues within [the debate about anonymity]' in the 1850s and beyond ['Literary' 111], which indicates the phrase's common use.) Stephen sees more than surface similarities between her own situation and those of Miss Williams and Burke: they struggle to learn and write in the face of obstacles. But recognising those similarities does not erase the advantages she knew she had, either. Classic insider/outsider tension, dilemma.
12. In her draft, she adds, 'My father spent perhaps £100 on my education' (*L6* 419).
13. I found no evidence Stephen understood why Morley offered both liberal arts and catch-up skills classes (and asked her to teach both) or what classes at Morley were supposed to add up to, if anything, or how her own classes connected to any others being taught. Morley's mission, its commitment to students who wanted to sample courses, learn something about various topics and have collegial experiences while doing so seems obvious to us (Richards 5), but that mission does not seem to have been clearly communicated to her. Her perception that at least some Morley students wanted more structure to their learning may also relate to her experience of taking various entry-level and intermediate courses at King's College London; she experienced more sequence in the Ladies' Department than they did at Morley, but she may have wondered what it all added up to as well.
14. As Clara Jones's study of Virginia Woolf's 'ambivalent activism' demonstrates, Woolf worked more as an ally than as a traditionally understood activist: advocated rather

than crusaded; suggested rather than dictated; worked behind the scenes rather than on the front lines.
15. Richard Gilbert calls reading a potential or virtual classless space, 'formed and united by shared enquiry and artistry' (in conversation). See also Detloff, who proposes 'imagin[ing a commons instead of a canon' and hopefully asks, 'Perhaps literature has the capacity to provide a commons not because of its content, but because it has the ability to exist between us – temporally, geographically, and culturally?' ('Iconic Shade' 215).
16. Woolf refused to impose her ideas on or imaginatively occupy the working class; as Jean Mills points out, if Woolf had tried to speak from within working-class consciousness, 'her motives and her aesthetics would be questioned and discredited ... and her work far more easy to dismiss' ('Politics' 226). Subtly and convincingly, Madelyn Detloff argues that Woolf's insistence on an uncertain and unjust world co-existing with her 'conscious self-positioning' is an ethical chosen stance ('Snob' 185). See Pat Laurence, Andrea Adolph, Patrick Brantlinger and Maren Linett for other nuanced readings of Woolf and class.
17. See, however, Michelle M. Tokarczyk for obstacles to this ideal's fulfilment.
18. See Alex Zwerdling, 'Coterie', and Jonathan Rose on Leonard Bast, 393–438.

Part III

Apprentice, 1904–1912: Writing for Newspapers

[A]nd still it is a matter of the very greatest interest to a writer to know what an honest and intelligent reader thinks about his work.
– 'Reviewing' (*E6* 201)

To know whom to write for is to know how to write.
– 'The Patron and the Crocus' (*E4* 214)

With the move to Bloomsbury in 1904, Virginia Stephen declared her independence.[1] Recovering from a breakdown after her father's death, she was determined to find her way.[2] Between the ages of 22 and 30, she continued to practise writing in her letters and diary, but also travelled extensively for the first time and wrote a few essays and numerous book reviews, most of them anonymous. Although in summer 1907 she began drafting the novel that became *The Voyage Out*, Stephen became a professional writer through her non-fiction. Andrew McNeillie argues that if you were a young writer in the early 1900s and wanted to make some money, which Stephen did ('I dont in the least want Mrs L's candid criticism; I want her cheque!' [*L1* 154]; see also *L1* 155, 160), the best route was writing reviews (xi; see also Brosnan 43). But John Mepham points out that as Stephen moved into the world of letters through the book review, she 'had no specialised education to call upon. She had no training in any discipline in the modern sense – no introduction to the conceptual foundations of any field of scholarship, no knowledge of methods of research' (18). Like her education at home and her work as a teacher, then, her apprenticeship in letters was, in the main, a solitary pursuit.

To understand Virginia Woolf as an essayist, we must first understand the context within which Virginia Stephen began her work as a writer,[3] the periodicals she wrote for and the lessons she learned from them. Building on lessons learned during her home and Morley schooling, Stephen learned how to establish and maintain a writer's discipline, prepare for and write a book review or an essay, and work with editors. During her writing apprenticeship, she did literary exercises in her journal, wrote about her travels, took notes, and most significant, published 158 reviews and essays, most of them in seven different periodicals: the *Guardian*'s Women's Supplement, *The Academy*, the *National Review*, *Cornhill*, the *Speaker*, the *Nation* and the *Times Literary Supplement*. More than anything else, as she wrote and saw her work into print, she learned how to think about and write for various audiences.

Education for Writers

When Virginia Woolf published her 1939 essay 'Reviewing', she provoked immediate disagreement. Leonard Woolf questioned her argument in a note appended to the Hogarth Sixpenny Pamphlet (number 4) and included himself on the cover and title page.[4] W. Denham Sutcliffe, writing an Oxford dissertation on book reviewing, wrote to say the roots of modern reviewing lay in the early eighteenth-century essayists who combined criticism with publicity in their attempt to 'guide the public taste' (Daugherty, 'You' 172).[5] Critics have noted its portrayal of a writer exposed, class implications, tensions between journalism and criticism, and ambiguity about the reviewer's role (Brosnan 70–6, 120–1; Collier, *Modernism* 73–9; Bowlby, 150–4). But these persuasive interpretations overlook the educational nature of what Woolf calls for.[6] Valuing the dialogue between reviewer and author growing out of an author's desire 'to be told why [the reviewer] likes or dislikes his work' and a reviewer's desire 'to tell them why I either like or dislike their work' (*E6* 201), Woolf calls for a private meeting between 'doctor and writer' – 'for an hour they would consult about the book in question. They would talk, seriously and privately' – so the writer could gain 'the opinion of an impersonal and disinterested critic' outside publicity glare and market concerns (*E6* 202–3).[7]

Woolf's 1939 proposal reflects not only the unease about commercial journalism many writers shared between the wars,[8] but also a gap in Stephen's apprenticeship at the start of her career. Her call for a private discussion with a disinterested reader reveals what she and other young writers lacked in 1904: instruction, attention to first efforts, and 'coming into touch with a well-stored mind, housing other books and even other literatures, and thus other standards' (*E6* 203). What she asks for, her sister had at the Cope School of Art and the Royal Academy's Painting School. Vanessa learned her art in a group setting where instructors and other students viewed and commented on her work and she viewed and commented on theirs. Woolf's request bears a striking resemblance not only to Vanessa's education, but also to the workshop and conference method practised in many US creative writing programmes today.[9] Woolf pleads for what novice writers who can afford higher education now routinely have, a formalised apprenticeship including consultations with readers who focus on the work itself, comment on the writing without regard for reputation or commerce, and diagnose and suggest. Nothing parallel to such an apprenticeship was available to young writers in the early twentieth century and certainly not to Virginia Stephen. As she writes to Madge Vaughan in 1906, 'I have had so very little criticism upon my work that I really dont know what kind of impression I make' (*L1* 227).

Stephen entered a world of burgeoning journalism where battle lines were being drawn between it and the academy[10] and women were making their mark. Although Walter Besant uses the male pronoun in his 1899 *The Pen and the Book*, he does, when considering the 'modern man of letters – not a great genius, not a popular author: but a good steady man of letters', qualify 'man' by acknowledging 'many women now belong to the profession' (24); he wants readers to assume he includes women throughout. He also traces the reading public's growth – from perhaps 30,000 readers in 1750 when the population was ten million and 'none of the working classes could read at all', to perhaps 50,000 readers in 1830 when the population was twenty-four million and the increase stemmed from women's beginning to read, to 120 million possible readers at the end of the nineteenth century when the population in the British Isles was forty million and the population in the colonies, Canada and the United States could be reached by the book market (27–9). Schools trained students to read and desire reading, 6,000 free libraries existed in America, Britain and the colonies, and 'reading, which [had] always been the amusement of the cultivated class, [had] now become the principal amusement of every class' (29–30). Anyone wanting the 'Literary Life', he concludes, must consider that change in the audience's size and the writer's resulting influence and responsibility (33–6).

Larger, diverse audiences and technological advances meant many more books. Peter Keating says the combined adult/juvenile novel totals between 1895 and 1914 averaged 1,618 a year or 4.4 a day, with the peak being 1906 when 2,108 novels were issued, 5.7 a day, including Sunday (32–3). Add to that non-fiction, drama, poetry and periodicals, and Virginia Stephen's use of 'monster' for the British public's print desire does not seem overblown (*E1* 25). Gillian Sutherland notes the same phenomenon: writing as an occupation grew from 1,500 authors, editors and writers in the 1861 Census to just under 14,000 in the 1911 Census, and the 'number of weekly, monthly and quarterly magazines quadrupled' between 1875 and 1903 (*NW* 64).[11] Such output also meant many more reviews. Discussing the development of the *Times Literary Supplement* in 1902, Philip Waller notes that in 1901, '*The Times* had devoted 260 columns to book reviews, fifty-five of these to novels', and as the newspaper of record, it literally could not continue to print entire parliamentary reports and also keep up with the 'expanding literary market' (114–15). Somebody else had to take up the slack, and thus papers of all political, religious and social stripes had book review columns or pages or sections.[12] Henry Nevinson, the *Daily Chronicle*'s literary editor from 1899 to 1903, said 'Three whole columns of the paper were nearly always given to review or other literary subjects every day' (qtd in Waller 117).

Anthea Trodd says the 'new journalism' of the 1880s and 1890s had expanded women's chances to enter the profession (38), and Sutherland agrees: journalism still 'offered the best opportunities' for women who wanted to write, and one could survive without having 'a cushion of private money' (Sutherland, *NW* 12). But as Barbara Onslow notes, for women in journalism at the end of the nineteenth century, being a freelance journalist meant 'extremely variable' pay that depended on the paper, one's contribution, one's reputation and the current competition level; it also meant worrying about cash flow as one waited months to be paid or discovered no pay was forthcoming because a publication had folded (87–8). At least a tradition of female journalists existed, with Frances Power Cobbe, Margaret Oliphant, Anne Thackeray Ritchie, Alice Meynell and countless other sung and unsung female journalists and reviewers participating in and influencing the periodical world Virginia Stephen would enter in late 1904.[13] It was a thriving, competitive, even ruthless atmosphere, a world of possibility for advancement and influence, but filled with hard work, incredible pressure and inevitable abuse: short cuts, puffery, slating (Waller 116–74; Sutherland, *NW* 64).[14]

Virginia Stephen differed from peers who had formal schooling, including university education, and from peers who had teacher training, but she was similar to them in not having any instruction in learning to write or to write book reviews.[15] Though Virginia Woolf would say in 'The Leaning Tower' that 'a writer has to be taught' his or her art just as painters, musicians or architects have to be taught theirs (*E6* 266), as Virginia Stephen, she said not much could be taught about writing (*E1* 116). Her youthful claim reflected her society's belief, and writers coming of age in the early twentieth century received little guidance in learning how to write. The editorial for *The Times* on 29 May 1911 wryly questions the establishment of a Chair of English Fiction by the Royal Society of Literature, claiming the best English novelists 'have owed little to their predecessors' and asserting the 'critic cannot teach authors how to write' ('A Chair' 11F). David Anderson opened a London School of Journalism in 1887, charging one hundred guineas ($500) for a year-long course: 'a limited number of educated young men' could learn 'the whole bag of tricks' with daily assignments and working as though on a newspaper staff ('European Gossip' 2). F. L. Green, in 'Journalism as a Profession for Women', says women could read individually with Anderson; the course consisted of 'paragraphs, reviewing, shorthand, interviewing, special and war correspondence, preparing telegrams, leaders, art and dramatic criticism, sub-leaders, sub-editing, and the writing of stories and magazine articles' (qtd in Onslow 32). When Harold Child writes about the course in *The Academy*, he discusses it in the past tense and says Anderson could not have had more than a 'score of pupils', Mr Robert Hichens, Mr Francis Gribble, Mr Herbert Vivian and several others. He mentions no women ('Literary Week', 26 August 1905: 867).[16] Creative writing courses or programmes simply did not exist at either the secondary or the university level.

Virginia Stephen might have picked up an instructional book or manual. Indeed, instructional books were available in increasing numbers. As Keating notes, the birth of literary agency and founding of the Society of Authors in the late nineteenth century meant that 'literary advice had become a marketable commodity', and as agency influence grew, so did the 'publication of literary handbooks, manuals, guides, reference works and periodicals' (71). Onslow suggests aspiring journalists at the end of the nineteenth century were 'overwhelmed with advice' (86). But the quality and usefulness of the advice in books such as Percy Russell's *The Literary Manual* (1886) and *The Authors' Manual* (1891), John Oldcastle's *Journals and Journalism: With a Guide for Literary Beginners* (1880) or Eustace H. Miles's *How to Prepare Essays, Lectures, Articles, Books, Speeches and Letters with Hints on Writing for the Press* (1905) were questionable, much of the advice being 'little more than belletristic chat' (Keating 71) or advice about how to break into publishing.[17] Russell begins his reviewing chapter in *The Author's Manual* with the discouraging conclusion that 'no department of journalism is so badly done as reviewing' (45), then discusses humiliating errors made through ignorance, notes the importance of actually reading the book being reviewed and not waiting for other reviews to come up with ideas,[18] and offers a formula: 'find out *what* the book to be reviewed says, and *how* it says it' (45–55, emphasis in original).

Stephen might also have consulted some better manuals – such as George Henry Lewes's *The Principles of Success in Literature* (articles originally in *The*

Fortnightly Review in 1865), Walter Besant's *The Pen and the Book* or Arnold Bennett's *Journalism for Women: A Practical Guide* (1898) and *How to Become an Author: A Practical Guide* (1903) – but they, too, did not offer much help to a novice wanting to learn the writer's craft. According to Monika Brown, Lewes's articles were meant to be a 'self-help guide for aspiring authors', an attempt to explain literature's psychological appeal through three principles, Vision (intellectual), Sincerity (moral) and Beauty (aesthetic). They outline a basic literary theory, 'offer sensible advice for avoiding common pitfalls' (137; Lewes 35), identify principles 'under[lying] *all* successful writing', and conclude with style laws (Lewes 21, emphasis in original; 126–59). Besant, chief founder of the Society of Authors and first chairman, was, says Clinton Machann, one of the first to call for creative writing courses, and although *The Pen and the Book* is 'the most complete exposition of his ideas on writing and publishing', it is also full of 'many incongruities and unsupported statements' (45). His most useful section is on literary agents, editors and copyright.

If Stephen consulted Bennett's *Journalism for Women*, she might have been angered by his warning women to avoid their reputation for unreliability, inattention to detail and lack of restraint. He blames these traits on lack of training, not biology (9–20), so Trodd thinks he intervened to help women put their 'inappropriate training for an exclusively domestic sphere' behind them and become professionals (39). But Onslow notes Bennett did not seem to realise women would find it difficult to obtain training and would not have had the education men could receive (32), and Rosenbaum calls his guide 'condescending' (147). Bennett's books are indeed practical and include chapters on style, by which he seems to mean spelling and grammar. But they focus more on breaking into the market, earning a living and preparing manuscripts than on writing craft. The same is true of Frances Low's *Press Work for Women: A Text Book for the Young Woman Journalist* (1904), geared to the young middle-class woman with an average secondary education 'and the faculty for presenting her matter in readable form (which latter comes for the most part with practice)' (4–7). Such a woman, with five years of hard work, may reach a stage where she earns £120 a year. She warns young women against writing book notices paid in inferior journals at 'sweating prices'; 'as a stepping-stone to reviewing of a cultivated kind no more disastrous method could be conceived' (12–13).[19] Such advice is useful, just not about writing.

Virginia Stephen probably did not consult such a manual, given her 1906 review of Adam Lorimer's *The Author's Progress*. Lorimer emphasises increasing the wage for writing and downplays learning how to write (E1 116–17). Although he ostensibly addresses the 'dear young writer', he shows off for and winks at the older writer who already 'knows' what he says is true. He begins by noting the etymological connection between the words 'author' and 'auctioneer', and with his second maxim, reveals why Stephen uses the word 'jocular' in her reading notes (VS notes 139): 'the master of all is the Public, the great Public which buys books, determines Parliamentary Elections, and consumes Patent Medicines' (33).[20] Lorimer's guide is 'the ugliest form of "shop" expounded', writes Stephen, focusing only on what 'make[s] a book successful independently of the book itself' (E1 117). She confesses to Nelly Cecil, 'it is a most depressing and ugly book, and treats Literature like a trade' (*L1* 176).²¹ Her opinion may have been coloured by the assumptions Keating says quickly grew up around advice manuals – only failed authors would write such manuals and only people beyond help would buy one (71–2) – but she does not argue against helping people learn how to write.²² Rather, it is, in fact, a depressing book, and not just because 'the confusion between art and trade must always be ugly ... and ... inevitable' (*E1* 117). Lorimer assumes writing ability counts for so little that novices need tricks, and he has an arch and cynical tone, especially about readers:

> Henceforward it is to be feared the Writer who writes because he has thought profoundly, or had visions which seem to him inspirations, will be heard of no more. There is no Publisher for him; a little longer and there will be no Magazine for him. There never was much of a Public for him, and it seems there will be less of such a Public as we progress farther into the halfpenny newspaper age. (272)

Manuals, then, did not offer Stephen the sort of help she needed.

For the specialised craft of book reviewing, advice was even sparser. Brosnan cites the 1901 publication *How to Write an Essay* (46, 68 n17), volume 10 of a 'How to' series; it devotes a lot of space to actual essay writing, along with listing ninety-two essay subjects in an appendix (105–8). She also mentions Miles's *How to Prepare Essays ...*, but it is geared mainly toward improving schoolboy essays and teaching composition in schools. Discussions in Bennett's books and these sources clearly show that contributions a young writer could make to periodicals were ultimately governed by a circumstance Onslow also notes: 'Reviewers needed a track record or influential introduction to gain entrée to a journal' (81). Low advises beginners to

> abandon all thought of reviewing, which is the prize of the journalistic profession, and sought after by University men of high distinction .... Reviewing can, as a rule, only be secured through a literary reputation or by intimate acquaintance with an editor. (12–13)

When Arnold Bennett recommends writing something and sending it to a paper as a freelance contribution, he means articles, not book reviews, which the public was not invited to submit. McNeillie may be right that the best way to make a little money in the early 1900s was by reviewing (xi), but it was not an easy way. Also, as Onslow says, the genre was 'a motley crew', varying widely: 'some mere summaries padded out with extracts' and others '"dissertations" under the guise of reviewing books' (63). A beginner might read many reviews but not know which ones were best to learn from.

In addition, although numerous ads for correspondence writing courses appear in *John O'London's Weekly*, launched in 1919, such courses do not seem to have been prevalent before the war, at least in England,²³ or so Harold Child's surprise and amusement in 'The Literary Week' of *The Academy* on 26 August 1905 suggests. (Stephen may have read his remarks since her review of *Some Famous Women of Wit and Beauty* appeared in that issue.) He reports on a contributor's receiving a letter from what he understood to be an American literary agency.... Imagine his respectful amazement when there came from Indianapolis, Indiana, a proposal that he should pay two dollars a week, for a term of fifteen weeks, for a course of instruction in journalism! (867)

After quoting extensively from the letter, Child contrasts American industry in the journalism instruction area with the 'educational experiment on a much smaller and more costly scale' as conducted by David Anderson in the London School of Journalism, only to undercut the idea that any education occurred:

> though none of the pupils would admit that David Anderson ever did anything for them except smoke cigars in one room while they smoked cigarettes in another, several of them have got on just as well as if he had taught them everything that he unquestionably knew. (867)

Ads in the *Guardian*, *TLS*, *The Academy* and *Speaker* during her apprenticeship years do not include correspondence courses or schools,[24] and advice manuals do not mention such courses, which suggests they were not plentiful enough either to recommend or to warn against. Perhaps, as Onslow suggests, there was 'general agreement that journalists needed wide interests, curiosity, good physique, stamina and persistence', but 'less certainty' about 'those qualities which might be acquired' (33).

In any case, Harold Child's reaction suggests the idea of teaching someone to write by correspondence was laughable.[25] But an ad in the 1908 *Writers' and Artists' Year-Book* features a School of Journalism, Art and Secretarial Training for Women that provided individual tuition, manuscript criticism by post, and lessons by correspondence for a fee of five guineas.[26] Miss Cartwright, the editress (her term) of *Home Life*, was the principal, and Mrs T. P. O'Connor is listed as a patron. Testimonials in the ad were dated 1904 and 1905, interviews were required for admission, a full curriculum is listed (including article writing and book reviewing), and practical experience could be gained through the small papers issued by the school (v). By 1914, the ad featured a broader curriculum that added research, indexing and English Literature, for example, and included the line 'Lady Journalists in the Making' (iv). Right above it appears an ad for the Quill Club (established 1898), and although its heading is 'Literary Aspirants' and although it does not say men only, the president and all the officers are men, including T. P. O'Connor, Hilaire Belloc and G. K Chesterton. For a yearly fee of ten shillings and sixpence, the Club provided a lending library of instructional volumes, supplied criticism of articles and short stories, and met monthly for discussion. The juxtaposition of journalism with secretarial work in the name of Miss Cartwright's school suggests women needed basic training, practice and lots of paying options – journalism as an offshoot of secretarial work – whereas the juxtaposition of a fine writing implement with a club suggests men needed conversation, privacy and advice – journalism as an offshoot of 'the study and practice of Literature'.

When Stephen came of age as a writer, then, creative writing courses were not available in formal educational settings, and correspondence opportunities were rare and mocked by the literary establishment. She could not learn the reviewing craft with others, read other young reviewers' work in draft stages, or receive comments from other writers or an instructor. How-to manuals had begun to proliferate but were not necessarily helpful. Thus, as was true for much of her education, Virginia Stephen had to do her learning on the job and on her own.

Notes

1. James Wood says her first 'escape' was out of her father's house at Hyde Park Gate into Bloomsbury, but her 'second escape was into literary journalism .... For Woolf, I think, became a great critic, not simply a "great reviewer"' (92).
2. Ironically, just as her book reviewing career took off, reviews of F. W. Maitland's *The Life and Letters of Leslie Stephen* (1906) appeared. See the literary causerie by F. W. Hirst in the *Speaker* on 5 January 1907 (405–6) and reviews in *The Academy* on 10 November 1906 (463–5), *TLS* on 16 November 1906 (384) and *Guardian* on 9 January 1907 (55). In *The Academy*, the reviewer distinguishes between journalism and criticism, says 'it is impossible to place [Stephen] in the first rank' as a critic since his works lack 'the illumination of a really first-class mind' (464), and highlights his drawbacks as a writer and editor.
3. Leila Brosnan provides a great deal of that context and calls for more attention to it. My work here and in *Virginia Woolf's Essays: Being a Teacher* builds on her thorough study of Woolf's reviews and essays.
4. Gualtieri says Leonard took the reviewer's part against Woolf's defence of the author's interests (66–7), and Collier suggests Leonard could not ignore the contradiction between his wife's proposal and her position as a reviewer ('Journalism' 193). But Snaith comments, 'What should, perhaps, have been a private discussion becomes a public denunciation' (*PPN* 51), thus ironically denying the essay's request.
5. Woolf replied she was grateful to him 'for taking the question seriously'. See *L6* 370–1. R. C. K. Ensor, however, argues 'the fate of books was not decided by reviewers' in the eighteenth century (qtd in Waller 117), and Waller distinguishes between the eighteenth and nineteenth centuries, arguing that the 'advent of the reviewer as a power in literature' came in the early nineteenth century and continued to grow thereafter.
6. Bowlby does offhandedly suggest that what Woolf proposes is '[s]omewhere between a counseling session and a tutorial' (151). Anthony Curtis says Woolf 'anticipated events: the relationship she envisaged is essentially one that many authors have nowadays with their editors and their agents' (178). In *T. P.'s Weekly*, begun in late 1902, a 'Literary Help' column offered appraisals of readers' literary work for a fee (Waller 96).
7. Woolf evidently practised what she preached. Rose Macaulay notes that if a person talking with Woolf had written a book, 'he might, if lucky, get a verbal review of it, an analysis, appreciation and criticism that was worth more than any printed review' (Macaulay 165).
8. Collier and Brosnan both note this modernist ambivalence (Collier, *Modernism* 11–38, 'Journalism', and 'O'London's'; Brosnan, especially 70–91), but it predates modernism. Kelly Mays says the tension between art and commerce dates from at least the 1880s and 1890s (12, 25–8); Laurel Brake sees Matthew Arnold's 1887 attack on New Journalism as an attempt to raise his journalism to the status of criticism and thus literature ('Old Journalism' 1–2; see also Wiener, 'How New?'); and Onslow traces 'the interdependent if sometimes uneasy relationship' (201) between writing novels and writing for periodicals in an even earlier generation of women writers, Ward, Gaskell and Eliot (200–10). Brake, in 'Literary Criticism and the Victorian Periodicals', examines journalism from the 1860s forward, discusses Victorian jour-

nalistic practice in periodicals, including Leslie Stephen's, focuses on debates about anonymity and concludes,

> The frequent and articulate Victorian critical discourse concerning its own nature and means of production reveals tellingly the cultural, economic, aesthetic, and ideological underpinnings of Victorian criticism: its origins in the sway and bustle of the marketplace as well as in the tower. (116)

That cultural tension surrounded Virginia Stephen as she grew up, and as Brosnan notes, was directly communicated to her by her aunt, Caroline Emelia Stephen, who warned her against going into journalism (*L1* 166) and whose legacy was meant to help her escape it, and by Leslie Stephen, who felt ambivalent about his work (78–9). See Collier, 'Woolf' 321–2, for how journalism's reputation changed over Leslie Stephen's lifetime. His daughter's ambivalence about journalism is hardly surprising, given such historical, cultural and familial underpinnings. See Corbett for an astute and thorough study of this complex ambivalence and its effects.

Frank Swinnerton shared Woolf's desire that reviewers stand outside the commercial fray. In a dream perhaps as 'fanciful' and 'utopian' as Collier calls Woolf's ('Journalism' 193), Swinnerton isolates reviewers from cliques, professors, authors and publishers, and takes authors' names off books so they can be judged solely on merit (*Authors* 120–3). In his *The Reviewing and Criticism of Books* (1939), he also indicates a reviewer has some responsibility to the author: it is the reviewer's 'business to find the vital speck in that author, in that book' (41).

Collier persuasively argues that Woolf's sense of audience vacillates and that, late in life, she despairs about readers' abilities and abandons the possibility of public communication (*Modernism* 71–106). But Woolf's later concern does not seem surprising in the context of propaganda being successfully used in Nazi Germany and Great Britain to promote violence and war. Anxiety about the media does not necessarily mean being anti-democratic; one can believe in readers' acumen and still worry the media may overwhelm the ability to think critically. Such anxiety about the media's power to sway citizens puts more pressure on a writer to make herself heard and to do so responsibly.

9. Danell Jones comes to the same conclusion, seeing Woolf's proposal as the forerunner to today's creative writing programs (34–5). Current enrolment indicates Woolf's question, 'would they pay the doctor's fee of three guineas?' to get 'criticism and advice' (*E6* 213), has been answered with a resounding 'Yes'. See also Louis Menand's history of US writing programmes.

Critics attack the university workshop method with arguments (and fears) similar to those expressed by Stephen's society and sometimes by Woolf: (1) creative writing cannot be taught and (2) creative writing programmes produce sameness and conformity. See especially Anis Shivani and Donald Hall. However, Arielle Greenburg points out benefits that sound remarkably like what Woolf desires in 'Reviewing', and the five creative writers who posted 'Creative Writing Is Not a Fast Food Nation' in *Inside Higher Ed* remind readers that anti-creative writing programme arguments are not new or particularly salient and that such programmes attract students to the humanities and English Departments who seek something other than 'theory-laden literary analysis' (Mayers et al.). Heather McHugh, a poet, makes a similar argument.

10. See Valentine Cunningham on Churton Collins and Edmund Gosse.
11. See also Patrick Leary and Andrew Nash.
12. See Waller's exhaustive study for more detail about specific newspapers.
13. See Talia Schaffer's study of female aesthetes whose reputations equalled that of their male counterparts in the 1890s but were subsequently forgotten (6–7). See also Nicola Diane Thompson on Victorian literary criticism's strictures on women's writing, its use of 'masculine' and 'feminine' as evaluative terms, and its harsh judgements of

female writers and readers alike (8–24). Virginia Stephen had quite a minefield to navigate.

14. Slating means severe critical attacks. Patrick Collier's extensive work (on journalism and reviewing, 'What Is Modern Periodical Studies?', editorship of the *Journal of Modern Periodical Studies*, and the Woolf in Periodicals, Woolf on Periodicals issue of the *Virginia Woolf Miscellany*); the Modernist Periodicals Project; and scholars Melissa Sullivan, Catherine Clay, Maria DiCenzo, Barbara Green, Fiona Hackney, Faith Binckes, Carey Snyder, Faye Hammill, Mark Hussey, Alice Staveley, Sean Latham and Robert Scholes have broadened the modernist periodicals definition to include more than little magazines. See also Brooker and Thacker, *The Oxford Critical and Cultural History of Modernist Magazines*, Vol. 1.

15. Though Winifred Bryan Horner argues many students in British secondary schools and universities received some direct instruction in writing essays or compositions in the eighteenth and nineteenth centuries (she gives the best marks to Scottish institutions and the Dissenting Academies in England), such instruction reached only male students who had such schooling (such as Thoby), and essays and compositions were not considered creative writing (121–49).

16. According to Waller, Anderson soon closed his academy and went back to the *Daily Telegraph*; his students did not speak highly in their memoirs of what Waller calls a 'racket' (399–401). He had died by the time Child wrote about the course.

17. Oldcastle and the author of *How to Write an Essay* provide lists of periodicals, an early version of *Writers' Market*, and Oldcastle's is annotated. Some American titles were: C. E. Heisch, *The Art and Craft of the Author: Practical Hints upon Literary Work* (1906); Alice R. Mylene, comp., *To Write or Not to Write: Hints and Suggestions Concerning All Sorts of Literary and Journalistic Work* (1891); and George Bainton, *The Art of Authorship: Literary Reminiscences, Methods of Work, and Advice to Young Beginners* (1890). Mylene and Bainton compiled authors' statements, with Bainton playing 'an elaborate confidence trick' on authors to get their contributions (Keating 73).

18. See Collier, *Modernism* 82–3, for a discussion of this practice. Miss Williams, Virginia Stephen's Morley student, was not alone.

19. Again, one cannot help thinking of Miss Williams.

20. F. T. Dalton's note in the 'List of New Books and Reprints: Literary', in the *TLS* on 23 February 1906, reads: 'Amusing, knowing, and practical talks about authors and their prospects, publishers, reviewers, editors, the public, "booms", and other matters' (67). Lorimer's line conflates readers' choices and democracy in its definition of the public as duped.

21. The editors suggest January [?] 1905 for this letter, but the review of *The Author's Progress* appeared in the *Guardian* on 25 July 1906; perhaps this letter, in which she thanks Nelly for asking her to 'come some time', belongs with the editorially dated July 1906 letter in which she says she has returned home safely and thanks Nelly for her stay there (*L1* 231).

22. Some of the disdain may be class-based as well. See Catherine Mitchell's dissertation, 'Professions of Exclusivity: Authorship and the Anxiety of Expertise, 1880–1940'.

23. But see Waller 401–3.

24. *Cornhill* and *National Review* ads had been removed from the copies I examined; the same was true of more popular magazines, such as *Punch* and the *Strand*. *Bookman* had no such ads between 1903 and 1904, and 1904 and 1905 (vols 25–8), but from 1905–6 up until 1907–8 (vols 29–34), a regular notice on the *Bookman* Young Authors' Page told authors they could receive criticism of their submitted manuscripts by enclosing coupons and a stamped addressed envelope; they could also apply for 'fuller opinion'. In the September 1907 issue, an ad for Barry Pain's Literary Correspondence College appeared, and it was repeated sporadically after that.

25. Although correspondence courses have a long history within adult education (Noffsinger, Glatter and Wedell), have ties to examinations for degrees and the Open University in the UK (Glatter and Wedell, Bell and Tight), and have metamorphosed into Massive Open Online Courses and low-residency creative writing programmes, they also have long been associated with shady dealings and scams (Byrne). Indeed, some of the current suspicion about online education may stem from the notorious reputation of past correspondence schemes.
26. See Keating 72 about the Year-Book's evolution. How easily available would this increasingly useful yearbook have been? An eighty-page booklet costing a shilling in 1906 ('Writers' & Artists' Year-Book'), it may have been available in the British Museum Reading Room and the London Library since the 1898–1901 *Literary Year-Book* (its predecessor) is listed in the 1903 *Catalogue of the London Library* (873; Julia King, email 4 December 2017). But did public libraries purchase it annually?

Chapter 10

Becoming a Professional

Finding Work

Virginia Stephen had the advantage, as Leila Brosnan points out, of having family and friends who could help her find work in her apprenticeship's early days (44).[1] She did not, however, have the Cambridge associations with journals her male friends did (Brosnan 46; Rosenbaum 152; Mepham 17; Low 12–13) or access to male literary clubs and societies that had proliferated in London during the Victorian era, some created by and for literary men of the lower classes (Kent, Intro xviii; see also Mays 21). It would have been foolhardy not to use whatever advantage she had – certainly, her female predecessors had done so (Onslow 83–4) – and Jeanne Dubino notes how hard she worked to prove herself and sustain journal connections once made ('VW' 28). As already mentioned, reviewers needed introductions (Onslow 81). Though her father's literary standing may have helped her, it did not make acceptance automatic, as Reginald Smith's rejection of her unsolicited Boswell piece for the *Cornhill* in 1905 makes clear. Indeed, later typecasting of her work at the *Cornhill* suggests her father's reputation may have hindered her. Fittingly, Stephen's first influential introduction came through friendship – her own with Violet Dickinson, and Violet Dickinson's with Mary Kathleen Lyttelton – not through the world of letters.[2]

Although she knew to provide writing samples, Virginia Stephen had never sought work before, and she seemed unsure about how to proceed. In May 1904, when she and others were beginning to realise she was ill, she wrote to Violet Dickinson, almost pleading, 'Oh my Violet if you could only find me a great solid bit of work to do when I get back that will make me forget my own stupidity I should be so grateful. I *must* work' (*L*1 140, her emphasis). Between then and the end of October 1904, Violet most likely took her friend's desire for work seriously and approached Mrs Arthur Lyttelton, the *Guardian*'s Women's Supplement Editor, about Stephen's possibly writing for the paper. In turn, Violet probably mentioned Mrs Arthur Lyttelton to Virginia and suggested she try writing for the editor as she recovered from the breakdown after her father's death, which explains why, when Stephen wrote to Violet from the Porch, her Quaker Aunt's home, she seemed to be following up on a suggestion: 'Would Mrs Lyttelton like a description of a Q[uaker]. Meeting from my gifted pen, d'you think. I dont know if I shall have time, but it might be amusing' (*L*1 148). Perhaps already thinking about her potential audience, she proposed an essay about religion, but nothing seems to have come of it.³ Writing to Violet on 8 November to thank her for the inkpot 'with all his holes, and a well for ink deep enough to write a dozen articles for the Guardian' (*L*1 153), she sounded confident about having future work there, but the language underlined in the letter below, written only two days later, reveals her anxieties:

> I came upon <u>this kind of</u> essay which I wrote at Manorbier. It <u>aint up to much</u>, as I was writing then to prove to myself that there was nothing wrong with me – which I was already beginning to fear there was. Also I wrote <u>very quick and hasty</u> – without thought, as they say, of publication. But the Quakers words bear fruit; and I think I <u>may as well</u> send this to Mrs Lyttelton to show her the kind of thing I do. Of course <u>I dont for a moment expect her to take</u> *this* <u>which is probably too long or too short, or in some way utterly unsuitable</u>. I only want to get <u>some idea</u> as to whether <u>possibly</u> she would like me to write something in the future – at Giggleswick for instance. Could you address this to her office address, which I dont know. I dont want her to think that she has got to show me the *least* favour, because of you! (*L*1 154, her emphasis; my underlining)

Virginia Stephen, though willing to ask her friends to introduce her writing to editors, did not want the editors to feel pressured to accept her work uncritically.

Kitty Maxse, again on the basis of writing samples Virginia Stephen provided (this time via Vanessa), asked her to submit something to the *National Review*, which her husband, Leo, edited, and, according to S. P. Rosenbaum's reading of Virginia's 16 January 1905 diary entry, 'passed [Stephen's] writing on to the head of the foreign department of *The Times*, Valentine Chirol, to see if it were suitable for the *Times Literary Supplement*, for which he also reviewed' (152). According to Derwent May, Bruce Richmond then arranged for a dinner invitation from Walter and Ella Crum to be issued to Stephen so the two could meet (50). Richmond, though he had Stephen's work with him at the 26 January dinner, did not say anything to her then. Only through Kitty Maxse did Stephen discover that both 'the great Mr Chirol' and Richmond 'approve, & I am to come & meet them to discuss' (*PA* 228). Not, however, until 8 February, at a tea party where she knew nobody except Richmond, did he ask her, first, about writing for the *Outlook*, which never materialised, and second, for *The Times*, which did: 'might [we] send on books for review also' (*PA* 234), he asked. *Guardian*, *National Review* and *Times Literary Supplement* editors may have looked at Stephen's work at the request of friends, and it could not have hurt she was Leslie Stephen's daughter,⁴ but in fact, her writing garnered the invitations to submit to their papers.

Next, on 17 February 1905, came a letter 'from Literature & the Academy asking me to write' (*PA* 239), a request Rosenbaum suggests may have started with Richmond (157), which makes sense since Harold Child, its editor, was writing light leaders for *The Times*, working in the *TLS* office as well, and contributing to it (Roll-Hansen 218; Kent 'Academy' 5).⁵ Rosenbaum suggests Desmond MacCarthy may have been behind the December request from the *Speaker* to write for them (173; *L*1 214), which also makes sense, given his theatre columns for the journal. But we have no definitive evidence for these surmises or for whether her writing was shown to Harold Child or Arthur Clutton-Brock, literary editor of the *Speaker*, before the invitations were issued (although Bruce Richmond had read it and perhaps Desmond MacCarthy had as well).

Although she had considered the *Cornhill* for 'longer and better articles' in late 1904 (*L1* 156), when she sent a short piece on Boswell's letters in January 1905, it was rejected with a printed slip (*L1* 171), perhaps reflecting Bennett's warning that 'Fleet Street at this moment is simply running with women who are writing fanciful essays and not selling them' (*Journalism* 61–2). She did not write for the magazine her father had edited until 1908. Less is known about how *Cornhill*'s 'The Book on the Table' column, which she and Nelly Cecil alternated monthly, came to be – McNeillie suggests Smith had lots of space and 'invited' Stephen and Cecil to share it (xiv), whereas Rosenbaum says she and Cecil 'persuaded' him to start the column (365). In any case, she moved rapidly from having no work in October 1904 (other than writing her note for the Maitland biography) to boasting to Emma Vaughan in February 1905 of writing for the *TLS*, *Academy*, *National Review* and *Guardian* (L1 180). She added the *Speaker* at the end of 1905 and *Cornhill* in 1908 and had single submissions to the *Englishwoman* in 1910 (ghosting for Marjorie Strachey) and the *Nation* in 1911.

Virginia Stephen's letters and diary show she fully participated in that practical world where young writers have to prove themselves, anxiously calling on friends to help establish herself ('If you see Mrs Lyttelton try to find out how often I may write for her with a chance of being accepted' [L1 164]), sending out both solicited and unsolicited materials and dealing with acceptances ('Leo is *delighted* to accept my *charming* article—so there!' [L1 178, her emphasis]) and rejections:

> (I am so cross today, crosser than ever – that fool of a man, the Cornhill editor, sends me back my Article – Boswells letters – without a word, but a printed slip. I never expected him to take it, . . . but I thought he might say so. [L1 171])

She veered between confidence (thinking she can write 'better stuff than that wretched article you sent me. Why on earth does [Mrs Lyttelton] take such trash?' [L1 155]) and anxiety ('I have an article for you to criticise: . . . I dont know if its any good or not' [L1 160]). She borrowed a proof-correcting book from Violet Dickinson (*L1* 169), kept (and lost) a 'MS. book' with article ideas (*L1* 155), and discovered the 'satirical fact that when I am allowed ½ a column I can always fill 2, & when I am to have as much space as I like, I cant screw out words at any price' (*PA* 252). She also returned to her *Hyde Park Gate News* discipline to set up productive routines.

Establishing Routines

Once Virginia Stephen had an invitation from an editor or a paper, she worked hard to fulfil her obligation. Arrangements made when she was ill are unknown – the letters we have never refer to them – but Bruce Richmond, after a slowdown from 1910 to 1913 and hiatus in 1914–15, had Virginia Woolf write fourteen reviews in 1916 – the quality of her work and habits meant he did not hesitate to return to her as soon as she was well (Dubino, 'VW' 32). Nothing in her letters or diaries indicates she was ever late with a review; she conscientiously wrote to Vanessa from Dresden in August 1909, 'I got my Holmes article done in time, and sent it, so I didn't think I need write to Bruce Richmond' (*L1* 410). She did not request extensions; she turned down no assignments. As Quentin Bell puts it, 'She would turn her hand to almost anything' (1 94). Warning Richmond when he asked her to review Edith Sichel's *Catherine de Medici and the French Revolution* that she was not 'learned in Mediaeval French' (*PA* 250), she tried to 'find out something about France of the Reformation from other histories' (*PA* 251) and thought the review bad, expecting 'to have it thrown back in my hands' (*PA* 253). Sure enough, he rejected it: *TLS* wanted 'a serious criticism from a historical point of view' (*L1* 187–8).[6] She sometimes complained to her friends, particularly about editorial changes she was not consulted on, but she never ended her working relationships with papers. When asked to make cuts, she did so. Like many a neophyte before and since, she wanted the work, the cheque and a reputation ('I should like more steady work at reviews, for the sake of my purse' [*PA* 232]), so she diligently read (keeping records of books read and work done at the back of her 1905 journal [*PA* 274–7] and listing additional reading in the entries), took notes, drafted, revised, submitted her work, listened to suggestions and criticism, and responded to editorial demands. Her efforts led to more introductions and more work, such as when the *Guardian* editor, perhaps because of Mrs Lyttelton's recommendation, sent her poetry and drama volumes to review for the paper's regular pages (*L1* 217) or when Richmond began to 'pelt' her with novels (*PA* 252).

The novice also established the 'pattern of work that was to last her the rest of her life' (Dubino, 'VW' 29). Virginia Stephen created or slipped easily into the writing life discipline, devoting a certain number of hours to reading her 'review books', writing, revising and proofing when necessary ('Leo prints badly' [*PA* 239]; see also *L1* 169). She discovered writer's blocks – 'words wouldn't come' (*PA* 250); learned revising takes time – 'It takes me almost as long to rewrite one page, as to write 4 fresh ones' (*PA* 239); and learned everything takes longer than expected – the 'reading and copying' of letters for Fred Maitland she thought 'would take 2 days' took six (*L1* 151). Self-deprecating in her 28 February 1905 diary entry about the 'barely two mornings work' she spent on 'Street Music' (*PA* 244), she says in her earlier entries and a letter to Violet: 'Wrote all the morning at a paper which may, with luck do for Leo' (30 January; *PA* 229); 'Finished my possible Nat. Review article – about which I am doubtful' (31 January; *PA* 230); 'I send you [. . .] the miserable article which I have screwed out with a view to Leo: say if it wont do' (February 1905; *L1* 177); 'Bothered some about the article for Leo, after Violets criticism' (*PA* 232). She consistently worked very hard to prepare her work for publication:

> Wrote . . . all the morning at my Times Review. . . . pegged away at my review; as I am allowed 1500 words; of course they wont come – so I had to beat my brains a little. However I finished it in the course of the day, & made it fairly good I hope. . . . I sent my review off by 7 o'clock Post, to reach tonight if possible. (*PA* 240)

She also kept working at Greek and Latin on her own, setting assignments for herself (Thucydides, Aristotle's *Poetics*, the Georgics, Sophocles' *Oedipus Tyrannus*) and completing them. She taught from 1905 to 1907 and committed herself to preparing for classes ('Scribbled some pages about Florence for my working women' [*PA* 233]). Furthermore, she added the writing of her 'imaginative work' (*The Voyage Out*) to the routine from autumn 1907 onward ('I am struggling with my work of the Fancy and the Affections' [*L1* 331]). Illness, travel, holidays and social obligations, old and new, might interrupt, but for the most part, Virginia Stephen maintained a rhythm of reading, drafting and revising that served her well. She had a daily rhythm – in her diary, she repeatedly wrote some variation on the following:

> Worked all the morning at miscellaneous jobs – at my Cellini which I finished . . . then I finished my Essay article & typewrote it. Then, . . . I found a letter from Mrs. L. enclosing that wretched review, & asking me to cut it down, & send it back as soon as possible. So I set to work with literal & metaphorical scissors & somehow patched it together, having cut out all the plot & a good deal else, so that it wont take more than 800 words . . . Walked home, read 2 review books sent by the Times – & to my girls club. (*PA* 237–8)

– and a weekly one, which she noted in a letter to Nelly Cecil on 10 November 1905:

> It is the busy season, and I have never been without 3 books in hand since I came back. The Times sends me one novel every week; which has to be read on Sunday, written on Monday, and printed on Friday. In America, as you know, they make sausages like that. Mrs Lyttelton asked me to tea, and gave me a prize of 4 books afterwards; the Academy thinks I can write about Wilhelmina, Margravine of Bayreuth. (*L1* 211–12)

In early 1905 mornings, she generally worked on Greek, her classes or a review; afternoons, she walked to the London Library or with Gurth, the dog, typed or proofed; evenings, she read, went to social events or taught. As she says, 'Read, wrote, cursed, & walked – all as usual' (*PA* 216).

Her hard work also earned her some money.[7] Virginia Stephen was organised about keeping track of how much she wrote for whom, payments she received, and reviews that appeared in print. She delighted in being paid ('Found this morning on my plate my first instalment of wages – £2.7.6. for Guardian articles, which gave me great pleasure' [*PA* 219]); paying bills ('Pass book, & my balance better than I expected, so I paid some bills!' [*PA* 268] and 'made a 1905 vow to keep myself in pocket money at least this year by my writing!' [*L1* 172]); being able to afford small luxuries ('Out & bought fire irons of wrought iron, to match my fender, which is a source of real joy to me. Also I bought that great looking glass, which will just fill the space over my writing table, & liven up the room. . . . bought James Thomsons poems . . . – also a note book; & got some of Renan' [*PA* 242; see also Dubino, 'VW' 28–9]); and saving copies of her reviews ('Would you keep me a copy of the [*Times*] supplement with my Sterne in it?' she writes to Vanessa from Bayreuth. 'It comes out on Thursday: also wd. you keep my Holmes on the 26th. I paste them in a book' [*L1* 406]). She toted up her literary and financial achievements. A cheque for £5 from Leo for 'Street Music' made her feel overpaid (*PA* 244), and a cheque for £9 7s. from *The Times* in July of 1906 was 'the largest sum I have ever made at one blow' and a 'gift' (*L1* 232). McNeillie estimates, basing his figures on her Reading Notebook log of nine *Guardian* contributions, that she probably earned £17 10s. 0d. over the course of her employment there (xviii n12; Silver 176). Rosenbaum says some figures in her Reading Notebooks suggest her assignments with and payments from the *Guardian* and *TLS* may have been based on columns (172). And he points out that in her notes for 'Professions for Women', she recalled making approximately a guinea per thousand words and a total of fifty guineas her first full year (496 n8; *P* 163).[8]

After Virginia Stephen moved to Bloomsbury in November 1904, she began pursuing work seriously ('I am a lady in search of a job at present,' she wrote to Nelly Cecil in December 1904 [*L1* 168]). 'I cant help writing,' she wrote to Madge Vaughan on 1 December 1904 (*L1* 162), but certain material conditions made it easier to do so – separation from older family members and friends, space, privacy, light, beauty.[9] Indeed, during her recovery at Caroline Stephen's that autumn, she yearned for the house the Stephens had rented and Vanessa had already decorated and furnished at 46 Gordon Square in Bloomsbury. She complained to Violet that Dr Savage and others

> dont realise that London means my own home, and books, and pictures, and music, from all of which I have been parted since February now.... I long for a large room to myself, with books and nothing else, where I can shut myself up, and see no one, and read myself into peace. (*L1* 147)

When she arrived there in November, Violet's present, the large ink pot, was in her room, and in her thank you letter, she says 'The house is a dream of loveliness after the Quaker brown paper' (*L1* 153). By mid-December, she wrote to Madge Vaughan,

> I wish you could see my room at this moment, on a dark winter's evening – all my beloved leather backed books standing up so handsome in their shelves, and a nice fire, and the electric light burning, and a huge mass of manuscripts and letters and proof-sheets and pens and inks over the floor and everywhere. Tomorrow week they will be bad enough for a general clearance; then I start tidy and gradually work myself up into a happy frenzy of litter. (*L1* 167)

Surrounded by the tools of her trade, Virginia Stephen learned to write book reviews.

Notes

1. Not all accounts of Stephen's early work agree. Quentin Bell says Bruce Richmond, editor of the *TLS*, approached her, not vice versa (1 104). Derwent May suggests Stephen sent some work to Valentine Chirol at *The Times*, who approached Richmond, who then set up a social engagement with her (the timing of letters and diary entries support his account on 50). Frank Swinnerton, whom Brosnan contrasts with Stephen (45), did work to make contacts. But he made them early and used them assiduously, as did Stephen. His work at Chatto & Windus as a publisher's reader meant he met many writers, published a book annually for years, and formed a network of friends whose operations and support seem no different from Bloomsbury's (Langenheim; Lusty). Brosnan is correct, class matters, but it was no more unusual for Stephen to use whatever contacts she had than it was for Swinnerton to seek and use those he fostered. Not all her friends' efforts on her behalf succeeded, either. Rosenbaum points out

Stephen thought she might do an edition of Boswell's letters and write the introduction. Despite Lytton Strachey's recommendation, she was passed over for Thomas Seccombe (and had to review his edition) (352).

2. See also Rosenbaum 152. Would Leslie Stephen have introduced her to editors? Or would he have steered her away from journalism? At first, she could have easily used her father's *Cornhill* connections to succeed there as a reviewer. Instead, she did what others did and simply submitted an article.
3. Her last piece for the *Guardian* was her aunt's obituary on 21 April 1909. In it, she discussed Caroline Emelia Stephen's faith and her aunt's need to express it in writing.
4. Julia Stephen had encouraged Kitty Maxse, who then encouraged Virginia. Marion Dell argues that Julia Stephen should receive more recognition for her role in the direction Virginia Stephen's early career (and Woolf's later one) took. Dell not only discusses Julia's literary tending in *Influential* (see especially Chapters 1 and 5), but also argues Madge Vaughan acted as a 'mother-substitute' in her nurturing of Stephen's first work (43). Dell has continued to pursue the 'elusive Julia Stephen'; see the results of her ongoing biographical research at https://www.theelusivejuliastephen.wordpress.com.
5. *The Times* used to have four leaders (editorials), with the fourth generally light or humorous, an 'essaylet' loosely connected to a day's event that gave writer and reader the chance to '[turn] aside from preoccupations of the moment to meander down agreeable by-paths' (Foreword v; Stuart N. Clarke email communication 5 December 2017).
6. Rosenbaum says Stephen would not have known Edith Sichel 'was one of the few other women reviewing for the *TLS* at the time' (161). See *L1* 182 for Stephen's misgivings about accepting this assignment in the first place.
7. She did not receive the now-famous bequest from her Aunt Caroline until 1909.
8. In 1908, *The Writers' and Artists' Year-Book* says *Cornhill* paid a guinea a page (450 words) for short stories and articles, but no reviewing fee is noted (14). Periodical descriptions include information about content, length, fees and whether a preliminary letter is required, but only for article submissions; nothing is said about reviews.
9. Whether Virginia Stephen made the conscious connection at the time, Virginia Woolf made it later in *A Room of One's Own*. Though Woolf's book has been read as saying art can be produced only under good circumstances (Daugherty, 'You' 81–2), she knew art had been created under abominable conditions but that artists desired good conditions and struggled against pressures to conform under such bad circumstances. Would not space, privacy and financial security help artists sustain work and maintain freedom? Woolf wrote *A Room of One's Own* out of a visceral understanding of space and privacy needs; see also her essay on Donne, *E5* 349–66, especially 356. She was indeed privileged to have space and privacy early in her career. But she did not always have such conditions, and circumstances other than poverty can lead to such understanding: Stephen grew up in a house where rooms were not sanctuaries, and she recovered from mental strain in other people's houses.

Chapter 11

Learning from Editors

Teachers

Virginia Stephen's letters and diaries reveal a young woman who needs encouragement above everything, as do all young writers – 'Do you feel convinced I *can* write?' she writes to Violet in July 1905 (*L1* 202, her emphasis) – but also questions, suggestions for revision, and challenges without the imposition of constraints. In other words, a good teacher. As an apprentice, Stephen learned from a student, her reading, and her friends' occasional and informal critiques, but her main teachers, the ones who taught her how to be a professional, were the editors and journals she wrote for.

When Virginia Stephen talked about reviewing with a Morley student, she discovered Miss Williams had to turn pages 'with a keen eye' for 'quotations picked up at random', link them together with 'a connecting word', and rapidly pull it all together in an unfavourable or favourable notice having nothing to do with the author. She knew Miss Williams had potential, but she also understood Miss Williams's situation meant she had no time to read the books she reviewed and must handle words like another woman might '[manipulate] the bottles of a patent mouth wash'.[1] This conversation may have been the impetus for the 'Gutter and Stamp system' Virginia Woolf sarcastically proposed in 'Reviewing', in which the 'gutter' will 'write out a short statement of the book; extract the plot . . . ; quote a few anecdotes', and the 'taster' will stamp it with 'an asterisk to signify approval, a dagger to signify disapproval' (*E6* 209).[2] At the time, her student taught Stephen she wanted to avoid becoming 'a writing machine' controlled by an editor ('Report' 202). Indeed, literary manuals warned against such a practice.

Virginia Stephen also picked up guidance from her reading. Her 'youthful training' on the *Hyde Park Gate News* (Brosnan 23) reveals her imitating journalistic style as early as age 9 (*QB1* 28). Her parents probably subscribed to the *Cornhill* and *Nineteenth Century* (Gillespie, 'Essays' 198, 211),[3] and she could have read reviews there, in other magazines, and in newspapers, where, Waller notes, 'the review had become ubiquitous' (117). Although Dubino argues Leslie Stephen did not actively provide his daughter with practical or instructional assistance ('VW' 27), Virginia may have learned from reading her father's work – his earlier pieces and the biographical essays he continued to write up until 1902 for the *National Review* that became the basis for his four-volume *Studies of a Biographer* (Fenwick 179, 213–20). Rosenbaum concurs, suggesting she learned the art of the essay from reading Leslie Stephen, Aristotle and Pater (164).[4]

She also sought out literary models for learning how to write book reviews, writing on 13 March 1905, 'Out to Hatchards to buy [Robert Louis] Stevenson & [Walter] Pater – I want to study them – not to copy, I hope, but to see how the trick's done. Stevenson is a trick – but Pater something different & beyond' (*PA* 251). The Stevenson titles published in 1905 or before in the Library of Leonard and Virginia Woolf are not related to essays or reviewing (see Appendix 2), though she might have purchased Stevenson volumes in March 1905 that have not survived. The more instructional Stevenson collection, *Essays in the Art of Writing*, with its helpful 'Technical Elements of Style', was published in 1905, but in September according to a *Guardian* review (13 September 1905 1508). The comment about Pater is also puzzling since the bookplates in her Pater volumes show Stephen bought most of them in 1902–3, including *Miscellaneous Studies* and *Appreciations* (K&M-V 172), the books most connected to essays and possibly reviewing; only her copy of *Plato and Platonism* has a bookplate dated 1905, and it does not model reviewing.

Who knows what Virginia Stephen bought that day, but she distinguished between Stevenson and Pater, so we know she was meeting neither for the first time. Mitchell Leaska surmises she was interested in Stevenson's *Virginibus Puerisque* (For Girls and Boys), which contains familiar or personal essays, and *Familiar Studies of Men and Books* (*PA* 251 n27), a collection of biographical studies. Honest and self-deprecating, calling himself a 'literary vagrant' in his *Familiar Studies* preface, Stevenson discusses the disadvantages inherent in compressing an entire lifetime and many published volumes into something 'logical and striking': 'keep[ing] his eye steadily' on his 'point of view' means many omissions by necessity (7–11). Leslie Stephen praises Stevenson's avoidance of 'orthodox standards', his 'freshness and the genuine ring of youthful enthusiasm' (*RLS* 40), and Glenda Norquay focuses on his emphasis on pleasure, interest in patterns, curiosity about psychology, and most important, awareness of readers: 'the reader of the essay and the reader figured in the essay are both activated; the author as writer and as part of a reading community is in continual play' (15–23). Thus, Stevenson may have contributed to Stephen's (and later Woolf's) essay tone and approach, but his possible relationship to her book reviewing remains a mystery.

Perhaps Virginia Stephen bought Walter Pater's *Essays from 'The Guardian'* that day in 1905?[5] Although not in the Library of Leonard and Virginia Woolf or Stephen's library, Pater's essays, after appearing anonymously in the *Guardian*, were collected and published in a private edition in 1896 and then by Macmillan in 1901, so could have been in Hatchards.[6] In these nine true reviews, Pater writes about contemporary books, four anthologies for English literature students, a reprinted book about the English stage called *Their Majesties' Servants*, Mrs Humphry Ward's *Robert Elsmere*, editions of Wordsworth and Gosse, a study of Browning by Arthur Symons, two French works, and a translation of Amiel's *Journal intime* by Mrs Ward. Though tempting to think Virginia Stephen bought and read this volume, we know only that she seemed to have consulted literary models rather than manuals.

Her letters and journal indicate she also occasionally shared work with friends.[7] As early as 1903, she probably shared literary exercises from her journal with Violet (*L1* 82 and n1, 103 and n2). She sometimes received comments before revising, as from Violet, probably about her piece on Haworth (*L1* 160) or 'Street Music' (*PA* 232), or from Kitty Maxse, Violet and Nelly Cecil about the note for Fred Maitland (*PA* 230: *L1* 176, 177), or from Madge Vaughan (*L1* 226–27). Saxon Sydney-Turner offered 'all sorts of proprieties' as she worked on her *Guardian* articles (*L1* 201). She sent her 'unpublished works' to Walter Headlam for his 'sober criticism' and 'the truth' in December of 1906 (*L1* 259, 261, 272), and it seems he commented (*L1* 293), but we do not know what she sent or what he said. She also sometimes received or solicited comments about something in print, from Nelly, probably about her review of Howells (*L1* 167), or from Violet about 'Literary Geography' (*L1* 182) or her Henry James review (*L1* 234). Violet and Kitty, however, were not professional writers; Madge focused her criticism on domestic experience Virginia lacked (*L1* 226–7), and Nelly, although a reader of fiction and non-fiction for John Murray publishers and thus attuned to editors and trends, became increasingly difficult to communicate with because of her extreme deafness, inhabited a world Virginia often 'scorned', and in a review, tied the aesthetic worth of May Sinclair's *The Helpmate* to morality without giving her reasons for doing so (*L1* 215, 229; McNeillie xix; *L1* 317).[8] Headlam, a classics translator and sixteen years older, was in the midst of a flirtation with her, and Sydney-Turner's 'regular suggestions' may have curbed some of her unconventional stylistic impulses.

As a novice, Virginia Stephen had not yet developed an internal gauge for her writing. She knew 'literary advice is a very ticklish thing', realised the more candid the criticism the better, and understood she needed to '[sit] down solidly every morning' and make her work 'thoroughly substantial all through', but she struggled to figure out how to improve: 'I always think I might write so much better if I took time or trouble – or something else which I never do take' (*L1* 82). Pleased that Vanessa and Thoby liked her note about their father, she was rasped by Kitty's criticism, perhaps because Kitty wanted cuts 'to make it printable' (*PA* 230), a phrase suggesting censorship. In 1905, she said she did not take criticism well (*PA* 232), but she heard and internalised it, coming to agree with Violet, for example, that 'Street Music' was not as good as 'Plague of Essays' (*PA* 239, 240) and worrying about the lack of 'heart' Madge saw (*L1* 226–8). She also thanked Nelly Cecil for her comments about her piece on Jane Carlyle's letters for the *Guardian*, noted she 'actually attended to them', and tried to explain her views more clearly. When she sent the same piece to Violet, she says she 'altered words to suit' Nelly in response to Nelly's lack of enthusiasm and repeated Nelly's probable opinion: 'not much good I am afraid' (*L1* 200). Stephen sent a piece to Violet for her 'remarks' because 'I dont know if its any good or not' (*L1* 160). She needed, in other words, someone to tell her whether her writing was 'well, very well, or indifferently done' (*PA* 226).[9]

Soon after starting to review, however, irked at receiving 'nothing but criticism' from Violet and needing to develop accurate assessments of her own work, Virginia Stephen made the practical decision to 'send things straight to the editors, whose criticism is important' (*PA* 232). After all, editors, not friends, determined whether something saw print or not. From editors, she learned specific 'how-to's'. From editors, she learned the 'knack of writing for newspapers' she saw as differing from 'literary merit' (*L1* 155). From editors, she learned to adapt her writing to a variety of audiences, a skill fuelling Virginia Woolf's later creation of a common reader.

Virginia Stephen's most important teachers during this part of her apprenticeship, then, were the papers she published her early work in.[10] There, she moved from being a student to a teacher, a trainee to a skilled practitioner, an amateur to a professional.[11] There, she practised her craft, and although her practice was generally anonymous, she saw her words become public. Her editors, though sometimes irritating to the young woman trying to become independent, taught her that 'knack' she knew she had to learn – she realised the importance of their criticism even when she did not agree with it. Since periodicals at the time did not use mastheads and she did not always reveal editors' names, we cannot always be certain for whom Stephen worked or with whom she corresponded.[12] None of these periodicals published guidelines or issued public calls for publications, either, so it is hard to know their editorial requirements. We have, in some instances, her comments to friends or in her journal about guidelines or restrictions, but we do not have her correspondence with her editors or their correspondence with her.[13] However, as Louis James points out in his essay about methodology in periodicals studies, a journal

> communicates through its layout, its selection, arrangement and general presentation, the use or absence of illustrations, the size of columns, paragraphs, the type itself . . . . A journal's format thus becomes a tone of voice . . . . A periodical, because it selects and orders information in a specific way, becomes a microcosm, to a lesser or greater extent, of a cultural outlook. (350–1)[14]

Similarly, Arnold Bennett advised novices to study newspapers and magazines carefully: 'Each paper has its own public,' he writes in *Journalism for Women*, 'its own policy, its own tone, its own physiognomy, its own preferences, its own prejudices' (79).[15] If '[t]ailoring one's style to types of periodical had long been the key to journalistic success', as Onslow notes (84), then Stephen succeeded by tailoring her reviews and essays to seven different periodicals.[16]

Although Stephen wrote an anonymous memoir for Maitland's Leslie Stephen biography, reviewed a performance of *Lysistrata* for Marjorie Strachey that appeared above Strachey's name in the *Englishwoman*,[17] and placed two essays about Wagner's operas in *The Times*, she published the bulk of her 158 apprenticeship reviews and essays in seven periodicals: the *Guardian*, whose women's pages were edited by Mary Kathleen Lyttelton (thirty-nine reviews and essays, from 1904 to 1906, and one each in 1907, 1908 and 1909); the *National Review*, edited by Leo Maxse (one essay in 1905); the *Academy and Literature* or *The Academy*, edited by Harold Child (four reviews and essays in 1905–6); the *Speaker*, whose literary editor was Arthur Clutton-Brock (three reviews in 1906); *Cornhill Magazine*, edited by Reginald Smith (six reviews in 1908); the *Nation*, whose literary editor may have been A. W. Evans (one review in 1911); and the *Times Literary Supplement*, edited by Bruce Richmond (100 reviews and essays from 1905 to 1912). These seven papers range from narrow and defined audiences to broad and open ones; they include two monthlies and five weeklies; one religious, one general, three political and two literary; and in circulation, four small, two medium and one large. These newspapers and editors, representing varied cultural outlooks, taught Virginia Stephen to review.

Mrs Arthur Lyttelton – *Guardian*

The daughter of two agnostics, Virginia Stephen writes to Violet in mid-February 1905 that she 'cant conceive' how the *Guardian*, the High Anglican weekly newspaper for clergy, 'ever got such a black little goat into their fold' (*L*1 178). Andrew McNeillie agrees, writing it is 'difficult to imagine a more unlikely outlet' for the writer who would become Virginia Woolf (xii), and Anthony Curtis notes it seems 'an incongruous platform for the future *doyenne* of Bloomsbury' (148). According to Henry Charles Moore's article on the religious press in the *Newspaper Press Directory* (hereafter *NPD*), the *Guardian* was founded in 1846 because the Anglo-Catholic High Church party wanted a 'high-class paper to represent it in the same way that the *Record* represented the Evangelicals' (12).[18] Its 1904 *NPD* ad notes the *Guardian* had incorporated *The Churchwoman* and is

> a weekly journal of Politics, Literature, Education, and the Fine Arts, for Churchmen and Churchwomen, dealing with the Ecclesiastical and many of the secular sides of social and industrial activity. Whilst Ecclesiastical and Political subjects are treated from a definite Church standpoint, its Correspondence columns are open to all shades of opinion. Special reports are given of all important matters connected with the Church and Education. (*NPD*, 1904 151)

The paper saw itself as aiming to establish 'a clear view of the ground taken by the High Church party on matters religious and political' and to provide articles about social reforms in the public eye. It calls itself 'a well-printed, large-sized paper; devoting much space to reviews of books, and to educational matters', along with 'well-written criticisms on music, and the arts' (*NPD*, 1904 78). In 1907, 'It is an influential journal' was added (*NPD*, 1907 66).[19] Mainly Conservative in national politics, it was also seen as not hewing to any particular party line (H. C. Moore 12); according to Alvar Ellegård, it appealed to 'liberal-minded and Liberal churchmen, especially clergy', perhaps because 'it looked with some favour on the Broad Church position', perhaps because it featured a large and well-written literary section (12).

An examination of the *Guardian* from 1904 to 1909, the years Virginia Stephen placed reviews and essays in the Supplement, shows that editors (and readers) were interested in understanding Parliamentary bills related to education; turning moral beliefs into charitable, Church and/or public policy; appreciating literature, art and music; experiencing travel; and knowing more about the colonies and other cultures. The content of the newspaper's main portion – on 8 February 1905, for example, a column called 'The Church at Home and Abroad', an article on 'Church Differences and the Appeal to Antiquity' and a review of 'Dr Plummer's English Church History', along with correspondence about the Athanasian creed, theological hoods and the misuse of the offertory – shows most *Guardian* readers were Church of England members and many were clergy. Numerous ads for domestic servants indicate a primarily middle-class readership, and articles about working-class life are written from a middle-class perspective, though Supplement writers sometimes attempt to indicate how working-class people themselves might view something like cottage-building schemes (14 December 1904, 'The Trials of the Cottager' 2121). Its three-columned 11 × 17 pages of fine print, news and commentary about political events, extensive review sections, lecture reprints by Church leaders, and attention to social issues from a moral point of view all point to an educated, serious, involved audience.

Though Andrew McNeillie calls the paper 'pretty dull' (xii),[20] many articles – religion in education, poverty solutions, education reform, the rights of women and children, attempts to understand other religions, the rights of workers – and correspondence discussions reveal some of the same debates and arguments we currently have. *Guardian* readers cared about these issues, wanted to be informed about them and agreed on the need for both individual and collective action. When the Church of England was concerned about the Education Bill of 1906 and its restrictions on the Anglican presence in schools, leaflets were printed, sold at 1 shilling per hundred, and widely distributed (see Supplement, 9, 16, 23 and 30 May 1906). The *Guardian*'s perspective is Christian, assumes British superiority to the colonies and is far from radical. On the other hand, it is open to varying views, questions the class system, includes columns written from inside the colonies and calls for the reform of various institutions, including the Church.

Clerical content aside, the *Guardian* did in fact provide a fitting beginning to Virginia Stephen's professional career as a reviewer and essayist. As G. Martin Murphy notes about R. W. Church, a *Guardian* founder, the paper was 'written for laymen, not churchmen', so thoughtful articles on science, history and the arts appeared frequently amid Church news and reports. Plus, Anthony Curtis suggests

> it hardly matters where the novice-reviewer first appears in print. What does matter is that she should receive a regular flow of books, establish an amicable working relation with a lit[erary] ed[itor] whom she respects, and that the reviews she writes should appear without inordinate delay. (148)

In Mrs Arthur Lyttelton, supervisor of the Supplement replacing *Churchwoman*, Stephen had an editor who met Curtis's criteria.[21] She also generously allowed Virginia Stephen 'any subject' (*L1* 155), giving her the chance to write essays, not just reviews, taking her unsolicited Haworth piece and liking it (*L1* 166).[22] Furthermore, although deeply religious, the Honourable Mrs Lyttelton was, as her *Times* obituary noted, 'a considerable student of literature' who 'devoted much of her life to fighting for the improvement of women's lives in general, and for the extension of suffrage to women in particular' (S. Kelly). Virginia Stephen sensed that early, saying Mrs Lyttelton was 'broad minded, a refreshing & inspiriting woman' on 26 January 1905 (*PA* 228).[23]

The seven pages of Mrs Lyttelton's Supplement (three for ads) came at the end of every week's 24–32-page newspaper, were designated 'Notes' in the paper's table of contents and were not identified anywhere as 'women's pages'. She filled the four pages 'under [her] supervision' with reports and commentary about women's social and political activism of the period, such as a column-and-a-half notice/review of a pamphlet by Margaret Llewelyn Davies on the Women's Co-operative Guild in the 10 August 1904 issue (1333) and a long article about 'How Working Women Govern Themselves' by Davies in the 12 April 1905 issue (626). Although the pages certainly contained home-related articles such as those on furniture or gardening, along with charity-related articles on women missionaries or homes for waifs and strays, much space is also given to (1) women's education (Alice Zimmern's 'What the Older Universities Do for Women' [21 December 1904 2158] and Wilmer Cave France's 'The Career of the College-Bred Woman in America' [19 April 1905 68]); (2) suffrage ('The Woman's Suffrage Convention' [30 November 1904 2017] and a report on the public demonstration for 'The Parliamentary Vote for Women' [22 March 1905 508]); (3) women's work in the middle and working classes (a review of *Women in the Printing Trades: A Sociological Study* [17 August 1904 1366] and letters about 'Sweating and Women's Labour' [13 June 1906 1004 and 20 June 1906 1045]); and (4) homeless women ('The Tramp Ward' [6 July 1904 1138]). There are stories about inebriation and drug abuse, columns on ladies' sports (lawn tennis, croquet, hockey and golf) and reviews of books from America, such as Upton Sinclair's *The Jungle* (4 April 1906 591) and Gene Stratton Porter's *Freckles* (10 May 1905 803). Mrs Lyttelton's 'Notes' begin the section, followed by series articles such as Zimmern's on women's unpaid professions or Constance Smith's on women workers (26 October 1904 1806 and 2 November 1904 1850), or articles such as Clementina Black's on 'The "Pocket-Money" Worker' (27 July 1904), in which she calls it 'curious' that critics of women who work even though they have an income do not 'see anything reprehensible ... when the income-possessing money-earner is a man' (1258), and then literature, music, art and correspondence have regular space.

The Supplement gives a remarkable amount of space to suffrage. Mrs Lyttelton's sudden death in January 1907 makes it clear how much her attitudes about women had permeated the Supplement's pages because an obvious shift occurs after her death toward more articles about beauty, fashion and housekeeping (including recipes), and the tenor of the Supplement becomes more overtly religious. Soon after Mrs Lyttelton's death, Eveline B. Mitford of the Women's Franchise Declaration writes to the *Guardian* to explain that working-class women will also benefit from the enfranchisement, to which Penderel-Brodhurst appends a note stating 'We cannot embark on a correspondence upon this subject' (3 April 1907 567). And the 29 July 1908 issue of the Supplement gives space to a notice of a Women's National Anti-Suffrage League meeting and a summary of its manifesto (1294). Virginia Stephen's increasing *TLS* work likely caused her to reduce *Guardian* submissions to one piece a year for 1907–9 (one in the regular pages), but just as likely, the Supplement's new editor did not give Stephen work or Stephen did not want to work for Mrs Lyttelton's successor.[24]

It is hard to know how many people read the *Guardian* during Virginia Stephen's association with it; she herself did not 'suppose the most sensitive of authors cares what the Guardian says of him – preaching the charities of the parish in the next breath' (*L1* 197). The *WDENP* lists a 6,000-per-week circulation in 1865, as does Ellegård for 1870 (11), but perhaps the later addition of 'influential' to its description meant it was read outside its target audience and thus reached larger and more diverse numbers, making authors care more about the paper's reviews than Stephen thought. Thirty-two of the books she reviewed in her apprenticeship between 1904 and 1912 had reviews in both the *Guardian* and the *TLS*, so an author who cared enough to cut out *TLS* reviews might also want *Guardian* clippings. At the same time, it is easy to see why Stephen thought of her readers as do-gooders and the paper as 'righteous' (L1 178): her review of W. D. Howells's *The Son of Royal Langbrith* follows a full page of likenesses of Christ painted from the time of the Apostles to the present day (14 December 1904 2119) and appears next to a report about missionary study and letters about training midwives, hiring widows as charwomen and needing money for a poor children's Christmas gathering (2120; see also McNeillie xii). See Figure 11.1.

Not only did a women's network help Virginia Stephen break into the literary world, but she started out by writing for a female editor and audience. Rosenbaum observes that 'The Value of Laughter' assumes a readership of active women as it offers an 'early feminist analysis of the comic spirit' and ridicules masculine solemnity (158–9). Stephen may have described her readers as 'a Governess, and maiden Lady, and high church Parson mixed' (L1 178), but anyone who writes that women are probably 'looked upon with such disfavor in the learned professions' because their laughter at the 'pomps and conventions and dreary solemnities' of modern men 'shrivels them up and leaves the bones bare' (E1 60) is relying on women with a sense of humour.

Under Mrs Lyttelton, Virginia Stephen was able to practise writing personal essays: about the Stephen dog, Shag ('On a Faithful Friend'), or a pilgrimage to the Brontë parsonage ('Haworth, November, 1904'), or women's humour ('The Value of Laughter'). But Stephen also practised more prosaic skills, such as meeting length requirements. Because Mrs Lyttelton had only four pages to work with, she had to ask for short reviews. When she tells Stephen to cut from a third to a half of her review of Henry James's *The Golden Bowl*, Stephen responds angrily, writing to Violet, 'It was quite good before the official eye fell upon it; now it is worthless, and doesn't in the least represent all the toil I put into it' (L1 178). In her journal, she blames having to cut it on 'the worthy Patronesses' who 'want to read about midwives' (PA 237), and the Association for Promoting Training and Supply of Midwives does report its annual meeting on the page opposite her review (22 February 1905 338). But she neglects to mention her assignment, also written down in her journal, which was to boil 550 pages of 'Henry James print' into '7 or 800 words' (PA 234–5), the length of the published review, the result of her 'cut[ting] two sheets to pieces, [writing] a scrawl to mend them together, and ... sen[ding] the maimed thing off' (L1 178). What she 'forgets' in her diary and letter, though, she learns in her professional life. As she confides about a later review, 'I hadn't much difficulty ... – not that I over flowed my limit. I shant waste words again!' (PA 251). Noting in her 1905 journal that a typewritten foolscap sheet has approximately 450 words and that a page of her manuscript book equals 400 (PA 277), she paid attention to page lengths and word count averages for the rest of her life, often jotting down estimates and predictions on fiction and non-fiction drafts alike.

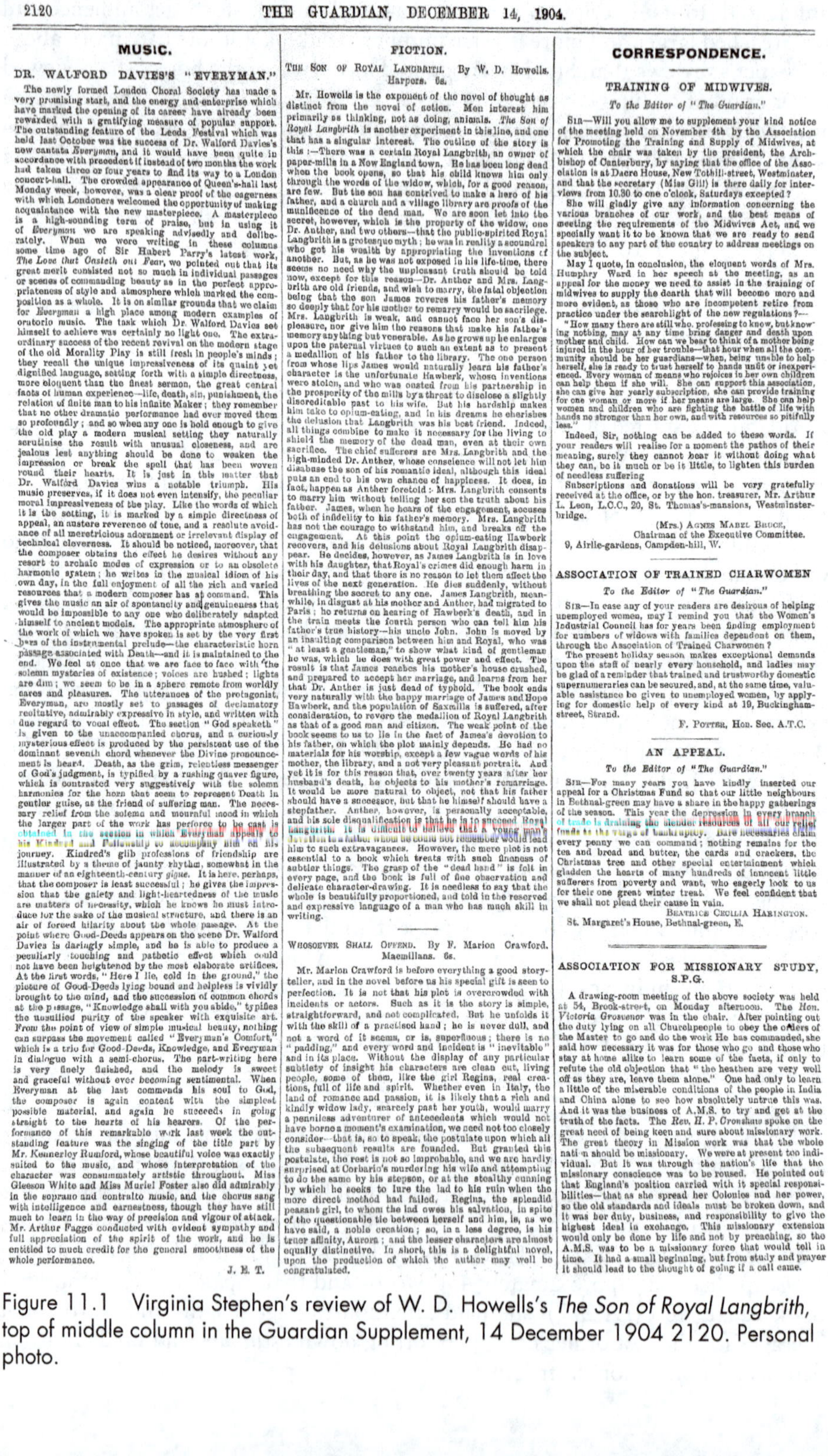

2120 THE GUARDIAN, DECEMBER 14, 1904.

MUSIC.

DR. WALFORD DAVIES'S "EVERYMAN."

The newly formed London Choral Society has made a very promising start, and the energy and enterprise which have marked the opening of its career have already been rewarded with a gratifying measure of popular support. The outstanding feature of the Leeds Festival which was held last October was the success of Dr. Walford Davies's new cantata *Everyman*, and it would have been quite in accordance with precedent if instead of two months the work had taken three or four years to find its way to a London concert-hall. The crowded appearance of Queen's-hall last Monday week, however, was a clear proof of the eagerness with which Londoners welcomed the opportunity of making acquaintance with the new masterpiece. A masterpiece is a high-sounding term of praise, but in using it of *Everyman* we are speaking advisedly and deliberately. When we were writing in these columns some time ago of Sir Hubert Parry's latest work, *The Love that Casteth out Fear*, we pointed out that its great merit consisted not so much in individual passages or scenes of commanding beauty as in the perfect appropriateness of style and atmosphere which marked the composition as a whole. It is on similar grounds that we claim for *Everyman* a high place among modern examples of oratorio music. The task which Dr. Walford Davies set himself to achieve was certainly no light one. The extraordinary success of the recent revival on the modern stage of the old Morality Play is still fresh in people's minds; they recall the unique impressiveness of its quaint yet dignified language, setting forth with a simple directness, more eloquent than the finest sermon, the great central facts of human experience—life, death, sin, punishment, the relation of finite man to his infinite Maker; they remember that no other dramatic performance had ever moved them so profoundly; and so when any one is bold enough to give the old play a modern musical setting they naturally scrutinise the result with unusual closeness, and are jealous lest anything should be done to weaken the impression or break the spell that has been woven round their hearts. It is just in this matter that Dr. Walford Davies wins a notable triumph. His music preserves, if it does not even intensify, the peculiar moral impressiveness of the play. Like the words of which it is the setting, it is marked by a simple directness of appeal, an austere reverence of tone, and a resolute avoidance of all meretricious adornment or irrelevant display of technical cleverness. It should be noticed, moreover, that the composer obtains the effect he desires without any resort to archaic modes of expression or to an obsolete harmonic system; he writes in the musical idiom of his own day, in the full enjoyment of all the rich and varied resources that a modern composer has at command. This gives the music an air of spontaneity and genuineness that would be impossible to any one who deliberately adapted himself to ancient models. The appropriate atmosphere of the work of which we have spoken is set by the very first bars of the instrumental prelude—the characteristic horn passage associated with Death—and it is maintained to the end. We feel at once that we are face to face with the solemn mysteries of existence; voices are hushed; lights are dim; we seem to be in a sphere remote from worldly cares and pleasures. The utterances of the protagonist, Everyman, are mostly set to passages of declamatory recitative, admirably expressive in style, and written with due regard to vocal effect. The section "God speaketh" is given to the unaccompanied chorus, and a curiously mysterious effect is produced by the persistent use of the dominant seventh chord whenever the Divine pronouncement is heard. Death, as the grim, relentless messenger of God's judgment, is typified by a rushing quaver figure, which is contrasted very suggestively with the solemn harmonies for the horn that seem to represent Death in gentler guise, as the friend of suffering man. The necessary relief from the solemn and mournful mood in which the larger part of the work has perforce to be cast is obtained in the section in which Everyman appeals to his Kindred and Fellowship to accompany him on his journey. Kindred's glib professions of friendship are illustrated by a theme of jaunty rhythm, somewhat in the manner of an eighteenth-century *gigue*. It is here, perhaps, that the composer is least successful; he gives the impression that the gaiety and light-heartedness of the music are matters of necessity, which he knows he must introduce for the sake of the musical structure, and there is an air of forced hilarity about the whole passage. At the point where Good-Deeds appears on the scene Dr. Walford Davies is daringly simple, and he is able to produce a peculiarly touching and pathetic effect which could not have been heightened by the most elaborate artifices. At the first words, "Here I lie, cold in the ground," the picture of Good-Deeds lying bound and helpless is vividly brought to the mind, and the succession of common chords at the passage, "Knowledge shall with you abide," typifies the unsullied purity of the speaker with exquisite art. From the point of view of simple musical beauty, nothing can surpass the movement called "Everyman's Comfort," which is a trio for Good-Deeds, Knowledge, and Everyman in dialogue with a semi-chorus. The part-writing here is very finely finished, and the melody is sweet and graceful without ever becoming sentimental. When Everyman at the last commends his soul to God, the composer is again content with the simplest possible material, and again he succeeds in going straight to the hearts of his hearers. Of the performance of this remarkable work last week the outstanding feature was the singing of the title part by Mr. Kennerley Rumford, whose beautiful voice was exactly suited to the music, and whose interpretation of the character was consummately artistic throughout. Miss Gleeson White and Miss Muriel Foster also did admirably in the soprano and contralto music, and the chorus sang with intelligence and earnestness, though they have still much to learn in the way of precision and vigour of attack. Mr. Arthur Fagge conducted with evident sympathy and full appreciation of the spirit of the work, and he is entitled to much credit for the general smoothness of the whole performance.

J. E. T.

FICTION.

THE SON OF ROYAL LANGBRITH. By W. D. Howells. Harpers. 6s.

Mr. Howells is the exponent of the novel of thought as distinct from the novel of action. Men interest him primarily as thinking, not as doing, animals. *The Son of Royal Langbrith* is another experiment in this line, and one that has a singular interest. The outline of the story is this:—There was a certain Royal Langbrith, an owner of paper-mills in a New England town. He has been long dead when the book opens, so that his child knows him only through the words of the widow, which, for a good reason, are few. But the son has contrived to make a hero of his father, and a church and a village library are proofs of the munificence of the dead man. We are soon let into the secret, however, which is the property of the widow, one Dr. Anther, and two others—that the public-spirited Royal Langbrith is a grotesque myth; he was in reality a scoundrel who got his wealth by appropriating the inventions of another. But, as he was not exposed in his life-time, there seems no need why the unpleasant truth should be told now, except for this reason—Dr. Anther and Mrs. Langbrith are old friends, and wish to marry, the fatal objection being that the son James reveres his father's memory so deeply that for his mother to remarry would be sacrilege. Mrs. Langbrith is weak, and cannot face her son's displeasure, nor give him the reasons that make his father's memory anything but venerable. As he grows up he enlarges upon the paternal virtues to such an extent as to present a medallion of his father to the library. The one person from whose lips James would naturally learn his father's character is the unfortunate Hawberk, whose inventions were stolen, and who was ousted from his partnership in the prosperity of the mills by a threat to disclose a slightly discreditable past to his wife. But his hardship makes him take to opium-eating, and in his dreams he cherishes the delusion that Langbrith was his best friend. Indeed, all things combine to make it necessary for the living to shield the memory of the dead man, even at their own sacrifice. The chief sufferers are Mrs. Langbrith and the high-minded Dr. Anther, whose conscience will not let him disabuse the son of his romantic ideal, although this ideal puts an end to his own chance of happiness. It does, in fact, happen as Anther foretold:—Mrs. Langbrith consents to marry him without telling her son the truth about his father. James, when he hears of the engagement, accuses both of infidelity to his father's memory. Mrs. Langbrith has not the courage to withstand him, and breaks off the engagement. At this point the opium-eating Hawberk recovers, and his delusions about Royal Langbrith disappear. He decides, however, as James Langbrith is in love with his daughter, that Royal's crimes did enough harm in their day, and that there is no reason to let them affect the lives of the next generation. He dies suddenly, without breathing the secret to any one. James Langbrith, meanwhile, in disgust at his mother and Anther, had migrated to Paris; he returns on hearing of Hawberk's death, and in the train meets the fourth person who can tell him his father's true history—his uncle John. John is moved by an insulting comparison between him and Royal, who was "at least a gentleman," to show what kind of gentleman he was, which he does with great power and effect. The result is that James reaches his mother's house crushed, and prepared to accept her marriage, and learns from her that Dr. Anther is just dead of typhoid. The book ends very naturally with the happy marriage of James and Hope Hawberk, and the population of Saxmills is suffered, after consideration, to revere the medallion of Royal Langbrith as that of a good man and citizen. The weak point of the book seems to us to lie in the fact of James's devotion to his father, on which the plot mainly depends. He had no materials for his worship, except a few vague words of his mother, the library, and a not very pleasant portrait. And yet it is for this reason that, over twenty years after her husband's death, he objects to his mother's remarriage. It would be more natural to object, not that his father should have a successor, but that he himself should have a stepfather. Anther, however, is personally acceptable, and his sole disqualification is that he is to succeed Royal Langbrith. It is difficult to believe that a young man's devotion to a father whom he could not remember would lead him to such extravagances. However, the mere plot is not essential to a book which treats with such fineness of subtler things. The grasp of the "dead hand" is felt in every page, and the book is full of fine observation and delicate character-drawing. It is needless to say that the whole is beautifully proportioned, and told in the reserved and expressive language of a man who has much skill in writing.

WHOSOEVER SHALL OFFEND. By F. Marion Crawford. Macmillans. 6s.

Mr. Marion Crawford is before everything a good story-teller, and in the novel before us his special gift is seen to perfection. It is not that his plot is overcrowded with incidents or actors. Such as it is the story is simple, straightforward, and not complicated. But he unfolds it with the skill of a practised hand; he is never dull, and not a word of it seems, or is, superfluous; there is no "padding," and every word and incident is "inevitable" and in its place. Without the display of any particular subtlety of insight his characters are clean cut, living people, some of them, like the girl Regina, real creations, full of life and spirit. Whether even in Italy, the land of romance and passion, it is likely that a rich and kindly widow lady, scarcely past her youth, would marry a penniless adventurer of antecedents which would not have borne a moment's examination, we need not too closely consider—that is, so to speak, the postulate upon which all the subsequent results are founded. But granted this postulate, the rest is not so improbable, and we are hardly surprised at Corbario's murdering his wife and attempting to do the same by his stepson, or at the stealthy cunning by which he seeks to lure the lad to his ruin when the more direct method had failed. Regina, the splendid peasant girl, to whom the lad owes his salvation, in spite of the questionable tie between herself and him, is, as we have said, a noble creation; so, in a less degree, is his truer affinity, Aurora; and the lesser characters are almost equally distinctive. In short, this is a delightful novel, upon the production of which the author may well be congratulated.

CORRESPONDENCE.

TRAINING OF MIDWIVES.

To the Editor of "The Guardian."

SIR—Will you allow me to supplement your kind notice of the meeting held on November 4th by the Association for Promoting the Training and Supply of Midwives, at which the chair was taken by the president, the Archbishop of Canterbury, by saying that the office of the Association is at Dacre House, New Tothill-street, Westminster, and that the secretary (Miss Gill) is there daily for interviews from 10.30 to one o'clock, Saturdays excepted?

She will gladly give any information concerning the various branches of our work, and the best means of meeting the requirements of the Midwives Act, and we specially want it to be known that we are ready to send speakers to any part of the country to address meetings on the subject.

May I quote, in conclusion, the eloquent words of Mrs. Humphry Ward in her speech at the meeting, as an appeal for the money we need to assist in the training of midwives to supply the dearth that will become more and more evident, as those who are incompetent retire from practice under the searchlight of the new regulations?—

"How many there are still who, professing to know, but knowing nothing, may at any time bring danger and death upon mother and child. How can we bear to think of a mother being injured in the hour of her trouble—that hour when all the community should be her guardians—when, being unable to help herself, she is ready to trust herself to hands unfit or inexperienced. Every woman of means who rejoices in her own children can help them if she will. She can support this association, she can give her yearly subscription, she can provide training for one woman or more if her means are large. She can help women and children who are fighting the battle of life with hands no stronger than her own, and with resources so pitifully less."

Indeed, Sir, nothing can be added to these words. If your readers will realise for a moment the pathos of their meaning, surely they cannot bear it without doing what they can, be it much or be it little, to lighten this burden of needless suffering

Subscriptions and donations will be very gratefully received at the office, or by the hon. treasurer, Mr. Arthur L. Leon, L.C.C., 20, St. Thomas's-mansions, Westminster-bridge.

(Mrs.) AGNES MABEL BRUCE,
Chairman of the Executive Committee.
9, Airlie-gardens, Campden-hill, W.

ASSOCIATION OF TRAINED CHARWOMEN

To the Editor of "The Guardian."

SIR—In case any of your readers are desirous of helping unemployed women, may I remind you that the Women's Industrial Council has for years been finding employment for numbers of widows with families dependent on them, through the Association of Trained Charwomen?

The present holiday season makes exceptional demands upon the staff of nearly every household, and ladies may be glad of a reminder that trained and trustworthy domestic supernumeraries can be secured, and, at the same time, valuable assistance be given to unemployed women, by applying for domestic help of every kind at 19, Buckingham-street, Strand.

F. POTTER, Hon. Sec. A.T.C.

AN APPEAL.

To the Editor of "The Guardian."

SIR—For many years you have kindly inserted our appeal for a Christmas Fund so that our little neighbours in Bethnal-green may have a share in the happy gatherings of the season. This year the depression in every branch of trade is draining the slender resources of all our relief funds to the verge of bankruptcy. Bare necessaries claim every penny we can command; nothing remains for the tea and bread and butter, the cards and crackers, the Christmas tree and other special entertainment which gladden the hearts of many hundreds of innocent little sufferers from poverty and want, who eagerly look to us for their one great winter treat. We feel confident that we shall not plead their cause in vain.

BEATRICE CECILIA HARINGTON.
St. Margaret's House, Bethnal-green, E.

ASSOCIATION FOR MISSIONARY STUDY, S.P.G.

A drawing-room meeting of the above society was held at 54, Brook-street, on Monday afternoon. The *Hon. Victoria Grosvenor* was in the chair. After pointing out the duty lying on all Churchpeople to obey the orders of the Master to go and do the work He has commanded, she said how necessary it was for those who go and those who stay at home alike to learn some of the facts, if only to refute the old objection that "the heathen are very well off as they are, leave them alone." One had only to learn a little of the miserable conditions of the people in India and China alone to see how absolutely untrue this was. And it was the business of A.M.S. to try and get at the truth of the facts. The *Rev. H. P. Cronshaw* spoke on the great need of being keen and sure about missionary work. The great theory in Mission work was that the whole nation should be missionary. We were at present too individual. But it was through the nation's life that the missionary conscience was to be roused. He pointed out that England's position carried with it special responsibilities—that as she spread her Colonies and her power, so the old standards and ideals must be broken down, and it was her duty, business, and responsibility to give the highest ideal in exchange. This missionary extension would only be done by life and not by preaching, so the A.M.S. was to be a missionary force that would tell in time. It had a small beginning, but from study and prayer it should lead to the thought of going if a call came.

Figure 11.1 Virginia Stephen's review of W. D. Howells's *The Son of Royal Langbrith*, top of middle column in the Guardian Supplement, 14 December 1904 2120. Personal photo.

Like most novices craving approval and money, she also admits that Mrs Lyttelton's criticism, 'however stringent will be worth attending to' (L1 155). Perhaps visits from the *Guardian*'s Supplement editor in mid-December 1904 and January 1905, soon after Stephen's first efforts were published, contributed to the extraordinary progress she made between her second (or first) and sixth reviews. Her *Son of Royal Langbrith* review has all the marks of a beginner: one long paragraph, three-quarters of it plot summary; three passive sentences in a row; a vague 'this'; unclear referents; and a 'needless to say' (E1 3–5).[25] Virginia Stephen was a quick study, though.[26] In her *Feminine Note in Fiction* review, she evaluates from the start, noting W. L. Courtney has made a 'laborious' attempt to define the feminine note in fiction; ends where he begins; and provides detailed plot outlines she would have gladly foregone

> in exchange for some definite verdict; we can all read Mrs Humphry Ward, for instance, and remember her story, but we want a critic to separate her virtues and her failings, to assign her right place in literature and to decide which of her characteristics are essentially feminine and why, and what is their significance. (E1 15)

Stephen thus confidently goes beyond the book's content to define what readers want from critics. Plus, she asks, 'Is it not too soon after all to criticise the feminine note in anything? And will not the adequate critic of women be a woman?' (E1 15). When he claims that women 'are seldom artists, because they have a passion for detail which conflicts with the proper artistic proportion of their work', she replies with mild sarcasm, 'We would cite Sappho and Jane Austen as examples of two great women who combine exquisite detail with a supreme sense of artistic proportion' (E1 16). She also will not let him get away with saying that because more and more novels are written by women for women, the novel as a work of art is disappearing. If more and more novels are being written by women for women, she says, that means 'Women having found their voices have something to say which is naturally of supreme interest and meaning to women.' But the 'assertion that the woman novelist is extinguishing the novel as a work of art seems ... more doubtful' (E1 16).[27] Mrs Lyttelton, the *Guardian* and women readers gave Virginia Stephen a foundation that became a launch pad.

Leo Maxse – *National Review*

Although the *National Review* might seem a more likely outlet for Virginia Stephen's early work, given her father's contributions and her mother's friendship with Kitty,[28] Leo Maxse did not, in fact, supply her with a steady stream of books or assignments. If the *Guardian* provided the novice with an amenable female context and audience, the *National Review* was a male preserve, with primarily male contributors and a patriarchal, bellicose tone. Even its own 1908 *Writers' and Artists' Year-Book* listing snarls, 'General articles of all kinds' will be 'gladly considered', but these articles 'must be original, hackneyed work is not appreciated' (39). In 1905, when Stephen published there, only Jane Findlater had a regular feature; few other women appear, and they generally endorse traditional perspectives, such as in Carmen Sylva's 'Vocation of Women' (45 611–24) or in Miss K. Bathurst's 'Some Children's Essays' (44 478–88).

A monthly quarto with one wide column of a fairly large font, the *National Review* took on the impress of Leo Maxse, editor from 1893 to 1932; under him, the literary disappeared, and the journal shifted from describing itself in the *NPD* as 'Political (Conservative), Literary, and General' in 1905 to 'Political and General' in 1907 (*NPD*, 1905 297; 1907 277).[29] Andrew Thompson says Maxse was 'an incredibly energetic and committed editor, who attracted articles from many well-known personalities', and the paper had published literary contributions by writers such as Andrew Lang, George Saintsbury, Violet Paget and Edmund Gosse under the previous editor, Alfred Austin, but it never aspired to have a voice in literary matters (Victor, 'National Review' 243–4). Up until World War I, Carol Victor notes, literary criticism, personal essays, some fiction and some poetry appeared in its pages; Leslie Stephen contributed 'The Choice of Books' in 1895 and critical articles on Shakespeare, Trollope, Stevenson and Godwin, along with autobiographical essays called 'Some Early Impressions' (published in 1903), and so did Austin Dobson and H. C. Biron (Victor, 'National Review' 245). But as John A. Hutcheson, Jr, notes, articles of general interest and literary studies were 'merely a garnish to the meat-and-potatoes diet of serious politics that became the *National Review*'s main fare' (56).[30]

Those politics were Conservative, Tory, Rightist, Imperialist.[31] As Victor says, Disraeli was the magazine's 'spiritual father', eight out of ten articles had Conservative views, and although a few writers might wonder what the proper Conservative stance was on a particular issue and even fewer might have a more radical point of view, the journal stood as 'a long-lived, eloquent, and self-confident Tory spokesman' ('National Review' 243). Maxse's 'imperialism put him in the political mainstream', says Thompson, and Kazuko and Harold Dailey describe the review as 'a lively journal of Conservative tendencies': it was 'sometimes hated and not seldom feared, but under Maxse, at least, no one ever called it either dull or mediocre' (532, 534).

In 1905, when issues were close to 200 pages long, Maxse's 'Episodes of the Month' often ran forty-five to fifty, and his 'Greater Britain' covering colonial matters was at least twenty, the magazine was read, quoted and influential. According to Hutcheson, Maxse strove above all to be frank and unequivocal, to make his writing immune to any chance of misinterpretation. Like his father (Admiral Frederick August Maxse, who had bought him the magazine), he saw the world in black and white, with no indeterminate grey areas (48).[32] Dailey and Dailey note that 'for all [Maxse's] intransigence he exerted a strong public influence because his motives were regarded as unfailingly patriotic and his facts were known to be highly accurate' (533). Maxse meant his 'Episodes' to inform and persuade simultaneously, and Hutcheson calls their content 'commentary, commendations, castigations, warnings, admonitions, lamentations, and rejoicings' (40). By 1905, the circulation was probably up to an average of 7,000 a month, and its highest average was somewhere around 10,000–12,000, but its impact went beyond circulation (Hutcheson 37, 38). An ad down the left-hand side of the *TLS* first page on 4 January 1907 attempted to increase influence as well as circulation. Linking *Times* readers, whose minds have 'already been prepared by the news given in [the] daily paper', to the monthly review readers, who read to enlarge their outlooks about the day's important subjects (1), Maxse offered *Times* subscribers a deal: the *National Review* for only 20s. a year instead of the usual 30s. Its strong political opinions, Maxse's well-written and provocative commentary, and its focus on current events both at home and abroad meant it was read by politicians outside the Tory Party, but as Hutcheson points out, the *National Review* was never located on Fleet Street, but instead in the 'affluent West End – Westminster, the clubs, Mayfair' (36), the part of London that was 'a large part of the *National Review*'s readership'. As a result, 'it made no attempt to reach a mass audience' (37).

Virginia Stephen's only piece in the paper is an essay called 'Street Music', about vagrant musicians and their contributions to art, and it seems out of place tucked between 'Man-Power as a Measure of National and Imperial Strength' and 'The Industrial Condition of the Country'. *National Review* readers had probably demanded the signs for London squares saying 'Street musicians are counted a nuisance' in the first place, and one suspects they did not want to be bothered by art of any kind, let alone art practised by the homeless (E1 27). Anna Snaith outlines the anti-street nuisance campaigns of the time, making clear their anti-immigrant, classist and racist bias, and she shows how Woolf's essay 'seems almost a point-by-point rebuttal of key elements of the campaigns' ('Years' 7).[33] In March 1905 when Stephen's essay appeared, the 'Episodes' column was followed by 'The Command of the Sea in Danger' (Britain's naval power was one of Maxse's fervent causes, along with creating animosity against Germany [Dailey and Dailey 533]); pieces about Canada, 'Agnosticism and National Decay', America and an Eton correspondence; and features such as 'The Auxiliary Forces and the War Office'. Clearly, 'the literary appeal [the journal] had enjoyed in its Victorian years' was becoming a thing of the past (Victor, 'National Review' 248). In a letter to Nelly in May 1908, Stephen sees the paper's intent to fight and destroy the opposition and reveals she must have occasionally skimmed periodicals she was published in:

> The National Review is here, polluting my room with its abuse of the late Sir Henry C[ampbell] B[annerman] .... politicians and journalists must be the lowest of Gods creatures, creeping perpetually in the mud, and biting with one end and stinging with the other ... Mary Coleridge [poet] is in odd company. (*L1* 332)

If she had not known it in 1905, she certainly realised by 1908 that she and her 'Street Music' had been in odd company as well.

With Leo Maxse at the *National Review*, Virginia Stephen practised patience. Two years after he published 'Street Music', Leo was supposedly '"constantly trying to think of subjects that would be likely to appeal to [her]"' (*L1* 309), but he never followed up. Perhaps this was because he knew what had appealed to her – equating street musicians with Beethoven – had not appealed to his readers. She also learned to consider audience. Perhaps assuming *National Review* readers would be similar to *Guardian* ones, perhaps not thinking about it much at all, she experienced the practical consequences of misreading readers: no more work.

Harold Child – The Academy

If the *Guardian* provided Virginia Stephen with her first women readers, *The Academy* provided her with her first literary ones. It had also requested work from her rather than vice versa (*PA* 239). In contrast to the *Guardian*'s religious and social emphasis and the *National Review*'s political focus, *The Academy* concentrated solely on literature. In 1902, the then *Academy and Literature* had taken over *Literature*, the first literary supplement from *The Times*, and it was an important model for the *TLS*, 'which took over its format and style' (J. Sutherland, *Longman* 6). Founded in 1869 by a group advocating liberal reform at Oxford (Fader and Bornstein 104–5) and edited by Charles Appleton from 1869 to 1879 and J. S. Cotton from 1881 to 1896 (*WDENP*), the magazine was '[p]roud of its contributors', such as Arnold, the Rossettis, Pater and Swinburne, and 'fought against anonymous reviewing and for the regular identification of authors' (Fader and Bornstein 107). During Charles L. Hind's editorship (1896 to October 1903), he 'betray[ed] its original aims', according to Fader and Bornstein, making the journal 'reputable and popular if no longer elite' (108). But Christopher Kent asserts that, under Hind, the journal may have become 'the liveliest literary journal in England' as he awarded prizes for best books of the year (like Joseph Conrad's *Tales of Unrest*), discovered Arnold Bennett and brought in regular contributors such as E. V. Lucas and the Meynells (4–5). Roll-Hansen says Hind 'knew how to produce a marketable paper', and he gained readers beyond 'bookworms at respectable school libraries'; he adds that *The Times* credited him with creating 'a new kind of journalism . . . "combining a reasonably high standard of criticism with a popular appeal in a remarkable way"' (214–15; 217).

After Hind left, the paper entered a period of turmoil and fast turnover, with its name changing seven times between 1903 and 1914 (Roll-Hansen 217 n23 and n24; Kent 5–6). William F. Teignmouth Shore edited the paper from 10 October 1903 until 28 January 1905; Peter Anderson Graham and Harold H. Child edited it from February 1905 until May 1907;[34] Lord Alfred Bruce Douglas, assisted by Thomas W. H. Crosland, edited it until 25 June 1910; Cecil Cowper, assisted by E. Ashmead-Bartlett, edited it until July 1914; and Henry Savage edited it, with Crosland and his 'venomous and conservative' literary opinions (Pondrom 40), until it folded in 1915 (Roll-Hansen 217). But in 1906, when Stephen published two pieces in it, it said in the *NPD*:

> Weekly review of literature, science and art. It contains reviews of books, literary news, and articles on subjects of interest to all readers and writers.
> The opinion of *Academy and Literature* has weight in the world of letters, and its favourable criticism is one of the prizes the author of a book values most, all work being taken strictly on its own merits by this review. Specialists in every branch of thought are included among its contributors, and one may always feel that its views on any subject are based on a thorough acquaintance with the facts. (64)

Roll-Hansen credits Child with energetically trying 'to shake off more than eight years mainly of literary gossip', arguing for the return of anonymous reviews in the interests of integrity and quality, and succeeding in re-establishing some of the paper's former dignity (218–19).

A weekly of generally twenty-four double-columned 8½ × 11-inch pages, the paper under Child had 'less gossip, less book trade emphasis, and less copy' (Kent 5). Its white space and somewhat larger print intimidate less than the *Guardian*, and though it does not shut out politics or social issues, Child's changes make literature primary, other things secondary. In the 26 August 1905 issue, for example, when the paper is called *The Academy: A Weekly Review of Literature, Science & Art*, a table of contents follows two pages of ads. 'The Literary Week', Child's column, comes next, followed by a Literature section that includes long reviews of the *Selected Essays of Henry Fielding*, Jules Derocquigny's *Charles Lamb*, John Fyvie's *Some Famous Women of Wit and Beauty* (Stephen's review, 'Their Passing Hour' 871–2), a book on the Spanish historian Mariana, Benjamin Constant's *Adolphe*, and *The Nun's Rule*. An article on Madame de Staël's early writings, essays on simplicity and dullness, and reviews of ten novels in a Fiction section come next. Sections on Drama, Fine Art and Music are followed by Books Received, Correspondence and The Bookshelf, where readers learn about a book called *Ethiopia in Exile* by M. Pullen-Burry, who had returned to Jamaica to follow up on previous work and 'study the Negro in the United States'. He collected statistics, visited Booker T. Washington, and tried 'to arrive at the true view of the present and future of a much debated people' (886).

The Academy added a column called The Library Table in 1906; paid attention to bibliographical work; printed the occasional poem; followed the American literary scene, reviewing W. E. B. Du Bois's *Souls of Black Folk*, for example; and published correspondence, including an exchange about 'one' as a pronoun used by women, not men (5 May 1906 434–5), and another about the university education of women that included a plea for funds for the Bedford College for Women (8 April 1905 402–3). Ads for pens, paper, authors' agencies and typewriting services, along with full-page ads for the Williams typewriter (£12 12s.) and its instalment plan, appeared, as well as ads for books and publishers, schools and universities, booksellers, cocoa and Mudie's.

Before becoming co-editor of *The Academy*, Harold Child obtained an Oxford degree in Classics, worked in a law firm and was an actor. He was drama critic of *The Observer* from 1912 to 1920, shared the dramatic criticism of *The Times* with A. B. Walkley, and wrote the stage histories for many volumes in *The New Shakespeare*, edited by Arthur Quiller-Couch and John Dover Wilson. He spent most of his career writing for the *TLS*, however, and his well-respected work there meant he contributed several chapters to the *Cambridge History of English Literature* (Roberts and Peach). At *The Academy*, he reveals the era's gender anxiety underlying his attempts to improve the magazine when he approvingly quotes Irving Babbitt, the US Modern Language Association President, who blamed excessively cultivated feminine virtues for turning criticism into impressionism instead of science and called for a return to a fixed standard against which to judge literature (13 October 1906 363). Virginia Stephen published only four pieces in *Academy and Literature/The Academy* between early 1905 and mid-1906, one essay (on essays) and three reviews. She had 'more space and time' for those pieces, but Child 'seem[s] to have typecast her as their reviewer of books about notable women of the past' (Rosenbaum 173). In a 5 May 1905 diary entry, she refers to a Lisbon Protestant Cemetery piece, 'possibly for the Academy', but the essay/draft has not been traced and we do not know whether she sent it (*PA* 271; see K&C 301). We do know she sent them a piece called 'Magic Greek', which they rejected in March 1905 (*PA* 252–6).[35]

Child's attempt to reform *The Academy* may have influenced his editing of 'A Plague of Essays'. Stephen's essay would have arrived soon after Child became editor on 28 January 1905 and was preparing to announce changes in a manifesto in 'The Literary Week' on 11 March 1905. In that piece, he bemoans the decay of journalism since the 1860s and 1870s, decries the influence of American 'slang and colloquial expressions' in the 1880s, and criticises the use of 'I' – writers have been encouraged 'to be as personal and egotistical as ... possible'. His conclusion contrasts the old style with the new journalism and again includes the word 'decay' (225). So perhaps it is not surprising that three weeks earlier, Child changed Stephen's title to 'The Decay of Essay-writing' (25 February 1905 165–6), cut the piece in half, and added and altered words without consulting her (*L1* 181; *PA* 243), this after having sent a proof 'word for word as [she] had written' (*L1* 180–1; *PA* 240)! To add insult to injury, 'what purports to be my article' appeared above her signature without her approval, which she learns from Gerald (*PA* 243).[36] Since the draft has not survived, we cannot know exactly how he edited it, but what he printed is playful enough to make one suspect he turned a combination of thoughtful and 'tongue-in-cheek' criticism into serious comments about decay. Virginia Stephen questions the use of 'I' as well, but for different reasons, arguing that writers are 'inclined to run away' when '[c]onfronted with the terrible spectre of themselves' (*E1* 26; see also Rosenbaum 157–8).

Circulation figures do not seem to be available after the 16,000 noted in 1869 (*WDENP*) and a drop to less than 3,000 after its first year (Fader and Bornstein 106). Ellegård estimates the 1870 circulation at around 8,000 (13) and describes its Victorian readers as 'educated middle to upper class' (13). Child seems to have succeeded in making the paper more literary in the early twentieth century, but his efforts to 'rehabilitate the old *Academy*' were 'not particularly successful' (Kent 5), and he moved to the *TLS* as a sub-editor in 1907 after being a contributor there since that paper's beginnings in 1902. As Roll-Hansen notes, he soon realised he was 'banking on the wrong journal' (218). The readers he sought were subscribing to the *TLS*, and Virginia Stephen was in the process of making the same move.

Submitting work to *Academy and Literature*, Virginia Stephen practised dealing with rejection (her piece on 'magic Greek') and with being edited without her consent. Stephen had unknowingly submitted an essay about writing essays to an editor anxious about the state of journalism, particularly its impact on his own journal. One suspects his changes to her essay had much more to do with his apprehensions about journalism's direction and his plans to bring the journal back to its former dignity than with her ideas. Our perplexity about her treatment of the genre in this essay may stem from him, not from her. *He* worries the essay is decaying (and thus changes her title), and although she does include concerns about the essay in her piece, particularly in relationship to newspapers and schooling, one suspects she also made other points. Furthermore, her worry does not relate to the use of the personal but to the depth of personal revelations. In any case, Stephen gained newfound respect for Mrs Lyttelton, who became 'really angelic in comparison' (L1 181). Stephen learned that if cuts must be made, it is better to make them yourself.

Arthur Clutton-Brock – *Speaker*

Asked to write for the *Speaker* (Rosenbaum 173), Virginia Stephen again had the opportunity to work on longer pieces, but also to write on things she cared about and would return to later in her career: essays (Canon Ainger's criticism); Elizabethan explorers (Raleigh's study of sixteenth-century English voyages); and women's letters (Elizabeth Barrett Browning's letters). The *Speaker* was Liberal, a political paper at the other end of the spectrum from the *National Review*. It also had a more general thrust, a wider framework and more writers' opinions than the *National Review* did. Literature and art do not seem alien since this weekly has proportionately more about them in each issue than the monthly *National Review* does.[37] When founded in 1890, its sub-title was 'A Review of Politics, Letters, Science and the Arts', but John Hammond changed it to 'The Liberal Review' in 1899 when he became editor (Weaver, *Hammonds* 57). In 1904, the *Speaker's NPD* annotation reads, 'it has already secured for itself a position in the front rank of English journalism' (87), but in 1907, the description simply reads 'The *Speaker* is a weekly journal of politics, literature, science, art and finance' (74).

The *Speaker* differs from the *National Review* about as much as possible. Edited by John L. Hammond, the liberal author who later co-authored with his wife the influential titles *The Village Labourer* (1911), *The Town Labourer* (1917) and *The Skilled Labourer* (1919), the *Speaker* was under his stewardship until 1907, when the paper became the *Nation* under H. W. Massingham. Whereas Maxse thought Asquith was the devil, Hammond saw him and Lloyd George as possible saviours. Whereas Maxse lauded imperialism, Hammond critiqued it – Desmond MacCarthy describes the *Speaker* as 'vigorously anti-Imperialistic' in his memoir of his early working years (15). Pro-Boer, Hammond joined with Francis Hirst and Gilbert Murray in writing *Liberalism and the Empire* (1900), which was, according to Stewart Weaver, 'a lonely protest in the name of reason against the imperialist excesses of the age' ('Hammond'). Although not pacifist, he would later work hard for reconstruction after the Great War and, like John Maynard Keynes, denounce the Treaty of Versailles for its vengefulness. Whereas Maxse supported his paper with his own funds and looked to influence Conservative opinion, Hammond looked to the Rowntree Trust (founded by the Quaker businessman in chocolates, Joseph Rowntree) for backing and attempted to influence Liberal opinion (Havighurst 143). 'In politics', the paper writes of itself in the 1904 *NPD*,

> the *Speaker* advocates the great principles which are common to all sections of the Liberal party – political and social reform, free trade, the extension of a truly national system of education, the development of the principle of local self-government, and the maintenance of individual and popular rights under the protection of the law. (87)

Whereas Maxse gave less and less space to literature, Hammond gave a lot to literature, music and the arts. Whereas Maxse wrote more and more of his paper's copy, Hammond wrote some copy, but also gave J. A. Hobson, L. T. Hobhouse, John Morley and James Bryce a chance to write articles from the Liberal point of view. Whereas Disraeli was the *National Review*'s spiritual father, Gladstone was the *Speaker*'s. Hammond was also pro-Home Rule: the *Speaker* will 'give its strenuous support to a policy of conciliation towards Ireland, and to the attempt to govern that country rather with than against the consent of its people' (*NPD*, 1904 87).[38] Maxse's monthly had 160–200 pages, whereas Hammond's weekly averaged 24–8 pages with an additional 4–6 pages of ads. The *National Review* seems narrow because of Maxse's obsession with right-wing politics; the *Speaker* seems wider in scope because literature, art and differing political opinions co-exist. It also has more regular and predictable sections and columns.

The *Speaker* used two columns on its grey 8½ × 11-inch pages. White space and markers between paragraphs denote a change of subject in the 'This Week' column, and lines and white space are used between titled articles, but print fills the articles themselves. The overall sombre look communicates a desire to be taken seriously. Ads are for insurance companies, cocoa, books, other periodicals, schools and hotels, but one hinting at ghost-writing appeared under Miscellaneous in the 11 April 1906 issue: 'Extempore speaking, Writing, Press Articles, &c. Postal instruction. Introductions. Speeches prepared. Articles written. – Professor Lewis, 269, Regent-street, W.' (v). The *Speaker* may have 'looked dull' (Swinnerton qtd in Havighurst 143), but it ranged freely over many topics, including middle-class complaints, man versus motorist, and *The Times*'s boycotting of books in the Book War; devoted many pages to literature, including Arthur Clutton-Brock's essays on Ibsen and Coventry Patmore and MacCarthy's drama reviews; and generated passionate correspondence about topics such as militarism in boys' schools, lynching in America, suffrage, and higher education for working men and women.

At the *Speaker*, Virginia Stephen would have submitted her work to the literary editor, Clutton-Brock. When he left it after being there from 1904 to 1906, he became an art critic and general essayist for the *TLS* and *Times Educational Supplement*, where he based his work on three principles: (1) critics must be judged, first, as writers; (2) the critic should provoke thought, not suppress it; and (3) since art is for people, not just artists, the critic's job is to 'enrich' his readers' experience by 'expressing his own experience of the art' (Blank 72). In his reviews, G. K. Blank says, he addressed the general topics in books, '[read] authors from their works', included 'general speculation of a more personal nature' and invited the reader's participation; his reviews 'inform at least as much as they criticize' (71). Although Stephen never mentions him, it seems likely Clutton-Brock communicated such principles to his *Speaker* reviewers.

On 21 April 1906, when Virginia Stephen's signed 'Poets' Letters' appeared, 'The Week' section opens with 'San Francisco is in flames' (45). Her review, of Percy Lubbock's *Elizabeth Barrett Browning in Her Letters* and Frederic G. Kenyon's edition of letters, *Robert Browning and Alfred Domett*, appears between reviews of *Dick*, a book about the average Rugby boy, and a book about Rubens. Each week's Literature section begins with a causerie, and on 21 April, the literary 'chat' focuses on Richard Garnett, who had died recently. Then come reviews of Hilaire Belloc's *Algerian Impressions*, a book about Mrs Fitzherbert and George IV, the already-mentioned books and a book about English watercolours. Two much briefer reviews follow these longer ones, on a translation of two Dumas texts and on *Some Irish Essays* by A. E.

In the 11 August 1906 issue, when Stephen's unsigned 'Trafficks and Discoveries' appeared, the contents are evenly divided between politics and literature, with some literary material mixed in with politics in the 'Middle Articles' and some recent economics books reviewed in 'Literature'. Clutton-Brock has an article on 'Art for Art's Sake', and H. W. Massingham writes about 'Persons and Politics', followed by correspondence about the Irish Railway Commission, the use of rhyme in poetry, and military training at Clifton College. The causerie, a review discussion about the Eighth Duke of Argyll's autobiography, comes before Madge Vaughan's review of Francis Marion Crawford's *Gleanings from Venetian History* and a review of *Lord Curzon in India*. Stephen's review is sandwiched between the latter and the economics books review. Next are reviews of books on the Greek world, art in the nineteenth century, and western culture in eastern lands. In the section on Fiction, two reviews assess two novels apiece. Finally, finances, particularly new laws on insurance in the United States and a note on losses related to the fire in San Francisco, fill the last two-and-a-half pages. Among the widely diverse pages of the *Speaker*, Virginia Stephen's essays seem at home.

At the *Speaker*, Arthur Clutton-Brock's assignments allowed Virginia Stephen to try out her own aesthetic ideas; every essay she placed there evolved into later, more well-thought-out pieces. She discovered affinities or practised developing affinities for subjects such as essays, the Elizabethans, women and their letters, practised some of Arthur Clutton-Brock's aesthetic principles for reviewing, and strove for balance between informing and criticising.

Reginald Smith – *Cornhill Magazine*

For Virginia Stephen, the *Cornhill*, founded in 1860, would have had the most Leslie Stephen associations. William Makepeace Thackeray was its first editor. Leslie Stephen edited it from 1871 to 1882, and Smith, Elder, the magazine's publisher, also published the *Dictionary of National Biography*, Stephen's mammoth editorial project. In 1908, when Virginia Stephen had six long reviews in the magazine as part of its 'Book on the Table' series, Professor James Sully, a friend of her father she mentions in her diary (*PA* 260), had a piece in the January issue called 'Reminiscences of the Sunday Tramps', an article recalling Leslie Stephen with great fondness (44 76–88). Ironically, those Leslie Stephen associations may have worked against her.

For Reginald Smith, who became editor in 1898, the *Cornhill* had traditions – 'national pride, serialized novels, literary essays, and remembrances of past glories' (Huxley and Schmidt 'Smith') – among which were Thackeray and Stephen, brilliant editors who had nonetheless censored or rejected writers like Ruskin, Trollope, Arnold and Hardy because they were 'anxious to avoid publishing any material that might offend' (Vann 82). Jennifer Phegley argues the early *Cornhill* bucked the trend of dismissing or demeaning women readers, made a conscious effort to attract them and often included articles arguing women should be educated and encouraged to move into some professions; such goals would not only help the family and the 'newly defined "professional gentleman"', but would help the nation (23–4, 32). She also notes strong support for education and the professional life from contributors like Harriet Martineau and Anne Thackeray Ritchie (32–7; see also Janice Harris). But Sara Ferrell and Mary Wallace suggest *Cornhill* became 'more military and nationalistic', with a heavier emphasis on '"human documents" – memoirs, autobiographies, and diaries' (323), under John St Loe Strachey, editor from 1896 to 1897; Reginald Smith then 'perpetuated most of Strachey's innovations in the face of continuous financial loss' (323). Barbara Schmidt also says Smith 'emphasized patriotism' (103), and 1908 articles like 'Nationality in Horses' (June 781–92) and 'The Battle of Agincourt' (December 789–93) reveal such nationalism.

A quarto-sized monthly with 144 pages of one-column print (excluding ads), its 1905 *NPD* ad featured four quotations from *Punch*, *The World*, the *Manchester Guardian* and the *Guardian* ('*Cornhill* is really full of good reading from beginning to end. There is nothing to skip') and noted each number contained instalments of 'serial stories by popular authors' and 'Short Stories and Articles by the Best Writers' (553). Its ad unchanged in 1907, its directory listing said it was devoted to Fiction and General Literature (256). Early on, according to the *WDENP*, it included departments on literary reviews, roundabout papers, natural history articles, personal adventure and observation, and reports of scientific discovery. In 1908, table of contents items seem to reflect those departments, along with history, memoirs, education, politics, sports and driving ('The Moderate Motorist'). But because the periodical did not use department headings, readers would have had trouble knowing what departments were where. Few regular columns appeared, though one was 'The Provincial Letters' by Sylvanus Urban, travel pieces about England's small towns.

It had been, according to John Sutherland, the 'premier fiction-carrying magazine of the [nineteenth] century' (*Longman* 150),[39] and in the twentieth century, it continued to serialise two novels, one at the beginning and one at the end of each issue, even though most magazines were no longer doing so. Between those 'bookends', it seems confused about its identity. Even its format is not consistent. Sometimes bylines are below a piece's title; other times, they appear at the end. Sometimes a review has a footnote with the title of the book reviewed along with publication information; other times it does not. Sometimes the Book on the Table section, which alternated between Nelly Cecil and Virginia Stephen, gives the title of the book underneath the heading; other times it does not. Most confusing, however, is that headings do not tell readers whether they are reading fiction or non-fiction. Onslow says this 'blurring of fictional and non-fictional genres' gave general periodicals like *Cornhill* the opportunity to expand the scope of subjects and treatments – '[N]arrative forms became a widespread mechanism' for making subjects like economics and science popular (85) – but it seems odd that a magazine specialising in fictional forms did not help readers know if they were reading a short story or an article.

Because Smith had independent means and was connected to the publishing house of Smith, Elder, he could focus on good literature without worrying about profits (Huxley and Schmidt 'Smith'). But Vann and also Ferrell and Wallace question whether the literature was good any longer: according to them, Smith published 'second-rate essays' (Vann 83), the 'meager descendants' of the declining literary essay (Ferrell and Wallace 323). When Leslie Stephen left the editor's chair, circulation was down to 12,000, and Ferrell and Wallace note it went down even further under James Payn with financial losses continuing under Smith (323). The early *Cornhill* was innovative, publishing 'outstanding writers' and enjoying a 'readership of unprecedented size' (Vann 83–4), but after its forty-year heyday, Michael Stanton comments, 'it did not always fully live up to [its reputation]' (18). By 1909, Virginia Stephen labelled it 'singularly dull' (*L1* 390) and ended her association with it.

Some issues with Stephen's work in them illuminate the era's race and class attitudes. In the February 1908 issue, a story by L. M. Cooke follows Stephen's review of the *Memoirs of Sarah Bernhardt*; titled 'His Excellency the Governor' (197–212), it is about Blacks electing a governor. Its dialect, stereotypical names, and amusement at the idea of Blacks holding an election (an election which a woman wins, making it even more amusing, of course) reveals in a way nothing else can the casual, bigoted attitude toward Blacks in Britain. Another juxtaposition, in the June 1908 issue, sheds light on class attitudes. Stephen's essay on John Delane, *The Times* editor, follows an essay on Eton and its graduates called 'An Eton Portrait Gallery' and precedes a short story called 'Harriet Dixon's Afternoon Off' by Mary Mann (771–80), in which class differences between Harriet and her cousin Sarah, and a deeply engrained need to maintain appearances, contribute to assisted euthanasia.

Reginald Smith was a lawyer, and according to Leonard Huxley and Barbara Schmidt, his legal work was 'distinguished for his painstaking care, lucid arrangement of material, and invincible courtesy' ('Smith'). He was also known for his care in the publishing firm, reading everything that came to it (Schmidt 104). Such attention to detail may be why Virginia Stephen thought him rigid in his assignments, meticulous in his instructions (*L1* 327) and infuriating in his editing (*L1* 332). Known for being a conscientious, considerate editor, often sending a 'letter of kindly criticism' with rejected manuscripts (Huxley and Schmidt 'Smith'), Smith sent a printed rejection slip to Leslie Stephen's daughter when she submitted an unsolicited essay about Boswell's letters in 1905 (McNeillie xiv; *L1* 171; Rosenbaum 152). Perhaps he assumed she would continue submitting work simply because her father had edited the magazine. McNeillie says Smith seems to have generally 'lacked tact and to have been at times more than a little condescending' (xiv), ending his instructions for her John Delane review by saying 'I really believe, dear Miss Stephen, that if you will put heart and head into it, you will make a mark in reviewing' (*L1* 327). Even more curious, Smith rejected her 'Memoirs of a Novelist' and her proposed series of imaginary portraits in 1909 (*L1* 413) – its blurred boundaries between fiction and non-fiction seem aligned with Onslow's perception about such genre blending and the magazine's own casual mix of the two genres. But he, like Harold Child at *The Academy*, may have typecast her, confusing her with her father, and thus assigned memoirs and biographies rather than the literature she wanted (A. Curtis 149; Rosenbaum 366; *L1* 324–5, 327). Plus, he did not give her imaginary portraits a chance: 'My feeling is that you have impaled not a butterfly, but a bumblebee, upon a pin. It is cleverness itself, but ... ' (*QB1* 154 and 269n); his attempt at a conciliatory tone only showed he had forgotten his earlier rejection of her piece on Boswell's letters (Rosenbaum 371). Stephen used the rejection to break with the Victorian tradition the *Cornhill* increasingly seemed to represent and never tried to publish there again.

With Reginald Smith, Virginia Stephen learned to stand up to a controlling editor by being quietly subversive: 'I have also been writing about President Roosevelt, for Smith, at his command,' Stephen writes to Violet Dickinson, and, she continues, 'The sublety [sic] of the insinuations is so serpentine that no Smith in Europe will see how I jeer the President to derision, seeming to approve the while' (*L1* 337). So infuriating in his editing that she threatened to resign (*L1* 332), he would not let her become anyone other than her father's daughter. But she could practise using reviews as pretexts for essays in the ample space Smith gave her, so her *Cornhill* pieces blend the subject's biography, the era's history and culture, and the work's content and almost ignore the author's execution. In her review of the John Delane biography, she makes us respect the integrity of *The Times* and see and understand the famous editor whose political sway she found depressing (*L1* 326) while simultaneously exposing the masculine world of power.

A. W. Evans – *Nation*

Virginia Stephen published only one essay in the *Nation*, a review of C. Lewis Hind's book about the post-impressionists on 14 October 1911 (Hind was *Academy and Literature* editor before Harold Child). The *Nation* existed between 1907 and 1921, supplanting the *Speaker* as the liberal weekly, then being supplanted by the *Nation and Athenaeum* with Hubert Henderson as editor and Leonard Woolf as literary editor. Thus, Stephen and then Woolf published reviews and essays across the three linked papers. From 1907 to 1921, H. W. Massingham edited what Henry Nevinson and A. J. A. Morris call a 'livelier, more comprehensive, and much more controversial' publication than 'its predecessor or most of its contemporaries'. James D. Startt says 'Massingham had a reputation for making the papers he served more readable and interesting', and his 'blend of features of the New Journalism' with 'his radical passion' made the *Nation* significant (284). In addition, as Alfred Havighurst makes clear, Massingham served literature well by 'open[ing] up the columns of the *Nation*' to 'celebrated men of letters', 'those not so successful' and 'the young aspiring to fame' (174).[40] He assembled a 'brilliant' editorial team and complemented those editors with excellent writers (Nevinson and Morris).

Havighurst says Edward Garnett and Holbrook Jackson were rejected as candidates for literary editor (147–8), and Desmond MacCarthy was not retained (148); Stanton says William Archer wrote drama criticism early and Frank Swinnerton later (45). The 'World of Books' or 'Books in Brief' sections were under A. W. ('Penguin') Evans during the early years and Henry W. Nevinson 'dominated the literary side of the *Nation* in its first years' (Havighurst 147–9). But neither Evans nor Nevinson is called the literary editor in Havighurst's account, and in Nevinson's autobiography, he discusses being literary editor for the *Daily Chronicle*, not for the *Nation*. He mentions A. W. Evans, saying he was assistant editor for Massingham until the war, when he resigned (see also Waller 408). According to Nevinson, Evans's 'knowledge of literature, especially of last century's literature, was intimate and peculiar', which meant he 'for many years wrote a weekly page of literary discussion on those varied subjects which are always so difficult to choose'. He translated the works of Anatole France and had a 'strongly marked sympathy with France and French literature' (*Fire* 217). But whether Virginia Stephen submitted her work to him as assistant editor remains a mystery.[41]

Although the *Nation* placed most of its emphasis on politics and public affairs, moving from a radical Liberal to a more Labour position over the years, it included original fiction and poetry, book and drama reviews, and literary and art articles. It looks a great deal like the *Speaker*, continuing with two columns, 8½ × 11-inch pages, but with a line between columns and a table of contents on the first page. In the Saturday issue on 14 October 1911, when Stephen's review appears, the Diary of the Week is followed by sections on Politics and Affairs; Life and Letters; The Drama; Short Study (which Stanton says was fiction [44]); Letters from Abroad; Communication; Letters to the Editor; Poetry; Reviews; Books in Brief; and The Week in the City. Stephen's paragraph-long review of Hind's book, in which she focuses on his ability to reconcile his taste for the old masters with his appreciation for the post-impressionists, occurs in the context of Roger Fry's reviews and articles about art that appeared in the *Nation* between 3 November 1910 and 26 September 1914. In November and December 1910, Fry's articles had been all about the post-impressionist exhibition at the Grafton Gallery that was causing such an uproar (see also Stanton 45). The thorough and well-organised *Nation* index for volume 10 (7 October 1911 to 30 March 1912) demonstrates how open the paper was to a wide variety of subjects and genres, and the 14 October 1911 issue reflects that diversity: political articles about China, Churchill, the Congo and India, along with the minimum wage, women ('The New Wife') and miners; literary articles ('What England Reads'), fairy tales by Gorky, poetry by D. H. Lawrence; articles about Home Rule, insurance, nature, science, drama, music and other countries; and extensive reviews and correspondence sections.

Circulation was not large – the periodical continued to lose money – but correspondence reveals an engaged readership across a wide liberal spectrum. Clive Bell wrote about the 'Old Master at the Grafton Galleries' on 7 October 1911, and a letter from Margaret Llewelyn Davies about higher education on 19 August 1911 (741–2) appeared amid a long, heated discussion of universities and the working classes that began with S. A. Barnett's article, 'What Use Are the Universities to the Poor?', on 29 July 1911 and ended with the editor's note, 'This correspondence must now cease' on 9 September (843). Ethel Smyth (16 September 1911 877–8) and Ethel Jonson of New York (14 October 1911 96–7) discussed their support of women's suffrage from two different positions – Smyth thinks having the vote will allow women to rid the earth of several evils whereas Jonson thinks women 'are human beings in exactly the same way as men' (96). R. Dyce Sharp in Sussex, who wrote to Woolf about *Roger Fry* in 1940–1 (Daugherty, 'You' 199–201; 210–12),[42] writes as a freethinker about an Anglican theological controversy in which a Bishop deprived a Mr Thompson of his licence (98). Virginia Stephen's review is at the end of Books in Brief, following reviews of E. V. Lucas's book of essays, *Old Lamps for New*, a prose translation of *The Clouds of Aristophanes*, Henry James's *The Outcry* and A. A. Jack's *Poetry and Prose: Being Essays on Modern English Poetry*. The *Nation* continued the *Speaker*'s lively and diverse outlook, communicating curiosity about a wide range of topics, including modern art and education.

Receiving a book about the post-impressionists to review for the *Nation*, Virginia Stephen could ponder another art form and formulate her own ideas a year after outraged critics had savaged the London exhibit at the Grafton Gallery. Praising C. Lewis Hind's defence of post-impressionism, his ability to reconcile the conventional with the new, and his suggestions about point of view (E1 379–80), she begins to define her own modernism.

Bruce Richmond – *Times Literary Supplement*

The *TLS* (or Lit Supp, Bruce Richmond's preferred abbreviation) would in time become a main outlet for Virginia Woolf's essays. But when Stephen submitted her first review in March 1905, it was still a fairly new venture.[43] It grew out of the short-lived *Literature* (1897–1902),[44] begun in the late days of the nineteenth century, but it was a new literary review for the new century, on the cusp between a past of weekly, monthly and quarterly reviews and a future of little magazines and academic journals. The *TLS* gave Virginia Stephen a much larger audience of readers, neither mass nor coterie, not allied to a particular church or party line, and devoted to literature and reading. According to Harold Child's anniversary account,[45] the Lit Supp exceeded the daily circulation of *The Times* in 1904 because, up until 1914, it was literally folded within *The Times*; for example, it reached the 38,000 people subscribing to the newspaper in 1908 (WDENP), but also non-subscribers or purchasers who could buy it for a penny (33). In 1914, when a separate publication and selling for 1d, its circulation ranged between 35,000 and 45,000 (35).[46] Contrasting the *TLS* with the *Egoist*, Michael Kaufmann mentions a circulation of 20,000 (138), but Derwent May says the average weekly circulation was back up to 31,864 in 1919 (123).

Writing for the *TLS*, Stephen could assume reader interest in both the literary tradition and the new. 'The Notes', very brief notices of published books or short paragraphs about upcoming publications, and the 'List of New Books and Reprints', at least four columns on new books, with publication information, prices and often a short annotation by F. T. Dalton (something he wrote week after week for years) (May 15), communicate both a respect for and a courting of readers. According to May, Augustine Birrell's review of *More Letters of Edward Fitzgerald* in the first issue of the *TLS* set the tone:

literature was for keen general readers, not for specialists, and though the new paper would be scholarly and critical, its role would above all be like that of an educated reader, helping other such readers to find the books that were most worth reading. (11)

That 'voice' probably contributed to Stephen's budding sense of a common reader. The *TLS*, its origins anything but stable,[47] had a remarkably stable editor in Bruce Richmond, whose tenure lasted thirty-five years. He gave Stephen steady apprenticeship work, keeping her supplied with books and steadily moving her toward a lead article/review, the first of which was about Laurence Sterne, published on 12 August 1909 (*E1* 280–8; see also Rosenbaum 345–6).

Beginning in a quiet and inauspicious way, *TLS* gained a foothold in the era's incredible mix of reviews, magazines and papers. Tellingly, both Harold Child, who had worked for *The Academy*, and Arthur Clutton-Brock, who had worked for the *Speaker*, migrated to the *TLS* and spent the rest of their lives there, and Richmond once commented that 'Clutton-Brock had done more to ensure the success of the *Literary Supplement* than any other person' (May 122). In its early days, the Contents box led off with Literature, with Fiction as a separate heading; according to May, 'literature' was defined very broadly – 'from politics and history to travel and cookery, and indeed including the criticism of fiction – while fiction, formally at any rate, was not conceived of as part of "literature" at all' (11). Drama, Correspondence, Notes, a List of New Books and Reprints (which became the Book List), and Chess followed these headings. Using half a full newspaper-sized page, easily inserted into *The Times*, the *TLS* had three columns, with a thin rule between them. Usually eight pages, but occasionally twelve or sixteen before Christmas, *TLS* was given away, part of *The Times* copy price, 3d. Although *The Times* had various orientations during its long history, it was an independent newspaper, not the mouthpiece of any party (Startt 286–7), and its ad in the 1904 *NPD* proudly claims, 'It deals out its denunciations with equal force and freedom on all parties in their turn' (63). It had a primarily middle-class and upper-middle-class audience, but as views of those classes changed, so did *The Times*. However, as J. O. Baylen clarifies, the concentration of the press into fewer hands and the start of war in 1914 meant that 'the press, which normally provided information and comment, was now expected to purvey propaganda' (41–2); *The Times* was no exception.[48]

Simon Nowell-Smith and Rebecca Mills say Richmond had a gift for discovering and encouraging new talent, for making the Lit Supp a forum for discussion of literature, literary history and textual criticism. As they also point out, although Woolf and T. S. Eliot both 'fretted in the strait-jacket of "*The Times*'s style"', Eliot called Richmond a 'great editor' (17) and Woolf acknowledged how much his mentorship had meant to her when young (*D5* 145). Accounts of his time at the *TLS* make it clear he did in fact edit, assigning books, controlling contributors, editing, copyediting. Eliot said he learned from Richmond that an editor should 'know his contributors personally, . . . keep in touch with them and . . . make suggestions to them . . . . And I learnt from Richmond that I must read every word of what was to appear in print' (17). Richmond rarely came in for the criticism Stephen reserved for the *Guardian* editor, and she writes to Violet, perhaps remembering Smith's 'printed slip', that Richmond, in rejecting her Sichel review, calls it 'excellent', just 'not what they want', is sending more books, 'and is polite' (*L1* 187–8). (Later, Virginia Woolf would fume at not being allowed to use the word 'lewd' in a Henry James review [*D2* 152].) But because her letters to him have not survived, only secondhand reports and occasional references to him in other correspondence reveal any details of his work with her.[49]

Virginia Stephen appears in the *TLS* for the first time in the 10 March 1905 issue with 'Literary Geography'. The paper opens with a list of the publisher Messrs Constable's List down the left-hand side of the page, where Edith Sichel's book about Catherine de Medici is advertised, along with a pocket edition of *The Works of George Meredith*, Augustine Birrell's edition of *Boswell's Life of Johnson* and a new twelve-volume edition of *An English Garner* edited by Professor Arber (Stephen rebound an earlier edition [K&M-V 7]). Marie Corelli, several six-shilling novels, and *Resurrection* by Leo Tolstoy all appear in the same list. (The next week, when Virginia Stephen reviewed *Barham of Beltana*, the ad belongs to Chatto & Windus, and the lead article is about Edmund Gosse's *Coventry Patmore*.) Illustrating May's comment about the broad definition of the term 'literature', Stephen's 'Literary Geography' appears in the Literature section and has a separate headline (10 May 1904 81); it keeps company with a review of *Chatham* by Frederic Harrison; *Christus in Ecclesia* by Hastins Rashdall; *Spanish Influence in English Literature* by Martin Hume; *The Mammals of Great Britain and Ireland* by J. G. Millais; *Matilda, Countess of Tuscany* by Mrs Mary E. Huddy; and *The Yellow War* by O. The fiction reviewed in the issue includes Mrs Humphry Ward's new novel, *The Marriage of William Ashe*, *Shining Ferry* by Q (Arthur Quiller-Couch), *Mrs Galer's Business*, also by Q, and *The Child: Andrea* by Karin Michaelis (translated from the Danish). *Auguste Rodin: The Man, His Ideas, His Works* by M. Camille Mauclair and translated by Clementina Black earned a shorter notice. Thus, although Stephen would later do numerous short reviews of novels near the back of the paper, she started out writing a somewhat longer piece for the Lit Supp 'middle'.

The *TLS* has a clear identity, in contrast to *Cornhill*; it is serious about books. Everything in it is related to reading, readers, books and reviews (except for the issue-ending column on Chess). But it does not include gossip about the book world or editorial commentary as in *The Academy*. As a result, the *TLS* communicates integrity, respect for writers and readers, and a belief in literature's permanence. It was fortunate in its editor, who communicated the same 'love of literature and seriousness of purpose' (Eliot 17). T. S. Eliot, in his 13 January 1961 tribute to Bruce Richmond on his ninetieth birthday, also praises Richmond's editing, particularly when reviews were unsigned; his choice to remain anonymous himself; and his efforts to know and cultivate his reviewers' specialities and interests. He also notes how many of his 'troupe of regular contributors ... produced some of their most distinguished critical essays as leaders for the *Literary Supplement*'. And he explains why: 'For Bruce Richmond we wanted to do our best' (17). One suspects Virginia Woolf, remembering Virginia Stephen, would have agreed.

Finally, in Bruce Richmond and the *TLS*, Virginia Stephen had steady, frequent work ('I am glad that the Times shows signs of keeping me on to do reviews' [*PA* 246]), which gave her the time and security to learn how to take notes and revise, practise and improve. From Richmond, she learned what Eliot called 'the discipline of anonymity' (17). She was 'pelted', reviewing fifty popular novels between 1905 and 1908 (*PA* 252), but the experience helped her hone aesthetic principles, and Richmond praised her work. Plus, paying those dues meant that when she protested she did not want to review current fiction any more (*L*1 331; Rosenbaum 340), Richmond began assigning her new editions or letters of canonical authors such as Sidney or Rossetti, and she could practise a more expansive criticism. By the time he gave Stephen her first *TLS* 'lead review' on Laurence Sterne in 1909, she was ready.

Since an individual periodical functions as 'a microcosm ... of a cultural outlook' (L. James 351), together, the seven periodicals Virginia Stephen worked for provided a variety of opportunities, audiences and lessons. She wrote for women and men, the reform-minded and the traditional, the general and the literary. She wrote for editors with guidelines and editors without, editors who actively changed her work and editors who were hands-off. From the established *Guardian* to the new *Times Literary Supplement*, from the imperialist *National Review* to the liberal *Speaker* and *Nation*, from the old-fashioned *Cornhill* to the constantly changing *Academy*, Stephen learned to consider editor, paper and audience, adapt to diverse expectations, adjust: from short to long, from review to essay, from critical to complimentary. Under the varied tutelage of her editor teachers, she practised, learned and became an expert reviewer.

Between late 1904 and the end of 1912, Virginia Stephen practised being a professional writer. She obtained work and met obligations, created the material conditions she needed, and established a working life's productive routines. As she practised, she read a lot of fiction, became more independent and learned what she wanted to say. She also practised particular writing skills for each editor and newspaper she wrote for, gaining experience in writing for different audiences, a skill that would foster Virginia Woolf's creation of a common reader and her ability to reach out to that reader (see also Rosenbaum 146; Dubino, 'VW' 26). Her toughest lesson, though, involved handling every novice's dilemma: how to balance one's creative integrity and an editor's practical expertise? how to meet editorial demands yet say what one wants to say?[50]

Early in her apprenticeship, Virginia Stephen details her anger at some of her editors' strictures yet knows those editors' 'criticism is important' (*PA* 232). They determine whether she is published. Much later, in 'Professions for Women', Virginia Woolf describes the internal critic, the Angel who speaks with the authority of traditional gender roles and expectations, and she calls for the Angel's murder. Later still, in 'A Sketch of the Past', she worries her tea-table training had unduly influenced the tone of some *TLS* essays. But she also notes her 'surface manner' has allowed her to say things that would not have been heard if spoken directly and out loud (150). Julia Briggs notes Woolf's pleasure, in fact, in circumventing censorship's obstacles: 'Restrictions have their own contribution to make to the creative process' (*RVW* 6). In the context of learning to write, these statements identify the paradox all writers wrestle with: the editor's views are important, but the writer must also resist the Angel in the House. If the writer writes just for herself and lets no editor tell her anything, she risks not being published or having only a coterie audience; the editor, after all, represents readers. If the writer considers only the audience, internalises its assumptions and takes all editorial suggestions, she risks compromising her integrity, having only a mass audience, or not being taken seriously. Keeping one's balance is difficult.

During her apprenticeship, Virginia Stephen's work was cut without permission by *The Academy*; changed without permission by the *Guardian* ('Mrs. L or Margaret L rather cobbled my poor Shag between them' [*L1* 172]), by *The Academy* (the editor changed a title and altered words after having sent unchanged proofs [*L1* 180–1]), by the *Cornhill* ('Smith has added words to my sentences, cut out others' [*L1* 332]) and by the *TLS* ('the Times have cut ... down and tamed' an 'originally long and vigorous' review [*L1* 295]); and signed without permission by *The Academy* ('I shouldn't so much mind if they hadn't clapped on my name in full at the end—to which I do object' [*L1* 181]). She perceived herself as needing to '[water] down' a review for the *TLS* (*PA* 255); she wished she 'could be brave & frank in my reviews, instead of having to spin them out elaborately' (*PA* 270); and she felt Mrs Lyttelton '[stuck] her broad thumb into the middle of my delicate sentences and improve[d] the moral tone' (*L1* 214). Finally, many of the books she reviewed were chosen for her by the editors.

But it is also true Virginia Stephen fully understood the *Guardian*'s moral perspective and told Mrs Lyttelton to 'do what she liked with my articles' (*L1* 170; see also *L1* 169). When she wrote to Violet Dickinson she did not mean 'to ask [Mrs L] to do all the dirty work of correcting and polishing for me', she needs to tell her editor so (*L1* 169), and 'I wish they would let me do it if it has to be done' (*L1* 172), it seems to have had an effect: the next time Mrs Lyttelton wanted changes, she asked Stephen to make them. Although she was angry at having to cut her review of James, she controlled those cuts and ended up comparing Mrs Lyttelton favourably to *The Academy*. It is also true she experienced seeing her work come to her in proofs just as she had written it: 'After dinner I got my proof from the Times, printed word for word, so I only hope they wont cut out at the last moment' (*PA* 244). Her comment about needing to water down strong negative opinions comes as she sits down to write her third review for the *TLS* – perhaps she was not responding to a specific dictum from the editor but stating a more general assumption about book reviewing? (The 'ouch!' written in my margin of that review long ago indicates she did not drown her opinions.) Her criticism of other writers was often harsher in her notes than in her reviews, but such revision occurred consistently, across various publications, and cannot be attributed solely to repressive editorial policy. Distrust of her own critical attitude may be why she 'make[s] [her] criticism less abrupt' when she receives the proofs of her review of the Spanish books for the *TLS* (*L1* 190) (but see Brosnan 62) or notices a short review for the *Guardian* is 'a shade more scornful than I mean' (*L1* 197), for example. Finally, it was standard practice for literary editors to assign reviews, and it is also true that when she said she did not want to review contemporary novels any longer for *TLS*, Bruce Richmond complied.

Given the number of pieces she produced during her apprenticeship, if the specific changes Stephen records are the only ones that caused her ire, editors did not tamper with her work very often; she did well for a novice. Stephen followed a common trajectory: as she gained confidence and skill and her career progressed, she gained more control. Her editors' suggestions and changes can be seen as common in an apprentice's learning process, not attempts to silence or stifle. Eric Sandberg agrees, saying 'Woolf's early journalism was written without excessive editorial interference or self-censorship' (13).⁵¹ Virginia Stephen does what is required of her, yes, but not slavishly. Her editors collectively taught her to imagine different readers, to shift according to publication and audience, to aim beyond a coterie; but as she learned to do that, she retained and strengthened her own voice, as the next chapters show. Louis James suggests periodicals can function as a genre, giving fiction and non-fiction 'their sense of being a dialogue between writer and reader', and Stephen used her apprenticeship in different periodicals, a form of literature James calls 'particularly intimate' (352), to develop her own voice but also establish that dialogue with voices unlike her own – authors, editors, readers – within a conversational community. When Virginia Woolf later positioned herself as a common reader, an amateur writing for other amateurs, she did so as a strategy designed to invite a variety of readers into the conversation. She had learned her lessons well.

Notes

1. See Collier, *Modernism* 79–83, for facts about the pressures on book reviewers.
2. A. Curtis understands Woolf's gutter and stamp system 'anticipated the modern listings page' (178), but John Sutherland quotes this system as though Woolf thought it existed. He does not identify it as a proposal, see its sarcasm, or identify its source (*Fiction* 86). Waller also assumes Woolf was describing current practice (152), perhaps because, though she meant it as parody, it was not that unusual, according to Collier, for reviewers to produce columns 'covering 10 to 12 books in 1,000 words' (*Modernism* 81).
3. See also Gillespie's 'The Elusive Julia Stephen'. John Mason argues that essays in the monthly reviews were 'well suited to the conditions of the nineteenth century: the new, well-educated, middle-class reader was eager for cultural guidelines in an age of expanding scientific knowledge, religious doubt and the approach of democracy' (282).
4. Rosenbaum says Stephen was reading Aristotle's *Poetics* with growing absorption and excitement at the end of February 1905 (159), thinking it 'will fit me for a reviewer!' (*PA* 240).
5. Or *The Renaissance: Studies in Art and Poetry* (K&M-V 172)? In his study of Virginia Woolf as an essayist, Perry Meisel asserts she 'is very likely without peer in this [twentieth] century' (xi) and argues she represses a debt to Pater. In his relentless application of Harold Bloom's 'anxiety of influence' to Woolf's supposed debt (Hill, 'Review' 118–19), he attempts, James Gindin says, to '[confer] the status of exclusive truth on what might be interesting and suggestive speculation' (153).
6. According to a *Guardian* notice, the third edition of this collection was issued by Macmillan in summer 1905 (16 August 1905 1359).
7. Rosenbaum mentions Violet Dickinson, her sister and brothers, and Bloomsbury friends (164).
8. As A. Curtis notes, that question would occupy Bloomsbury a great deal (149). See his 'Gissing' 161–2 for further perspective on Nelly's attitudes. See also Rosenbaum 365–6.
9. Virginia Stephen makes this remark about her note on Leslie Stephen for Maitland's biography, but it could just as easily apply to her need about all her writing at the time.

10. My study of these periodicals follows Brosnan's call for more critical attention to the historical, cultural and material context of Woolf's essays and journalism (1–15).
11. I agree with Pat Collier that Woolf's attitude toward the word 'professional' is not easy or relaxed (*Modernism* 73), but from our point of view, she becomes a professional, and as a professional, maintains the persona of an amateur.
12. Stephen mentions Mrs Lyttelton, Leo Maxse, Reginald Smith and Bruce Richmond by name, but not Harold Child, Arthur Clutton-Brock or A. W. Evans. Perhaps she mentions the first four because she knew or had been introduced to them. Or we may not have the letters in which she mentions the latter three. But it seems odd she would mention getting a letter from *The Academy* asking her to write and not mention the editor's name (*PA* 239). Or complain about the editor's changes to her 'Plague of Essays' without using a name; indeed, she says 'they' changed it (*L1* 180–1). Perhaps correspondence from *The Academy*, the *Speaker* and the *Nation* was signed with a generic term such as Editors or Literary Editor.
13. As far as I know, no letters from Virginia Stephen to these editors or periodicals exist. In his *Letters* 1 introduction, Nigel Nicolson notes the 'total destruction' of Woolf's letters to Bruce Richmond, calling the loss of her letters to him during her apprenticeship 'particularly unhappy' (xiii). The index entry for Richmond reads 'destroyed V.'s letters to him' (521). Documentation in *The Times* archive for Richmond's editorship (1902–37) is sparse, though a few papers remain (May xiii). Nick Mays, current News UK archivist, says the 'concept of retaining important documentation' was in place at *The Times* during Richmond's tenure, though Richmond seems not to have kept copies of his outgoing correspondence and destroyed incoming correspondence once it was no longer required (email 13 December 2018). Correspondence with almost all contributors from Richmond's time is gone.
14. This work builds on the snapshots and sources McNeillie provides in his 'Notes on the Journals', Appendix IV of *Essays* 1, and that Clarke provides in his 'Notes on the Journals', Appendix VII of *Essays* 6. I relied heavily upon the *NPD*, the online version of the *WDENP*, the *Wellesley Index to Victorian Periodicals 1824–1900*, *British Literary Magazines*, volumes 3 and 4, the online *ODNB*, and individual studies of editors or papers. Victorian scholars devoted dozens of years to compiling periodical press records and were far ahead of modernist scholars in preserving and evaluating magazines and journals. But Sean Latham and Robert Scholes's call in 'The Rise of Periodical Studies' for more attention to the role of periodicals in modernism has begun to bear fruit. The database and Cover-to-Cover Initiative in the Modernist Journals Project undertaken by Brown University and the University of Tulsa aim not to lose the resource that periodicals provide to modernist and cultural studies. The University of Sussex and De Montfort University also sponsor a Modernist Magazines Project. Up until recently, the modernist focus has been on little magazines, but periodical studies now includes newspapers, magazines and journals of all kinds. See 208 n14 and studies by Avery and Brantlinger, Laurel Brake, and Pat Collier, whose work and defining articles are particularly helpful to beginners in the field.
15. Novices could not easily undertake this study at the turn of the century, as noted in Chapter 10. Although *The Literary Year-Book* appeared in 1897, it was not at first helpful. The publishers' directory is only twenty pages long, and it has some useful glossaries of terms, information about libraries and literary clubs, and articles about printing and the book trade, but is mainly filled with portraits and 'puffing' biographical sketches that promote certain authors. The closest thing to what Bennett suggests young writers find out is in the short chapter 'On Magazine Articles', which includes a three-page chart listing the style, length, fees and other information about twenty-six magazines, and the only part devoted to reviews is a 3½-page long chapter on review copies. Once it became *The Writers' and Artists' Year-Book* in 1906, it gradually, year by year, 'gave a greater amount of space to solid information' (P. Keating 72).

16. Brosnan says Stephen often 'speaks in the voice required and often demanded by the editorial policy of the relevant journal' (61). The editorial policies for these particular journals are difficult to find and reconstruct, however, and such adaptation to editor, house style and audience does not seem unusual for a novice, as Eric Sandberg points out (12–13).
17. I have not included *Englishwoman* in my discussion because of the odd circumstances under which Stephen's review appeared. As Kirkpatrick and Clarke note (249), the review is signed by Marjorie Strachey, but according to Elizabeth Boyd, Miss Strachey told her she had been unable to review the Laurence Housman adaptation of *Lysistrata* and that Virginia Stephen reviewed it on her behalf (see *E6* 374 n1). Probably this arrangement was made at the last minute, with Stephen having no dealings with the periodical herself – Strachey simply signed Stephen's work and submitted it. It is noteworthy Stephen saw *Lysistrata* in late 1910 and had the confidence to step in and review a play, but it does not seem likely the *Englishwoman* committee of editors (including Mary Lowndes and Frances Balfour) functioned as a teacher the way the other periodical editors did. See Stuart Clarke's note (*E6* 374 n1) and Steven D. Putzel for a detailed study of Woolf's 'multi-faceted relationship to the theater' (xiii).
18. See also Frank Webster on the religious press and see the *Guardian* 18 January 1946 centenary articles for more information about the founding and subsequent life of *The Guardian* (30–5).
19. The papers themselves supplied the *NPD* with the descriptions for their listings. Many papers also placed more overtly commercial ads on advertisers' pages.
20. See McNeillie's full description of the paper, xi–xiii. His comment refers more to the paper as a whole than to its supplement because the latter gives a fascinating glimpse into women's issues at the turn of the century and cries out for further study.
21. The Rev. Walter Hobhouse (1862–1928) edited the *Guardian* from 1899 to 1905 (H. C. Moore 13), when James George Joseph Penderel-Brodhurst (1859–1934) became editor (*Who's Who 1909* 1490). Because Stephen mentions Mrs Lyttelton's daughter, who did some work for the *Guardian* Supplement, in her letters, McNeillie and others have conflated the two women. But Stephen refers to her editor as Mrs Lyttelton (or Mrs L) and to her daughter as Margaret.
22. Brosnan's discussion of the complex, unstable relationship between supposedly 'high' essays and 'low' journalism (5–7) makes my privileging the essay problematic, especially since F. Elizabeth Gray, citing Oldcastle, says reviewing 'was perceived as demanding, intellectual, and closer to literature than other forms of journalism' at the end of the nineteenth century (6). Brosnan warns against conflating Woolf's reviews and essays (41), but perhaps that tendency also acknowledges the aesthetic qualities of reviews and the commercial underpinnings of literature, thus undercutting the division of non-fiction into 'high' and 'low', 'literature' and 'journalism'. See 297 n5.
23. See Ann Kennedy Smith's posts, 'Kathleen Lyttelton and Virginia Woolf' on the *Something Rhymed* blog and 'A Public Space: Kathleen Lyttelton's Campaigning Journalism' on her *Cambridge Ladies' Dining Society* blog.
24. The supplement heading does not identify an editor after Mrs Lyttelton's death, and I could not discover who took it over. Early twentieth-century publications often lack mastheads, thwarting such investigation; decisions made by microfilmers and volume reprinters to omit ads also frustrate.
25. Stephen's review of Howells opens *Essays* 1, but Kirkpatrick and Clarke, using evidence from Stephen's journal, list 'Social England' as a 'Doubtful contribution' (300), making it possibly her first review (see *E1*, App. II, 269–71).
26. In his 1992 dissertation, 'Contesting Discourses in the Essays of Virginia Woolf, James Baldwin, Joan Didion, and E. B. White', Kenneth Alan Smith makes the same point and uses the same words, 'a quick study' (125), after detailing the immaturity

of the early Howells review (118–19) and noting the growth evident in 'The Value of Laughter' (121–5).

27. Although not discussing the gender issue in the same way, Lucas Malet in the *Bookman* had similar criticisms (December 1904 116–18). Courtney would later review Woolf's *Jacob's Room* in 1922, recognising its modernism and comparing its prose style to jazz (105).

28. Julia Stephen had encouraged the courtship of Leo Maxse and Kitty Lushington, and Kitty was Woolf's model for Clarissa Dalloway.

29. The *National Review* is part of the *Directory*'s listing but is not included in the fuller annotations section. It also did not place an ad.

30. Victor says Leslie Stephen's essays may count as 'the most significant group of literary essays published in the *National Review* during Maxse's editorship' ('National' 246).

31. See Hutcheson's introduction (xiii–xx) for a brief discussion of the complexity of Conservative politics at the time.

32. Admiral Maxse was in the Crimea, George Meredith's *Beauchamp's Career* was a study of his character, and Ridgway published his *Reasons for Opposing Woman Suffrage* in 1884. He purchased the *National Review* for his son in 1893.

33. Virginia Woolf would also support the public use of space. In a letter to the *Nation* on 24 June 1933 ('London Squares'), she proposes that while people around the squares are away for the summer, why not open the gates and allow everyone to have some respite from the August and September heat (843; E6 3–4)?

34. Graham edited *Country Life*, to whose offices *The Academy* moved during this period (Kent 5). They were joint editors, but it seems as though Child did most of the actual editing.

35. Rosenbaum suggests that twice in March 1905, Stephen 'had failed to satisfy the academic standards of the men who were her editors', first when Richmond rejected her review of Sichel's book and then when Child turned down her 'Magic Greek' essay (162).

36. His policy seems to have been to sign essays, but not reviews, since he wanted to go back to anonymous reviews to ensure integrity. Roll-Hansen says Child 'gladly allowed the more eminent contributors to sign their articles, Andrew Lang and Bernard Shaw, for example, or Arthur Symons and Virginia Stephen' (219). But Virginia Stephen was not an 'eminent contributor' in 1905–6 unless Roll-Hansen thought her father made her so. (Of course, Roll-Hansen could not consult Woolf's *Letters* or adolescent journal when he published his book in 1957.) Furthermore, Child did not 'allow' her to sign; he signed without her permission.

37. Oddly enough, the *National Review* is part of *British Literary Magazines* (primarily because of its earlier incarnation), but the *Speaker* is not. However, both Frank Swinnerton and Edward Garnett seem to have thought the *Speaker* was largely political (Havighurst 143).

38. To grasp some of the complexity of the Liberal point of view, see Stewart Weaver's *The Hammonds* and Michael Bentley. In the complex world of newspapers, ideologies and political positions, the *Speaker* was an alternative to the Liberal Unionist *Spectator*. Weaver argues Hammond's supplements to the *Nation* in 1921 helped change Lloyd George's mind about negotiations with Ireland (18).

39. According to Sutherland, it was modelled after the US *Harper's Magazine* (Longman 150); its title came from the street on which the publishing firm had its offices (Herd 212). It combined, says Huxley, the 'popular lure of the serial with the literary work of the more serious reviews' (*House* 89), and its first issue sold 110,000 copies.

40. Leonard Woolf replaced H. N. Brailsford on the staff when Brailsford left to become the editor of the *New Leader* in 1922, though he had been writing and reviewing for the paper since 1920. See *Downhill All the Way*, 91–8, for his description and impressions of the paper's backers, political leanings and editor, H. W. Massingham.

41. I could find no biographical information about him.
42. Her brother, Clifford Sharp, was editor of the *New Statesman* from 1913 to 1931. Her sister, Evelyn Sharp, was married to Henry W. Nevinson.
43. Christopher Kent says the *Times Literary Supplement* editor 'wanted Leslie Stephen but settled for his daughter, Virginia Woolf, who became a *TLS* regular as early as 1905' (Intro xxiv). See also QB1 104; McNeillie xviii n24; and Dubino, 'VW' 27–8.
44. Carol de Saint Victor explains that *Literature* first appeared in October 1897 and filled a niche that did not yet exist: 'a critical literary weekly'. Meant 'to serve as a record of current publications', to engage with literary topics and to provide readers with 'critical reviewing', it also self-consciously explored reviewing: 'the role of mediator between reader and writer, whether as literary critic or as teacher, became the subject of a number of articles' ('Literature' 199). Its basic organisation, with a leading article followed by a long middle section of reviews, correspondence and a new book list (200), became the *TLS* format's backbone. The last issue of *Literature* appeared on 11 January 1902, and the first issue of the *TLS* appeared on 17 January (202).
45. Harold Child died in 1945, but he had already written the history of the *TLS*'s origins and early years that was then used in the 18 January 1952 issue (33–9).
46. May reports that in 1914, the average weekly circulation was 41,974; during 1918, the last year of the Great War, the average circulation was 29,106 (123).
47. The *TLS* was originally conceived as a supplement that would run while Parliament was in session so *The Times* did not have to use space on book reviews. When Parliament adjourned, the idea that book reviewing should shift back into *The Times* seems to have faded away. As Child writes, 'Like some other English things the *Literary Supplement* was started as a makeshift and continued through an oversight' ('Times' 33). But see May, 7–10, for a more detailed and complex history of the supplement's origins. Although Richmond experienced the origins as determined by chance, much planning was going on behind the scenes.

    Lord Northcliffe wanted to stop publishing the *TLS* in April 1922, but the supplement continued to appear because, Diego Saglia reports, the 'order had not reached all the departments concerned.' When Northcliffe died in August, the *TLS* was spared (845). See also May 123–53.
48. See Baylen's description of the loss of civil liberties in Britain and the manipulation of the press by political leaders and owners. Independent editors like A. G. Gardiner, Baylen writes, denounced the British press for becoming 'almost completely partisan – either committed to a political party or to a political personality'. According to Gardiner, Lloyd George had facilitated the concentration of almost all press opinion into the hands of six men (Baylen 46).
49. We know that at the end of both his career and her involvement with the *TLS*, a working relationship spanning over thirty years, they expressed mutual respect and gratitude. Richmond, replying to her letter at his retirement, expressed his deep pride in her work for the Supplement and noted its early beginnings (Letter to Virginia Woolf, SxMs–18/1/D/123/2; see also D5 144–5).
50. Brosnan asks similar questions (41), but sees Stephen developing a 'language of duplicity' in a battle against self-censorship (62), not navigating a typical novice's progress.
51. Sandberg argues the 'textual evidence' of the early reviews and essays suggests Stephen's struggles are simply 'part of the common experience of writing' (13). Brosnan, citing Woolf's manuscript notes (P 163), says the male author Woolf refers to in 'Professions for Women' is Henry James (58). Rosenbaum claims, citing the speech typescript (P xxxi), that the author was Arnold Bennett (147). Virginia Stephen reviewed Henry James on 22 February 1905 (E1 22–4); Virginia Woolf reviewed Arnold Bennett on 5 July 1917 (E2 128–32).

Chapter 12

Essay-writing and Book-reviewing Skills

Practice

In 'The Leaning Tower', Virginia Woolf calls a writer's education 'so much less definite' than the education of others, then defines it as a mix of '[r]eading, listening, talking, travel, leisure' (*E6* 266), a combination many women, ethnic minorities and working-class people could not easily gain. Beyond that 'less definite' schooling, many practising writers, then and now, recommend what Robert Louis Stevenson suggests in 'A College Magazine' (57–76). As did others, Virginia Stephen learned to be a writer by following that advice, whether she had read it or not: read widely, set oneself exercises, imitate models and practise consistently. If she was going to break into the world of letters through reviewing and essay writing, Stephen knew she had to learn the 'knack of writing for newspapers' (*L1* 155), and we can see her practising that skill in her observations, journal entries, reading notes, and reviews of popular fiction.

Observing

From the start, Virginia Stephen's writing revealed acute powers of observation, but as she grew older, she worked to improve both her writing and the observations it rested on. Her first request for criticism from a friend, a letter to Emma Vaughan dated 11 September 1899, coincidentally came when she was in Warboys, where she had begun, says Leaska, 'practising the art of essay writing for the first time' in her summer holiday journal (*L1* 28; *PA* 135). From that date forward, although dated entries still appear, Stephen fills her journal with literary exercises, some titled, in which she describes nature and people, place and time, society and culture, home and away. What she explains in 'Retrospect' (30 July 1903) about her Hyde Park diary book applies to all her 1899–1909 pieces: they 'serve for a sketch book; as an artist fills his pages with scraps & fragments . . . . It is an exercise – training for eye & hand –' (*PA* 186–7).

Learning to write for papers, Virginia Stephen apprenticed as a book reviewer who practised reading books, but also as an essayist who practised reading the world. She trains eye and hand, recording what she sees with 'an honest desire to put down the truth with whatever materials one has to hand', knowing 'roughness' may result (*PA* 187), but also realising interpretation, evaluation or remedy require such an observational foundation. As she says in her travel books review, 'Journeys in Spain', successful authors in the genre succeed because of their 'faculty of seeing' and 'interpreting the sight to others' (*E1* 44), and her many set pieces demonstrate Stephen's fidelity to surfaces and concurrent eagerness to delve beneath them. She exercises in her journal to expand her ability to see, describe clearly and 'read' what she sees.

In 'Street Haunting', Virginia Woolf declared that upon leaving the house on a winter evening, 'We are no longer quite ourselves'; the resulting freedom and anonymity break the 'shell-like covering' protecting the soul and leave only 'a central oyster of perceptiveness, an enormous eye' (*E4* 481). In numerous journal entries,[1] Virginia Stephen develops overlapping layers of skill that Woolf reveals in this and other essays: observing the mind as it observes; opening one's senses; identifying perspective; seeing relationship and paradox; and fusing perception with interpretation of what is perceived, the double meaning of observation.

Whether it was dashed off or time was taken over it, whether it was drafted in a familiar or strange room, or on a train or boat or in a carriage, when Stephen sits down to write an 'assignment' she relies on memory – 'We have this moment come in from a sunset expedition – an account of which I must at once write down, or I shall never attempt it'[2] – to record not only what she saw but also how her mind moved. After a windy and stormy day, she notes how slowly the sun was sinking, but then realises within a minute, they were 'in the midst of the performance. [So] quickly did the clouds catch the glory, glow, & fade, that our eyes & mind had ample work merely to register the change' (*PA* 155; Leaska brackets). Her central perception, that 'Everything is done by different shades & degrees of light – melting & mixing infinitely', changes again 'when our eyes found an instant to leave it' and see 'another glory, reflected indeed but no less glorious & perfect of its kind than the original, all round' (*PA* 156). In one of several Acropolis entries in her Greece and Turkey travel journal, she notices how

> when you have gazed at the patterned colours [white & blue & tawny red] of the Parthenon an image of such life is left there that all other buildings seem mean & frigid as tho' cut out by brainless machines 'in comparion'.

Indeed, she finds it constructive to glance down at the streets, the Palace, the Exhibition, 'just to have that sight instantly corrected – or rather erased altogether – by one look at the Temple'. Comparing the two sights seems spontaneous because 'the eye was acted upon unconsciously, as though it had to choose between red & green. This is beauty – that nothing at all' (*PA* 328). Describing shepherds she sees on the way to Stonehenge, she hesitates, 'half afraid of over picturesqueness', but then proceeds to record the picture: 'they wear long black cloaks reaching down to their heels, . . . [and] they grasp a real shepherds staff' (*PA* 204). She likes the 'stupendous mystery' that confronts her at Stonehenge – 'no one in the world can tell you anything about it' (*PA* 199) – but her mind likes to 'imagine those toiling pagans doing honour to the very sun now in the sky above me' (*PA* 200). In her short piece 'The Downs', she confesses her mind keeps likening the downs to the long curved waves of the sea. It is as though the land here, all molten once, & rolling in vast billows had solidified while the waves were still swollen & on the point of breaking. (*PA* 192)

Moving from a lovely description of the 'almost liquid' stone of the Hermes statue at Olympia, she quotes the guidebook about what seems to be a 'very disorderly pagan graveyard', only to conclude, 'Still this is not what the vagrant mind dwells on most; there was thyme growing by the pillars, & fine grass' (*PA* 319). Trying to capture Mycenae on the page, she confesses

> There never was a sight ... less manageable; it travels through all the chambers of the brain, wakes odd memories & imaginations; forecasts a remote future; retells a remote past. And all the while it is – let me write it down – but a great congeries of ruined houses, on a hill side. (*PA* 331)

These passages reveal what her eye, 'vagrant mind' and ultimately her hand actually do as they observe.

Virginia Stephen often finds language, hers or in general, unequal to the task. She admits she uses 'words implying some thing handed down to me' about the 'gift' of two-and-a-half hours of solitary happiness 'bestowed' on her at Giggleswick so she can delay writing about her walk 'because I shall get no nearer the words by making a direct search for them than by thus dallying upon the outskirts' (*PA* 306). Trying to avoid guidebook writing in describing the Hermes statue, she admits 'So we pile words; but it is a pretence. You must see him, & let the eye spring like a creature set free along those curves & hollows' (*PA* 319). About Olympia and Corinth, she writes 'I cannot lay my hands on any words but those that come uppermost [tonight], & it is peculiarly purposeless to belabour such a perfect image with ill fitting adjectives' (*PA* 320). She confesses that 'Such words as I have hastily & barbarously applied to Epidauros are singularly inadequate; & when I consider Mycenae, my next attempt, I might well leave a blank page' (*PA* 331). Near the end of her Turkey trip, she wonders,

> But can we make this plain on a white sheet of paper? You must remember not only the morning veil of mist, & the stately domes that shine through, & all the gold & white & blue of the town at midday, but you must also think of the little streets crowded with live people, you must remember the turbans & the veiled women, the arab horses & the yellow dogs; & finally you must return to the great mosques, & see them filled once more with a dark crowd that kneels & rises & cries its faith aloud. (*PA* 357–8)

Words on paper cannot portray the images in her brain, yet 'pile words' she must.

Constantly exercising her senses in her journal training, Stephen realises all observation is like going to Stonehenge, 'a drive which needed open eyes' (*PA* 198). In the passage about Turkey above, her eye notices colour, shape, light and movement among much else, but then she shifts from eye to ear:

> you must see all this, & hear the clamour of the street & the bazaar; in the night when the dogs even are silent, you must hear the muffled beat of a drum, & listen to a voice that neither falls nor rises, but pleads always, in earnest & in confidence, for something that is given to the faithful who spend the night in prayer. (*PA* 358)

Similarly, at the end of her Giggleswick tramp, she blends sound, sight and touch: 'I . . . listened to the queer cries & laments of plovers & curlews, wheeling close above my head, for the afternoon was almost cloudless, & singularly warm' (*PA* 307). She emphasises taste in a Greek coachman's vineyard when she experiences 'sitting on the ground & eating grapes from the tree in the open air. The skins were warmed through, & that made the globe of juice within all the sweeter & more cool' (*PA* 320–1). Highlighting touch, she contrasts 'a beautiful polished foot which you may stroke with your own soft flesh' (*PA* 319). Later, she explores a bodily experience of language: she has the

> taste of Homer . . . in my mouth. Indeed, this is the pearl of seeing things here; the words of the poets begin to sing & embody themselves. This is no pretence, moreover, as it may so easily be at home, in a London room; it needs no effort; but if statues & marble are solid to the touch, so, simply, are words resonant to the ear. (*PA* 331)

When Stephen describes the transition from summer to autumn before leaving Warboys, she focuses on smell:

> the definite touch that has spelt autumn is the subtle difference in the air. It brings with it odours of burning wood & weeds; & delicious moisture from the shaven earth; it is cleaner & more virile; it is autumn in its youth . . . . (*PA* 161)

Detailing what her senses tell her, Stephen practises an essential skill for the writer who later suspects 'scene receiving' lies at the core of her 'writing impulse' ('Sketch' 142).

Virginia Stephen opens all her senses, but her 'enormous eye' does predominate (*E4* 481). So, in Greece, on an evening climb, the air is 'blue with daylight still, though the lamps are pouring yellow into it' (*PA* 326). Or, in her 'study' of the shift from summer to fall, Stephen writes

> Where the corn stood yellow & luxuriant, there are now fields of brown clods, which leave a decided impression on ones eyes when one sees the country spread beneath one. The still days of haze & blue distance are over; a sharp wind comes racing over the plain, & brown coveys of partridges rise from the stubble that yet stands . . . . The hedges all along the roads are laden with scarlet berries . . . The little brown birds rise in a cloud & go twittering high up in the air over the brown fields. There is that mellow clearness in the air, which softens & matures the land & the mens faces who till it . . . . Brown & ruddy colours have stolen across what was green & gold; a thousand delicate vivid hues have supplanted the prevailing luxuriant green in hedge & grass & leaf & plant. (*PA* 161)

Full of such passages, Stephen's exercises affirm her reflection in 'An Artistic Party': 'Still I could have been well content to take my evening's pleasure in observation merely' (*PA* 176).

Reminding herself how observer affects observed, Virginia Stephen includes perspective in her descriptions. She may identify a simple location, such as when she says her view of the 'flowing' Downs comes '[f]rom a height' (*PA* 192). But more often, she specifies a cultural or social difference, such as noting the gap between tourist and native views in her travel journals. After admiring discoveries made on archaeological digs for days, she admits such digs seem like a 'curious mania' when a Greek man wonders why he is not digging up potatoes instead of ancient fragments (*PA* 337). She implicitly contrasts her visitor status (and writing life) with the Wilton Carpet Factory girls when she describes them, 'the youngest was twelve I suppose', as having 'the pale preoccupied look of people who sit long hours over hard work, from which their attention can never stray, though the depths of the mind are unstirred' (*PA* 201–2). In another telling commentary on her class, she writes about her second trip to Stonehenge and the farm where they stayed:

> we had the rare experience of managing entirely for ourselves – & if you want to feel a fool try to do for yourself what you have always paid a servant to do for you. I have always thought that grooms were an uneducated race – but they might have truthfully laughed at me today. Everybody ought to know how to unharness a horse – lead him to his stable – fasten him there – & provide with corn without a moments doubt. Otherwise not only the whole race of grooms but of horses likewise is for the time your superior. (*PA* 204)

Feeling detached at the Royal Academy's Annual Reception, she notes her tendency to gawk, 'constantly' shocked when she sees 'some face well known in photograph or caricature suddenly fronting me in the life' and 'wish[es] to point' (*PA* 176). Visiting Stonehenge, she articulates the impact of time on perspective:

> [the stones] have seen sunrise & moonrise over those identical swells & ridges for – I know not how many thousand years . . . . & for some perverse reason I find this a more deeply impressive temple of Religion . . . than that perfect spire [of Salisbury Cathedral] whence prayer & praise is at this very moment ascending. (*PA* 200)

Her most extensive description of context's power comes, however, near the end of her travels in Greece. She realises she is homesick for English places such as a 'great London square, where the lamps are just lit, & all the windows stand out red' at the very same time she cares little about English people or their concerns: 'Out here . . . traitors & imperialists are nothing more than names. The Times loses its stately proportions: it is the private sheet of a small colony of islanders, whose noise is effectually shut up in their prison' (*PA* 346, 345). Being elsewhere has created a longing for place, but an amused and indifferent perspective on England's politics.

Virginia Stephen frequently employs comparison, combination or paradox in her observations. So, travelling to Stonehenge, she passes 'only those few men & women to whom the openness of the fields is as natural as the enclosure of my room is to me' (*PA* 204). Or she notices an evening in Greece when 'the moon was rising before the sun had set; so you had a curious marriage of two lights; the soft silver of the moon, & the ruddiness of the sun' (*PA* 333). Or she points out that when an expression of 'serene immutability' rarely seen on living faces appears on a carved boy's 'face that is otherwise young & supple', it makes the viewer ponder beauty's immortality and 'breathe a higher air' (*PA* 322). In a contrast that also encompasses different perspectives, Stephen writes that the

> poorer people of Athens . . . have a pleasant habit of lounging up here [at the Acropolis] in the evening when their work is done; just as we stroll in our parks. They sit about on

classic marble, chatting & knitting; but they do not vulgarise the place as we Tourists must do; but rather make it human & familiar. (PA 328)

In another passage about Greece, Stephen monitors herself on the page and paradoxically describes the Bay of Salamis as seen from train windows:

Take, for instance, the little journey from Corinth to Athens; I say 'take' & then stop. For there never was a scene less easy to fit with words, though it is also true that, like all Greek things – poems & temples & statues – there is a certain form & finish even in the landscape that makes separate views of it detach themselves like pictures. (PA 333)

Observing similarities and differences, seeing unlikely combinations and acknowledging paradoxes, Stephen practises what would become Woolf's metaphor habit.

Stephen's youthful observations often blend description with commentary, sometimes subtle, sometimes blatant, on what she has observed. In a Greek hotel lobby patronised by Greeks, she notices a mother and daughter who, she imagines, are there to buy clothes. Description – 'directly [the daughter's] meal is finished, she hastens to the drawing room' – shades into interpretation – '& there alone belabours the small sharp piano with merciless fists. It is to do her bidding, you hear at every stroke.' The sketch expands further into statements about women, education and the search for a husband: 'there is no doubt that she can do her hair; but there is no reason to suppose that she can read, write or talk', and 'if you meet her, sitting by herself in the drawing room, dull, vacant, pallid, & infinitely bored, you can even pity her' since she perhaps 'cant marry into the circle above her own' and the young man from Patras with whom the mother talks 'may represent the ambition of her life' (PA 339). In Wells, her landlady has lodged theological students for thirty years and is exactly what Stephen expects, 'wavering about in the passage with clasped hands & bent shoulders, ready to welcome me, but keeping her distance'. But in an injunction to herself that occurs fairly frequently in Stephen's journal, she decides Mrs Wall 'deserves a little closer attention' (PA 377). Again, description – a woman always sewing or cleaning – shades into 'a woman of patient, deft & indefatigable industry' – passes into interpretation – 'a widow, who for 30 years has paid her rent, & kept her house going, must have come by a certain insight & tact' that we might imagine as 'shrewd wisdom' – evolves into comment on class – 'in spite of this sharpness, she is not one of the rulers' (PA 377–8). In her two-page 'Hampstead', Stephen moves from country to house, furniture and crockery, to two women and their visitor, and ultimately, to beliefs. Emphie Case, Janet Case and Margaret Davies 'together [make] an harmonious picture'. The Case sisters 'are of a piece with the house', one 'pale and fresh, and rather shabby like the furniture', and the other . . . 'fine and rather austere' with 'solid works and her Greek archaeology' filling the rooms, and Miss Davies's 'eyes have a way of growing dark, as though clouds crossed them, when she is in earnest' (CH 10–11). Stephen, observing women twenty years older than she, thus sets up a group portrait that depicts, labels, compares and evaluates. When these three women meet,

they generally surprise me by their likeness to schoolgirls. They were at [Girton] together, and they like to recall the attitude which was theirs then; they tell humorous and affectionate stories about each other; have the familiarity of a loose, well worn glove. At the same time they drop easily into what I suppose is their shop; they describe the last problem play; they discuss the last development in the fight for the franchise. It is all admirably sane, altruistic, and competent; save for a certain sharpness of edge, it might be the talk of capable members of parliament. I was struck by the conviction with which they spoke; a conviction that justice ought to be done, not to them or their children,[3] but to the whole of womankind. (CH 11)

Virginia Stephen's observations have deepened her ability to read people and construct meaning.

During her apprenticeship, then, Stephen assigns herself set pieces in which she develops, sustains and improves her skill in observing the mind, sensory data, place, affinity or paradox, and implications. Using her journals, she meets her goals: observe, ensure the ensuing mental pictures are not obliterated (PA 203–4), and 'read' for deeper significance. She also begins to revise on the spot, changing the general 'life flows past' in her Greece journal (Travel, end of second Acropolis entry, BL Add MS 61837), for example, to the specific 'people come swarming down [the streets], happy & garrulous, in crowds' (PA 326). Progressing from a self-conscious Warboys beginning in August 1899 ('I must make some mark on paper to represent so auspicious an occasion' [PA 135] to a detailed November 1909 account of a 'passionate dispute' in the divorce courts involving a crucifix, a candlestick and a bowl (CH 18), Virginia Stephen 'train[ed] the eye & hand' the essayist Virginia Woolf would need.

Using a Journal

Along with practising observation, Virginia Stephen learns to mine her journal for notes that become published work. So, a brief five-sentence journal entry on Sunday, 16 April 1905 (PA 265), becomes 'An Andalusian Inn' (E1 49–52) in the *Guardian* on 19 July 1905 and a much longer paragraph from the Cornwall 1905 journal (PA 297–8) becomes 'A Walk by Night' (E1 80–82), also in the *Guardian*, on 28 December 1905. As Stephen transforms these 'drafts' into published essays, she expands simple observations through description and detail, but also deepens significance. Travel – walking, moving from place to place, encountering the strange – becomes the basis for learning and insight. She ultimately creates a persona and uses the essay's rambling form to find meaning in personal reactions to ordinary events.

On 25 March 1905, before Virginia and Adrian Stephen left on their journey to the Iberian Peninsula, Mrs Lyttelton asked her to write about her '"personal experiences" in Spain; which I suppose I must do' (PA 256). The next morning, she makes

> a paper book ... for my Spanish Diary, by means of which I hope to pay some at least of my travelling expenses. It is a Grub St. point of view – but all the same, rather a nice little bit of writing might be made out of the sea & land. (256–7)

Upon her return, she immediately begins drafting, making 'an effort to fix some kind of sketch of our journey ... but as usual the thing wont come – & after struggling 2 hours, I produced one scored page which has nothing to do with the subject' (*PA* 268). Richmond gives her three books about Spain to review and says he wants a general article, 'wh. means I suppose that I can be as silly & amateurish as I like' – 'Journeys in Spain' was in the *TLS* on 26 May 1905 (*E1* 44–6) – and she keeps working away at her 'Spanish Sketch'. She complains it 'wont resolve itself into words' (*PA* 268–9), so she tries 'a fresh one' a few days later, focusing on Granada, and says on 3 May she has 'three dry little sketches' done, 'but whether they have any conceivable use, even as wage earners, remains to be seen' (*PA* 269–70). On 4 May, she writes a fourth sketch, and on 5 May, mentions something on Lisbon's Protestant Cemetery for the *Academy* (*PA* 270–1). The latter piece has not been traced, and although she says she writes four sketches for Mrs Lyttelton, we know about only 'An Andalusian Inn' (*PA* 268 n27).

In a letter to Violet written after her journal entry, she says they stayed at 'a little country wayside inn' where there was a fire and Spanish peasants who 'sat round and drank and stared at us, and we expected to have knives in our throats every moment'. She mentions being given one room, 'the only sleeping room – with one bed – and a canvas door between us and the family who undressed outside, and we locked our door as best we could – and lay down delicately side by side in our clothes'. She ends her story by writing 'This all happened on the edge of an arid desert, lit by stars, smelling of meadow sweet beneath the shadow of a Moorish Castle' (*L1* 187). This letter is much more descriptive and fanciful than her journal account, where, in a log of their day's travels, she mentions arriving 'at a place called Amonhon where we were to sleep', not being prepared, even after '[m]aking all allowances for Spanish hotels as we did', for a 'little white cottage, a kind of public house, by the side of a desert & a Moorish castle', and lying in their clothes on the bed in the one room available. The published essay's focus becomes what the hotelkeeper in Granada said would be awaiting them: 'a "good second class hotel"' (*PA* 265).

Virginia Stephen makes all sorts of revisions as she moves from journal to essay: for example, changing her journal's statement about their 'long tiresome journey' into her essay's statement about 'a long day's loitering through the country', a day filled with 'joltings and fatigues' (*E1* 50). But when she shifts from her journal's phrase, 'good second class hotel', to what a tourist's imagination actually does with that phrase, she moves into an investigation of language and an indirect commentary on tourism. Being foreign in another land heightens one's awareness of language, of course, one's awareness of the difficulties of human communication, and those difficulties, along with the workings of the imagination, become her essay's true subject.

The Granada hotelkeeper had had an artist's imagination (*E1* 51), Stephen notes, when he had loyally (though not morally), called their upcoming night's quarters a 'good second-class inn, where we should be made comfortable and provided with beds of the cleanest' (*E1* 49–50). The hotelkeeper's word 'sound[ing] comfortable in our ears', the travellers 'dwelt much upon the terms of this recommendation', sure they will meet with true hospitality. The

> good second-class inn became an epitome of all that is desirable in life. Here we should meet with a simple-hearted welcome; we pictured the innkeeper and his wife coming

out to greet us, eager to take our bundles and our wraps – bustling about to prepare our rooms and catch the fowl who was to make our dinner.

They imagine a night's rest between 'clean and scented sheets', a 'plain but delicious dinner', and an 'excellent breakfast' before their early start the next day (*E1* 50).

In reality, porters are surprised to see two travellers with heavy luggage get off the train at 9.30 at night, and the tourists, instead of gawking, are gawked at: a crowd 'came running to stare at us', gaping 'when we produced the careful arrangement of Spanish words in which we signified our desire for an inn'. What follows is a slapstick description of hapless tourists trying to make themselves understood: 'A sentence in a conversation-book is something of the nature of an extinct monster in a museum: only the specially initiated can tell you that it is related to the live animal.' After Spanish, French and English 'clash unprofitably', the townspeople try 'the powers of gesticulation'. An official arrives who says he can speak French, and the travellers 'joyfully' translate their request

> into that language. 'The train goes no further tonight', answered the interpreter. 'We know that, and therefore we wish to sleep here', we said. 'To-morrow morning, at 5.30.' 'But to-night, an hotel', we insisted. The gentleman who spoke French produced a pencil with an air of resignation, and wrote large and very black the figures 5 and 30. We shrugged our shoulders, and vociferated 'hotel' first in French and then in three different kinds of Spanish. The crowd had by this time made a complete circle round us, and every one was translating for the benefit of his neighbour. (*E1* 50–1)

The travellers bring out a Spanish dictionary, pointing to words, but the interpreter starts searching 'feverishly for a word of his own among the Ss and the Zs'. So the Stephens repeat 'our solitary word in the chance that it might somewhere fall upon fertile soil'. Finally, she writes, 'when we were trying to define hotel with an umbrella', a small old man appears who lays his hand on his breast and bows profoundly every time they make their request. Eventually, they follow him into a small, solitary cottage, where, after being inspected by the people sitting around a fire, they are led 'into an ante-room, in whose honour that word "hotel" had been applied to the cottage' (*E1* 50–1).

Another kind of imagination begins to work when they try to sleep. As they lie in bed, listening to '[s]craps of vehement Spanish' that 'somehow seemed to be concerned with us', they perceive Spanish as 'a fierce and bloodthirsty language' and transform the small, old, bowing man into a sinister and ominous presence who seemed determined 'we should be parted from our luggage'. When they do finally fall asleep in their clothes, 'fortified' by a chair propped up against the canvas partition 'against the murderous assault' they expect, they dream they find 'the Spanish word for "inn"' (*E1* 52).

The essay gently mocks the tourists as well as the townspeople, but underneath the humorous surface, Stephen points out crowds of humanity, all talking, yet none capable of understanding or of finding words that lead to understanding. Formal language is useless, guidebooks, dictionaries, repetition, gesticulations and good intentions do not help. The gap between signifier and signified is huge, and the gap fills with fear. Unwarranted, it turns out, since the morning's noise at the door reveals a woman holding a bowl of goat's milk (*E1* 52).

'A Walk by Night' (*E1* 80–2) grows out of a detailed Cornwall journal entry (*PA* 297–8),⁴ both ending with the same metaphor: the walkers relieved to see the road and the town's lamps at journey's end, but paradoxically, feeling 'caged' by such comforts. In both, Stephen mentions keeping to the road even when one cannot see it, a walker leading the way, a farmer calling out a greeting, and light from lamps, carts and town. She writes in her journal that 'The road when we reached it was of a vague white mist upon which our feet struck hard, even to our surprise' (297) while in the essay, she writes 'In half-an-hour's time even the white surface beneath us swam like mist, and our feet struck somewhat tentatively as though they questioned the ground' (80). In her journal, she says of the village 'all was silent though not asleep' (298); in her essay, she writes, 'The village was quiet, but not asleep, as though it lay wide-eyed in tacit conflict with the dark' (82). The journal's 'long black figures leaning against the walls quiescent' (298) that the walkers can barely see become 'forms leaning against the house-walls, men apparently, who could not sleep with that weight of night pressing against their windows, but must come forth and stretch their arms in it' (82). She mentions 'great swarms of lights which spring up in the dark where by day there is nothing' in her journal (298), which become houses that 'were sparks of fire' in her essay (82). Differences between journal and essay are not as extreme as those in the inn piece, but Stephen generalises references to particular places and people and uses much more imagery, detail and metaphoric language as essayist. She moves from a personal experience of a night walk to the human experience of being in the dark, not sure of your footing: not lost exactly, but disoriented by your surroundings.

Adrian's 'figure stalking ahead' in the journal (297) becomes 'one strode on alone, conscious of the pressure of the dark all around' in the essay (81). In her journal, Stephen does not report distance, whereas in the essay, she adds to a sense of vast space and time by noting six or seven miles 'must yet be traversed on foot' (80). The journal entry is almost all about sight, or its lack, and how darkness turns shapes vague, whereas in the essay, 'Both eyes and ears were fast sealed' and 'our voices sounded strange to each other' (81). The essayist adds mood, noting that 'insensibly we glided into such topics as are suitable to sombre and melancholy places' (81), and then says once 'accustomed to the strange element' of seeming to be in water, 'there was great peace and beauty in it' (82). A body's resistance to the 'pressure of the dark' decreases, and 'the body carried forward over the ground was some thing separate from the mind which floated away as though in a swoon' (81): 'some thing', two words. She questions language, using the word 'struck' and then observing, 'if a word implying definite action can be used of anything as indefinite as our course now became'. She parallels testing language's adequacy to their identity as walkers who occasionally 'test the ground beneath the feet in order that its substance might be proved indisputably' (81).

The journal describes a walk home, capturing the 'mystification' of walking through something familiar turned strange: we 'stepped into a vast trackless country, without mark or boundary' (297): the essay's kernel. But the essay takes more time with sensations, the mind's movements and questions, meetings with people. Plus, ship and water images do not appear in the journal but abound in the essay. Rather than step 'into a vast trackless country, without mark or boundary'

(297), the walkers in the essay leave 'the fields of the daytime' to cross 'the trackless ocean of the night' (81). The essay begins with looking out to sea with a clear vision of Atlantic waves, but within half an hour, the walkers' feet begin to 'question' the ground and 'A figure withdrawing itself some yards wavered for a moment and was then engulfed as though the dark waters of the night had closed over it, and the voice sounded like one reaching across great depths' (80). The walkers feel 'submerged', the farmer's voice bidding them good night 'recalled us as though a firm hand had grasped ours, to the shores of the world', but it takes only two strides for 'the immense flood of darkness and silence' to be over them again (81). Lamps' rays are puny 'against the immeasurable waves of darkness surging round them!'. The little village, 'anchored to the desolate earth and exposed every night, alone, to the unfathomed waters of darkness', is lonelier than any lonely ship at sea (82).[5]

In her journal, Virginia Stephen describes the strangeness of walking through a familiar landscape in the dark. In her essay, she depicts an earth 'with its infinity of detail... dissolved into ambiguous space', a sense of 'ships passing at sea' (82, 81) as people pass each other, and a 'pilgrimage' that ends with the recognition of 'great peace and beauty' in this strange element that makes it seem as 'though only the phantoms and spirits of substantial things were now abroad'. Tentative, frightened and melancholy at first, the essayist ultimately finds pleasure in a 'bathe[d] and refresh[ed]' vision, one that reveals how the solid walls and bright lamplight of home trap and blind us (82). Daytime muffles the reality in which we do not really know where we are going. Or perhaps we know full well where we are going, toward the 'unfathomed waters of darkness', because, after all, we *do* have someone striding ahead of us.

'An Andalusian Inn' and 'A Walk by Night' are seemingly simple essays about common events: finding lodgings one does not expect, walking home in the dark. But Stephen discovers that meaning accrues as she rambles and describes ordinary events. A hotelkeeper's phrase becomes a disquisition on language and a walk at night becomes a metaphor for seeing and living. Woolf learned from Stephen's discovery, going out for a pencil on a winter's night to explore empathy and its limits in 'Street Haunting' or gazing at the world during a solar eclipse and a fish in an aquarium to examine humanity's minute role in the universe in 'The Sun and the Fish'. Learning to speak from a common human position about small, ordinary, obscure things informs Woolf's later long, thoughtful pieces on books and writers as well. In these early apprenticeship essays, developed out of journal entries, Virginia Stephen distinguishes between personal and egoistic, the challenge she identifies in 'The Decay of Essay-writing', and teaches Virginia Woolf a strategy and a stance she can use throughout her career as an essayist.

Taking Notes

When it came to book reviewing, Virginia Stephen learned from all the editors and publications she wrote for, but Virginia Woolf later acknowledged direct instruction from Bruce Richmond at the *Times Literary Supplement*. According to her 1938 self, she learned from Richmond 'a lot of my craft writing;... & also

... to read with a pen & notebook, seriously' (*D5* 145). If the reading notes for her early reviews housed in the Monks House Papers at the University of Sussex are the first such notes she made, they support her later comment. Only two of the seven reviews she published before her work for the *TLS* began have notes, whereas after starting with the *TLS*, forty-two of the forty-six 1905–6 reviews have notes.[6]

One can watch Virginia Stephen learn her reviewing craft because books she reviewed are in libraries or digitised, her reading notes are in archives and her early reviews have been published – with one caveat. Any tracing must be partial because we do not have reading notes for all her early reviews, and we do not have all the steps she took between notes and publication – drafts, revisions, typescripts. But a representative sample of Stephen's early work – three 1905 reviews and two early 1906 ones, published in the *Guardian*, the *Speaker* and the *TLS* – illustrates her early writing and revising process to some degree. Henry James's *The Golden Bowl* and Edith Wharton's *House of Mirth* are canonical, whereas Beatrice Harraden's *The Scholar's Daughter* and Canon Alfred Ainger's *Lectures and Essays* are not; Ada Sterling's *A Belle of the Fifties: Memoirs of Mrs Clay of Alabama* is historical. Reading notes for *Belle of the Fifties*, *The Golden Bowl* and the *Lectures and Essays* are extensive, whereas notes for Harraden and Wharton are brief.[7] Reviews of Wharton, James and Sterling are positive, while reviews of Harraden and Ainger are negative. These reviews also tangentially touch on some of Woolf's later essay interests – Beatrice Harraden was a feminist who supported the suffragette cause, Alfred Ainger wrote about literature, and Ada Sterling wrote a memoir of a woman living through a war – and fiction strategies – Edith Wharton and Henry James could be Stephen's literary aunt and uncle.

Virginia Stephen's reading notes would not seem unusual to anyone who writes book reviews. Not following the practice of her father, who wrote in book margins, she uses a notebook; notes the date, publication venue, and title and author of book at the top of a new page; and keeps a tally of chapter and/or page numbers down the left-hand side with generally short descriptive phrases or quotations and paraphrases to the right of the page numbers. These notes reveal what she notices, her first impressions, which she then depends on in her reviews when she uses some of the quotations: neutral notes used in a straightforward way. But the notes also occasionally include comments, such as, for example, Ainger 'almost always begins by saying that he has nothing new to tell' and 'won't say anything decided "probable" ["]likely enough"' (VS notes 113, 111). In the reading notes for these review samples, she makes almost no comments about *A Belle of the Fifties*, but becomes comfortable commenting on Henry James as she proceeds further into his novel; for the other books, her ratio of comments to description ranges from about one in ten to one in three. Naturally, Stephen comments the least on Mrs Clay's memories of the Civil War era – she knows little about United States history and does research on the 1850s by consulting the *Cambridge Modern History of the United States*. Only when she tries to fit the United States into her own frame of reference, calling Washington society 'a kind of democratic Court' (VS notes 2), does she interpret at all. In the review, she makes the same move, turning Mrs Clay into 'an American version of our European "great lady"' (*E1* 17).

Studies of Virginia Woolf's writing and revising practice often focus on her cuts and a resulting loss of critique,[8] but Virginia Stephen's movement from notes to reviews reflects a more complex process. For example, Stephen's notes for *Belle of the Fifties* contain details of wartime deprivations – scarce food, leather cut off furniture to make shoes, coffee made from potatoes, wallpaper used for writing paper (VW notes 6–7) – but her review emphasises the gaiety of a certain class's pre-war social life. That choice reflects a general shift from her notes' neutrality to her review's evaluation: her focus on fashion, gossip and parties implies a critique. Stephen does not use Mrs Clay's belief that slavery 'civilises the slave' in her review (VS notes 7), but she clearly says it is 'according to Mrs Clay' that slaves had lives of 'idyllic peace and prosperity', and she calls the Southern woman's use of 'insolent' for emancipated Negroes the 'conclusion of the deposed aristocrat' (E1 20). Stephen's notes simply record Mrs Clay's descriptions and perceptions, but her review makes clear the belle's enthusiasm for the Southern cause means the reader is 'not allowed to weigh the questions which separated the two sides' (E1 20).[9]

The negative reactions Virginia Stephen has to Henry James's novel in her reading notes appear in her basically positive review, including an analogy between James and the artist who, because he knows anatomy, 'paints every bone and muscle in the human frame' (E1 23). Her impatience in the notes – 'two chapters of solid explanation always follows on any conversation or action' (E1 385) – shows up in the review when she notes the book's length three times and writes 'we suffer from a surfeit of words' (E1 22–3). She was not afraid to call James 'vague and difficult' in her notes (E1 386) or to say he lacked genius in her review (E1 23–4). Stephen changes notes about Edith Wharton's novel being 'too long and minute' (VS notes 69) into a positive yet critical comment: the writer has 'spared no pains to make her delineation exact' (E1 67–8). The reader knows what to expect.

In her Ainger review, Virginia Stephen begins to draw the line between the nineteenth- and twentieth-century views of things that Virginia Woolf would later emphasise, and she carves out what not to do in essays. But the young reviewer does not use her notes about Ainger's claim to have no special knowledge or his attempt to write criticism from the average reader's point of view (VS notes 108). She notes his 'definition of criticism' (VS notes 119) but does not copy this passage from the same page: 'When we read we lose much by not standing side by side with the writer.... To understand some writers we must change our planet and wait patiently till we are acclimatized' (Ainger 2 331). Ideas like these appear later, though, when Woolf positions herself as an amateur (E4 19) and articulates her view that readers should read first as fellow-workers in 'How Should One Read a Book?' (E5 573).

In her notes for Harraden's *The Scholar's Daughter*, Stephen seems unaware of the similarity between her own life and Harraden's motherless Geraldine, whose father is engaged in dictionary making. But her review acknowledges that '[t]he picture of a girl, young, beautiful, and gifted, brought up solely among learned scholars who are preparing a colossal dictionary of the English language attracts attention at the outset' (E1 92). Stephen's review of Harraden's novel is critical – 'if we consider the book as a serious novel its superficiality irritates us, or if we take it as a short story we are wearied by the protracted explanations' (E1 92) –

but her notes are more direct: 'theres no one to care for after 10 minutes absurdly unreal. She has not realised her characters. Obvious Emotions a very weak novel' (VS notes 135–6). Stephen softens that criticism in her review, suggesting

> Miss Harraden might have concentrated her powers upon the sufficiently amusing intricacies of the plot and turned out a well-filled short story, or, had she chosen to expound the characters more elaborately, she might have given us an interesting study of the conflict of one temperament with another. (E1 92)

She also ends with a compliment and a comment about potential:

> If it is said that in spite of this it is easy to read *The Scholar's Daughter* with interest and amusement it is obvious how much more might have been expected of the writer than she has given us here. (E1 92)

Early in her book-reviewing career, Virginia Stephen writes to Madge Vaughan that her 'real delight in reviewing is to say nasty things',[10] but that she has to be 'respectful' (L1 166–7). In her 1905 review of W. L. Courtney's *The Feminine Note in Fiction*, Stephen is both respectful and nasty when she ends the review this way: 'Mr Courtney has given us material for many questions such as these, but his book has done nothing to prevent them from still remaining questions' (E1 16). Later, Virginia Woolf would worry her 'tea-table training' caused her to take a 'sidelong approach' ('Sketch' 150). Such statements suggest that changes made between reading notes and reviews stem from internal censorship (tea-table training) or external oppression (editorial intervention) (Brosnan 58–68). However, Stephen follows her letter to Vaughan with one to Nelly Cecil on 22 December 1904, in which she says 'I hate the critical attitude of mind because all the time I know what a humbug I am, and ask myself what right I have to dictate whats good and bad, when I couldn't, probably, do as well myself!' (L1 167), and Woolf follows her 'tea-table training' remark with an 'on the other hand': she realises her 'surface manner' allowed her 'to slip in things that would be inaudible if one marched straight up and spoke out loud' ('Sketch' 150). Such statements imply she distrusts her nasty impulses, expresses respect out of self-awareness and says what she wants in a non-confrontational way. Repression alone cannot explain all her revisions.[11]

Stephen's reading notes reveal she is impatient and quick to judge, but her reviews indicate she knows that. For example, in her notes for Louise Kenny's *The Red-Haired Woman*, she writes: 'quite shapeless. no characterisation . . . stories wh. lead nowhere . . . no pretence of telling the story . . . Her humans seem dead failures . . . No notion of writing a novel' (VS notes 105, 107). As a reviewer, she consciously steps back, but without sacrificing her basic judgement. She writes:

> The writer seems to have absorbed a strange miscellany of facts, legends, and theories, which she has poured out without any regard to form or coherency. Why, we ask, did Miss Kenny burden herself with the pretence of a plot or the pretence of characters? For we are constantly tantalized by signs of an original mind stored with interesting knowledge struggling to express itself in an uncongenial medium. A patient reader, however, will find much that illuminates the Irish character in the labyrinths of Miss Kenny's novel. (E1 79)

Readers of 'Two Irish Novels' know Miss Kenny's work has been sharply criticised – we do not need the damning phrases in Stephen's notes – but Stephen also includes some praise and blames the problem on genre choice, not on the author's intelligence, a strategy allowing the author to consider other possibilities for later work. Stephen also implies a critique of her own reading when she imagines a patient reader unlike herself. As a young reviewer, she slowly and consciously trains herself to follow the reading process she later recommends in 'How Should One Read a Book?' – read first as a friend, then as a judge. Furthermore, she may remove personal attacks, but she does not say one thing in her notes and something entirely different in her reviews.

True, she sometimes tones her notes down. But something besides 'tea-table training' or editorial intervention contributes to McNeillie's description of Woolf as a generally 'generous reviewer' (xvi). Maybe Virginia Stephen learns from Ainger's suggestions about reading and reviewing. Maybe she just does what novices learn to do: create a reviewing persona that allows her to be herself and communicate her judgements yet acknowledge another writer's efforts and convey professional respect. Stephen's reviewing practice reveals a typical arc for a young person learning to negotiate between the approval of the reader/teacher/editor and the integrity of one's self/ideas/voice. Or maybe Stephen's lack of a teacher/student relationship in her apprenticeship leads her to create such a relationship in her reviews. *Belle* is an American memoir about a time long past; James is a well-established great author; Wharton is American; Ainger is dead – they do not need instruction. Indeed, Stephen plays the student to these authors – discovering how Sterling's memoir uncovers women who 'did really exist beneath [a] mass of artificialities' (*E1* 19); thumbing her nose at the great James when she comments that genius would have dissolved the fatigues of reading him, but genius 'is precisely what we do not find' (*E1* 23–4); noticing how Wharton leaves the moral up to the reader (*E1* 68); and learning from Ainger that 'certain defects are almost inherent in the [lecture's] form' (*E1* 83–4). But in the reviews of Harraden and Kenny, the living, writing women in England and Ireland, Stephen plays the teacher she asks for in 'Reviewing', answering their underlying cry for advice, saying precisely why she dislikes their work and noting how flaws might be addressed – in effect, putting her 'well-stored mind' and 'other standards' at their disposal (*E6* 203).

Comparing reading notes to reviews during Stephen's apprenticeship provides evidence of her growing ability to present her views with professional respect, avoid the slating noted in contemporary accounts, and be both the sympathetic and judging reader Woolf later describes in 'How Should One Read a Book?'. Thus, Virginia Stephen does not bow to Henry James in her *Golden Bowl* review. Yes, he is a great writer, he deserves more words than she has,[12] and she remains basically positive. But Stephen points out his flaws, firmly stating he does not have the genius to pull it off and complaining about the novel's level of detail and length.[13] Stephen never takes one stand in her notes and another in her reviews. She may soften her criticism or reconsider it within a different frame; she may add something encouraging or kind to a negative review or something critical or pointed to a positive review; she may mute the strength or intensity of first impressions recorded in her notes. But she never undercuts her integrity or conceals her judgements – the reader knows when she likes a book, when she does not, and why.

Reviewing Popular Fiction

Perhaps most important to Virginia Stephen's growth as a writer, she developed independence, a stance and a voice of her own while she reviewed popular fiction. As part of paying her apprenticeship dues, Stephen read and reviewed five collections of short stories and one set of novellas by popular authors and fifty of what we would now call popular novels. When she writes about the *TLS* in her journal on 14 March 1905 that 'They pelt me now' (*PA* 252), she exaggerates a bit since her reviewing career was just getting under way, but the statement soon became accurate. She writes to Nelly Cecil on 10 November 1905, for example, that *The Times* 'sends me one novel every week; which has to be read on Sunday, written on Monday, and printed on Friday' (*L1* 211–12). In fact, three of her reviews appeared in the 17 November 1905 edition of the *TLS*. Two years after her journal comment, she writes to Violet Dickinson that 'The old Times sends me a novel every week' (*L1* 280), so they continued to pelt her with current fiction. Between March 1905, when Stephen felt pelted by novels, and the moment in May 1908 when she felt secure enough in her *TLS* position to tell Bruce Richmond she refused to review current fiction anymore (*L1* 331; Rosenbaum 340), she averaged three pieces a month, writing seventeen essays and reviewing 101 books, more than half of which were light fiction.

It has become commonplace to categorise these popular works as 'dross' (A. Curtis 150), 'ephemeral novels' (Rosenbaum 172; May 51) or 'mediocre' (Mepham 21; Rosenbaum 341). Minor and mediocre they may be, but an examination of the 1904–9 *Guardian*, the 1905–6 *Academy*, 1906–7 *Speaker* and the 1905–8 *TLS*, the years Stephen reviewed popular fiction for those papers, shows that twenty-five of the fifty-six books she reviewed were covered in two of the papers, eleven were reviewed in three of them, and three were reviewed in all four. Given that almost six novels a day were published in 1906 (P. Keating 33) and that many novels must not have been reviewed at all, these reviews in common suggest a fairly high level of agreement among literary editors about which novels, or at least which authors, deserved a review.[14] Some authors were simply 'in the air',[15] and editors themselves read. In a letter to Mary Gladstone on 16 October 1906, for example, Mrs Lyttelton praises Mary Cholmondeley's *Prisoners-fast bound in Misery and Iron*, briefly compares it to *Red Pottage*, mentions liking and reviewing the American Winston Churchill's *Coniston*, though others are bored by its length, and is disappointed by Anthony Hope's new book (Letter, BL Add MS 46235). Stephen did not review Cholmondeley's work but she knew it, based on a quotation she uses in a letter to Violet in May 1907 (*L1* 294); she reviewed *Coniston* for the *TLS* (*E1* 115–16); and she reviewed a book by Hope in September 1907 ('Tales of Two People', *E6* 336–7).

Although labelled ephemeral, all the popular fiction Virginia Stephen reviewed is listed in WorldCat, with some books available in only three or four libraries. Almost half can be read on Google.Books, while a few have only one hit on

Google, Stephen's review. Seventeen of the authors are in the *ODNB* (albeit one as part of his wife's entry),[16] and eleven have primary sources in Gale's database, Literary Reference Center Plus. The most frequent word used in the *ODNB* entries for these authors is 'prolific', applied to James Owen Hannay (writing under the name George A. Birmingham) (Bellasis and Taylor), Dorothea Gerard (Perkins), Gilbert Parker (Atkinson), W. Pett Ridge (Johnson), and Margaret Campbell Long (Malpezzi). Long was excruciatingly poor as a child and continued to support her mother and sister long after she left home; she wrote as Marjorie Bowen, Joseph Shearing (mysteries), George Preedy (historical novels), John Winch and Robert Paye (children's literature), as well as Margaret Campbell (in her autobiography). These pseudonyms helped her separate her creative personalities (Malpezzi), but they also ensured a steady income stream. Algernon Gissing, however, published twenty-five novels and never earned more than a 'mere pittance' for them; one of his sons 'equated his father's clinging to unsuccessful novel-writing with a curse on the family' (Coustillas).

Some *ODNB* biographers, however, do not stop at popular, successful or prolific. Patrick Maume calls Shan F. Bullock 'undervalued', Clare Taylor says some of Anthony Hope's fiction beyond *The Prisoner of Zenda* 'deserves reassessment', and Frances Malpezzi cites several supporters of Bowen 'who believe she should be taken seriously as a literary writer'. And then there is Mrs Hamilton Synge, whose *A Supreme Moment* Stephen unequivocally likes (E1 92–3). It reads easily, has a heroine who slowly recognises another self underneath her rigidly controlled exterior, and then understands the same is true of others, including her brother Bertram:

> 'Have I ever really known Bertram?' she thought to herself. She had lived with him all her life, but did she know him? The man she knew, who liked a well-considered entrée, and regular hours, and the history of the Middle Ages, was not all there was of Bertram. (307)

Mrs Synge is not in the *ODNB* but is part of Montana history because she travelled to Yellowstone National Park around 1890 and published *A Ride through Wonderland* in 1892 as Georgina Synge. In other words, though we may dismiss these writers now, during their lifetimes, many of them had good reputations and some measure of fame.

In her current fiction reviews, Virginia Stephen sometimes, one assumes unknowingly, fully or partially agreed with other reviewers, whether the assessment was positive or negative. (In my review sampling, her reviews appeared before the others did.) So, for example, the *Guardian* reviewer, the *Academy* reviewer and Stephen all agree Beatrice Harraden could do a lot better than she does in *The Scholar's Daughter*. Stephen and the *Academy* reviewer both suggest another genre would have been more conducive to the story, and the *Guardian* reviewer and Stephen both note how easy the novel is to read. From the beginning, though, Stephen went her own way, disagreeing with other reviewers. For example, in one of her earliest reviews, she calls W. Pett Ridge 'an open-eyed and interested observer' whose short stories, 'if stories they can be called', are no more than of 'ephemeral interest' (E1 11). The *Academy* reviewer, however, calls Ridge a 'great artist' who has produced a collection of 'real tales of the people' even better than his previously strong work (7 January 1905 14). The *Guardian* reviewer of W. E. Norris's *Barham of Beltana* 'upholds the author's well-deserved reputation' and thus commends it (3 June 1905 755), but both the *Academy* reviewer and Stephen are more tepid. The *Academy* reviewer knows that Norris's large following will welcome this book, but whether it is 'worth reading is another matter. It has all the drawbacks and the advantages of a strictly non-alcoholic beverage' (11 March 1905 240), and Stephen concludes, the novel 'will not sadden; it will not excite; but it will provide an hour or two of healthy entertainment; and that, we imagine, is a result with which the author would declare himself content' (*E*1 37). Indicating she occasionally read other reviewers of works she reviewed, though perhaps only after she wrote her own, she writes to Violet in May 1907 that she had reviewed Marjorie Bowen's *The Glen o' Weeping* in the *TLS* and 'damned it' – she writes that the 'slightly grandiloquent magnificence' of Bowen's prose provides 'a rich cloak, but it does not take the place of bones and flesh' (*E*1 139) – 'and now all the other reviewers are exclaiming, and there is a 2nd edition' (*L*1 295).

As she grows in skill, Virginia Stephen more confidently mixes criticism and praise. In these early reviews, her nuggets of praise seem like an encouraging gesture to writers doing the hard work she has begun to realise goes into writing fiction, a reflection of how conscious she was of being unpublished herself (*L*1 167) rather than a feature of a 'tea-table' manner.[17] So, for example, the *Guardian* reviewer of Louise Kenny's *The Red-Haired Woman* thinks it is a 'remarkable book' with lifelike characters and vivid atmosphere (20 December 1905 2172), whereas Stephen thinks the characters and plot are a pretence and that finding the Irish character in Kenny's novel requires a patient reader. But she also says Kenny's work reflects a struggle between 'an original mind stored with interesting knowledge' and 'an uncongenial medium' (*E*1 79). In other words, Kenny's problem may be the genre she chose. The *Academy* reviewer of Ella Fuller Maitland's *Blanche Esmead* wonders if Maitland really believes refined women are as 'defenceless and incapable' as portrayed in this novel (7 April 1906 336), whereas Stephen notes how content Maitland is with the conventional patterns of village life, how 'facile and frivolous' the style is, and how shallow the people and plot are. But she also says that 'within its limits – the limits of a fashionable drawing-room – this is a graceful and entertaining novel, and the action is swift and sparkling from first to last' (*E*1 95–6). The *Guardian* reviewer says G. A. Birmingham's historical novel *The Northern Iron* is 'full of adventure, pathos, and humour, for, indeed, Mr Birmingham is an artist' (29 January 1908 187), whereas Stephen criticises how loosely held together the different scenes are before noting the value of the book lies elsewhere, 'in the broad view it gives of the mass of the struggle'. She says Mr Birmingham writes, 'if not with brilliancy, still with a thorough grasp of his time and an enthusiasm for his subject which interest and satisfy' (*E*6 347). Stephen calls Stanley Weyman's *Chipping* a 'safe undertaking' because you can trust that you are in 'able hands', but thinks the novel's political conflict overshadows individuals' characters (*E*6 301). The novel is memorable as a picture of a crowd rather than of separate people, but '[n]ovels that urge you along with them as *Chipping* does are not so common that you can afford to quarrel with the means by which they do it' (*E*6 302). The *Guardian* reviewer of Maarten Maartens's *The New Religion: A Modern Novel* yawned over the various characters and incidents (25 September 1907 1564), but Stephen writes, 'We have not believed in the loves or the diseases; nor have we profited by the satire; but we have been very much entertained, and wit and fantasy are good, call them what you will' (*E1* 149). She makes fine distinctions, saying that Anthony Hope 'knows his craft; and the present volume [of sixteen stories] will satisfy all who admire that achievement; and will cause even those who distrust it to applaud the ingenuity and good workmanship with which it is done' (*E6* 337). She seems scrupulously fair, often wanting more from writers but acknowledging the limitations the authors themselves have set and admitting that, within those limitations, works succeed.

Virginia Stephen can, however, tilt toward the negative or be totally devastating. The *Guardian* reviewer of Gilbert Parker's *The Weavers* has some of the same reservations about it as Stephen does – it is 'difficult reading' and 'over-conscientious[ly]' wrought (23 October 1907 1760) – but says we should be thankful for Parker's 'minute and conscientious labour' (1760). Stephen, on the other hand, though admitting it seems ungrateful to say this about such an earnest book, says it anyway: 'it is not easy to follow this long drama with any keen interest or to feel that the people in it are any more sensitive than the props that sustain old-fashioned draperies' (*E6* 340). The *Guardian* reviewer of Bak's *Outrageous Fortune* calls the novel 'pleasant reading' and says it 'seems to contain the promise of better things' (23 October 1907 2761). But Stephen writes:

> The only reason why this conscientious work can be read, for it is neither witty nor subtle, is for the sake of that prosaic good sense which gives it the appearance of truth and solidity, on the surface at any rate. You derive from it that sense of instruction in unimportant matters which you get by looking from the train window at a flat stretch of the countryside. (*E6* 343)

By 1908, Virginia Stephen has expanded beyond evaluation to explore bigger questions: the nature of plot, generic demands, literary reception. The *Guardian* reviewer of H. A. Hinkson's *Father Alphonsus* calls it ground-breaking, a 'wonderfully clever and vivid tale' and 'a real work of art' (3 June 1908 936); Stephen says it has the sort of merit that 'implies a capacity for better work' (*E6* 356) because Hinkson tackles an ambitious theme, the conflict between flesh and spirit in a priest's life. But the plot is familiar, conventional, inevitable and sensational, making the strife 'unconvincing' (*E6* 357). Although she agrees with the other reviewer about Hinkson's ability to portray ordinary people and Irish life, she deplores his use of 'sudden dramatic action which always comes at the right moment' to change everything (*E6* 357). (History has agreed with Stephen; Peter van de Kamp, the *ODNB* biographer of Kathleen Tynan, notes her husband 'produced mediocre historical adventure novels'.) The *Guardian* reviewer of K. L. Montgomery's *Colonel Kate* calls it an 'excellent and powerful story', whose human interest, not historical background, drives the reader to finish it (20 May 2008 851–2), but in her review, Stephen looks at the larger issue of the imaginative restrictions the historical novelist willingly accepts. How does, in fact, a novelist capture a world where 'the customs are different from ours and the speech is only to be guessed at' (*E6* 358)? Is using 'obsolete or Gaelic words' that need translation in notes the best way to recapture a bygone era (*E6* 359)? The *Guardian* reviewer of Marjorie Bowen's *The Sword Decides* focuses on a falling off since her book *The Viper of Milan* (17 June 1908 1034), whereas Stephen examines the phenomenon of blurbs and the nature of Bowen's popularity (*E6* 362–4).

It can be tempting to regret the years Virginia Stephen spent reviewing so much now-forgotten fiction. But under the pressure of reviewing dozens of popular authors, she learned to trust her own perceptions and developed the point of view, critical vocabulary and insights that would make Virginia Woolf's essays so delightful. Derwent May points out, for example, that Virginia Stephen 'almost invariably found something memorable to say' about the popular works the *TLS* felt obligated to notice briefly (51). As Stephen gained more independence, she also honed her aesthetic principles and imagined how her future fiction might differ from what she was reading. Reading and reviewing popular fiction gave her dual training, shaping both her non-fiction's persona and her fiction's aesthetic standards. Being pelted, however aggravating, boring or pressure-filled at the time, turned out to be useful, ensuring Stephen learned her craft.

Building on her homeschooling, concurrently teaching at Morley and reviewing books, Virginia Stephen practised on her own and with editors. She read, observed, consistently took notes, wrote, revised and wrote some more: exercises, personal essays, travel pieces and reviews. Without training or much experience in receiving feedback, Stephen increasingly trusted her own assessments as she learned how to write a review, gained skill in capturing a book's complexity and learned how to praise and criticise. Taking her place in a long tradition of reviewers and writers who both learned from editors and pushed back against them, Stephen developed her own approach at the same time she met the expectations of the assignments she was given. The practice, the almost weekly repetition, the reward of seeing her hard work in print – all of it taught Virginia Stephen not only the 'knack' of writing for newspapers but lessons she would use as the essayist Virginia Woolf.

Notes

1. For this discussion, I use this representative sample: the 1899 'A Chapter on Sunsets' (*PA* 155–6) and a farewell to summer (*PA* 160–2); some 1903 pieces, 'An Artistic Party' (*PA* 175–7), 'The Downs' (*PA* 191–2), 'Stonehenge' (*PA* 198–200), 'The Wilton Carpet Factory' (*PA* 200–2) and 'Stonehenge Again' (*PA* 203–5); a 1906 segment from her Giggleswick journal (*PA* 306–7); a 1906 travel journal on Greece and Turkey (*PA* 317–62); a 1908 description of Mrs Wall (*PA* 377–8); and the 1909 'Hampstead' (*CH* 10–11).
2. Although she kept notebooks all her life, she did not seem to carry one at all times or take notes on the spot, though entries often sound that way.
3. All three were unmarried, with no children; perhaps relatives' children? all children?
4. Because the distinction between the journal and the essay is clear in this discussion, I use only page numbers in the citations.
5. In a paper presented at the Thirtieth Annual International Conference on Virginia Woolf, Diana Royer noted that throughout the essay, Stephen uses 'metaphors of the sea to convey the insignificance of humanity amidst the forces of nature' (6).

6. We have only Virginia Stephen's 1905–6 reading notes and one set from 1907. Given the numerous reading notebooks catalogued by Brenda Silver, however, Stephen may have taken other early notes that did not survive.
7. All subsequent in-text references to these notes cite 'VS notes' except for those for *The Golden Bowl*, which cite McNeillie's transcription of her reading notes in *Essays 1*, Appendix III (381–8). In Virginia Stephen's notebook, see the reading notes for Sterling's *Belle*, 1–9; James's *The Golden Bowl*, 10–22; Kenny's *The Red-Haired Woman*, 104–7; Wharton's *House of Mirth*, 68–9; Ainger's *Lectures and Essays*, 108–19; and Harraden's *The Scholar's Daughter*, 135–6.
8. See my survey of such studies ('Readin" 168–9).
9. James Stephen (1758–1832) fought against Britain's slave trade and Leslie Stephen supported the North, criticising *The Times* for its slanted Civil War coverage in *The 'Times' on the American War: An Historical Study*.
10. Stephen's practice belies her words, suggesting she exaggerates for her recipient's amusement. Waller quotes Stephen's letters to describe her reviewing practice, implying they accurately reflect it (152–3), but his bibliography suggests he did not consult her reviews.
11. Brosnan may overstate the case when she suggests oppressive editorial policies 'demanded' Virginia Stephen speak in a certain way (61). Today's writing teachers advise students to study publications and consider audience when revising work; learning to 'develop a voice that managed to keep the vocabulary and tone of the journal yet import her own meanings' is exactly the skill Stephen was learning (Brosnan 61; see also 67–8).
12. Brosnan criticises Mrs Lyttelton for 'deem[ing] 7–800 words equally sufficient to deal with the likes of *The Son of Royal Langbrith* . . . and Henry James' (62), but Mrs Lyttelton could not have predicted our current canonical hierarchy, especially since Howells was, as McNeillie notes, 'one of the leading literary figures of his generation in the United States' (5 n2); at the time, he was quite as well known as James, if not more. See Rachel Cohen, Chapters 2, 4 and 6, on Howells, his work and his influence.
13. If Henry James is the great man Virginia Woolf blames for inhibiting her young self's thought in 'Professions for Women', perhaps she remembers something from the portion she had to cut for length reasons. Or perhaps she conflates that early time with her later fury at not being able to use the word 'lewd' in a James review for the *TLS*. Or most likely, her metaphor's individual represents a composite of oft-repeated experiences with real mental barriers.
14. Further examination of all the runs of the other papers Stephen reviewed for between 1904 and 1912, including *Cornhill* and the *Nation*, would almost certainly bring more reviews in common to light. Checking other reviewing periodicals such as *Bookman* for agreement (or disagreement) among literary editors would also be instructive.
15. Multiple reviews also occur of more well-known authors reviewed by Virginia Stephen, such as Henry James and Edith Wharton, and of other genres, such as biography (Arthur Irwin Dasent's life of his uncle, John Delane), memoir (*The Belle of the Fifties*), diaries (*Journal of Lady Holland*), art history (C. L. Hind's *The Post-Impressionists*) and essays (Canon Ainger's *Lectures and Essays*).
16. The popular fiction writers in the *ODNB* are: Rose Macaulay, Stanley J. Weyman, Dorothea Gerard, Horace Annesley Vachell, Algernon Gissing, Jane Barlow, Gilbert Parker, Anthony Hope [Anthony Hope Hawkins], Shan Fadh Bullock, George A. Birmingham [James Owen Hannay], Mrs Edmee Elizabeth Monica de la Pasture Dashwood [E. M. Delafield], Beatrice Harraden, Marjorie Bowen [Margaret Gabrielle Campbell Long], Will Pett Ridge, Robert Hugh Benson, Elizabeth Robins and H. A. Hinkson (as part of his wife's, Kathleen Tynan's, entry). Some

might question Rose Macaulay's being on this list, but Stephen reviewed her first novel.
17. As Rosenbaum puts it, she can be critical, though 'not often dismissive' and 'usually able to rescue something of value from wrecks of books' (172).

Chapter 13

Outcomes: Writing for Newspapers

'[L]onging to begin work' as she recovers from a breakdown in September 1904 (*L1* 144),[1] Virginia Stephen uses her editors' assignments and guidance over the next eight years to learn the 'knack' of writing for papers and move from being a novice to an expert book reviewer and essayist. By the end of 1911, she has moved to 38 Brunswick Square with Adrian, welcomed Leonard Woolf into the household,[2] and written and revised, though not for the last time, her *Melymbrosia* manuscript, which would become *The Voyage Out*. That year saw three essays, too, one of them two columns in the three-columned *TLS* on the Duke and Duchess of Newcastle-upon-Tyne, whom she would revisit as Virginia Woolf. From now on, her non-fiction weaves itself through all her work as a writer, sometimes prominently, sometimes not, but never absent.

By the time she writes 'The Novels of George Gissing', her last review essay as Virginia Stephen before her thirtieth birthday in 1912, she has produced a large body of work: between 7 December 1904 and 11 January 1912, Virginia Stephen published 158 book reviews, review essays, and essays, according to Andrew McNeillie, B. J. Kirkpatrick and Stuart N. Clarke (see Appendix 5, a chronological, descriptive table). Some doubtful or untraced periodical contributions also exist.[3] She published the most in 1905 and 1907, thirty-seven pieces each, successfully breaking into newspapers at the same time as she was teaching at Morley. She reveals her enthusiasm for the writing life in a letter to Violet Dickinson on 1 October 1905: 'Writing is a divine art, and the more I write and read the more I love it,' and then adds she hopes Mrs Lyttelton will 'send more work' (*L1* 209). She published twenty-five reviews and essays in 1906 and thirty in 1908. Never shunning hard work,[4] she did publish fewer book reviews and essays as she dedicated more time to drafting her novel: seventeen in 1909, five in 1910, three in 1911, and one in 1912 before marrying Leonard.

Fifteen of her 158 published pieces were essays – travel, personal, or responses to music or literature, 9.5 per cent – and 143 were reviews, 90.5 per cent, fifteen of those being review essays.[5] As an apprentice, Stephen reviewed several genres, learning how other authors used and challenged genre and its demands.[6] Her only review of a poet's work appeared in 'Thomas Hood' (*E1* 159–64) when she evaluated his *Poems* in the context of his biography, though comments about poetry also appear in reviews focused on other genres, such as 'The Poetic Drama', 'Poets' Letters' and 'Shelley and Elizabeth Hitchener'. She reviewed a performance of *Lysistrata* and nineteen plays spread out over three drama reviews, 'The Poetic Drama', 'Some Poetic Plays' and 'Some Poetical Plays', 2.8 per cent of her total. Sixty-nine of her 143 reviews were of fiction, 48.2 per cent, eight on short story collections (5.6 per cent) and sixty-one on novels (42.6 per cent). Despite feeling pelted by contemporary fiction, Stephen reviewed slightly more non-fiction than fiction, 49 per cent, ranging over various *kinds* of non-fiction: essays (six, 4.2 per cent), memoir (ten, 7 per cent), diaries (five, 3.5 per cent), letters (thirteen, 9.1 per cent), biography (twenty-three, 16.1 per cent), history (nine, 6.3 per cent), travel (six, 4.2 per cent), and literary, social or cultural criticism (twelve, 8.4 per cent).[7]

Tangibly productive, Virginia Stephen also learned intangible lessons during her reviewing apprenticeship. She increased her knowledge of genre and placed what she knew about literary tradition against and within a contemporary context. She began to express her aesthetic principles and state her cultural attitudes. She also clarified the writer/reader relationship for herself, gaining an understanding of the writing process and emerging with a clear stance and sense of audience. Virginia Stephen's apprenticeship as a book reviewer, combined with her homeschooling and teaching, meant Virginia Woolf would become an inclusive educator essayist who saw her readers as reading and learning with her.

Learning the 'Knack': Virginia Stephen's Reviews and Essays

Although Virginia Stephen's apprenticeship as a reviewer and essayist cannot be easily reduced to a linear path, it falls into roughly three stages, early (1904–5), middle (1906–7) and late (1908–12).[8] She publishes forty works as a novice, three in late 1904 and thirty-seven in 1905. In them, she calls on what she already knows about literary tradition, gender and genre to clarify her cultural attitudes and aesthetic stance. During her middle practitioner period, while her Morley teaching is in full swing, Virginia Stephen writes sixty-two reviews and essays in which she extends her cultural analysis, strengthens her aesthetic positions, and becomes aware of the review and the essay *as* genres; she begins to chart her critical path. More skilled and confident, she uses her knowledge of literary history; delves into genre complexities; values character development, narrative's power and language's nature; praises reader engagement; and articulates her dislike of moral instruction. During her last five expert years, Virginia Stephen receives six declarations of love, ends her teaching career, begins working on a novel in earnest, and writes fifty-six essays and reviews, most in 1908–9. She reviews mainly non-fiction after being 'pelted' by fiction in her early and middle stages and being absorbed by fictional and autobiographical narratives in her middle stage. In these later essays and reviews, many of them longer, Stephen examines the construction of literary history, identifies genre repercussions and solidifies aesthetic positions. She also sharpens a reviewing method of her own as her cultural emphases and critical habits become stronger. Honing her essay writing craft even as she begins drafting her first novel, Virginia Stephen matures, extends her range and practises what she has learned as a reviewer, assembling the attitudes, strategies and skills she would later use as Virginia Woolf, essayist.

The thirty-five reviews and six essays examined below span the three stages of Virginia Stephen's development, represent a quarter of her output and illustrate her training's intangible outcomes: what she learned as she read widely, explored multiple genres and practised her critical stance as a reader.

Literary tradition

Virginia Stephen could immediately use and comment on the literary tradition in her apprentice work because of her wide reading, but her reviewing also taught her how literary history could fail and how it could expand. In 'Literary Geography' and 'The Value of Laughter', she displays her grasp of a literary tradition that includes Victorian Britain and the Greeks. In the first, Stephen distinguishes between the fictional places of Dickens and Thackeray that live in our brains and the places the writers inhabited. Her remarks on two books about the Victorian authors include discussion of Scott, Hardy and Meredith, and she reminds readers of a women's literary tradition when she refers to Brontë Country, hinting the canon of writers deserving such attention could be enlarged (E1 32–3). 'The Value of Laughter' rests on Aristotle's *Poetics* (Rosenbaum 158–9), a work whose clarity about 'the rudiments' of literature and criticism had impressed Stephen (PA 240–1). By bringing in Shakespeare and Bunyan, and defining tragedy as 'pictur[ing] men as greater than they are', comedy as 'represent[ing] the failings of human nature', and humour as 'strik[ing] a mean between the two' (E1 58), she implicitly claims Aristotle and the Greeks as part of her British literary tradition just as male writers did.

Stephen also reveals her ease with British literary history in 'Trafficks and Discoveries', a review of Walter Raleigh's *The English Voyages of the Sixteenth Century*, a study of Hakluyt's *Principal Navigations, Voyages, and Discoveries of the English Nation*; 'William Allingham' about the poet's diary; and 'Poet's Letters' about Percy Lubbock's selection of Elizabeth Barrett Browning letters and excerpts. She focuses on Raleigh's linking of Elizabethan poets to Elizabethan voyagers and claims the sailors' writing is poetic (E1 121–2); makes sure we share Allingham's walks and overhear his talk about works by Leigh Hunt, Carlyle, Dickens, Browning, Tennyson, Swinburne, Whistler, Whitman, Shakespeare and George Eliot (E1 155–6); and glances at John Ruskin, Joseph Arnould, Alfred Domett, Shakespeare and, of course, Robert Browning in her determination to cut through the too-familiar story of Elizabeth Barrett Browning's room-bound youth to a clear awareness of 'a thing that did really happen and that had an immense but calculable influence on the victim's life' and work (E1 102).

Constance Hill's attempt at literary history in *Maria Edgeworth and Her Circle* provoked one of Virginia Stephen's most negative reviews, however. Neither Hill's rationale nor her terminology pass muster. Hill does not justify her book's existence through a discussion of Edgeworth's novels or their reception, so does not encourage readers to read or reread them. Undercutting the book's rationale even further, Hill calls other women writers who simply lived and wrote at the same time a 'circle' and exaggerates their impact on Edgeworth. Yes, Edgeworth knew and visited Joanna Baillie, but would she have put the great beauty Mme Récamier in her circle (E1 316)? Worse, Hill relies on Mme de Staël for descriptions of London and Mme d'Arblay (Frances Burney) for 'faded exclamations' about Waterloo rather than finding out what Edgeworth observed about the peasants living on her estate (E1 317). Finally, Hill's catalogue of clothes, possessions and furniture does not clarify or add to readers' knowledge of Edgeworth's times or works; rather, it leaves readers with 'visual impressions – of turbans and chariots with nothing inside them' (E1 316).

Books by Robert Ross and Walter Jerrold, on the other hand, taught Virginia Stephen to consider typical absences in traditional literary history: any era's various purposes and styles, any era's many publishing writers. When Robert Ross, in 'Masques and Phases', says a literary movement is 'going on among us' even if we cannot see it, she suggests that only when we look back at the history of literature does it seem to fall into literary movements motivated 'by a single aim', whereas 'the more one reads of books the more one distrusts the history of them'. More likely, she argues, books then, just like books now, are 'written in separate garrets, from different points of view', so any 'classifications' should be made only 'from a height and with very nervous fingers' (E6 370). Reviewing Walter Jerrold's biography of Thomas Hood, she notes, 'A student of letters is so much in the habit of striding through the centuries from one pinnacle of accomplishment to the next that he forgets all the hubbub that once surged round the base' (E1 159). Jerrold makes the reader see that when John Keats and Charles Lamb were writing, there were probably 'hundreds of Thomas Hoods, sons of middle-class parents, apprenticed to engravers, with a turn for writing verse or prose' who 'fill[ed] endless columns satisfactorily' (E1 160). That hubbub, she continues, had its 'effect upon things that we are wont to look upon as isolated births' (E1 159), a point Woolf would later make in *A Room of One's Own*. Virginia Stephen's reviewing heightened her awareness of literary history's underlying complexity.

Genre

Exposed to all the major genres, though mainly fictional and non-fictional ones, Virginia Stephen uses her apprenticeship reviews and essays to formulate, explore, and question genre definitions, boundaries and potentials. Genre choice has consequences, as she notes in her review of Mary E. Wilkins [Freeman's] *The Debtor*. Wilkins uses the same method in her novel that she used in her 'very brief and delightful' short stories;[9] although her characters are elaborately and subtly conceived in what could be good stand-alone stories, the 'effect is that of a succession of disconnected studies of character rather than of a single and well-proportioned whole' (E1 68–9). Stephen thus suggests Wilkins's genre choice undercuts her talent and skill in writing short stories. Because she does not always emphasise genre, however, pithy comments about the memoir, journal and letters genres can be obscured by captivating descriptions of Lady Dorothy Nevill's, Lady Holland's and Boswell's lives. Stephen notes that when an aristocrat picks up a pen to reflect on life within the high walls of privilege, readers may discover that 'whatever genuine test [they] apply to [the aristocracy], it goes to pieces directly' (E1 182). Memoir exposes more than Lady Nevill intends. Stephen is grateful for Lord Ilchester's edition of Lady Holland's diary because before, we knew only what others thought of her 'and had to guess what she had been feeling herself' (E1 230). Diaries make it difficult for later ages to pretend a writer did not exist (E1 238). Stephen notes that Boswell's letters to Temple, beginning when he was 18 and continuing right up to a few months before his death, show he 'existed independently of Johnson', and furthermore, 'To read a man's letters after reading his works has much the same effect as staying with him in his own house after meeting him in full dress at dinner-parties' (E1 249–50). Letters foster intimacy with a writer.

Ostensibly focusing on documents, diaries and letters in 'Trafficks and Discoveries', 'William Allingham' and 'Poets' Letters', Stephen pays more attention to poetry's evocative qualities, particularly in everyday locations. Not only did '"poets and dramatists [go] abroad"' in spirit, succeeding, like Drake and Cavendish, in '"rifl[ing] foreign nations"', but sailors, dipping their 'laborious pens' into the 'stately vocabulary ... common to seaman and poet', produced lists of commodities and descriptions of landscapes that 'buil[t] up such a noble structure of words ... that the effect is as rich and more authentic than that got by more artistic processes' (E1 121–2). William Allingham evaluates Victorian poets, recalls hearing his own poems read aloud by Tennyson in a '"rich slow solemn chant"', and fills his diary with poetic imagery (E1 154–6). Stephen suspects if Percy Lubbock treated Elizabeth Barrett Browning's poetry the way he treats her letters – combing through all the volumes, 'prompting her ... to speak just those words which explain herself and connecting them with admirably intelligent comments of his own' – she would not be proclaimed 'a bad poet' or 'an extravagant freak of early Victorian taste' (E1 101–2).[10]

Virginia Stephen often highlights fiction's ability to delve beneath appearances. Typical is her review of the short stories in *Old Hampshire Vignettes* by Lanoe Falconer (Mary Elizabeth Hawker),[11] in which Stephen gently asks readers not to '[shoot] past' the inhabitants of a Hampshire valley, not to be a 'tourist with a crude eye', not to believe strangers who claim village dwellers are dull, apathetic and lazy. If readers view the characters, their lives and their speech within the 'delicate framework of suggestion' and tender bantering Falconer creates, they will 'see how differently things look in the valley to one who knows' (E6 310–11).

Virginia Stephen also establishes distinctions to evaluate genre. In her review of R. J. Farrer's *The House of Shadows*, Stephen identifies two approaches to writing a novel: focusing on character or focusing on an idea and making characters serve it. Farrer does the latter, which makes the book 'remarkable for its force and continuity' (E1 93–4). Paradoxically, Stephen shows, this strength also limits: Farrer's steady focus on how physical pain conquers the soul means he 'is a writer to be remembered', but he 'harangues us on occasion as though he were speaking from the pulpit' (E1 94).

In her review essay on George Gissing's *The Private Papers of Henry Ryecroft* and her review of Ashton Hilliers's *Memoirs of a Person of Quality*, Virginia Stephen examines the blurred lines between autobiography and fiction, whether blurred by writer or reader.[12] Both are novels, but Hilliers pretends to edit a British nobleman's memoir and takes 'little advantage of his artistic right to arrange and amend' (E6 306), whereas Gissing, early readers assumed, was writing about himself (E1 131). Stephen praises Hilliers's ability to give his invented Mr Fanshawe all 'the faults and the virtues' a son of an earl who sat down in the eighteenth century to write his memoirs would have had; approves his decision to let the memoir flow in a lifelike way rather than impose a plot; admires his writing skill in the 'very vigorous' scene in which Mr Fanshawe 'convicts Mr Vyze of playing with loaded dice'; and lauds the excellent English: 'Without affectation, it has a pleasant flavour of sedate Georgian prose, and its polish and lucidity reflect the best qualities of that period' (*E6* 306–7). This 'admirable' novel succeeds because it reads like a plausible autobiography from the past.

Her discussion of genre blurring in Gissing's novel starts from a different premise, given its author's fame, but concludes similarly. Stephen thinks reading *The Private Papers* no longer requires readers to align the life and personality of George Gissing with Henry Ryecroft since Ryecroft as a character 'stands solidly on his own feet', 'needs no exterior support' and 'wrote down what he thought'. Stephen concludes that the novel succeeds because it reads as 'the most genuine of all autobiographies'. Its excellent writing, sweet humour and wisdom pale in comparison to the 'impression that it leaves of a live, human creature, who has not scrupled to let us know his foibles, and his failings, and his imperfect human shape' (*E1* 131–2). Virginia Stephen evaluates both novels for their plausibility: readers, persuaded they are reading memoirs, engage with the characters' lives and insights; the fictions succeed through another fiction, seeming to be memoirs.

With non-fiction, Virginia Stephen considers the genre's aims and scope, privileges imagination's power and sees potential for cultural and social analysis. In 'Literary Geography', she questions the need for 'pilgrimage' books, the need for journeys to authors' homes and haunts, the need for guidance from F. G. Kitton and his overwhelming 'storehouse of facts about Dickens' when writers, their worlds and the characters in them 'live most certainly in our brains' (*E1* 32–5). Stephen considers the context for such pilgrimages (sentiment or science) and prefers Lewis Melville's approach: he at least selects the most important Thackeray sites from many possibilities (*E1* 34). But by questioning why books exist that 'try to impress upon the mind the fact that great men were once alive because they lived in this house or that' (*E1* 35), she disconcertingly implies why review them?[13]

Virginia Stephen elevates fictional portrayals of historical women over biographical ones in 'Their Passing Hour'. Reviewing *Some Famous Women of Wit and Beauty*, short biographies of eight Georgian women by John Fyvie, Stephen articulates a paradox, the contrast between the conversational wit and charm claimed by contemporaries and the flatness of reported conversations. Readers cannot account for what Fyvie cites because the women's power does not translate into print: 'The secret of the spell seems to have died in each case with its possessor; it could not be transmitted to another' (*E1* 61). Their own literary efforts do not help, either: Mrs Norton's novels had 'enormous vogue', but now rest in 'rubbish-heaps of tarnished finery' (*E1* 62). One may see such women's influence in current hostesses, salons and literary criticism, but Stephen argues that only George Meredith's novelistic genius preserves 'the wit that has been spoken and the beauty that has long faded, by creating [Mrs Norton] afresh' in his portrayal of Diana in *Diana of the Crossways* (*E1* 63).

With Elizabeth McCracken's study of the American woman, however, Virginia Stephen sees non-fiction's potential for enquiry. Admiring McCracken's decision not to portray individual American women but to take 'snapshots' of fourteen *types* based on extensive travel, interviews, research and notes, Stephen focuses on McCracken's method and praises her ability to initiate 'many interesting lines of thought', including her insight into the brevity of America's past and the short story genre, the American writer's 'province' (*E1* 46–8). Stephen also records some McCracken findings: women founded most small-town public libraries, often became librarians, and taught Blacks to participate in public life after the Civil War (*E1* 47). Most intriguing, McCracken's non-fiction teaches Stephen something different about charity. Stephen typifies an English woman's charity as personal, ending when she becomes ill or dies, whereas McCracken reports an American woman founds a 'society' to confront a problem, but then, 'not satisfied with relieving suffering', determines to learn more, persuades the government to become involved in training programmes, and works to eliminate the suffering's cause (*E1* 47–8). Sceptical about personal philanthropy, Stephen learns about both a different approach and non-fiction's capacity to capture readers with social analysis.[14]

In 'Impressions of Sir Leslie Stephen' and 'Mary Christie', Virginia Stephen puts her reading of memoirs to use as she writes one and critiques another. What she called her note about her father, perhaps because she did not intend it to be printed (*PA* 219, 226, 229, 230, 246), appears almost at the end of F. W. Maitland's full-length biography (474–6), whereas Maud Withers's memoir introduces a collection of Christie's miscellaneous essays. Neither memoir is meant to stand alone; each appears soon after the loved person has died, making it difficult to write – Stephen's letters show she agonised over hers, and she praises Withers's 'gallantry' in hers (*E6* 312). Because her somewhat anonymous impressions of her father (by 'one of his daughters') are folded into someone else's biography, however, Stephen need not provide dates or times; she can focus on memories that add to Maitland's portrayal. Withers, in contrast, must recount the contours and facts of Christie's whole life. Stephen applauds Withers's attempt to record the testimony of Christie's friends ('[h]ow she helped and cheered and praised them'), catalogue her influence, and raise a 'monument' with the publication of papers, but questions using a memoir to justify a collection of essays; it manipulates the reviewer (and reader) who must evaluate essays based on a plea for 'a kind of sympathy which it is painful not to give': how can you not praise a work following the memoir of a well-loved friend (*E6* 311–12)? The function of a memoir matters.

Autobiography and memoir also crisscross Stephen's review of William Allingham's diary. Barbara Lounsberry calls it a 'memoir-diary' (106) since Allingham planned to use it to write his memoirs; it combines an autobiographical fragment about his childhood and youth with a diary of 'short spontaneous notes' (*E1* 155). Stephen identifies an autobiographical habit of imaginative people: they treat childhood and early youth happily because 'events of inexplicable interest ... sum up long trains of thought and experience in some quaint symbol, persistent all through life' (*E1* 154–5). Allingham remembers certain trees, describing them beautifully, and such things 'shaped and coloured his life with their odd meanings far more than the real people about him' (*E1* 155).[15] Stephen shares some of Allingham's assessments of his contemporaries' work, concluding his stories are 'true in the best sense of the word'. That is, his diary captures both the man and his time, serving future biographers who will 'want to know exactly what Carlyle said of Browning, or how it was that he disposed of his old pipes!' (E1 156). This 'writer's diary' (Lounsberry 105) thus becomes a source not only for later biographers and historians but also for apprentice writers like Virginia Stephen who want to learn about the diary genre for their own professional and personal reasons.

In her review essay on Thomas De Quincey, Stephen tackles a substantial essayist whose body of work then existed in fourteen volumes and reveals her growing knowledge of the genre. A 'somewhat altered or embellished platitude' about how a 'true book dictates the mood and season in which it shall be read' gives Stephen a 'starting point for some reflections radiating in very different directions', showing she understands the essay's meandering quality (E1 365). She claims De Quincey really should be read outdoors, not inside 'with a clock ticking'; considers De Quincey's past and present reputation (the former determined by '[m]en who were old in the early days of the nineteenth century' and the latter determined by the 'opinions of two or three elderly people'); compares his work to that of Stevenson and Pater, who would have cut, 'clipped and combed' each sentence and 'freshly ordered and established' the essay's structure; and argues, as she often does, that the writer's 'chief fault ... is one that under other circumstances becomes his chief virtue': he sees 'everything a size too large' and then conveys his vision in 'words which are also a size too large' (E1 366). This leads to his tendency to provide 'precise and unnecessary information' – he 'cannot pass by an allusion or a statement that is capable of further explanation without setting down the whole burden of the story and proceeding to remove the imperceptible pebble, elaborately, from the reader's path' (E1 366–7).[16] Stephen clearly enjoys detailing this bad habit while simultaneously advising readers to be 'callous' in skipping such notes, especially when in the midst of a 'rushing sentence' about the speeding mail coach or an 'eloquent passage' about the emotions of a young man and woman in a pony carriage with that mail coach bearing down on them. Her last two paragraphs move to De Quincey's 'writing at its best', and Stephen writes eloquent passages of her own about the 'obvious relation between [his] use of language and a musician's use of sound'. His frequent use of the word 'orchestral' and images that combine sound and infinite space leads her to envision his writing as 'an organ booming down the vast and intricate spaces of a cathedral'. When she returns to her opening and places a 'generous reader' outside, 'where the view between hedges is of a vast plain sunk beneath an ocean of air', a De Quincey page is 'no mere sheet of bald signs, but part of the pageant itself' (E1 367–8). It is a lovely, rambling essay about essay rambling.

As with Stephen's deepening command of the essay, when she reviews *The Countess of Huntingdon and her Circle*, she pushes at a review's boundaries. She describes Sarah Tytler's biography as 'serious and conscientious' (E1 315), but would rather inform readers about the book's subject than evaluate Tytler's treatment of it. She uses her two paragraphs to comment on Lady Huntingdon's ability to 'not lose the world while she kept her soul in all austerity'. But Tytler's biography succeeds in making the agnostic Stephen respect an aristocratic woman who becomes a Methodist proselytiser and confronts her class about its spiritual wellbeing.[17] Lady Huntingdon's hard work impresses Stephen, who notes that had Lady Huntingdon lived in another time, she might have 'embraced a strenuous cause' such as women's franchise (E6 316). Stephen's interest in Lady Huntingdon and her co-worker, Lady Glenorchy, 'a remarkable pair'; her fascination with a 'masterful' woman who kept her aristocratic standing while promoting a religion that cared little for high rank and good breeding; her delight in Lady Huntingdon's persistence, inviting Wesley and Whitefield 'to instruct a curious crowd, in which fashion and wit and infidelity were gathered together in her drawing-room at Chelsea' (E6 316); and her involvement in the narrative, all imply admiration. Without overtly assessing Tytler's biography, Stephen not only recommends it, but shows how biography should engage readers. As she reads and reviews multiple genres, then, Virginia Stephen learns about the constraint, power and impact genre has on both writers and readers.

Critical values

Virginia Stephen consistently uses what a reader wants, needs or appreciates to frame her evaluations. Though sometimes referring to herself as a reviewer, she typically establishes herself as a reader among readers, though with some distinctive habits of mind. For example, she wants to be involved, not controlled, commenting in her review of Vincent Brown's *Mrs Grundy's Crucifix* that he lays out his novel's intent early by denouncing a 'portentous old lady' who turns a community into 'abject devotees' and thus creates readers who do not care about the 'injured woman', though she is a 'victim of harsh social laws', or her rescuer, who is 'a tract which has been put somewhat crudely into a human case' (E1 111–12). His sermon overwhelms narrative and any potential aesthetic pleasure or wisdom: a novel that 'undertakes a crusade' and 'insist[s] upon [a] crucifix and [a] crucified' dangerously sacrifices 'much of natural human nature ... , much truth' (E1 112). Similarly, in 'Mary Christie', although Stephen responds positively to Christie's love of the world and her ardour in exploring it in essays, her pursuit of a theory about moral virtue has 'the high pitch of a scolding voice' (E6 312).

Stephen often calls attention to how readers' needs change, depending on what they are reading. As she continues her remarks about Mary Christie's essays, for example, she notes that Christie's voice, her 'zealot's bigotry', may add 'zest' to a magazine article, but it becomes 'monotonous' in a collection of essays (E6 312). In her review of *Next-Door Neighbours*, she suggests the book format creates expectations that do not serve its short pieces. The characters in Pett Ridge's stories, she notes, do not stir the reader's sympathies, and the 'ephemeral interest' of the stories suits 'the columns of a daily paper' but is not worth preserving in a book (E1 11). Readers expect books to work as coherent wholes, not be a hotchpotch of hastily collected short pieces published elsewhere.

Stephen also insists on a both/and approach. Lady Holland, for example, could be both unhappy and unfair to her first husband (E1 231–2), proud in her happiness yet suffering (E1 234), hard yet strong and courageous (E1 238), and a powerful woman with no real power (E1 236). Or Thomas Hood could be both 'one of a class' and 'typical of it' (E1 160). Studying Elizabeth Barrett Browning's life through letters, Virginia Stephen asserts in 'Poets' Letters', enlarges our sense of Browning as both artist and woman, helping readers see her strength and genius. Browning replied to critics of her poetry not by pleading, but by using straightforward and authoritative argument – she was 'almost obstinate when her literary independence was attacked'. Stephen also criticises Elizabeth Barrett Browning for tacitly claiming that 'the cause of truth would be demeaned by a more scrupulous regard for literary form' in her poetry (E1 103), asserting it is not an either/or situation: an artist can both tell the truth and craft the form that contains it.

In reviews of two novels, A. J. Dawson's *The Fortunes of Farthings* and W. E. Norris's *Lone Marie*, Stephen skewers conventionality and distinguishes first-rate from what is not. *The Fortunes of Farthings*, she says, is an old-fashioned novel: conventional in plot, character and attitude, and set in the early eighteenth century (E1 38). Dawson's scrupulous citations of contemporary sources for the villain's cruelties 'divert our sympathies from the characters themselves', and his 'pleasant and diffuse' style is more suited to describing 'simple country life' than to developing complex characters the reader cares anything at all about. Furthermore, 'he easily lapses into sentimentality and a patriotism which tends to be ridiculous' (E1 39).

W. E. Norris, in contrast, is an entertaining, skilled and above-average writer. He has, Stephen says, 'rare and indisputable gifts for his calling'. So why has he never 'achieved any work of first-rate importance'? She distinguishes between his evident skill and his unwillingness to test it, and she argues Norris skims the surface of characters in *Lone Marie*, only hinting at depths that 'remain unrevealed'. Believing he could achieve more since he has 'the same economy of incident, and restraint of treatment' as Henry James, Stephen says Norris seems 'ready to stop when Mr James is just prepared to begin' (E1 66). To answer her question about quality, Stephen indicates Norris knowingly chooses ease over a struggle to delve below a character's surface.[18]

In a review of *The Wingless Victory*, she openly searches for better language to articulate her complex judgement of the novel, 'some emphatic word that shall signify a book that is not a season's masterpiece' but is 'worth keeping on the shelves, even by the classics, for [it is] painted in colours that do not fade' (E6 314–15). She explains that Miss Willcocks's novel falls among the books for which 'rules of measurement seem a little out of place' because it is 'like other living things; we have no need to test the degree of life' (E6 314). She admits her dilemma – the difficulty of assessing books that do not fit the usual critical categories – and proposes another standard, admittedly amorphous, as a result.

During her apprenticeship, Stephen's extensive reading of contemporary fiction tells her most of it does not model a path she wants to follow: it lacks reality and depth or is marred by the customary and conventional. R. J. Farrer lacks coherence in his novel, *The Ways of Rebellion*, and his hero's antagonists are 'clumsy', unworthy (E6 359). '[U]naccountable episodes' interrupt a tract-like story, the hero's feelings and actions are implausible, and the plot and final solution 'bewildering'. It is 'disappointing work' compared to Farrer's earlier *The House of Shadows* because it 'has so much more in common with the ordinary novel' (E6 360). Similarly, J. E. Buckrose (Annie Edith Jameson) relies on stock situations, stock attitudes and an 'obsolete form of humour' in *The Wolf* to reinforce the stereotype that people in country villages are as simple and elementary as the trees, fields and farmyards they live among (E6 360–1).[19] H. Fielding Hall creates allegorical, cardboard men and women to discuss eastern and western thought and views of love in *One Immortality*, but the conversations seem 'neither accurate nor profound', and the book neither functions like a novel nor entertains serious claims about the theories put forward (E1 255–6). Reviewing Henry Normanby's collection of stories, *Destinies*, Stephen grasps the short-story genre: 'in so narrow a space you must choose your note and strike it firmly, and in so doing you must eliminate much, and make much subservient'. The writer must choose 'some incident of emotion like Mr Henry James' or 'boldly pluck the brightest incidents', Normanby's choice. As a result, however, he introduces violent or shocking events without any connection to the past or future, making his plots neither 'ingenious [n]or credible', and his melodramatic formulas 'do not disturb the mind' – his stories are 'like pageants that pass across the eye and leave little trace' (E6 365–6). Openly impatient with the formulaic and the typical, Stephen craves substance, significance, innovation.

In 'A Description of the Desert' (E1 72–4), a travel book review, the interplay of fact and fiction fascinates her. In her reading notes for *The Voice of the South*, she writes, 'A good book; well written & imaginative – Some very good description' (VS notes 74), and that assessment permeates her review in which she likes Gilbert Watson's open attitude to his journey from Biskra to Tougourt on the edge of the Sahara – he 'trust[s] to his own powers of observation'. His style is 'leisurely and graceful', he paints 'little pictures of real beauty', and travelling on a camel provides him with 'philosophic calm' and a 'humorous sense of ... incongruities' (E1 72). He breaks what might be monotonous about the 'immense solemnity' of consistently comparing the desert to the sea by giving voices to Athman, the guide, and Abdullah, the camels' owner. Through Athman, we learn about internalising racism, hear poetry and observe religious practices. Stephen weaves her reading notes question – 'How much true, & how much fiction?' (VS notes 74) – into her review's end when, according to Watson, Athman falls in love with a dancer and rides away with her: 'Whether we accept this and much that is like it as fact or fiction, there is no doubt that Mr Watson has managed to convey to us something of the mystery and charm of the strange land' he journeys across (E1 73). She has begun an exploration of fact, fiction and the nature of truth that would last her entire life.

Virginia Stephen's non-fiction reviews of Alfred Ainger's *Lectures and Essays*, 'A Nineteenth-Century Critic', Percy Lubbock's *Elizabeth Barrett Browning in Her Letters* and Professor Walter Raleigh's study of Hakluyt's *Principal Navigations* stake out a twentieth-century approach to literature, a biographical method and a goal of criticism. She criticises Ainger for allowing his ethical judgements of writers' morals to cloud his evaluations of their art, identifies that point of view as nineteenth-century and contrasts it with a more aesthetic twentieth-century one (E1 83–5).[20] She praises Lubbock's method of composing a 'finished and brilliant' biographical portrait by weaving excerpts from Browning's letters with his own commentary; his method encourages readers to re-examine Elizabeth Barrett Browning's poetry and resist the quick judgement that relegated her to a secondary place in literary history (*E1* 101–2). And she compliments Raleigh's ability to organise the gorgeous and chaotic volumes of Hakluyt and help readers 'see the whole pageant in its proper proportions'. Furthermore, his 'luminous and authoritative comment' increases this miscellaneous world's beauty rather than impoverishes it (*E1* 121, 123). Criticism, then, can use textual analysis to increase not only a reader's understanding, but also a text's beauty and value.

Virginia Stephen's non-fiction reviews reveal her curiosity about lives and a search for depths.[21] Whether she reviews memoirs, journals, letters or biographies, she invariably turns to subjects' lives rather than to authors' editing or execution. The inquisitive Stephen appreciates books that open windows on earlier times and writers, and delights in sharing illuminating literary titbits, thus spurring readers to read the work being reviewed. For 'The Genius of Boswell' and 'The Duke and Duchess of Newcastle-Upon-Tyne', Stephen establishes a lifelong habit, pulling stories from review books, but also from related materials,[22] so readers learn why Boswell may have continued to write to the Rev. W. J. Temple – they both had literary ambitions, Temple 'had received the earliest of Boswell's confidences' and he 'reflected the image of what Boswell would like to be'. We learn what an 'adventurous history' the letters had (they wrapped a parcel purchased in Boulogne in 1850!); we discover what Macaulay and Carlyle thought of Boswell, and what Boswell thought of himself – 'a Newmarket courser yoked to a dung-cart; . . . "a sad dupe – a perfect Don Quixote"'; a romantic; a Don Juan; a 'friend of Johnson and Paoli' (*E1* 249–50). By the end of her review of Thomas Seccombe's edition of Boswell's letters to Temple, readers know about Boswell's hopes and dreams, repeated vows to do better, failures, vanity, vitality and, ultimately, genius. 'He was always', Stephen writes, 'imagining himself' (*E1* 250), and her tracing of his creations and re-creations charms us.[23]

Virginia Stephen brings the remarkable Duke and Duchess of Newcastle alive: a rich nobleman who loves the arts, fights for King Charles I and trains horses, and a maid of honour for Queen Henrietta Maria who loves science and philosophy, writes fiction, poetry and drama, and is thirty-one years younger. As Stephen notes, Restoration society was 'as intolerant of eccentricity as the society of boys at a public school', and the curious Duchess (wondering whether snails have teeth or trying to explain a spider's web), with her writing, odd clothes and even odder habits, was a laughing stock. The Duke, occupied with his equestrian concerns and possessing a deep affection for his wife, let her investigate, write and do what she wanted, all 'without bullying her, although she brought him no children' (*E1* 348). Readers, intrigued by what Stephen shares of their endearing foibles and quirks – the Duke 'teaching a horse to dance' (*E1* 349) or the Duchess having an idea in bed about the 'destiny of mankind' and calling for a servant to write it down (*E1* 348) – and by the quotations she selects – a friend said '"[The Duke's] edge . . . had too much razor in it"' (*E1* 347) or the Duchess observed that '"Women live like Bats or Owls, labour like Beasts, and die like Worms"' (*E1* 349) – painlessly pick up knowledge about the past, literary context and an often-overlooked woman writer.

But non-fiction disappoints Virginia Stephen when it seems empty clutter, signifying nothing. She criticises Vernon Lee in some of her *Sentimental Traveller* essays for veering off into 'egotistical diversions' about what a place awakens in her mind (people she has known, childhood, music, books or 'some deep question of life or morality') instead of trying to see a place or an object 'as exactly as it can be seen' (E1 157). Constance Hill, in her Edgeworth biography, misses the 'opportunity of getting the truth' when she describes simplistic husks of people, who are 'more amusing to believe in and much easier to write about', but surely were 'quite different in the flesh, and as ugly, as complex, and as emotional as we are' (E1 318). Stephen concludes that *Modes and Manners of the Nineteenth Century* 'is not a history of ourselves, but of our disguises'. For her, 'Only great artists [that is, poets and novelists], giving their minds to nothing else, represent their age; dressmakers and cabinet-makers generally caricature it or say nothing about it' (E1 334). Stephen prefers both fiction and non-fiction that delve beneath self and surface.

In her essay on 'Caroline Emelia Stephen', then, Virginia Stephen aims to grasp her aunt's essence, the peace at the heart of an inward life devoted to Quaker thought. In the process, she pays her aunt a high compliment: 'the secret of her influence and of the deep impression she made even upon those who did not think as she did was that her faith inspired all that she did and said'. And even though she wished 'to make others share her peace', she was 'no solitary mystic': she was practical, had common sense and displayed a 'wonderful command of language'. Stephen traces the bare outline of her aunt's life, especially the critical junctures when Caroline Stephen moved toward independence; describes her publications;[24] and recognises her quiet, 'almost maternal' influence on the people around her (E1 268). Indeed, the obituary's calm matches Caroline Stephen's key trait: her aunt's life 'had about it the harmony of a large design' (E1 269). As Stuart N. Clarke reports, this obituary was reprinted in Philadelphia's *The Friend: A Religious and Literary Journal* with the caveat that, even though '"the author of it is not a Friend, and ... the article appeared in a Journal not conducted by Friends"', it seemed to the editor '"so true to our apprehension of [Caroline Stephen's] character, that we have believed the readers of *The Friend* might welcome it"' (E6 630). Readers of *Light Arising: Thoughts on the Central Radiance* believed the obituary had successfully captured its author.

As Virginia Stephen wrote her apprenticeship reviews and essays, the principles underlying her judgements emerged – she clarified them for herself and her readers. She mocks sentimentality and surface emptiness, and values plausibility and character development. She abhors preaching and values complexity, paradoxes and 'both/and' thinking. She praises vivid scene-making and effective language. She enjoys confronting aesthetic questions such as the nature of truth in fiction. She criticises convention and values significance and depth. Most important, she learns to make her critical values explicit.

Cultural attitudes

Virginia Stephen's cultural attitudes about gender and class also strengthened as her apprenticeship progressed. She often comments on women writers' use of genre and introduces feminist arguments. She mildly mocks 'the spirit of solemnity' in the 'Value of Laughter' by noting 'there is no doubt that it is masculine'. She also turns 'silly women' and children, supposedly defective observers, into crucial ones: they make sure we do not 'lose our sense of reality' by seeing things as they are and laughing (E1 58–60). Laughter achieves ethical, feminist value. Such budding feminist thought also weaves through her genre exploration in 'The Letters of Jane Welsh Carlyle'. For one thing, Stephen implies letters should be part of the literary tradition and worthy of study. Stephen writes that although Jane Carlyle may have 'sometimes resent[ed] the fate which had driven her to squander all her gifts on such apparently trivial ends', her letters are brilliant studies of human nature that reveal her 'insight into character and a power of seizing on the essential, which is creative as well as critical, and, in her, amounted to genius' (E1 57, 54). Her letters are 'genuine', capturing 'an active and practical human being' writing letters with specific purposes to specific people (E1 54–5). In Jane Carlyle, Virginia Stephen sees an intelligent woman studying and learning through domestic means, and she elevates Carlyle's letters to art – Jane Carlyle does the same thing 'over her teacups' that her husband did in his 'sound-proof room' as he 'decipher[ed] the motives and characters of the actors in some long-forgotten drama' (E1 55).[25] Thus, '[u]nder other conditions she might have written more; she could hardly have written better' (E1 57).

Virginia Stephen acknowledges the role of class in Hilliers's *Memoirs of a Person of Quality* – the 'writer', the second son of a fifth earl, is disowned, must leave his regiment and 'tramp the country as a farm labourer' (E6 306) – but she grapples with it in Gissing's *The Private Papers of Henry Ryecroft*. Henry Ryecroft barely makes his living by writing until a friend dies and leaves him an annuity of £300, giving him a modicum of stability and allowing him to spend his later years in a cottage reading and writing all he wishes. The resulting book details the thoughts and books 'which came in the end to mean most to him', and it documents the effects of poverty: 'It seems as though Henry Ryecroft had pared down every emotion, every thought, and every book until the pith of it only remained – as if poor men may not afford to feel or to think insincerely.' Stephen praises Ryecroft's singular talents, and her words for his response to his poverty – integrity, austerity, heroic – show her unqualified admiration for him (E1 132). But she wonders if his painfully won gifts are bound up with his deprivation. Could he have developed the same values and talent if he had 'learnt even unconsciously to buy things with money' (E1 133)? Yet his paring-down included selling his brains: 'if he had had the means to use them respectfully they might have kept their value undiminished' (E1 132). In spite of that, his prior poverty combined with his current ease buys him a delightful freedom – his mind and books are sufficient in the face of death. The novel suggests such freedom 'lies within the grasp of most of us. A book, a pen, a cottage in the country, and the world is at your feet' (E1 134). Yet the cottage, both Stephen and readers know, was *not* in Ryecroft's grasp before the annuity. Stephen openly shares her non-conclusive, back-and-forth thought process about class and its impact.

As she sharpens gender and class observations, Stephen also shows what such bias costs. Her aunt's obituary includes this comment: with 'health and opportunity', Caroline Emelia Stephen might have 'ruled and organised' (E1 268). In her essay about the Duke and Duchess of Newcastle, Stephen asks readers to consider the effects the accidents of gender and era have on life. The Duchess had an untrained though 'active mind', a 'dangerous possession if you were a woman and a Duchess and lived in the time of Charles the Second'. She also had the misfortune 'to live either too late or too soon'. She might have taught Greek in Elizabeth's time; now, 'we should turn her energy on to a thousand committees' (*E1* 348). If, Stephen notes, there had been 'a literary society such as we have now in the provinces – something might have come of her ideas' (*E1* 349). Instead, this immensely curious, intelligent and prolific writer was laughed at, ignored, ostracised. Lady Elizabeth Holland, on the other hand, defied society, moved freely in it even as a divorced and remarried woman, and created an atmosphere in Holland House for intense literary and political discussions. Able to fearlessly turn her home into a '"political council chamber"', according to Lloyd Sanders's *Holland House Circle*, she still could not '[inspire] ministers, or [be] the secret author of policies that have changed the world' (*E1* 236). Impersonal, 'brilliant and outspoken', and with a head for business, Stephen says, Lady Holland could do no more than rule a house, command people to visit and dash off numerous assured 'likenesses' in her diary. With more thought about what it all meant, with more concentration, 'she might have shaped a cynical reflection in which a lifetime of observation was compressed' (*E1* 235–7). Society loses female leaders and writers because women lack opportunity and training, Stephen demonstrates, and implicit expectations and assumptions hobble even upper-class and seemingly free women.

In her review essay of Thomas Hood's biography and poetry, Virginia Stephen emphasises the detrimental effect economic struggles had on his work. Hood managed to 'travel the whole course that slighter men trod partly' and thus achieve something significant, but 'the ceaseless pressure of money cares' and ill health forced him to continue using the comic style the public wanted, and the editorial appointment that might have allowed him to do better work never materialised. The 'sharp blade of his own circumstance' wounds even his most solid work (*E1* 160, 162–3). In Stephen's review of a memoir and a notebook of Lady Dorothy Nevill, she subtly condemns Lady Nevill's unwarranted pride, her regret for a past when class demarcations were even more rigid, and her 'sublimely insolent disrespect for art' (*E1* 182). The lady's belief in her privilege means 'No one, so far as we can discover, of natural rather than hereditary gifts ever found his way into these dining-rooms' (*E1* 180); it guarantees Nevill sees the relationship between lord and tenant as 'picturesque inequality' (*E1* 181–2). Stephen analyses why the English might believe 'a handful of us should grow up with Greek statues round us, Titians on our walls, spacious gardens to walk in, time for reading and music and talk' – shouldn't there be 'sanctuaries where all that is high-minded and witty and fair can live happily' (*E1* 179)? – but then skewers this justification by showing how Lady Nevill reveals it serves no purpose: life in her world is far from high-minded, conversation far from witty and society far from fair. Perhaps some consolation accrues from being granted a glimpse of aristocratic life, but the privilege portrayed behind 'the stout walls of their parks, the locked doors of their galleries' could become 'intolerable to any one possessed of pen and ink or dynamite' (*E1* 179).[26] Both poverty and privilege curtail insight and thus insightful work. Virginia Stephen has learned how to subtly weave social and cultural commentary into her work.

Reader awareness

In her early fiction reviews, Virginia Stephen cared most about characters and their depth, unified purpose and reader interest. Lack of such interest stemmed from writers being implausible, conventional, sentimental, argumentative or focused on glib surfaces at the expense of complex depths. So, for example, Stephen wishes Pett Ridge would dig deeper and make her care about the characters in his 'brief lantern-slides' (E1 11). In contrast, 'every page interests' the reader in Elizabeth Robins's novel, *A Dark Lantern* (E1 42). The novel is suspenseful, the characters intense and the work strong and sincere. Although she dislikes the novel's pervasive sick-room atmosphere, the pronounced criticism of nurses that becomes argument, not art, and the implausible hospital relationship between doctor and patient, Stephen commends Robins's talent and ability to engage the reader and concludes 'few living novelists are so genuinely gifted as Miss Robins' (E1 43).

In her concern that readers learn, understand and enjoy, Stephen often probes beneath surfaces of all kinds. Increasingly impatient with creative work with nothing at its heart, she frequently conveys an essential kernel of significance about a book or person through scene, story or snippet of dialogue. This compulsive search, Virginia Woolf would later say in 'A Sketch of the Past', marked all her writing:

> I almost always have to find a scene; either when I am writing about a person, I must find a representative scene in their lives; or when I am writing about a book, I must find the scene in their poems or novels. (142)

Likewise, she often isolates one or two pieces within a collection to justify her evaluation of the whole, as she does with the *Masques and Phases* essays – 'yet we seem to discover in the last and longest fragment an eminence from which to survey the rest' (E6 369–70). She quickly summarises three story plots in *Destinies* to point out the improbability of all twenty-five (E6 366). She often summarises a book's contents, too, before isolating a scene or assessing a work, noting the central conflict between concern for the poor and incomprehension about privilege in *The Ways of Rebellion* and then summarising the novel's implausible plot (E6 359–60) or quickly running through the major events of Thomas Hood's personal and professional life before focusing on his writing's distinctive qualities (E1 160). Stephen also enjoys moving from the seemingly simple to the complex, such as when, after dashing off some brief character sketches of people living in Maria Edgeworth's world, she confronts our need to see our ancestors as charming, simple, humorous or strange rather than as complicated (E1 318) or questions J. E. Buckrose's assumption that villagers are as simple as the land they live on (E6 360–1). Most important, she repeatedly calls attention to people's inward selves and their attempts to communicate that inner world in language, as her aunt did through her books and her 'interest in [her friends'] lives and in her own' (E1 268) and as Thomas Hood, 'supersensitive to the surface inflections of language', did through 'wild and incongruous associations', including numerous puns (E1 162, 161). Virginia Stephen, like Boswell, 'was not content ... with a view of a "visible progress through the world"; it was "a view of the mind in letters and conversation" that [s]he sought' (E1 251).

As Virginia Stephen matures as a book reviewer, she establishes consistent strategies to aid the reader and stimulate thought. She uses common beliefs, sayings or imaginary readers, for example, to set up her commentary, as she does in '*One Immortality*' by quoting a poet's lines about not feeling at home in the world and imagining the audience who will thus find consolation in Fielding Hall's book: 'The need for such a book as this . . . is not obvious, unless one bears these considerations in mind' (*E1* 255). Or when she imagines a walker and an omnibus driver observing a 'swinging crystal box' bearing a Lord and Lady to a 'great white hall' where 'the ladies have space to spread their trains like peacocks, and the lords toy gently with their silver swords' before she comments on what Lady Dorothy Nevill reveals in her memoirs (*E1* 178–9). She sometimes sets up an opposition to overturn it, such as when she identifies the 'necessary relationship' between Thomas Hood's fun and his tragedy: 'You could not have the one without the other – if he laughed in this way he must cry in that' (*E1* 162). Or when she anticipates an objection to a contradiction she is about to state: 'Will it seem inconsistent with what we have said of Mr Ross's modernity if we now insist that his style . . . belongs to yesterday rather than to the present?' (*E1* 371). Stephen implies, of course, that both things are true.

Finally, Stephen strengthens other reader-friendly strategies, such as quoting from a work to enrich context, add literary detail or capture voice. She also sometimes quotes to expose an author's flaws, doing so to devastating effect in 'The Sentimental Traveller'. She admits she can fall back only on her taste (while suspecting readers will agree) to explain why one Vernon Lee metaphor satisfies – '"That melancholy sunset, the smell of torn-up seaweed and wet sands, has always remained in my mind as symbolical of a soul's shipwreck"' – whereas another seems 'forced and unimaginative': '"Of such quivering slime we also are made up; and our microscopic realities steep in our living liquids as these creatures in the sea"' (*E1* 158). Most important, Stephen often helps readers, subtly defining 'pathetic fallacy' in '*The Wolf*' or casually explaining *Genius Loci* in her opener to 'The Sentimental Traveller' (*E6* 360–1; *E1* 157). Is it perhaps because she faults work that turns readers into outsiders? She castigates Robert Ross for reprinting college magazine essays in which the

> true meaning is to be enjoyed only by those who are behind the scenes; they will enjoy it all the more no doubt because we, the public, are outside . . . . We are flattered to be told so much; at the same time, feeling that we are not really initiated, it is natural to protest that this is not the whole of life, nor (since it excludes us) the best of it.[27]

Preferring essays that 'do not depend upon allusion for their wit' (*E6* 371), Virginia Stephen calls for the writer to be the reader's ally.

Culmination: 'Sterne'

When Virginia Stephen writes her first *TLS* lead essay for the 12 August 1909 issue, a review of Wilbur Cross's biography of Laurence Sterne that becomes an essay about Sterne and his work, she weaves these habits of mind and critical concerns together and comes closer to creating the signature essay that would mark Virginia Woolf's mature essay career. Her first sentence identifies a custom, that of 'draw[ing] a distinction between a man and his works'. She then identifies a common formula: biographers, 'having delivered judgement upon his work, . . . state that "a few facts about his life" may not be inappropriate, or, writing from the opposite standpoint, proclaim that their concern is "with the man and not with his works"'. Her whole essay strives to overturn this customary opposition; in her last paragraph, she declares 'we must combine a life of extraordinary flightiness and oddity with the infinite painstaking and self-consciousness of an artist' (E1 280; 286). She employs summary for Sterne's childhood, his life before he began writing and his reading (E1 282–3). She plucks numerous scenes from his life, such as when Sterne, helping his wife who believed for a while she was Queen of Bohemia, 'drove her through the stubble fields with bladders fastened to the wheels of her chaise to make a noise "and then I told her this is the way they course in Bohemia"', and from his works, such as the account of Uncle Toby shooing the fly out a window in *Tristram Shandy* (E1 282, 285). Seeking Sterne's essential perspective, she decides

> the spirit which inspires his humours and connects them is the spirit of the humorist; the world is an absurd place, and to prove it he invents absurdities which he shows to be as sensible as the views by which the world is governed. (E1 283)

Sterne can hardly be called a simple man, but Stephen relishes unearthing complexity after complexity ('a real life is wonderfully prolific' [E1 281]), and she argues for biographies that do not emphasise either the life or the art, but acknowledge how they intertwine:

> This thin, excitable man, who was devoured by consumption, who said of himself that he generally acted on the first impulse, and was a bundle of sensations scarcely checked by reason, not only kept a record of all that he felt, but could sit close at his table, arranging and rearranging, adding and altering, until every scene was clear, every tone was felt, and each word was fit and in its place. (E1 286)

Virginia Stephen also moves inward, describing the workings of Sterne's mind, noting the 'fever heat' of writing the first books of *Tristram Shandy*, the '"quaint demons grinning and clawing at his head"', the ideas coming fast and furious on his walks, and the resulting run back home to get them down on paper. '[T]he first books still impress us,' she writes; 'a wonderful conception, long imprisoned in the brain and delicately formed, seems to leap out, surprising and intoxicating the writer himself. He had found a key to the world' (E1 283). She frequently quotes his works to make her points, such as when she supports her idea about Sterne's absurdity with his *Tristram Shandy* passage about the stranger's nose: it '"just served as a frigate to launch them into a gulf of school divinity, and then they all sailed before the wind"' (E1 283). Or when she follows her point about Sterne's precise revising and editing with this passage:

> 'How do the slight touches of the chisel', he exclaimed in *Tristram Shandy*, 'the pencil, the pen, the fiddle stick, et cetera, give the true swell, which gives the true pleasure! O, my fellow countrymen! – be nice; be cautious of your language – and never, O! never let it be forgotten upon what small particles your eloquence and your fame depend.' (E1 286)

Though pursuing Sterne's essence, she also resists generalising, noting no matter how hard we try to figure Sterne out, much remains speculative. Even her conclusions include paradoxes: 'there is no life which it is harder to judge; its eccentricities are often genuine, and its impulses are often premeditated' (E1 286). Stephen does not use terms in this essay that require definition or translation, but she acknowledges a 'common complaint' readers have about biography, that 'it is "not like"', and her long first paragraph, in which she ponders the nature of biography and its differences from fiction, invites readers to work with her to puzzle out a different definition of the genre (E1 280–1). Also, by providing so much intriguing detail from Cross's biography and so many bits and pieces from *Tristram Shandy* and *A Sentimental Journey*, Stephen shows her admiration for both Cross and Sterne and asks readers to share it.

Most important, this biography impresses Virginia Stephen because it 'makes excellent reading from start to finish and persuades us that we know Sterne better than we did before' (E1 281). Her achievement impresses, too. She discusses the art of biography and the false separation between a man and his work, compares biographies to novels, and argues 'no novelist could wish for finer material than the life of Sterne affords him' (E1 281). She spends two paragraphs on Sterne's life, then links that life to his writing: 'He was forty-five before it occurred to him that these vivid experiences ... had given him a view of the world which it would be possible to put into shape' (E1 283). Delighting in Sterne's absurdities, humour, indecency, eccentricities, passions and style, she shows how his life and art mingle, paragraph after paragraph. When she concludes his 'fame depends partly upon that inimitable style, but rests most safely upon the extraordinary zest with which he lived, and upon the joy with which his mind worked ceaselessly upon the world' (E1 286), she has demonstrated, through both argument and method, her premise: the distinction between life and art in biography is false. Stephen has written a 'modern' essay, moving closer to the Woolfian work that would combine (1) review and essay, (2) biography, era and work, (3) writer's aesthetic and reader's response, and (4) the personal and the impersonal. In 'The Novels of George Gissing', discussed in the Conclusion, Virginia Stephen, apprentice, makes the full transition to Virginia Woolf, essayist.

Writing for the newspapers, Stephen received on-the-job training and produced a tangible outcome, 158 reviews, review essays, and essays. She moved from novice through practitioner to expert, used and gained knowledge about literary history, aesthetic standards and genre, and discovered her own way forward. During this training's early novice stage, she felt her way and began to think and write for herself. She bloomed in her middle practitioner stage, focusing more clearly on her craft and its possibilities. In her late expert stage, she gained confidence, strengthened her positions and extended her critical skills. Most important, Stephen learned from the reading her reviewing required of her and established the path she wanted to take as novelist and essayist. She decided to break from the conventions she had observed in contemporary fiction and to create essay reviews that reached out to readers with a blend of intriguing narrative, satisfying information and subtle evaluation. Virginia Stephen worked diligently during her apprenticeship, and the effort spent learning the 'knack' would serve Virginia Woolf well. See Figure 13.1, near the end of her apprenticeship.

Figure 13.1 Virginia Stephen with Adrian Stephen (left, standing) and Duncan Grant (front, seated). Originally misidentified as being with Thoby and thus misdated as before 1906. Photo probably taken during 38 Brunswick Square days, 1911-12. © British Library Board, add_ms_58120_b_f133v.

Virginia Stephen's Lessons: Access and Readers

Virginia Stephen loved to read. As she wrote to Violet Dickinson in early January 1905, 'reading makes me intensely happy'. She educated herself through reading and learned from Morley students the intellectual and cultural impact of being deprived of that foundation. Reading meant access and learning.[28] She continued to Violet that her reading 'culminates in a fit of writing always' (*L1* 172). As Jeanne Dubino observes, Stephen established from the beginning what would be 'a lifelong connection between reading and writing', 'eagerly and quickly [seeking] to be published' in book reviews, the main way she could at the time ('VW' 25). Writing meant communication. Reading and writing formed a joyous loop of learning and communicating, listening and talking, being educated and sharing that education.

Virginia Stephen was aware of readers' reactions to her writing from a young age, excited when her mother 'liked something I had written' in the *Hyde Park Gate News* ('Sketch' 95; VB 64–5),[29] and addressing the reader in that publication. In her August 1899 Warboys journal, she confesses she 'suppose[s] a reader sometimes for the sake of variety when I write; it makes me put on my dress clothes such as they are' (*PA* 144); she understands the difference between her self and the self who writes and attempts to communicate with a reader. A later entry in the same journal indicates she also understands revising. Describing the events of a 'somewhat grim day of pleasure' with Stephen relatives takes her a long time: 'such a relation of details is extraordinarily difficult, dull & unprofitable to read. However there is no end to writing, & each time I hope that I may make better stuff of it' (*PA* 149–50). Her Morley College teaching introduced her to a different audience, an audience that gave her immediate feedback on her classroom work and indirectly revealed its lack of prior interactions with literature, history and other printed materials. As she began her book reviewing apprenticeship, she sought feedback from relatives, friends and editors because, as she wrote to Madge Vaughan in December 1904, 'I am no judge; and honestly dont know from hour to hour whether my gifts are first – second or tenth rate. I go from one extreme to another' (*L1* 162).

Virginia Stephen's homeschooling in 22 Hyde Park Gate and teaching at Morley College made her profoundly aware of how gender and class often prevented or hindered access. That homeschooling and teaching meant she noticed gender and class implications in what she reviewed during her newspaper writing apprenticeship, and her awareness of those threats to access meant she ultimately developed a writing persona who assumed readers wanted to learn and participate in the literary conversation. As she learned and practised the book reviewing craft, Virginia Stephen learned and used intangible lessons about stance, access and audience.

Clues to her developing attitude are scattered through her apprenticeship reviews and essays. Stephen provides descriptions, definitions and plot summaries, along with explaining her evaluation criteria. She consistently emphasises reader interest. She suggests Adam Lorimer condescends to the '"dear young author"' he addresses in *The Author's Progress* (*E1* 116–17), implying she hopes her relationship with readers will be more than a financial transaction. 'Trafficks and Discoveries' shows she appreciates books that encourage readers to 'be [their] own poet[s]' (*E1* 123). Disapproving of the essays by Robert Ross that exclude readers by using inside information (*E6* 370–1), Stephen implicitly calls for essays that invite readers in. She shares her ruminations, as in 'Sterne' when she 'talks' through the web of life and work she thinks a biography should present. Or she divulges her questions, such as those about class in her review essay about *The Private Papers of Henry Ryecroft*. As Virginia Stephen learned to write for the papers, she also imagined her persona, her readers and the relationship between the two.

Virginia Stephen's apprenticeship also taught her to adapt to different audiences. Writing for the *Guardian* Supplement's audience of women, she quarrels with W. L. Courtney's assertion that because more and more novels are written by women for women, the novel as a work of art is disappearing. Yes, 'women [have] found their voices [and] have something to say which is naturally of supreme interest and meaning to women', but to link that development with a decline in the novel is 'more doubtful' (*E1* 16). She thinks her *National Review* Tory audience is more radical and interested in art than it is, but her discussion of the essay in *The Academy* is on target – it attempts to define the form, refers to Montaigne, and humorously equates improved 'manual dexterity with a pen' with the proliferation of essays in the newspapers (*E1* 26). 'Trafficks and Discoveries', written for the liberal and anti-imperialist *Speaker*, focuses on the concealed poetry in the sailors' lists and highlights Raleigh's description of the age as '"a carnival of plunder"' (*E1* 122). Writing about Louise de La Vallière, one of Louis XIV's mistresses, Stephen wonders whether the *Cornhill*, with its prudish readers, including its editor, will allow her to 'call a prostitute a prostitute, or a mistress a mistress' (*L1* 343). A model of discretion on the surface, the essay includes neither word, and focuses on love, but subversively leaves readers in no doubt about de La Vallière's role while also making us sympathise with her (*E1* 215–20). When she praises Hind's book on post-impressionists, she counts on the *Nation*'s liberal and debate-oriented readers to appreciate her modernist arguments: post-impressionists both follow the masters and break with them, viewers can 'respect even where [they] cannot like' (*E1* 380), and point of view influences what is seen. Because she suspects *TLS* readers are probably most interested in how Thackeray and Dickens 'live most certainly in our brains', she risks asking in 'Literary Geography', once we know all about Dickens's houses, do we really know any more about Dickens (*E1* 35)?

Mitchell Leaska says Virginia Stephen was 'expert in identifying herself with her audience', which he attributes to her 'preoccupation with pleasing others' (Intro xxxviii). However, wanting to please others cannot fully explain her extraordinary skill at understanding or anticipating readers. Imagination, empathy and reading probably strengthened that ability, but her practice in interacting with various audiences at this early career stage may have contributed even more. Having to move back and forth between her real audience at Morley College and an imaginary one at her desk, Stephen had to consider how to reach the audience in both situations. Having to imagine, respond to and write for the 'Governess, and maiden lady, and high church Parson mixed' who was reading the Anglo-Catholic and 'pretty dull' *Guardian* (*L1* 178; McNeillie xii), the right-wing and anti-German imperialists interested mainly in politics in the *National Review*, the reform liberals reading the lively *Academy*, the anti-imperialistic liberals keeping up with literature and politics in the *Speaker*, the more literary types (similar to Leslie Stephen) reading the old-fashioned *Cornhill*, the feminists reading the *Englishwoman*, the left-wing readers of the *Nation* and the large numbers reading the still fairly new *Times Literary Supplement* built on what Stephen was learning from her working-class students and gave her further practice in thinking about common readers, wider audiences – indeed, the varied nature of any audience. From the experience of writing for different periodicals, Stephen learned to adapt her writing to a variety of audiences, a skill fuelling Woolf's creation of a common reader and her ability to reach out to that reader (see also Rosenbaum 146; Dubino, 'VW' 26). Virginia Stephen's apprenticeship as a book reviewer supported, along with her homeschooling and her teaching of working-class adults, her development into an essayist who used her essays to teach, not by lecturing her readers, but by connecting and sharing.

As with her homeschooling and Morley teaching, Virginia Stephen's apprentice writing had its curriculum, pedagogy, lessons and communities. Her curriculum as a novice newspaper writer included no classes and probably no manuals or how-to books, but instead, past models and current periodical contributors. She also probably read or skimmed the papers she began to write for, to learn what they expected. But her assigned review books provided the main curriculum: she learned to build reviews around what she noticed while reading and taking notes. More and more often, she supplemented her review books with other sources, mainly letters, diaries and biographies. Also, reading and assessing numerous books, mainly popular and canonical fiction and non-fiction, expanded Stephen's considerable knowledge of the British literary tradition as it introduced her to contemporary writers' work. Such 'homework' taught her about genre, its restrictions, challenges and possibilities, about gender and class issues, and about historical and cultural contexts for various times, including her own. This curriculum served Stephen as a book reviewer, increasing her knowledge of current publishing and trends, but also as would-be writer, widening her knowledge of contemporary thought and her literary moment.

Her editors' pedagogical methods varied from direct and helpful to demanding and maddening. Virginia Stephen experienced those who taught through correction and consultation (Mrs Lyttelton) and condescension (Reginald Smith); through rejection (Leo Maxse) and encouragement (Bruce Richmond); through alterations (Harold Child) and principles (Arthur Clutton-Brock). Knowing she needed to learn how to write for papers to break in, Stephen paid attention to what her editor teachers said and did, complained to friends when she thought them unfair and learned how to meet different expectations and maintain her own perspective. Her editors also taught her about everything from word limits to periodical style and constraints, from being rejected to meeting deadlines, from cutting and revising to working as a professional. Each editor taught different lessons, so she learned to write for individual papers but also for papers in general. Stephen also learned from her readers, if only in imagining them. She might chafe at the restrictions and mock the staid, respectable and religious underpinnings of the *Guardian* and its readers, but she thought about finding the 'right' things for it (*L*1 148, 154, 171). Why? Yes, she wanted to be published, but she also knew she could count on both Mrs Lyttelton and those readers to take her seriously.

During her apprenticeship, Stephen learned how to write reviews and essays, moving from tentative novice to confident expert. But reviewing so many popular novels also deepened her knowledge of fiction, revealed what the stakes were and caused her to hone her own artistic standards. Reviewing so much non-fiction – letters, diaries, memoirs, biographies, essays – deepened her knowledge of those genres, showed her how to move beyond her father's practice and led her to forsake lecture for exploration. She increased her knowledge of literary tradition and became more sharply aware of working people's and women's exclusion from it in Britain. Stephen's reading notes show she struggled to learn how to read as a friend and accomplice before reading as a judge, the process Woolf would later recommend in 'How Should One Read a Book?'. (Virginia Woolf would substantially revise that essay to reach three very different audiences, illustrating how well Virginia Stephen learned her audience lessons.)

Stephen learned to meet length requirements, use summary more sparingly, think about her audience carefully, take control of editorial changes when she could, formulate and state her aesthetic values, move beyond the work to consider biographical and cultural issues, refuse to compromise her integrity, and work with an editor. Between 1904 and 1912, she also learned how to be a professional: she found work and met her obligations; created the material conditions she needed; established the routines of a working life; gained confidence in her critical opinions; and responded to her editors' demands while developing her own views, persona and voice.

Perhaps most important, however, becoming a book reviewer brought Virginia Stephen into the community of writers and readers she so wanted to enter as a practitioner rather than as an observer. All her patient study, hard work and diligent practice meant she was doing what she loved, reading and writing, learning and teaching, entering a world in which writers communicated with her and she communicated with readers. In this world, she belonged.

Having grown up with few formal teachers and no writing groups, Virginia Stephen seems to have considered her students, readers and friends her informal teachers, or at least partners in learning. Thus, as she developed her essayist persona during her apprenticeship, she sensed that presenting herself as a learner just like her readers would ultimately make her a more effective writer (and teacher). Rather than being seen as an authority, she preferred to present herself as a reader working to put together what she would later call a 'ramshackle' and flexible framework for reading and understanding literature, one open to constant revision (*E*4 19), a common reader reaching out to other common readers, an amateur writing for other amateurs.

Virginia Stephen's development of her persona as an amateur reader meant adopting a receptive tone, open to thought, learning and trespass. The intangible outcome of her book-reviewing apprenticeship, this predilection for providing access and nurturing an atmosphere in which literature thrives, in turn created community. As she entered the community of writers and readers through publishing, she also worked to use reading to create such a community. Because

Virginia Stephen knew what it felt like to learn on her own, Virginia Woolf's essays would share rather than withhold, open up rather than shut out, welcome rather than intimidate.

Notes

1. She continues, 'I know I can write, and one of these days I mean to produce a good book'; she adds shortly thereafter, 'writing is I know my natural means of expression' (*L1* 144). Coming back from illness, she knows what she wants to practise, and she has a goal.
2. At 38 Brunswick Square, near the Foundling Hospital in Bloomsbury, Maynard Keynes had a ground-floor room for occasional use that Duncan Grant could also use as a studio, Adrian Stephen had the first floor, Virginia Stephen the second and Leonard Woolf the top (QB1 175).
3. See K&C 300–4, for information about doubtful and untraced contributions. As additional discoveries have been made, marked periodical files found or archival research reported on, contributions have been added or subtracted. For example, Michael Whitworth's research led to a couple of reviews about poetic drama being added to Virginia Stephen's canon by Stuart N. Clarke in *E6*, 'Additional Essays 1906–1924' (301–400), and the untraced item Cb 3 in K&C, 301, refers to work being done for Stephen's Morley teaching.

   Another essay can be added to the untraced contributions list. Two letters from Harold Child to Lord Northcliffe discuss a piece called 'The Matron' that Virginia Stephen submitted to him for a weekly *Woman's Supplement* to *The Times* he was editing. In a letter dated 28 October 1910, he asks for Lord Northcliffe's opinion of the piece, adding 'Miss Stephen is a daughter of Leslie Stephen and does a good deal for the Literary Supplement. I think this article brilliantly clever and likely to cause discussion' (Letter 7–8, BL Add MS 62256). Writing on 9 November 1910, he says he encloses several article proofs, including 'The Matron' (Letter 15, BL Add MS 62256). However, nothing with that title, related to that title or with her name on it exists in the November or December issues of the short-lived *Woman's Supplement* (housed in the British Library News Room).

   Other searches turn up two letters to Clive Bell, dated 4 and 8 September 1910, when she mentions writing and talking to Harold Child, and says 'I'm now pledged to do a good deal of work' (*L1* 434–5). On 29 December, she writes to Clive, 'The Lit. Sup^t. doesn't print my single review; and the Womans Sup^t. I take to be dead, and giving off odours.' Nicolson and Trautmann identify the Woman's Supplement as the *Guardian*'s (*L1* 446), but Stephen, no longer writing for the *Guardian*, surely refers to Child's weekly. It was discontinued in December and not rejuvenated the next year, though a *Woman's Times* and a *Woman's Supplement* (associated with *The Times*) had short runs starting in June 1920 (see K&C, Cb 19, 302). The 'single review' probably refers to her Duke and Duchess of Newcastle piece, which she was writing the week of 14 November (*L1* 438). She may have sent it in late November or early December, thinking it would be published then, but it did not appear until early 1911.

   Nick Mays, News UK Archivist, provided access to letters related to the *Woman's Supplement*, including anything by or about Harold Child, and the periodical's marked copies (SSI/1/1–14). Though plenty about the supplement's contents and its financial difficulties can be gleaned from these sources, 'The Matron' never appears. Neither the title nor Virginia Stephen appears in The Times Digital Archive, either. Stephen evidently wrote 'The Matron' and the 'brilliantly clever' piece reached proof stage at the *Woman's Supplement*, but it was never published. Presumably, *The Times*

threw it away, and perhaps Stephen did, too, since no draft exists in Sussex or the Berg, and she never mentions it again or seems to have tried to publish it elsewhere. A tantalising dead end.
4. See *L1* 172, where Virginia writes to Violet in early January 1905 that 'I want to work like a steam engine, though editors wont take what I write.'
5. Terms for Virginia Stephen's non-fiction can be confusing. McNeillie uses notices (for very short reviews), reviews, articles (about literature or culture, but not reviews) and essays in his endnotes. Brosnan cautions that giving all of Virginia Stephen's and then Woolf's published non-fiction the label 'essay' tends to position that work as art without acknowledging its role in commercial journalism (41). On the other hand, emphasising the distinction suggests journalistic work cannot be art. In this chapter, I aimed to call Stephen's evaluative pieces 'reviews', choose 'review essays' for longer pieces that ostensibly review but become essays, and use 'essays' for non-fiction work with no reviewing function, thus taking Brosnan's point. However, I should note that 'essay' has in fact come to function as an umbrella term for both journalism and creative non-fiction, a development I take up in more detail in *Virginia Woolf's Essays: Being a Teacher*.
6. Jeanne Dubino also notes that during her book reviewing apprenticeship, Stephen 'became more familiar with a wide range of books' that 'pulled her away from the mostly canonical literature and history with which she had nourished her imagination' ('VW' 26).
7. These numbers add up to 84 and 58.8 per cent (rather than 70 and 49 per cent) because Stephen's reviews sometimes fall into two non-fiction categories: both biography and history, for example, or both essays and criticism, or both biography and letters.
8. Dubino follows McNeillie's periodisation to define Woolf's apprenticeship's span and uses 1918, after Woolf's move to short fiction and the 1917 acquisition of Hogarth Press, as its end. Dubino also divides Woolf's apprenticeship into three: 1904–9, 1910–15 and 1916–18 ('VW'). Leaska divides her apprenticeship into two, seeing 1897–1904 as her journalism apprenticeship and 1905–9 as her fiction apprenticeship (Intro xliii n14). My choice of 1912 as the endpoint of Virginia Stephen's apprenticeship is biographically convenient and logical, though not quite precise since features typical of 'Woolf' essays appear in the last few pieces Stephen wrote before her thirtieth birthday.
9. Stephen's language indicates she either has done research or is familiar with Wilkins's work, and she hints at a similar familiarity in her review of Edith Wharton's *House of Mirth*. She knows Henry James's work and she reviews W. D. Howells; her inscription indicates she bought Edgar Allen Poe's *The Fall of the House of Usher and Other Tales* in Florence in 1903. Although Stephen (and later Woolf) would never travel to America, she seems to have had her father's curiosity about Americans.
10. Similarly, Stephen's reviews of poetic drama focus on the poetry but occasionally veer into considering the difference between reading such a play and seeing it staged (*E1* 97–101; *E6* 318–23; *E6* 347–55).
11. It is difficult to discern from Stephen's review or Peter Rowland's introduction to *The Collected Stories of Lanoe Falconer* whether these vignettes are fiction or non-fiction, another kind of genre blurring. Rowland calls them 'reminiscences' (6) and has endnotes identifying the real people behind invented names, but includes them in a collection of stories. Stephen calls them 'sketches' (*E6* 311). Since the literary definition of 'sketch' covers both possibilities, I used 'short stories' for the purpose of my genre numbers and percentages.
12. Stephen must have read these two genre-bending works at nearly the same time: her *Guardian* essay about Gissing (13 February 1907) appears within a week of her *TLS* review of Hilliers's work (8 February 1907).

13. See May 50 for his sense of her achievement in this review.
14. Stephen's distinction between English and American women's approaches here evokes the difference between her mother's charitable nursing and Margaret Llewelyn Davies's work with the Co-operative Women's Guild.
15. What Stephen sees in Allingham, Woolf would do in 'A Sketch of the Past'.
16. Stephen's full description of this habit will remind contemporary readers of David Foster Wallace's essays and their copious footnotes.
17. Stephen notices that Lady Huntingdon did the usual thing at first, address the poor. But she soon went beyond charity, perhaps in her own way doing what Stephen had noticed American women did in McCracken's book, dig into poverty's causes and relate the religious poverty of the upper classes to the material poverty of the lower classes.
18. This perception may stem from her having reviewed several Norris books. In her review of his earlier *Barham of Beltana*, Stephen says Norris said 'somewhere' that he does not want 'to discuss motives and analyse emotions' (*E1* 36); she calls this attitude a lack of ambition in her 4 March 1905 reading notes, but accepts that he 'evidently knows his own limits, & does not attempt to go beyond them' (VS notes 29). In this 1 November 1905 review of *Lone Marie*, she uses comparison to challenge him to push beyond limits. In her 1907 review of *The Square Peg*, she expresses more frustration, openly 'protesting' about why Mr Norris is so content to stay inside the limits he has set for himself. She sees 'an almost sardonic air' that 'hint[s] ... he knows his boundary line as well as others and recognises that it is a narrow one, while at the same time he refuses pleasantly to push beyond it' (*E6* 340–1). Not surprisingly, Virginia Stephen, who would challenge herself, test genre boundaries and use her gifts to experiment throughout her career, does not understand W. E. Norris.
19. Stephen's long one-paragraph reviews of *The Wolf* and *The Ways of Rebellion* appeared on the same day in the *TLS*, 12 March 1908, demonstrating what she meant by 'pelted'.
20. See Rosenbaum's astute analysis of this review, including his insight into the connection between Ainger's work and Leslie Stephen's literary essays (173–4).
21. Leslie Stephen, of course, wrote numerous biographical essays and biographies, including 283 signed entries and many more unsigned ones (unfortunately, identification-related paperwork was destroyed) for the *Dictionary of National Biography* (Fenwick 245), which he also edited.
22. Endnotes in McNeillie and Clarke identify these sometimes extensive supplemental materials. Stephen, and later Woolf, seemed compelled to read, review or at least skim anything that might enlarge her overall knowledge about an author or subject.
23. As Dubino notes, Stephen portrays Boswell as 'a man of many contradictions; self-obsessed yet largely sympathetic and understanding; exuberant toward life but unable to settle down to any one project' ('VW' 37).
24. Caroline Stephen's *Light Arising* and *Quaker Strongholds* remain important to Quakers to this day.
25. Woolf would make the same feminist move with Clarissa Dalloway and Mrs Ramsay.
26. Virginia Woolf would intensify the class critique in her revision of this essay for *The Common Reader* by shifting to a maid's point of view; inequality is not picturesque to the maid (*CR* 196–200).
27. In fact, Ross identifies two of his essays, 'The Brand of Isis' and 'How We Lost the Book of Jasher', as written for two 'defunct undergraduate publications' (Acknowledgement iv), and the imaginary dialogue in 'The Jaded Intellectuals', set in a smoking room of a club, reads like an exaggerated version of undergraduate talk (248–55). Ross attended King's College, Cambridge.
28. Elizabeth Gordon Willson, building on Melba Cuddy-Keane's discussion of a '"pedagogical Woolf" concerned about making highbrow intellectual culture available to all'

(*VW* 2), notes Woolf's 'lifelong intellectual, emotional, and ethical engagement with the interconnectedness of democracy, education, and sites of reading' (89).
29. Woolf continues, 'Never shall I forget my extremity of pleasure – it was like being a violin and being played upon – when I found that she had sent a story of mine to Madge Symonds' ('Sketch' 95).

Conclusion: Implications

> Literature is no one's private ground; literature is common ground.
> – 'The Leaning Tower' (*E6* 278)

This study has sought to demonstrate what Virginia Stephen's apprenticeship as an essayist was like, how she educated herself, and what she learned that contributed to Virginia Woolf's later attempts to reach out to readers through her essays.

Broadly speaking, Virginia Stephen's homeschooling taught her about gender isolation and its impact on learning; her work at Morley College taught her about class exclusion and its impact on learning but also teaching; and her years as a reviewer taught her about different audiences and their impact on writing. This overall education affects Virginia Stephen's development as an essayist, but as she educated herself, she learned many other specific lessons, both positive and negative.

As Virginia Stephen explored her father's library and absorbed her mother's training, she experienced, quite literally, tension between two feminist views of education (separatist and non-compromising). Perhaps most important, Virginia Stephen experienced access *and* exclusion, was both inside *and* outside. Her class meant she had access to the wealth of her father's library, but her gender excluded her from a formal education outside that library. With no systematic curriculum framing her education, she practised learning from everyone, including her brother Thoby, and did so mainly through talking with others, reading everything she could put her hands on, attending classes at King's College London Ladies' Department as a non-matriculated student, and being tutored in Greek and Latin, the English patriarchy's nomenclature. She learned the importance of libraries and began using them and creating her own. She read widely among the classics, explored a wide variety of genres and had a glimmer of a woman's literary tradition. She watched her father and aunt live professional writing lives, observed the connection between writing and periodicals, and practised producing a periodical herself. Her reading taught her both what she was being excluded from and what some previous women had done in response. She developed discipline in her Greek studies, watched her aunt negotiate with the patriarchal culture, and absorbed the obligation to remember literary foremothers. Because both her father and Janet Case took her and her ideas seriously (though in different ways), used questions and discussion, and gave her freedom, she absorbed a pedagogy.

She discovered a male community of writers in her father's library and may also have discovered a community of female readers in *Atalanta*, but those communities existed only on paper. In many ways, she received an education well suited to a writer, but crucially, she experienced that education as isolating, fragmented and partial, and she perceived herself as uneducated.

When Virginia Stephen crossed Waterloo Bridge to teach at Morley College, she confronted another class, saw the impact of a very different kind of poor education, and observed the barriers to learning put up by the lack of a coherent curricular and historical framework. She saw a similarity between herself and others trying to educate themselves, identified with her students, and struggled to help them piece together their learning. While practising her teaching, she discovered she had little control over the curriculum, lectures did not work very well, and students were eager not only to learn, but also to establish a relationship with the teacher. She took her students and her teaching seriously, attempting to share what she knew with students, and in so doing, learned to engage them in conversation, use vivid detail, provide plenty of context, encourage access through biography, explain allusions and provide lists and handouts. She participated in a community of learners that faced formidable obstacles.

Virginia Stephen began writing reviews and the occasional essay for the *Guardian* in 1904, and by 1905, had begun working for the *Times Literary Supplement* as well. Between then and 1912, she created the conditions necessary for a writing life, worked with editors and learned how to conduct herself as a professional. Reviewing popular fiction meant she added contemporary fiction to her reading curriculum and practised writing almost every day. Learning to take notes, acknowledge the author's efforts and judge work on its merits, Stephen also learned to revise, particularly for different audiences. She developed a persona and a voice, learned how important independence was, and attempted to address both reader and writer in her reviews. As her apprenticeship progressed, she took her role and her readers more seriously, learning how to express both positive and negative reactions, to expand reviews into essays, and to state her aesthetic principles. In working with editors, she also learned how to navigate that dynamic, when to push back, and how to respond to editorial demands without losing her voice. She joined a community of writers trying to reach a community of readers.

The multiple lessons of Virginia Stephen's apprenticeship helped Virginia Woolf grow into an essayist who adopted the persona of a common reader addressing other common readers, who valued independence, pleasure and access, and who provided tools and strategies to readers for learning how to think, read and write. Virginia Stephen's isolated, fragmented education, spread over thirty years and consisting of reading, teaching and writing, shaped Virginia Woolf into an essayist who taught, as evidenced by an essay canon that reveals a philosophy of education, a curriculum and a pedagogy.[1]

Virginia Woolf responded to the lessons of her younger self's homeschooling with an appreciation for conversation, an acceptance of fragmentation paradoxically co-existing with a desire for coherence, and an admiration for inclusive strategies. She perceived herself as an unschooled outsider, and that perception influenced her positioning of herself as an amateur, a common reader speaking to other common readers. Although one of the best read of writers, Woolf chose to address her reader as a friend and equal, not as an inferior. Stephen gained a great deal of discipline as she worked on her own, and that, combined with her growing ability to use libraries, led to the massive research and reading behind most of Woolf's essays. Because reading was so crucial to Virginia Stephen, Woolf worked to communicate her love and enthusiasm for it throughout her career. Stephen's intense awareness of being shut out because she was female meant Woolf never lost her resentment about her lack of education, but even as she strongly identified with similar angers in others, she also saw the damage such anger could do to communication and art and tried to manage it. Ultimately, the division between her parents about education for women coloured her own attitudes, and Woolf embodied those contradictions at the same time she attempted to move beyond them.

Virginia Woolf responded to the lessons of her younger self's teaching experience by identifying with other outsiders, widening her definition of the reader and attempting to create a community of readers. Stephen saw and understood, more fully than before, her middle-class privilege, even though she did not, perhaps could not, consistently act on that understanding, and she chose to fight oppression as an ally through writing rather than as an activist through traditional political venues. She became more aware of the necessity of context, particularly of historical and cultural frameworks. Stephen's teaching reinforced her conviction, gained from her homeschooling, that inclusive strategies were important, and she eschewed the authoritative lecture for the exploratory conversation, for reaching out, for making connections. She learned the power of narrative and the telling detail. For her, reading and learning brought pleasure, and she wanted all readers to experience that enjoyment, not just those who had the luxury or leisure to do so. In fact, part of Woolf's later success in reaching the reader lies in her acknowledgement of readers' fears, obstacles and genuine responses, whether negative or positive.

Finally, Virginia Woolf responded to the lessons of her younger self's book reviewing experience with a fierce belief in independence for the writer and the reader and a strong need to make her non-fiction accessible. Stephen called on her literary tradition and saw the gaps in her literary education; gained a sense of genre's power and its capacity for blending; observed the hold of convention and its vulnerability to courageous overthrow; and learned from writers who submitted to or struggled against threats to aesthetic vision. She became increasingly adept at expressing her opinion in her own voice without attracting an editor's ire and without lecturing or preaching. Most important, she enlarged her definition of the reader even further, revising to meet various audiences and varying her approach when necessary. Stephen emerged from her apprenticeship understanding her obligations and role as a professional, which included creating a relationship with her reader based on respect, mutual learning and access, something Virginia Woolf succeeded in doing.

The lessons Virginia Stephen learned, then, led to Virginia Woolf's creation of the common reader, an emphasis on the pleasure of reading, a belief in democratic principles, great respect for the reader, an inclusive pedagogy and an attempt to teach without being didactic.[2] Her overall goal, to have readers become critics with voices of their own, to help students become independent of the teacher, also reveals an underlying desire to remove or at least lower class barriers. As Michael Kaufmann notes, in comparing Woolf to Eliot, Woolf aimed to enlighten, not mystify, the reader (140). Because of Stephen's apprenticeship, Woolf becomes an educator who brings components of the familiar essay to bear on literary topics or subjects, or as Melba Cuddy-Keane puts it, 'integrate[s] the intellectual and the personal'. Cuddy-Keane continues,

> While her commitment to a common readership and her rejection of an authoritative voice link her essays in style and approach to the familiar essay and forms of everyday writing, the literary issues that she addresses connect her essays in content with the academic professional article beginning to emerge. ('Woolf' 907)

Woolf also demonstrated, through her method in essays, *how*: how to be a female intellectual, how to develop and use a public voice, how to read, research, write and criticise (Johnston in conversation; Fernald, 'Pleasure' 194, 210; Cuddy-Keane, *VW* 1). After all, the essay as a genre lends itself to education, and Woolf, according to Jeanne Dubino, uses the essay as the vehicle for her role as an educator (Intro 9) and teaches in a gentle way,[3] which recalls Virginia Woolf's memory of Leslie Stephen's teaching. Virginia Stephen's education taught her lessons that influenced the attitudes, content and methods of Virginia Woolf's essays.

The lessons Virginia Stephen learned during her apprenticeship turned Virginia Woolf into an essayist compelled to teach. Virginia Stephen published 158 reviews and essays during her apprenticeship (see Appendix 5), and Virginia Woolf wrote or published 500 more, for an essay canon total of 658.[4] Stephen and Woolf wrote 102 essays that can be called overtly pedagogical (about reading, writing and/or education), 15.5 per cent of her total output.[5] Anne Fernald notices this marked pedagogical content, commenting that Woolf's literary essays 'attempt to teach readers how to read' ('Pleasure' 194), and Danell Jones shows what a good creative writing teacher Woolf can be. Woolf's essays model the kind of education she wishes for her readers; indeed, the essays become an education, imbued with a philosophy, curriculum and pedagogy. Woolf thus both comments on education and educates. As she points out at the end of her essay on Sterne's *A Sentimental Journey*, most great writers are, in their own way, teachers (*E5* 407). That insight certainly applies to her own work. Reading Woolf's essays through an educational lens reveals a teacher at work: teaching by example, by suggestion, through conversation, through method, through relationship. Portrayals of teachers and students, comments about teaching and learning, and advice about reading and writing emerge everywhere. One can most easily see this educational presence or thrust when Woolf overtly writes about reading and readers, but it surfaces elsewhere as well. Most significantly, Virginia Stephen's education means that education – as subject, rationale, underlying philosophy, implied curriculum and strategic pedagogy – permeates Virginia Woolf's essays.

By the time Virginia Stephen publishes her last review two weeks before her thirtieth birthday in 1912, she has become the essayist we recognise as Virginia Woolf. Not only does 'The Novels of George Gissing' show all the marks of a Woolf essay, combining review and essay; biography, era and work; writer's aesthetic and reader's response; and the personal and the impersonal, it reveals maturity, an ability to '[range] freely' across her subject's life, time and works, and a 'command of her medium' (McNeillie xv). On the face of it, her essay does not seem pedagogical at all. Yet it illustrates a pervasive educational quality.

Virginia Stephen marks the publication of a new edition, Sidgwick and Jackson's reprint of Gissing's eight later works, to write an essay about Gissing. Other than noting that the publishers have produced these works 'well and cheaply' and making sure readers know they can buy *Born in Exile* at 'railway bookstalls for sevenpence' (*E*1 355–6), she barely, as McNeillie points out, refers to the edition or the works reprinted in it. Rather, she 'celebrates her subject at length and in depth' (xv). Her assignment becomes an excuse to educate her readers about George Gissing's reputation, work and point of view and to ensure, even in the face of some high barriers, that they walk away from her 'review' wanting to read him.

Over the course of the essay, she crafts a definition of Gissing's readers, and in so doing, encourages her readers to become part of that group. Carefully remaining tentative ('If this is at all true of his readers . . . '), she acknowledges Gissing 'does not appeal to a great multitude' – he is not popular or famous, though respected – but she also lists a wide variety of people who will purchase this new edition: those who live in 'houses where very few novels are kept', '[o]rdinary cultivated people', and

> governesses who scarcely ever read; mechanics; working men who despise novels; dons who place him high among writers of English prose; professional men; the daughters of farmers in the North. We can imagine that he is the favourite novelist of a great many middle-aged, sceptical, rather depressed men and women who when they read want thought and understanding of life as it is, not wit or romance. (*E*1 356)

Readers reaching the end of a Gissing novel may try to deflect its despair, 'exclaiming, "After all, this is only one side"' (*E*1 357), readers used to identifying with heroes and heroines are 'completely baffled' by the harshness with which Gissing treats his poverty-stricken characters (*E*1 358–9), and yet readers cannot dismiss him as a cynic because 'the real cynics are the writers who have a trivial merry view of life, and make people easily content and drugged with cheap happiness' (*E*1 359). When she expresses her certainty that Gissing's novels will not perish because there will always be a few readers who exclaim '"This man understood!"' (*E*1 361), she in effect urges her readers to join those few.

Stephen acknowledges why readers have difficulty reading Gissing – his books are sad, they detail the overwhelmingly bleak and degrading costs of poverty, they prevent the 'ordinary excitement of guessing the end', they are sometimes dull and have a low tone (*E*1 356, 359) – but without castigating those readers who recoil, she keeps giving readers reasons to keep at it. 'You have to read from the first page to the last to get the full benefit of his art' (*E*1 359), she writes, but if you do, 'the low almost insignificant chapters gather weight and impetus' and you discover 'a kind of flameless fire' glowing at the heart of his 'terse workman-like prose' (*E*1 359–60). Most important, she helps readers 'grasp his point of view', particularly his focus on men and women who think, which allows him to highlight different kinds of pleasures, 'of reading, companionship, and a few comfortable evenings', within different kinds of relationships: among friends, or between those who like the same books, or between 'one man and men in general'. Out of those relationships, she writes,

> he makes the texture of his works. Loves have exploded; tragedies have fired up and sunk to ashes; these quiet, undemonstrative feelings between one man and another, one woman and another, persist; they spin some kind of thread across the ravages; they are the noblest things he has found in the world. (E1 359)

Pedagogically, to point out only some examples, Stephen uses narrative, outlining the basic plot underlying all Gissing's novels; lists, such as types of characters used by novelists; and context, using a letter Gissing wrote about what publishers thought of him and building a detailed cultural framework about poverty and its effects. She presents and explains paradoxes, asks questions and uses quotations, all while employing vivid, moving details. But most important, she provides some principles and a model for evaluating literature.

When all that is left of a writer are works and editions ('twelve volumes of dead leaves!'), Virginia Stephen writes, our task is to 'grasp [the author's] point of view' and 'stand where he stood' (E1 355–6). In her view, 'what Gissing proves is the terrible importance of money, and, if you slip, how you fall and fall and fall' (E1 357). She also thinks most novelists have 'one great theme', and that Gissing's is 'the life of a man of fine character and intelligence who is absolutely penniless and is therefore the sport of all that is most sordid and brutal in modern life' (E1 356). Positing that Gissing's misery and Meredith's magnificence are both true because we believe both, she contends, 'The thing that really matters, that makes a writer a true writer and his work permanent, is that he should really see' (E1 361). But how can readers tell true books from false? Rather than assert, she suggests a possible answer through 'two figures':

> You clasp a bird in your hands; it is so frightened that it lies perfectly still; yet somehow it is a living body, there is a heart in it and the breast is warm. You feel a fish on your line; the line hangs straight as before down into the sea, but there is a strain on it; it thrills and quivers. That is something like the feeling which live books give and dead ones cannot give; they strain and quiver. But satisfactory works of art have a quality that is no less important. It is that they are complete. A good novelist, it seems, goes about the world seeing squares and circles where the ordinary person sees mere storm-drift .... Here is a little world for us to walk in with all that a human being needs. (E1 361)

Once she has helped her readers see by using 'figures', she concludes: when books have these two essential qualities, life and completeness, as Gissing's books do, they will not perish. She has taught us what she knows.[6]

Perhaps I see Virginia Stephen's apprenticeship so strongly in Woolf's essays because of that long-ago reaction to reading them as a fledgling graduate student. As I asked in my Preface, why, when this woman had clearly read more, knew more and wrote better than any English literature graduate from Yale, Princeton or Johns Hopkins ever could, was I not intimidated by *her*? Why did I feel as though Virginia Woolf herself was giving me permission to read her, study her, write about her? Why, when background, class and education should have made me feel excluded from the world of those essays, did I feel included instead?[7] I have spent most of my scholarly career trying to answer those questions, and for me, much of the answer lies in Stephen's homeschooling and in her teaching at Morley College at the same time as she began writing reviews for publication.

But it is not just me who sees this connection. Woolf herself links her education, her work at Morley College and her essays. Near the end of her life, she writes the following draft of a letter to Ben Nicolson, trying to answer his charges against Bloomsbury:

> I never went to school or college. My father spent perhaps £100 on my education. When I was a young woman I tried to share the fruits of that very imperfect education with the working classes by teaching literature at Morley College; by holding a Womens Cooperative Guild meeting weekly; and, politically, by working for the vote. It is true I wrote books and some of those books, like the Common Reader, A Room of One's Own and Three Guineas . . . have sold many thousand copies. That is, I did my best to make them reach a far wider circle than a little private circle of exquisite and cultivated people. And to some extent I succeeded. (L6 419–20)

The young, lonely and insecure Virginia Stephen absorbed lessons from her homeschooling, her teaching and her reviewing as she struggled to come into voice. Those lessons, those struggles, leave traces in Virginia Woolf's essays, traces that encourage others working, learning and struggling to come into *their* voices. She told Ben Nicolson in the same letter that she 'ought to have been able to make not merely thousands of people interested in literature; but millions' (L6: 420). Yearning to communicate, Virginia Woolf could not have known her essays would go a long way toward achieving that desire.

Notes

1. See, for example, Daugherty, 'Streets'; Yoshida; Hagen; and Detloff's *Virginia Woolf Miscellany* issue devoted to Woolf and Pedagogy, 73 (Spring–Summer 2008).
2. See Desmond Pacey, who writes, 'Her critical approach is modest and unassuming. Her essays read like conversation . . . She never . . . speaks with academic condescension' (34).
3. Shannon Lakanen, in conversation.
4. This total includes extended essays such as *A Room of One's Own* and *Three Guineas*, variant and much-revised essays, broadcast and talk transcripts, and extensive drafts published in the *Essays*, and I suspect the total is provisional.
5. I use these general topics to categorise Stephen and Woolf's essays: (1) history, political, social, class; (2) literature, literary history; (3) women; (4) aesthetics, genre, other arts, criticism; (5) contemporary literature; (6) travel, place, cultures; (7) personal, family; (8) science, philosophy, economics; (9) reading, writing, education, pedagogical; and (10) miscellaneous. Overlap between and among these topics of course exists, so an essay that falls into literature and literary history, for example, might also fall into women or pedagogical or class.
6. Pierre Coustillas, writing about Gissing in Woolf's works and papers for the *Gissing Newsletter*, thinks this essay, 'as warmly and lucidly appreciative as the first [on *The Private Papers of Henry Ryecroft*], appears the best of the four she was to write [on Gissing]' (6).
7. Anne Fernald, discussing 'Woolf's surprisingly resonant appearance in the works of three mid- to late-twentieth century African writers', cites Wai Chee Dimock's point that 'one mark of literary endurance is the continuing resonance of a literary work for

"the reader not implied, not welcome"'. Then noting, as Stephen and Woolf often do, the congruence of a flaw with an asset, she writes, 'One of Woolf's limitations may have been her inability to imagine African readers or writers; one of her strengths, however, is their ability to imagine, revise, and respond to her' (*Feminism* 14). Woolf continues to connect with readers quite unlike herself because she models what Fernald calls an 'at once generous and critical' reading of her own literary tradition, encouraging us to read her work in the same way (15).

Appendices

Appendix 1

Virginia Stephen's King's College Department for Ladies Class Schedule

This class schedule derives from Christine Kenyon Jones and Anna Snaith's detailed 'Tilting at Universities'; the King's College for Women Register listing instructors and numbers of students taking courses each term from 1879 to 1910, including tutors and fees (KWA/R2); the Address Books for Courses at King's College for Women, KWA/RAD 3–7; and the *King's College Syllabus of Lectures* volumes 1–3 for 1878–89, 1889–1900 and 1900–9. Annual Reports for previous years at the back of each year's *Syllabus of Lectures* and the King's College London annual *Calendars* provided much corroborating information.

1897–8

Michaelmas (autumn) – M, 11 October to F, 17 December

Greek Elementary, Prof. George C. W. Warr

Mondays, 2–3.30 p.m.
Mayor, *Greek for Beginners*
Morice, *Stories in Attic Greek*

Continental History, Prof. John Knox Laughton

Tuesdays, 10–11 a.m.[1]
1660–1702 (no listed texts)
subject prescribed for London B.A. exam

English History, Prof. John Knox Laughton

Fridays, 10–11 a.m.
1660–1702 (no listed texts)
subject prescribed for London B. A. exam

Lent (spring) – M, *17 January to F, 25 March*

    Greek Elementary, Prof. George C. W. Warr

Mondays, 2–3.30 p.m.
presumably with texts above

    Continental History, Prof. John Knox Laughton

Tuesdays, 10–11 a.m.
1702–1748
subject prescribed for Cambridge Higher Local exam

    English History, Prof. John Knox Laughton

Fridays, 10–11 a.m.
1702–1748
subject prescribed for Cambridge Higher Local exam

Easter (summer) – M, *2 May to F, 8 July*

    Greek Elementary, Prof. George C. W. Warr

Mondays, 2–3.30 p.m.
presumably with texts above

    Continental History, Prof. John Knox Laughton

Tuesdays, 10–11 a.m.
1748–1789
subject prescribed for Cambridge Higher Local exam

    English History, Prof. John Knox Laughton

Fridays, 10–11 a.m.
1748–1789
subject prescribed for Cambridge Higher Local exam

1898–9

Michaelmas (autumn) – M, *17 October to F, 23 December*

    Advanced Greek, Reading and Composition, Prof. George C. W. Warr

Mondays, 3.30–4.30 p.m.
Sophocles, *Oedipus Coloneus*; Greek prose
subject prescribed for Final Pass B.A., London

> *Intermediate Latin, Reading,* Miss Pater

Tuesdays, 2–3 p.m.
Virgil, *Aeneid*, IX, X
subject prescribed for Intermediate B.A., London

> *English History,* Prof. John Knox Laughton

Fridays, 10–11 a.m.
Accession of Elizabeth to Essex

Lent (spring) – M, 16 January to F, 24 March

> *Advanced Greek, Reading and Composition,* Prof. George C. W. Warr

Mondays, 3.30–4.30 p.m.
Demosthenes, *Medias and Androtion*; Greek prose
subject prescribed for Final Pass B.A., London

> *Intermediate Latin, Reading,* Miss Pater

Tuesdays, 2–3 p.m.
Livy, IX
subject prescribed for Intermediate B.A., London

> *English History,* Prof. John Knox Laughton

Fridays, 10–11 a.m.
Accession of James I to Laud

Easter (summer) – M, 1 May to F, 7 July[2]

> *Intermediate Greek, Reading,* Miss Pater

Tuesdays [Mondays?], 11–12 a.m.[3]
Revision and Unseen Translation
(Euripides' *Hippolytus* in Lent term, Plato's *Laches* in Michaelmas)
subject prescribed for Intermediate B.A., London

> *Intermediate Latin, Reading,* Miss Pater

Tuesdays, 2–3 p.m.
Revision of Virgil, Livy texts used in Michaelmas and Lent terms
subject prescribed for Intermediate B.A., London

1899–1900

Michaelmas (autumn) – M, 9 October to F, 15 December

Elementary German, Miss Emma Sophia Buchheim

Mondays, 12–1 p.m.
Aue, *Elementary German Grammar*
Buchheim, C. A., *Modern German Reader*, part 1
Buchheim, E. S., *German Poetry for Beginners*
Class II pass (course exam)

Intermediate Greek, Reading, Miss Pater

Tuesdays, 11–12 a.m.
Plato, *Ion*
subject prescribed for Intermediate B.A., London

Greek, private tuition, Miss Pater

Intermediate Latin, Reading, Miss Pater

Tuesdays, 2–3 p.m.
Horace, *Odes* I–III
subject prescribed for Intermediate B.A., London

Lent (spring) – M, 15 January to F, 23 March

Elementary German, Miss Emma Sophia Buchheim[4]

Mondays, 12–1 p.m.
presumably with texts above

Advanced Greek, Reading and Composition, Prof. Warr [Miss Pater][5]

Mondays, 3.30–4.30 p.m.
Thucydides, Book II; Greek prose
subject prescribed for Final Pass B.A., London

Intermediate Latin, Reading, Miss Pater

Tuesdays, 2–3 p.m.
Horace, *Odes* IV and *Epodes*
subject prescribed for Intermediate B.A., London

Easter (summer) – M, 30 April to F, 6 July

Elementary German, Miss Emma Sophia Buchheim

Mondays, 12–1 p.m.
presumably with texts above
[Miss Buchheim's father, Prof. C. A. Buchheim, died on 4 June 1900]

Intermediate Greek, Reading, Miss Pater

Tuesdays, 11–12 a.m.[6]
Revision and Unseen Translation
(taught Sophocles' *Antigone* Lent Term, Plato's *Ion* in Michaelmas)
subject prescribed for Intermediate B.A., London

Intermediate Latin, Reading, Miss Pater

Tuesdays, 2–3 p.m.
Cicero *de Officiis*, III
subject prescribed for Intermediate B.A., London

1900–1

Michaelmas (autumn) – M, 8 October to F, 14 December

German Grammar and Reading, Miss E. S. Buchheim

Mondays, 11–12 a.m.
Buchheim, C. A., ed., Lessing's *Minna von Barnheim* [comedy]
subject prescribed for matriculation, London
Class II pass (course exam)

[Two Greek classes, perhaps these two[7]]

Intermediate Reading, Miss Pater [Miss Lucas]

Mondays [Wednesdays?], 3–4 p.m.
Lysias, *Eratosthenes and Agoratus*
subject prescribed for Intermediate B.A., London

Advanced Reading and Composition, Prof. Warr [Miss Lucas]

Mondays, 3.30–4.30 p.m.
Homer, *Iliad*, XXII–XXIV, Greek prose
subject prescribed for Final Pass B.A., London
[Professor Warr died on 21 February 1901]

316   Virginia Woolf's Apprenticeship

Lent (spring) – M, 14 January to F, 22 March

German Grammar and Reading, Miss E. S. Buchheim

Mondays, 11–12 a.m.
presumably with text above
subject prescribed for matriculation, London

[One Greek class, probably this one[8]]

Intermediate Reading, Miss Pater and Miss Clay

Mondays, 3–4 p.m.
Aeschylus, *Septem contra Thebas*
Subject prescribed for Intermediate B.A., London
[Miss Pater resigned in February]

Easter (summer) – M, 29 April to F, 5 July[9]

Greek, private tuition, probably from Miss Clay[10]

1901

Michaelmas (autumn) – M, 7 October to F, 13 December

Greek, private tuition, probably from Professor Flamstead Walters[11]

Notes

1. The Syllabus generally specified a beginning time only, but given the earliest syllabi Timetables that also provided an ending time and the focus on attendance hours, Virginia Stephen's classes must have been an hour long; exceptions, such as Professor Warr's Greek Elementary, were noted on the Syllabus.
2. Jenkins has Stephen enrolled in English History as well (29), but the 1898–9 Address Book (KWA/RAD 4) shows that was not the case; see also Jones and Snaith 9 (Fig. 1b) and 41.
3. The King's Ladies Department Address Book for 1898–9 (KWA/RAD 4; Jones and Snaith 9 [Fig. 1b]) has ditto marks under 'Greek adv Rd.' and 'Latin Int. Rd.' for Easter Term 1899, indicating that the registration person knew Miss Stephen was not signing up for Elementary Greek in Easter Term. But Professor Warr offered Advanced Greek, Reading and Composition only in Michaelmas and Lent Terms and is not listed for any Easter Term Greek courses in the *Syllabus of Lectures for 1898–99* (22; Time Table 58). He was scheduled to teach Greek History (under Ancient History and Literature) in Easter Term on Mondays at 3 p.m. (13–14; Time Table 58), but he does not appear in the Easter Term list as having taught at all (KWA/R2 71), so perhaps not enough students signed up or perhaps he was ill, as Jenkins suggests (29). The only non-elementary Greek course left in the 1898–9 *Syllabus of Lectures* for Easter Term is Miss Pater's, Intermediate rather than Advanced, and is listed as Revision and

Unseen Translation meeting on Tuesdays from 11 to 12 (22). Virginia Stephen's letters at the time confirm she was taking both Latin and Greek from Miss Pater (*L1* 23, 26), but in a Tuesday letter, she says we have been 'to our Latin this afternoon; and yesterday was Greek' (*L1* 26). Since the Register term list records Miss Pater as having five students in Greek and twenty in Latin (KWA/R2 71), perhaps she and the students in Greek agreed to change the meeting day. Or perhaps Virginia Stephen simply had the day of her letter (or her course) wrong.

4. The seeming discrepancy between the text in Jones and Snaith (28 n24) and Figures 5a and 5b (32–3) – did Virginia Stephen pass course exams in Michaelmas and/or Lent Terms? – stems from the use of two different sources. KWA/R1 listed exam results in 1899 and 1900 as they occurred; the K/SER1/170 source (*King's College Magazine, Ladies' Department*) folded those class lists into their publication. So the *Magazine* printed exam results for Michaelmas Term in Lent Term.

5. Since Warr is not listed in the staff register for this term (KWA/R2), Jenkins wonders whether Stephen stayed in this class and studied Thucydides with Pater or whether she joined Pater's Intermediate Reading Greek class, which met on Tuesdays from 11 to 12, and studied Sophocles' *Antigone* (30 n8). Perhaps the latter? See 107.

6. The same situation occurs in this Easter Term as in the previous one. The Address Book shows a ditto mark for 'Grk. Ad.' in Easter Term. But no Advanced Greek course is listed in the *Syllabus of Lectures* for Easter Term 1900 (*SL 1899–1900* 22; Time Table 62), and Professor Warr is not listed in the King's College London term list register as having taught Greek of any kind in 1899–1900. Miss Pater is listed for Latin, with four students, and Greek, with two (KWA/R2 77).

7. Gwyn Jenkins plausibly suggests the two courses could be Intermediate Greek Reading and Intermediate Grammar, both taught by Miss Pater, and since the latter course was offered on Thursdays at 11, the possible time conflict noted on p. 69 would not have existed (31). On the other hand, Stephen enrolled in no other Greek (or Latin) Grammar classes, her 23 October [1900] letter also erases the time conflict, and Stephen had been struggling with Homer in the summer of 1898 (*L1* 19).

8. Miss Pater resigned her post as classical tutor at King's in February 1901 (AR 1901–2, *SL 1902–3* 50). In the Register of term lists, Miss Pater and Miss Clay are listed together in Lent Term as having two classes in Greek, with seven students, and two classes in Latin, with seven students (KWA/R2 81), along with having two Greek private tuition students and two Latin private tuition students (KWA/R2 82). Such evidence suggests Miss Pater started the term and Miss Clay finished it when Miss Pater was forced to resign due to illness. Virginia Stephen's reference to Miss Clay in her 1903 journal sketch of Janet Case (*PA* 182) makes it more likely she was enrolled in Miss Pater's Intermediate Greek Reading than in Professor Warr's Advanced Greek Reading, as Jenkins also suggests (31). Also, although the Annual Report calls Professor Warr's death a 'grievous loss' and 'sudden' (*SL 1901–2* 48), he had not taught in Michaelmas Term (KWA/R2 79).

Jenkins suggests the King's College Ladies' Department 'was keen to keep George Warr's name on the *Syllabus of Lectures* even when in 1900–01 he was too ill to teach' because he was a 'male, lettered academic' (32). But the Department's willingness to continue scheduling George Warr's classes probably had more to do with his support of their existence than with his credentials. Also, as a practical matter, schedules are determined far in advance and if beloved professors say they think they will be well enough to teach, a Department's affection may outweigh evidence to the contrary. After all, the Department had also scheduled Miss Pater's 1900–1 classes not knowing she would become ill, need Miss Lucas and Miss Clay to take her classes, and then resign.

9. The 1900–1 Address Book (KWA/RAD6) shows that Stephen was not enrolled in German Grammar Easter Term, as Jenkins suggests (31); see also Jones and Snaith 12 (Fig. 1e) and 41.

10. Miss Clay, according to the King's College for Women term list, taught a Greek class (KWA/R2 83) and had five private tuition students in Latin and six in Greek (KWA/R2 84). See 70, Figure 3.1.

Evidence in the King's College London archives corroborates Virginia Stephen's belief that she can judge her Greek teachers' merits because of her 'varied experience' (*PA* 182); that experience included extensive work with Professor Warr, Clara Pater and Janet Case, but also some exposure to Miss Lucas, Professor Walters (who became Professor Warr's replacement in the Department) and Miss Clay. Miss Clay made enough of an impression to be named in Stephen's sketch: '[Miss Case] was more professional than Miss Pater though perhaps not so cultivated – she was more genial than Miss Clay & as good a scholar' (*PA* 182). Stephen substituted 'cultivated' for the original 'sympathetic' ([Diary] 50), and deleted a phrase after 'as good a scholar –': 'of course dear old Professor Warr with his courtesy & deliberation would soon have' (*PA* 412), perhaps hinting at a judgement of both Miss Case and Miss Clay.

But who was Miss Clay? Almost certainly Agnes Muriel Clay, who was awarded a scholarship (£30 in Classics) at Lady Margaret Hall, Oxford, in 1895–6 (*AR for LMH*, I, no. 17 5), received a Class II in Classical Moderations as part of the University Honour Schools in 1898 (*AR for LMH*, II, no. 19 5), and earned a Class I in Literae Humaniores, a B.A. diploma, in 1900 (*AR for LMH*, II, no. 21 4). She also was awarded a Class I MA degree in 1920 when women were admitted to degrees (*AR for LMH*, V, no. 43 5 and 'Students of LMH, 1879–1922'). She was a Resident Tutor at Lady Margaret Hall from 1901 to 1910 (when she married E. H. N. Wilde), served as the Librarian for a short period, tutored for the Association for Education of Women at Oxford, which made lectures and coaching available to 'members of all the Women's Societies' (Gwyer 30), and worked with both the Oxford Mission to Calcutta (Gwyer 30–1) and the St Pancras Charity Organisation Society (*AR for LMH*, IV, no. 36 after page 11). She was the Oxford correspondent for the *Brown Book: The Lady Margaret Hall Chronicle*, served on the Lady Margaret Hall Council in various capacities from 1915 until its replacement by a College Governing Body in 1953 (Lannon 29), and left a bequest to the Buildings Endowment Fund on her death in 1962 (letters, Mrs A. M. Wilde folder).

Her scholarship was solid, particularly in Latin; she and A. H. J. Greenidge published *Sources for Roman History 133–70 BC* in 1903. When reissued by Clarendon Press in 1960 and 1986, the second edition editor noted he did not change the original editors' selection (Gray v). Miss Clay was also one of thirty-five women contributors out of 1,500 total to the eleventh *Britannica*, furnishing all the entries on Roman law (Thomas 18, 36). Furthermore, she lived at 3 Gordon Street, Gordon Square, in 1907 (*The Brown Book: Lady Margaret Hall Chronicle*, November 1907 6) and was at 35B Mecklenburgh Square in 1921–2 (*AR for LMH*, Vol. V, no. 43 2). Perhaps she literally crossed paths with Virginia Stephen and then Virginia Woolf. (Both Miss Buchheim and Miss Clay [Mrs Wilde] outlived Virginia Woolf. Did they ever realise Woolf had been their student? Did they ever read Woolf or write to her?)

Most pertinent to Stephen's comment in her sketch, however, is that Agnes Muriel Clay was born in 1878. Thus, when she taught and tutored Virginia Stephen at King's College Ladies' Department, she was just four years older than her student and teaching for the first time. Her subsequent work – teaching Lady Margaret Hall students, coaching Oxford women and serving the Charity Organisation Society – indicates an effective and caring teacher. But presumably she would have been nervous, aware of her inexperience and thus perhaps overly stern when she walked into the beloved Miss Pater's classrooms in the middle of a term? No wonder she may have seemed less genial than Miss Case.

11. Jones and Snaith surmise these private tuition lessons were with Miss Pater, but neither Miss Pater nor Miss Clay is listed as a tutor in the King's College for Women Register

for Michaelmas Term 1901 (KWA/R2 85), and Miss Pater had resigned. Professor Flamstead Walters, who would begin teaching Greek in Lent Term 1902 and taught Latin and Greek at King's College from then on, contrary to Jenkins's assertion about the Classics at King's after Professor Warr's death (32), taught Latin in Michaelmas, with five students, and had fifteen private tuition students in Latin and Greek (KWA/R2 86), so if Stephen followed up on the private tuition she signed up for, her private lessons were probably from him.

Tangentially, Jones and Snaith say Vanessa Stephen took Art in Michaelmas Term 1900 (7). But an examination of the handwriting of other entries in the Registration book suggests she registered for Amb (KWA/RAD 6; Jones and Snaith, Fig. 1e 12) or Ambulance Lectures, the First Aid course, taught by Peyton T. B. Beale, assistant surgeon at King's College Hospital. Why Vanessa took a course that covered treatments for fractures, wounds, burns, fainting and so forth (*SL 1900–1* 32–3) has not been discovered. Perhaps she wanted to have some nursing knowledge in her role as female head of the household?

Appendix 2

Virginia Stephen's Library

Books listed below are in the Library of Leonard and Virginia Woolf (LLVW), Manuscripts Archives and Special Collections (MASC), Holland/Terrell Libraries, Washington State University, Pullman, WA, unless otherwise noted with the abbreviations below:

F1 or F2 – Funke catalogue: *Virginia & Leonard Woolf* (F1); *This Perpetual Fight* (F2)
HRC – Harry Ransom Center, University of Texas, Austin, TX
PO – Private owner
S – Sotheby's sale, 27 July 1970
– Book purchased or received, as noted in *L1* or *PA*, but not in LLVW[1]

Proof that books located in the Library of Leonard and Virginia Woolf belonged to Virginia Stephen include an inscription to or by her, a monogram, a bookplate, a date or other clear identification marks. Books in the LLVW listed below have such evidence except those marked with these symbols:

* Almost surely a VS book; convincing contextual reasons, but no proof
+ Possibly a VS book; contextual reasons exist, but not entirely convincing

Not listed here are books inherited from Stephen's parents, Thoby and so forth. In other words, Virginia Stephen's Library, as I have constructed it here, does not include all the books that would have filled those boxes in 46 Gordon Square. Books published in 1912 or before with a 'VW – binder' designation but no other corroborating journal or letter evidence have also not been included because although AVS certainly bound many books, so did VW, making it impossible to determine when a book was bound. See, for example, George Gissing's *The Nether World*, published in 1907 (K&M-V 86).

Brackets at end of entries provide either source or source page numbers for ownership information. Endnotes describe exceptions or add information.

HRC Abercrombie, Lascelles. *Emblems of Love; Designed in Several Discourses.* London: J. Lane, the Bodley Head, 1912.
* Aeschylus. *The Prometheus Bound of Aeschylus.* Ed. and trans. Janet Case. London: Dent, 1905.

+ Aeschylus. *Aischylou Agamemnon = Aeschyli Agamemnon ad fidem manuscriptorum emendavit notas et glossarium adjecti Carolus Jacobus Blomfield*. 4th ed. London: B. Fellowes, 1832.
+ Apuleius. *The Golden Ass*. Trans. William Aldington. Ed. George Sampson. London: George Bell & Sons, 1904. [L1 325]
[*Arabian Nights*] *Le Livre des Mille nuits et une nuit: Traduction littérale et complète du texte arabe*. Trans. J. C. Mardrus. 8 vols. Paris: E. Fasquelle, 1908–12. Vol. 1 only.
Arber, Edward, comp. *An English Garner: Ingatherings from Our History and Literature*. 7 vols. London: E. Arber, 1877–83.
Arnold, Matthew. *The Study of Celtic Literature*. London: Smith, Elder & Co., 1891.
* Bacon, Francis. *The Essays or Counsels, Civil and Moral, of Sir Francis Bacon, Lord Verulam, Viscount St. Alban: With a Table of the Colours of Good and Evil: Whereunto is Added the Wisdom of the Antients*. Trans. Arthur Gorges. London: Samuel Mearne, 1680. [L1 66]
# Baedeker, Karl. *Greece. A Handbook for Travellers*. 3rd rev. and enl. ed. London: Dulau, 1905. [PA 319, 331]
Baedeker, Karl. *Northern France, from Belgium and the English Channel to the Loire, excluding Paris and Its Environs: Handbook for Travellers*. 3rd ed. New York: C. Scribner's Sons, 1899.
Balzac, Honoré de. *Eugénie Grandet*. [PA 222]
Bible. English. Authorized. *The Book of Common Prayer and The Holy Bible: Containing the Old Testament and the New, Translated out of the Original Tongues and with the Former Translations Diligently Compared and Revised by His Majesties Speciall Command: Appointed to be Read in Churches*. Cambridge: John Hayes, 1683.
Bible. English. Authorized. *The Holy Bible: Containing the Old Testament and the New, Translated out of the Original Tongues and with the Former Translations Diligently Compared and Revised by His Majesty's Special Command: Appointed to be Read in Churches*. Oxford: Oxford UP, 1900.
+ Bible. N. T. Greek. *He Kaine Diatheke = The Greek New Testament: With the Readings Adopted by the Revisers of the Authorized Version*. Oxford: Clarendon, 1888.
+ Boswell, James. *The Journal of a Tour to the Hebrides with Samuel Johnson, LL.D.* 3rd ed. London: J. M. Dent, 1902.[2]
Brown, Horatio Robert Forbes. *Venice: An Historical Sketch of the Republic*. 2nd and rev. ed. London: Rivington, Percival and Co., 1895.
Browning, Robert. *Pocket Volume of Selections from the Poetical Works of Robert Browning*. London: Smith, Elder, & Co., 1890.
Browning, Robert. *Pocket Volume of Selections from the Poetical Works of Robert Browning*. London: Smith, Elder, & Co., 1894.
Burton, Robert. *The Anatomy of Melancholy*. 8th ed. London: Peter Parker, 1676.
Bury, J. B. *A History of Greece to the Death of Alexander the Great*. 1st ed. London: Macmillan, 1900.
Bury, Richard de. *The Love of Books: The Philobiblion of Richard de Bury*. Trans. E. C. Thomas. London: A. Moring, De la More, 1902.
Butcher, Samuel Henry. *Harvard Lectures on Greek Subjects*. London: Macmillan, 1904.
Butcher, Samuel Henry. *Some Aspects of the Greek Genius*. 2nd ed. London and New York: Macmillan, 1893.
Butcher, Samuel Henry and A. Lang. *The Odyssey of Homer Done into English Prose*. London: Macmillan, 1897.
Butler, Samuel. *The Way of All Flesh*. 2nd ed. London: A. C. Fifield, 1908.
Byron, George Gordon Byron. [L1 376–7][3]
Cassell's German Dictionary: In Two Parts, German–English – English–German. Ed. Elizabeth Weir. London: Cassell, 1906.

Chaucer, Geoffrey. *The Complete Works of Geoffrey Chaucer*. Ed. Rev. Walter W. Skeat. Oxford: Clarendon Press, 1901.

Clough, Arthur Hugh. *Poems*. London: Macmillan, 1898.

+ Cockerell, Douglas. *Bookbinding and the Care of Books, A Text-Book for Bookbinders and Librarians*. London: John Hogg, 1901. [L1 45, 56]

HRC Conrad, Joseph. *Some Reminiscences*. London: E. Nash, 1912.

Creighton, Mandell. *Queen Elizabeth*. London, Paris and Edinburgh: Boussod, Valadon & Co., 1896. [L1 3]

Dante Alighieri. *La Divina Commedia*. New ed. Florence: G. Barbèra, 1898.

Dostoevsky, Fyodor. *The Brothers Karamazov*. Trans. Constance Garnett. London: William Heinemann, 1912.[4]

Eliot, George. *The Popular Short Tales of George Eliot*. London: Simpkin, Marshall, Hamilton, Kent, & Co., n.d.

Euripides. *Euripides Translated into English Rhyming Verse*. Trans. Gilbert Murray. London: George Allen, 1902. Volume 3 of The Athenian Drama series (*Hippolytus, The Bacchae, The Frogs*).

+ Euripides. *The Hippolytus of Euripides*. Trans. Gilbert Murray. 2nd ed. The Athenian Drama for English Readers. London: G. Allen, 1904.

Evelyn, John. *The Life of Margaret Godolphin*. The King's Classics. London: A. Moring, De la More, 1904.

Fabre, Jean Henri. *Souvenirs entomologiques:(cinquième série): Études sur l'instinct et les mœurs des insectes*. Paris: Librarie Ch. Delagrave, 1897. [PA 38]

Fisher, Herbert Albert Laurens. *Studies in Napoleonic Statesmanship: Germany*. Oxford: Clarendon Press, 1903.

FitzGerald, Edward. *Letters and Literary Remains of Edward FitzGerald*. 7 vols. London: Macmillan, 1902.

FitzGerald, Edward. *Polonius: A Collection of Wise Saws and Modern Instances*. London: Methuen, 1903.

Ford, Richard. *Murray's Hand-Book for Travellers in Greece*. [PA 326]

Foxe, John. *The Book of Martyrs: Containing an Account of the Sufferings and Death of the Protestants in the Reign of Queen Mary the First*. London: H. Trapp, 1776.

Froude, James Anthony. *History of England from the Fall of Wolsey to the Defeat of the Spanish Armada*. 12 vols. London: Longmans, Green, 1870–5.[5]

Froude, James Anthony. *Short Studies on Great Subjects*. New ed. 4 vols. London: Longmans, Green, 1897–8.

F1,2 Gallichan, Walter M. *The Story of Seville*. London: J. M. Dent, 1903. [55, 22]

Gardner, Edmund Garratt. *The Story of Florence*. 6th ed. London: J. M. Dent & Co., 1903.

Gibbon, Edward. *The History of the Decline and Fall of the Roman Empire*. New ed. 12 vols. London: T. Cadell and W. Davies, 1820.

+ Gosse, Edmund. *Sir Thomas Browne*. English Men of Letters. London: Macmillan, 1905.[6]

Granville-Barker, Harley. *Waste: A Tragedy in Four Acts*. London: Sidgwick & Jackson, 1909.

PO Green, John Richard. *Letters of John Richard Green*. Ed. Leslie Stephen. London: Macmillan, 1897. [VW Daybook xvi]

Hakluyt, Richard. *Hakluyt's Collection of the Early Voyages, Travels, and Discoveries of the English Nation*. New ed. 5 vols. London: R. H. Evans, 1809–12.

HRC Hardy, Thomas. *The Dynasts: A Drama of the Napoleonic Wars*. 3 vols. London: Macmillan, 1904–9.

F1 Hardy, Thomas. *Far from the Madding Crowd*. London: Macmillan, 1908. [57]

F1 Hardy, Thomas. *A Group of Noble Dames*. London: Macmillan, 1903. [58]

F2 Hardy, Thomas. *A Laodicean*. London: Macmillan, 1912. [21–2]

F1 Hardy, Thomas. *Life's Little Ironies*. London: Macmillan, 1903. [58]
F1,2 Hardy, Thomas. *The Mayor of Casterbridge: The Life and Death of a Man of Character*. London: Macmillan, 1908. [57–8; 21–2]
F1,2 Hardy, Thomas. *A Pair of Blue Eyes*. London: Macmillan, 1910. [58; 21–2]
F1 Hardy, Thomas. *Tess of the D'Urbervilles*. London: Macmillan, 1909. [57]
HRC Hardy, Thomas. *Time's Laughingstocks and Other Verses*. London: Macmillan, 1910.
Hardy, Thomas. *Two on a Tower*. 1882. [PA 386–7]
F1 Hardy, Thomas. *Under the Greenwood Tree*. London: Macmillan, 1907. [58]
F1 Hardy, Thomas. *The Well-Beloved*. London: Macmillan, 1903. [58–9]
F1 Hardy, Thomas. *Wessex Tales*. London: Macmillan, 1903. [58]
Hare, Augustus. *Walks in London*. 6th ed. 2 vols. London: George Allen, 1894.
Hare, Augustus J. C. and St Clair Baddeley. *Venice*. 6th ed. London: G. Allen, 1904.
Harte, Anthony. *These Thoughts Were Written by Anthony Harte*. No place: no pub., 1905.[7]
Hazlitt, William. *The Round Table*. London: S. Low, Son and Marston, 1869.
Headlam, Walter George, ed. and trans. *A Book of Greek Verse*. Cambridge: Cambridge UP, 1907.[8]
Heine, Heinrich. *The Prose Writings of Heine Heinrich*. Ed. Havelock Ellis. London: W. Scott, 1887.
Henley, William Ernest. *Poems*. Rev. 4th ed. London: D. Nutt, 1900.
+ Herodotus. *Heroditou Halikarnesseos Historioe Logoi 9 = Herodoti Halicarnassei historiarum libri IX: Codicem sancrofti manuscriptum*. Ed. Thomas Gaisford. 3rd ed. Oxford: T. Combe, 1840.
Herodotus. *Herodotus*. Trans. William Beloe. 2nd ed., corr. and enl. 4 vols. London: L. and S. Sotheby, 1806.
* Holinshed, Raphael. *Chronicles*. [L1 67]
Holland, Mary Sibylla. *Additional Letters of Mary Sibylla Holland*. Ed. Bernard Holland. Edinburgh: R. & R. Clark, 1899.
Holland, Maud Constance Walpole. *Verses*. London: E. Arnold, 1898.
Homer. *Homeri Opera et reliquae*. Ed. D. B. Monro. Oxford: Clarendon Press, 1901.
Homer. *HomerouIlias, kai Odysseia: Estin alethos basilikon pragma he Homerou poiesis*. Ed. Thomas Grenville. 4 vols. Oxford: Oxford UP, 1800.
Hope, Anthony. *The Heart of Princess Osra*. 1896. [PA 57]
S James, Henry. *The American Scene*. London: Chapman & Hall, 1907.
James, Henry. *The Golden Bowl*. 1st British ed. London: Methuen, 1905.[9]
James, Henry. *Partial Portraits*. London: Macmillan, 1894.
Jefferies, Richard. *The Life of the Fields*. London: Chatto & Windus, 1902.
Johnson, Samuel. *Lives of the Most Eminent English Poets: With Critical Observations on Their Works* ... London: F. Warne & Co., n.d. With a sketch of the author's life by Sir Walter Scott.
Keats, John. *Letters of John Keats to Fanny Brawne* ... Ed. Harry Buxton Forman. London: Reeves & Turner, 1878.
F1,2 Keats, John. *The Poetical Works*. Ed. H. Buxton Forman. Oxford: Oxford UP, 1906. [62–3; 20–1] [L1 263, 269, 272].
Kingsley, Charles. *Andromeda, and Other Poems*. 3rd ed. London: Parker, Son, and Bourn, 1862.
S Lee, Sidney. *A Life of William Shakespeare*. London: Smith, Elder. 1899.
Lee, Sidney. *Principles of Biography: The Leslie Stephen Lecture Delivered in the Senate House, Cambridge, on 13 May 1911*. Cambridge: Cambridge UP, 1911.
Lennox, Sarah. *The Life and Letters of Lady Sarah Lennox, 1745–1825* ... Ed. Countess of Ilchester and Lord Stavordale. 2 vols. London: Murray, 1901.

Litchfield, Henrietta Emma Darwin. *Emma Darwin, Wife of Charles Darwin; A Century of Family Letters by Her Daughter.* 2 vols. Cambridge: Cambridge UP, 1904.
Lockhart, John Gibson. *Memoirs of Sir Walter Scott.* 10 vols. Edinburgh: A. & C. Black, 1882.
Lowell, James Russell. *The Complete Poetical Works of James Russell Lowell.* Boston: Houghton Mifflin, 1896.
Lowell, James Russell. [PA 60]
Lowell, James Russell. [PA 60]
Lubbock, Percy. *Elizabeth Barrett Browning in her Letters.* London: Smith, Elder, 1906.[10]
Lucan. *Marci Annaei Lucani Pharsalia, cum supplemento Thomae Maii.* Paris: Typis Barbou, 1767.
Lucas, St John. *The Oxford Book of French Verse, XIIIth Century – XIXth Century.* Oxford: Clarendon, 1908. [L1 375, 377]
Lucretius Carus, Titus. *Titi Lucreti Cari De rerum natura libri sex.* Trans. H. A. J. Munro. 2 vols. Cambridge: Deighton, Bell, 1864.
Mackail, J. W., ed. *Select Epigrams from the Greek Anthology.* London: Longmans, Green, and Co., 1890.
* Maitland, Frederic William. *The Life and Letters of Leslie Stephen.* London: Duckworth & Co., 1906.
+ Meredith, George. *The Adventures of Harry Richmond.* London: Constable, 1902. [PA 391–2]
Meredith, George. *An Essay on Comedy and the Uses of the Comic Spirit.* 2nd ed. Westminster: Constable, 1898.
Meredith, George. *Poems Written in Early Youth (Published in 1851), Poems from 'Modern Love' (First Edition), and Scattered Poems.* London: Constable, 1909.
Mérimée, Prosper. *Lettres à une inconnue.* Paris. [PA 340–5]
+ Michelet, Jules. *Histoire de France.* 19 vols, only vols 12 and 13. Paris: Marpon et Flammarion, 1879. [L1 398 and n2]
S Milton, John. *Paradise Lost.* London: J. and R. Tonson, 1750.
* Montaigne, Michel de. *Essays of Michael Seigneur de Montaigne, Translated into English.* 7th ed. 3 vols. Vol. 3 only. London: Ballard and Clarke, 1759.[11]
Moore, George. *'Hail and Farewell!'* 3 vols. London: W. Heinemann, 1911–14.[12]
+ Morris, William. *The Defence of Guenevere and Other Poems.* Ed. Robert Steele. London: De La More, 1904. [PA 275 and n11]
Norway, Arthur Hamilton. *Highways and Byways in Devon and Cornwall.* London: Macmillan, 1907.
Omar Khayyam. *Rubaiyat of Omar Khayyam; the Astronomer-Poet of Persia.* Trans. Edward FitzGerald. 5th ed. London: Macmillan, 1899.
Osborne, Dorothy. *The Love Letters of Dorothy Osborne to Sir William Temple.* Ed. Israel Gollancz. London: Moring, 1903.
The Oxford Book of English Verse, 1250–1900. Ed. A. T. Quiller-Couch. Oxford: Clarendon, 1900.
F1,2 Paston, John and Margaret and family. *The Paston Letters 1422–1509 A. D.* Ed. James Gairdner. Westminster: Constable, 1901. [63–5; 22–3]
Pater, Walter. *Appreciations; with an Essay on Style.* London: Macmillan and Co., 1900.
Pater, Walter. *Gaston de Latour: An Unfinished Romance.* Ed. Charles L. Shadwell. New ed. London: Macmillan, 1902.
Pater, Walter. *Greek Studies: A Series of Essays.* 2nd ed. London: Macmillan, 1901.
Pater, Walter. *Imaginary Portraits.* 4th ed. London: Macmillan, 1901.
Pater, Walter. *Marius the Epicurean: His Sensations and Ideas.* 4th ed. London: Macmillan, 1900.

Pater, Walter. *Miscellaneous Studies: A Series of Essays*. Ed. Charles L. Shadwell. London: Macmillan and Co., 1900.
Pater, Walter. *Plato and Platonism: A Series of Lectures*. 2nd ed. London: Macmillan, 1902.
Pater, Walter. *The Renaissance: Studies in Art and Poetry*. 6th ed. London: Macmillan, 1904.
Patmore, Coventry. *The Poetry of Pathos and Delight, from the Works of Coventry Patmore*. Ed. Alice Meynell. London: William Heinemann, 1896.
Payn, James. *The Backwater of Life, Or, Essays of a Literary Veteran*. Intro Leslie Stephen. London: Smith, Elder and Co., 1899.
Peel, Robert. *Sir Robert Peel: From His Private Papers*. Ed. Charles Stuart Parker. 3 vols. London: J. Murray, 1891–9.
Phillips, Stephen. *The Sin of David*. London: Macmillan, 1904.
Plato. *Platonos Phaidon = The Phaedo of Plato*. Ed. R. D. Archer-Hind. 2nd ed. London: Macmillan, 1894.
Poe, Edgar Allan. *The Fall of the House of Usher, and Other Tales and Prose Writings of Edgar Allan Poe*. Ed. Ernest Rhys. Camelot Series. London: W. Scott, 1889.
+ Rabelais. [PA 223]
Ritchie, Anne Thackeray. *Blackstick Papers*. London: Smith, Elder, 1908.[13]
Roget, Peter Mark. *Thesaurus of English Words*. [L1 5–6]
Romanes, George John. *Thoughts on Religion*. Ed. Charles Gore. London: Longmans, Green, 1899.
Rossetti, Christina Georgina. *The Family Letters of Christina Georgina Rossetti: With Some Supplementary Letters and Appendices*. Ed. William Michael Rossetti. London: Brown, Langham, 1908.[14]
Rossetti, Christina Georgina. *The Poetical Works of Christina Georgina Rossetti*. Ed. William Michael Rossetti. London: Macmillan, 1906.
Rossetti, Dante Gabriel. *The Collected Works of Dante Gabriel Rossetti*. 2 vols. London: Ellis and Elvey, 1901.
Saint-Simon, Louis de Rouvroy, duc de. *Memoires de Saint-Simon*. Abridged version. [L1 374 n2]
Saunders, Howard. *An Illustrated Manual of British Birds*. 2nd ed., rev. and enl. London: Gurney and Jackson, 1899.[15]
Shelley, Percy Bysshe. *The Complete Poetical Works of Shelley, Including Materials Never Before Printed in any Edition of the Poems*. Ed. Thomas Hutchinson. Oxford: Clarendon Press, 1904.
Smith, Goldwin. *The United Kingdom: A Political History*. London: Macmillan & Co., 1899.
Smith, Miriam. *Poems*. London: G. Richards, 1908.
Sophocles. *Sophocles, for the Use of Schools*. Ed. Lewis Campbell and Evelyn Abbott. New rev. ed. 2 vols. Oxford: Clarendon Press, 1886–99.
Sophocles. *The Tragedies of Sophocles*. Trans. Richard C. Jebb. Cambridge: Cambridge UP, 1904.
* Stephen, Caroline Emelia. *Light Arising: Thoughts on the Central Radiance*. Cambridge: Heffer, 1908. [L1 331]
Stephen, Caroline Emelia. *Quaker Strongholds*. 3rd ed. London: E. Hicks, 1891.
Stephen, Harry Lushington, ed. *State Trials, Political and Social*. 4 vols. London: Duckworth and Co., 1899–1902.
Stephen, Leslie. *English Literature and Society in the Eighteenth Century: Ford Lectures, 1903*. London: Duckworth and Co., 1904.
Stephen, Leslie. *The English Utilitarians*. 3 vols. London: Duckworth, 1900.
Stephen, Leslie. *Hobbes*. English Men of Letters. London: Macmillan, 1904.
Stephen, Leslie. *Hours in a Library*. New ed., with additions. 3 vols. London: Smith, Elder & Co., 1892.

Stephen, Leslie. *Studies of a Biographer*. 4 vols. London: Duckworth, 1899–1902. [Vol. 3 only]
+ F2 Stevenson, Robert Louis. *Familiar Studies of Men and Books*. London: Chatto & Windus, 1912.[16] [81]
Stevenson, Robert Louis. *The Letters of Robert Louis Stevenson to His Family and Friends*. Ed. Sidney Colvin. 4th ed. 2 vols. London: Methuen and Co., 1901.
Stevenson, Robert Louis. *Poems by Robert Louis Stevenson, including Underwoods, Ballads, Songs of Travel*. St. Martin's Library. London: Chatto & Windus, 1906.
HRC Strachey, G. L. [Lytton] *Landmarks in French Literature*. Home University Library of Modern Knowledge. London: Williams & Norgate, 1912.
Strachey, Ray. *The World at Eighteen*. [Ray Costelloe] London: T. F. Unwin, 1907.
Swinburne, Algernon Charles. *A Channel Passage and Other Poems*. London: Chatto & Windus, 1904.
Symonds, John Addington. *Studies of the Greek Poets*. 3rd ed. 2 vols. London: A. and C. Black, 1902.
+ Symonds, Margaret. *Days Spent on a Doge's Farm*. 2nd ed. London: T. F. Unwin, 1908. [L1 373]
Tanska-Hofmanowa, Kementyna. *The Journal of Countess Françoise Krasinska, Great Grandmother of Victor Emmanuel*. Trans. Kasimir Dziekonska. London: K. Paul, Trench, Trübner & Co., 1897.
Tennyson, Alfred. *The Works of Alfred, Lord Tennyson, Poet Laureate*. London: Macmillan, 1902.
Tennyson, Hallam Tennyson, ed. *Tennyson and His Friends*. London: Macmillan, 1911.
Thomas à Kempis. *Of the Imitation of Christ in Four Books*. London: K. Paul, Trench, Trübner, 1898.
Thomson, James. *Biographical and Critical Studies*. London: Reeves and Turner and B. Dobell, 1896.
Thomson, James. *Poems, Essays and Fragments*. Ed. John M. Robertson. London: A. & H. B. Bonner; Reeves & Turner, 1892.
Thomson, James. *Poems, Essays & Fragments*. Ed. John M. Robertson. Cheaper ed. London: A. C. Fifield, 1905.
Thomson, James. *The Poetical Works of James Thomson . . .* Ed. Bertram Dobell. London: Reeves and Turner, 1895.
Thomson, James. *Satires and Profanities*. London: Progressive Pub. Co., 1884.
F1 Tolstoy, Leo. *A Landed Proprietor/The Cossacks/Sevastopol*. Trans. Leo Wiener. Vol. II of *Complete Works*. London: J. M. Dent, 1904. [66–7]
Vanbrugh, John. *Plays*. 2 vols. London: J. Rivington, 1776.
Virgil. *The Aeneid of Virgil*. Trans. J. W. Mackail. London: Macmillan, 1885.
Wells, H. G. *The New Machiavelli*. London: The Bodley Head, 1911.
White, Gilbert. *The Natural History and Antiquities of Selborne*. London: Methuen, 1901.
Whitten, Wilfred, comp. *London in Song*. London: G. Richards [1898].
Wilde, Oscar. *Poems, with the Ballad of Reading Gaol*. London: Methuen, 1909.
Wordsworth, William. *The Complete Poetical Works of William Wordsworth*. Intro John Morley. London: Macmillan, 1902.
F2 Yonge, Charlotte M. *The Little Duke. Richard the Fearless*. London and New York: Macmillan, 1895. [87]

Notes

1. For books mentioned by Virginia Stephen but not in MASC, it can be difficult to know whether she is referring to a purchase, a library book, or a book in her father's original library. For example, on 28 March 1905, she mentions packing several books, includ-

ing, among others, Green's *Conquest of England* and a couple of Hawthorne titles, *The House of the Seven Gables* and *The Scarlet Letter* (*PA* 257). Ownership is too uncertain to include them here.
2. Virginia Stephen mentions reading this book while in the country, at Netherhampton House, Salisbury, during the summer of 1903 (*PA* 206), where she has taken a 'precious box ... well crammed with books' (*PA* 186). Since evidence also exists for Virginia's owning this book – it is listed as 'VW – binder' in K&M-V 26 – I included it as possibly in her library.
3. Based on her letter's description, perhaps *The Works of Lord Byron*, ed. Ernest Hartley Coleridge et al. New and enlarged edition. 13 volumes. John Murray, 1905?
4. Leonard Woolf gave Virginia Stephen this book in April 1912, before their marriage (K&M-V 64). He gave her additional Dostoevsky titles after their marriage.
5. This set of books is signed by Leslie Stephen and has his annotations and drawings in it. But Virginia writes, on 30 June 1897, that 'He lent me 12 vols. of Froude's History of England, which he has not room for. I am to read 'em some time – at present they have a whole new bookshelf for themselves' (*PA* 108–9; see also *PA* 117). It seems safe to assume they resided in Virginia Stephen's library from then on.
6. Inscription reads 'From G L S' (Lytton Strachey; K&M-V 90).
7. Actually written by Violet Dickinson. See 110 and *PA* 221, *L1* 174–5 and 210.
8. Perhaps Virginia Stephen owned two other Headlam titles in the LLVW, though no direct evidence exists: *Greek Lyric Metre*, a reprint from the *Journal of Hellenic Studies*, 22 (1902) and *Walter Headlam: His Letters and Poems* (K&M-V 101). She may have given Headlam feedback about the first; see *L1* 259. She was asked to write impressions for the 1910 memoir Cecil Headlam wrote after Walter's sudden death in 1908, the second (*L1* 378); a rapid perusal shows she did not do so, but Cecil thanks her for lending him letters Walter wrote to her (162), and he mentions Leslie and/or Julia several times (84, 103, 141).
9. Book reviewed and kept; see *E1* 22–4.
10. Book reviewed and kept; see *E1* 101–5; the other book featured in the review, *Robert Browning and Alfred Domett*, ed. F. G. Kenyon, is not in the LLVW.
11. Of the editions of Montaigne in the LLVW, this one is the best candidate for what Thoby gave her on her 1903 birthday, even though only Vol. 3 is there. In her thank you letter (*L1* 66), she mentions buying a Florio translation once, but preferring this one because it is printed better and since there is not 'much to choose between the translations'.
12. Vol. 1, published in 1911, is inscribed Virginia Stephen.
13. Book reviewed and kept; see *E1* 228–9.
14. Book reviewed and kept; see *E1* 225–7.
15. Julia King confirmed that the 'VW – annotations' are dated 1901–5, so this book belongs in Virginia Stephen's Library (K&M-V 196; email message 24 August 2010).
16. This book clearly belonged to Virginia, but whether Stephen or Woolf is hard to determine given its publication date.

Appendix 3

Virginia Stephen's Morley College Teaching Schedule

Appendix sources include Morley College annual reports and the *Morley College Magazine* (both available at http://vle.morleycollege.ac.uk/course/view.php?id=1646#section-8); Morley College Executive Committee and other Committee Minutes located in the London Borough of Lambeth, Lambeth Archives at the Minet Library; Elaine Andrews, Learning Resources Manager at Morley College (Waterloo); perpetual calendars; and Virginia Stephen's letters and journals (*L1* and *PA*).

Annual reports were published at the end of each academic year in late summer, before the next academic year began. For example, the Council thanks Virginia Stephen, a voluntary teacher, for her service in the 1904–5 school-year report (6) that covered 1 August 1904 to 31 July 1905 (13). The list of Classes and Teachers at the report's end, headed October 1905 (15–17), applies to the upcoming year, 1905–6. Appended is this note:

> The above is to be regarded as a general outline of the work of the several classes. Much discretion is necessarily left to the teachers as to the actual ground covered, having regard to the amount of knowledge already possessed by the students. It cannot be guaranteed that every class will necessarily be formed or continued. This must depend on attendance and other circumstances. (17)

Earlier mistakes, including my own, about what Virginia Stephen taught when, stemmed from not understanding the distinction between the report (of the academic year just passed) and the list of Classes and Teachers (for the academic year ahead).

Firm ending dates for courses are impossible to determine from available documents; as noted below, some magazines are missing, and many magazine covers, which probably included calendars, were not copied by the binder years ago. Term opening soirée dates, usually given or reported on, occurred on Saturdays with the term (College) opening on the following Mondays. Morley established College opening and closing dates, but teachers, according to Elaine Andrews, probably determined which (and how many) weeks their courses would cover. Courses generally met 8–10 times a term, though shorter courses were sometimes offered. Exam dates for course certificates, grant funding and university matriculation were set by the College.

In the terms listed below, information about Virginia Stephen's class follows general information about the College term. In *MCM* references, the second set of Roman numerals, if there, refers to pages at the very end of the year's issues.

? [day/time] = questionable date/time; guess based on other calendars, other years
??? = no information; did not guess

1904–5

Michaelmas term

M, 3 October to Th, 22 December (*MCM*, xiv.1 1; *MCM*, xiv.3 ii)
Soirée on 1 October
[did not teach; not approached until late December (*PA* 217; *L1* 171, 173)

Lent term

M, 9 January to ?F, 24 March (*MCM*, xiv.4 ii; March to July *MCM* missing)
Soirée on 7 January

Culture Lecture Series

W 9 p.m. (dinner at 7.30, then ten-minute cab to Morley, *PA* 224)
Starts W, 18 January and ends W, 22 March; drafts sketch of experience on 25 March (*PA* 256), which we do not have

Easter term

?M, 1 May to ?F, 30 June (March–July *MCM* missing; Easter on 23 April
Soirée on ?29 April

English History (from 'beginning' to King John)

?W 9 p.m. (probably W since Lent term students continued in Easter term and since W was her usual day until her last term; probably 9 p.m. because it was her usual time)
Starts after 24 April (*L1* 186; *PA* 269–72); drafts 'report' in July 1905, seemingly responding to criticism from Miss Sheepshanks on 29 June

1905–6

Michaelmas term

M, 18 September to ?F, 8 December (*MCM* xv.1 1; *MCM* xv.2 31; probable later calendars on covers not copied; because term started two weeks earlier, I speculate it ended two weeks earlier
Soirée on 16 September (*MCM* xv.2 31)

Composition

W 9 p.m. (*L1* 207; *L1* 210) – List of Courses, October 1905 (*MCAR* 1904–5 15)

Starts after Th, 5 October (*L1* 209n); observed by Miss Sheepshanks on 8 November (*L1* 210)

Lent term

M, 8 January to ?M, 9 April (*MCM* xv.4 53; *MCM* xv.7 101 [end date for College in general, or just for Archeological Society, as in announcement?])
Soirée on 6 January (*MCM* xv.4 53)

Composition

W 9 p.m. (List of Courses, October 1905 (*MCAR* 1904–5 15)

Easter term

M, 23 April to ?T, 2 July (Easter on 15 April; *MCM* xv.7 101; *MCM* xv.10 149; pertinent calendars sometimes referred to, probably on covers not copied)
Soirée on 21 April (*MCM* xv.7 101)

Composition

W 9 p.m. List of Classes and Teachers, October 1905 (*MCAR* 1904–5 15)

1906–7

Michaelmas term

M, 24 September to ?F, 7 December (*MCM* xv.10 149; *MCM* xvi.1 1; probable later calendars on covers not copied)
Soirée on 22 September
[did not teach; trip to Greece; Thoby died 20 November]

Lent term

M, 7 January to T, 26 March (*MCM* xvi.4 64 and *MCM* xvi.5 74; *MCM* xvi.6 81)
Soirée on 5 January (*MCM* xvi.4 64 and *MCM* xvi.5 74)

Composition (Advanced)

W 9 p.m. List of Classes and Teachers (*MCAR* 1905–6 15)

Easter term

M, 8 April to M, 1 July (*MCM* xvi.6. 81; *MCM* xvi.7 97; *MCM* xvi.10 ii; Easter on 31 March)
Soirée on 6 April (*MCM* xvi.7 97)

Composition (Advanced)

W 9 p.m. List of Classes and Teachers (*MCAR* 1905–6 15)

1907–8

Michaelmas term

M, 23 September to ?F, 6 December (*MCM* xvi.10 ii; probable later calendars on covers not copied)
Soirée on 21 September (*MCM* xvii.1 13)

Keats, Shelley, Browning Reading Circle

M 9 p.m. (*MCM* xvi.10 iii; *MCAR* 1906–7 18)
Starts on ?30 September (*L1* 312 editorial letter dating)

Lent term

M, 6 January – S, 11 April (*MCM* xvii.4. 68; soirée for Easter term on last day of *this* term *MCM* xvii.7 101; probable calendars on covers not copied)
Soirée on 4 January (*MCM* xvii.4 68)
[did not teach; gives up teaching at Morley in December 1907 (*L1* 320)]

Easter term

??? – ??? (Easter on 19 April; no covers available; soirée held at end of previous term; *MCM* xvii.10 149)
[did not teach, though Executive Committee Minutes for the 18 May meeting indicate she was going to be asked to take another literature circle in 1908–9 (*MCECM3* 132)]

Appendix 4

Virginia Stephen's Lectures

These two lectures exist in a thirty-eight-page 'mutilated exercise book', with Virginia Stephen's page numbers beginning on 73. Besides the pieces about Benvenuto Cellini and the dramatic, the notebook contains a fragment that seems to be about Violet Dickinson at Fritham, some notes on Aeschylus and Euripedes, and a fragment of what seems to be an unfinished novel.

S. P. Rosenbaum discovered these works and identified them as lectures. In 1994, he sent his clean transcriptions to me, along with an introduction, both of which had been intended for *The Charleston Magazine* but were never published there; instead, his introduction was folded, with revisions, into sections of *Edwardian Bloomsbury* (152, 165–7). Pat generously allowed me to use his transcriptions to check and sometimes correct my own, though any remaining errors are mine. To suggest the look of Stephen's manuscripts, I have retained her line lengths and spacing and reproduced marginal and interlinear inserts where they occur. All grammitical slips and word underlinings are hers.

Symbols used in transcription of lectures

~~word~~	cancelled word or passage
word [?]	questionable transcription
———	illegible word or passage
═══	illegible cancellation
word word	interlinear or marginal revision

Autobiography of Benvenuto Cellini

Monks House Papers, University of Sussex Special Collections at The Keep
SxMs–18/2/A/26/B
VS Early Writings c. 1902
VS numbers pages 85–91; no 88, but page not missing; [archive numbers 6–11]

Life
Autobiography of Benvenuto Cellini ---
Mr Symonds has translated this book ~~so that~~ in a way which produces ~~the curious effect~~ a curious & rather contradictory effect: one realises one forgets his skill altogether. But, as ~~everyone~~ knows, afterwards that is ~~exactly the~~ precisely his great merit; ~~he has achieved a task even h of supreme difficulty for it calls for~~ He ~~has~~ is forgotten because your ~~attention is so closely fixed on the subject whi the~~ whole attention is taken up with the man himself-- ~~Ben~~ Cellini - ~~who writes this autobiography~~ you are scarcely once conscious that ~~Cellini~~ there is a writer medium between you & the ~~speaker:~~ that another voice is speaking his words in a language different from that in which they were written originally. ~~This~~ This translation is rightly held to be a masterpiece— entirely 'rightly' those ~~most ignorant~~ who are ignorant of ~~a word~~
e
of Italian can say, from th~~is~~ very fact that I have
Italian or
noted – that one does not think of ~~translation or~~
English
~~translator:~~ only those who are versed in the original & know something of the exceeding difficulties of translation - of 'pouring from the golden cup to the silver' only those, ~~I say,~~ can give Mr Symonds his due meed of praise –
~~The ignorant reader offers however a tribute which is~~

~~no translator would~~   ~~is perhaps the best a~~
     or
~~From~~   both these reasons, I ~~pas~~ say no more of the
                          &
translators part of the book; ~~Mr Symonds~~ I am sure

                              is   valuable
~~there could be~~ no praise ~~says~~ more than my silence.
B Cellini, without the Autobiography would be merely
the   a
~~a~~ name of ~~the man who made the certain beautiful little~~
~~gold & silver ornaments — plates of~~ a famous 16th century
goldsmith.   There are but few of his works in
                      took ~~of~~ on
existence - inasmuch as they ~~were for the most~~
                      form
~~part~~ a very perishable ~~kind~~ for the most part –
settings for jewels - little table ornaments - seals &
                    trifles
medals - ~~all of which~~ things that rarely survive
into another age.   It is true that he made one
                              was his only success in that line
famous statue - the Perseus - ~~which~~ — but this
was ~~the work of his later age~~; he ~~is best known~~ is best
~~his fame is~~ known as a goldsmith - a maker of
        ~~& elaborate~~   &
exquisite ~~designs, of~~ minute ~~work~~ jewel work –
enamels & so forth - but, as I say, few survive –
& his fame is half kept alight by this Autobiography.
One quickly perceives that ~~this~~ he is a ~~great~~
        much
~~deal~~   more than a goldsmith; a man of
endless versatility - he plays the flute (against
his will it is true) knows all the crafts of
                      the draughtsman
the goldsmith, the sculptor, the enameller - ~~the~~ writes
verses 'in terza rima' - & ~~is above all a~~
& is proficient - & more - in most of them. But this
                                                87
is only the artist side of him; which one suspects that
he thinks ~~les~~ of less importance, less befitting a man,

than the other - It is true he thinks very well of both
                                          'Bravado'
~~sides [?]~~   The other side is the sportsman side - the ~~'Blood~~ ---
the man of the world: 'I have only two murders on my
conscience' he writes, about the middle of his life, & I think ~~they~~
  he   improved upon [?] that
were multiplied before the end; indeed he was a
good fighter, invariably in the right - invariably getting
the best of it (so he says) - though to a modern reader
he seems to have had a turn for picking quarrels.
~~He is a full-blooded sensual, man of genius –~~

His Life is chock full of adventures - He went
through the streets of Rome with a coat of mail under his
doublet; he had so many enemies - spiteful & malicious
creatures - waiting at the corners to spring out upon him.
                              down the middle of the street
But he goes forth courageously prepared to beat
them all single handed.   He shows himself most in
this guise of fighter; a quarrelsome turbulent
man, not over-squeamish in any way.   He
inveighs against his 'Fortune' which had made up her
mind to try & baffle him ~~in every way~~. We
more than suspect that this fortune lay in his own
heart; ~~he is for ever suspecting slights & injuries~~

he was for ever suspecting slights & injuries –
& did not wait to inquire coolly into things before
drawing his sword -   Yet there is something fine &
                                              89
generous about all this -- ~~He sto~~ ~~did not~~   He ~~knew no fear~~
dashed into his brawls without any reckoning of
costs to himself or anyone else. ~~Once he spent
some time (how long it is not stated) in a Dungeon –
through some not clearly defined piece of~~ & it follows
that if you think yourself a God   many people will ~~fail~~
fall short of the right degree of reverence.   Cellinis
quarrels, I think, were mostly brought about by ~~innocent~~
unwitting acts of irreverence of this kind - ~~Once however~~
However
He made silver salt cellars for the Pope which pleased
his Holiness so much that ~~the two 'homicides' were
Cellinis sins were absolved.   Once, though the cause
seems~~   the murders did not matter -   Once, though
the cause ~~of~~ seems to me ~~rather –~~ obscure, Cellini
fell into such disfavour with the Pope that he
was clapped into a dungeon - ~~a da~~ & had for
gaoler a eccentric gentleman who thought himself a bat.
~~He stood on the battlements of the castle, procl - calling
out this fact, & saying that he was going to fly.~~
                    leading
His madness unfortunately ~~led~~ him to a peculiar
prejudice against Cellini, who was ~~thrust into one from
one mean lodging to another~~   finally thrust into an
                                            pitch
underground cellar, which was ~~pitch~~ dark ~~for 2~~
save for two hours of every day, & full of worse evils
than this - But here Cellini shows at his best.
His hot bloodedness was after all not a bad quality, & under these

circumstances it turned to a fine kind of courage. He ~~he was naturally religious~~ = was by nature ~~full of an almost superstitious~~ religious to the verge of superstition; & in this imprisonment he began to have visions & trances of ecstasy - ~~thinking that he was visited by angels. & held converse with beings of another world. his talks with them are recorded with great minuteness~~ & seeing beings from another world & holding talk with them. But ~~his time was spent~~ he was not wholly given over to this: his great ~~res~~ skill of hand & ~~resourcefulness~~ ingenuity stood him in good stead. He made ink from powder which he scraped from the bricks & moistened; & with this he wrote a ~~the~~ long ~~disserta~~ a description of his experiences in rhyme. Also he scratched faces & ~~he~~ figures on the walls — of sacred meaning.   In the end the mad gaoler died, & Cellini was released —

The experience does not seemed to have damped his spirits. He migrated to Florence — then to Paris, ~~where he worked for the 1~~ at the invitation of the King of France.   The enthusiasm ~~with~~ these which great people ~~were ready to cultivate one so~~ felt for a mere goldsmith & desire to get him to produce work for themselves alone — is noteworthy. We can hardly conceive anything like it nowadays — though Cellini complains that the great were very fickle & sometimes forgot to pay their debts. ~~But~~ It must be observed that Cellini ~~was finely [?] an~~ had a fine disregard for ~~the~~ mere profit; he ~~spared no~~ thought each thing that he produced worked with his whole heart, & ~~thought the~~ had an a masterpiece without a rival -- overweening conceit of himself - but as often as not his he gave the finished work to ~~the comm~~ employer — sometimes not even ~~asking~~ asking or getting ~~the~~ back the sums he had ~~paid out~~. spent upon it.   He went back to Florence after a time, & entered the service of the Duke of Florence — for whom he cast the famous Perseus, & while still in his service the book ends.

In summing up it must be said that however great his

&heat
faults, the picture of this man is full of life ~~& power.~~
He put into his work as an artist all the vigour of his
great animal strength. Mr Symonds says that ~~his~~ the works
~~surviving~~ [?] of his that remain are teeming with invention
& ingenuity - though as a whole wanting in expression – in
human feeling – in refinement. ~~It is hard to require
of one man that he shall be at the same time a
first rate craftsman - a expert gunner [?] - & a sportsman &~~
These are faults which a study of his life leads one to
           Cellini remains
expect. Yet when all is said & done - ~~the man as~~ a
full blooded sensual man of genius, practised in
many arts - expert in some - & through all time
    &
vigorous convincing – very palpable flesh & blood in
the midst of shadows.
   Autobiography of Benvenuto Cellini
   1 vol.   Translated fresh by J. A. Symonds.

The Dramatic in Life & Art

Monks House Papers, University of Sussex Special Collections at The Keep
SxMs–18/2/A/26/C
VS Early Writings c. 1902
VS numbers pages 92–6 [archive numbers 12–16]

              92

   ~~Drama in Life~~
   The Dramatic in Life & Art.

 What a play depends upon to be good drama
  does not exist in real life.
 Very little Drama in real life.
~~The art of the~~ Yet the sense of drama is strongly
developed in us. & the playwright caters to this.
~~It is b~~ There is drama in life – mostly of the
emotions – not much happens.
What the playwright has to do is to give
these invisible dramatic emotions a form – a body –
  is is
~~they~~ often carried to ridiculous lengths in melodrama.
But even the best plays are more exaggerated than
Life. more exaggerated than novels. In writing it is
possible to ~~go through~~ represent ~~a~~ much of what
passes through the mind. In play writing any subtlety

of thought or character that you wish to express must
take the form of action. This is a coarser process, but
more dramatic than the other.
~~Three ways~~ Three ~~ways of~~ processes - Life – fiction –
drama: ~~The Life not self conscious~~
The liver: the novelist: the dramatist: all reproducing
thought & emotion in different shapes: ~~Life is a~~
we are all trying to speak parts - to translate what

passes in our brains into language & action. This is
the first & simplest ~~way of~~ kind of drama: nevertheless
people differ in their ways of doing this as much as in
their ways of doing anything else.
2ndly the novelist who rearranges, revises, omits, but does
not (if he be a good one) put into the mouths of his
characters anything that they would not have said or do
a great deal of his work is copied literally from life –
but the tendency, indeed the necessity is to epitomise,
to give you the sum of life without its details
Thus, purporting to tell the history of a mans life as
Thackeray in Pendennis for instance, we get only selected
scenes from it, each of which is meant to illustrate ~~the~~ some new phase
of the heroes character. ~~There is no repetition; when the hero has been shown in every conceivable light the The action of the book is all subservient to this purpose~~-- we are shown only
the picked moments of some crisis - which throws light on
the character; a great novelist will contrive that these
crises are very simple & natural such as happen to everybody –
but no novelist can do without them - no novelist that is
can ~~go back to a step~~ put his own ~~simple 'past' into~~
life straight into a novel.
3rdly the dramatist. The drama is more conventional than the
novel - that is it cannot keep so close to the reality. The
necessity of a plot is greater for the ~~novelist~~ dramatist than the
novelist. ~~For~~ A play ~~generally~~ to be good drama must be

full of action, & dramatic moments. There is never the same
subtlety of character drawing in a play as in a novel –
The dramatist takes one simple passion generally & embodies it in
a character - the ~~whole~~ character only exists to emphasise
this passion: (this is exaggerated) Hamlet &c proof to the
contrary) ~~but no such subtlety~~ Reasons for this are –
~~shortness~~ space in which the character is acted – shorter
than a novel – must be still more epitomised.
~~Shortness a great eleme~~
But Dramatist has really a different object from a novelist

~~He sees that it is possible to represent but very little of~~
~~life in the compass of one play.~~
What is the difference between them?
~~Mainly~~ a play really the simplest way of reproducing life –
the oldest - & of course far the most <u>real</u>.   The only
means of ~~getting real people to   to~~ embodying ideas in
            ·   the drama is
real people: But ~~a~~ very limited: a play ~~must~~ cannot
last more than 2 or 3 hours:
~~from~~   That real people act it – That it is a reproduction of
                                                        make it essentially
life that its length is very limited, ~~determine the~~
~~peculiar quality of the~~ dramatic.
Dramatic – things <u>done</u> – <u>action</u>   <u>done</u> as opposed to thought.
That the essence of drama –
Another meaning – <u>dramatic</u> drama -- by dramatic we
understand ~~the essence of~~   exaggerated drama
A good play differs from a good novel in that the play's

                                                            95

excellence lies in its being dramatic – ~~presenting several~~
~~lives which are on the face of it dramatic~~   which is but a
2ndary ~~value~~ quality in a novel – no novel can be as
dramatic as a play.   Take a Dramatic moment -----
in a play - you find it is done ~~by leading up to some~~
generally by some sudden surprise as when a pistol
is raised to the head. This is tame in reading, dramatic

when seen.   On the other hand the novelist gains immensely
                                     complicated
over the dramatist in   scenes ~~where~~ of thought or
emotion. These cannot be reproduced literally on the stage
They must be translated into action – as by a pistol.
          To sum up then.
The playwright & the novelist are both trying ~~the~~ to
express the same thing in different ways.
~~Drama~~ [There ~~is~~ are dramatic moments in life, but they
come mostly from the emotions – without definite
action – only to be realised by the people themselves – not
translated into words (much) or action perhaps at all –
not visible to outsiders – therefore not possible for a play –
————   Drama in life depends upon the actors sense of
drama. A dramatic situation not ~~dramat~~   realised unless the
            feel
actors ~~realise~~ it to be dramatic.   Really nothing in life <u>is</u>
dramatic – too coarse a word. <u>Dramatic</u> ~~must~~ ~~implies~~ understands
'doing' This ~~limits~~ makes the dramatic possibilities of life
very limited. Yet there is a dramatic instinct in us –

& such a thing as drama in life – even in thought – intensified

96

There is a dramatic [doing] element in thought even though nothing happens which makes some situations in life dramatic – this doing element translated into action in a play.

Thought or emotion in contact with something ~~exter~~ external is ~~dramatic~~ almost rightly to be called dramatic. Translate this into action, make it stronger & coarser & visible to the bodily eye & you have a play --- Thought which does something becomes dramatic. ~~Of course all seems~~ Internal & external drama – the play & real life. Dramatic ~~thoughts~~ emotion always has indirectly its dramatic action - only perhaps perceptible to the actor –

emotion
In a play ~~it must~~ ~~action~~ must be clearly followed by ~~emot~~ actions. 2 ways of ~~doin~~ making drama in a play: ~~mak~~ bring about a ~~dramatic~~ an arrangement of external circumstances totally <u>unexpected</u> (this a great element in drama) the commonest way – emotions follow, of a simple kind – Wife discovered in cupboard in another mans room by her husband – that coarse drama – but dramatic & easily perceived --- Reverse this process: make it internal drama. Lover says to Lady -- ⸺ What if your husband shd. find us?' ~~very~~ Lady thinks the same thing – silence, ought to be dramatic – finally results in getting into cupboard. If you could see on stage whole emotions in Ladys mind when Lover says this, it would be far finer drama than the rude shock of being discovered by the husband -- In real life you would say – what will happen if your husband comes – have emotions - but the husband very rarely would come – These emotions must be embodied (leaving out half) in a play by the entrance of the husband; turn the emotion into action – dramatic thought into dramatic action.

Appendix 5

Virginia Stephen's Reviews and Essays

Reviews and essays are chronologically arranged, based on the most recent information. Some may be in Appendices within the *Essays* volumes noted. Early reviews and essays are split between *Essays* 1 and *Essays* 6 because many of those found after Andrew McNeillie had gone to press with *Essays* 1 are in *Essays* 6, edited by Stuart N. Clarke.

In addition to depending upon the editorial work of Andrew McNeillie and Stuart N. Clarke, I have relied on B. J. Kirkpatrick and Stuart N. Clarke's *A Bibliography of Virginia Woolf*, 4th ed. (1997). See also Jeanne Dubino, 'VW', 26–33, and Table 1.1, 35.

Key to Table

italics   book title is also title of review
[ ]   possibly by Virginia Stephen, but not confirmed

Original publication location
A&L   *The Academy / Academy & Literature*
C   *Cornhill*
EW   *Englishwoman*
G   *Guardian*
M   Maitland biography of Leslie Stephen
N   *Nation*
NR   *National Review*
S   *Speaker*
T   *Times* (London)
TLS   *Times Literary Supplement*

Current publication location
E1   *The Essays of Virginia Woolf*, vol. 1
E6   *The Essays of Virginia Woolf*, vol. 6

Key to other information
A   book by an American, about an American, or both
B   Berg Collection, New York Public Library

d	draft available
e	essay
K&C	Kirkpatrick and Clarke, *A Bibliography of Virginia Woolf*, 4th ed.
L1	*The Letters of Virginia Woolf*, vol. 1
PA	*A Passionate Apprentice: The Early Journals, 1897–1909*
r	review
rn	reading notes available
S	University of Sussex Special Collections, The Keep
w	book by a woman, about women, or both

Genre key for reviews

dr	drama
f	fiction
f(n)	novel
f(ss)	short stories
nf	non-fiction
nf(b)	biography
nf(c)	criticism (literary, social or cultural)
nf(d)	diary
nf(e)	essay
nf(h)	history
nf(l)	letters
nf(m)	memoir
nf(t)	travel
p	poetry

Table Appendix 5.1

Title of review or essay	Publication, location	Review, essay	Other information
	1904		
[Social England] K&C	G E1	r	nf(h)
The Son of Royal Langbrith	G E1	r	f(n) A
Haworth, November, 1904	G E1	e	w
	1905		
Next-Door Neighbours	G E1	r	f(ss)
On a Faithful Friend	G E1	e	
The Feminine Note in Fiction	G E1	r	nf(c) w
A Belle of the Fifties	G E1	r	rn, S nf(m) w A
Mr Henry James's Latest Novel	G E1	r	rn, S f(n) w A
[The Story of the Mutiny] K&C	G E1	r	nf(h)
The Decay of Essay-writing	A&L E1	e	
Street Music	NR E1	e	
Literary Geography	TLS E1	r	rn, S nf(c)
Barham of Beltana	TLS E1	r	rn, S f(n)
By Beach and Bogland	G E1	r	rn, S f(ss) w
The Fortunes of Farthings	TLS E1	r	rn, S f(n)
Nancy Stair	G E1	r	rn, S f(n) w
Arrows of Fortune	G E1	r	f(n)
A Dark Lantern	G E1	r	rn, S f(n) w A
Journeys in Spain[a]	TLS E1	r	rn, S nf(t)
The American Woman	G E1	r	nf(c) w A
[The Oxford History of Music] K&C	G E1	r	nf(h,c)
Rose of Lone Farm	G E1	r	rn, S f(n) w
An Andalusian Inn	G E1	e	d, L1, PA
A Priory Church	G E1	e	
The Letters of Jane Welsh Carlyle	G E1	r	nf(l) w
The Value of Laughter	G E1	e	w
Their Passing Hour	A&L E1	r	rn, S nf(b) w
The Letter Killeth	TLS E1	r	rn, S f(n)
Lone Marie	G E1	r	rn, S f(n)
The Devil's Due	G E1	r	rn, S f(n)
The House of Mirth	G E1	r	rn, S f(n) w A

Title of review or essay	Publication, location	Review, essay	Other information
The Debtor	TLS E1	r	rn, S f(n) w A
A Flood Tide	TLS E1	r	rn, S f(n) w
The Making of Michael	TLS E1	r	rn, S f(n) w
A Description of the Desert	G E1	r	rn, S nf(t)
The Brown House and Cordelia	G E1	r	rn, S f(ss) w
Delta	G E1	r	rn, S f(n)
Two Irish Novels[b]	TLS E1	r	rn, S f(n) w
The Tower of Siloam	G E1	r	rn, S f(n) w
A Walk by Night	G E1	e	d, B, PA
1906			
A Nineteenth-century Critic	S E1	r	rn, S nf(e)
After His Kind	G E1	r	rn, S f(ss) w
The Sister of Frederic the Great	A&L E1	r	rn, S nf(b) w
The Scholar's Daughter	TLS E1	r	rn, S f(n) w
A Supreme Moment	TLS E1	r	rn, S f(n) w
The House of Shadows	TLS E1	r	rn, S f(n)
Blanche Esmead	TLS E1	r	rn, S f(n) w
The Face of Clay	TLS E1	r	rn, S f(n)
The Poetic Drama[c]	G E1	r	rn, S dr
Poets' Letters[d]	S E1	r	rn, S nf(l) w
[Fenwick's Career] K&C	G E1	r	rn, S f(n) w
Wordsworth and the Lakes[e]	TLS E1	r	rn, S nf(t)
The Compromise	TLS E1	r	rn, S f(n) w
Mrs Grundy's Crucifix	TLS E1	r	rn, S f(n) w
The Bluest of the Blue	G E1	r	rn, S nf(h,c) w
Coniston	TLS E1	r	rn, S f(n) A
The Author's Progress	G E1	r	rn, S nf(c)
Sweetness – Long Drawn Out	A&L E1	r	rn, S nf(b) w
Trafficks and Discoveries	S E1	r	rn, S nf(h)
The English Mail Coach	G E1	e	rn, S
Portraits of Places	G E1	e	A
Impressions of Sir Leslie Stephen	M E1	e	
Chippinge	TLS E6	r	f(n)
Occasion's Forelock	TLS E6	r	f(n) w
Abbots Verney	TLS E6	r	f(n) w

Title of review or essay	Publication, location	Review, essay	Other information
	1907		
The Lonely Lady of Grosvenor Square	TLS E6	r	f(n) w
Memoirs of a Person of Quality	TLS E6	r	f(n)
The Private Papers of Henry Ryecroft	G E1	e	rn, S f(n)/nf(m)
Temptation	TLS E1	r	f(n)
Disciples	TLS E6	r	f(n) w
Carlyle and the London Library	TLS E6	r	nf(h,l)
Old Hampshire Vignettes	TLS E6	r	f(ss) w
Mary Christie	TLS E6	r	nf(e,m) w
The Wingless Victory	TLS E6	r	f(n) w
Lady Huntingdon	TLS E6	r	nf(b) w
In Playtime	TLS E6	r	nf(e)
Some Poetic Plays^f	G E6	r	dr
The Longest Journey	TLS E6	r	f(n)
The Call of the East	TLS E6	r	f(ss) w
Fräulein Schmidt and Mr Anstruther	TLS E1	r	f(n) w
Mrs Sellar's Recollections	TLS E6	r	nf(m) w
The Glen o' Weeping	TLS E1	r	f(n) w
Letters of a Betrothed	TLS E6	r	nf(l) w
Philip Sidney	TLS E1	r, e	nf(b)
Venice	TLS E6	r	nf(t) w
A Mirror of Shalott	TLS E6	r	f(ss)
The Feast of Bacchus	TLS E6	r	f(n)
The Red Sphinx	TLS E6	r	f(n)
Lady Fanshawe's Memoirs	TLS E1	r	nf(m) w
Love the Judge	TLS E6	r	f(n)
The New Religion	TLS E1	r	f(n)
Tales of Two People	TLS E6	r	f(n)
Mam Linda	TLS E6	r	f(n) A
The Weavers	TLS E6	r	f(n)
The Square Peg	TLS E6	r	f(n)
Outrageous Fortune	TLS E6	r	f(n) w
The Last Days of Marie Antoinette	TLS E1	r	nf(h) w

Title of review or essay	Publication, location	Review, essay	Other information
A Swan and Her Friends	TLS E1	r	nf(l) w
The Desert Venture	TLS E6	r	f(n)
The Forest Playfellow	TLS E6	r	f(n)g w
The Northern Iron	TLS E6	r	f(n)
William Allingham	TLS E1	r	nf(d)
1908			
Some Poetical Plays[h]	G E6	r	dr
Rachel Gurney of the Grove	TLS E6	r	nf(l) w
The Sentimental Traveller	TLS E1	r	nf(e) w
Thomas Hood	TLS E1	r, e	nf(b),p
Father Alphonsus	TLS E6	r	f(n)
Colonel Kate	TLS E6	r	f(n) w
The Memoirs of Sarah Bernhardt	C E1	r, e	nf(m) w
The Inward Light	TLS E1	r	nf(c)
Shelley and Elizabeth Hitchener	TLS E1	r	nf(l) w
The Ways of Rebellion	TLS E6	r	f(n)
The Wolf	TLS E6	r	f(n)
The Memoirs of Lady Dorothy Nevill	C E1	r	nf(m) w
Wordsworth Letters	TLS E1	r	nf(l)
The Sword Decides	TLS E6	r	f(n) w
The Red Neighbour	TLS E6	r	f(n) w
Destinies	TLS E6	r	f(ss)
Marotz	TLS E6	r	f(n)
John Delane	C E1	r, e	nf(b)
Between the Twilights	TLS E6	r	nf(b) w
The Diary of a Lady in Waiting	TLS E1	r	nf(d) w
The Stranger in London	TLS E1	r	nf(t)
A Week in the White House	C E1	r, e	nf(b,h) A
Scottish Women	TLS E1	r	nf(b,h) w
Louise de La Vallière	C E1	r, e	nf(b,m,l) w
A Room with a View	TLS E1	r	f(n)
Château and Country Life	TLS E1	r	nf(m) w
Letters of Christina Rossetti	TLS E1	r	nf(l) w
Blackstick Papers	TLS E1	r	nf(e) w

Title of review or essay	Publication, location		Review, essay	Other information		
The Journal of Elizabeth Lady Holland	C	E1	r, e	nf(d)		w
A Vanished Generation	TLS	E1	r	nf(b)		w
1909						
Venice	TLS	E1	r	nf(t,h)		
The Genius of Boswell	TLS	E1	r, e	nf(l)		
One Immortality	TLS	E1	r	f(n)		
More Carlyle Letters	TLS	E1	r	nf(l)		w
Gentlemen Errant	TLS	E1	r	nf(b,c)		w
Caroline Emelia Stephen	G	E1	e			w
The Opera	T	E1	e			
A Friend of Johnson	TLS	E1	r, e	nf(b)		
Art and Life	TLS	E1	r	nf(e,c)		w
Sterne	TLS	E1	r, e	rn, B	nf(b)	
Impressions at Bayreuth	T	E1	e			
Oliver Wendell Holmes	TLS	E1	r, e	rn, B	nf(b)	A
Masques and Phases	TLS	E6	r	nf(e)		
A Cookery Book	TLS	E1	r	nf(c)		w
Sheridan	TLS	E1	r, e	nf(b,d)		w
Maria Edgeworth and Her Circle	TLS	E1	r	nf(b)		w
The Girlhood of Queen Elizabeth	TLS	E1	r	nf(b,l)		w
1910						
Lady Hester Stanhope	TLS	E1	r	nf(b,m)		w
Modes and Manners of the Nineteenth Century	TLS	E1	r	nf(h,c)		w
Emerson's Journals	TLS	E1	r, e	rn, B	nf(d)	A
Mrs Gaskell	TLS	E1	r	nf(b)		w
Lysistrata (performance)	EW	E6	r	dr		w
1911						
The Duke and Duchess of Newcastle-upon-Tyne	TLS	E1	r, e	nf(b)		w
Rachel	TLS	E1	r	nf(b)		w
The Post-Impressionists	N	E1	r	nf(c)		
1912						
The Novels of George Gissing	TLS	E1	r, e	f(n)		

Table Appendix 5.1 Notes

a. The two books reviewed were *Letters from Catalonia and Other Parts of Spain* and *The Land of the Blessed Virgin: Sketches and Impressions*.
b. The two novels reviewed were *Dan the Dollar* and *The Red-Haired Woman*.
c. The seven plays reviewed were *King William I*; *Aurelian: A Drama of the Later Empire*; *Sir Thomas More: An Historical Play in Five Acts*; *The Little Mermaid: A Play in Three Acts*; *The City: A Poem-Drama, and Other Poems*; *Plays & Poems*; and *The Two Arcadias: Plays and Poems*.
d. The books reviewed were *Elizabeth Barrett Browning in Her Letters* and *Robert Browning and Alfred Domett*.
e. The books reviewed were *Wordsworth's Guide to the Lakes* and *Months at the Lakes*.
f. The five plays reviewed were *Constantine the Great: A Tragedy*; *King Arthur Pendragon*; *Three New Plays*; *Apotheosis: A Poem*; and *Desiderio: A Drama in Three Acts*.
g. A children's book.
h. The seven plays reviewed were *Deirdre: Being Volume Five of Plays for an Irish Theatre*; *Prunella: or, Love in a Dutch Garden*; *The Romance of King Arthur*; *Sir Walter Ralegh: A Drama in Five Acts*; *The Goddess of Reason*; *Scorn of Women*; and *The Virgin Goddess: A Tragedy*.

Adding It All Up

158 reviews and essays:

100 in *TLS*
39 in *G*
6 in *C*
4 in *A&L*
3 in *S*
2 in *T*
1 in *M*
1 in *NR*
1 in *N*
1 in *EW*

 3 in 1904
37 in 1905
25 in 1906
37 in 1907
30 in 1908
17 in 1909
 5 in 1910
 3 in 1911
 1 in 1912

13 reviewed books by or about Americans
80 reviewed books by or about women
15 essays
143 reviews, 15 of which are review essays
   4 drama reviews
   69 fiction reviews (61 novels, 8 collections of short stories)
   70 non-fiction reviews* (9 history; 23 biography; 12 criticism; 10 memoir; 6 travel; 13 letters; 5 diaries; 6 essays)
     8 of these reviews include some discussion of poetry (3 overlap with drama)

* Types of non-fiction add up to 84, not 70, because in many cases, Stephen was reviewing more than one work or works that fit into more than one kind of non-fiction.

Sources

Archival Sources

Archives of American Art, Smithsonian Institution

Stephen, Leslie. Letter to George Warr. 1 November 1897. MS. Microfilm 3480.

British Library

Atalanta: the Victorian Magazine. Vols 1–4. Ed. L. T. Meade, Alicia A. Leith and John C. Staples. London: Hatchards. 1887–91.
Cecil, Lord Robert. The Cecil of Chelwood Papers. Correspondence and papers of Edgar Algernon Robert Gascoyne-Cecil, Viscount Cecil of Chelwood. 1893–1953. Add MS 51071–51204.
Child, Harold Hannyngton. Letter to Lord Northcliffe. 28 October 1910. Northcliffe Papers, Vol. CIV. ff. 4–8. Add MS 62256.
Child, Harold Hannyngton. Letter to Lord Northcliffe. 9 November 1910. Northcliffe Papers, Vol. CIV. ff. 12–16. Add MS 62256.
Lyttelton, Kathleen Mary. Letter to Mary Gladstone. 16 October 1906. Mary Gladstone Papers, Vol. XVII. ff. 159–60. Add MS 46235.
School Reports, Stories. 1888–94. Thoby Stephen's Papers. Stephen Family Papers. Add MS 88954/3/2.
Stephen, Julian Thoby. Papers of Thoby Stephen. c1900–6. Add MS 89118.
Stephen, Leslie. Letters to Thoby and Adrian. 1888–1903. Stephen Family Papers. Add MS 88954/1/1.
—. *The 'Mausoleum Book'*. Vol. I. The 'Mausoleum Book'. 21 May 1895–14 November 1903. Add MS 57920.
—. *The Mausoleum Book Notebook*. Vol. III. 'Calendar of Correspondence'. 1895. Add MS 57922.
Woolf, Virginia. *Travel and Literary Notebook*. Visits to Greece, Turkey and Italy. Comments on Hardy, Meredith, Merimée. 1906–9, n.d. Add MS 61837.
Worsley, G. T. Letters to Julia Stephen. 1891–4. Stephen Family Papers. Add MS 88954/1/2.

Cambridge University Library Reading Room

The Cambridge University Calendar. Cambridge: Deighton Bell, 1883–5.
The Cambridge University Reporter. Cambridge: University Press, 1880–5.

Center for Research Libraries

Guardian. Vols 59–64. 1904–9.

Eberly Family Special Collections Library, Pennsylvania State University

Woolf, Virginia. Letter to Dear Madam. 15 August 1935. MS. The Allison-Shelley Collection, the Pennsylvania State University Libraries. University Park, PA.

Girton College Archives and Special Collections, University of Cambridge

'Classical Club'. *The Girton Review* 7 (March 1884): 19. PDF file. GCCP 2/1/1.
'The Classical Tripos'. *The Girton Review* 3 (December 1882): 4–5. PDF file. GCCP 2/1/1.
Girton College Register. 1869–1946. Janet Case entry, 1881. PDF file.
Long, Marjorie. 'In Memoriam: Janet Elizabeth Case'. *Girton Review* 105 (Michaelmas 1937): 41–2. PDF file. GCCP 2/1/3.

King's College London College Archives

Class List-Exam Results 1899 and 1900. KWA/R1.
Delegacy Minutes. January 1910–19. December 1929. KA/D/M1, 7.
King's College London Calendar. 1899–1900.
King's College Magazine, Ladies' Department. K/SER1/170.
Register of Matriculated Students. 1902–20. KWA/R4.
Register of Term Lists. KWA/R2.
Registration Records. 1897–1901. KWA/RAD 3 7.
Syllabus of Lectures. Vols 1–3. 1878–89; 1889–1900; 1900–9. Annual Reports for previous years in Appendices. KW/SYL 6–9.

Lady Margaret Hall Archives, University of Oxford

Annual Reports for LMH. Vols I–V (1880–1925).
The Brown Book: Lady Margaret Hall Chronicle. June 1906. November 1907.
Clay, Agnes Muriel (Wilde). Lady Margaret Hall Register 1879–1990.
Gwyer, B. E. 'Agnes Muriel Wilde (née Clay), 1878–1962'. *The Brown Book: The Lady Margaret Hall Chronicle.* Oxford, December 1962: 30–1.
Lannon, Frances. *Lady Margaret Hall, Oxford: The First 125 Years, 1879–2004.* Oxford: Lady Margaret Hall, 2004.
Wilde, A. M. Clay. Letters. *LMH Cuttings, Album 4.*

Lambeth Archives, London Borough of Lambeth, Minet Library

Morley College Executive Committee Minutes. Vol. 1, IV/224/1/3/1/1 (1891–5); Vol. 2, IV/224/1/3/1/2 (1895–1901); Vol. 3, IV/224/1/3/1/3 (1901–12).

The London Library Archive, The London Library

Catalogue of the London Library, 5th ed., 1888.
Harrison, Robert. Preface. *Catalogue of the London Library, St. James's Square*, 3rd ed. London: London Library, 1865. vii–xii.
London Library Annual Reports. 8 July 1937; 16 July 1941.
London Library: Minutes of the Committee. 29 May 1890; 28 May 1891; 9 May 1894; 14 June 1894; 9 January 1899; 11 March 1901; 14 January 1935.
Wright, C. T. Hagberg and the London Library, comp. *Catalogue of the London Library, St. James's Square, London.* London: Williams & Norgate, 1903.

Manuscripts, Archives and Special Collections, Washington State University Libraries

Case, Janet. Letter to Marion Rathbone. 3 April 1937. MS. Cage 4591.
Stephen, Julia Duckworth. ['Agnostic Women']. 1880? MS Julia Stephen Folder 13.
Stephen, Julian Thoby. Annotations in Lucretius Carus, Titus. *T. Lucreti Cari De rerum natura libri I–III.* Ed. and intro. by J. H. Warburton Lee. Macmillan's School Class Books. London: Macmillan, 1893.
Stephen, Leslie. Annotations in:
   Morley, John. *On Compromise.* London: Chapman and Hall, 1874.
   Newman, John Henry. [six of eight titles]
   Richardson, Samuel. *The Correspondence of Samuel Richardson.* London: Phillips, 1804. 6 vols [lacking vol. 1]
   Stephen, Leslie. *Hours in a Library.* London: Smith, Elder, 1874–9. 3 vols.
Woolf, Virginia. Annotations in:
   Lucretius Carus, Titus. *T. Lucreti Cari De rerum natura libri I–III.* Ed. and introd. by J. H. Warburton Lee. Macmillan's School Class Books. London: Macmillan, 1893.
   Martial. *M. Val. Martialis Epigrammata selecta.* Ed. F. A. Paley and W. H. Stone. Grammar School Classics. London: G. Bell, 1896.

Morley College Library

Morley College Annual Reports. 1893–1919. See link.
Morley College Archive. https://vle.morleycollege.ac.uk/course/view.php?id=1646#section-8
Morley College Magazine. May 1892-present. Index, 1892–1940. See link.
Morley College. Programme of Classes. 1910–11.

New York Public Library, Berg Collection

Woolf, Virginia. [Diary] Holograph notebook. Unsigned. June 3–October 1, 1903? No. 2.
—. 'How Should One Read a Book?' 'Articles, essays, fiction, and reviews'. Volume 1: 21 April 1925. MS 177–249.

The Ohio State University

The Academy. Vols 68–75. 1905–08. Microform.
Atalanta: the Victorian Magazine. Vols 3–5. Ed. L. T. Meade, Alicia A. Leith, and John C. Staples. London: Hatchards. 1889–1892.
Cornhill Magazine. Vols 24–25 (series 3). 1908.
The Literary Year-book. Vols 1–24. 1897–1923. Microform.
Lorimer, Adam. *The Author's Progress; or the Literary Book of the Road*. London: Blackwood and Sons, 1906. The Ohio State University Rare Book and Manuscript Library.
Nation. Vol. 1, 1907–1918. Microform.
National Review. Vols 44–45. 1905.
Times Literary Supplement. 1902–1912. 1952. 1961. Microfilm.

Special Collections, University of Sussex Library, The Keep

Richmond, Bruce. Letter to Virginia Woolf. MHP. TS. SxMs–18/1/D/123/2.
Stephen, Adrian. Diary of Adrian Stephen. MHP. TS. SxMs–18/4/9/1.
Woolf, Virginia. 'Autobiography of Benvenuto Cellini' [1905?] Early Writings by Virginia Stephen. c. 1902. MHP. MS. SxMS–18/2/A/26/B.
—. 'The Dramatic in Life and Work'. [1905?] Early Writings by Virginia Stephen. c. 1902. MHP. MS. SxMS–18/2/A/26/C.
—. 'Janet Case'. [1937]. Miscellaneous Published Articles. MHP. MS. SxMs–18/2/B/26/C.
—. 'Notes of Virginia Woolf. "Authorities. The English Kingdoms"'. Miscellaneous Materials Relating to Virginia Woolf. LWP. MS. SxMS–13/2/D/17/A.
—. 'Notes on circa 45 books read in review for "The Guardian", "The Academy", "Times" and "The Speaker"'. 1905–6. MHP. MS. SxMs 18/2/B/1/A.
—. ['Report on Teaching at Morley College']. July 1905. MHP. MS. SxMS–18/2/A/22.
—. 'A Sketch of the Past'. 19 July 1939. Reminiscences of Family and Childhood by Virginia Woolf. MHP. MS and TS. SxMS–18/2/A/5/C.
—. ['Writing in the Margin']. 22 May n.y. Fragment. Manuscripts by Virginia Stephen. MHP. MS. SxMS–18/2/A/23/C.

Times Newspapers Ltd Archive, News Corp UK and Ireland Ltd

Bell, C. F. Moberly. Letters. Vol. 56. 20 October 1910–18 October 1912. Manager's Letter Books. 2nd series.
Child, Harold. Letter to Lord Northcliffe. 7 November 1910. ALS. NOR/1/1/041.
The Woman's Supplement to *The Times*. October–December 1910. Marked copies. SSI/1/1–14.

University of Cincinnati

Speaker. Vols 1–15 (new series). 1899–1907. Microform.

Women's Library@London School of Economics

Sheepshanks, Mary. *The Long Day Ended*. 1952–3. Papers of Mary Sheepshanks. TS. 7MSH.

Virginia Woolf Sources

Books

The Captain's Death Bed and Other Essays. Ed. Leonard Woolf. New York: Harvest/HBJ, 1950.
Carlyle's House and Other Sketches. Ed. David Bradshaw. London: Hesperus, 2003.
Collected Essays. Ed. Leonard Woolf. 4 vols. New York: Harcourt, 1967.
The Common Reader. 1925. Ed. Andrew McNeillie. Annotated ed. San Diego: Harvest/HBJ, 1984.
The Crowded Dance of Modern Life: Selected Essays: Volume Two. Ed. Rachel Bowlby. London: Penguin, 1993.
The Death of the Moth and Other Essays. Ed. Leonard Woolf. 1942. New York: Harvest/HBJ, 1970.
The Diary of Virginia Woolf. Ed. Anne Olivier Bell and Andrew McNeillie. 5 vols. New York: HBJ, 1977–84.
The Essays of Virginia Woolf. Ed. Andrew McNeillie and Stuart N. Clarke. 6 vols. Vols 1–3 (McNeillie) New York: HBJ, 1986–98; Vol. 4 (McNeillie) London: Hogarth, 1994; Vols 5–6 (Clarke) London: Hogarth, 2009–11.
Granite & Rainbow: Essays. Ed. Leonard Woolf. 1958. New York: Harvest/HBJ, 1975.
Hyde Park Gate News: The Stephen Family Newspaper. With Vanessa Bell and Thoby Stephen. Ed. Gill Lowe. London: Hesperus, 2005.
The Letters of Virginia Woolf. Ed. Nigel Nicolson and Joanne Trautmann. 6 vols. New York: HBJ, 1975–80.
The Moment and Other Essays. Ed. Leonard Woolf. 1948. New York: Harvest/HBJ, 1974.
Moments of Being: A Collection of Autobiographical Writing. Ed. Jeanne Schulkind. 2nd ed. San Diego: Harcourt, 1985.
Moments of Being: Unpublished Autobiographical Writings. Ed. Jeanne Schulkind. 1st ed. New York: Harvest/HBJ, 1976.
Mrs. Dalloway. 1925. Ed. Bonnie Kime Scott. Annotated ed. Orlando: Harvest/Harcourt, 2005.
The Pargiters: The Novel-Essay Portion of The Years. Ed. Mitchell A. Leaska. New York: Harvest/HBJ, 1977.
A Passionate Apprentice: The Early Journals 1897–1909. Ed. Mitchell A. Leaska. San Diego: HBJ, 1990.
A Room of One's Own. 1929. Ed. Susan Gubar. Annotated ed. Orlando: Harvest/Harcourt, 2005.
The Second Common Reader. 1932. Ed. Andrew McNeillie. Annotated ed. San Diego: Harvest/HBJ, 1986.
Three Guineas. 1938. Ed. Jane Marcus. Annotated ed. Orlando: Harvest/Harcourt, 2006.

To the Lighthouse. 1927. Ed. Mark Hussey. Annotated ed. Orlando: Harvest/Harcourt, 2005.
Virginia Woolf: Selected Essays. Ed. David Bradshaw. Oxford World's Classics. Oxford: Oxford UP, 2008.
The Voyage Out. 1920. New York: Harvest, 1948.
A Woman's Essays: Selected Essays: Volume One. Ed. Rachel Bowlby. London: Penguin, 1992.
The Years. 1937. Ed. Eleanor McNees. Annotated ed. Orlando: Harvest/Harcourt, 2008.

Reviews, Essays, Memoirs, Short Stories

'22 Hyde Park Gate'. *MoB* 162–77.
'The American Woman'. *E1* 46–8.
'An Andalusian Inn'. *E1* 49–52.
'Anon' and 'The Reader'. *E6* 580–607.
'The Author's Progress'. *E1* 116–17.
'Barham of Beltana'. *E1* 36–7.
'A Belle of the Fifties'. *E1* 17–22.
'Blackstick Papers'. *E1* 228–9.
'Blanche Esmead'. *E1* 95–6.
'Byron and Mr Briggs'. *E3* 473–99 (Appendix II).
'Carlyle and the London Library'. *E6* 308–10.
'Caroline Emelia Stephen'. *E1* 267–9.
'Chippinge'. *E6* 301–2.
'Colonel Kate'. *E6* 358–9.
'The Common Reader'. *E4* 19.
'A Dark Lantern'. *E1* 42–3.
'The Debtor'. *E1* 68–9.
'The Decay of Essay-writing'. *E1* 24–7.
'A Description of the Desert'. *E1* 72–4.
'Destinies'. *E6* 365–6.
'Divorce Courts'. *CH* 16–18.
'Donne after Three Centuries'. *E5* 349–66.
'The Duke and Duchess of Newcastle-Upon-Tyne'. *E1* 345–51; *E6* 632.
'The Enchanted Organ'. *E3* 399–403.
'The English Mail Coach'. *E1* 365–8; *E6* 632–3.
'Father Alphonsus'. *E6* 356–7.
'The Feminine Note in Fiction'. *E1* 15–17.
'The Fortunes of Farthings'. *E1* 38–9.
'The Genius of Boswell'. *E1* 249–54.
'George Eliot'. *E4* 170–81.
'The Glen o' Weeping'. *E1* 138–9.
'The Golden Bowl Reading Notes'. *E1* 381–8 (Appendix III).
'Hampstead'. *CH* 10–11.
'Haworth, November, 1904'. *E1* 5–9.
'The House of Mirth'. *E1* 67–8.
'The House of Shadows'. *E1* 93–4.
'How Should One Read a Book?' *E5* 572–84.
'Impressions of Sir Leslie Stephen'. *E1* 127–30.
'Introductory Letter to Margaret Llewelyn Davies'. *E5* 225–41.
'Jane Austen'. *E4* 146–57.

'J. M. S.: Notes (1929?)'. *The Platform of Time: Memoirs of Family and Friends*. Ed. and intro. S. P. Rosenbaum. Expanded ed. London: Hesperus, 2008. 125–7.
'John Delane'. E1 188–94.
'*The Journal of Elizabeth Lady Holland*'. E1 230–9.
'The Journal of Mistress Joan Martyn'. *The Complete Shorter Fiction of Virginia Woolf*. Ed. Susan Dick. 2nd ed. San Diego: Harcourt, 1989. 33–62, 295–6.
'Journeys in Spain'. E1 44–6.
'Julia Margaret Cameron'. E4 375–86.
'Lady Dorothy Nevill'. CR 196–200; E4 200–4.
'Lady Huntingdon'. E6 315–17.
'Lady Ritchie'. E3 13–20.
'The Leaning Tower'. E6 259–83.
'Leslie Stephen, the Philosopher at Home: A Daughter's Memories'. E5 585–93.
Letter to Eva Hubback. Ed. Stephen Barkway. *Virginia Woolf Bulletin* 48 (January 2015): 5–9.
'The Letters of Jane Welsh Carlyle'. E1 54–8.
'Literary Geography'. E1 32–6.
'London Squares'. *Nation* 24 June 1933: 843. Letter. E6 3–4.
'*Lone Marie*'. E1 66.
'Louise de La Vallière'. E1 215–20.
'Maria Edgeworth and Her Circle'. E1 315–19.
'Mary Christie'. E6 311–13.
'*Masques and Phases*'. E6 369–72.
'*Memoirs of a Person of Quality*'. E6 306–7.
'The Memoirs of Lady Dorothy Nevill'. E1 178–83.
'The Memoirs of Sarah Bernhardt'. E1 164–71.
'Middlebrow'. E6 470–9.
'Miss Janet Case: Classical Scholar and Teacher'. E6 111–14.
'Miss Ormerod'. E4 131–40, 144–5.
'The Modern Essay'. E4 216–27.
'Modes and Manners of the Nineteenth Century'. E1 330–5.
'Moments of Being: "Slater's Pins Have No Points"'. *The Complete Shorter Fiction of Virginia Woolf*. 2nd ed. Ed. Susan Dick. San Diego: Harcourt/Harvest, 1989. 215–20, 305–6.
'Mr Bennett and Mrs Brown'. E3 384–9.
'Mr Henry James's Latest Novel'. E1 22–4.
'*Mrs Gaskell*'. E1 340–44.
'*Mrs Grundy's Crucifix*'. E1 111–12.
'The New Biography'. E4 473–80.
'*The New Religion*'. E1 148–50.
'Next-Door Neighbours'. E1 11–12.
'A Nineteenth-Century Critic'. E1 83–6.
'*The Northern Iron*'. E6 346–7.
'The Novels of George Gissing'. E1 355–62.
'Old Bloomsbury'. MoB 181–201.
'*Old Hampshire Vignettes*'. E6 310–11.
'On a Faithful Friend'. E1 12–15.
'On Being Ill'. E4 317–29.
'On Not Knowing Greek'. E4 38–53.
'*One Immortality*'. E1 255–6.
'*Outrageous Fortune*'. E6 342–3.
'The Patron and the Crocus'. E4 212–15.
'The Perfect Language'. E2 114–19.

'The Poetic Drama'. *E1* 97–101.
'Poetry, Fiction and the Future'. *E4* 428–41.
'Poets' Letters'. *E1* 101–5.
'*The Post-Impressionists*'. *E1* 379–80.
'*The Private Papers of Henry Ryecroft*'. *E1* 131–4.
'Professions for Women'. *E6* 479–84.
'A Professor of Life'. *E4* 342–8.
'Reminiscences'. *MoB* 28–59.
['Report on Teaching at Morley College']. *QB1* 202–4 (Appendix B).
'Reviewing'. *E6* 195–209.
'The Russian Point of View'. *E4* 181–90.
'*The Scholar's Daughter*'. *E1* 92.
'The *Sentimental Journey*'. *E5* 401–10.
'*The Sentimental Traveller*'. *E1* 157–9.
'A Sketch of the Past'. *MoB*. Ed. Jeanne Schulkind. 1st ed. New York: HBJ, 1976. 64–137.
'A Sketch of the Past'. *MoB*. Ed. Jeanne Schulkind. 2nd ed. San Diego: Harvest/Harcourt, 1985. 63–159.
['*Social England*']. *E1* 369–71.
'Some Poetic Plays'. *E6* 318–23.
'Some Poetical Plays'. *E6* 347–55.
'*The Son of Royal Langbrith*'. *E1* 3–5.
'The Square Peg'. *E6* 340–2.
'Sterne'. *E1* 280–8.
'Street Haunting: A London Adventure'. *E4* 480–91.
'Street Music'. *E1* 27–32.
'The Sun and the Fish'. *E4* 519–24.
'A Supreme Moment'. *E1* 92–3
'*The Sword Decides*'. *E6* 362–4.
'Tales of Two People'. *E6* 336–7.
'Their Passing Hour'. *E1* 61–5.
'Thomas Hood'. *E1* 159–64.
'Trafficks and Discoveries'. *E1* 120–4.
'Two Irish Novels'. *E1* 77–9.
'Two Women'. *E4* 419–26.
'The Value of Laughter'. *E1* 58–60.
['Virginia Woolf and the Authors of *Euphrosyne*'.] *QB1* 205–6 (Appendix C).
'A Walk by Night'. *E1* 80–2.
'*The Ways of Rebellion*'. *E6* 359–60.
'The Weavers'. *E6* 339–40.
'A Week in the White House'. *E1* 204–10.
'Why?' *E6* 30–6.
'William Allingham'. *E1* 154–6.
'*The Wingless Victory*'. *E6* 313–15.
'The Wolf'. *E6* 360–2.

Other Sources

Please note: All sources are print unless otherwise indicated.

Adam, Ruth. *A Woman's Place: 1910–1975*. 1975. London: Persephone Books, 2003.

Adolph, Andrea. 'Luncheon at "The Leaning Tower": Consumption and Class in Virginia Woolf's *Between the Acts*'. *Women's Studies* 34 (2005): 439–59.

Ainger, Alfred. *Lectures and Essays*. Ed. H[enry]. C. Beeching. 2 vols. 1905. New York: AMS, 1972.

Alcoff, Linda. 'The Problem of Speaking for Others'. *Cultural Critique* (Winter 1991–2): 5–32.

Alexander, Christine. 'Play and Apprenticeship: The Culture of Family Magazines'. *The Child Writer from Austen to Woolf*. Ed. Christine Alexander and Juliet McMaster. Cambridge: Cambridge UP, 2005. 31–50.

—. 'Victorian Juvenilia'. *A Companion to the Victorian Novel*. Ed. William Baker and Kenneth Womack. Westport, CT: Greenwood, 2002. 223–38.

— and Juliet McMaster. Introduction. *The Child Writer from Austen to Woolf*. Ed. Christine Alexander and Juliet McMaster. Cambridge: Cambridge UP, 2005. 1–7.

Allen, Judith. *Virginia Woolf and the Politics of Language*. Edinburgh: Edinburgh UP, 2010.

—. 'Virginia Woolf's Essayistic Practice as Cultural Critique'. Diss. University of Delaware, 1994.

Alley, Henry. 'A Rediscovered Eulogy: Virginia Woolf's "Miss Janet Case: Classical Scholar and Teacher"'. *Twentieth Century Literature* 28 (Fall 1982): 290–301.

Altick, Richard D. *The English Common Reader: A Social History of the Mass Reading Public, 1800–1900*. 1957. 2nd ed. Foreword Jonathan Rose. Columbus: Ohio State UP, 1998.

—. 'The Sociology of Authorship: The Social Origins, Education, and Occupations of 1,100 British Writers, 1800–1935'. *Writers, Readers & Occasions: Selected Essays on Victorian Literature and Life*. Columbus, OH: Ohio State UP, 1989. 95–109.

Anderson, Chris. 'Hearsay Evidence and Second-Class Citizenship'. *College English* 50 (1988): 300–8.

Anderson, G. L. 'The Social Economy of Late-Victorian Clerks'. *The Lower Middle Class in Britain 1870–1914*. Ed. Geoffrey Crossick. London: Croom Helm, 1977. 113–34.

Annan, Noel. *Leslie Stephen: The Godless Victorian*. New York: Random House, 1984.

Arata, Stephen. '1897'. *A Companion to Victorian Literature and Culture*. Ed. Herbert F. Tucker. Oxford: Blackwell, 1999. 51–65.

Argyros, Ellen. 'The Angel in the House Had a Pen: Julia Duckworth Stephen on the Sympathetic Imagination and Maternal Absence'. Midwest Modern Language Association. Marriott City Center, Minneapolis. 5 November 1999. Address.

Armstrong, Isobel. *Victorian Poetry: Poetry, Poetics, and Politics*. London: Routledge, 1993.

Aronsfeld, C. C. 'German Jews in Victorian England'. *Publications of the Leo Baeck Institute: Year Book VII*. London, Jerusalem and New York: Leo Baeck Institute, 1962. 312–29.

Ashton, Rosemary and Deborah Colville. 'London School of Ethics and Social Philosophy'. *UCL Bloomsbury Project*. Leverhulme Trust. 2007–11. Web. 7 December 2018.

Atkinson, Damian. 'Parker, Sir (Horatio) Gilbert George, baronet (1860–1932), novelist and politician'. *ODNB*. Oxford UP, 6 January 2011. doi.org/10.1093/ref:odnb/35384. Web. 9 June 2017.

Avery, Todd and Patrick Brantlinger. 'Reading "Mind Hungers" Common and Uncommon'. *A Concise Companion to Modernism*. Ed. David Bradshaw. Malden, MA: Blackwell, 2003. 243–61.

Baggs, Chris. '"In the Separate Reading Room for Ladies Are Provided Those Publications Specially Interesting to Them": Ladies' Reading Rooms and British Public Libraries 1850–1914'. *Victorian Periodicals Review* 38.3 (Fall 2005): 280–306.

Bainton, George, comp. and ed. *The Art of Authorship: Literary Reminiscences, Methods of Work, and Advice to Young Beginners*. New York: D. Appleton, 1890.

Baker, William. *The Early History of the London Library*. Lewiston, NY: Mellen, 1992.

Bamford, T. W. *Rise of the Public Schools: A Study of Boys' Public Boarding Schools in England and Wales from 1837 to the Present Day*. London: Nelson, 1967.

Banks, Olive. *Faces of Feminism: A Study of Feminism as a Social Movement*. Oxford: Martin Robertson, 1981.

Barkevicius, Jocelyn. '"That peculiar form": On Virginia Woolf and a Poetics of the Essay'. Diss. University of Iowa, 1994.

Barkway, Stephen, ed. Front matter. *The Virginia Woolf Daybook*. Southport: Virginia Woolf Society of Great Britain, 2007. i–xvi.

Barwick, G. F. *The Reading Room of the British Museum*. London: Ernest Benn, 1929.

Basbanes, Nicholas. *Patience & Fortitude: Wherein a Colorful Cast of Determined Book Collectors, Dealers, and Librarians Go about the Quixotic Task of Preserving a Legacy*. New York: Perennial, 2003.

Baylen, J. O. 'The British Press, 1861–1918'. *The Encyclopedia of the British Press, 1422–1992*. Ed. Dennis Griffiths. New York: St. Martin's, 1992. 33–46.

Beer, Gillian. *Virginia Woolf: The Common Ground*. Edinburgh: Edinburgh UP, 1996.

Beetham, Margaret and Kay Boardman, eds. *Victorian Women's Magazines: An Anthology*. Manchester: Manchester UP, 2001.

Bell, Alan. Introduction. *Sir Leslie Stephen's Mausoleum Book*. Ed. Alan Bell. Oxford: Clarendon, 1977. ix–xxxiii.

—. 'The London Library'. *The Cambridge History of Libraries in Britain and Ireland. Volume III: 1850–2000*. Ed. Alistair Black and Peter Hoare. Cambridge: Cambridge UP, 2006. 160–8.

Bell, Anne Olivier. Introduction. *The Diary of Virginia Woolf*. By Virginia Woolf. Vol. 1: 1915–1919. New York: HBJ, 1977. xiii–xxviii.

Bell, Barbara Currier and Carol Ohmann. 'Virginia Woolf's Criticism: A Polemical Preface'. *Critical Inquiry* 1.2 (1974): 361–71.

Bell, Matthew. 'Seventy Years On, Woolf Reveals a New Character'. *The Independent* 6 March 2011. Independent.co.uk. Web. 3 August 2011.

Bell, Quentin. *Virginia Woolf: A Biography*. 2 vols in 1. New York: Harcourt/Harvest, 1972.

Bell, Robert and Malcolm Tight. *Open Universities: A British Tradition?* Ballmoor, UK: Open UP, 1993.

Bell, Vanessa. 'Notes on Virginia's Childhood'. *Sketches in Pen and Ink: A Bloomsbury Notebook*. Ed. Lia Giachero. London: Hogarth, 1997. 55–65.

Bellamy, Joan, Anne Laurence and Gill Perry, eds. Postscript. *Women, Scholarship and Criticism: Gender and Knowledge c. 1790–1900.* Manchester: Manchester UP, 2000. 222.

Bellasis, M. R. and Brian Taylor. 'Hannay, James Owen [pseud. George A. Birmingham] (1865–1950), novelist'. *ODNB.* Oxford UP, 23 September 2004. doi.org/10.1093/ref:odnb/33686. Web. 9 June 2017.

Benjamin, Sarah. *A Castle in Tuscany: The Remarkable Life of Janet Ross.* Millers Point, NSW, Australia: Murdoch Books, 2006.

Bennett, Arnold. *How to Become an Author: A Practical Guide.* London: C. Arthur Pearson, 1903.

—. *Journalism for Women: A Practical Guide.* London: John Lane, 1898.

Bentley, Michael. 'The Liberal Party, 1900–1939: Summit and Descent'. *A Companion to Early Twentieth-Century Britain.* Ed. Chris Wrigley. Oxford: Blackwell, 2003. 23–37.

Berman, Jessica. Rev. of *How to Make It as a Woman: Collective Biographical History from Victoria to the Present.* By Alison Booth. *Virginia Woolf Miscellany* 70 (Fall 2006): 38–9.

Bernstein, Susan David. 'Radical Readers at the British Museum: Eleanor Marx, Clementina Black, Amy Levy'. *Nineteenth-Century Gender Studies* 3.2 (Summer 2007): 20 par. ncgsjournal.com. Web. 9 June 2011.

—. *Roomscape: Women Writers in the British Museum from George Eliot to Virginia Woolf.* Edinburgh Critical Studies in Victorian Culture. Edinburgh: Edinburgh UP, 2013.

—. 'Too Common Readers at the British Museum'. *Victorian Vulgarity: Taste in Verbal and Visual Culture.* Ed. Susan David Bernstein and Elsie B. Michie. Farnham: Ashgate, 2009. 101–17.

Besant, Walter. *The Pen and the Book.* London: Thomas Burleigh, 1899.

Best, Geoffrey. *Mid-Victorian Britain: 1851–1875.* New York: Schocken Books, 1972.

Bicknell, John W. Notes. *Selected Letters of Leslie Stephen.* Vol. 2. 1882–1904. Basingstoke: Macmillan, 1996. *passim.*

Binckes, Faith and Carey Snyder, eds. *Women, Periodicals, and Print Culture in Britain 1890s–1920s.* Edinburgh: Edinburgh UP, 2019.

Birch, Dinah. 'The Child Writer'. Rev. of *The Child Writer from Austen to Woolf,* ed. Christine Alexander and Juliet McMaster and *The Hyde Park Gate News: The Stephen Family Newspaper,* ed. Gill Lowe. *The Times Literary Supplement* 6 February 2006. *Times Online.* Web. 25 July 2006.

Bishop, Edward. 'Metaphor and the Subversive Process of Virginia Woolf's Essays'. *Style* 21.4 (Winter 1987): 573–88.

Black, Alistair. 'The People's University: Models of Public Library History'. *The Cambridge History of Libraries in Britain and Ireland: Volume III, 1850–2000.* Ed. Alistair Black and Peter Hoare. Cambridge: Cambridge UP, 2006. 24–39.

Black, Naomi. *Virginia Woolf as Feminist.* Ithaca, NY, and London: Cornell UP, 2004.

Blain, Virginia, Isobel Grundy and Patricia Clements, eds. *The Feminist Companion to Literature in English: Women Writers from the Middle Ages to the Present.* New Haven, CT: Yale UP, 1990.

Bland, Lucy. 'The Married Woman, the "New Woman" and the Feminist: Sexual Politics of the 1890s'. *Equal or Different: Women's Politics, 1800–1914.* Ed. Jane Rendall. Oxford: Basil Blackwell, 1987. 141–64.

Blank, G. K. 'Arthur Clutton-Brock'. *Modern British Essayists, First Series.* Ed. Robert Beum. *DLB* 98. Detroit: Gale, 1990. 69–72.

Bond, Robin. 'Virginia Woolf's *Antigone:* An Analysis of Woolf's Marginalia in Her Text of Sophocles's Plays from The Library of Leonard and Virginia Woolf'. 27th Annual International Conference on Virginia Woolf. University of Reading, Reading, UK. 29 June 2017. Address.

Boose, G. C. 'Gordon, Lucie or Lucy, Lady Duff-Gordon'. *Dictionary of National Biography*. Ed. Leslie Stephen. Vol. 22. London: Smith & Elder, 1885–1901. 220–1.

Booth, Alison. *How to Make It as a Woman: Collective Biographical History from Victoria to the Present*. Chicago and London: U of Chicago P, 2004.

Borer, M. C. *Willingly to School: A History of Women's Education*. Guildford and London: Lutterworth, 1976.

Borwick, F., ed. *Clifton College Annals and Register, 1862–1912*. Bristol: Arrowsmith, 1912.

Bowlby, Rachel. 'Meet Me in St. Louis: Virginia Woolf and Community'. *Virginia Woolf and Communities: Selected Papers from the Eighth Annual Conference on Virginia Woolf*. Ed. Jeanette McVicker and Laura Davis. New York: Pace UP, 1999. 147–60.

Boyd, Elizabeth French. *Bloomsbury Heritage: Their Mothers and Their Aunts*. New York: Taplinger, 1976.

Bradshaw, David. Introduction. *Carlyle's House and Other Sketches*. By Virginia Woolf. Ed. David Bradshaw. London: Hesperus, 2003. xiii–xxv.

— and Kevin J. H. Dettmar, eds. *A Companion to Modernist Literature and Culture*. Oxford: Blackwell, 2006.

Brake, Laurel. 'Literary Criticism and the Victorian Periodicals'. *The Yearbook of English Studies* 16 (1986): 92–116.

—. 'A Moment of Being: Miss Marx, Miss Pater, "Miss Ambient"'. *Eleanor Marx (1855–1898): Life, Work, Contacts*. Ed. John Stokes. Farnham: Ashgate, 2003. 145–55.

—. 'The Old Journalism and the New: Forms of Cultural Production in London in the 1880s'. Wiener. 1–24.

—. 'Pater, Clara Ann (bap. 1841, d. 1910), tutor and promoter of the higher education of women'. *ODNB*. Oxford UP, 23 September 2004. doi.org/10.1093/ref:odnb/48505. Web. 26 September 2007.

Brantlinger, Patrick. '"The Bloomsbury Fraction" Versus War and Empire'. *Seeing Double: Revisioning Edwardian and Modernist Literature*. Ed. Carola M. Kaplan and Anne B. Simpson. New York: St. Martin's, 1996. 149–67.

Breay, Claire. 'Women and the Classical Tripos 1869–1914'. *Classics in 19th and 20th Century Cambridge: Curriculum, Culture and Community*. Ed. Christopher Stray. Supplementary volume no. 24. Cambridge: Cambridge Philological Society, 1999. 49–70.

Briggs, Julia. *Reading Virginia Woolf*. Edinburgh: Edinburgh UP, 2006.

—. *Virginia Woolf: An Inner Life*. Orlando: Harcourt, 2005.

Brittain, Vera. *On Being an Author*. New York: Macmillan, 1947.

Brooker, Peter and Andrew Thacker, eds. *The Oxford Critical and Cultural History of Modernist Magazines*, Vol. 1 (Britain and Ireland, 1880–1955). Oxford: Oxford UP, 2009.

Brosnan, Leila. *Reading Virginia Woolf's Essays and Journalism: Breaking the Surface of Silence*. Edinburgh: Edinburgh UP, 1997.

Brown, Julia Prewitt. *The Bourgeois Interior*. Charlottesville: U of Virginia P, 2008.

Brown, Monika. 'George Henry Lewes, 1817–1878'. *Victorian Prose Writers Before 1867*. Ed. William B. Thesing. *DLB* 55. Detroit: Gale, 1987. 128–41.

Bruley, Sue. *Women in Britain since 1900*. Social History in Perspective. Basingstoke: Macmillan, 1999.

Bryant, Margaret. *The Unexpected Revolution: A Study in the History of the Education of Women and Girls in the Nineteenth Century*. London: U of London Institute of Education, 1979.

Bryson, Bill. *Shakespeare: The World as Stage*. Eminent Lives Series. New York: Harper, 2007.

Buchheim, C. A., ed. Preface. *Modern German Reader: A Graduated Collection of Prose Extracts from Modern German Writers*. Part 1. 6th rev. ed. Oxford: Clarendon, 1890. v–viii. *Internet Archive*. PDF file.

'Buchheim, Charles Adolphus'. *Who Was Who: A Companion to 'Who's Who' Containing the Biographies of Those Who Died During the Period 1897–1916*. London: A. & C. Black, 1920. 99. *Internet Archive*. Web. 9 August 2011.

Buchheim, E. S. 'C. A. Buchheim: A Biographical Sketch'. *Hermann und Dorothea*. By Johann Wolfgang von Goethe. Ed. C. A. Buchheim. Oxford: Clarendon, 1901. v–x. *HathiTrust*. Web. 22 July 2011.

Buck, Claire, ed. *The Bloomsbury Guide to Women's Literature*. London: Bloomsbury, 1992.

Buffon, Georges Louis Leclerc. *Œuvres choisies de Buffon: précédées d'une notice sur sa vie et ses ouvrages*. New ed. Tours: A. Mame, 1858.

Bullock, Shan F. *Robert Thorne: The Story of a London Clerk*. London: T. Warner Laurie, 1907.

Bunyan, Alix. 'The Children's Progress: Late Nineteenth-Century Children's Culture, the Stephen Juvenilia, and Virginia Woolf's Arguments with Her Past'. Diss. Oxford U, 2001.

Burnett, John, ed. *The Annals of Labour: Autobiographies of British Working-Class People, 1820–1920*. Bloomington: Indiana UP, 1974.

—, ed. *Destiny Obscure: Autobiographies of Childhood, Education, and Family from the 1820s to the 1920s*. London: Allen Lane, 1982.

—, ed. *Useful Toil: Autobiographies of Working People from the 1820s to the 1920s*. London: Routledge, 1974.

Burstyn, Joan N. 'Education and Sex: The Medical Case Against Higher Education for Women in England, 1870–1900'. *Proceedings of the American Philosophical Society* 117.2 (April 1973): 79–89.

—. *Victorian Education and the Ideal of Womanhood*. Totowa, NJ: Barnes & Noble, 1980.

Byerly, Alison. 'From Schoolroom to Stage: Reading Aloud and the Domestication of Victorian Theater'. *Culture and Education in Victorian England*. Ed. Patrick Scott and Pauline Fletcher. Lewisburg, PA: Bucknell UP, 1990. 125–41.

Byrne, Robert. *Writing Rackets*. New York: Lyle Stuart, 1969.

Calder, Jenni. *The Victorian Home*. London: B. T. Batsford, 1977.

Calisch, Edward N. *The Jew in English Literature, as Author and as Subject*. Richmond, VA: Bell Book and Stationery, 1909. *Google Books*. Web.

Callender, G. A. R. and Andrew Lambert. 'Laughton, Sir John Knox (1830–1915), naval educator and historian'. *ODNB*. Oxford UP, 4 October 2007. doi.org/10.1093/ref:odnb/34420. Web. 29 July 2011.

Cannadine, David, Jenny Keating and Nicola Sheldon. *The Right Kind of History: Teaching the Past in Twentieth-Century England*. New York: Palgrave Macmillan, 2011.

Carey, John. *The Intellectuals and the Masses: Pride and Prejudice among the Literary Intelligentsia, 1880–1939*. London: Faber and Faber, 1992.

Case, Janet, ed. and trans. *Prometheus Bound*. Aeschylus. London: J. M. Dent, 1905.

Caughie, Pamela L. *Virginia Woolf & Postmodernism: Literature in Quest & Question of Itself*. Urbana and Chicago: U of Illinois P, 1991.

Caygill, Marjorie. *The British Museum Reading Room*. London: Trustees of the British Museum, 2000.

'A Chair of Engligh [sic] Fiction'. *Times* [London, England] 29 May 1911: 11. Editorial. *The Times Digital Archive*. Web. 13 December 2018.

Chernaik, Judith. 'The Most English Library in All of England'. *New York Times Book Review* 30 June 1991: 24. *EBSCOhost Academic Search Complete*. Web. 6 July 2011.

Child, Harold. 'The Literary Week'. *The Academy: A Weekly Review of Literature, Science & Art* 11 March 1905: 225–6. Microfilm.

—. 'The Literary Week'. *The Academy* 26 August 1905: 867–9. Microfilm.

—. 'The Times Literary Supplement: A Record of its Beginnings'. *Times Literary Supplement* 18 January 1952: 33–9. Microfilm.
Childers, Mary. 'Virginia Woolf on the Outside Looking Down: Reflections on the Class of Women'. *Modern Fiction Studies* 38 (1992): 61–79.
—. *Welfare Brat: A Memoir*. New York and London, 2005.
Childs, Michael J. *Labour's Apprentices: Working-Class Lads in Late Victorian and Edwardian England*. Montreal: McGill-Queen's UP, 1992.
Chiles, E. E. 'Oral Composition a Basis for Written'. *English Journal* 3.6 (June 1914): 354–61.
Clark, Beverly Lyon. 'Cracking the Code of the School Story: Telling Tales about Telling Tales'. *Culture and Education in Victorian England*. Ed. Patrick Scott and Pauline Fletcher. Lewisburg, PA: Bucknell UP, 1990. 108–24.
—. *Regendering the School Story: Sassy Sissies and Tattling Tomboys*. New York: Routledge, 1996.
Clarke, Stuart N., ed. Introduction. Notes. Appendices. *The Essays of Virginia Woolf*. By Virginia Woolf. Vols 5–6. London: Hogarth Press, 2009–11. ix–xxi and xi–xxiii; *passim*; 601–68 and 403–674.
Clay, Catherine, Maria DiCenzo, Barbara Green and Fiona Hackney, eds. *Women's Periodicals and Print Culture in Britain, 1918–1939*. Edinburgh: Edinburgh UP, 2018.
A Clifton Boy. 'A Chat about Clifton College'. *Chums* no. 7 26 October 1892: 102–3.
Cohen, Rachel. *A Chance Meeting: Intertwined Lives of American Writers and Artists*. New York: Random House, 2004.
Collier, Patrick. '*John O'London's Weekly* and the Modern Author'. *Transatlantic Print Culture, 1880–1940: Emerging Media, Emerging Modernisms*. Ed. Ann Ardis and Patrick Collier. New York: Palgrave Macmillan, 2008. 98–113.
—. 'Journalism Meets Modernism'. *Gender in Modernism: New Geographies, Complex Intersections*. Ed. Bonnie Kime Scott. Urbana: U of Illinois P, 2007. 186–96.
—. *Modernism on Fleet Street*. Farnham: Ashgate, 2006.
—. 'Virginia Woolf and the Art of Journalism'. *Virginia Woolf and the Arts*. Ed. Maggie Humm. Edinburgh: Edinburgh UP, 2012. 314–31.
—. 'What Is Modern Periodical Studies?' *Journal of Modern Periodical Studies* 6.2 (2015): 92–111.
Collier, William. *History of the British Empire*. London: T. Nelson & Sons, 1884.
Collins, Philip. *Reading Aloud: A Victorian Métier*. Lincoln, NE: Tennyson Society, 1972.
Copeland, Ian. 'The Making of the Dull, Deficient, and Backward Pupil in British Elementary Education, 1870–1914'. *British Journal of Educational Studies* 44 (1996): 377–94.
Corbett, Mary Jean. *Behind the Times: Virginia Woolf in Late-Victorian Contexts*. Ithaca, NY, and London: Cornell UP, 2020.
A correspondent. 'Obituary for C. A. Buchheim'. *Times* [London, England] 11 June 1900: 9. *The Times Digital Archive*. Web. 13 December 2018.
Cotton, James Sutherland. 'Morris, Richard (1833–1894)'. *Dictionary of National Biography*, 1901 Supplement. Vol. 3. *Wikisource*. 24 October 2020. Web. 10 January 2021.
Courtney, W. L. 'W. L. Courtney, review, *Daily Telegraph* [10 November 1922, 4]'. *Virginia Woolf: The Critical Heritage*. Ed. Robin Majumdar and Allen McLaurin. London: Routledge & Kegan Paul, 1975. 103–5.
Coustillas, Pierre. 'Gissing, Algernon Fred (1860–1937), novelist'. *ODNB*. Oxford UP, 23 September 2004. doi.org/10.1093/ref:odnb/38643. Web. 9 June 2017.
—. '"A Voice that Spoke Straight and Shapely Words": Gissing in the Works and Papers of Virginia Woolf'. *Gissing Newsletter* 23.3 (July 1987): 1–30.

Crane, David Lisle, ed. Notes. Appendices. Commentary. *Letters Between a Victorian Schoolboy and His Family, 1892–1895*. Intro. Julie Crane. Durham, UK: Jean Wrangham, 1999.
Cross, Nigel. *The Common Writer: Life in Nineteenth-Century Grub Street*. Cambridge: Cambridge UP, 1985.
Crossick, Geoffrey. 'The Emergence of the Lower Middle Class in Britain: A Discussion'. *The Lower Middle Class in Britain 1870–1914*. Ed. Geoffrey Crossick. London: Croom Helm, 1977. 11–60.
Cuddy-Keane, Melba. 'Inside and Outside the Covers: Beginnings, Endings, and Woolf's Non-Coercive Ethical Texts'. *Woolfian Boundaries: Selected Papers from the Sixteenth Annual International Conference on Virginia Woolf*. Ed. Anna Burrells, Steve Ellis, Deborah Parsons and Kathryn Simpson. Clemson, SC: Clemson U Digital P, 2007. 172–80.
—. 'Pedagogical Woolf: Between the Academic Devil and the Mass-Culture Sea'. MLA Annual Convention, Toronto. 28 December 1997. Address.
—. 'Virginia Woolf and the Public Sphere.' *The Cambridge Companion to Virginia Woolf*. Ed. Susan Sellers. 2nd ed. Cambridge: Cambridge UP, 2010. 231–49.
—. *Virginia Woolf, the Intellectual, and the Public Sphere*. Cambridge: Cambridge UP, 2003.
—. 'Woolf, Virginia'. *Encyclopedia of the Essay*. Ed. Tracy Chevalier. Chicago: Fitzroy Dearborn, 1997. 905–8.
Cuddy-Keane, Melba, Adam Hammond and Alexandra Peat. *Modernism: Keywords*. Malden, MA: Wiley Blackwell, 2014.
Cunningham, Valentine. 'Darke Conceits: Churton Collins, Edmund Gosse, and the Professions of Criticism'. *Grub Street and the Ivory Tower: Literary Journalism and Literary Scholarship from Fielding to the Internet*. Ed. Jeremy Treglown and Bridget Bennett. Oxford: Clarendon, 1998. 72–90.
Curtis, Anthony. 'Gissing and the Lushingtons'. *A Garland for Gissing*. Ed. Bouwe Postmus. Costerus New Series 138. Amsterdam and New York: Rodopi, 2001. 153–62.
—. *Lit Ed: On Reviewing and Reviewers*. Manchester: Carcanet, 1998.
Curtis, S. J. *History of Education in Great Britain*. 1948. London: University Tutorial Press, 1967.
Curtis, Vanessa. 'Thoby Stephen (Asquith's House 1894–1899) and the Origin of the Bloomsbury Group'. *The Clifton [College] Magazine*. 2008: 21–4.
Dailey, Kazuko and Harold E. Dailey. 'The National Review, 1883–1900: Introduction'. *The Wellesley Index to Victorian Periodicals, 1824–1900*. Ed. Walter E. Houghton. Vol. 2. Toronto: U of Toronto P, 1972. 529–35.
Dalgarno, Emily. *Virginia Woolf and the Migrations of Language*. Cambridge: Cambridge UP, 2012.
—. *Virginia Woolf and the Visible World*. Cambridge: Cambridge UP, 2001.
Dalsimer, Katherine. *Virginia Woolf: Becoming a Writer*. New Haven, CT, and London: Yale UP, 2001.
Dalton, F. T. 'List of New Books and Reprints: Literary'. *Times Literary Supplement* 23 February 1906: 67. Microfilm.
Daugherty, Beth Rigel. 'Learning Virginia Woolf: Of Leslie, Libraries, and Letters'. *Virginia Woolf and Communities: Selected Papers from the Eighth Annual Conference on Virginia Woolf*. Ed. Jeanette McVicker and Laura Davis. New York: Pace UP, 1999. 10–17.
—. 'Morley College, Virginia Woolf and Us: How Should One Read Class?' *Virginia Woolf and Her Influences: Selected Papers from the Seventh Annual Conference on Virginia Woolf*. Ed. Laura Davis and Jeanette McVicker. New York: Pace UP, 1998. 125–39.

—. 'Readin', Writin', and Revisin': Virginia Woolf's "How Should One Read a Book?"' Rosenberg and Dubino 159–75.

—. 'The Streets of London: Virginia Woolf's Development of a Pedagogical Style'. *Woolf and the City: Selected Papers from the Nineteenth Annual Conference on Virginia Woolf*. Ed. Elizabeth Evans and Sarah Cornish. Clemson, SC: Clemson U Digital P, 2010. 190–4.

—. 'Taking a Leaf from Virginia Woolf's Book: Empowering the Student'. *Virginia Woolf Miscellanies: Proceedings of the First Annual Conference on Virginia Woolf*. Ed. Mark Hussey and Vara Neverow-Turk. New York: Pace UP, 1992. 31–40.

—. 'Virginia Stephen's Uneasy Heritage: Lessons, Readers, and Class'. *Virginia Woolf and Heritage: Selected Papers from the Twenty-Sixth Annual International Conference on Virginia Woolf*. Ed. Jane de Gay, Tom Breckin and Anne Reus. Clemson, SC: Clemson UP, 2017. 30–5.

—. 'Virginia Woolf Teaching/Virginia Woolf Learning: Morley College and the Common Reader'. *New Essays on Virginia Woolf*. Ed. Helen Wussow. Dallas: Contemporary Research Press, 1995. 61–77.

—, ed. 'Virginia Woolf's: How Should One Read a Book?"' *Woolf Studies Annual* 4 (1998): 123–85.

—, ed. '"You see you kind of belong to us, and what you do matters enormously": Letters from Readers to Virginia Woolf'. *Woolf Studies Annual* 12 (2006): 1–212.

—. '"Young writers might do worse": Anne Thackeray Ritchie, Virginia Stephen and Virginia Woolf'. *Virginia Woolf's Bloomsbury, Volume 1: Aesthetic Theory and Literary Practice*. Ed. Gina Potts and Lisa Shahriari. Basingstoke: Palgrave Macmillan, 2010. 20–36.

David, Deirdre. *Intellectual Women and Victorian Patriarchy: Harriet Martineau, Elizabeth Barrett Browning, George Eliot*. Ithaca, NY: Cornell UP, 1987.

Davidson, William and Joseph Crosby Alcock. *English Composition*. London: Allman & Son, 1884. *Google Books*. Web. 31 May 2015.

'Death of Sir J. K. Laughton, A Great Naval Historian'. *Times* [London, England] 15 September 1915: 9. Obituary. *The Times Digital Archive*. Web. 13 December 2018.

Deem, Rosemary. *Schooling for Women's Work*. London: Routledge & Kegan Paul, 1980.

de Gay, Jane. *Virginia Woolf and Christian Culture*. Edinburgh: Edinburgh UP, 2018.

Delamont, Sara. 'The Contradictions in Ladies' Education'. *The Nineteenth-Century Woman: Her Cultural and Physical World*. Ed. Sara Delamont and Lorna Duffin. London: Croom Helm, 1978. 134–63.

—. 'The Domestic Ideology and Women's Education'. *The Nineteenth Century Woman: Her Cultural and Physical World*. Ed. Sara Delamont and L. Duffin, 1978. 164–87.

Dell, Marion. 'The Elusive Julia Prinsep Stephen'. https://www.theelusivejuliastephen.wordpress.com.

—. *Virginia Woolf's Influential Forebears: Julia Margaret Cameron, Anny Thackeray Ritchie, and Julia Prinsep Stephen*. Basingstoke: Palgrave Macmillan, 2015.

—. 'Writing Back through Our Mothers: Julia Stephen's Influence on the Work of Virginia Woolf'. *Virginia Woolf Bulletin* 46 (May 2014): 18–27.

DeSalvo, Louise. '1897: Virginia Woolf at Fifteen'. *Virginia Woolf: A Feminist Slant*. Ed. Jane Marcus. Lincoln: U of Nebraska P, 1983. 78–108.

—. 'As "Miss Jan Says": Virginia Woolf's Early Journals'. *Virginia Woolf and Bloomsbury: A Centenary Celebration*. Ed. Jane Marcus. Bloomington: Indiana UP, 1987. 96–124.

—. *Virginia Woolf: The Impact of Childhood Sexual Abuse on Her Life and Work*. Boston: Beacon, 1989.

Detloff, Madelyn. '"Am I a Snob?" Well, Sort of: Socialism, Advocacy, and Disgust in Woolf's Economic Writing'. *Contradictory Woolf: Selected Papers from the Twenty-First Annual International Conference on Virginia Woolf*. Ed. Derek Ryan and Stella Bolaki. Clemson, SC: Clemson U Digital P, 2012. 181–5.

—. 'Iconic Shade ... and Other Professional Hazards of Woolf Scholarship'. *Women Making Modernism*. Ed. Erica Gene Delsandro. Gainesville: UP of Florida, 2020. 203–19.
Diamond, Michael. *'Lesser Breeds': Racial Attitudes in Popular British Culture, 1890–1940*. London: Anthem, 2007.
Digby, Anne and Peter Searby. *Children, School and Society in Nineteenth-Century England*. London: Macmillan, 1981.
Dixon, Diana. 'Children and the Press, 1866–1914'. *The Press in English Society from the Seventeenth to Nineteenth Centuries*. Ed. Michael Harris and Alan Lee. London and Toronto: Associated University Presses, 1986. 133–48.
—. 'Deprived and Oppressed: Victorian and Edwardian Magazines for Girls'. *Newspaper Library News* 25 (Winter 1998/9). The British Library. Web. 13 August 2007.
Doughty, Terri, ed. *Selections from* The Girl's Own Paper, *1880–1907*. Broadview Reprint edition. Peterborough, ON: Broadview, 2004.
Douglas, R. K. 'The Forgotten Graces: From a Man's Point of View'. *Atalanta* 3 (1889–90): 459–61.
Drabble, Margaret, ed. *The Oxford Companion to English Literature*. 6th ed. New York: Oxford UP, 2000.
Dubino, Jeanne. Introduction. *Virginia Woolf and the Literary Marketplace*. Ed. Jeanne Dubino. New York: Palgrave Macmillan, 2010. 1–23.
—. 'The Politics of Exclusion: The Literary Criticism of Virginia Woolf'. Diss. University of Massachusetts, 1992.
—. 'Virginia Woolf: From Book Reviewer to Literary Critic, 1904–1918'. Rosenberg and Dubino 25–40.
Dunn, Jane. *A Very Close Conspiracy: Vanessa Bell and Virginia Woolf*. Boston: Little, Brown, 1990.
Dusinberre, Juliet. *Virginia Woolf's Renaissance: Woman Reader or Common Reader?* Iowa City: U of Iowa P, 1997.
Dyhouse, Carol. *Girls Growing Up in Late Victorian and Edwardian England*. London: Routledge & Kegan Paul. 1981.
—. 'Good Wives and Little Mothers: Social Anxieties and the Schoolgirl's Curriculum, 1890–1920'. *Oxford Review of Education* 3.1 (1977): 21–35.
—. 'Miss Buss and Miss Beale: Gender and Authority in the History of Education'. *Lessons for Life: The Schooling of Girls and Women, 1850–1950*. Ed. Felicity Hunt. Oxford: Blackwell, 1987. 22–38.
—. *No Distinction of Sex? Women in British Universities, 1870–1939*. London: UCL Press, 1995.
—. 'Towards a "Feminine" Curriculum for English Schoolgirls: The Demands of Ideology 1870–1963'. *Women's Studies International Quarterly* 1 (1978): 297–311.
'Edward Augustus Freeman'. *Wikipedia, The Free Encyclopedia*. Wikipedia, The Free Encyclopedia. 4 July 2018. Web. 2 August 2018.
Eliot, T. S. 'Bruce Lyttelton Richmond'. *Times Literary Supplement* 3072 (13 January 1961): 17. Microfilm.
Ellegård, Alvar. 'The Readership of the Periodical Press in Mid-Victorian Britain'. *Victorian Periodicals Newsletter* 4.3 (September 1971): 3–22.
Engelman, Herta. 'The Ideal English Gentlewoman in the Nineteenth Century: Her Education, Conduct, and Sphere'. Diss. Northwestern U, 1956.
Epstein, Joseph. 'The Personal Essay: A Form of Discovery'. *The Norton Book of Personal Essays*. Ed. Joseph Epstein. New York and London: Norton, 1997. 11–24.
Eschbach, Elizabeth Seymour. *The Higher Education of Women in England and America, 1865–1920*. New York: Garland, 1993.
Esdaile, Arunell. *The British Museum Library: A Short History and Survey*. London: George Allen, 1946.

'European Gossip'. *The New York Times* 6 April 1887: 2. *ProQuest Historical Newspapers: The New York Times (1851–2008) with Index (1851–1993)*. Web. 2 August 2012.

Evans, Colin. *English People: The Experience of Teaching and Learning English in British Universities*. Buckingham: Open UP, 1993.

Ezell, Margaret. *Writing Women's Literary History*. Baltimore: Johns Hopkins UP, 1993.

Fader, Daniel and George Bornstein. *British Periodicals of the 18th and 19th Centuries*. Ann Arbor, MI: University Microfilms, 1972.

Faithfull, Lilian M. *In the House of My Pilgrimage*. London: Chatto & Windus, 1924.

Falke, Cassandra. *Literature by the Working Class: English Autobiographies, 1820–1848*. Amherst, NY: Cambria, 2013.

Fenwick, Gillian. *Leslie Stephen's Life in Letters: A Bibliographical Study*. Aldershot: Scolar, 1993.

Ferebee, Robert Steven. 'Bridging the Gulf: The Reader in and Out of Virginia Woolf's Literary Essays'. *College Language Association Journal* 30.3 (March 1987): 343–61.

—. 'Virginia Woolf as an Essayist'. Diss. University of New Mexico, 1981.

Fernald, Anne. 'The Memory Palace of Virginia Woolf'. *Virginia Woolf: Reading the Renaissance*. Ed. Sally Greene. Athens: Ohio UP, 1999. 89–114.

—. 'Pleasure and Belief in "Phases of Fiction"'. *Virginia Woolf and the Essay*. Ed. Beth Carole Rosenberg and Jeanne Dubino. New York: St. Martin's, 1997. 193–211.

—. '*A Room of One's Own*, Personal Criticism, and the Essay'. *Twentieth Century Literature* 40.2 (1994): 165–89.

—. *Virginia Woolf: Feminism and the Reader*. New York: Palgrave Macmillan, 2006.

Ferrell, Sara and Mary Wallace. 'The Cornhill Magazine, 1860–1900: Introduction'. *The Wellesley Index to Victorian Periodicals 1824–1900*. Ed. Walter E. Houghton. Vol. 1. Toronto: U of Toronto P, 1966. 321–4.

Fisher, Jane. 'The Seduction of the Father: Virginia Woolf and Leslie Stephen'. *Women's Studies* 18 (1990): 31–48.

Flanders, Judith. *Inside the Victorian Home: A Portrait of Domestic Life in Victorian England*. New York: Norton, 2004.

Flint, Kate. *The Woman Reader, 1837–1914*. Oxford: Clarendon Press, 1993.

Foreword. *'The Times' Fourth Leaders*. Edinburgh: Penguin, 1945. v.

Forrester, Wendy. *Great-Grandmama's Weekly: A Celebration of The Girl's Own Paper 1880–1901*. Guildford and London: Lutterworth, 1980.

Fowler, Rowena. 'Moment and Metamorphoses: Virginia Woolf's Greece'. *Comparative Literature* 51.3 (Summer 1999): 217–42.

—. '"On Not Knowing Greek": The Classics and the Woman of Letters'. *The Classical Journal* 78 (1983): 337–49.

Fox, Alice. *Virginia Woolf and the Literature of the English Renaissance*. Oxford: Clarendon, 1990.

Freeman, Edward Augustus. *The History of the Norman Conquest of England: Its Causes and Its Results*. 3rd ed. 6 vols. Oxford: Clarendon, 1877–79.

Friedman, Susan Stanford. *Mappings: Feminism and the Cultural Geographies of Encounter*. Princeton: Princeton UP, 1998.

Froula, Christine. *Virginia Woolf and the Bloomsbury Avant-Garde: War, Civilization, Modernity*. New York: Columbia UP, 2005.

Fryer, Peter. *Staying Power: The History of Black People in Britain*. 1984. Intro. Paul Gilroy. London: Pluto, 2010.

Fuller, Hester Thackeray and Violet Hammersley, comps. *Thackeray's Daughter: Some Recollections of Anne Thackeray Ritchie*. Dublin: Euphorion Books, 1951.

Funke, Sarah, ed. *Virginia & Leonard Woolf*. New York: Glenn Horowitz Bookseller, 2002.

— and William Beekman, eds. *This Perpetual Fight: Love and Loss in Virginia Woolf's Intimate Circle*. New York: The Grolier Club, 2008.

Garnett, Angelica. Prologue. *Sketches in Pen and Ink: A Bloomsbury Notebook.* By Vanessa Bell. Ed. Lia Giachero. London: Hogarth Press, 1997. 1–39.

Garnett, Henrietta. *Anny: A Life of Anne Isabella Thackeray Ritchie.* London: Chatto & Windus, 2004.

Geertz, Clifford. 'Thick Description: Toward an Interpretive Theory of Culture'. *The Interpretation of Cultures: Selected Essays.* New York: Basic Books, 1973. 3–30. E-book. https://hdl.handle.net/2027/heb.01005.

Gere, Anne Ruggles. *Writing Groups: History, Theory, and Implications.* Carbondale: Southern Illinois UP, 1987.

Gerzina, Gretchen Holbrook. 'Bushmen and Blackface: Bloomsbury and "Race"'. *South Carolina Review* 38.2 (Spring 2006): 46–64.

Gillespie, Diane F. 'The Elusive Julia Stephen'. Gillespie and Steele 1–27.

—. 'Essays for Adults'. Gillespie and Steele 195–213.

—. Introduction. *The Library of Leonard and Virginia Woolf: A Short-title Catalog.* Comp. Julia King and Laila Miletic-Vejzovic. Pullman: Washington State UP, 2003. vii–xx.

— and Elizabeth Steele, ed. *Julia Duckworth Stephen: Stories for Children, Essays for Adults.* Syracuse, NY: Syracuse UP, 1987.

Gindin, James. Rev. of *The Absent Father* by Perry Meisel and *Continuing Presences* by Beverly Ann Schlack. *Journal of English and Germanic Philology* 80.1 (1981): 151–6.

Glatter, Ron and E. G. Wedell, with W. J. A. Harris and S. Subramanian. *Study by Correspondence.* London: Longman, 1971.

Golden, Amanda. 'Textbook Greek: Thoby Stephen in *Jacob's Room*'. *Woolf Studies Annual* 23 (2017): 83–108.

—. 'Virginia Woolf's Marginalia Manuscript'. *Woolf Studies Annual* 18 (2012): 109–17.

Goldman, Jane. *The Feminist Aesthetics of Virginia Woolf: Modernism, Post-Impressionism, and the Politics of the Visual.* Cambridge: Cambridge UP, 1998.

Goldman, Mark. *The Reader's Art: Virginia Woolf as Literary Critic.* The Hague and Paris: Mouton, 1976.

Gordon, Lyndall. *Virginia Woolf: A Writer's Life.* Oxford: Oxford UP, 1984.

Gorham, Deborah. 'The Ideology of Femininity and Reading for Girls, 1850–1914'. *Lessons for Life: The Schooling of Girls and Women, 1850–1950.* Ed. Felicity Hunt. Oxford: Blackwell, 1987. 39–59.

Gosden, P. H. J. H., comp. *How They Were Taught: An Anthology of Contemporary Accounts of Learning and Teaching in England 1800–1950.* Oxford: Blackwell, 1969.

Gourvish, T. R. 'The Rise of the Professions'. *Later Victorian Britain, 1867–1900.* Ed. T. R. Gourvish and Alan O'Day. London: Macmillan, 1988. 13–35.

Grant, Duncan. 'Duncan Grant'. Noble 17–22.

Gray, E. W. Preface to the Second Edition. *Sources for Roman History, 133–70 B.C.* Comp. A. H. J. Greenidge and A. M. Clay. Oxford: Clarendon, 1960. v.

Gray, F. Elizabeth. Introduction. *Women in Journalism at the* Fin de Siècle: *Making a Name for Herself.* Ed. F. Elizabeth Gray. Palgrave Studies in Nineteenth-Century Writing and Culture. Basingstoke: Palgrave Macmillan, 2012. 1–20.

Green, Andy. *Education and State Formation: The Rise of Education Systems in England, France and the USA.* London: Macmillan, 1990.

Green, John Richard. *History of the English People.* 4 vols. New York: Harper & Brothers, 1900.

—. *A Short History of the English People.* London: Macmillan, 1877. *HathiTrust.* Web.

Green, Laura Morgan. *Educating Women: Cultural Conflict and Victorian Literature.* Athens: Ohio UP, 2001.

Greenburg, Arielle. 'A (Slightly Qualified) Defense of MFA Programs: Six Benefits of Graduate School'. Academy of American Poets. https://poets.org. Web. 2 August 2018.

Griffiths, Devin. 'The Radical's Catalogue: Antonio Panizzi, Virginia Woolf, and the British Museum Library's *Catalogue of Printed Books*'. *Book History*. Vol. 18. Ed. Greg Barnhisel, Beth le Roux and Jonathan Rose. Baltimore: Johns Hopkins UP, 2015. 134–65.

Grindea, Miron, ed. *The London Library*. London: Boydell/Adam, 1978.

Gualtieri, Elena. *Virginia Woolf's Essays: Sketching the Past*. Basingstoke: Macmillan, 2000.

Hagen, Benjamin. 'Feeling Shadows: Virginia Woolf's Sensuous Pedagogy'. *PMLA* 132.2 (March 2017): 266–80, 495.

Hager, Kelly. Description of *The Daisy Chain. amazon.com*. Web. 7 December 2018.

Hall, Donald. 'Poetry and Ambition'. *Poetry and Ambition: Essays, 1982–1988*. Ann Arbor: U of Michigan P, 1988. 1–19.

Hall, Edith and Fiona Macintosh. *Greek Tragedy and the British Theatre, 1660–1914*. Oxford: Oxford UP, 2005.

Hall, Theophilus Dwight. *A Manual of English Composition, With Copious Illustrations and Practical Exercises*. London: John Murray, 1880. HathiTrust. Web.

Hallsworth, Joseph and Rhys J. Davies. *The Working Life of Shop Assistants: A Study of Conditions of Labour in the Distributive Trades*. 1910. London: Forgotten Books, 2015.

Hamilton, Cicely. *Diana of Dobson's*. Broadview Literary Texts. Ed. Diane F. Gillespie and Doryjane Birrer. Peterborough, ON: Broadview Press, 2003.

Hammill, Faye and Mark Hussey. *Modernism's Print Cultures*. London: Bloomsbury Academic, 2016.

Hammond, Mary. '"The Great Fiction Bore": Free Libraries and the Construction of a Reading Public in England, 1880–1914'. *Libraries & Culture: A Journal of Library History* 37.2 (Spring 2002): 83–108.

Hardyment, Christina. *Perfect Parents: Baby-Care Advice Past and Present*. Oxford: Oxford UP, 1995.

'Harley Granville Barker and Waste at the Almeida Theatre London'. *Almeida Theatre*. Web. 21 February 2011.

Harris, Janice H. 'Not Suffering and Not Still: Women Writers at the *Cornhill Magazine*, 1860–1900'. *Modern Language Quarterly* 47 (1986): 382–92.

Harris, P. R. *A History of the British Museum Library 1753–1973*. London: The British Library, 1998.

—. *The Reading Room*. London: British Library, 1979.

Harrison, Brian. *Separate Spheres: The Opposition to Women's Suffrage in Britain*. New York: Holmes & Meier, 1978.

Harrison, Frederic, ed. *Carlyle and the London Library: Account of Its Foundation: Together with Unpublished Letters of Thomas Carlyle to W. D. Christie, C. B. Arranged by Mary Christie*. London: Chapman & Hall, 1907.

Harrison, J. F. C. *The English Common People: A Social History from the Norman Conquest to the Present*. London: Croom Helm, 1984.

Harvey, Benjamin. 'The Twentieth Part: Word and Image in Woolf's Reading Room'. *Woolf and the Art of Exploration: Selected Papers from the Fifteenth International Conference on Virginia Woolf*. Ed. Helen Southworth and Elisa Kay Sparks. Clemson, SC: Clemson U Digital P, 2006. 103–11.

Havighurst, Alfred F. *Radical Journalist: H. W. Massingham*. Cambridge: Cambridge UP, 1974.

Hearnshaw, F. J. C. *The Centenary History of King's College London*. London: Harrap, 1929.

Heisch, C. E. *The Art and Craft of the Author: Practical Hints upon Literary Work*. New York: Grafton, 1906.

Heller, Michael. *London Clerical Workers, 1880–1914: Development of the Labour Market*. London: Pickering & Chatto, 2011.

Herd, Harold. *The March of Journalism: The Story of the British Press from 1622 to the Present Day*. London: George Allen & Unwin, 1952.
Herman, William. 'Virginia Woolf and the Classics: Every Englishman's Prerogative Transmuted into Fictional Art'. *Virginia Woolf: Centennial Essays*. Ed. Elaine K. Ginsberg and Laura Moss Gottlieb. Troy, NY: Whitston Publishing Co., 1983. 257–68.
Heyck, Thomas William. 'Educational'. *A Companion to Victorian Literature and Culture*. Ed. Herbert F. Tucker. Oxford: Blackwell, 1999. 194–211.
Hill, Katherine C. 'Virginia Woolf and Leslie Stephen: History and Literary Revolution'. *PMLA* 96.3 (May 1981): 351–62.
—. 'Virginia Woolf: A Review Essay'. Rev. of *The Absent Father: Virginia Woolf and Walter Pater* by Perry Meisel, *Virginia Woolf's Major Novels: The Fables of Anon* by Maria DiBattista, and *The Letters of Virginia Woolf, Volume Six* ed. by Nigel Nicolson and Joanne Trautmann. *English Literature in Transition: 1880–1920* 25.2 (1982): 117–22.
Hilliard, Christopher. *To Exercise Our Talents: The Democratization of Writing in Britain*. Cambridge, MA: Harvard UP, 2006.
Hill-Miller, Katherine C. '"The Skies and Trees of the Past": Anne Thackeray Ritchie and William Makepeace Thackeray'. *Daughters and Fathers*. Ed. Lynda E. Boose and Betty S. Flowers. Baltimore: Johns Hopkins UP, 1989. 361–83.
Hirst, F. W. 'Literary Causerie'. *The Speaker* 5 January 1907: 405–6. Microfilm.
Hoberman, Ruth. *Museum Trouble: Edwardian Fiction and the Emergence of Modernism*. Charlottesville: U of Virginia P, 2011.
—. '"A Thought in the Huge Bald Forehead": Depictions of Women in the British Museum Reading Room, 1857–1929'. *Reading Women: Literary Figures and Cultural Icons from the Victorian Age to the Present*. Ed. Janet Badia and Jennifer Phegley. Toronto: U of Toronto P, 2005. 168–91.
—. 'Women in the British Museum Reading Room during the Late-Nineteenth and Early-Twentieth Centuries: From Quasi- to Counterpublic'. *Feminist Studies* 28 (2002): 489–512.
Hodder, Edwin. *The Life of Samuel Morley*. 5th ed. London: Hodder and Stoughton, 1889.
Hodgson, John Tweedale. 'Changes in English Teaching: Institutionalisation, Transmission and Ideology'. Diss. Institute of Education, University of London, 1974.
Hoffman, P. C. *They Also Serve: The Story of the Shop Worker*. London: Porcupine, 1949.
Holcombe, Lee. 'Women in the Classroom: The Teaching Profession'. *Victorian Ladies at Work: Middle-Class Working Women in England and Wales, 1850–1914*. Hamden, CT: Archon, 1973. 34–67.
Holleyman, M. G. *Catalogue of Books from the Library of Leonard and Virginia Woolf*. Brighton: Holleyman & Treacher, 1975.
Holtby, Winifred. *Virginia Woolf: A Critical Memoir*. 1932. Chicago: Academy, 1978.
Honey, J. R. de S. *Tom Brown's Universe: The Development of the English Public School in the Nineteenth Century*. New York: Quadrangle, 1977.
—. 'Tom Brown's Universe: The Nature and Limits of the Victorian Public Schools Community'. *The Victorian Public School: Studies in the Development of an Educational Institution*. Ed. Brian Simon and Ian Bradley. Dublin: Gill and Macmillan, 1975. 19–33.
Hopkins, Eric. *A Social History of the English Working Classes, 1815–1945*. London: Edward Arnold, 1979.
Horn, Pamela. 'The Education and Employment of Working-Class Girls, 1870–1914'. *History of Education* 17 (1988): 71–82.
Horner, Winifred Bryan. 'Writing Instruction in Great Britain: Eighteenth and Nineteenth Centuries'. *A Short History of Writing Instruction from Ancient Greece to Twentieth-Century America*. Ed. James J. Murphy. Davis, CA: Hermagoras, 1990. 121–49.

Hosgood, Christopher P. '"Mercantile Monasteries": Shops, Shop Assistants, and Shop Life in Late-Victorian and Edwardian Britain'. *Journal of British Studies* 38.3 (July 1999): 332–52. *JSTOR*. https://www.jstor.org/stable/176059. Web. 21 October 2016.

Hotho-Jackson, Sabine. 'Virginia Woolf on History: Between Tradition and Modernity'. *Forum for Modern Language Studies* 27.4 (October 1991): 293–313.

Howard, Anthony. 'Strict but Fair'. Rev. of *Headmaster: The Life of John Percival, Radical Autocrat*. By Jeremy Potter. *The Sunday Times*. 4 January 1998. *Factiva*. Web. 24 May 2011.

Howard, Ursula. *Literacy and the Practice of Writing in the 19th Century: A Strange Blossoming of Spirit*. Leicester: National Institute of Adult Continuing Education, 2012.

How to Write an Essay. (By the author of *How to Write a Novel*). London: Grant Richards, 1901.

Howe, Florence. 'Introduction: T. S. Eliot, Virginia Woolf, and the Future of "Tradition"'. *Tradition and the Talents of Women*. Ed. Florence Howe. Urbana and Chicago: U of Illinois P, 1991. 1–33.

Hughes, Thomas. *Tom Brown's School Days. By an Old Boy*. The World's Classics. Ed. Andrew Sanders. Oxford: Oxford UP, 1989.

Hunt, Felicity. 'Divided Aims: The Educational Implications of Opposing Ideologies in Girls' Secondary Schooling, 1850–1940'. *Lessons for Life: The Schooling of Girls and Women, 1850–1950*. Ed. Felicity Hunt. Oxford: Blackwell, 1987. 3–21.

Hunt, William. 'Freeman, Edward Augustus'. *Encyclopædia Britannica*. Ed. Hugh Chisholm. 11th ed. Cambridge: Cambridge UP, 1911. 76–7.

Hurst, Isobel. '"A fleet of . . . inexperienced Argonauts": Oxford Women and the Classics, 1873–1920'. *Oxford Classics: Teaching and Learning 1800–2000*. Ed. Christopher Stray. London: Duckworth, 2007. 14–27.

Hurt, J. S. *Elementary Schooling and the Working Classes 1860–1918*. London: Routledge & Kegan Paul, 1979.

Hussey, Mark. 'Mrs. Thatcher and Mrs. Woolf'. *Modern Fiction Studies* 50.1 (2004): 8–30.

—. *Virginia Woolf A to Z: A Comprehensive Reference for Students, Teachers and Common Readers to Her Life, Work and Critical Reception*. New York: Oxford UP, 1995.

Hutcheson, John A., Jr. *Leopold Maxse and the National Review, 1893–1914*. New York: Garland, 1989.

Huxley, Leonard. *The House of Smith Elder*. London: William Clowes & Sons, for private circulation. 1923. *Internet Archive*. Web.

— and Barbara Quinn Schmidt. 'Smith, Reginald John (1857–1916), barrister and publisher'. *ODNB*. Oxford UP, 23 September 2004. doi.org/10.1093/ref:odnb/36154. Web. 27 September 2007.

Inwood, Stephen. *A History of London*. New York: Carroll & Graf, 1998.

Isaac, Alan. *Virginia Woolf, the Uncommon Bookbinder*. London: Cecil Woolf, 2000.

Jackson, H. J. *Marginalia: Readers Writing in Books*. New Haven, CT: Yale UP, 2001.

Jackson, Kate. 'George Newnes and the "loyal Tit-Bitites": Editorial Identity and Textual Interaction in *Tit-Bits*'. *Nineteenth-Century Media and the Construction of Identities*. Ed. Laurel Brake, Bill Bell and David Finkelstein. Basingstoke: Palgrave, 2000. 11–26.

—. *George Newnes and the New Journalism in Britain, 1880–1910: Culture and Profit*. Farnham: Ashgate, 2001.

—. 'The *Tit-Bits* Phenomenon: George Newnes, New Journalism and the Periodical Texts'. *Victorian Periodicals Review* 30.3 (1997): 201–26.

James, Louis. 'The Trouble with Betsy: Periodicals and the Common Reader in Mid-Nineteenth-Century England'. *The Victorian Periodical Press: Samplings and Soundings*. Ed. Joanne Shattock and Michael Wolff. Toronto: U of Toronto P, 1982. 349–66.

James, Walter. Introduction. *Selections from Her Essays*. By Virginia Woolf. London: Chatto and Windus, 1966. 7–20.
Jann, Rosemary. *The Art and Science of Victorian History*. Columbus: Ohio State UP, 1985.
—. 'Breeding, Education, and Vulgarity: George Gissing and the Lower-Middle Classes'. *Victorian Vulgarity: Taste in Verbal and Visual Culture*. Ed. Susan David Bernstein and Elsie B. Michie. Farnham: Ashgate, 2009. 85–100.
Jenkins, Gwyn. 'Pater's Pins Stuck: Virginia Woolf and Clara Pater at King's College Ladies' Department'. *Woolf Studies Annual* 27 (2021): 23–45.
Johnson, Audrey. D. '"This may be true or it may be false—who can say?": Resistance to the Professionalization of History in *A Room of One's Own*'. Profession & Performance: Thirtieth Annual International Conference on Virginia Woolf. Virtual. 13 June 2021. Address. TS.
Johnson, George Malcolm. 'Ridge, William Pett (1859–1930), novelist and short story writer'. *ODNB*. Oxford UP, 23 September 2004. doi.org/10.1093/ref:odnb/56888. Web. 9 June 2017.
Johnston, Georgia. 'The Whole Achievement in Virginia Woolf's *The Common Reader*'. *Essays on the Essay: Redefining the Genre*. Ed. Alexander J. Burtrym. Athens: U of Georgia P, 1989. 148–58.
Jones, Christine Kenyon and Anna Snaith. '"Tilting at Universities": Woolf at King's College London'. *Woolf Studies Annual* 16 (2010): 1–44.
Jones, Clara. *Virginia Woolf: Ambivalent Activist*. Edinburgh: Edinburgh UP, 2016.
Jones, Danell. *The Virginia Woolf Writers' Workshop: Seven Lessons to Inspire Great Writing*. New York: Bantam, 2007.
Joseph, Gerhard. 'The Antigone as Cultural Touchstone: Matthew Arnold, Hegel, George Eliot, Virginia Woolf, and Margaret Drabble'. *PMLA* 96.1 (January 1981): 22–35.
Kamm, Josephine. *Hope Deferred: Girls' Education in English History*. London: Methuen, 1965.
Kaufmann, Michael. 'A Modernism of One's Own: Virginia Woolf's *TLS* Reviews and Eliotic Modernism'. Rosenberg and Dubino 137–55.
Keating, Jenny. 'Government Policy Towards English Elementary Schools and History Teaching 1900–1910'. *History in Education Project*. 2009. 1–16. https://www.history.ac.uk/history-in-education/project-papers/school-history.html. Web.
Keating, Peter. *The Haunted Study: A Social History of the English Novel 1875–1914*. London: Secker & Warburg, 1989.
Keigwin, R. P. 'Some Recollections of Sport at Clifton'. *Centenary Essays on Clifton College*. Ed. N. G. L. Hammond. Bristol: Arrowsmith, 1962. 129–53.
Kelly, Serena. 'Lyttelton [née Clive], Mary Kathleen (1856–1907), women's activist'. *ODNB*. Oxford UP, 23 September 2004. doi.org/10.1093/ref:odnb/50712. Web. 22 September 2007.
Kelly, Thomas. *A History of Adult Education in Great Britain from the Middle Ages to the Twentieth Century*. Liverpool: Liverpool UP, 1962.
—. *A History of Public Libraries in Great Britain, 1845–1965*. London: Library Association, 1973.
Kent, Christopher. 'The Academy'. *British Literary Magazines: The Victorian and Edwardian Age, 1837–1913*. Ed. Alvin Sullivan. Vol. 3. Westport, CT: Greenwood, 1984. 1–7.
—. Introduction. *British Literary Magazines: The Victorian and Edwardian Age, 1837–1913*. Ed. Alvin Sullivan. Vol. 3. Westport, CT: Greenwood P, 1984. xii–xxvi.
King, Julia and Laila Miletic-Vejzovic, comps. *The Library of Leonard and Virginia Woolf: A Short-title Catalog*. Pullman: Washington State UP, 2003.
Kirkland, Elizabeth. 'Mothering Citizens: Elite Women in Montreal, 1890–1914'. Diss. McGill U., 2011.

Kirkpatrick, B[rownlee]. J. and Stuart N. Clarke. *A Bibliography of Virginia Woolf*. 4th ed. Oxford: Clarendon, 1997.

Klein, Viola. 'The Emancipation of Women: Its Motives and Achievements'. *Ideas and Beliefs of the Victorians: An Historic Revaluation of the Victorian Age*. Ed. Harman Grisewood. London: Sylvan, 1949. 261–7.

Knighton, C. S., ed. *Clifton College: Foundation to Evacuation*. Vol. 65. Bristol: Bristol Record Society, 2012.

—. 'Thoby Stephen at Clifton College: A Closer View'. *Virginia Woolf Bulletin* 51 (January 2016): 24–9.

Kolocotroni, Vassiliki. '"This Curious Silent Unrepresented Life": Greek Lessons in Virginia Woolf's Early Fiction'. *The Modern Language Review* 100.2 (2005): 313–22.

Kopley, Emily. *Virginia Woolf and Poetry*. Oxford: Oxford UP: 2021.

Koulouris, Theodore. *Hellenism and Loss in the Work of Virginia Woolf*. Burlington, VT: Ashgate, 2011.

—. 'Virginia Woolf's "Greek Notebook" (VS Greek and Latin Studies): An Annotated Transcription'. *Woolf Studies Annual* 25 (2019): 1–72.

Kranzler, Laura. 'The Moth and the Moth-Hunter: The Literary Criticism of Virginia Woolf'. *The British Critical Tradition: A Re-evaluation*. Ed. Gary Day. New York: St. Martin's, 1993. 92–107.

Lamb, Walter [W. R. M. L.]. 'J. T. Stephen'. *The Cambridge Review* 28 (1906–07): 118. Google Books. Web. 10 August 2014.

Langenheim, Ralph L., Jr. 'Frank Swinnerton'. *Cyclopedia of World Authors*. Ed. Frank N. Magill. 4th rev. ed. Pasadena, CA: Salem, 2004. EBSCOhost Literary Reference Center Plus. Web. 9 July 2007.

Larson, Victoria Tietze. 'Classics and the Acquisition and Validation of Power in Britain's "Imperial Century" (1815–1914)'. *International Journal of the Classical Tradition* 6.2 (Fall 1999): 185–225.

Latham, Monica. '"Virginia Woolf Practising": *Hyde Park Gate News* and the Beginning of Woolf's Career as a Writer, Critic and Reader'. *Woolf as Reader/Woolf as Critic, Or, The Art of Reading in the Present*. Ed. Catherine Bernard. Montpellier: Presses Universitaires de la Méditerranée. 2011. 139–54.

Latham, Sean. *Am I a Snob? Modernism and the Novel*. Ithaca, NY: Cornell UP, 2003.

—. 'The Mess and Muddle of Modernism: The Modernist Journals Project and Modern Periodical Studies'. *Tulsa Studies in Women's Literature* 30.2 (Fall 2011): 407–28.

Latham, Sean and Robert Scholes. 'The Rise of Periodical Studies'. *PMLA* 121.2 (2006): 517–31.

Laurence, Patricia. '"Holding Her Pen Like a Broom": Virginia Woolf's Anxieties about Working-Class Women'. *Etudes Britanniques Contemporaines: Revue de la Société d'Etudes Anglaises Contemporaines (EBC)* Fall 1999: 5–18.

Leary, Patrick and Andrew Nash. 'Authorship'. *The Cambridge History of the Book in Britain, vol. 6: 1830–1914*. Ed. David McKitterick. Cambridge: Cambridge UP, 2009. 172–213.

Leaska, Mitchell. *Granite and Rainbow: The Hidden Life of Virginia Woolf*. New York: Farrar, Straus and Giroux, 1998.

—. ed. Introduction and Notes. *A Passionate Apprentice: The Early Journals, 1897–1909*. By Virginia Woolf. San Diego: HBJ, 1990. xv–xlv and *passim*.

Leavis, Q. D. 'Caterpillars of the Commonwealth Unite!' Rpt. in *Virginia Woolf: Critical Assessments*. Vol. 2. Ed. Eleanor McNees. Mountfield, UK: Helm Information, 1994. 272–81.

Lee, Hermione. '"Crimes of Criticism": Virginia Woolf and Literary Journalism'. *Grub Street and the Ivory Tower: Literary Journalism and Literary Scholarship from Fielding to the Internet*. Ed. Jeremy Treglown and Bridget Bennett. Oxford: Clarendon, 1998. 112–34.

—. Foreword. *Hyde Park Gate News: The Stephen Family Newspaper*. By Virginia Woolf, Vanessa Bell, with Thoby Stephen. Ed. Gill Lowe. London: Hesperus, 2005. vii–x.
—. 'How to End It All'. *Virginia Woolf's Nose: Essays on Biography*. Princeton, NJ: Princeton UP, 2005. 95–122.
—. *Virginia Woolf*. New York: Knopf, 1997.
—. 'Virginia Woolf and Offence'. *The Art of Literary Biography*. Ed. John Batchelor. Oxford: Clarendon, 1995. 129–50.
—. 'Virginia Woolf's Essays'. *The Cambridge Companion to Virginia Woolf*. Ed. Sue Roe and Susan Sellers. Cambridge: Cambridge UP, 2000. 91–108.
Lehmann, John. *Virginia Woolf*. New York: Thames and Hudson, 1975.
Lehmann, R. C. *In Cambridge Courts: Studies of University Life in Prose and Verse*. London: Henry and Co., 1891.
Leinster-Mackay, Donald. 'Old School Ties: Some Nineteenth Century and Early Twentieth Century Links Between Public and Preparatory Schools'. *British Journal of Educational Studies* 32.1 (February 1984): 78–83. *JSTOR*. Web. 19 May 2011.
Leonard, Arthur N. 'German Literature'. Rev. of Goethe's *Hermann und Dorothea*, ed. C. A. Buchheim. *Modern Language Notes* 19.2 (February 1904): 58–61. *JSTOR*. Web. 22 July 2011.
Levenback, Karen L. *Virginia Woolf and the Great War*. Syracuse, NY: Syracuse UP, 1999.
Levine, Philippa. *The Amateur and the Professional: Antiquarians, Historians and Archaeologists in Victorian England, 1838–1886*. Cambridge: Cambridge UP, 1986.
—. *Feminist Lives in Victorian England: Private Roles and Public Commitment*. Oxford: Basil Blackwell, 1990.
—. '"The Humanising Influence of Five o'Clock Tea": Victorian Feminist Periodicals'. *Victorian Studies* 33.2 (1990): 293–306.
Levy, Amy. 'James Thomson: A Minor Poet'. Rpt. in *The Complete Novels and Selected Writings of Amy Levy, 1861–1889*. Ed. Melvyn New. Gainesville: U of Florida P, 1993. 501–9, 559–60.
—. 'Readers at the British Museum'. *The Romance of a Shop*. Ed. Susan David Bernstein. Peterborough, ON: Broadview, 2006. 220–7.
Lewes, George Henry. *The Principles of Success in Literature*. 2nd ed. Ed. Fred N. Scott. Boston: Allyn and Bacon, 1892.
Lewis, Jane. *Women and Social Action in Victorian and Edwardian England*. Aldershot: Edward Elgar, 1991.
Light, Alison. *Mrs. Woolf and the Servants: An Intimate History of Domestic Life in Bloomsbury*. New York: Bloomsbury, 2008.
Lindsay, Geoff. 'Be Substantially Great in Thy Self: Getting to Know C. E. W. Bean; Barrister, Judge's Associate, Moral Philosopher'. *The Francis Forbes Society for Australian Legal History (forbessociety.org)*. 2011: 1–133, Appendices I–XI. Web. PDF file.
Linett, Maren. 'From Supernova to Manuscript Page: Circling Woolf'. *Modern Fiction Studies* 50.2 (Spring 2004): 224–40.
London Library. 'Join Online'. https://www.londonlibrary.co.uk/join/join-online. 2021. Web. 27 September 2021.
'The London Library, The annual meeting'. *Times* [London, England] 31 May 1890: 9. *The Times Digital Archive*. Web. 19 August 2018.
Lopate, Phillip, ed. *The Art of the Personal Essay: An Anthology from the Classical Era to the Present*. New York: Doubleday, 1994.
Lounsberry, Barbara. *Becoming Virginia Woolf: Her Early Diaries & the Diaries She Read*. Gainesville: UP of Florida, 2014.
Love, Jean O. *Virginia Woolf: Sources of Madness and Art*. Berkeley: U of California P, 1977.

Low, Frances H. *Press Work for Women: A Text Book for the Young Woman Journalist. What to Write, How to Write It, and Where to Send It*. London: L. Upcott Gill, 1904.

Lowe, Gill. Biographical Notes. *HPGN*. 221–39.

—. 'A Brief History of *The Hyde Park Gate News*, the Family Newspaper of the Stephen Children'. *Virginia Woolf Miscellany* 68 (Fall 2005): 15–17.

—. 'Hyde Park Gate News'. *Woolf and the Art of Exploration: Selected Papers from the Fifteenth International Conference on Virginia Woolf*. Ed. Helen Southworth and Elisa Kay Sparks. Clemson, SC: Clemson U Digital P, 2006. 38–43.

—, ed. *Hyde Park Gate News: The Stephen Family Newspaper*. By Virginia Woolf, Vanessa Bell, with Thoby Stephen. London: Hesperus, 2005.

—. '"I am fast locked up", Janus and Miss Jan: Virginia Woolf's 1897 Journal as Threshold Text'. *Virginia Woolf: Twenty-First Century Approaches*. Ed. Jeanne Dubino, Gill Lowe, Vara Neverow and Kathryn Simpson. Edinburgh: U of Edinburgh P, 2015. 17–33.

—. Introduction. *HPGN*. xi–xvii.

—. Note on the Text. *HPGN*. xix–xxi.

—. Notes. *HPGN*. 203–4.

—. Notes on the Manuscript. *HPGN*. 202.

Luedeking, Leila. 'Contents of the Woolf Library'. *Virginia Woolf Miscellany* 22 (Spring 1984): 2.

Lusty, Robert. 'Swinnerton, Frank Arthur (1884–1982), writer and publisher's reader'. *ODNB*. Oxford UP, 23 September 2004. doi:10.1093/ref:odnb/31741. Web. 4 October 2007.

McAleer, Joseph. *Popular Reading and Publishing in Britain, 1914-1950*. Oxford: Clarendon, 1992.

Macaulay, Rose. 'Rose Macaulay'. Noble 164–6.

MacCarthy, Desmond. 'Apprenticeship'. *Humanities*. Pref. Lord David Cecil. London: MacGibbon & Kee, 1953. 15–22.

MacCarthy, Mary. *A Nineteenth-Century Childhood*. 1924. London: Hamish Hamilton, 1948.

McClellan, Ann K. 'Adeline's (Bankrupt) Education Fund: Woolf, Women, and Education in the Short Fiction'. *Journal of the Short Story in English* 50 (2008): 85–101.

McCoy, Garnett. *Reading Records: A Researcher's Guide to the Archives of American Art*. Washington, DC: Archives of American Art, Smithsonian Institution, 1997.

McDermid, Jane. 'Women and Education'. *Women's History: Britain, 1850–1945*. Ed. June Purvis. New York: St. Martin's, 1995. 107–30.

McDonald, Peter D. *British Literary Culture and Publishing Practice, 1880–1914*. Cambridge: Cambridge UP, 1997.

Macdonell, John. 'Austin, Sarah'. *Dictionary of National Biography*. Ed. Leslie Stephen. Vol. 2. London: Smith & Elder, 1885–1901. 270–1.

McGee, Patrick. 'Woolf's Other: The University in Her Eye'. *Novel* 23.3 (Spring 1990): 229–46.

MacGibbon, Jean. *There's the Lighthouse: A Biography of Adrian Stephen*. London: James and James, 1997.

Machann, Clinton. 'Sir Walter Besant, 1836–1901'. *British Short-Fiction Writers, 1880–1914: The Realist Tradition*. Ed. William B. Thesing. *DLB* 135. Detroit: Gale, 1994. 38–46.

McHugh, Heather. 'On Creative Writing Programs'. *The American Scholar* 76.2 (2007): 6.

McIntyre, Tony. *Library Book: An Architectural Journey Through the London Library, 1841–2006*. London: The London Library, 2006.

MacKay, Carol Hanbery. 'Biography as Reflected Autobiography: The Self-Creation of Anne Thackeray Ritchie'. *Revealing Lives: Autobiography, Biography, and Gender*. Ed. Susan Groag Bell and Marilyn Yalom. Albany: State U of New York P, 1990. 65–79.

—. Introduction. 'Anne Thackeray Ritchie's Centenary Biographical Introductions to The Works of William Makepeace Thackeray'. *The Two Thackerays: Anne Thackeray Ritchie's Centenary Biographical Introductions to the Works of William Makepeace Thackeray*. Ed. Carol Hanbery MacKay, Peter L. Shillingsburg and Julie Maxey. Vol. 1. New York: AMS, 1988. xi–lxxxvii.

—. 'The Thackeray Connection: Virginia Woolf's Aunt Anny'. *Virginia Woolf and Bloomsbury*. Ed. Jane Marcus. Bloomington: Indiana UP, 1987. 68–95.

McMahon, Michael. 'Beastly Boys'. Rev. of *Letters Between a Victorian Schoolboy and His Family, 1892–95*. New Statesman 5 July 1999. NewStatesman.com. Web. 1 June 2011.

McManus, Patricia. 'The "Offensiveness" of Virginia Woolf: From a Moral to a Political Reading'. *Woolf Studies Annual* 14 (2008): 91–138.

McNeillie, Andrew. Introduction and Notes. *The Essays of Virginia Woolf: Vol. 1, 1904–1912*. Ed. Andrew McNeillie. San Diego: Harcourt, 1986. ix–xviii and *passim*.

Madden, Mary. 'Woolf's Interrogation of Class in *Night and Day*'. *Woolf in the Real World: Selected Papers from the Thirteenth International Conference on Virginia Woolf*. Ed. Karen V. Kukil. Clemson, SC: Clemson U Digital P, 2005. 56–63.

Maddison, Isabel, comp. *Handbook of Courses Open to Women in British, Continental and Canadian Universities*. New York: Macmillan, 1896.

Maitland, Frederic William. *The Life and Letters of Leslie Stephen*. 1906. Detroit: Gale, 1968.

Malet, Lucas. 'The Feminine Note in Fiction'. *Bookman* 27 December 1904: 116–18.

Maloney, Stella and Gerald S. Argetsinger. 'Harley Granville-Barker'. *Critical Survey of Drama, Second Revised Edition* (2003): 1–5. EBSCOhost Literary Reference Center Plus. Web. 21 February 2011.

Malpezzi, Frances M. 'Long [née Campbell] Margaret Gabrielle Vere [pseuds. Marjorie Bowen, Joseph Shearing, George Preedy (1885–1952), writer'. *ODNB*. Oxford UP, 23 September 2004. doi.org/10.1093/ref:odnb/40902. Web. 9 June 2017.

Marcus, Jane. *Hearts of Darkness: White Women Write Race*. New Brunswick, NJ: Rutgers UP, 2004.

—. 'The Niece of a Nun: Virginia Woolf, Caroline Stephen, and the Cloistered Imagination'. *Virginia Woolf: A Feminist Slant*. Ed. Jane Marcus. Lincoln: U of Nebraska P, 1983. 7–36.

—. 'Virginia Woolf and Her Violin: Mothering, Madness and Music'. *Virginia Woolf: Centennial Essays*. Ed. Elaine K. Ginsberg and Laura Moss Gottlieb. Troy, NY: Whitston, 1983. 27–49.

Marks, Pauline. 'Femininity in the Classroom: An Account of Changing Attitudes'. *The Rights and Wrongs of Women*. Ed. Juliet Mitchell and Ann Oakley. Harmondsworth: Penguin, 1976. 176–98.

Martin, Jane. *Women and the Politics of Schooling in Victorian and Edwardian England*. London: Leicester UP, 1998.

Martin, Lindsay. 'Virginia Woolf at Morley College'. *The Charleston Magazine* 4 (Winter/Spring 1991-2): 20-5.

Mason, Charlotte M. *Home Education: A Course of Lectures to Ladies*. London: Kegan Paul, 1886.

Maume, Patrick. 'Bullock, Shan Fadh [formerly John William Bullock] (1865–1935), novelist'. *ODNB*. Oxford UP, 23 September 2004. doi.org/10.1093/ref:odnb/64463. Web. 9 June 2017.

May, Derwent. *Critical Times: The History of the Times Literary Supplement*. London: HarperCollins, 2001.

Mayer, Louie. 'Louie Mayer'. Noble 154–63.

Mayers, Tim, Dianne Donnelly, Tom Hunley, Anna Leahy and Stephanie Vanderslice. 'Creative Writing Is Not a Fast Food Nation'. *Inside Higher Ed.* https://www.insidehighered.com. 5 July 2013. Web. 2 August 2018.

Mays, Kelly J. 'The Publishing World'. *A Companion to the Victorian Novel.* Ed. Patrick Brantlinger and William B. Thesing. Oxford: Blackwell, 2002. 11–29.

Meade, L. T. 'Preface to Employment for Girls'. *Atalanta* 1 (1887–8): 63.

Meiklejohn, J. M. D. *The Art of Writing English: A Manual for Students: With Chapters on Paraphrasing, Essay-Writing, Précis-Writing, Punctuation, and Other Matters.* London: A. M. Holden, 1899. *Google Books.* Web.

Meisel, Perry. *The Absent Father: Virginia Woolf and Walter Pater.* New Haven, CT: Yale UP, 1980.

Menand, Louis. 'Can You Teach Creative Writing?' *The New Yorker* 8 and 15 June 2009: 106–12.

Mepham, John. *Virginia Woolf: A Literary Life.* New York: St. Martin's, 1991.

Midgley, Nicholas. 'Virginia Woolf and the University'. *Woolf Studies Annual* 2 (1998): 147–59.

Miles, Andrew. *Social Mobility in Nineteenth- and Early Twentieth-Century England.* Basingstoke: Macmillan, 1999.

Miles, Eustace H. *How to Prepare Essays, Lectures, Articles, Books, Speeches and Letters, With Hints on Writing for the Press.* London: Rivingtons, 1905.

Miletic-Vejzovic, Laila. *A Library of One's Own.* London: Cecil Woolf, 1997.

Miller, E. J. 'The British Museum'. *Education.* Ed. Celina Fox and Gillian Sutherland. Government and Society in Nineteenth-Century Britain: Commentaries on British Parliamentary Papers Series. Dublin: Irish UP, 1977. 112–24.

—. 'Public Libraries'. *Education.* Ed. Celina Fox and Gillian Sutherland. Government and Society in Nineteenth-Century Britain: Commentaries on British Parliamentary Papers Series. Dublin: Irish UP, 1977. 125–36.

Miller, Jean Baker. *Toward a New Psychology of Women.* Boston: Beacon, 1976.

Mills, Jean. 'Virginia Woolf and the Politics of Class'. *A Companion to Virginia Woolf.* Ed. Jessica Berman. Blackwell Companions to Literature and Culture. Hoboken, NJ: John Wiley, 2016. 219–33.

—. *Virginia Woolf, Jane Ellen Harrison, and the Spirit of Modernist Classicism.* Columbus: Ohio State UP, 2014.

Mitchell, Catherine. 'Professions of Exclusivity: Authorship and the Anxiety of Expertise, 1880–1940'. Diss. U of California, Berkeley, 2004.

Mitchell, Sally. 'Children's Reading and the Culture of Girlhood: The Case of L. T. Meade'. *Browning Institute Studies.* Spec. issue on Victorian Popular Culture, ed. Anne Humpherys. 17 (1989): 53–63.

—. 'Girls' Culture: At Work'. *The Girl's Own: Cultural Histories of the Anglo-American Girl, 1830–1915.* Ed. Claudia Nelson and Lynne Vallone. Athens: U of Georgia P, 1994. 243–58.

Moore, Henry Charles. 'The Religious Press'. *Newspaper Press Directory.* London: C. Mitchell & Co., 1904. 12–13.

Moore, Madeline. *The Short Season Between Two Silences: The Mystical and the Political in the Novels of Virginia Woolf.* Boston: George Allen, 1984.

Morris, Richard. *English Grammar.* Literature Primers. New York: Appleton, 1888.

Mourão, Manuela. 'Delicate Balances: Gender and Power in Anne Thackeray Ritchie's Non-fiction'. *Women's Writing* 4.1 (1997): 73–91.

—. 'Interrogating the Female Bildungsroman: Anne Thackeray Ritchie's Marriage Fictions'. *Nineteenth-Century Feminisms* 3 (2000): 73–87.

—. 'Negotiating Victorian Feminism: Anne Thackeray Ritchie's Short Fiction'. *Tulsa Studies in Women's Literature* 20 (2001): 57–75.

Muir, Dorothy. *Lift the Curtain.* London: Jonathan Cape, 1955.

Murdoch, Lydia. *Daily Life of Victorian Women*. The Greenwood Press Daily Life Through History Series. Santa Barbara, CA: Greenwood, 2014.
Murphy, G. Martin. 'Church, Richard William (1815–1890), dean of St Paul's'. *ODNB*. Oxford UP, 23 September 2004. doi.org/10.1093/ref:odnb/5389. Web. 26 September 2007.
Murphy, Paul Thomas. *Toward a Working-Class Canon: Literary Criticism in British Working-Class Periodicals, 1816–1858*. Columbus: Ohio State UP, 1994.
Murray, Janet, ed. *Strong-Minded Women and Other Lost Voices from Nineteenth-Century England*. New York: Pantheon, 1982.
Mylene, Alice R., ed. *To Write or Not to Write: Hints and Suggestions Concerning All Sorts of Literary and Journalistic Work*. Boston: Morning Star Publishing House, 1891.
Nafisi, Azar. *Reading Lolita in Tehran: A Memoir in Books*. New York: Random House, 2003.
Nagel, Rebecca. 'Virginia Woolf on Reading Greek'. *The Classical World* 96.1 (Fall 2002): 61–75.
Nesfield, J. C. *Junior Course of Composition*. London: Macmillan, 1901. *Internet Archive*. Web.
—. *Oral Exercises in English Composition*. London: Macmillan, 1901. *Internet Archive*. Web.
Nevinson, Henry W. *Fire of Life*. With Ellis Roberts. Pref. John Masefield. New York: Harcourt, 1935.
Nevinson, H. W. and A. J. A. Morris. 'Massingham, Henry William (1860–1924), journalist'. *ODNB*. Oxford UP, 23 September 2004. doi.org/10.1093/ref:odnb/34923. Web. 26 August 2008.
Newman, Hilary. *Anne Thackeray Ritchie: and Her Influence on the Work of Virginia Woolf*. London: Cecil Woolf, 2008.
Newspaper Press Directory. London: C. Mitchell & Co., 1904–7.
Nicolson, Harold. Foreword. *Offspring of the Vic: A History of Morley College*. By Denis Richards. London: Routledge, 1958. xv–xix.
Nicolson, Nigel and Joanne Trautmann, eds. Introduction and notes. *The Letters of Virginia Woolf*. Vol. 1: 1882–1912. By Virginia Woolf. New York: HBJ, 1975. xiii–xxi and *passim*.
Noble, Joan Russell, ed. *Recollections of Virginia Woolf by Her Contemporaries*. Athens: Ohio UP, 1972.
Noffsinger, John S. *Correspondence Schools, Lyceums, Chautauquas*. New York: Macmillan, 1926.
Norquay, Glenda, ed. *R. L. Stevenson on Fiction: An Anthology of Literary and Critical Essays*. Edinburgh: Edinburgh UP, 1999.
Norton, Rictor. *Mistress of Udolpho: The Life of Ann Radcliffe*. London: Leicester UP, 1999.
Nowell-Smith, Simon and Rebecca Mills. 'Richmond, Sir Bruce Lyttelton (1871–1964), journal editor'. *ODNB*. Oxford UP, 23 September 2004. doi.org/10.1093/ref:odnb/35742. Web. 26 August 2008.
Oakeley, Hilda D. 'King's College for Women'. *The Centenary History of King's College London*. By F. J. C. Hearnshaw. London: Harrap, 1929. 489–509.
O'Day, Rosemary. 'Women and Education in Nineteenth-Century England'. *Women, Scholarship and Criticism: Gender and Knowledge c. 1790–1900*. Ed. Joan Bellamy, Anne Laurence and Gill Perry. Manchester: Manchester UP, 2000. 91–109.
Oldcastle, John [Wilfrid Meynell]. *Journals and Journalism: With a Guide for Literary Beginners*. London: Field & Tuer, 1880.
Oldfield, Sybil. 'Mary Sheepshanks Edits an Internationalist Suffrage Monthly in Wartime: Jus Suffragii 1914–19'. *Women's History Review* 12.1 (2003): 119–34. dx.doi/pdf/10.1080/13664530300200350. Web. PDF file.

—. *Spinsters of This Parish: The Life and Times of F. M. Mayor and Mary Sheepshanks*. London: Virago: 1984.
—. 'Virginia Woolf and Antigone – Thinking Against the Current'. *Virginia Woolf International*. Ed. Wayne Chapman. Spec. issue of *The South Carolina Review* 29.1 (Fall 1996): 45–57.
O'Neill, Helen. 'London Library Women: Virginia Woolf and George Eliot'. Blog. *The London Library*. 13 December 2013. Web. 7 December 2018.
Onslow, Barbara. *Women of the Press in Nineteenth-Century Britain*. New York: St. Martin's, 2000.
Pacey, Desmond. 'Virginia Woolf as Literary Critic'. *The University of Toronto Quarterly* 18 (April 1948): 234–44.
Pagnamenta, Peter and Richard Overy. *All Our Working Lives*. London: BBC, 1984.
Palmer, Kimberly. 'The First Feminist.' Rev. of *Vindication: A Life of Mary Wollstonecraft*. By Lyndall Gordon. *Women's Review of Books* 25.4 (July/August 2006): 30–1.
Parkes, S. M. 'Steamboat ladies, (*act*. 1904–1907)'. *ODNB*. Oxford UP, 4 October 2007. doi.org/10.1093/ref:odnb/61643. Web. 20 August 2021.
Parry, Jonathan. 'Morley, Samuel (1809–1886), businessman, politician, and philanthropist'. *ODNB*. Oxford UP, 23 September 2004. doi.org/10.1093/ref:odnb/19291. Web. 13 October 2017.
Pater, Walter. *Essays from 'The Guardian'*. London: Macmillan, 1901.
Paterson, Alexander. *Across the Bridges: Or, Life by the South London River-side*. New York: Garland, 1980.
Paul, Janis. *The Victorian Heritage of Virginia Woolf: The External World in Her Novels*. Norman, OK: Pilgrim Books, 1987.
Paulin, Tom. *J'Accuse: Virginia Woolf*. Dir. and prod. Jeff Morgan. Fulmar Productions for BBC Channel Four, London, 29 January 1991. Television.
Pawlowski, Merry M., ed. Introduction. 'The Virginia Woolf and Vera Douie Letters: Woolf's Connections to the Women's Service Library'. *Woolf Studies Annual* 8 (2002): 3–8.
—, ed. *Virginia Woolf and Fascism*. New York: Palgrave, 2001.
Pay and Record Office, Great Britain Army. *List of Officers and Men Serving in the First Canadian Contingent of the British Expeditionary Force, 1914*. London. Web. https://www.archive.org/details/listofofficersme00greauoft. PDF file.
Pedersen, Joyce Senders. 'Life's Lessons: Liberal Feminist Ideals of Family, School, and Community in Victorian England'. *The Girl's Own: Cultural Histories of the Anglo-American Girl, 1830–1915*. Ed. Claudia Nelson and Lynne Vallone. Athens: U of Georgia P, 1994. 194–215.
—. 'Schoolmistress and Headmistress: Elites and Education in Nineteenth-Century England'. *Women Who Taught: Perspectives on the History of Women and Teaching*. Ed. Alison Prentice and Marjorie R. Theobald. Toronto: U of Toronto P, 1991. 37–70.
—. 'Some Victorian Headmistresses: A Conservative Tradition of Social Reform'. *Victorian Studies* 24 (Summer 1981): 463–88.
'Penderel-Brodhurst, James George Joseph'. *Who's Who, 1909*. London: Adam and Charles Black, 1909. 1490.
Percival, Alice. 'Some Victorian Headmasters'. *The Victorian Public School: Studies in the Development of an Educational Institution*. Ed. Brian Simon and Ian Bradley. Dublin: Gill and Macmillan, 1975. 72–94.
Perkin, Joan. 'That Won't Earn a Gal a Living: Education for Girls'. *Victorian Women*. By Joan Perkin. New York: New York UP, 2005. 27–50.
Perkins, Pam. 'Gerard [married name de Laszowska], (Jane) Emily (1849–1905), novelist'. *ODNB*. Oxford UP, 23 September 2004. doi.org/10.1093/ref:odnb/33375. Web. 9 June 2017.

Perry, Kate. 'Case, Janet Elizabeth (1863–1937)'. *The Dictionary of British Classicists.* Vol. 1. Ed. Robert B. Todd. Bristol: Thoemmes Continuum, 2004. 161–3.
—. 'Case, Janet Elizabeth (1863–1937), classics teacher and journalist'. *ODNB.* Oxford UP, 23 September 2004. doi.org/10.1093/ref:odnb/51784. Web. 6 June 2011.
Phegley, Jennifer. 'Clearing Away "The Briars and Brambles": The Education and Professionalization of the "Cornhill Magazine's" Women Readers, 1860–65'. *Victorian Periodicals Review* 33.1 (Spring 2000): 22–43. *JSTOR.* Web. 5 August 2012.
Phelps, Tom. *The British Milkman.* Oxford: Shire Publications, 2010.
Phipps, Christopher. 'The London Library'. *Indexer* 25.3 (April 2007): 190–1. *EBSCOhost Library, Information Science & Technology Abstracts with Full Text.* Web. 6 July 2011.
Pipher, Mary. *Reviving Ophelia: Saving the Selves of Adolescent Girls.* New York: Putnam, 1994.
Pippett, Aileen. *The Moth and the Star: A Biography of Virginia Woolf.* New York: Viking, 1957.
Polack, A. I. 'Clifton and Anglo-Jewry'. *Centenary Essays on Clifton College.* Ed. N. G. L. Hammond. Bristol: Arrowsmith, 1962. 51–71.
Pollentier, Caroline. 'Virginia Woolf and the Middlebrow Market of the Familiar Essay'. Dubino 137–49.
Pondrom, Cyrena Norman. 'English Literary Periodicals: 1885–1918'. Diss. Columbia University, 1965.
Poole, Andrea Geddes. *Philanthropy and the Construction of Victorian Women's Citizenship: Lady Frederick Cavendish and Miss Emma Cons.* Toronto: U of Toronto P, 2014.
Poole, Lorna. 'Recreational Libraries for Victorian and Edwardian Shop-assistants'. *Library History* 2.2 (Autumn 1970): 41–5.
Popowich, A. S. 'Carlyle, Panizzi, and the Public Library Ideal'. *Library Student Journal* 2.1 (February 2007): 1–7. *EBSCOhost Library, Information Science & Technology Abstracts with Full Text.* Web. 6 July 2011.
Porter, D. S. 'Smith, Lucy Toulmin (1838–1911), literary scholar and librarian'. *ODNB.* Oxford UP, 23 September 2004. doi.org/10.1093/ref:odnb/36151. Web. 26 December 2007.
Potter, Jeremy. *Headmaster: The Life of John Percival, Radical Autocrat.* London: Constable, 1998.
Prins, Yopie. 'The Sexual Politics of Translating *Prometheus Bound*'. *Cultural Critique* 74 (Winter 2010): 164–80. *Project Muse.* Web. PDF file.
'Professor George Charles Winter Warr'. Obituary. *London Times* 23 February 1901: 12. Microfilm.
Purvis, June. *Hard Lessons: The Lives and Education of Working-class Women in Nineteenth-century England.* Oxford: Polity-Blackwell, 1989.
—. *A History of Women's Education in England.* Milton Keynes: Open UP, 1991.
Putzel, Steven D. *Virginia Woolf and the Theater.* Madison, NJ: Fairleigh Dickinson UP, 2012.
Quinn, Laurie. 'A Woolf with Political Teeth: Classing Virginia Woolf Now and in the Twenty-First Century'. *Virginia Woolf: Turning the Centuries: Selected Papers from the Ninth Annual Conference on Virginia Woolf.* Ed. Ann Ardis and Bonnie Kime Scott. New York: Pace UP, 2000. 325–30.
Raby, Alister. *Virginia Woolf's Wise and Witty Quaker Aunt: A Biographical Sketch of Caroline Emelia Stephen.* London: Cecil Woolf, 2002.
Ransome, Cyril. *A Short History of England from the Earliest Times to the Present Day.* London: Longmans Green, 1899.
Read, Donald. 'Introduction: Crisis Age or Golden Age?' *Edwardian England.* Ed. Donald Read. New Brunswick, NJ: Rutgers UP, 1982. 14–39.

Reed, Christopher. 'Bloomsbury Bashing: Homophobia and the Politics of Criticism in the Eighties'. Rpt. as '"Bloomsbury Bashing" Revisited' in *Queer Bloomsbury*. Ed. Brenda Helt and Madelyn Detloff. Edinburgh: Edinburgh UP, 2016. 36–63.

—. 'Critics to the Left of Us, Critics to the Right of Us'. *Charleston Magazine* 12 (2000): 35–39.

—. 'A Tale of Two Countries'. *Charleston Magazine* 22 (Autumn/Winter 2000): 35–39.

Rees, Peter. *Bearing Witness*. Sydney: Allen & Unwin, 2015.

Reid, Panthea. *Art and Affection: A Biography of Virginia Woolf*. Oxford: Oxford UP, 1996.

Reimer, Mavis. 'Elizabeth Thomasina Meade'. *British Children's Writers, 1880–1914*. Ed. Laura M. Zaidman. *DLB* 141. Detroit: Gale, 1994. 186–98.

—. '"These two irreconcilable things – art and young girls": The Case of the Girls' School Story'. *Girls, Boys, Books, Toys: Gender in Children's Literature and Culture*. Ed. Beverly Lyon Clark and Margaret R. Higonnet. Baltimore: Johns Hopkins UP, 1999. 40–52.

—. 'Worlds of Girls: Educational Reform and Fictional Form in L. T. Meade's School Stories'. *Culturing the Child, 1690–1914*. Ed. Donelle Ruwe. Lanham, MD: Children's Literature Association and Scarecrow, 2005. 199–217.

Rev. of F. W. Maitland's *The Life and Letters of Leslie Stephen*. *The Academy* 10 November 1906: 463–5. Microfilm.

Rev. of F. W. Maitland's *The Life and Letters of Leslie Stephen*. *Guardian* 9 January 1907: 55.

Rev. of F. W. Maitland's *The Life and Letters of Leslie Stephen*. *TLS* 16 November 1906: 384. Microfilm.

Rev. of *Schillers Ausgewählte Briefe* edited by Pauline Buchheim. 'Literary Criticism'. *The Princetonian* 11.36 (6 October 1886): 4. *Larry DuPraz Digital Archives: Papers of Princeton*. https://library.princeton.edu/resource/4803. Web. 13 December 2018.

Rev. of *Schillers Ausgewählte Briefe* edited by Pauline Buchheim. 'Notes'. *The Nation* 43.12 (August 1886): 139. *Google Books*. 11 August 2011.

Rex, Ida. 'Ida Rex, School teacher'. *Working Lives: A People's Autobiography of Hackney*. Vol. 1, 1905–1945. London: Hackney WEA with Centerprise Publishing Project, 1976. 23–30.

Rhine, Joseph Jacobs A. 'Buchheim, Charles Adolphus'. 1901–6. *JewishEncyclopedia.com*. 2002–21. Web. 22 July 2011.

Rich, Mark. 'James Thomson (1834–1882)'. *Critical Survey of Poetry, Second Revised Edition* (September 2002): 1–4. *EBSCOhost Literary Reference Center Plus*. Web. 21 February 2011.

Richards, Denis. *Offspring of the Vic: A History of Morley College*. London: Routledge, 1958.

Risolo, Donna. 'Feminist Utopian Visions in Julia Stephen's Stories for Children: Toward a New Reading of Julia Stephen'. Woolf Across the Generations: The Twelfth International Conference on Virginia Woolf. Sonoma State University, Rohnert Park, CA. 9 June 2002. Address.

Ritchie, Anne Thackeray. *A Book of Sibyls: Mrs Barbauld, Miss Edgeworth, Mrs Opie, Miss Austen*. 1883. Folcroft, PA: Folcroft Library Editions, 1974.

—. 'Fairies in the Box'. *Atalanta* 4 (1890–1): 334–7.

—. 'Jane Austen'. *Atalanta* 1 (1887–8): 226–30.

—. 'Jane Austen'. *Toilers and Spinsters and Other Essays. The Works of Miss Thackeray*. Vol. 7. London: Smith, Elder, 1876. 84–122.

—. 'Miss Edgeworth'. *Atalanta* 2 (1888–9): 57–61.

—. 'More about Miss Edgeworth'. *Atalanta* 3 (1889–90): 13–15.

—. 'On Fashions in Manner'. *Atalanta* 3 (1889–90): 336–38.

—. 'Reminiscences'. *Lord Tennyson and His Friends: A Series of 25 Portraits and Frontispiece from the Negatives of Mrs Julia Margaret Cameron and H. H. H. Cameron*.

By Julia Margaret Cameron and H. H. Cameron. London: T. Fisher Unwin, 1893. 8–16.

—. 'Toilers and Spinsters'. *Toilers and Spinsters and Other Essays. The Works of Miss Thackeray*. Vol. 7. London: Smith, Elder, 1876. 1–35.

'Robert Cecil, 1st Viscount Cecil of Chelwood. *Wikipedia, The Free Encyclopedia*. Wikipedia, The Free Encyclopedia. 30 November 2019. Web. 24 December 2019.

Roberts, R. D. 'A.D. 1873–1889 University Extention in England'. *History for Ready Reference*. Ed. Josephus Nelson Larned. 5 vols. Vol. 1 (A to ELBA). Springfield, MA: C.A. Nichols, 1895. 746–7.

Roberts, Sydney C. and Annette Peach. 'Child, Harold Hannyngton (1869–1945), writer and theatre critic'. *ODNB*. Oxford UP, 23 September 2004. doi.org/10.1093/ref:odnb/32398. Web. 26 August 2008.

Robertson, Linda K. *The Power of Knowledge: George Eliot and Education*. New York: Peter Lang, 1997.

Roll-Hansen, Diderik. *The Academy: 1869–1879, Victorian Intellectuals in Revolt*. Copenhagen: Rosenkilde and Bagger, 1957.

Rose, Jonathan. *The Intellectual Life of the British Working Classes*. New Haven, CT: Yale UP, 2001.

Rose, Phyllis. *Woman of Letters: A Life of Virginia Woolf*. New York: Oxford UP, 1978.

Rosenbaum, S[tanford]. P[atrick]. *Edwardian Bloomsbury: The Early Literary History of the Bloomsbury Group*. New York: St. Martin's, 1994.

Rosenberg, Beth Carole. *Virginia Woolf and Samuel Johnson: Common Readers*. New York: St. Martin's, 1995.

— and Jeanne Dubino. Introduction. Rosenberg and Dubino 1–22.

— and Jeanne Dubino, ed. *Virginia Woolf and the Essay*. New York: St. Martin's, 1997.

Rosner, Victoria. *Modernism and the Architecture of Private Life*. New York: Columbia UP, 2005.

Ross, Janet. *Three Generations of English Women: Memoirs and Correspondence of Mrs. John Taylor, Mrs. Sarah Austin, and Lady Duff Gordon*. 2 vols. London: John Murray, 1888.

Ross, Robert. *Masques and Phases*. London: Arthur L. Humphreys, 1909.

Rossum, Deborah J. '"A Vision of Black Englishness": Black Intellectuals in London, 1910–1940'. *Stanford Electronic Humanities Review* 5.2 (1997). stanford.edu/group/SHR/5-2/rossum.html. Web. 23 August 2014.

Rowland, Peter, ed. *The Collected Stories of Lanoe Falconer*. Palo Alta, CA: Academica, 2010.

Royer, Diana. 'The Literary and Philosophical Performances of Woolf's Walking Narratives'. Profession & Performance: Thirtieth Annual International Conference on Virginia Woolf. Virtual. 13 June 2021. Address. TS.

Russell, Percy. *The Authors' Manual: A Complete and Practical Guide to All Branches of Literary Work*. 6th ed. London: Digby & Long, 1893.

—. *The Literary Manual, Or, A Complete Guide to Authorship*. London: London Literary Society, 1886.

Sacks, Janet, ed. *Morley College: A 125th Anniversary Portrait*. London: Third Millennium, 2015.

Sadler, John. 'Percival, John (1834–1918), headmaster and bishop of Hereford'. *ODNB*. Oxford UP, 23 September 2004. doi.org/10.1093/ref:odnb/35471. Web. 16 June 2011.

Sadler, M. E. *Continuation Schools in England and Elsewhere: Their Place in the Educational System of an Industrial and Commercial State*. Manchester: Manchester UP, 1908.

Saglia, Diego. 'Times Literary Supplement'. *Encyclopedia of the Essay*. Ed. Tracy Chevalier. Chicago: Fitzroy Dearborn, 1997. 844–6.

Saloman, Randi. *Virginia Woolf's Essayism*. Edinburgh: Edinburgh UP, 2012.

Sandberg, Eric. 'A Certain Phantom: Virginia Woolf's Early Journalism, Censorship, and the Angel in the House'. *Virginia Woolf Miscellany* 76 (Fall 2009): 12–13.

Sanders, Andrew. Introduction. *Tom Brown's Schooldays*. By Thomas Hughes. Oxford: Oxford UP, 1989. vii–xxv.

Sanderson, Kay. '"A Pension to Look Forward to . . . ?": Women Civil Service Clerks in London, 1925–1939'. *Our Work, Our Lives, Our Words*. Ed. Leonore Davidoff and Belinda Westover. Totowa, NJ: Barnes & Noble, 1986. 145–60.

Schaffer, Talia. *The Forgotten Female Aesthetes: Literary Culture in Late-Victorian England*. Charlottesville: UP of Virginia, 2000.

Schmidt, Barbara Quinn. 'The Cornhill Magazine'. *British Literary Magazines: The Modern Age, 1914–1984*. Ed. Alvin Sullivan. Vol. 4. Westport, CT: Greenwood, 1986. 103–10.

Schneer, Jonathan. *London 1900: The Imperial Metropolis*. New Haven, CT: Yale UP, 1999.

Scholes, Robert and Carl Klaus. *Elements of the Essay*. New York: Oxford UP, 1969.

Schulkind, Jeanne. Editor's Note. 'A Sketch of the Past'. *Moments of Being: A Collection of Autobiographical Writing*. By Virginia Woolf. San Diego: Harcourt, 1985. 61–3.

Schwartz-McKinzie, Esther. Introduction. *Mrs Dymond*. By Anne Isabella Thackeray. 1885. Stroud: Sutton, 1997. ix–xiii.

—. Introduction. *The Story of Elizabeth* and *Old Kensington*. By Anne Isabella Thackeray. 1876. Bristol: Thoemmes, 1995. v–xxxii.

Scott, Bonnie Kime, ed. *Gender in Modernism: New Geographies, Complex Intersections*. Urbana: U of Illinois P, 2007.

—, ed. *The Gender of Modernism: A Critical Anthology*. Bloomington: Indiana UP, 1990.

Shankman, Lillian F. Introduction, Section 8. *Anne Thackeray Ritchie: Journals and Letters*. By Anne Thackeray Ritchie. Ed. Lillian F. Shankman, Abigail Burnham Bloom and John Maynard. Columbus: Ohio State UP, 1994. 258–71.

Sharma, Vijay L. *Virginia Woolf as Literary Critic*. New Delhi: Arnold-Heinemann, 1977.

Shattock, Joanne, ed. *The Oxford Guide to British Women Writers*. Oxford: Oxford UP, 1993.

—., ed. *Women and Literature in Britain, 1800–1900*. Cambridge: Cambridge UP, 2001.

Shivani, Anis. *Against the Workshop: Provocations, Polemics, Controversies*. Huntsville: Texas Review, 2011.

Silver, Brenda. *Virginia Woolf's Reading Notebooks*. Princeton: Princeton UP, 1983.

Simon, Brian. Introduction. *The Search for Enlightenment: The Working Class and Adult Education in the Twentieth Century*. London: Lawrence and Wishart, 1990. 9–13.

—. Introduction. *The Victorian Public School: Studies in the Development of an Educational Institution*. Ed. Brian Simon and Ian Bradley. Dublin: Gill and Macmillan, 1975. 1–18.

Small, Ian. *Conditions for Criticism: Authority, Knowledge, and Literature in the Late Nineteenth Century*. Oxford: Clarendon, 1991.

Smith, Ann Kennedy. 'Kathleen Lyttelton and Virginia Woolf'. Ed. Clêr Lewis. *Something Rhymed*. 12 July 2018. https://somethingrhymed.com. Web. 26 January 2020.

—. 'A Public Space: Kathleen Lyttelton's Campaigning Journalism'. *Cambridge Ladies' Dining Society*. 20 July 2018. https://akennedysmith.com. Web. 26 January 2020.

Smith, Catherine F. '*Three Guineas*: Virginia Woolf's Prophecy'. *Virginia Woolf and Bloomsbury: A Centenary Celebration*. Ed. Jane Marcus. Bloomington: Indiana UP, 1987. 225–41.

Smith, C. Fell. 'Taylor, John and Susannah'. *DNB* 55. Ed. Sidney Lee. London: Smith & Elder, 1885–1901. 444–5.

Smith, Frank. *A History of English Elementary Education, 1760–1902*. London: U of London P, 1931.

Smith, Goldwin. *The United Kingdom: A Political History*. London: Macmillan, 1899.
Smith, John T. '"No Subject . . . More Neglected": Victorian Elementary School History, 1862–1900'. *Journal of Educational Administration and History* 41.2 (May 2009): 131–49.
Smith, Kenneth Alan. 'Contesting Discourses in the Essays of Virginia Woolf, James Baldwin, Joan Didion, and E. B. White'. Diss. University of Iowa, 1992.
Snaith, Anna. '"Stray Guineas": Virginia Woolf and the Fawcett Library'. *Literature and History* 12.2 (Autumn 2003): 16–36.
—. *Virginia Woolf: Public and Private Negotiations*. New York: St. Martin's, 2000.
—. 'The Years, Street Music, and Acoustic Space'. *Woolf and the City: Nineteenth Annual Conference on Virginia Woolf*. Fordham U, New York. 5 June 2009. Plenary address. TS.
Snape, Robert. 'The National Home Reading Union 1889–1930'. *Journal of Victorian Culture* 7.1 (2002): 86–110.
Soffer, Reba N. 'Authority in the University: Balliol, Newnham and the New Mythology'. *Myths of the English*. Ed. Roy Porter. Cambridge: Polity, 1992. 192–215.
Sotiropoulos, Carol Strauss. *Early Feminists and the Education Debates: England, France, Germany 1760–1810*. Teaneck, NJ: Fairleigh Dickinson UP, 2007.
Spender, J. A. and Cyril Asquith. *Life of Herbert Henry Asquith, Lord Oxford and Asquith*. London: Hutchinson, 1932.
Spiropoulou, Angeliki. '"On Not Knowing Greek": Virginia Woolf's Spatial Critique of Authority'. *Interdisciplinary Literary Studies: A Journal of Criticism and Theory* 4.1 (Fall 2002): 1–19.
Stanton, Michael N. *English Literary Journals, 1900–1950: A Guide to Information Sources*. Detroit: Gale, 1982.
Startt, James D. 'Good Journalism in the Era of the New Journalism: The British Press, 1902–1914'. Wiener 275–98.
Staveley, Alice. '"Pulling Back the Covers": Virginia Woolf's Undiscovered "Bedde's Head" Reading Lists'. *Interdisciplinary/Multidisciplinary Woolf: Twenty-Second Annual International Conference on Virginia Woolf*, Saskatoon, SK. 9 June 2012. Address.
Steele, Elizabeth. 'Stories for Children'. Gillespie and Steele 29–35.
Stemerick, Martine. 'Virginia Woolf and Julia Stephen: The Distaff Side of History'. *Virginia Woolf: Centennial Essays*. Ed. Elaine Ginsberg and Laura Moss Gottlieb. Troy, NY: Whitston, 1983. 51–80.
Stephen, Ann. 'Ann Stephen'. Noble 15–17.
Stephen, James, Sir. 'On Desultory and Systematic Reading'. *Lectures Delivered before the Young Men's Christian Association at Centenary Hall and Freemasons' Hall, 1854*. YMCA. London: Green, 1854. 2–43. *Google Books*. Web.
Stephen, Julia Duckworth. ['Agnostic Women']. Gillespie and Steele. 241–7.
—. 'The Black Cat or the Grey Parrot'. Gillespie and Steele 115–37.
—. 'Cat's Meat'. Gillespie and Steele. 166–87.
—. ['Domestic Arrangements of the Ordinary English Home']. Gillespie and Steele 253–5.
—. 'The Duke's Coal Cellar'. Gillespie and Steele 188–93.
—. 'Julia Margaret Cameron'. Gillespie and Steele 214–15.
—. 'The Mysterious Voice'. Gillespie and Steele 89–106.
—. *Notes from a Sick Room*. Gillespie and Steele 216–40.
—. 'Tommy and His Neighbours'. Gillespie and Steele 36–46.
—. 'The Wandering Pigs'. Gillespie and Steele 138–65.
Stephen, Julian Thoby. 'The Cambridge Muse'. *The Cambridge Review* 19 October 1905: 8.
—. 'Compulsory Chapel: An Appeal to Undergraduates on Behalf of Religious Liberty and

Intellectual Independence'. 1904. Rpt. (Ed. Stuart N. Clarke) in *Virginia Woolf Bulletin* 53 (September 2016): 44–50.

[—.] 'Euphrosyne'. *The Cambridge Review* 5 November 1905: 49.

Stephen, Leslie. 'The Redundancy of Women'. *The Saturday Review* 27.704 (24 April 1869): 545–6.

—. *Robert Louis Stevenson: An Essay*. New York and London: G. P. Putnam's Sons, 1902. HathiTrust. Web. 12 December 2017.

—. *Selected Letters of Leslie Stephen*. Ed. John W. Bicknell. 2 vols. Basingstoke: Macmillan, 1996.

—. *Sir Leslie Stephen's Mausoleum Book*. Ed. Alan Bell. Oxford: Clarendon, 1977.

—. *The 'Times' on the American War: An Historical Study*. London: Ridgway, 1865. Digital rpt. The Times *on the American War and Other Essays*. Cambridge: Cambridge UP, 2012.

Stevenson, Robert Louis. 'A College Magazine'. *Essays of Robert Louis Stevenson*. Ed. William Lyon Phelps. New York: Charles Scribner's, 1906. 143–58. Google Books. Web.

—. *Familiar Studies of Men and Books*. New York: Charles Scribner's, 1895.

Stewart, Victoria. 'Q. D. Leavis: Women and Education under Scrutiny'. *Literature and History* 13.2 (Autumn 2004): 67–85.

Strachey, Ray. *'The Cause': A Short History of the Women's Movement in Great Britain*. London: G. Bell, 1928.

Stray, Christopher. 'Classics'. In 'What the Victorians Learned: Perspectives on Nineteenth-Century Schoolbooks'. Roundtable with Leslie Howsam, Christopher Stray, Alice Jenkins, James A. Secord and Anna Vaninskaya. *Journal of Victorian Culture* 12.2 (Autumn 2007): 263–7.

—. *Classics Transformed: Schools, Universities, and Society in England, 1830–1960*. Oxford: Clarendon, 1998.

—. 'Schoolboys and Gentlemen: Classical Pedagogy and Authority in the English Public School'. *Pedagogy and Power: Rhetorics of Classical Learning*. Ed. Yun Lee Too and Niall Livingstone. Cambridge: Cambridge UP, 1998. 29–46.

Sullivan, Melissa. 'The "Keystone Public" and Virginia Woolf: *A Room of One's Own*, *Time and Tide*, and Cultural Hierarchies'. *Virginia Woolf and the Literary Marketplace*. Ed. Jeanne Dubino. New York: Palgrave Macmillan, 2010. 167–79.

Sully, James. 'Reminiscences of the Sunday Tramps'. *The Cornhill Magazine* 44 (January 1908): 76–88.

Suskind, Ron. *A Hope in the Unseen: An American Odyssey from the Inner City to the Ivy League*. New York: Broadway Books, 1999.

Sutherland, Gillian. 'Anne Jemima Clough and Blanche Athena Clough: Creating Educational Institutions for Women'. *Practical Visionaries: Women, Education and Social Progress 1790–1930*. Ed. Mary Hilton and Pam Hirsch. Harlow: Pearson Education, 200. 101–14.

—. 'Education'. *The Cambridge Social History of Britain 1750–1950. Vol. 3: Social Agencies and Institutions*. Ed. F. M. L. Thompson. Cambridge: Cambridge UP, 1990. 119–69.

—. 'Emily Davies, the Sidgwicks and the Education of Women in Cambridge'. *Cambridge Minds*. Ed. Richard Mason. Cambridge: Cambridge UP, 1994. 34–47.

—. '"Girton for Ladies, Newnham for Governesses"'. *Teaching and Learning in Nineteenth-Century Cambridge*. Ed. Jonathan Smith and Christopher Stray. Woodbridge, UK: Boydell, 2001. 139–49.

—. *In Search of the New Woman: Middle-Class Women and Work in Britain, 1870–1914*. Cambridge: Cambridge UP, 2015.

—. 'Self-education, Class and Gender in Edwardian Britain: Women in Lower Middle-

Class Families'. *Oxford Review of Education* 41.4 (August 2015): 518–33. https://doi.org/10.1080/03054985.2015.1048118. Web. 12 October 2016.

Sutherland, John A. *Fiction and the Fiction Industry*. London: Athlone, 1978.

—. *The Longman Companion to Victorian Fiction*. Harlow: Longman, 1988.

Swinnerton, Frank. *Authors and the Book Trade*. 1932. Freeport, NY: Books for Libraries, 1970.

—. *The Reviewing and Criticism of Books*. Ninth Dent Memorial Lecture. New York: Oxford UP, 1939.

Synge, Mrs Hamilton. *A Supreme Moment*. London: T. Fisher Unwin, 1905.

Taylor, Clare L. 'Hawkins, Sir Anthony Hope [pseud. Anthony Hope] (1863–1933), novelist'. *ODNB*. Oxford UP, 23 September 2004. doi.org/10.1093/ref:odnb/33769. Web. 9 June 2017.

'teach, v'. *OED Online*. Oxford UP, December 2018. Web. 19 December 2018.

Thane, Pat. 'Late Victorian Women'. *Later Victorian Britain, 1867–1900*. Ed. T. R. Gourvish and Alan O'Day. London: Macmillan Education, 1988. 175–208.

Thomas, Gillian. *A Position to Command Respect: Women and the Eleventh Britannica*. Metuchen, NJ: Scarecrow, 1992.

Thompson, Andrew S. 'Maxse, Leopold James (1864–1932), journalist and political activist'. *ODNB*. Oxford UP, 3 January 2008. doi.org/10.1093/ref:odnb/34956. Web. 26 August 2008.

Thompson, Nicola Diane. *Reviewing Sex: Gender and the Reception of Victorian Novels*. New York: New York UP, 1996.

Todd, Janet, ed. *British Women Writers: A Critical Reference Guide*. New York: Continuum, 1989.

Tokarczyk, Michelle M. 'Facing Gender/Class Conflicts: A Theory of Working-Class Women Reading'. *Phoebe: An Interdisciplinary Journal of Feminist Scholarship, Theory and Aesthetics* 4.2. (Fall 1992): 1–12.

Tomalin, Claire. *Jane Austen*. New York: Knopf, 1997.

Tratner, Michael. *Modernism and Mass Politics: Joyce, Woolf, Eliot, Yeats*. Stanford: Stanford UP, 1995.

Trodd, Anthea. *Women's Writing in English: Britain 1900–1945*. New York: Longman, 1998.

Tunstall-Behrens, Tankred. *Letters between a Victorian Schoolboy and his Family, 1892–1895*. Ed. David Lisle Crane. Durham, UK: Jean Wrangham, 1999.

Turnbull, Annmarie. 'Learning Her Womanly Work: The Elementary School Curriculum, 1870–1914'. *Lessons for Life: The Schooling of Girls and Women, 1850–1950*. Ed. Felicity Hunt. London: Basil Blackwell, 1987. 83–100.

Turner, Barry. *Equality for Some: The Story of Girls' Education*. London: Ward Lock Educational, 1974.

van de Kamp, Peter. 'Tynan [married name Hinkson], Katharine (1859–1931), poet and novelist'. *ODNB*. Oxford UP, 23 September 2004. doi.org/10.1093/ref:odnb/33887. Web. 9 June 2017.

Vann, J. Don. 'The Cornhill Magazine'. *British Literary Magazines: The Victorian and Edwardian Age, 1837–1913*. Ed. Alvin Sullivan. Vol. 3. Westport, CT: Greenwood, 1984. 82–5.

Venn, J. A., comp. 'Warr, George Charles Winter'. *Alumni Cantabrigienses: A Biographical List of All Known Students, Graduates and Holders of Office at the University of Cambridge, from the Earliest Times to 1900*. Part II (1852–1900). Vol. 6. Cambridge: Cambridge UP, 1954. 356.

Venn, John. *Annals of a Clerical Family: Being Some Account of the Family and Descendants of William Venn, Vicar of Otterton, Devon, 1600–1621*. London: Macmillan, 1904. *Internet Archive*. Web. 5 September 2011.

Vicinus, Martha. *Independent Women: Work and Community for Single Women, 1850–1920*. Chicago: U of Chicago P, 1985.

—. *The Industrial Muse: A Study of Nineteenth-Century British Working-Class Literature*. London: Croom Helm, 1974.

Victor, Carol de Saint. 'Literature'. *British Literary Magazines: The Victorian and Edwardian Age, 1837–1913*. Ed. Alvin Sullivan. Vol. 3. Westport, CT: Greenwood, 1984. 199–203.

—. 'The National Review'. *British Literary Magazines: The Victorian and Edwardian Age, 1837–1913*. Ed. Alvin Sullivan. Vol. 3. Westport, CT: Greenwood, 1984. 242–50.

Vincent, David. *Literacy and Popular Culture: England 1750–1914*. Cambridge: Cambridge UP, 1989.

Virginia Woolf Miscellany. The Leonard and Virginia Woolf Library. Ed. Diane Gillespie. 22 (Spring 1984): 1–8.

Virginia Woolf Miscellany. Woolf and Pedagogy. Ed. Madelyn Detloff. 73 (Spring–Summer 2008): 1–2, 11–34.

Virginia Woolf Miscellany. Woolf in Periodicals/Woolf on Periodicals. Ed. Patrick Collier. 76 (Fall–Winter 2009): 1–2, 9–19.

Waller, Philip. *Writers, Readers, and Reputations: Literary Life in Britain 1870–1918*. Oxford: Oxford UP, 2006.

Walton, J. Michael. 'Benson, Mushri, and the First English *Oresteia*'. *Arion* 14.2 (Fall 2006): 49–67. *JSTOR*. Web. 23 July 2011.

Wardle, David. *English Popular Education 1780–1970*. Cambridge: Cambridge UP, 1970.

'Warr, George Charles Winter'. *Who Was Who: A Companion to 'Who's Who' Containing the Biographies of Those Who Died During the Period 1897–1916*. London: A. & C. Black, 1920. 743. *Internet Archive*. Web. 9 August 2011.

Warr Memorial Prize. King's College Department of Classics, School of Arts and Humanities. https://www.kcl.ac.uk/artshums/depts/classics/study/handbook/programmes/prizes.aspx. Web. 9 August 2011.

Weaver, Stewart A. 'Hammond, (John) Lawrence Le Breton (1872–1949), historian and journalist'. *ODNB*. Oxford UP, 23 September 2004. doi.org/10.1093/ref:odnb/33673. Web. 26 August 2008.

—. *The Hammonds: A Marriage in History*. Stanford: Stanford UP, 1997.

Webb, R. K. 'Working Class Readers in Early Victorian England'. *The English Historical Review* 65 (1950): 333–51.

Webster, F. A. M. 'Clifton College'. *Our Great Public Schools: Their Traditions, Customs and Games*. London: Ward, Lock & Co., 1937. 79–86.

Webster, Frank. 'The Religious Press of To-day. Interviews with Editors of Leading Journals'. *The Quiver* March 1906: 386–93.

Weinstein, Arnold. *Recovering Your Story: Proust, Joyce, Woolf, Faulkner, Morrison*. New York: Random House, 2006.

Wells, John. *Rude Words: A Discursive History of the London Library*. London: Macmillan, 1991.

—. 'Some Previous Librarians'. *Founders & Followers: Literary Lectures Given on the Occasion of the 150th Anniversary of the Founding of the London Library*. London: Sinclair-Stevenson, 1992. 150–74.

Whitaker, Joseph. *An Almanack for the Year of Our Lord 1917*. London: Almanack Office, 1916.

Whitaker, Wilfred B. *Victorian and Edwardian Shopworkers: The Struggle to Obtain Better Conditions and a Half-Holiday*. Newton Abbot, UK: David & Charles, 1973.

Whitworth, Michael. *Virginia Woolf*. Oxford and New York: Oxford UP, 2005.

Wiener, Joel H. 'How New Was the New Journalism?' Wiener 47–71.

—., ed. *Papers for the Millions: The New Journalism in Britain, 1850s to 1914*. New York: Greenwood, 1988.
Wild, Jonathan. *The Rise of the Office Clerk in Literary Culture, 1880–1939*. Basingstoke: Palgrave Macmillan, 2006.
Williams, Holly. 'Thoroughly Modern Virginia'. *The Independent* 6 March 2011. *Independent.co.uk*. Web. 3 August 2011.
Williams, Perry. 'Pioneer Women Students at Cambridge, 1869–81'. *Lessons for Life: The Schooling of Girls and Women, 1850–1950*. Ed. Felicity Hunt. Oxford: Blackwell, 1987. 171–91.
Willson, Elizabeth Gordon. 'Digital Humanities in the Classroom'. *Scholarly Adventures in Digital Humanities: Making the Modernist Archives Publishing Project*. Ed. Claire Battershill, Helen Southworth, Alice Staveley, Michael Widner, Elizabeth Willson Gordon and Nicola Wilson. New Directions in Book History. Cham, Switzerland: Palgrave Macmillan, 2017. 89–109.
Wilson, J. J. 'My First Visit to the Woolf Library and Bloomsbury Collection in Pullman'. *Virginia Woolf Miscellany* 22 (1984): 6.
Wilson, Keith. 'Benson, A. C'. *Encyclopedia of the Essay*. Ed. Tracy Chevalier. Chicago: Fitzroy Dearborn, 1997. 84–5.
Wilson, Mary. *The Labors of Modernism: Domesticity, Servants, and Authorship in Modernist Fiction*. Burlington, VT: Ashgate, 2013.
Winterbottom, Derek. *Clifton After Percival: A Public School in the Twentieth Century*. Bristol: Redcliffe, 1990.
—. *Dynasty: The Polack Family and the Jewish House at Clifton, 1878–2005*. Isle of Man: Polack's House Educational Trust, 2008.
—. *John Percival: The Great Educator*. Local History Pamphlets 81. Bristol: Bristol Branch of the Historical Association, University, 1993.
—. *A Season's Fame: How A. E. J. Collins of Clifton College in 1899 Made Cricket's Highest Individual Score*. Local History Pamphlets 77. Bristol: Bristol Branch of the Historical Association, University, 1991.
Winterson, Jeanette. 'A Veil of Words (with reference to *The Waves*)'. *Art Objects: Essays on Ecstasy and Effrontery*. 1995. New York: Vintage, 1997. 79–99.
Wood, James. 'Virginia Woolf's Mysticism'. *The Broken Estate: Essays on Literature and Belief*. New York: Random House, 1999. 89–102.
Woolf, Leonard. *Downhill All the Way: An Autobiography of the Years 1919 to 1939*. 1967. New York: Harvest/Harcourt, 1975.
—. Editorial Note. *Death of the Moth and Other Essays*. By Virginia Woolf. London: Hogarth, 1942. 7–8.
—. Note [appended to 'Reviewing']. *The Essays of Virginia Woolf*. By Virginia Woolf. Ed. Stuart N. Clarke. Vol. 6. London: Hogarth, 2011. 205–7.
—. *Sowing: An Autobiography of the Years 1880–1904*. 1960. New York: Harvest/Harcourt, 1975.
Worth, George J. *Thomas Hughes*. English Authors Series. Boston: Twayne, 1984.
Wright, Anne. 'Harley Granville-Barker'. *Modern British Dramatists, 1900–1945*. Ed. Stanley Weintraub. DLB 10, Part 1: A–L. Detroit: Gale Research, 1982. 25–31.
The Writers' and Artists' Year-Book. Ed. G[eraldine]. E[dith]. Mitton. London: Adam and Charles Black, 1908, 1914.
'Writers' & Artists' Yearbook'. *Wikipedia, The Free Encyclopedia*. Wikipedia, The Free Encyclopedia. 17 July 2017. Web. 2 August 2018.
Yaldwyn, Cyril. 'In Memoriam: George Meredith'. *Morley College Magazine* xviii.10 (July 1909): 151.
—. 'Love's Best Way'. *Morley College Magazine* xvii.6 (March 1908): 89.
—. 'The Mortality of Feeling'. *Morley College Magazine* xvii.4 (January 1908): 59.
—. 'The Passing of Swinburne'. *Morley College Magazine* xviii.9 (June 1909): 143.

—. 'The Poetic Principle'. *Morley College Magazine* xix.4 (January 1910): 65.
—. 'Three Poets'. *Morley College Magazine* xix.4 (January 1910): 57–8.
—. 'Two Ways of Love'. *Morley College Magazine* xvii.5 (February 1908): 73.
Yoshida, Erika. '"The Leaning Tower": Woolf's Pedagogical Goal of the Lecture to the W.E.A. Under the Threat of the War'. *Virginia Woolf: Art, Education, and Internationalism: Selected Papers from the Seventeenth Annual Conference on Virginia Woolf*. Ed. Diana Royer and Madelyn Detloff. Clemson, SC: Clemson U Digital P, 2008. 33–9.
Young, Damon. *The Art of Reading*. London: Scribe, 2017.
Zimmern, Alice. 'The Daughters of London'. *The Guardian* (Women's Supplement) 59.2 (7 September 1904): 1486–7.
Zwerdling, Alex. 'The Common Reader, the Coterie and the Audience of One'. *Virginia Woolf Miscellanies: Proceedings of the First Annual Conference on Virginia Woolf*. Ed. Mark Hussey and Vara Neverow-Turk. New York: Pace UP, 1992. 8–9.
—. *Virginia Woolf and the Real World*. Berkeley: U of California P, 1986.

Index

The Academy (Academy and Literature), 199, 202, 204, 205, 206n2, 212, 213, 215, 232, 237, 238, 241, 242, 244, 246n12, 248n34, 257
  audience for, 230, 232, 243, 293, 294
  comparison of reviews, VS, *Guardian*, *TLS*, 265–7
  description and perspective of, 230–4, 242
  VS's work in, 142, 199, 221, 231–2, 237–8, 244, 343–4, 348
  see also Stephen, Virginia, teachers of: Child, Harold
Acland, Arthur, 32n4
Acton, Florence, 127, 144, 155n29, 166
Adam, Ruth, 80n8, 151–2n2
Adams, Charles Francis, Jr, 81–2n18
Adams, William Henry Davenport, 82n21
Addison, Joseph, 30
Adolph, Andrea, 197n16
Aeschylus, 68, 69, 70, 75, 76, 77, 85n38, 88nn58,60, 107, 316, 320, 321, 332
Ainger, Canon Alfred, 233, 261, 262, 264, 270nn7,15, 282, 298n20
Alcoff, Linda, 123n2
Alexander, Christine, 96, 97, 98, 99, 102, 104n21, 104–5n22, 105n28
Alexander, Christine and Juliet McMaster, 102
Allen, Judith, xxiii
Altick, Richard
  on authors, 3, 10n18
  on libraries, 58–9, 61, 79nn2,5, 131
  on working-class education, 121, 126, 128, 131, 133n14, 152n4
  amateur, 6, 15, 19n11, 31, 47, 65, 73, 76, 77, 179n18, 180–1n24, 194, 221, 245, 246n11, 262, 295, 301
Anderson, Chris, 7
Anderson, David, 202, 205, 208n16

Anderson, G. L., 133n18
Andrews, Elaine, 127, 181–2n30, 328
Angel in the House, 49, 93, 105n26, 114, 243
Annan, Noel, 14–15, 19n8, 23, 25, 28, 41, 52–3n12, 54n24, 64, 67, 68
anti-suffrage, 15, 19n12, 105n28, 116n6, 224
Arata, Stephen, 121, 130
Arber, Edward, 112, 242, 321
Archer, William, 238
Argyros, Ellen, 33n16, 34n23, 34nn23,25
Aristophanes, 36, 77, 240
Aristotle, 87n55, 155n30, 158, 177–8n6, 188, 214, 219, 245n4, 274
Armstrong, Isobel, 112
Arnold, Matthew, 25, 47, 49, 50, 56n46, 91, 206–7n8, 230, 235, 321
Arnold, Thomas, 91
Arnould, Joseph, 274
Aronsfeld, C. C., 86n49
art/commerce tension, 49–51, 56nn46,47, 57n48, 102, 170, 183n42, 200, 203–4, 206–7n8, 256
'Arthur's Education Fund', 17, 35, 36, 92, 196n12, 306
Ashton, Rosemary and Deborah Colville, 88n63
Asquith, Herbert Henry, 233
Asquith, W. W., 37, 38–9, 51n5, 53–4n22
Astell, Mary, 3, 107
Atalanta see Stephen, Virginia, teachers of
Austen, Jane, 4, 10n19, 25, 32n4, 44, 55n38, 99, 227
  Anne Thackeray Ritchie's essay on, 43, 44, 46
Austin, Alfred, 228
Austin, John, 94
Austin, Sarah, 93, 94, 103–4n11
Avery, Todd and Patrick Brantlinger, 246n14

Babbitt, Irving, 231
Bacon, Francis, 30, 37, 107, 110, 321
Baggs, Chris, 80–1n15
Baillie, Joanna, 274
Bainton, George, 208n17
Bairdsmith, Eleanor, 55–6n41
Bak (William Heinemann), 268
  reviews of, VS and *Guardian* compared, 268
Baker, William, 59, 61, 80n10
Ballantyne, R. M., 32n7
Bamford, T. W., 53n14
Banks, Olive, 16
Barbauld, Mrs, 28, 44
Barker, Joseph, 122
Barkevicius, Jocelyn, xxiii
Barkway, Stephen, 109, 152n9
Barnett, S. A., 239
Barwick, G. F., 63, 80–1n15
Basbanes, Nicholas, 80n11
Baylen, J. O., 241, 249n48
Baylis, Lilian, 132n3
Beale, Dorothea, 3, 14, 16, 17, 47
Beale, Peyton T. B., 318–19n11
Bean, C. E. W., 52–3n12, 53–4n22
Beer, Gillian, 9n7
Beerbohm, Max, 6
Beetham, Margaret and Kay Boardman, 55–6n41
Beethoven, 229
Behn, Aphra, 4, 24
Behrens, Leu and Min, 39, 52n11
Bell, Alan, 55n37, 60, 62, 80nn12,13
Bell, Anne Olivier, 96, 140
Bell, Barbara Currier and Carol Ohmann, xxiv n5
Bell, Clive, 1, 153n17, 239, 296–7n3
Bell, Matthew, 84n31
Bell, Quentin, 1, 14, 18n5, 23, 26–7, 35–6, 38, 42, 87n52, 95, 96–7, 99, 102–3, 103nn3,5, 116–17n7, 119, 142, 152n9, 154–5n26, 155n28, 180n23, 214, 216–17n1, 218, 238, 249n43, 296n2
  transcriptions, 183–4n44
Bell, Robert and Malcolm Tight, 209n25
Bell, Vanessa, 23, 24, 26, 28, 49, 61, 95, 96–7, 98, 103n4, 106, 133n12, 292
  VS's letters to, 72, 213, 215
Bellamy, Joan et al., 3
Belloc, Hilaire 6, 205, 235
Benjamin, Sarah, 103–4n11
Bennett, Arnold, 6, 203, 204, 213, 221, 230, 246n15, 249n51
Benson, A. C., 6

Bentley, Michael, 248n38
Berman, Jessica, 82n21
Bernstein, Susan David, 61, 62, 63, 80–1n15, 81n17, 82n19, 82–3n22
Besant, Walter, 48, 133n17, 184n51, 200–1, 203
Best, Geoffrey, 18n3
Bicknell, John, 20n25, 54n24, 81–2n18
Binckes, Faith, 208n14
Birch, Dinah, 102
Birmingham, George A., 266, 267, 270–1n16
  reviews of, VS and *Guardian* compared, 267
Biron, H. C., 228
Birrell, Augustine, 240–1
Bishop, Edward, 187, 195–6n7
Black Alistair, 79n2
Black, Clementina, 48, 61, 224
Black, Naomi, 9n7
Blain, Virginia, Isobel Grundy and Patricia Clements, 10–11n20
Blake, William, 112
Bland, Lucy, 20n20
Blank, G. K., 234
Bognor Library, 83n24
Bond, Robin, 77
Bookman, 208n24, 248n27, 270n14
Booth, Alison, 55n34, 82n21, 104n12
Booth, Charles, 127
Borer, M. C., 10n15
Boswell, James, 211, 213, 216–17n1, 237, 238, 275–6, 283, 287, 298n23, 321
Bowen, Marjorie, 266, 267, 269, 270–1n16
  reviews of, VS and *Guardian* compared, 269
Bowlby, Rachel, xxiv n6, 200, 206n6
Boyd, Elizabeth, 44, 247n17
The Boy's Own Paper, 48–9
Bradshaw, David, xxiv n6, 103n1
Bradshaw, David and Kevin Dettmar, xxiv n6
Brailsford, H. N., 248n40
Brake, Laurel, 70, 196n11, 206–7n8, 246n14
Brantlinger, Patrick, 197n16, 246n14
Breay, Claire, 87n53
Briggs, Julia, 9nn2,7, 11nn21,23,27, 37, 98, 104n17, 138, 140, 243
British Literary Magazines, 246n14, 248n37
British Museum Reading Room *see* Stephen, Virginia, teachers of
Brittain, Vera, 5

Brontë, Charlotte, 4, 44, 47, 110, 117n9, 225, 274
Brontë, Emily, 4, 225, 274
Brosnan, Leila, xxii, xxiii, 6, 97, 99, 101, 102, 103n3, 104nn15,16, 104–5n22, 105n31, 199, 200, 204, 206n3, 206–7n8, 211, 216–17n1, 218, 244, 246n10, 247nn16,22, 249nn50,51, 263, 270nn11,12, 297n5
Brown, Julia Prewitt, 20n26
Brown, Monika, 203
Brown, Vincent, 280
Browne, Thomas, 30, 148, 158, 188, 191
Browning, Elizabeth Barrett, 4, 44, 77, 111, 233, 234, 274, 276, 280–1, 282–3, 327n10, 344, 348n d
Browning, Robert, 47, 109, 110, 141, 156, 172, 173, 174, 175, 219, 234, 274, 279, 321, 327n10, 331, 344, 348n d
Bruley, Sue, 10n17
Bryant, Margaret, 10n15
Bryson, Bill, 52n7
Buchanan, Robert, 121, 175
Buchheim, C[harles] A[dolphus], 71–2, 86nn46,47,49, 314–15
Buchheim, E[mma], S[ophia] see Stephen, Virginia, teachers of
Buchheim, Pauline (née Hermann), 72, 86nn46,48,49
Buck, Claire, 10–11n20
Buckrose, J. E. (Annie Edith Jameson), 281–2, 287
Bullen, George, 81n17
Bullock, Shan Fadh, 130, 266, 270–1n16
Bulwer-Lytton, Edward, 48, 110
Bunyan, Alix, 28, 32n4, 56n45, 96, 102, 103n6, 104nn15,21, 105n31
Bunyan, John, 274
Burke, 149, 150, 170, 171, 174, 191–2, 196n11
Burne-Jones, Edward, 48, 136
Burnett, John, 121, 123, 124n7, 171
Burney, Fanny, 4, 275
Burrow, J. W., 162, 179n18
Burstyn, Joan, 10n15, 16, 19n16
Burton, Robert, 109
Bury, J. B., 111, 321
Buss, Frances, 3, 14, 16–17
Butcher, S. H., 111, 321
Butler, Samuel, 112, 321
Buxton, Charles Roden, 137, 139, 140, 169, 172
Byerly, Alison, 32n9
Byrne, Robert, 209n25
Byron, George Gordon, 30

Cahill, Ellen, 81–2n18
Calder, Jenni, 20n26, 123n4
Calisch, Edward N., 86n49
Callender, G. A. R. and Andrew Lambert, 71, 83n29
Cambridge University, 14, 15, 19n8, 20n25, 24, 35, 36, 37, 38, 40, 41, 51n5, 52n10, 54–5n30, 55nn31,32, 75, 77, 84n31, 85n37, 99–100, 103n9, 114, 130–1, 136, 187, 211, 298n27
  qualifying examinations for, 52–3n12, 67–8, 169, 182n39, 209n25, 312
  see also Girton; Newnham
Cameron, Julia Margaret, 31, 42, 43, 44, 55n33
Cannadine, David et al., 181n25
Carey, John, 9n7
Carlyle, Jane, 191, 220, 285
Carlyle, Thomas, 25, 59, 60, 79n5, 80n10, 94, 99, 105n26, 162, 274, 279, 283
Carnegie, Andrew, 79nn1,2
Cartwright, Miss, 205
Case, Emphie, 255
Case, Janet see Stephen, Virginia, teachers of
Caughie, Pamela, xxii, 151–2n2
Caygill, Marjorie, 61, 62
Cecil, David, 81–2n18
Cecil, Nelly, 144, 158, 175, 177–8n6, 213, 220, 236, 245n8
  VS's letters to, 119, 128–9, 133n17, 146, 174–5, 184n48, 203–4, 208n21, 215, 216, 220, 229, 237, 238, 244, 263, 265, 267
Cecil, Robert, 158, 175, 177–8n6, 184n52
Cellini, Benvenuto, 142, 158, 159, 160, 177–8n6, 187–8, 189, 190–1, 195nn5,6, 195–6n7
Chaucer, Geoffrey, 191, 322
Cheltenham Ladies' College, 14, 17
Chernaik, Judith, 63, 64, 80n12
Chesterton, G. K., 205
Child, Harold see Stephen, Virginia, teachers of
Childers, Mary, 11n22, 123n2
Childs, Michael J., 133n18, 178n11
Chiles, E. E., 182n38
Chirol, Valentine, 212, 216–17n1
Cholmondeley, Mary, 265
Christie, Mary, 278, 280
Church, A. J., 48, 116n2
Churchill, Winston (UK), 133–4n21, 239
Churchill, Winston (US), 265
Cicero, 93, 315
Clark, Beverly Lyon, 91, 92, 103n8

Clarke, Stuart N., 217n5, 246n14, 284, 296–7n3, 298n22, 341
Clarke, Stuart N. and B. J. Kirkpatrick, 247nn17,25, 272, 341
classics, 36, 38–9, 40, 51–2n5, 52nn6,8, 52–3n12, 53n14, 69, 75, 85nn37,39, 86n41, 88n59, 111, 130–1, 220, 231, 318n10, 318–19n11; see also Greek; Latin
Clay, Agnes Muriel, 69, 70, 316, 317n8, 318n10, 318–19n11
Clay, Catherine, 208n14
clerks, 121, 128, 129, 130, 133n17, 166, 169, 175, 184n51
A Clifton Boy, 39
Clifton College, 35, 37, 38–9, 40, 51n5, 52nn9–11, 53nn14,16–18,20,21, 53–4n22, 54n23, 65, 136, 235
Clough, Anne, 16, 17
Clutton-Brock, Arthur see Stephen, Virginia, teachers of
Cobbe, Frances Power, 201
Cobden-Sanderson, T. J., 112
Cockerell, Douglas, 112, 322
Cohen, Rachel, 270n12
Coleridge, Mary, 229
Coleridge, Samuel, 5, 24, 29, 36, 48, 172
Coleridge, Sara, 4
Collier, Pat[rick], 12n30, 102, 200, 206n4, 206–7n8, 208nn14,18, 245n1,2, 246nn11,14
Collier William, 160
Collins, Churton, 207n10
Collins, Philip, 32n9
common reader, xxiv n5, 2, 6, 8, 11nn23,25,27, 12n30, 36, 49–50, 64–5, 77, 146, 148, 177, 186, 190, 191, 192, 194, 221, 241, 243, 245, 294, 295–6, 301, 302, 303, 306
Conrad, Joseph, 230
Cons, Emma, 125–6, 128, 132n3, 133n11
Cooke, L. M., 237
Cooper, Thomas, 122
Copeland, Ian, 10n14, 121, 122
Corbett, Mary Jean, 32n8, 206–7n8
Cornhill, 31, 199, 208n24, 211, 213, 217nn2,8, 218, 221, 244, 270n14
audience for, 235–6, 237, 293, 294
description and perspective of, 235–8, 242, 243, 248n39
VS's work in, 199, 213, 221, 235, 237, 238, 244, 293, 346–7, 348
see also Stephen, Virginia, teachers of: Smith, Reginald
Cotton, James Sutherland, 182n35
Courtney, W. L., 227, 248n27, 263, 293

Coustillas, Pierre, 266, 306n6
Cowley, Abraham, 30
Cox, Frederick, 60–1, 80n11
Crane, David Lisle and Julie, 38, 52n11, 53n13
Creighton, Mandell, 109, 322
Cross, Nigel, 3, 10n18, 183–4n44
Cross, Wilbur, 288, 290
Crossick, Geoffrey, 130, 133n18
Crum, Ella (née Sieveking), 140, 146, 156, 212
Cuddy-Keane, Melba, xxiii, 9n7, 9–10n10, 10n11, 12n30, 56n46, 65, 83n25, 123n2, 131, 143, 174, 180n22, 194, 298–9n28, 303
Cuddy-Keane, Melba and Adam Hammond, Alexandra Peat, 105n25
Cunningham, Valentine, 207n10
Curtis, Anthony, 206n6, 222, 223, 237–8, 245nn2,8, 265
Curtis, S. J., 122, 130
Curtis, Vanessa, 37, 38–9, 54n23

Dailey, Kazuko and Harold, 228, 229
Dalgarno, Emily, 42, 83n28, 88n62
Dalsimer, Katherine, 1–2, 9n5
Dalton, F. T., 208n20, 240
Daniel, Miss, 72
Dante, 109, 322
Daugherty, Beth Rigel, 11n25, 14, 20n22, 33n11, 55n39, 174, 190, 192, 193, 195n1, 200, 217n9, 240, 270n8, 306n1
David, Deirdre, 3
Davidson, William and Joseph Crosby Alcock, 167, 169
Davies, Emily, 3, 16–17, 25, 133n20
Davies, Margaret Llewelyn, 75, 124n8, 151–2n2, 153n14, 224, 239, 255–6, 298n14
Davies, Rhys J., 133n16
Davies, Theodore Llewelyn, 139, 140
Davies, Tony and Teresa, 103n1
Dawson, A. J., 281
Day's Library, 64, 83n24
Deem, Rosemary, 10n15
de Gay, Jane, 51n1
Delamont, Sara, 10n15, 17
Dell, Marion 34n25, 51n1, 105nn29,30, 217n4
Demosthenes, 36, 313
De Quincey, Thomas 29, 279
DeSalvo, Louise, 1–2, 9n5, 9–10n10, 18nn2,7, 24, 33n10, 93, 95–6
Detloff, Madelyn, 197nn15–16, 306n1

Diamond, Michael, 151n1
DiCenzo, Maria, 208n14
Dickens, Charles, 32n4, 71, 94, 110, 127, 274, 277, 293
Dickinson, G. Lowe, 14, 19n8
Dickinson, Violet, 87n52, 107, 110, 119, 140, 178n7, 211, 213, 216, 220, 245n7, 327n7, 332
  VS's letters to, xxi, 6, 37, 41, 52n10, 54–5n30, 60, 63, 74, 75, 76, 87n52, 90, 107, 110–11, 116n1, 119, 128, 129, 140, 141, 142, 144, 149, 154n22, 155n27, 156, 157, 158, 159, 161, 163, 164, 165, 169, 171–2, 173, 174, 177n3, 178n14, 179n17, 180nn22–3, 182nn31,33, 183n41, 184nn47,48, 199, 211, 212, 213, 214, 215, 216, 217n6, 218, 220, 221, 222, 223, 224, 225, 227, 229, 232, 233, 237, 238, 241–2, 243, 244, 246n12, 250, 257, 265, 267, 272, 288, 292, 293–4, 295, 296nn1,3, 297n4, 324, 327n8, 329, 330, 331
Dictionary of National Biography (*DNB*), 31, 83n29, 93, 106, 235, 298n21
Digby, Anne and Peter Searby, 19n14, 121, 124n6
Disraeli, Benjamin, 228, 234
Dixon, Diana, 49, 56nn43,44
Dobson, Austin, 228
Domett, Alfred, 274
Doughty, Terri, 49, 56n45
Douglas, R. K., 47
Drabble, Margaret, 10–11n20
Dr Williams' Library, 64, 83n24, 161, 178n14
Dryden, John, 5
Dubino, Jeanne, xxii, xxiii, xxiv nn4,5, 11n26, 195n2, 211, 213, 214, 215, 218, 243, 249n43, 292, 294, 297nn6,8, 298n23, 303, 341
Du Bois, W. E. B., 135, 151n1, 231
Duckworth, George, 15, 30, 35, 36, 57n49, 75, 101, 103n4, 106, 110
Duckworth, Gerald, 15, 30, 35, 36, 57n49, 101, 106, 109, 232
Duckworth, Herbert, 29, 33n19, 106
Duckworth, Stella, 15, 30, 36, 66, 83n24, 94, 119, 140
Duff-Gordon, Lucie, 93, 94–5, 103–4n11
Duncan, Sara Jeanette, 48
Dunn, Jane, 142, 149
Dusinberre, Juliet, 179n18
Dyhouse, Carol, 5, 10n15, 16, 19n14, 20n20

Edgeworth, Maria, 44, 46, 47–8, 274–5, 284, 287
Education Acts
  1870, 49, 56n47, 120, 121–2, 123n3, 130, 136
  1880, 1891 and 1918, 122
  1902, 3
education, boys and men, 14, 18n5, 19n8, 20n18, 30–1, 33n10, 51–2n5, 52nn8,11, 52–3n12, 53n21, 53–4n22, 101, 115
  public schools, 20n24, 33n10, 35–9, 42, 75, 91–2, 115, 137
education, girls and women, 14–18, 20n18, 31, 51n4, 75, 93–5, 114, 124n6, 133n20, 137, 191, 196n12
  Atalanta articles about, 47–8
  barriers to, 10n17, 11n21, 113, 114, 115, 133n20
  debates about, 14–18, 94, 114
  history of, 3–5, 14–15, 16–17, 18nn3,4, 19n14, 20n21
  Leslie and Julia Stephen debates about, 15–16, 17–18, 302
  for women writers, 4–5, 10–11n20
  see also Stephen, Virginia, homeschooling
education, working classes, 3, 95, 120–3, 126, 130, 131, 132n6, 133n18, 136–7, 152n4, 170, 190, 196n11
  adult education, 126, 130
  autobiographies, 122–3, 124nn7,8, 171, 178n11, 181n25
  barriers to, 121, 122, 123n4, 133nn18,20, 152n4, 181n25, 194, 196n11, 301
  debates about, 125, 126
  levels, 130, 132n6, 133n19
  schools, 120, 121, 123n3, 132n6
  Workers' Educational Association Tutorial Class, 178n9, 181n26
  see also Morley College for Working Men and Women; Stephen, Virginia, Morley College teaching
education for writers, 7–8, 170, 200–6
  see also Stephen, Virginia, book reviewing and essay writing
Edwards, John Passmore, 79n2
Eliot, George, 4, 30, 43, 44, 47, 110, 206–7n8, 274
Eliot, T. S., xxii, xxiv n4, 6, 112, 241, 242–3, 303
Ellegård, Alvar, 222, 224, 232
Ellis, A. I., 81n17
Emerson, Ralph Waldo, 24, 30
Engelman, Herta, 19n9

Englishwoman, 213, 221, 247n17, 294
Ensor, R. C. K., 206n5
Epstein, Joseph, xxiv n6
Eschbach, Elizabeth, 19n14
Esdaile, Arunell, 80–1n15
Eton, 36, 52n10, 52–3n12, 229, 237
Euripides, 29, 36, 76, 77, 111, 181n27, 313, 322
Evans, A. W., *see* Stephen, Virginia, teachers of
Evans, Colin, 157–8
Evelyns Prep School, 20n24, 32n7, 35, 36, 38, 52n10, 54n24, 65
Ewart, William, 79nn2,5
Ezell, Margaret, 24–5, 32n6

Fader, Daniel and George Bornstein, 230, 232
Faithfull, Lillian, 66, 67, 68, 73, 83n29, 84n32, 85nn34,36, 86–7n51, 195n3
Falconer, Lanoe (Mary Elizabeth Hawker), 276, 297n11
Falke, Cassandra, 123
Fanshawe, Lady, xxi
Farrer, R. J., 276, 281
Fawcett, Henry, 15
The Fawcett Library, 64, 80n9, 82n20
Fenwick, Gillian, 33n22, 219, 298n21
Ferebee, Steve, xxiv n5
Fernald, Anne, xxiii, 10n11, 11n24, 62, 63, 64, 88n62, 184n46, 303, 306–7n7
Ferrell, Sara and Mary Wallace, 236, 237
Fielding, Henry, 24
Findlater, Jane, 227
Fisher, Jane, 83n28, 84n32, 86n45, 93, 113
Fisher, Mary, 52n8
Fisher, Mr [Herbert], 81–2n18, 98, 322
FitzGerald, Edward, 111, 322
Flanders, Judith, 20n26
Flint, Kate, 79n3, 80–1n15
Forrester, Wendy, 48–9, 56n45
Forster, E. M., 81–2n18
Fowler, J. H., 37
Fowler, Rowena, 88n62
Fox, Alice, 9n6
Foxe, John, 109, 322
Frasier, George MacDonald, 91
Freeman, Edward Augustus, 142, 162, 179n7
French language, culture, 23, 25, 26, 30, 33nn13,21, 94, 107, 143, 163, 167, 214, 219, 239, 258
Friedman, Susan Stanford, 10n11
Froude, James Anthony, 109, 116n5, 322, 327n5

Froula, Christine, 10n11
Fry, Roger, 2, 11n25, 53n21, 239
Fryer, Peter, 151n1
Funke, Sarah, 111, 320
Funke, Sarah and William Beekman, 111, 320
Fyvie, John, 231, 277

Galsworthy, John, 6
Galton, Francis, 24
Galway, Lady, 80n11
Garnett, Angelica, 103n4
Garnett, Edward, 238, 248n37
Garnett, Henrietta, 55n37
Garnett, Richard, 81n17, 235
Gaskell, Elizabeth, 4, 43–4, 206–7n8
Geertz, Clifford, 12n28
George, Lloyd, 233, 248n38, 249n48
Gerard, Dorothea, 266, 270–1n16
Gere, Anne Ruggles, 182n38
German language, culture, 70, 86nn46–9, 94
  VS's study of, 65, 67, 69, 71–2, 73, 314–16, 317n9, 321
Gerzina, Gretchen Holbrook, 151n1
Gibbon, Edward, 109, 110, 322
Gibbs, Mrs F. W., 109
Giffen, Robert, 60, 80n8
Gilbert, Richard, 197n15
Gillespie, Diane, 16, 20n26, 28, 30, 31, 31–2n2, 32n5, 33nn12,15,19, 34n25, 218, 245n3
Gindin, James, 245n5
Girls' Best Friend, 56n44
The Girl's Own Paper, 46, 48–9, 55–6n41, 102
Girls' Public Day Schools Company, 15
Girton, 16, 20n21, 25, 68, 75, 76, 78, 84n31, 115–16, 255; *see also* Cambridge University
Gissing, Algernon, 266, 270–1n16
Gissing, George, 191, 245n8, 272, 276, 277, 285, 290, 297n12, 303–5, 306n6, 320
Gladstone, Mary, 265
Gladstone, William, 59, 82n11, 94, 234
Glatter, Ron and E. G. Wedell, 209n25
Glazebrook, Michael, 39, 51n5, 53n13
Godwin, William, 228
Golden, Amanda, 33n12, 88n62
Goldman, Jane, 10n11
Goldman, Mark, xxiv n5
Goldsmith, Oliver, 24
Gordon, Lyndall, 1, 9nn3,4, 14, 15, 19n15, 40
Gorham, Deborah, 17

Gosden, P. H. J. H., 124n7
Gosse, Edmund, 6, 48, 207n10, 219, 228, 242
Gourvish, T. R., 19n11
Graham, Peter Alexander, 230, 248n34
Grand, Sarah, 4
Grant, Duncan, 155n28, 170, *291*, 296n2
Granville-Barker, Harley, 112–13, 322
Gray, F. Elizabeth, 247n22
Gray, E. W., 318n10
Gray, Thomas, 30
Greek language, culture, 9n3, 35, 39, 40, 41, 42, 69, 74, 84n31, 85n39, 87n55, 88nn58–60, 92, 94, 149, 158, 159, 160, 167, 177n4, 196n11, 235, 251–6, 274, 286; see also classics
    VS's study of, 1, 9nn2,3, 26, 33n12, 37, 38, 40, 41, 42, 54–5n30, 58, 65, 66, 67, 68–70, 71, 72, 73–8, 83n28, 84n33, 85nn39,40, 87nn52,56, 87–8n57, 88n62, 89, 90, 92, 107, 109, 110, 111, 113–14, 115, 136, 214, 215, 300, 311–16, 316–17n3, 317nn4–8, 318n10, 318–19n11
    VW's use of, 41, 88n62, 95, 107
Green, Alice Stopford, 63, 81–2n18, 178n14, 179n19
Green, Andy, 19–20n17, 38
Green, Barbara, 208n14
Green, F. L., 202
Green, John Richard, 109, 154n24, 162, 178n14, 179nn16,18
Green, Laura Morgan, 4, 10n15, 20n23
Greenburg, Arielle, 207n9
Greenwood, Thomas, 83n23
Grey, Maria (Mrs William), 68
Gribble, Francis, 202
Griffiths, Devin, 82–3n22
Grindea, Miron, 59, 79n5, 80n12
Grüner, Alice, 138
Gualtieri, Elena, xxiii, 123n2, 206n4
The Guardian, 205, 206n2, 214, 219, 222–3, 230, 231, 236, 245n6, 247nn18,20–1, 345–6
    audience for, 222–3, 224–5
    description and perspective of, 222–5, 231, 244
The Guardian (women's supplement), 1, 6, 66, 74, 119, 142, 199, 211, 212, 213, 215–16, 220, 227, 247n21, 265–9, 296–7n3
    audience for, 225, 227, 229, 230, 243, 244, 293–4, 295
    comparison of reviews, VS, *Academy*, *TLS*, 265–9
    description and perspective of, 223–5, 226, 244
    VS's work in, 199, 208n21, 217n3, 220, 221, 223, 224, 225, 226, 227, 241, 244, 256, 261, 265–9, 297n12, 301, 343–5, 347, 348
    see also Stephen, Virginia, teachers of: Lyttelton, Mrs Arthur

Hackney, Fiona, 208n14
Hagen, Benjamin, 306n1
Hager, Kelly, 116–17n7
Hakluyt, Richard, 59, 90, 109, 274, 282–3, 322
Hall, Donald, 207n9
Hall, Edith and Fiona Macintosh, 68–9, 85nn38,39
Hall, H. Fielding, 282, 288
Hall, Theophilus Dwight, 168
Hallsworth, Joseph, 133n16
Hamilton, Cicely, 133n16
Hamilton, Edith, 77, 88n58
Hammond, John, 233–4
Hammond, John, Francis Hirst and Gilbert Murray, 233
Hammond, Mary, 59, 79n3, 131
Hardwick, Lorna, 77
Hardy, Thomas, 26, 64, 109, 111, 112, 117n8, 235, 274, 322–3
Hardyment, Christina, 33n14
Hare, Augustus, 111, 323
Harraden, Beatrice, 261, 262–3, 264, 266, 270n7, 270–1n16
    reviews of, VS, *Guardian*, and *The Academy* compared, 266
Harris, Janice, 45, 236
Harris, Lilian, 141, 153n18
Harris, P. R., 63, 81n17
Harrison, Brian, 19n12, 116n6
Harrison, Frederic, 59
Harrison, Jane Ellen, 68, 73, 74, 76, 85n36
Harrison, J. F. C., 122–3
Harrison, Robert, 60
Harvey, Benjamin, 62
Havighurst, Alfred F., 233, 234, 238, 239, 248n37
Hawthorne, Nathaniel, 25, 47, 90
Hayes Court School, xx, 14, 18n6
Headlam, Walter, 220, 323, 327n8
Hearnshaw, F. J. C., 67
Heath Brow School, 75
Heine, Heinrich, 94
Heisch, C. E., 208n17

Heller, Michael, 133n18
Hemans, Mrs, 44
Hemingway, Ernest, 133–4n21
Henderson, Hubert, 238
Henley, W. E., 24, 49, 50, 64, 323
Herman, William, 88n62
Herodotus, 69, 111, 323
Heyck, Thomas William, 122, 130, 136, 137
Hichens, Robert, 202
Hill, Constance, 274–5, 284
Hill, Katherine, 2, 18n7, 20nn24,25, 24, 32n3, 84n32, 109, 161, 162, 245n5
Hill, Octavia, 119, 125, 128
Hilliard, Christopher, 123n2
Hilliers, Ashton, 276–7, 285, 297n12
Hill-Miller, Katherine, 42
Hills, Jack, 30, 57n49
Hind, Charles Lewis., 230, 238, 239, 240, 270n15, 293
Hinkson, H. A., 268, 270–1n16
  reviews of, VS and *Guardian* compared, 268
Hoberman, Ruth, 59, 61–3, 80–1n15, 83nn23,24
Hobsbawm, E. J., 120
Hodder, Edwin, 132n4
Hodgson, John Tweedale, 168
Hoffman, P. C., 133n16
Holcombe, Lee, 136, 137
Holland, Elizabeth, 270n15, 275–6, 280, 286
Holleyman, M. G., 32n5, 33n19, 116n3
Holst, Gustav, 152n8
Holtby, Winifred, 9n3
Homer, 36, 77, 253, 315, 317n2, 323
Honey, J. R. de S., 20n24, 53n20
Hood, Thomas, 48, 272, 275, 280, 286, 287, 288
Hope, Anthony, 265, 266, 268, 270–1n16, 323
Hopkins, Eric, 121, 123n3
Horn, Pamela, 10n14
Horner, Winifred Bryan, 208n15
Hosgood, Christopher P., 129, 133n16
Hotho-Jackson, Sabine, 178–9n15, 179n20
Howard, Anthony, 39
Howard, Ursula, 148, 169
Howe, Florence, xxiv n4
Howells, W. D., 220, 225, 226, 247n25, 247–8n26, 270n12, 297n9
Hubback, Eva, 133n14, 145–6, 152n9
Hughes, Harry, 103n9
Hughes, Thomas, 90, 91, 92, 93, 103n9
Hunt, Felicity, 10n15, 17

Hunt, Leigh, 274
Hunt, William, 162
Huntingdon, Lady, 279–80, 298n17
Hurt, J. S., 10n14, 121, 122, 127
Hussey, Mark, 9n7, 103n10, 123n2, 182n36, 208n14
Hutcheson, John A., 228, 229, 248n31
Huxley, Leonard, 248n39
Huxley, Leonard and Barbara Quinn Schmidt, 235, 237
Hyde Park Gate News 95–102; 48, 50, 59, 89, 292
  class in, 97, 99
  education in, 100–1
  gender in, 48, 97, 99, 100–1
  reader awareness in, 59, 98–9, 101–2
  writing skills practice, 89, 97, 102
  see also Stephen, Virginia, works, juvenilia

Ibsen, Henrik, 32n8, 107, 234
insider/outsider, VS's position, 2, 9–10n10, 51, 64–5, 73, 95, 113–14, 151–2n2, 192, 193–4, 196n11, 300, 301, 302
International Woman Suffrage Alliance, 139, 153n12
Inwood, Stephen, 59
Irwin, Sidney T., 37, 52n9
Isaac, Alan, 112
Italian language, culture, 94, 129, 158, 173, 333

Jackson, H. J., 33n12
Jackson, Holbrook, 238
Jackson, Kate, 49–50, 56nn46,47, 57n48, 99
Jackson, Maria, 19n10, 23, 28, 96
James, Henry, 26, 45, 117n9, 249n51, 261, 262, 264, 270nn12,13,15, 281, 282, 297n9
James, Louis 221, 243, 245
James, Walter, xxii
James, William, 26
Jann, Rosemary, 38, 179nn18,20
Jebb, R. C., 36, 52n6, 107
Jefferies, Richard, 111, 323
Jenkins, Gwyn, 83n26, 85n40, 86n42, 318–19n11
Jerrold, Walter, 275
Jewsbury, Geraldine, 191
John O'London's Weekly, 204
Johnson, Audrey, 179n18
Johnson, George Malcolm, 266
Johnson, Samuel, xxii, 5, 110, 181n25, 192, 276, 283, 323
Johnston, Georgia, 11n25, 190, 303

Jones, Christine Kenyon and Anna Snaith, 2, 18n6, 51n3, 66, 67–70, 72, 73, 83nn26,28, 84nn31–3, 85nn34,36, 86–7n51, 161–2, 311, 316n2, 316–17n3, 317nn4,9, 318–19n11
Jones, Clara, 71, 86n44, 141, 153n16, 154–5n26, 163, 178–9n15, 180n23, 180–1n24, 181nn27,28, 183–4n44, 184n45, 191, 193, 196n11, 196–7n14
 transcriptions by, 181, 183–4n44, 191, 193
Jones, Danell, 207n9, 303
Jonson, Ben, 54n28
Jonson, Ethel, 239–40
Joseph, Gerhard, 88n62
Joyce, James, xxii, 32n8
Jus Suffragii, 153n12
Juvenal, 77

Kamm, Josephine, 10n15
Kauffmann, Angelica, 44
Kaufmann, Michael, xxiv n4, 240, 303
Keating, Jenny, 160–1, 178nn10,13, 181n25
Keating, Peter, 201, 202, 204, 208n17, 209n26, 246n15, 265
Keats, John, 25, 29, 47, 107, 110–11, 112, 141, 156, 171, 172, 173, 174, 187, 275, 323, 331
Kelly, Serena, 223
Kelly, Thomas, 58, 59, 125, 126, 127, 136
Kemble, Fanny, 44
Kenny, Louise, 263–4, 267, 270n7
 reviews of, VS and *Guardian* compared, 267
Kent, Christopher, 211, 212, 230, 231, 232, 248n34, 249n43
Keynes, John Maynard, 233, 296n2
Khayyam, Omar, 51n5, 110, 324
King, Eleanor, 154n24
King, Julia, 31–2n2, 54–5n30, 79n6, 116n3, 209n26, 327n15
King, Julia and Miletic-Vejzovic, Laila (K&M-V), 24, 26, 29–30, 31–2n2, 32nn4,5, 33n12, 36, 40, 41, 43, 46, 51n5, 59, 61, 72, 80n12, 86n43, 103n10, 107, 109–12, 151n1, 179n16, 219, 242, 245n5, 320–6, 327nn2,4,6,8,15
King's College Department for Ladies, 65–73; 1, 2, 13, 18n6, 36, 42, 56 58, 83n26, 113, 114, 115, 136, 157, 161–2, 165, 187, 196n13
 Annual Reports and Delegacy Minutes, 68, 69, 70, 72, 311, 317n8

 policies, 66, 83n29, 86–7n51
 students: level and number, 68, 84nn30–32; matriculated and non-matriculated, 65, 66, 67–8, 73, 84n32, 113, 114, 181–2n30
 VS's class schedule, 311–16
 VS's courses, 51n3, 65, 66–7, 68, 69–70, 71
 as VS's teacher, 65, 73, 113–15, 300
 see also Stephen, Virginia, teachers of: Buchheim, Emma; Laughton, John Knox; Pater, Clara; Warr, George C. W.
Kingston Library, 64, 79n1
Kipling, Rudyard, 36
Kitton, F. G., 277
Klein, Viola, 18n4
Knighton, C. S., 52n9, 54n23
Kolocotroni, Vassiliki, 88n62
Kopley, Emily, 110, 179nn16,17
Koulouris, Theodore, 32nn5,8, 54n29, 76, 77, 78, 85n36, 88n61
Kranzler, Laura, xxii

Lady Margaret Hall (Oxford University), 70, 318n10
Lakanen, Shannon, 303, 306n3
Lamb, Charles, 6, 172, 275
Lamb, Walter, 38, 41
Lang, Andrew, 228, 248n36
Langenheim, Ralph L., 216–17n1
Lansdowne, Lord Henry, 94
Larson, Victoria, 51–2n5, 53n14
Latham, Monica, 105n23
Latham, Sean, 9n7, 123n2, 208n14
Latham, Sean and Robert Scholes, 246n14
Lathbury, Bertha, 51n4
Latin language, culture, 28, 29, 36, 52n6, 69, 70, 75, 85n39, 87n55, 92, 93, 94, 120, 167, 177n4, 196n11, 317nn6,8, 318–19n11; *see also* classics
 VS's study of, 23, 26, 33n13, 37, 38, 40, 54n26, 54–5n30, 55n31, 65, 67, 69, 70, 73, 77, 89, 109, 110, 111, 113, 115, 214, 300, 313–15, 316–17n3, 317n7, 318n10
Laughton, John Knox *see* Stephen, Virginia, teachers of
Laurence, Pat[ricia], 197n16
Lawrence, D. H., 6, 239
Leary, Patrick and Andrew Nash, 207n11
Leaska, Mitchell, 9n1, 25, 70, 86–7n51, 179n16, 180n23, 196n11, 219, 250, 251, 293, 297n8
Leavis, Q. D., 5, 11n21, 18n4, 56n46

Lee, Hermione, xxiv n6, 9n3, 32n7,
    33n12, 39, 40, 51n1, 52nn8,10,
    54n24, 64, 96, 97, 101, 102,
    104n21, 104–5n22, 105n28, 106,
    116n1, 140, 151–2n2, 153n17,
    174, 184n51
Lee, Sidney, 37, 40, 52n7
Lee, Vernon (Violet Paget), 228, 283–4,
    288
Lehmann, John, 9n1, 55n32
Lehmann, R. C., 55n32
Leinster-Mackay, Donald, 52n10
Leonard, Arthur N., 84n47
Levenback, Karen, 9n7
Levine, Philippa, 19n11, 29, 86n41
Levy, Amy, 48, 61, 117n10
Lewes, George Henry, 202–3
Lewes Free Library, 64, 65
Lewis, Jane, 153n16
libraries, 58–65; 13, 78, 82nn20,21, 131,
    133n16, 181n26, 230, 246n15,
    300, 302
  commercial, 4, 59, 64, 83n24, 131
  public, free, 58–9, 64–5, 79nn1–5,
    80–1n15, 83nn23,24, 131, 201,
    209n26, 278
  Public Libraries Act of 1850, 58–9, 79n3
  see also Stephen, Virginia, teachers of,
    British Museum Reading Room;
    London Library
Library of Leonard and Virginia Woolf,
    24, 32n4, 43, 46, 59–60, 86n44,
    103n10, 106, 151n1, 179n16, 219,
    320, 327nn8,10,11
  Julia Stephen's library, 29–30, 31,
    31–2n2
  Leslie Stephen's library, 23–6, 30–1,
    31–2n2, 33n12
  Thoby Stephen's library, 31–2n2, 36,
    40–1, 51–2n5
  Virginia Stephen's library, 31–2n2,
    106–13, 108, 116n3, 320–6
Light, Alison, 123n1
Lindsay, Geoff, 52–3n12, 53–4n22
Linett, Maren, 197n16
literacy, 56n47, 120, 122–3, 123n5, 131,
    138, 148, 169–70, 183n43
literature, orality of, 11n25, 25, 26, 32n9,
    40, 90, 98, 104n18, 157, 173, 174,
    177
lives of the obscure, 8, 12n28, 63, 77, 90,
    95
  Burke, 149, 150, 170, 171, 174, 191–2,
    196n11
  Clay, Agnes Muriel, 69, 70, 316, 317n8,
    318n10, 318–19n11
  Williams, Miss, 128, 129, 149, 150,
    170–1, 174, 183–4n44, 191–2,
    196n11, 208nn18,19, 218
  Yaldwyn, Cyril, 174–5; *176*, 177,
    184nn51,52, 185nn53,54, 193
Lockhart, J. G., 110, 111, 324
The London Library *see* Stephen, Virginia,
    teachers of
London School of Economics, 88n63
Lopate, Phillip, xxiv n6
Lorimer, Adam, 170, 203–4, 208n20,
    292–3
Lounsberry, Barbara, 83n27, 278–9
Love, Jean O., 1, 15, 19n10, 20nn24,25,
    23, 32n8, 35
Low, Frances, 203, 204, 211
Low, Sidney 81–2n18
Lowe, Gill, 40–1, 54n24, 83n27, 96, 98–9,
    101, 102, 104nn13,15, 104–5n22,
    105nn24,29
Lowell, James Russell, 24, 29, 54n24, 91,
    324
Lubbock, Percy, 111, 234, 274, 276,
    282–3, 324
Lucan, 111, 324
Lucas, Miss, 69, 85n40, 315, 317n8,
    318n10
Lucretius, 40–1, 54–5n30, 111, 324
Luedeking, Leila, 33n11
Lusty, Robert, 216–17n1
Lysias, 70, 315
Lyttelton, Margaret, 244, 247n21
Lyttelton, Mrs Arthur *see* Stephen,
    Virginia, teachers of

Maartens, Maarten, 267–8
  reviews of, VS and *Guardian* compared,
    267–8
McAleer, Joseph, 121–2, 131
Macaulay, Rose, 10–11n20, 11n20,
    206n7, 270–1n16
Macaulay, Thomas Babington, 162, 283
MacCarthy, Desmond, 81–2n18, 212,
    233, 234, 238
MacCarthy, Mary, 45
McClellan, Ann, 178n9
McCoy, Garnett, 83n28
McCracken, Elizabeth, 277–8, 298n17
McDermid, Jane, 14, 121
McDonald, Miss, 129
McDonald, Peter, 49–50, 57n48, 64
Macdonell, John, 94
McGee, Patrick, 20–1n27
MacGibbon, Jean, 35–6, 52n8, 52–3n12,
    54n24
Machann, Clinton, 203

McHugh, Heather, 207n9
McIntyre, Tony, 60, 63, 64, 80nn11,12
Mackail, J. W., 52n6, 55n31, 110, 324
MacKay, Carol Hanbery, 42, 43, 44, 45, 54n24, 55nn35,36, 81–2n18
McKeon, Josh, 81–2n18
McMahon, Michael, 52n11
McManus, Patricia, 151n2
McNeillie, Andrew, 6, 43, 55n33, 199, 204, 213, 215, 220, 222, 223, 225, 237, 246n14, 247nn20,21, 249n43, 264, 270nn7,12, 272, 293–4, 297nn5,8, 298n22, 303–4, 341
Madden, Mary, 151–2n2
Maddison, Isabel, 68
Mahan, Alfred T., 86n43
Maida Vale High School, 76
Maitland, Ella Fuller, 267
   reviews of, VS and *The Academy* compared, 267
Maitland, F[rederic] W[illiam], 178–9n15
   The Life and Letters of Leslie Stephen, 19n10, 20n24, 23, 32n4, 33n10, 60, 90, 103n2, 107, 119, 159, 206n2, 213, 214, 220, 221, 245n9, 278, 324
Malet, Lucas (Mary St Leger Kingsley), 248n27
Maloney, Stella and Gerald S. Argetsinger, 113
Manchester College (Oxford University), 55n40
The Manchester Guardian, 236
Mann, Mary, 237
Marcus, Jane, 9n7, 51n1, 54n24, 151n1
Marks, Pauline, 16, 17
Martial, 36, 41
Martin, Jane, 10n15
Martin, Lindsay, 133n13, 141, 149, 150, 152n9, 154nn19,22
Martineau, Caroline, 128, 139, 148
Martineau, Harriet, 4, 28, 236
Marx, Eleanor, 61
Mason, Charlotte, 28
Mason, John, 245n3
Massingham, F. W., 233, 235, 238, 239, 248n40
Maxse, Frederick August, 228, 248n32
Maxse, Kitty, 41, 212, 217n4, 220, 227, 248n28
Maxse, Leo *see* Stephen, Virginia, teachers of
May, Derwent, 212, 216–17n1, 240–1, 242, 246n13, 249nn46,47, 265, 269, 298n13
Mayer, Louie, 104n19

Mayers, Tim, et al., 207n9
Mayor, Flora M., 125, 139
Mays, Kelly, 206–7n8, 211
Mays, Nick, 246n13, 296–7n3
Meade, L. T., 46, 47, 55n40, 56nn42,44, 80n14
Mechanics' Institutes, 3, 126, 131, 132n6
Medeney, J. S. A., 30
Meiklejohn, J. M. D., 168–9, 183n40
Meisel, Perry, 9n6, 117n8, 245n5
Melville, Lewis, 277
Menand, Louis, 207n9
Mepham, John, 1, 9n4, 51n1, 199, 211, 265
Meredith, George, 24, 76, 103n10, 248n32, 274, 277, 305, 324
Meynell, Alice, 6, 201, 230
Midgley, Nicholas, 42, 195n3
Miles, Andrew, 169–70
Miles, Eustace H., 202, 204
Miletic-Vejzovic, Laila, 32n5, 33n11
Mill, John Stuart, 3, 44, 94
Mill, John Stuart and Harriet Taylor, 3
Miller, E. J., 61, 79n3
Miller, Jean Baker, 190
Mills, Jean, 74, 76, 77, 78, 87nn52,56, 88n60, 197n16
Mitch, D. F., 169
Mitchell, Catherine, 208n22
Mitchell, Sally, 14, 46, 56n42
Mitford, Mary Russell, 44
Montague, Basil, 94
Montaigne, xxiii, 6, 7, 37, 110, 171, 293, 324, 327n11
Montgomery, K. L., 268–9
   reviews of, VS and *Guardian* compared, 268–9
Moor, E. P. N., 38, 53n13
Moore, Henry Charles, 222, 247n21
Moore, Madeline, 51n1
More, Hannah, 16, 19n15
Morley College for Working Men and Women
   courses, 126, 127, 132n6, 132–3n9
   clubs, 132n6, 137–8, 152n6
   demographics, Lambeth/Southwark, 125, 127–8
   history, mission, 125–8; 132nn3–6, 152nn6,8, 168–9, 169–70, 196n13
   policies, 132n8, 137–8, 154n21, 154–5n26, 155n29, 181–2n30, 184n47
   pressures, administrative, 126–7, 144, 164
   teachers, 136, 137–8, 152nn3,8

Morley College, VS's teacher, 8, 120, 132, 135–6, 138, 145, 150–1, 157, 177, 186, 194–5; *see also* Stephen, Virginia, Morley College teaching; Stephen, Virginia, teachers of: Sheepshanks, Mary; students, Morley College
Morley, Samuel, 125, 126, 132n4
Morrell, Ottoline, 178n7
Morris, Richard, 167, 182n35
Mourão, Manuela, 44, 45
Mudie's Circulating Library, 59, 64, 83n24, 131, 231
Muir, Dorothy, 139
Munk, William, 81–2n18
Murdoch, Lydia, 153n16
Murphy, G. Martin, 223
Murphy, J. T., 178n11
Murphy, Paul Thomas, 123
Murray, Gilbert, 85n38, 233
Murray, Janet, 19n14
Mylene, Alice R., 208n17

Nafisi, Azar, 11n22
Nagel, Rebecca, 88n62
Nansen, Fridtjof, 187
The Nation, 199, 213, 221, 233, 246n12, 248nn33,38, 270n14
  audience for, 239–40, 243, 293, 294
  description and perspective of, 238–40, 248n38
  VS's work in, 199, 221, 238, 239, 240, 347, 348
  see also Stephen, Virginia, teachers of: Evans, A. W.
National Home Reading Union, 172, 173, 184n50
The National Review, 199, 208n24, 212, 213, 218–19, 221, 248nn29,32,37
  audience for, 228–9, 293, 294
  description and perspective of, 227–9, 230, 233, 234, 243, 248nn30,31
  VS's work in, 199, 221, 229, 343, 348
  see also Stephen, Virginia, teachers of: Maxse, Leo
National Union of Suffrage Societies, 139
Nesfield, J. C., 168, 182n39
Nevill, Dorothy, 275, 286, 288, 298n26
Nevinson, Henry, 201, 239, 249n42
Nevinson, Henry and A. J. A. Morris, 238
Newcastle, Duchess of, 191, 272, 283, 285–6
New Journalism, 49, 201, 206–7n8, 232, 238
Newman, Hilary, 51n1

Newman, John Henry, 24
Newnes, George, 49–50, 56nn46,47, 57n48, 99
Newnham, 15, 17, 20n21, 32n3, 68, 84n31, 115–16, 138, 191; *see also* Cambridge University
newspapers, as VS's teacher, 199, 220–2, 243–5, 269, 290, 293–6, 301, 302; *see also* *The Academy*, *Cornhill*, *Guardian*, *Nation*, *National Review*, *Speaker*, *Times Literary Supplement*; Stephen, Virginia, teachers of: Child, Harold; Clutton-Brock, Arthur; Evans, A. W.; Lyttelton, Mrs Arthur; Maxse, Leo; Richmond, Bruce; Smith, Reginald
Nicolson, Ben, 2, 145, 306
Nicolson, Harold, 126, 132n8, 143
Nicolson, Nigel and Joanne Trautmann, 9n8, 112, 178n14, 208n21, 246n13, 296–7n3
Nineteenth Century, 31, 51n4, 218
Noffsinger, John, 209n25
Normanby, Henry, 282, 287
Norquay, Glenda, 219
Norris, W. E., 267, 281, 298n18
  reviews of, VS, *Guardian* and *The Academy* compared, 267
Northcliffe, Lord (Alfred Harmsworth), 49, 249n47, 296–7n3
North London Collegiate School, 14, 16
Norton, Caroline, 277
Norton, Rictor, 4
Norway, Arthur Hamilton, 111, 324
Nowell-Smith, Simon and Rebecca Mills, 241
NPD (*Newspaper Press Directory*), 222, 224–5, 228, 230, 233, 234, 236, 241, 246n14, 247n19, 248n29

Oakeley, Hilda D., 67, 68, 73
O'Connor, T. P., 205
O'Connor, Mrs T. P., 205
O'Day, Rosemary, 5
Oldcastle, John, 202, 208n17, 247n22
Oldfield, Sybil, 88nn62,64, 125, 127–8, 132n1, 132–3n9, 137, 138–40, 142–4, 153nn10,12,15, 164, 168, 184n47
Oliphant, Margaret, 4, 44, 201
O'Neill, Helen, 80n8
Onslow, Barbara, 183–4n44, 201, 202, 203, 204, 205, 206–7n8, 211, 221, 236, 237
Opie, Amelia, 44

Orwell, George, 6
Osborne, Dorothy, 111, 191, 324
Ovid, 29
Oxford University, 4, 5, 39, 55n40, 67, 70, 75, 86n41, 99, 100, 114, 130–1, 182n39, 200, 230, 231, 318n10

Pacey, Desmond, 306n2
Pagnamenta, Peter and Richard Overy, 129
Pall Mall Gazette, 31
Palmer, Kimberly, 19n15
Panizzi, Antonio, 79n5
Pankhurst, Dr, 81–2n18
Parker, Gilbert, 266, 268, 270–1n16
  reviews of, VS and *Guardian* compared, 268
Parkes, S. M., 87n53
Parry, Jonathan, 132n4
Paston, John, 111, 191, 324
Pater, Clara *see* Stephen, Virginia, teachers of
Pater, Walter, 9n6, 36, 70, 107, 109, 112, 117n8, 219, 230, 245nn5,6, 279, 324–5
Paterson, Alexander, 124n7, 133n10
Patmore, Coventry, 29, 234
Paul, Janis, 32n8
Paulin, Tom, 9n7
Pawlowski, Merry, 9n7, 81–2n18
Payn, James, 107, 237
Pedersen, Joyce, 20n23
Penderel-Brodhurst, James George Joseph, 224, 247n21
Penson, Lillian, 81–2n18
Percival, John, 39, 53nn14,16,17,19
periodical studies, 208n14, 246n14
Perkin, Joan 19n9
Perry, Kate, 75, 76, 77, 78
Peters, Charles, 48
Phegley, Jennifer, 236
Phelps, Tom, 34n23
philanthropy, 16, 19n13, 30, 78, 145, 153n16, 278, 298n17; *see also* Stephen, Virginia, Morley College teaching, barriers
Phipps, Christopher, 60, 62, 64
Pilkington, Laetitia, 191
Pipher, Mary, 105n27
Pippett, Aileen, 9n1
Pizan, Christine de, 3
Plath, Sylvia, 133–4n21
Plato, 9n3, 36, 70, 77, 87n55, 111, 155n30, 181n27, 313–15, 325
Poe, Edgar Allen, 109, 112, 297n9, 325

Polack, A. I., 53n18
Poole, Andrea Geddes, 132n2, 152nn6,8
Poole, Lorna, 133n16
Pope, Alexander, 24
Popowich, A. S., 63
Porter, D. S., 55n40
Porter, Gene Stratton, 224
Potter, Beatrice, 81–2n18
Potter, Beatrix, 4
Potter, Jeremy, 39, 53n17
Power, Annie, 112
Power, Eileen, 63, 81–2n18
Prins, Yopie, 75, 77, 78, 87n54, 88n58
professional, 6, 15, 16, 19nn11,13, 31, 33n22, 42, 45, 49, 51, 61, 70, 71, 78, 93–5, 99, 102, 104n16, 113, 115, 130, 136–7, 138, 141, 142, 144, 178n14, 179n18, 180n22, 180–1n24, 199, 211–16, 218, 220, 221, 223, 225, 236, 243, 246n11, 264, 279, 287, 294, 295, 300–4, 318n10
professions, 18, 31, 52n8, 102, 125, 175, 200, 225
  for journalists, 47, 104n16, 165, 170, 178n14, 183n42, 183–4n44, 202, 204–5, 206–7n8, 208n14, 213, 247n22
  for teachers, 47, 136–7
  for women, 16, 19n11, 44, 47, 48, 93–5, 138, 183–4n44, 200, 201, 202, 203, 204, 205, 224, 236
Pullen-Burry, M., 231
Punch, 102, 208n24, 236
Purvis, June, 3, 10n14, 120
Putzel, Steven D., 247n17

Quill Club, 205
Quiller-Couch, Arthur, 231
Quinn, Laurie, 123n2

Raby, Alister, 51n1
racial attitudes, 94, 105n25, 190, 237
Rackham, Arthur, 72
Radcliffe, Ann, 4
Raleigh, Walter, 186–7, 233, 274, 282–3, 293
Ransome, Cyril, 86n44, 160
Rathbone, Marion, 74
Read, Donald, 130, 133n19
Récamier, Mme, 274
Reed, Christopher, 123n2
Rees, Peter, 53–4n22
Reid, Panthea, 1, 15, 23, 96, 97, 105n29
Reimer, Mavis, 20n18, 47, 55n40, 56nn42,43, 80n14, 133n20

Revised Code of 1862 (payment by results), 122, 131
  Standards I–VI, 122, 123n5, 127, 160
  three Rs, 120, 122, 126, 127, 132n6, 146, 190
Rex, Ida, 122, 131
Rhine, Joseph Jacobs, 86n49
Rhondda, Lady, 82n20
Rich, Mark, 112
Richards, Denis, 125–8, 130, 131, 132nn1,3,6–8, 133nn11,14, 136, 138, 139, 144, 148, 152n6, 154n23, 154–5n26, 161, 164, 166, 168, 169, 179n21, 193, 196n13
Richardson, Samuel, 24
Richmond, Bruce *see* Stephen, Virginia, teachers of
Ridge, Will Pett, 266–7, 270–1n16, 280, 287
  reviews of, VS and *The Academy* compared, 266–7
Risolo, Donna, 33n16
Ritchie, Anne Thackeray *see* Stephen, Virginia, teachers of
Ritchie, Richmond, 45
Roberts, L. J., 178n11
Roberts, R. D., 172
Roberts, Sydney C. and Annette Peach, 231
Robertson, Linda, 4
Robins, Elizabeth, 270–1n16, 287
Robinson, Anabel, 76
Roll-Hansen, Diderik, 212, 230, 232, 248n36
Roosevelt, Theodore, 133–4n21, 238
Rose, Jonathan, 9n7, 123, 123n2, 197n18
Rose, Phyllis, 1, 9–10n10, 68, 142
Rosenbaum, S[tanford] P[atrick], 37, 38, 177–8n6, 187, 188, 189, 195nn4,6, 203, 211, 212, 213, 215–16, 216–17n1, 217nn2,6, 219, 225, 231–2, 233, 237–8, 241, 243, 245nn4,7,8, 248n35, 249n51, 265, 271n17, 274, 294, 298n20, 332
Rosenberg, Beth, xxii–xxiii
Rosenberg, Beth and Jeanne Dubino, xxii, xxiii, xxiv nn4,5
Rosner, Victoria, 31n1, 33n17, 34n24, 51n2
Ross, Janet, 90, 92, 93–5, 103nn7,10, 103–4n11
Ross, Robert, 275, 288, 293, 298n27
Rossetti, Christina, 4, 111, 230, 243, 325
Rossetti, Dante, 136, 230, 325
Rossetti, William Michael, 111

Rossum, Deborah J., 151n1
Rowland, Peter, 297n11
Rowntree, Joseph, 233
Royer, Diana, 269n5
Ruskin, John, 47, 136, 235, 274
Russell, Bertrand, 88n63, 141, 144, 153n10
Russell, Percy 202

Sacks, Janet, 132n5
Sackville-West, Vita, 14
Sadler, John, 53n19
Sadler, M. E., 126
Saglia, Diego, 249n47
Saintsbury, George, 30, 228
Saloman, Randi, xxiii
Sandberg, Eric, 245, 247n16, 249n51
Sanders, Andrew, 91
Sanderson, Kay, 122
Sanger, Charles and Dora, 139, 153n13
Sappho, 227
Saunders, Howard, 109, 111
Savage, Dr, 157, 216
Schaffer, Talia, 207–8n13
Schmidt, Barbara Quinn, 235, 236, 237
Schneer, Jonathan, 135
Scholes, Robert, 208n14, 246n14
Scholes, Robert and Carl Klaus, 7
School of Journalism, Art and Secretarial Training for Women, 205
Schulkind, Jeanne, 115
Schwartz-McKinzie, Esther, 44, 45
Scott, Bonnie Kime, 10n11
Scott, Walter, 29, 32n8, 33n20, 274
  Waverley Novels, 25
Seccombe, Thomas, 216–17n1, 283
Servant's Magazine, 56n44
Seton, Dr, 19n16
Sévigné, Madame de, 44
Shakespeare, William, 25, 30, 32n4, 36–7, 38, 40, 41, 48, 52n7, 114, 172, 173, 174, 175, 228, 274
Shankman, Lillian, 45
Sharma, Vijay L., xxiv n5
Sharp, Rachel Dyce, 240, 249n42
Shattock, Joanne, 10–11n20
Shaw, George Bernard, 248n36
Sheepshanks, Mary *see* Stephen, Virginia, teachers of
Shelley, Mary, 4
Shelley, Percy Bysshe, 24, 112, 141, 156, 172, 272, 325, 331
Shirreff, Emily, 68
Shivani, Anis, 207n9
shop girls, 128–9, 130, 132, 133n16, 144, 169, 171, 182n33

shorthand, 89, 103nn2,4, 127, 128, 129, 130, 175, 202
Shorthouse, J. H., 172
Sichel, Edith, 214, 217n6, 241–2, 248n35
Sidgwick, Henry, 15, 17
Sidgwick, Nora, 17
Silver, Brenda, 77, 215–16, 270n6
Simon, Brian, 39, 123
Sinclair, May, 220
Sinclair, Upton, 224
Sladen, F. D., 81n17
Small, Ian, 19n11
Smith, Ann Kennedy, 247n23
Smith, Catherine, 51n1
Smith, C. Fell, 93
Smith, Frank, 10n14
Smith, George Barnett, 82n21
Smith, Goldwin, 109, 116n6, 325
Smith, John T., 178n11
Smith, Kenneth Alan, 247–8n26
Smith, Lucy Toulmin, 47, 55n40
Smith, Reginald *see* Stephen, Virginia, teachers of
Smyth, Ethel, 239–40
Snaith, Anna, xxiii, 10n11, 56n46, 59, 80n9, 81–2n18, 206n4, 229
Snape, Robert, 172, 173, 184n50
Snyder, Carey, 208n14
Society of Authors, 202, 203
Socrates, 70
Soffer, Reba 20n21
Somerville (Oxford University), 39, 70
Sophocles, 29, 36, 77, 107, 111, 158, 214, 312, 315, 317n5, 325
Sotiropoulos, Carol, 20nn19,23
spaces, rooms, 8, 13, 20n26, 23–4, 26, 29–31, 31n1, 33n17, 34n24, 35, 40, 41, 60, 61, 62, 64, 65, 73, 80n9, 82n19, 106, 116n5, 120, 126, 136, 140, 148, 150–1, 186, 190, 193, 194, 197n15, 215, 216, 217n9, 248n33, 259, 260, 279, 288
Spanish language, culture, 60, 139, 231, 244, 256, 257–8
The Speaker, 199, 205, 206n2, 212, 213, 238, 239, 241, 246n12, 248n37
  audience for, 234, 239, 243, 293, 294
  description and perspective of, 233–5, 239, 240, 248nn37,38
  VS's work in, 199, 221, 233, 234, 235, 261, 265, 344, 348
  see also Stephen, Virginia, teachers of; Clutton-Brock, Arthur
Spiropoulou, Angeliki, 88n62
Staël, Madame de, 231, 274–5
Stanton, Michael, 237, 238, 239

Startt, James D., 238, 241
Staveley, Alice, 208n14
Steele, Elizabeth, 28, 29, 33n15
Stelts, Sandra, 72
Stemerick, Martine, 54n24
Stephen, Adrian, 27, 32n7, 35, 52n10, 87n52, 97, 101, 103n6, 106, 110, 117n11, 152n9, 153n17, 162, 178n7, 256, 259, 272, 291, 296n2
Stephen, Ann, 191
Stephen, Caroline Emelia, 1, 51n1, 74, 89, 109, 116n1, 206–7n8, 216, 217nn3,7, 284, 285, 298n24, 325
Stephen, Dorothea, 109–10
Stephen, Harry Lushington, 109, 325
Stephen, James, 24, 32n4, 94, 270n9
Stephen, J. K., 68, 110
Stephen, Julia *see* Stephen, Virginia, teachers of
Stephen, Katherine, 15
Stephen, Laura Makepeace, 15, 36, 51n1
Stephen, Leslie *see* Stephen, Virginia, teachers of
Stephen, Minny, 42
Stephen, Thoby *see* Stephen, Virginia, teachers of
Stephen, Vanessa, 17, 27, 28, 29, 33n18, 41, 49, 52n10, 65, 96–7, 98, 101, 106, 110, 116n1, 116–17n7, 152n9, 158, 178n7, 200, 212, 216, 220, 318–19n11; *see also* Bell, Vanessa
Stephen, Virginia, book reviewing and essay writing
  context, education for writers, 200–6
  isolation, 199, 205–6
  lessons, 199, 214, 221, 225, 229, 232–3, 235, 238, 240, 242–3, 243–5, 250, 256, 260, 264, 265, 269, 273, 275, 280, 284, 286, 288, 290, 292–6, 301
  outcomes
    audience awareness, 199, 292–6, 298n27, 298–9n28, 299n29
    book reviews and essays, 273–90, 296–7n3, 297n5, 303–05, 341–9
  practice
    learning 'knack', 213, 221, 250, 269, 272, 273–90
    observing, 97, 250–6, 269nn1,2
    reviewing popular fiction, 265–9, 301
    taking notes, revising, 260–5
    using a journal, 256–60, 269n2
    professional, becoming one, 199, 211–16

Stephen, Virginia, (cont.)
  networks, 211–13, 216–17n1
    217nn2,4
  pay, 215–6, 217n8
  records, 214, 215
  routines, 213–5
  revising process
    notes, reading, 260–5, 270nn6,7, 282,
      298n18
    revision, 256–60
  reviews and essays
    critical values in, 280–4, 298n18
    cultural attitudes in, 284–6,
      298nn25,26
    genre in, 275–80, 297nn10–12
    literary tradition in, 274–5
    numbers, percentages of, 221, 225,
      265, 272–3
    popular fiction, 250, 265–9,
      270–1n16, 301
    reader awareness in, 287–8, 298n27,
      298–9n28
    rejections: Boswell's letters, 211,
      213, 237–8; Sichel review, 241–2,
      248n35; 'Magic Greek', 232,
      248n35; 'Memoirs of a Novelist',
      237–8; 'wildly romantic account',
      103n4
    table of, 341–9
  stages in, 273, 290, 297n8
  teachers, 218–45, 294–6
    friends, 220, 245n7
    literary models, 218–19, 245nn4–6
    Miss Williams, 218
    newspaper editors, 221–45
    see also Stephen, Virginia, teachers
      of: Child, Harold; Clutton-Brock,
      Arthur; Evans, A. W.; Lyttelton,
      Mrs Arthur; Maxse, Leo;
      Richmond, Bruce; Smith, Reginald
  teaching, concurrent with, 119, 138,
    141, 142, 145, 150, 161, 170,
    187, 195, 214, 269, 272–3, 293–4,
    306; see also Stephen, Virginia,
    works
Stephen, Virginia, homeschooling
  context, education for girls and women,
    2–5, 13–18
  gender, marked by, 25, 28–9, 55n32,
    61–4, 85n38, 90, 93, 100, 101,
    106, 113–16, 120, 292, 300, 302
  isolation, 7, 8, 13, 46, 79, 106, 114,
    115, 116, 300–1
  lessons, 13, 30–1, 35, 42, 45–6, 51,
    73, 78–9, 114–16, 117n11, 199,
    300–1

outcomes
  gender awareness, 113–15
  library, 106–13, 108, 320–6
practice
  bookbinding and design, 111–12
  notetaking, 40–41, 54–5n30, 55n31,
    78
  shorthand, 89, 103nn2,4
  writing, 89–90, 95–103
teachers, 13, 23–6, 26–31, 35–42,
    42–6, 46–51, 58–65, 65–73, 73–8,
    113–15; see also Stephen, Virginia,
    teachers of: Atalanta; British
    Museum Reading Room; Buchheim,
    Emma; Case, Janet; Laughton,
    John Knox; London Library; Pater,
    Clara; Ritchie, Anne Thackeray;
    Stephen, Julia; Stephen, Leslie;
    Stephen, Thoby; Tit-Bits; Warr,
    George C. W.
Stephen, Virginia, Morley College teaching
  barriers
    class assumptions, 9n7, 135,
      151–2n2, 170, 186, 190, 192, 193
    isolation, 120, 125, 138
    institutional constraints, 127, 144–6
    lack of knowledge: course aims,
      Morley mission, 165–6, 168–70,
      196n13; London demographic
      diversity, 135; working-class life,
      education, 119–20, 125, 132, 135,
      146, 151–2n2
    lack of training, 136, 141–2, 145,
      156, 194
    philanthropic framework, 135, 140–1,
      145, 153n16
    transitions, 136, 141, 165, 166, 172,
      173, 177
  class, marked by, 119–20, 123n2, 125,
    129–132, 135, 145, 148, 149–50,
    151–2n2, 170, 186, 190–5, 292,
    301, 302
  context, education for working classes,
    120–1, 126, 127–8, 146, 147,
    160–1, 190
  courses taught 141, 156–7
    composition, 165–72:
      autobiographical writing, 165,
      169, 170–1; curricular identity,
      165–6, 168–70; grammar emphasis,
      165, 166–9, 182nn35–9, 183n40;
      learning defined as, 171; pedagogy
      in, 171–2, 177, 181–2n30; possible
      lessons from, 172; textbooks
      167–9, 182nn35,39, 183n40; value
      of, 163, 165, 170

culture series, 157–60: curricular identity, 141, 157; evolving pedagogy in, 159–60, 177, 187; learning defined as, 158; lectures in, 187–9; lessons from, 160, 177; 'syllabus', 158; VS's lectures, 332–40

history (English), 160–5: curricular identity, 143–4, 161; learning defined as, 161; lessons from, 145, 177; pedagogy in, 143, 161, 162, 163, 164, 177, 178n13; sources for, 161–2, 178–9n15, 179nn16–18; textbooks, 160

literature (poetry), 172–4: curricular identity, 172–3; learning defined as, 174; lessons from, 177; pedagogy in, 173–4, 177; VS's curriculum suggestion for, 163–4, 174

criticism, Mary Sheepshanks of VS, 143, 144, 145

criticism, VS of Morley, 143–4, 148, 150, 163–4, 174, 180n23, 193

lessons, 120, 135–6, 138, 145–6, 150–1, 157, 170, 177, 186, 189, 190–5, 301

Morley College Annual Reports (MCAR), 129, 136, 137, 146, 147, 152n9, 154n19, 156, 157, 161, 164, 166, 167, 169, 172, 173, 177n4, 178nn7,9,12, 178–9n15, 180–1n24, 181n26, 328, 330–1

Morley College Executive Committee Minutes (MCECM), 137, 152nn3,5, 154n23, 155n29, 156, 161, 163, 164, 165, 168, 173, 174, 180–1n24, 328, 331

Morley College Magazine (MCM), 156, 157, 166, 170, 172, 175, 176, 181–2n30, 183–4n44, 328–31

outcomes,
class awareness, 190–5
lectures, 186–9, 332–40
reviewing, concurrent with, 119, 138, 141, 142, 145, 150, 161, 170, 187, 195, 214, 269, 272–3, 293–4, 306

students
compared to VS, 150, 191–2
educational barriers, 122, 146, 148, 149, 150, 151–2n2, 160–1, 190, 192, 193, 194, 196n11
educational potential, 146, 148, 150, 151, 192, 194
representative occupations *see* clerks; shop girls
VS's comments about, 146, 150, 151n2, 154nn22,25, 155n31, 180n22, 193
VS's interactions with, 144, 148–50, 159–60, 161, 171, 174–7, 191–4

teachers, other, 136–8, 155n29, 168, 172, 177n4, 179n21, 183–4n44

teaching potential, 9–10n10, 142, 148–50, 190–5

teaching schedule, 328–31

see also Stephen, Virginia, teachers of: Sheepshanks, Mary; students, Morley College

Stephen, Virginia, teachers of
Atalanta, 46–8; 35, 50, 51, 55n40, 55–6n41, 56n43, 57n48, 61, 78, 115, 116n2, 301; comparison with *Tit-Bits*, 50–1, 57n48; readers of, 47, 56n43; as teacher, VS's lessons 115

The British Museum Reading Room, 59, 60, 61–2, 63, 64, 79n5, 80n14, 80–1n15, 81nn16,17, 82n19, 82–3n22, 83n24, 92, 113, 209n26; comparison with London Library, 62–4; as teacher, VS's lessons, 58, 63–4; 115

Buchheim, E[mma] S[ophia], 71–2; 67, background, publications, 72, 86n46; class schedule with VS, 314–16, 317n4, 318n10; perspective on German, 71–2; as teacher, VS's lessons 72

Case, Janet, 73–8; 1, 9n2, 13, 40, 58, 65, 69, 70, 79, 87nn52–4,56, 87–8n57, 88nn63–4, 113, 115, 136, 154n20, 165, 181–2n30, 255, 300, 317n8, 318n10; attitudes about Greek, feminism, 77, 78; translation of *Prometheus Bound*, 77, 88n58,107; as teacher, VS's lessons, 36, 67, 74, 75, 76–7, 78, 79, 113, 114, 115, 165, 181–2n30

Child, Harold, 199, 202, 204–5, 212, 221, 231, 237, 238, 240, 241, 246n12, 248n36, 249nn45,47, 294, 296–7n3; as teacher, VS's lessons, 232–3, 243, 244, 293, 294

Clutton-Brock, Arthur, 199, 212, 221, 234, 235, 240, 241, 246n2, 294; as teacher, VS's lessons, 234, 235, 243, 293, 294

Evans, A. W., 199, 221, 238–9, 246n12, 249n41; as teacher, VS's lessons, 240, 243, 293, 294

Laughton, John Knox, 65, 67, 83n29, 86n43, 161–2, 178–9n15;

Stephen, Virginia, teachers of (*cont.*)
  Laughton, John Knox (*cont*)
    background, publications, 71; class schedule with VS, 311–13; recommended textbooks, 86n44; as teacher, VS's lessons, 71, 115, 178–9n15
  The London Library, 59–61, 62–3, 64, 79nn5,6, 80nn7,10, 81–2n18, 82n19, 82–3n22, 83n24, 157, 215, 209n26; Committee members, 81–2n18; comparison with British Museum Reading Room, 62–4; Annual Reports and Committee Minutes, 58, 61, 80n7, 81–2n18; as teacher, VS's lessons, 61, 63, 64–5, 115
  Lyttelton, Mrs Arthur, 119, 142, 199, 211, 212, 213, 215, 221, 223, 244, 247nn21–4, 256, 257, 265, 270n12, 272, 294, 295; as teacher, VS's lessons, 214, 225, 227, 233, 243, 244, 293, 294
  Maxse, Leo, 86n49, 199, 212, 213, 214, 215, 221, 228, 229, 233, 234, 246n12, 248nn28,30,32, 294; as teacher, VS's lessons, 229, 243, 293, 294
  Pater, Clara, 67, 69; background, 70; class schedule with VS, 313–16, 316–17n3, 317nn5–8, 318n10, 318–19n11; in 'Slater's Pins', 70–1, 86–7n51; as teacher, VS's lessons, 36, 67, 70–1, 73, 79, 86n42, 113, 114, 115, 165, 181–2n30
  Richmond, Bruce, 1, 140, 199, 212, 213, 214, 216–17n1, 221, 240, 241, 242, 244, 246nn12,13, 248n35, 249n47, 257, 265, 294; as teacher, VS's lessons, 1, 214, 241, 242–3, 244, 249n49, 260–1, 293, 294
  Ritchie, Anne Thackeray, 42–6; 1, 13, 26, 35, 47, 48, 51, 51n1, 55nn33–9, 58, 78, 80n8, 113, 114, 115, 201, 236; in *Atalanta*, 47, 48; comparison with VW, 44–5; as teacher, VS's lessons, 42, 43, 44–5, 51, 114, 115
  Sheepshanks, Mary, 138–45; 9n2, 119, 120, 125, 128, 132, 132n6, 132–3n9, 136, 137, 146, 148, 149, 150, 152n9, 153nn10–12,14–15,17, 154–5n26, 155nn27,28, 156, 157, 159, 161, 163, 164, 168, 180n23, 184n48, 186, 192, 196n11, 329, 330; as administrator, 139, 143, 144, 161, 164, 180–1n24, 181nn26,28; autobiography (*LDE*), 128, 132n6, 132–3n9, 139, 141, 153n10, 181n26, 196n11; and Bloomsbury, 139, 140, 153n17, 155n28; feminism, other causes, 139, 140, 153n12; philanthropic framework, 140–1, 145; professional relationship with VS, 141, 142, 144; as teacher, VS's lessons, 120, 136, 138, 142–3, 144–5, 146, 150, 159, 164, 184n4
  Smith, Reginald, 235–8; 211, 213, 221, 241, 244, 246n12, 294; as teacher, VS's lessons, 238, 243, 244, 293, 294
Stephen, Julia, 13–18, 26–31; 1, 19n9, 33n16, 34n23, 42, 45, 46, 54n24, 56n45, 56, 59, 97, 98, 101, 217n14, 245n3, 248n28; debate with Leslie Stephen about education, 14, 15–16, 17–18, 20n24, 23, 46; education budget of, 36, 51n4; education of, 19nn9,10, 29–30; library of, 29–30, 31–2n2, 33n20, 48, 106; relationship with servants, 119, 123n1; stories, 28–9, 33nn15,16; as teacher, VS's lessons, 13, 23, 26–30, 30–1, 33n18, 34n25, 93, 105n29, 114–15; as writer, 7, 16, 31, 34nn23,24, 51n4
Stephen, Leslie, 13–18, 23–6; xxii–iii; 1, 19nn8–11, 20nn25,26, 28, 30–1, 33nn12,22, 37, 38, 42, 45, 46, 51n1, 52–3n12, 54nn23,24, 55nn37,38, 56n45, 59, 66, 67, 73, 74, 75, 79n6, 83nn28,29, 84n32, 91, 93, 101, 103nn6,9,10, 104nn20,21, 107, 109, 112, 113, 116–17n7, 179n19, 206–7n8, 212, 217n2, 218–19, 228, 235, 237, 249n43, 270n9, 298nn20,21, 327n8; debate with Julia Stephen about education, 14, 15–16, 17–18, 20n24, 23, 46; education, youth, 14–15, 18n7, 33n10, 91; as lecturer, 136, 187; for essay, VS on, *see* Maitland, F[rederic] W[illiam]; Stephen, Virginia, works, 'Impressions'; essay, VW on, *see* Woolf, Virginia, works, 'Leslie Stephen: The Philosopher at Home'; library of, 23–6, 29, 30–1, 31–2n2, 32n4, 33nn11,12, 35, 42, 48, 58, 91, 92, 95, 106; 327n5; London

Library, 59–60, 61, 80nn8,12, and women on Committee, 81–2n18, 179 n19; as teacher, VS's lessons, 2, 13, 23–6, 30–1, 32n7, 54n28, 55n31, 64, 72, 78, 86n45, 90, 91, 92, 98, 103n2, 109, 114–15, 136, 161, 162, 173–4, 178–9n15, 184n49, 187, 218–19, 303; works: 'The Choice of Books', 32n3, 228; *English Literature and Society in the Eighteenth Century*, 110, 325; *Hours in a Library*, 33n12, 110, 325; *Mausoleum Book*, 54n24, 55nn31,38, 103n9; 'The Redundancy of Women', 45; *Robert Louis Stevenson*, 219; *Studies of a Biographer*, 218–19, 248n30, 326; 'The Times' on the American War: An Historical Study, 31, 270n9; *see also* Fenwick, Gillian

Stephen, Thoby, 35–42; 13, 15, 20nn24,25, 23, 27, 31–2n2, 32n7, 51n5, 52nn8–10, 52–3n12, 53nn13,18, 53–4n22, 54nn23–9, 54–5n30, 55nn31,32, 58, 62, 65, 77, 92, 96–7, 101, 103n6, 107, 110–12, 116n7, 136, 141, 152n9, 155n32, 181–2n30, 182n32, 184n51, 208n15, 220, 300, 320, 327n11, 330; comparison with Tankred Tunstall-Behrens, 38–9; education of, public schools, 20n24, 35–9, 42, 92, 115; essays of, 37–8; *HPGN* pieces, 96, 97, 99, 104n13; library of, 31–2n2, 36, 86n43, 106; notetaking, 40–1, 54–5n30; and sports, 38, 39, 54n23; as teacher, VS's lessons, 35, 36–7, 37–8, 40–2, 51, 78, 113–15, 300; VS letters to, 14, 36–7, 40, 41, 52n10, 66, 89, 107, 111, 112, 114, 116, 327n11

students, Morley College, 128–32; demographics, 147; diversity, occupational, 127–9, 130, 133n15; educational barriers, 131, 132, 133nn14,20, 133n20, 143–4, 146, 155n29, 160–1; educational potential, 131, 146, 148, 166; as teacher, VS's lessons, 136, 145–51, 190–5

Tit-Bits, 48–51; 35, 46, 58, 99, 102, 103n4; comparison with *Atalanta*, 50–1, 57n48; readers of, 49, 50; as teacher, VS's lessons, 49–50, 115

Warr, George C. W., 65, 67, 68–9, 73, 77, 84n33, 85nn37–9; attitudes about Greek, 68–9, 87nn37–9; background, publications, 68–9; class schedule with VS, 311–15, 316n1, 316–17n3, 317nn6,8, 318n10, 318–19n11; Leslie Stephen's letter to, 66, 83n28; as teacher, VS's lessons, 69

Stephen, Virginia, works

DRAFTS, NOTEBOOKS, PAPERS

'Agamemnon Notebook', 88n60

['Authorities, The English Kingdoms'], 142, 154n24, 163, 179n16

'Autobiography of Benvenuto Cellini', 142, 158–9, 160, 187–9, 195nn5,6, 215, 333–7

'The Dramatic in Life and Art', 142, 158–9, 177–8n6, 187, 188–9, 337–40

'Greek Notebook', 77, 88n61, 89

'The Libation Bearers Notebook, 77, 88n60

'The Matron', untraced, 296–7n3

'Notes on circa 45 books', 203, 261–5, 270nn6–7, 282, 298n18

['Report on Teaching at Morley College'] (MS) 141, 146, 163, 191, 193

['Report on Teaching at Morley College'] (QB), 128, 131, 138, 141–2, 143, 144, 146, 148, 149, 150, 154–5n26, 159, 161, 163–4, 165, 170–1, 180nn22,23, 183–4n44, 188, 191–3, 218, 329

['Virginia Woolf and the Authors of Euphrosyne'], 14, 18n4, 38

['Writing in the Margin'], 33n12

JUVENILIA

Hyde Park Gate News, 95–102; 32n3, 48, 50, 53n16, 59, 89, 103nn3,6, 104nn13–16,21, 104–5n22, 105nn23–31, 116–17n7, 213, 218, 292

missing, 89–90, 103n1

['wildly romantic account'], 103n4

LITERARY EXERCISES

'An Artistic Party', 253, 254, 269n1

'A Chapter on Sunsets', 251, 269n1

'The Country in London', 181n27

'Divorce Courts', 256

'The Downs', 251–2, 253, 269n1

['Farewell to Summer'], 253, 269n1

'Greece and Turkey Journal', 251, 252–6, 269n1

'Hampstead', 255–6, 269nn1,3

Stephen, Virginia, works (*cont.*)
  LITERARY EXERCISES (*cont.*)
    'Miss Case', 69, 74, 76–7, 78, 87–8n57, 317n8, 318n10
    ['Mrs Wall'], 255, 269n1
    'Retrospect', 250
    ['Short Expeditions'], 252, 269n1
    'Stonehenge', 252, 254, 269n1
    'Stonehenge Again', 251, 254, 269n1
    'Warboys 1899', 250, 256, 292
    'The Wilton Carpet Factory', 254, 269n1
  MEMOIRS
    'Caroline Emelia Stephen', 217n3, 284, 285, 287, 347
    'Impressions of Sir Leslie Stephen' (note for Maitland biography), 19n10, 60, 90, 107, 119, 159, 213, 220, 221, 245n9, 278, 344
    'Reminiscences', 23, 30, 31
  REVIEWS, ESSAYS
    'The American Woman', 277–8, 298n17, 343
    'An Andalusian Inn', 256–58, 260, 343
    'The Author's Progress', 170, 203–4, 208nn20,21, 292–3, 344
    'Barham of Beltana', 242, 267, 298n18, 343
    'A Belle of the Fifties', 261–2, 270n15, 343
    'Blackstick Papers', 43, 117n9, 325, 347
    'Blanche Esmead', 267, 344
    'Carlyle and the London Library', 60, 345
    'Caroline Emelia Stephen', 217n3, 284, 285, 287, 347
    'Chippinge', 267, 344
    'Colonel Kate', 268–9, 346
    'A Dark Lantern', 287, 343
    'The Debtor', 275, 297n9, 344
    'The Decay of Essay-writing' ('A Plague of Essays'), 6–7, 169, 171, 183nn41,42, 220, 232, 244, 246n12, 260, 293, 343
    'A Description of the Desert', 282, 344
    'Destinies', 282, 287, 346
    'The Duke and Duchess of Newcastle-Upon-Tyne', 272, 283, 285–6, 296–7n3, 347
    'The English Mail Coach', 279, 344
    'Father Alphonsus', 268, 346
    'The Feminine Note in Fiction', 227, 248n27, 263, 293, 343
    'The Fortunes of Farthings', 281, 343
    'Fraulein Schmidt and Mr Anstruther', 244, 345
    'The Genius of Boswell', 275–6, 283, 287, 298n23, 347
    'The Glen o' Weeping', 267, 345
    'Haworth, November, 1904', 220, 223, 225, 343
    'The House of Mirth', 261, 262, 264, 270nn7,15, 297n9, 343
    'The House of Shadows', 276, 281, 344
    'Impressions of Sir Leslie Stephen', 159, 220, 245n9, 278, 344
    'John Delane', 237, 238, 270n15, 346
    'The Journal of Elizabeth Lady Holland', 270n15, 275–6, 280, 286, 347
    'Journeys in Spain', 251, 257, 343, 348n a
    'Lady Huntingdon', 279–80, 298n17, 345
    'The Letters of Jane Welsh Carlyle', 220, 285, 343
    'Literary Geography', 220, 242, 274, 277, 293, 343
    'Lone Marie', 281, 298n18, 343
    'Louise de La Vallière', 293, 346
    'Lysistrata', 221, 247n17, 272–3, 347
    'Maria Edgeworth and Her Circle', 274–5, 284, 287, 347
    'Mary Christie', 278, 280, 345
    'Masques and Phases', 275, 287, 288, 293, 298n27, 347
    'Memoirs of a Person of Quality', 276–7, 285, 297n12, 345
    'The Memoirs of Lady Dorothy Nevill', 275, 286, 288, 298n26, 346
    'The Memoirs of Sarah Bernhardt', 237, 346
    'Modes and Manners of the Nineteenth Century', 284, 347
    'Mr Henry James's Latest Novel', 45, 117n9, 220, 225, 249n51, 261, 262, 264, 270n7, 343
    'Mrs Gaskell', 43, 347
    'Mrs Grundy's Crucifix', 280, 344
    'The New Religion', 268, 345
    'Next-Door Neighbours', 270–1n16, 266–7, 280, 287, 343
    'A Nineteenth-Century Critic', 233, 261, 262, 264, 270nn7,15, 282, 298n20, 344
    'The Northern Iron', 267, 346
    'The Novels of George Gissing', 272, 290, 303–5, 347

'Old Hampshire Vignettes', 276, 297n11, 345
'On a Faithful Friend', 225, 244, 343
'One Immortality', 282, 288, 347
'Outrageous Fortune', 268, 345
'The Poetic Drama', 272–3, 297n10, 344, 348n c
'Poets' Letters', 111, 233, 234, 272, 274, 276, 280–1, 282–3, 324, 344, 348n d
'The Post-Impressionists', 238, 239, 240, 270n15, 293, 347
'The Private Papers of Henry Ryecroft', 276, 277, 285, 293, 297n12, 306n6, 345
'The Red-Haired Woman' ('Two Irish Novels'), 263, 267, 270n7, 348n b
'The Scholar's Daughter', 261, 262–3, 264, 266, 270n7, 344
'The Sentimental Traveller', 283–4, 288, 346
'Shelley and Elizabeth Hitchener', 272, 346
'[Social England]', 247n25, 343
'Some Poetic Plays', 273, 296n3, 297n10, 345, 348n f
'Some Poetical Plays', 273, 296n3, 297n10, 346, 348n h
'The Son of Royal Langbrith', 220, 225, 226, 227, 247n25 247–8n26, 270n12, 343
'The Square Peg', 298n18, 345
'Sterne', 215, 241, 243, 288–90, 293, 347
'Street Music', 214, 215, 220, 229, 343
'A Supreme Moment', 266, 344
'The Sword Decides', 269, 346
'Tales of Two People', 265, 268, 345
'Their Passing Hour', 204, 231, 277, 343
'Thomas Hood', 48, 272, 275, 280, 286, 287, 288, 346
'Trafficks and Discoveries', 233, 235, 274, 276, 282–3, 293, 344, 348n b
'Two Irish Novels', 264, 344, 348n b
'The Value of Laughter', 225, 247–8n26, 274, 284–5, 343
'A Walk by Night', 256, 259–60, 269n5, 344
'The Ways of Rebellion', 281, 287, 298n19, 346
'The Weavers', 268, 345
'A Week in the White House', 238, 346
'William Allingham', 274, 276, 278, 298n15, 346
'The Wingless Victory', 281, 345
'The Wolf', 282, 287, 288, 298n19, 346

SHORT STORY
'The Journal of Mistress Joan Martyn', 9n4, 178–9n15

Sterling, Ada, 261–2, 264, 270n7
Sterne, Laurence, 9n4, 32n4, 215, 241, 243, 288–90, 293, 303, 347
Stevenson, Robert Louis, 107, 219, 228, 250, 279, 326
Stewart, Victoria, 11n21
Strachey, John St Loe, 236
Strachey, Lady, 54n28
Strachey, Lytton, 14, 42, 91, 216–17n1, 326, 327n6
Strachey, Marjorie, 213, 221, 247n17
Strachey, Ray, 15, 17
Strand, 49, 50, 208n24
Stray, Christopher, 38, 40, 51–2n5, 52n6, 75
Sullivan, Melissa, 208n14
Sully, James, 235
Suskind, Ron, 133–4n21
Sutherland, Gillian, xxiv n8, 5, 18n4, 19–20n17, 20n21, 84n31, 201
Sutherland, John, 230, 236, 245n2, 248n39
Swift, Jonathan, 191
Swinburne, Algernon Charles, 36, 38, 175, 230, 274, 326
Swinnerton, Frank, 206–7n8, 216–17n1, 234, 238, 248n37
Sydney-Turner, Saxon, 72, 88n59, 153n17, 220
Symonds, J. A., 187, 188, 326, 333, 337
Symons, Arthur, 219, 248n36
Synge, Mrs Georgina, 266

Taunton Commission, 16, 20n18
Tawney, Richard H., 169, 171, 178n9
Taylor, Henry, 95
Taylor, Susannah, 93–4
Temple, William, 111, 191, 276, 283, 324
Tennyson, Alfred, 25, 29, 32n7, 36, 47, 95, 109, 174, 274, 276, 326
Thackeray, William Makepeace, 24, 36, 42, 43, 95, 235, 274, 277, 293, 338
Thane, Pat, 16, 19n13, 30
Thomas, Gillian, 75, 318n10
Thomson, James, 38, 112, 117n10, 184n51, 215, 326
Thompson, Andrew S., 228

Thompson, Nicola Diane, 207–8n13
Three Generations of English Women, 90, 92–5, 102, 103nn7,10
  comparison with *Tom Brown's School Days*, 92–3
Thucydides, 214, 314, 317n5
The Times, 31, 60, 63, 68, 81–2n18, 201, 202, 212, 216–17n1, 217n5, 221, 223, 229, 230, 231, 234, 237, 238, 240, 241, 246n13, 249nn47–8, 254, 270n9, 296–7n3
The Times Literary Supplement (*TLS*), 74, 97, 112, 114, 117n9, 140, 142, 174, 183n42, 199, 201, 205, 206n2, 208n20, 212, 213, 215, 216, 216–17n1, 217n6, 221, 228–9, 231, 232, 234, 240, 246n13, 249n43, 260, 261, 269, 270n13
  audience for, 240–1, 249n46, 293, 294
  comparison of reviews, VS, *Academy, Guardian*, 265–9
  description and perspective of, 214, 230, 240–2, 243, 249nn44–5,47
  VS's work in, 60, 174, 199, 214, 215, 221, 224, 225, 241, 242–3, 244, 257, 261, 265, 267, 272, 288, 297n12, 298n19, 301, 343–7, 348
  see also Stephen, Virginia, teachers of, Bruce Richmond
Tit-Bits see Stephen, Virginia, teachers of
Todd, Janet, 10–11n20
Tokarczyk, Michelle M., 197n17
Tomalin, Claire, 4, 10n19
Tom Brown's School Days, 25, 90–2, 95, 102, 103nn8–10
  comparison with *Three Generations of English Women*, 92–3
Tratner, Michael, 9n7
Treasure Island, 25, 90
Trevelyan, G. M., 92, 154n23, 156, 163, 173, 180–1n24
Trinity College Dublin, 75, 87n53
Tripos (Classical), 15, 38, 52n8, 52–3n12, 75–6, 87nn53,55
Trodd, Anthea, 201, 203
Trollope, Anthony, 32n4, 228, 235
Tunstall-Behrens, Tankred, 38–9, 52n11, 53n15
Turnbull, Annmarie, 10n14
Turner, Barry, 3, 10n16, 17
Tweedsmuir, Lady, 58, 82n20
Tytler, Sarah, 279–80

university extension lectures, 78, 122, 126, 131, 132n6, 152n3, 166, 172, 179n21, 180–1n24
University of London, 67, 85n34, 88n63, 131, 181n26
Urban, Sylvanus, 236

Vann, J. Don, 235–6, 237
Vaughan, Emma, 70, 138, 152n9, 154n22, 213, 250
Vaughan, Madge (née Symonds), 89, 90, 103n3, 111, 217n4, 235, 299n29, 326
  VS's letters to, 89, 117n9, 146, 200, 216, 220, 263, 292
Vaughan, Marny, 69
Vaughan, Millicent, 99
Venn, J. A., 85n37
Venn, Jane, 103n2
Venn, John, 103n2
Verlaine, 38
Verrall, A. W., 77, 88n60
Vicinus, Martha, 10n16, 14, 19n14, 123
Victor, Carol de Saint, 228, 229, 248n30, 249n44
Vincent, David, 120, 122, 169, 183n43
Virgil, 29, 37, 54n26, 77, 93, 100, 111, 214, 313, 326
Virginia Woolf Miscellany
  Library of Leonard and Virginia Woolf issue, 31–2n2
  pedagogy issue, 306n1
  periodicals issue, 208n14
Vivian, Herbert, 202

Wace, Henry, 86n49
Walkley, A. B., 231
Wallace, David Foster, 298n16
Waller, Philip, 201, 206nn5,6, 207n12, 208nn16,23, 218, 239, 245n2, 270n10
Walters, Flamstead, 316, 318n10, 318–19n11
Walton, J. Michael, 85n38
Ward, Mrs Humphry, 4, 206–7n8, 219, 227, 242
Wardle, David, 10n14, 120, 121, 122
Warr, George C. W. *see* Stephen, Virginia, teachers of
Watson, Gilbert, 282
WDENP (*Waterloo Directory of English Newspapers and Periodicals*), 224, 230, 232, 236, 240, 246n14
Weaver, Stewart, 233, 248n38
Webb, R. K., 120
Webster, F. A. M., 53n20
Webster, Frank, 247n18

Weinstein, Arnold, 12n29
Wells, H. G., 109
Wells, John, 61, 62, 64, 79n5, 80n12, 81n18
Wesley, John, 280
Westminster School, 35
West, Samuel, 113
Weyman, Stanley J., 267, 270–1n16
Wharton, Edith, 261, 262, 264, 270nn7,15, 297n9
Whistler, James McNeil, 274
Whitaker, Joseph, 135
Whitaker, Wilfred B., 133n16
White, Gilbert, 111, 326
Whitman, Walt, 112, 274
Whitworth, Michael, 6, 9n2, 296–7n3
Wiener, Joel H., 206–7n8
Wild, Jonathan, 130, 133nn17,18, 184n51
Wilde, Oscar, 87n54, 109
Wilkins (Freeman), Mary E., 275, 297n9
Willcocks, Mary Patricia, 281
Williams, Holly, 84n31
Williams, Miss, 128, 129, 149, 150, 170–1, 174, 183–4n44, 191–2, 196n11, 208nn18,19, 218
Williams, Perry, 115–16
Willson, Elizabeth Gordon, 298–9n28
Wilson, J. J., 24
Wilson, John Dover, 231
Wilson, Keith, 6
Wilson, Mary, 123n1, 151–2n2
Wilson, Woodrow, 133–4n21
Winchester, Simon, 80n11
Winterbottom, Derek, 39, 53nn14,16–18,20
Winterson, Jeanette, xxii
Withers, H. L., 178n11
Withers, Maud, 278
Wollstonecraft, Mary, 3, 16, 19n15
Women's Service Library, 58
women writers, 2–5, 10–11n20, 24–5, 35, 42, 44, 45, 55n36, 61, 114, 206–7n8, 274, 284
Wood, James, 206n1
Woolf, Bella, 72
Woolf, Leonard, xxii, xxiv n4, 11n25, 42, 52n10, 53n18, 75, 104n19, 141, 142, 151n1, 151–2n2, 153n14, 154n24, 200, 206n4, 238, 248n40, 272, 296n2, 327n4
Woolf, Virginia, essayist, xx, 2, 7, 12n31, 13, 45, 73, 91, 97, 116, 119, 125, 138, 146, 151, 186, 190–5, 199, 223, 245n5, 256, 260, 269, 273, 290, 294, 295, 301–6
Woolf Virginia, works

BIOGRAPHY
Roger Fry, 11n25, 240
DRAMA
Freshwater, 7
ESSAYS
'Anon', and 'The Reader', 11n25
'Books and Persons', 249n51
'Byron and Mr Briggs', 11n23
'The Common Reader', 6, 8, 64, 148, 192, 194, 262, 295
'Donne After Three Centuries', 192, 217n9
'The Enchanted Organ', 43
'George Eliot', 43, 44
'Henry James's Ghost Stories', 242, 270n13
'How Should One Read a Book?' MS draft, xx, 14, 20n22
'How Should One Read a Book?', 1, 189, 196n10, 262, 264, 295
'Introductory Letter to Margaret Llewelyn Davies', 124n8
'Jane Austen', 99
'Janet Case' MS, 74, 75, 154n20
'Julia Margaret Cameron', 43, 44
'Lady Ritchie', 43, 45, 46, 55n38
'The Leaning Tower', 2, 7–8, 10n18, 13, 64–5, 79, 90–1, 92, 101, 189, 192, 195, 196n10, 202, 250, 300
'London Squares', 248n33
'Middlebrow', 170–1
'Miss Janet Case: Classical Scholar and Teacher', 74–6, 78
'Leslie Stephen: The Philosopher at Home', 15, 17–18, 23, 25, 26, 52n8, 64, 106, 115, 184n49
'Mr Bennett and Mrs Brown', 92, 189, 196n10
'Miss Ormerod', 101
'The New Biography', xxi
'The Modern Essay', 151
'The Novels of Thomas Hardy', 64
'On Being Ill', 55n33
'On Not Knowing Greek', xxi, 95, 107
'The Patron and the Crocus', 102, 199
'The Perfect Language', 74, 76, 77
'Poetry, Fiction and the Future', 189, 196n10
'Professions for Women', 95, 114, 189, 196n10, 216, 243, 249n51, 270n13
'A Professor of Life', 145, 186–7
'The Reader', 11n25

Woolf Virginia, works (*cont.*)
  ESSAYS (*cont.*)
    'Reviewing', 102, 199, 200, 207n9, 218, 264
    'The Russian Point of View', 95
    'The *Sentimental Journey*', 303
    'Street Haunting', 251, 253, 260
    'The Sun and the Fish', 260
    'Two Women', 101, 111
    'Why?' 119, 145, 186
  ESSAY COLLECTIONS
    The Captain's Death Bed and Other Essays, xxiv n3
    Collected Essays, xxi, xxiv n3
    The Common Reader, xxii, xxiv n5, 2, 11nn23,25,27, 14, 65, 190, 191, 192, 298n26, 306
    The Common Reader: Second Series, 11n25, 190, 191
    The Death of the Moth and Other Essays, xxiv n3, 11n25
    Granite & Rainbow: Essays, xxiv n3
    The Moment and Other Essays xxiv n3
  EXTENDED ESSAYS
    A Room of One's Own, xxii, 2, 6, 9n9, 10n18, 18, 19n8, 24, 32n6, 34n25, 41, 44, 64, 73, 82–3n22, 92, 93, 95, 101, 102, 163, 171, 179n18, 189, 191, 196n10, 217n9, 275, 306, 306n4
    Three Guineas, xxii, 2, 5, 6, 9n9, 11n21, 17, 18, 18n4, 20–1n27, 35, 41, 64, 73, 80–1n15, 92, 101, 114, 186, 195n3, 303, 306, 306n4
  MEMOIRS
    '22 HPG', 20n26, 29, 30, 34n24
    'J. M. S.: Notes (1929?)', 54n28
    'Old Bloomsbury', 41, 106
    'Sketch of the Past' (1st ed.), 35, 39, 40, 52–3n12, 76, 90
    'Sketch of the Past' (2nd ed.), 13–14, 15–16, 19n9, 20n26, 23, 24, 26, 29, 30, 31, 33nn13,18,20, 36, 37, 38, 39, 40, 41, 52n9, 53–4n22, 54nn25,27, 57n49, 65, 85n36, 89, 90, 92, 98, 99, 104nn17,20, 114, 115, 123n1, 181n27, 243, 253,
263, 287, 292, 298n15, 299n29
    'Sketch of the Past' MS, 103n5, 115
  NOVELS
    Between the Acts, 7
    Jacob's Room, 42, 248n27
    Mrs Dalloway, 14, 72, 174, 175, 248n28, 298n25
    The Pargiters, 70–1
    To the Lighthouse, 14, 33n18, 34n23, 100, 298n25
    The Voyage Out, 61, 110, 199, 215, 272
    The Waves, 72
    The Years, 11n21, 70–1
  STORY
    'Moments of Being: "Slater's Pins Have No Points"', 70–1, 86–7n51
Wordsworth, William, 25, 32n7, 48, 76, 109, 112, 172, 174, 219, 326
Workers' Educational Association, 53n19, 123, 131, 169, 178n9, 181n26, 192
Working Men's College, 92, 131, 132n6, 136, 169, 180–1n24
The World, 236
A World of Girls, 48, 56n42
Worsley, G. T., 52n10, 54n24
Worth, George J., 91, 92, 103n8
Wright, Anne, 112, 113
Wright, C. T. Hagberg, 61, 80nn12,13
Writers' and Artists' Year-Book, 205, 209n26, 217n8, 227, 246n15
writers, readers, as class, 193–4
writers, popular fiction, 265–9
  ODNB biographers of, 266, 268, 270–1n16

Yaldwyn, Cyril, 174–5; 176, 177, 184nn51,52, 185nn53,54, 193
Yonge, Charlotte M., 111, 116–17n7, 326
Yoshida, Erika, 306n1
Young, Damon, 155n30

Zeldwyn, Cyril *see* Yaldwyn, Cyril
Zimmern, Alice, 66, 67, 75, 84n32, 85nn34,36, 224
Zimmern, Helen, 48
Zwerdling, Alex, 33n15, 197n18

EU representative:
Easy Access System Europe
Mustamäe tee 50, 10621 Tallinn, Estonia
Gpsr.requests@easproject.com